JOURNAL FOR THE STUDY OF THE OLD TESTAMENT
SUPPLEMENT SERIES

93



JSOT Press
Sheffield

# JOSHUA 24
# as
# POETIC NARRATIVE

William T. Koopmans

Journal for the Study of the Old Testament
Supplement Series 93

Published by JSOT Press
JSOT Press is an imprint of
Sheffield Academic Press Ltd
The University of Sheffield
343 Fulwood Road
Sheffield S10 3BP
England

Printed in Great Britain
by Billing & Sons Ltd
Worcester

British Library Cataloguing in Publication Data Available

ISSN 0143-5108
ISBN 1-85075-247-8

# CONTENTS

# Preface

This book is my thesis submitted to the *Theological Academy* of the *Johannes Calvijnstichting* (Kampen, The Netherlands). It is a pleasure to thank all who contributed to its completion. I am particularly indebted to Professor Dr. J. C. de Moor for his inspiring and sympathetic guidance as supervisor of this study. His generous counsel and criticisms throughout the duration of this research was supplemented by innumerable pointers regarding employment of computer programs, including the layout of the camera-ready manuscript. Professor J. H. Stek graciously conceded to function as co-supervisor. His painstaking reading of the manuscript facilitated countless improvements. Dr. W. G. E. Watson generously agreed to evaluate the manuscript in the capacity of external referent during the process of its evaluation as a dissertation. I also gratefully acknowledge assistance from Professor Dr. E. Noort. He was instrumental in the selection of Josh. 24:1-28 as the topic of my research, and he offered valuable advise regarding the history of interpretation of this passage. My treatment of various topics was enhanced by conversations with students and colleagues at the Theological University of Kampen.

Professor Dr. C. H. W. Brekelmans generously gave me a prepublication copy of his paper ("Joshua xxiv: Its Place and Function") presented at the opening session of The 13th Congress of IOSOT (Leuven, Aug. 27–Sept. 1, 1989). Valuable assistance was offered by the library personnel in Kampen (Oudestraat and Broederweg) and Grand Rapids (Calvin Theological Seminary).

This study was made possible by funds from a Netherlands Government Scholarship administered via the Association of Universities and Colleges of Canada, a scholarship from Calvin Theological Seminary, and an appointment as Research Assistant at the Theological University of Kampen.

Friends and relatives in Canada and the Netherlands offered constant encouragement during the arduous task of this research. I wish to dedicate the final product to Louise, my covenant partner. Without her undaunted support this project would not have been possible. Her love supported a family that grew as rapidly as the present volume—with Amy and Rachel joining sisters Tina and Karissa in our international family. Above all, I express my thanks to the one God who inspired the verses upon which this study is based.

# Abbreviations

| | |
|---|---|
| *AA* | *Archäologischer Anzeiger, Beiblatt zum Jahrbuch des Archäologischer Instituts* (Berlin). |
| *AB* | *Anchor Bible* (Garden City). |
| *ABR* | *Australian Biblical Review* (Melbourne). |
| *AKAW* | *Abhandlungen der Kaiserlichen Akademie der Wissenschaften* (Wien). |
| *AnBibl* | *Analecta Biblica* (Rome). |
| ANET | J.B. PRITCHARD (ed.), *Ancient Near Eastern Texts Relating to the Old Testament*, 3rd ed., Princeton 1969. |
| *AnOr* | *Analecta Orientalia* (Rome). |
| *AnSt* | *Anatolian Studies* (London). |
| *AOAT* | *Alter Orient und Altes Testament* (Kevelaer/Neukirchen-Vluyn). |
| *ArOr* | *Archiv Orientální* (Prague). |
| *ASOR* | American School of Oriental Research. |
| *ASTI* | *Annual of the Swedish Theological Institute in Jerusalem* (Leiden). |
| *ATD* | *Das Alte Testament Deutsch* (Göttingen). |
| *AThANT* | *Abhandlung zur Theologie des Alten und Neuen Testaments* (Zürich). |
| *AThD* | *Acta Theologica Danica* (Århus). |
| *AUSS* | *Andrews University Seminary Studies* (Berrien Springs, MI). |
| *BA* | *The Biblical Archaeologist* (New Haven). |
| *BAR* | *Biblical Archaeology Review* (Washington, DC). |
| *BASOR* | *Bulletin of the American Schools of Oriental Research* (New Haven). |
| *BBB* | *Bonner Biblische Beiträge* (Bonn). |
| *BETL* | *Bibliotheca Ephemeridum Theologicarum Lovaniensium* (Leuven). |
| *BHS* | *Biblia Hebraica Stuttgartensia* (Stuttgart). |
| *Bibl* | *Biblica* (Roma). |
| *BiOr* | *Bibliotheca Orientalis* (Leiden). |
| *BIOSCS* | *Bulletin of the International Organization for Septuagint and Cognate Studies.* |
| *BKAT* | *Biblischer Kommentar Altes Testament* (Neukirchen-Vluyn). |
| *BN* | *Biblische Notizen* (Bamberg). |
| *BOT* | *De Boeken van het Oude Testament* (Roermond/Maaseik). |

| | |
|---|---|
| *BR* | *Biblical Research* (Chicago). |
| *BWANT* | *Beiträge zur Wissenschaft vom Alten und Neuen Testament* (Stuttgart). |
| *BZ* | *Biblische Zeitschrift* (Paderborn). |
| *BZAW* | *Beihefte zur ZAW* (Berlin). |
| *CAD* | *The Assyrian Dictionary of the Oriental Institute of the University of Chicago.* |
| *CAH* | *Cambridge Ancient History* (Cambridge). |
| *CB OTS* | *Coniectanea Biblica Old Testament Series* (Lund). |
| *CBQ* | *Catholic Biblical Quarterly* (Washington, DC). |
| *COT* | *Commentaar op het Oude Testament* (Kampen). |
| CTA | A. HERDNER, *Corpus des tablettes en cunéiformes alphabétiques découvertes à Ras Shamra-Ugarit de 1929 à 1939.* Paris, 1963. |
| *EA* | J.A. KNUDTZON (Hrsgb), *Die El-Amarna Tafeln.* 2 Teile. Aalen 1964. |
| *ErIs* | *Eretz-Israel, Archaeological, Historical and Geographical Studies* (Jerusalem). |
| *EstBib* | *Estudios Biblícos* (Madrid). |
| *EvTh* | *Evangelische Theologie* (München). |
| *FRLANT* | *Forschungen zur Religion und Literatur des Alten und Neuen Testaments* (Göttingen). |
| *Fs* | Festschrift. |
| *FzB* | *Forschung zur Bibel* (Würzburg). |
| *HAT* | *Handbuch zum Alten Testament* (Tübingen). |
| *HSM* | *Harvard Semitic Monographs* (Cambridge, Mass.). |
| *HSS* | *Harvard Semitic Studies* (Cambridge, Mass.). |
| *HTR* | *Harvard Theological Review* (Cambridge, Mass). |
| *HUCA* | *Hebrew Union College Annual* (Cincinnati). |
| *IDB(Sup)* | *The Interpreter's Dictionary of the Bible (Supplementary Volume)* (New York/Nashville). |
| *IEJ* | *Israel Exploration Journal* (Jerusalem). |
| *Interp* | *Interpretation* (Richmond, Virg.). |
| *IThC* | *International Theological Commentary* (Grand Rapids/ Edinburgh). |
| *JANES* | *Journal of the Ancient Near Eastern Society of Columbia University* (New York) |
| *JAOS* | *Journal of the American Oriental Society* (Boston/New Haven). |
| *JBL* | *Journal of Biblical Literature* (Philadelphia). |
| *JCS* | *Journal of Cuneiform Studies* (Chicago). |

| | |
|---|---|
| *JEA* | *Journal of Egyptian Archaeology* (London). |
| *JEOL* | *Jaarbericht Ex Oriente Lux* (Leiden). |
| *JLH* | *Jahrbuch für Liturgik und Hymnologie* (Kassel) |
| *JNES* | *Journal of Near Eastern Studies* (Chicago). |
| *JNSL* | *Journal of Northwest Semitic Languages* (Stellenbosch). |
| *JSOT* | *Journal for the Study of the Old Testament* (Sheffield). |
| *JSOTS* | *Journal for the Study of the Old Testament Supplement Series* (Sheffield). |
| *JSS* | *Journal of Semitic Studies* (Manchester). |
| *JThSt* | *Journal of Theological Studies* (Oxford) |
| KAI | H. DONNER, W. RÖLLIG, *Kanaanäische und aramäische Inschriften*, Bd.1-3, Wiesbaden 1966-1969. |
| *KAT* | *Kommentar zum Alten Testament* (Leipzig). |
| *KC* | *Kamper Cahiers* (Kampen) |
| *KeH* | *Kurzgefasstes exegetisches Handbuch* (Leipzig). |
| *KHC* | *Kurzer Hand-Commentar zum Alten Testament* (Tübingen/ Leipzig). |
| KTU | M. DIETRICH, O. LORETZ, J. SANMARTÍN, *Die keilalphabetischen Texte aus Ugarit*, Bd. 1, Neukirchen–Vluyn 1976. |
| *KuD* | *Kerygma und Dogma* (Göttingen). |
| *KV* | *Korte Verklaring der Heilige Schrift* (Kampen). |
| *LThQ* | *Lexington Theological Quarterly* (Lexington, Ky.). |
| *MAA* | *Mededeelingen der Koninklijke Akademie van Wetenschappen te Amsterdam* |
| *MDOG* | *Mitteilungen der Deutschen Orient-Gesellschaft* (Berlin). |
| *MIO* | *Mitteilungen des Instituts für Orientforschung* (Berlin). |
| *MVÄG* | *Mitteilungen der Vorderasiatisch-Ägyptischen Gesellschaft* (Leipzig) |
| *NCBC* | *The New Century Bible Commentary* (Grand Rapids/ Basingstoke). |
| *NICOT* | *The New International Commentary on the Old Testament* (Grand Rapids). |
| *NIV* | *New International Version* |
| *NThT* | *Nederlands Theologisch Tijdschrift* (Wageningen). |
| *OBO* | *Orbis Biblicus et Orientalis* (Freiburg/Göttingen). |
| *OLZ* | *Orientalische Literaturzeitung* (Berlin). |
| *Or* | *Orientalia.* Nova Series (Roma). |
| *OrAnt* | *Oriens Antiquus* (Roma). |

| | |
|---|---|
| *OTL* | *Old Testament Library* (London). |
| *OTS* | *Oudtestamentische Studiën* (Leiden). |
| *OTWSA* | *Die Ou Testamentiese Werkgemeenskap in Suid-Afrika* (Pretoria) |
| *PEQ* | *Palestine Exploration Quarterly* (London). |
| *POT* | *De Prediking van het Oude Testament* (Nijkerk). |
| *PRU* | *Le Palais Royal d'Ugarit publié sous la direction de C.F.A. Schaeffer*, Paris. |
| *QDAP* | *The Quarterly of the Department of Antiquities in Palestine* (London) |
| *RGG* | *Die Religion in Geschichte und Gegenwart*[3] (Tübingen, 1957-1965). |
| RS | Ras Shamra. |
| *RSP* | L. FISHER, ed., *Ras Shamra Parallels*, I-II; S. RUMMEL, ed., *Ras Shamra Parallels*, III, Roma 1972-1981. |
| *RSV* | *Revised Standard Version* |
| *RThPh* | *Revue de Théologie et de Philosophie* (Épalinges). |
| *RThR* | *The Reformed Theological Review* (Melbourne). |
| *SBB* | *Soncino Books of the Bible* (London). |
| *SBL Diss* | *Society of Biblical Literature Dissertation Series.* |
| *ScH* | *Scripta Hierosolymitana* (Jerusalem) |
| *SSN* | *Studia Semitica Neerlandica* (Assen). |
| *StANT* | *Studien zum Alten und Neuen Testament* (München). |
| *StBoT* | *Studien zu den Boğazköy-Texten* (Wiesbaden). |
| *StBTh* | *Studies in Biblical Theology* (London) |
| *StTh* | *Studia Theologica* (Lund). |
| *SVT* | *Supplements to Vetus Testamentum* (Leiden). |
| *Syria* | *Syria. Revue d'art oriental et d'archéologie* (Paris). |
| *TB* | *Tyndale Bulletin* (Cambridge). |
| *THAT* | E.JENNI C.WESTERMANN, eds., *Theologisches Handwörterbuch zum Alten Testament*, 2 vols. München/Zürich, 1971. |
| *ThB* | *Theologische Bucherei* (München). |
| *THB* | *The Tyndale House Bulletin* (Cambridge). |
| *TheolQuart* | *Theologische Quartalschrift* (Tübingen). |
| *ThPh* | *Theologie und Philosophie* (Freiburg). |
| *ThSt* | *Theologische Studien* (Zürich). |
| *ThT* | *Theologisch Tijdschrift* (Leiden). |
| *ThWAT* | *Theologisches Wörterbuch zum Alten Testament* (Stuttgart). |
| *ThZ* | *Theologische Zeitschrift* (Basel). |

| | |
|---|---|
| *TThZ* | *Trierer Theologische Zeitschrift* (Trier). |
| *TUAT* | *Texte aus der Umwelt des Alten Testaments* (Gütersloh). |
| *TvT* | *Tijdschrift voor Theologie* |
| *UBL* | *Ugaritisch-Biblische Literatur* (Altenberge). |
| *UF* | *Ugarit-Forschungen* (Neukirchen–Vluyn). |
| *VT* | *Vetus Testamentum* (Leiden). |
| *VuF* | *Verkündigung und Forschung* (München). |
| *WBC* | *Word Biblial Commentary* (Waco). |
| *WMANT* | *Wissenschaftliche Monographien zum alten und Neuen Testament* (Neukirchen-Vluyn). |
| *WTJ* | *Westminster Theological Journal* (Philadelphia) |
| *WZUH* | *Wissenschaftliche Zeitschrift Univ. Halle* (Halle). |
| *ZA* | *Zeitschrift für Assyriologie* (Berlin/Leipzig). |
| *ZAW* | *Zeitschrift für die Alttestamentliche Wissenschaft* (Gießen/Berlin). |
| *ZDMG* | *Zeitschrift der Deutschen Morgenländischen Gesellschaft* (Leipzig/Wiesbaden). |
| *ZDPV* | *Zeitschrift des Deutschen Palästina-Vereins* (Stuttgart/Wiesbaden). |
| *ZfA* | *Zeitschrift für Althebraistik* (Stuttgart). |
| *ZThK* | *Zeitschrift für Theologie und Kirche* (Tübingen). |

# 1 The History of Interpretation of Josh. 24:1-28

## 1.1 Introduction

This opening chapter presents a survey of the various methods of interpretation which have been employed in the study of Josh. 24:1-28.[1] Primary consideration is given here to two basic issues, namely, various theories about the diachronical composition of the text of Josh. 24:1-28, and secondly, the role which Josh. 24 has occupied in broader analyses of the the covenant concept in the OT. Since the history and significance of the concept of covenant has been one of the most productive seedbeds in recent OT scholarship, our survey cannot attempt to be exhaustive. It is hoped, rather, that a review of the broader outlines of these developments will help to focus upon the fundamental issues involved in the interpretation of Josh. 24:1-28.

Any presentation of a history of interpretation is confronted from the outset with methodological questions concerning the arrangement of material. Respective advantages and disadvantages can be listed for either a chronological or a thematic approach. A chronological delineation is advantageous insofar as it sketches major developments in the order they occurred, thereby offering a quick and natural overview of the historical stages through which a field of study has advanced. Such an approach also tends to elucidate lines of dependency of various scholars and schools of thought upon their predecessors. However, the danger in a chronological survey geared at revealing trends and developments is that such systematization threatens to either oversimplify historical connections, movements, and schools of thought, or conversely, in attempting to do justice to the individuality and uniqueness of the representatives, it becomes so detailed and extensive that the "quick overview" is sacrificed for a more burdensome thoroughness and accuracy. A thematic approach, by grouping similar positions together, is able to avoid some of the repetition which

[1] Due to obvious affinity with respect to content, various other passages such as Josh. 8:30-35; Deut. 11:29-32; 27 will also be considered, but their treatment here is kept secondary. For a previous sketch of the different approaches to Josh. 24 see J.P.Floss, *Jahwe dienen–Göttern dienen* (Bonn, 1975), 334-340. See too C.H.W.Brekelmans, "Joshua XXIV: Its Place and Function" (forthcoming in the publication of papers presented at The 13th Congress of the International Organization for the Study of the Old Testament, Leuven, Aug. 27–Sept. 1, 1989).

usually occurs in a chronological layout. In the light of these considerations it is desirable to begin with a brief historical survey of the major developments in our present field of study, followed by a more detailed thematic analysis.

## 1.2 A chronological overview

Our intention here is not to survey the general history of OT interpretation[2] but to focus specifically on the history of interpretation of Josh. 24:1-28, with select examples from the broader field of study. This specific focus is the primary factor governing our selection of representatives and works in what follows.

While it is not our desire to create the impression that OT study begins with Julius Wellhausen (1844-1918),[3] it is appropriate to begin our survey with a consideration of his influence upon our topic. Wellhausen presupposed a complex literary history behind Josh. 24. In his opinion, an original E source went through stages of redaction, notably to form a JE combination under influence from Dtistic editors.[4] Here, as elsewhere for Wellhausen, covenant theology betrayed the influence of the prophets. Wellhausen's conclusion regarding a Dtistically edited E source was echoed for numerous decades by a majority of commentators.[5]

A different approach to the source criticism of Josh. 24 was advocated by R.Smend,[6] followed by O.Eissfeldt.[7] Smend and Eissfeldt

[2]See conveniently R.E.Clements, *One Hundred Years of Old Testament Interpretation* (Philadelphia, 1976).

[3]Cf. B.S.Childs, *Biblical Theology in Crisis* (Philadelphia, 1970), 139f. See also his tribute to Calvin, Drusius, Rashi and Ibn Ezra, in *The Book of Exodus: A Critical, Theological Commentary* (Philadelphia, 1974), x. Nor do we intend to minimize the significance of theological scholarship pertaining to covenant previous to Wellhausen. Consider, e.g., developments within federal theology since the time of the Reformation, cf. M.W.Karlberg, "Reformed Interpretation of the Mosaic Covenant," *WTJ* 43 (1980-81) 1-57.

[4]J.Wellhausen, *Die Composition des Hexateuchs und der historischen Bücher des Alten Testaments*, 3rd ed. (Berlin, 1899; reprint ed. 1963), 133.

[5]See H.Mölle, *Der sogenannte Landtag zu Sichem* (Würzburg, 1980), 14-16.

[6]R.Smend *Die Erzählung des Hexateuch auf ihre Quellen untersucht* (Berlin, 1912), 334-339.

[7]O.Eissfeldt, *Hexateuch-Synopse. Die Erzählung der fünf Bücher Mose und des Buches Josua mit dem Anfange des Richterbuches* (Leipzig, 1922; reprinted Darmstadt, 1962), 79-81, 248-250, 284; *The Old Testament: An Introduction*, trans. P.R.Ackroyd (Oxford, 1965), 255.

questioned the theory that Josh. 24:1-28 was produced via Dtistic redaction of an original E source. They attempted instead to discern multiple original sources. M.Noth's original opinion, published in 1930, fundamentally agreed with their effort to distinguish various sources.[8] In his commentary of 1953, however, Noth in certain respects broke with all previous source-critical theories about the book of Joshua. He suggested that Josh. 24 bore evidence of a pre-Dtistic *Grundlage*,[9] but he no longer simply equated this with E. This important transition in Noth's approach must be attributed on the one hand to his originality. On the other hand, however, this development was a refinement of conclusions already prepared for in the work of, inter alia, S.Mowinckel and the related school of form criticism. Noth's search for cultic settings and pre-literary transmission of tradition alerted him to the possiblility of a cultic origin for Josh. 24 independent of the E source. Clearly, Noth's views were also a development of E.Sellin's theory regarding the cultic significance of Shechem. The supposed historical implications were developed most prominently in his theory of an amphictyony centered at Shechem.

It is thus evident that Noth stands as a critical transitionary figure at the crossroads of classical source analysis and form criticism. A similar observation must be made regarding G.von Rad.[10] In his theory of an ancient credo,[11] von Rad too claimed to find pre-Elohistic material derived from an original setting in local tradition and the cultic life of ancient Israel. Studies such as these by Noth and von Rad had the cumulative effect of redirecting analyses of Josh. 24:1-28 away from primarily source-critical questions, to include form-critical matters focusing upon *Sitz im Leben*, genre, and transmission of tradition, whether orally or literarily.

[8]M.Noth, *Das System der Zwölf Stämme Israels* (Stuttgart, 1930; reprinted Darmstadt, 1980), 133-144.

[9]M.Noth, *Das Buch Josua*, 2nd ed. (Tübingen, 1953), 15f.

[10]G.von Rad, "Das formgeschichtliche Problem des Hexateuch," (BWANT, 4th series, 26; Stuttgart, 1938); reprinted in *Gesammelte Studien zum Alten Testament* (München, 1958) (= *The Problem of the Hexateuch and Other Essays*, trans. E.W.T.Dicken [London, 1984], 1-78).

[11]H.-J.Kraus observes, "So ist die Arbeit G. v. Rad's 'Das formgeschichtliche Problem des Hexateuchs' ohne die in Mowinckels Werken gelegten Grundlagen gar nicht zu denken. Dieser Arbeit v. Rads aber gilt nun unsere Aufmerksamkeit im Anschluss an die formgeschichtlichen Untersuchungen Alts und unter Berücksichtigung der erwähnten Forschungen Mowinckels" (*Gottesdienst in Israel. Grundriss einer Geschichte des alttestamentlichen Gottesdienstes* [München, 1954], 51).

A subsequent shift in emphasis and methodology was stimulated by attempts to compare OT covenant texts with ancient NE treaty documents. Especially influential in this development were G.E.Mendenhall[12] and K.Baltzer;[13] their works, by appearing in English and German respectively, wrenched open the sluices for a veritable flood of comparative analyses. This heightened interest in comparing biblical and extra-biblical texts inaugurated a new period in the form criticism of Josh. 24. The central question now shifted away from the influence of the cultus or local traditions in the literary development of Israel's history writing, to questions of affinity with treaty texts and the implications such similarities might have for understanding covenant themes. This sort of form criticism diverges considerably from the *Gattungsgeschichtliche* studies inaugurated by Gunkel and Mowinckel. Here there is no attempt to move back to an antecedent oral tradition. To the contrary in fact, all emphasis now falls upon *textual* comparison and potential correlation of the text's final form with a particular *Sitz im Leben.*

In addition to the chronological progression sketched above, from source-critical analyses to various brands of form criticism, it is important to note the currently renewed interest in matters of Dtistic history and theology. While it is evident that ever since Wellhausen the theory of major Dtistic redaction of the historical material from Joshua–2 Kings has never been absent, the precise application of that thesis has been carried out in various ways. Characteristic of this movement in general is an attempt to utilize various critical methods to ferret various layers, both theological and textual, from the final form of the text. This present interest in Dtistic theology has stimulated a reappraisal of virtually every aspect of covenant in the OT. Previous claims regarding a close affinity between Josh. 24 and Hittite treaty texts of the 2nd millenium B.C., for example, have been called into question in numerous recent works.[14] Without at this point en-

[12]G.E.Mendenhall, *Law and Covenant in Israel and the Ancient Near East* (Pittsburgh, 1955) (= *BA* 17 [1954] 26-46, 50-76).

[13]K.Baltzer, *Das Bundesformular, sein Ursprung und seine Verwendung im Alten Testament* (Neukirchen, 1960) (= *The Covenant Formulary in Old Testament, Jewish and Early Christian Writings* [Oxford, 1971]). See also J.Muilenburg, "The Form and Structure of the Covenantal Formulations," *VT* 9 (1959) 347-365.

[14]See for example C.F.Whitley, "Covenant and Commandment in Israel," *JNES* 22 (1963) 37-48; L.Perlitt, *Bundestheologie im Alten Testament* (Neukirchen-Vluyn, 1969); M.Weinfeld, *Deuteronomy and the Deuteronomic School* (London, 1972);

tering into a discussion of the variety of approaches represented within recent studies under the general rubric of Dtistic theology, it will suffice our purpose here to simply note this development and wait until later with further illustration and elaboration.

However, it is necessary to comment upon the terminology employed. Some OT studies use the terms Dtic and Dtistic respectively for successive stages in Israel's historical writing. The term Dtic is often applied to the central portion of Deuteronomy,[15] while Dtistic is used in reference to later passages believed to have been influenced, whether in their original composition or their redaction, by an affiliated movement. However, some scholars also employ the term Dtic for texts thought to have been written at approximately the same time as the central part of Deuteronomy, and therefore prior to the Deuteronomistic history spanning Deuteronomy–2 Kings as a whole. This matter is important for the discussion of Josh. 24:1-28. For example, Perlitt considers Josh. 24:1-28 to be Dtic, but pre-Dtistic, i.e., prior to DtrH. For these reasons, even though it entails that at times the terms Dtic and Dtistic may be employed with various nuances, when summarizing the views of other authors the present study ordinarily retains the terminology they use. In the opinion of the present writer, the absence of objective criteria for distinguishing between Dtic and Dtistic texts in Joshua–2 Kings has led to considerable confusion in the employment of these terms. Since the present study does not attempt to systematically differentiate various historical periods or literary layers of Dtistic influence in the corpus from Deuteronomy–2 Kings, e.g., double or triple redactions of the Dtistic history, the term Dtistic is usually employed when discussing such characteristics in passages outside of Deuteronomy itself.

In addition to the methods mentioned above, numerous studies also permitted archaeological considerations to have a significant role in the interpretation of Josh. 24:1-28. Efforts to harmonize archaeological data and textual considerations may be divided chronologically into two periods; the first period corresponds with work at *tell balâṭah*

E.Kutsch, *Verheissung und Gesetz. Untersuchungen zum sogenannten "Bund" im Alten Testament* (Berlin, 1973); D.J.McCarthy, *Treaty and Covenant: A Study in Form in the Ancient Oriental Documents and in the Old Testament*, 2nd ed. (Rome 1978).

[15]E.g., McCarthy uses the term Dtic in reference to Deut. 4:44-26:19 and 28:1-46 (*Covenant and Treaty*, 12).

under the supervision of especially Sellin, primarily in the 1920's, and the second was stimulated by American expeditions at that site under the direction of G.E.Wright in the 1950's and 60's.[16]

While these major chronological progressions will serve adequately as a rough introductory sketch for the history of interpretation of Josh. 24:1-28, it is necessary to issue a firm caveat against viewing the different approaches outlined above as standing independent from each other either historically or methodologically. A search for literary sources persists throughout the entire history of interpretation. Similarly, attention to the role of the cultus in the shaping of Josh. 24 did not begin with Noth and von Rad, as is evident immediately in a perusal of Sellin's approach. The form-critical endeavors are neither homogeneous nor restricted to a certain period of interpretation. The question of Dtistic theology is to varying degrees present throughout the entire history of interpretation of this passage. The present blossoming of such efforts owes much to seed sown in the seminal studies of Noth, and this method's validity continues to be tested today. Finally, as is alluded above, archaeological details were already considered by Sellin, but not nearly to the extent of recent studies. With these considerations in mind it is possible to present a more detailed summary of the history of interpretation of Josh. 24:1-28 under six major headings:

1.3 Covenant and source-critical methodology
1.4 Covenant and cult in Israel's history writing
1.5 Covenant and treaty; new developments in form criticism
1.6 Covenant and Dtistic theology; writing history anew
1.7 Josh. 24:1-28 and archaeology
1.8 Textual criticism of Josh. 24:1-28

Inclusion of figures treated under these six headings is selective rather than exhaustive, based upon the significance of the representatives in the light of their influence upon the present state of scholarship in this area. The divisions here proposed have a clear affinity to the chronological developments, but our intention is to concentrate upon the specific contributions of the selected individuals rather than upon an elaboration of the historical developments or connections.

[16]For bibliographical references see 1.7.

## 1.3 Covenant and source-critical methodology

### 1.3.1 J.Wellhausen

Wellhausen's writings have functioned virtually as a canon by which subsequent views of covenant have often been measured.[17] Numerous recent scholars have in particular hastened to draw comparisons between Perlitt's recent study[18] and Wellhausen's view of covenant.[19] These observations will suffice to demonstrate the importance of dealing with Wellhausen's perspective.

Wellhausen's view of covenant is inseparable from his theory regarding a process of cultic development in Israel. To avoid misrepresenting his view of the relationship of covenant to law and cultus, however, a couple of observations are necessary. Summary statements passing Wellhausen's view off as essentially Hegelian[20] and evolutionistic are inadequate.[21] A clear understanding of Wellhausen's position

[17]See, e.g., Baltzer's comments regarding J.Pedersen and J.Begrich (*Bundesformular*, 14, 16). See also E.W.Nicholson, "Covenant in a Century of Study since Wellhausen," *OTS* 24 (Leiden, 1986), 54-69; *God and His People: Covenant and Theology in the Old Testament* (Oxford, 1986), 3ff.

[18]See n.14 above.

[19]D.J.McCarthy, "*Berît* in Old Testament History and Theology," *Bibl* 53 (1972) 111; C.F.H.Henry, *God, Revelation and Authority*. Vol. 2 (Grand Rapids, 1976), 263: "Lothar Perlitt returns almost the whole distance to Wellhausian notions by viewing covenant theology in Deuteronomy as a development in the seventh century B.C."; Nicholson, *God and His People*, 117; R.A.Oden, "The Place of Covenant in the Religion of Israel," in P.D.Miller et al., eds., *Ancient Israelite Religion: Essays in Honor of Frank Moore Cross* (Philadelphia, 1987), 429-447, esp. 436: "Many of Perlitt's affirmations are strikingly similar to those of Wellhausen."

[20]H.-J.Kraus, *Geschichte der historisch-kritischen Erforschung des Alten Testaments von der Reformation bis zur Gegenwart*, 4th ed. (Neukirchen-Vluyn), 1981, 264; *Gottesdienst in Israel*, 15; J.L.Koole, "Wellhausen," *Christelijke Encyclopedie* (Kampen, 1961), 6:579; D.R.Hillers, *Covenant: The History of a Biblical Idea* (Baltimore, 1969), 21.

[21]L.Perlitt, *Vatke und Wellhausen, Geschichtsphilosophische Voraussetzungen und historiographische Motive für die Darstellung der Religion und Geschichte Israels durch Wilhelm Vatke und Julius Wellhausen* (Berlin, 1965), esp. 153ff., 185ff. In a review of this book N.H.Ridderbos observes, "Wie Perlitts boek gelezen heeft, zal niet licht zo ongenuanceerd over Wellhausens 'Hegelianisme' spreken, als dikwijls gebeurd is" (*GThT* 65 [1965] 263). Cf. R.Smend, "Vorwort" in *Julius Wellhausen. Grundrisse zum alten Testament* (München, 1965), 7: "Man hat Wellhausen gern Beeinflussung durch Hegel nachgesagt. Nichts ist verkehrter als das; will man Namen, dann sind es vor anderen Carlyle und Burckhardt." But not everyone has found Perlitt's analysis convincing, cf. F.M.Cross, *Canaanite Myth and Hebrew Epic* (Cambridge, Mass., 1973), 82 n.9.

is fostered by keeping two crucial factors in mind. First, Wellhausen was attempting ***historical reconstructions*** of both events and interpretation. Thus, central to his concern were questions regarding what actually happened in history, and the extent to which narration of religious development in Israel accurately reflected that history. Second, his assessment of the respective merits of any given stage of Israelite religion was conducted first and foremost upon considerations of the relationship of the individual to the "divine."

Consequently, a blanket statement to the effect that prophecy in ancient Israel constituted for Wellhausen the highwater mark of Yahwism, needs immediate qualification.[22] It is true that in prophecy Wellhausen found an impetus towards a purer personal relationship between human and divine, an impetus towards an ideal which stood in sharp contrast to a legalistic, centralized cultus. Thus, Wellhausen viewed the central sanctuary as a positive step towards monotheism but he simultaneously considered it detrimental to the extent that it fostered subsequent legalism. The reverse side of the coin was his qualified appreciation of cultic activity in local "high-places" on the grounds that it reflected personalized rather than institutionalized religion. What was not endorsed was the polytheism that accompanied such practices. He considered Canaanite religion to be one historical stage in the development of monotheism,[23] but this does not entail that he sanctioned the polytheistic content which accompanied the cultic form. The opposite is in fact true, as becomes evident from his positive analysis of the role of the Israelite prophets.

It is therefore essential in discussing Wellhausen's view of covenant to distinguish between cultus as historical phenomenon on the one hand, and as an element of biblical narration on the other–a distinction which is clear from his own summary of the place of cultus in the various sources. He concludes that cultus was an element in the worship of Yahweh that originated from heathen practice, withstood the criticism of the prophets, underwent correction in the Deuteronomic reformation, and finally in the Priestly tradition was exalted to a prominence exceeding its original status.[24] Already in 1878 in

[22]See now Perlitt's analysis of Pedersen's criticisms of Wellhausen (*Vatke und Wellhausen*, esp. 193ff.).

[23]R.K.Harrison, *Introduction to the Old Testament* (Grand Rapids, 1969), 22; R.J.Thompson, *Moses and the Law in a Century of Criticism since Graf* (Leiden, 1970), 59.

[24]J. Wellhausen, "Die Israelitisch-Jüdische Religion," in P.Hinneberg, ed., *Ge-*

his *Geschichte Israels* he demonstrated the extent to which questions of cultus were critical for his designation of documentary sources. He suggested, "Es ist der alte volkstümliche Cultus, welcher sowol in J als in E durch die Patriarchen geheiligt wird."[25] While the sources J and E were mingled, "zu JE verschmolzen sind,"[26] by Dtistic redaction, to such an extent that Wellhausen questioned whether it was legitimate to separate them,[27] he nevertheless detected a different nuance regarding the extent of prophetic influence upon the narration of cultic activity. "Die zweite Quelle, E, lässt eine fortgeschrittenere und grundsätzlichere Religiosität erkennen; sie ist mindestens prophetisch angehaucht."[28]

As an example of this relative dependence upon prophetic influence in the E strand, Wellhausen includes a reference to Josh. 24:27 and the erection of a stone at Shechem.[29] The narration of this cultic action is comparable to the description of Abraham as a prophet (*nby'*), of Jacob burying the *teraphim*, and especially of the history of the golden calf.[30] By contrast, in J the prophetic influence has distantiated the patriarchs from such cultic activities in order to preserve Jerusalem's status as the central sanctuary. Thus, Josh. 24 could be assigned to JE, and vs.27 specifically betrayed the character of E. Wellhausen's source-critical treatment of Josh. 24 is cursory,[31] but from this final chapter of the Hexateuch he draws important conclusions for the reconstruction of the E source. He suggested that it provides evidence for the E source's knowledge of the patriarchs, descent to Egypt, plagues, exodus through the Reed Sea, wilderness sojourn, conquest of the eastern land of the Amorites, conflict with Balak and Balaam, conquest of Jericho, defeat of twelve kings, and division of the land.[32]

As terminology typical of E he listed Elohim (vs.1, with pl. adj.

*schichte der christlichen Religion* (Die Kultur der Gegenwart, I.iv.1; Berlin, 1909), 31.

[25]J.Wellhausen, *Geschichte Israels, I.* Berlin, 1878, 371 (later editions were entitled *Prolegomena zur Geschichte Israels*; = *Prolegomena to the History of Israel* (Edinburgh, 1885).

[26]Wellhausen, *Geschichte Israels, I*, 370.

[27]Wellhausen, *Geschichte Israels, I*, 370.

[28]Wellhausen, *Geschichte Israels, I*, 371.

[29]Wellhausen, *Geschichte Israels, I*, 371.

[30]Wellhausen, *Geschichte Israels, I*, 371.

[31]Wellhausen *Composition*, 133f.

[32]Wellhausen, *Composition*, 133f.

in vs.19; cf. Gen. 20:13), "Götter der Fremde" (vss.20,23), sword and bow (vs.12, cf. Gen. 48:22), and Amorites as a general designation for early inhabitants of Palestine. As thematic evidence of E, Wellhausen appeals to the role of Shechem (cf. Gen. 35:4), Joshua as a second Moses, Aaron's accompaniment of Moses just as Eleazar is associated with Joshua (vss.5,33), interest in Joseph's bones (vs.32, cf. Gen. 50:24f.), patriarchal worship of other gods (vs.14, cf. Gen. 25:2-4 [sic][33]), stress upon the uniqueness (*Einzigartigkeit*) of Israel's religion, and the presence of the massebah in the temple at Shechem. Later glosses, whether Dtistic or "Jehovistic" are detected in vs.1 (*wyqr' ... wlšṭryw*, cf. 23:2), the nations in vs.11, vs.12 (*w'šlḥ ... mpnykm*), all of vs.13, various elements in vss.17-19 (e.g., *'t-kl-h'mym w* in vs.18, and vs.19b), and vs.26a.[34]

Wellhausen thought that Amos and Elijah were instrumental in the formulation of a conception of covenant which placed greater emphasis upon the conditionality of Israel's relationship with Yahweh.[35] Torah had functioned originally as a guideline within a free and natural relation between people and Yahweh, a relationship in which Yahweh acted as the liberating helper of his people; but within the conditional covenant, law became the standard of obedience which determined their relationship more legalistically as parties of a covenant treaty.[36] Law as *Wegzeigens* shifted to treaty law. Historical experiences such as the Syrian and Assyrian threats, and the Babylonian exile, played crucial roles in the fostering of that conceptual shift to a definition of covenant typified essentially by the demand for Israel's strict obedience to law.[37]

In short, in Wellhausen's approach source-critical analysis and theological considerations together lead to the conclusion that Josh. 24 derived essentially from an original E document, but in a complex redactional process it was considerably reshaped, especially via Dtistic utilization of JE material.

[33]Error for 35:2-4?

[34]Wellhausen, *Composition*, 133f. His conclusion regarding this chapter's later redaction is also implicit in a passing remark regarding the "jehovistischen Zusammenhänge," i.e., JE, of 24:29 (200).

[35]J.Wellhausen, *Prolegomena zur Geschichte Israels*, 5th ed. (Berlin, 1899), 423.

[36]Wellhausen, *Prolegomena zur Geschichte*, 423.

[37]Wellhausen, *Prolegomena zur Geschichte*, 423f.

### 1.3.2 A.Kuenen

A.Kuenen stated that he originally accepted Graf's view that Deut. 27 in its entirety was inserted into its present position somewhat later than the surrounding material; but in 1878, upon closer study of the passage in connection with Josh. 8:30-35 and Deut. 11:29f., he revised his position.[38] Kuenen thought that the relationship between Josh. 8:30-35, Deut. 27, and 11:29f. provides a glance into the workroom where the present form of the Hexateuch was composed, thereby contributing essential clues pertaining to the methodology of the redactors there at work.[39] The significance placed by Kuenen upon Josh. 8:30-35 and its relationship to Josh. 24 as well as other texts related to Shechem, and the subsequent conclusions he thereby reached regarding the composition of Joshua and the Pentateuch in general, entails that his study of these passages warrants our consideration.

Kuenen split Deut. 27 into four parts, namely vss.1-8, 9f., 11-13, 14-26.[40] With respect to vss.1-8, he noted that vss.5-7, recounting the instruction to build an altar, at first glance seem to have nothing in common with the plastered stones on Mt. Ebal.[41] But upon closer inspection it is inextricably connected to vs.4 via the adverb *šm*, which in his opinion could only refer to Ebal. Kuenen concluded that vss.1-8 came from the same hand, but vss.5-7 incorporate an ancient tradition regarding altar building, as is attested in comparison with Ex. 20:25.[42] Vss.9f., in his judgment, do not connect well with either the antecedent or subsequent verses of Deut. 27, but they do fit well with Deut. 26 and 28. He accordingly asserts that they are older than 27:1-8, 11-13, 14-26, all of which are judged to have been inserted into the text at some point subsequent to the presence of 27:9f. as part of

[38] A.Kuenen, "Bijdragen tot de critiek van Pentateuch en Jozua: V. De godsdienstige vergadering by Ebal en Gerizim (Deut. XI:29,30; XXVII; Joz. VIII:30-35)," *ThT* 12 (1878) 298; *De godsdienst van Israël*, 2 vols. (Haarlem, 1869, 1870), 1:424.

[39] "Bovendien doet zij ons, zoo ik mij niet bedrieg, een blik slaan in de werkplaatsen, waaruit de Hexateuch in zijn tegenwoordigen vorm is te voorschijn gekomen, en in de motieven en de methode van hen, die daar arbeiden" ("Bijdragen tot de critiek," 298).

[40] Kuenen, "Bijdragen tot de critiek," 298; *Historisch-critisch onderzoek naar het ontstaan en de verzameling van de boeken des ouden verbonds, I*, 2nd ed. (Leiden, 1885), 123.

[41] Kuenen, "Bijdragen tot de critiek," 330.

[42] Kuenen, "Bijdragen tot de critiek," 300.

the original corpus of Deuteronomy.[43]

He maintains that the assignment of the six tribes to speak the curses on Mt. Ebal (vs.13), the same mount upon which the altar is to be constructed (vss.4-7), is unthinkable in view of the promise in Ex. 20:24f. where the altar law is associated with Yahweh's promise to bless Israel in the place where he chooses to reveal his name. Kuenen therefore asserts that Deut. 27:1-8 which incorporates the ancient altar law, and Deut. 27:11-13, must be from different hands.[44] The author of 27:11-13 had available to him both 27:1-8 and 11:29f., but he misunderstood the phrase *ntn ... ʿl* of 11:29, which according to Kuenen originally meant to place a curse or a blessing upon the mountains themselves.[45] Finally, despite the then prevalent consensus, he judged that vss.14-26 could not possibly belong originally to vss.11-13. His conclusion was based on the fact that vss.1-13 speaks of blessing and cursing, while vss.14-26 mentions only cursing; in vvs.11-13 six tribes bless and six tribes curse, while in vss.14-26 all the people stand opposite the Levites who utter the curse, and the people answer with the "Amen." In vs.12 Levi is included with the tribes who bless, but here they are the only group that speaks the curse.[46]

This detailed analysis of Deut. 27 is of importance for our present study because Kuenen concludes from it that the final redactor of Josh. 8:30-35 did not know Deut. 27:14-26.[47] This conclusion is especially founded upon an alleged contradiction of the actions of the Levites in Josh. 8:33 as compared to Deut. 27:14ff. Furthermore, Kuenen asserts that Josh. 8:30-32, 34 (except *hbrkh whqllh*), 35, was written by a Dtistic redactor who had available to him Deut. 27:1-8.[48] The reason for declaring vs.33 plus *hbrkh whqllh* to be a later interpolation is an alleged inconsistency between this phrase of "the blessing and the curse" and the preceding clause *ʾt-kl-dbry htwrh* for which it now stands inappropriately as an explication.[49] Kuenen reasoned that if the phrase *hbrkh whqllh* is from a later hand, vs.33 must be viewed as a contemporaneous interpolation by the same

[43]Kuenen, "Bijdragen tot de critiek," 301-304.

[44]Kuenen, "Bijdragen tot de critiek," 304-306.

[45]Kuenen, "Bijdragen tot de critiek," 309-315.

[46]Kuenen, "Bijdragen tot de critiek," 306; *Historisch-critisch onderzoek*, 1:123.

[47]Kuenen, "Bijdragen tot de critiek," 307; *Historisch-critisch onderzoek*, 1:15, 262, 263.

[48]Kuenen, "Bijdragen tot de critiek," 322f.; *Historisch-critisch onderzoek*, 1:134f.

[49]Kuenen, "Bijdragen tot de critiek," 318f.

author.

The localization of the events narrated in Josh. 8:30-35, which now stands rather artificially in the historical traditions of the book of Joshua,[50] was associated with Ebal and Gerizim because of older traditions associated with that locality, inter alia the pre-Dtistic account of Joshua's farewell (ch. 24).[51] Josh. 8:33 plus the phrase *hbrkh whqllh* of vs.34 was added to this passage after the insertion of Deut. 27:11-13.[52] This expansion was necessary in order to show the conformity of the actions in Josh. 8:30-35 with the now expanded prescription of all the laws in Deut. 27:1-13.

Kuenen's view of the literary connections between Deut. 11:29f.; 27 and Josh. 8:30-35 has been delineated at some length here because his study provides a clear example of the literary problems involved in the study of these texts. It will be seen in subsequent summaries of other scholars, especially Sellin, Simpson and Eissfeldt, that they too with their respective approaches stand in a long tradition of scholars grappling with the position of Josh. 8:30-35 in connection with these texts from Deuteronomy on the one side and Josh. 24 on the other. These scholars shared the common conviction that Deut. 11:29-32; 27:1-26; Josh. 8:30-35; 24:1-28 constitute crucial texts for understanding the composition of the Hexateuch. Why are these texts which focus on cultic activity in the area of Shechem permitted to play such a conspicuous place in the literary corpus which is alleged to have had as its *raison d'être* an apologetic for the centralization of the cultus in Jerusalem?

Kuenen viewed Josh. 24 as essentially a pre-Dtistic document collected by a priestly redactor, to whom he assigned the designation P2.[53] In agreement with Wellhausen and J.Hollenberg he stated that 24:1-27 is certainly not of Dtistic origin.[54] A major portion of it must be assigned to E, as is proven by reference to the con-

[50]"Bijdragen tot de critiek," 315: "De tocht van gansch Israël naar den Ebal en den Gerizim is bovendien in dit verband zoo te eenenmale misplaatst, dat hij wel moet geacht worden daarheen verdwaald te zijn," cf. also *Historisch-critisch onderzoek*, 1:48.

[51]Kuenen, "Bijdragen tot de critiek," 312.

[52]Kuenen, "Bijdragen tot de critiek," 323; *Historisch-critisch onderzoek*, 1:135.

[53]Kuenen, "Bijdragen tot de critiek," 312; *Historisch-critisch onderzoek*, 1:104 n. 51; 329.

[54]Kuenen, *Historisch-critisch onderzoek*, 1:134, 223; cf. "Bijdragen tot de critiek," 312.

quest of the land.[55] But vss.1,13,31 are Dtistic additions.[56] Furthermore, certain phrases betray typically Dtistic terminology, e.g., *'lhym 'ḥrym* (vss.2,16); *yhwh 'lhy yśr'l* (vss.2,23); *yrš* (vs.4); *ymym rbym* (vs.7); *šmd* in the Hiph. form (vs.8); *mbyt 'bdym* (vs.17); *wbqwlw nšm'* (vs.24).[57]

### 1.3.3 J.J.P.Valeton

A series of three articles by Utrecht professor J.J.P.Valeton in 1892-1893[58] heightened discussion concerning the precise definition of *bryt* in various parts of the OT, and played a significant role in subsequent discussions of *bryt*, especially in Germany.

His article regarding *bryt* in J, in Dtistic texts of the Hexateuch, and in related historical books, devoted particular attention to occurrences where *bryt* is used with the verb *krt*, as in Josh. 24:25.[59] Valeton divided these texts into three main categories. 1) Covenants between two equal parties. 2) Covenants in which a more powerful party apparently takes primary initiative in establishment of the covenant relationship. Valeton noted that here the prepositions *'m* or *'t* are usually employed.[60] 3) Covenants employing the formula *krt bryt l*, which are similar to the second category but go a step further by clearly protraying that the covenant is for the benefit of the second party.

Valeton noted that Josh. 24:25 and 2 Kgs 11:4 are anomalous within his categorization because both employ the structure *krt bryt l*, but the contexts suggest a meaning closer to the second category where the prepositions *'m* and *'t* are utilized. Without attempting a

[55]Kuenen, *Historisch-critisch onderzoek*, 1:139.

[56]Kuenen, *Historisch-critisch onderzoek*, 1:129; note that the original reading on page 129 also includes vs.9, but this is emended in the list of corrections on page 553.

[57]Kuenen, *Historisch-critisch onderzoek*, 1:130f. n.26; cf. his list of "voornaamste uitdrukkingen en wendingen" found in Deut. 12-26, and beyond that found almost exclusively in Dtistic material (109-111, 114-116, 119f., 130f.), by which he determines what is and what is not "deuteronomistische spraakgebruik" (109).

[58]J.J.P.Valeton, "Bedeutung und Stellung des Wortes *bryt* im Priestercodex," *ZAW* 12 (1892) 1-22; "Das Wort *bryt* in den jehovistischen und deuteronomischen Stücken des Hexateuchs, sowie in den verwandten historischen Büchern," *ZAW* 12 (1892) 224-260; "Das Wort *bryt* bei den Propheten und in den Ketubim –Resultat," *ZAW* 13 (1893) 245-279.

[59]Valeton, "Das Wort *bryt*," 1892, 225.

[60]Valeton, "Das Wort *bryt*," 1892, 228.

detailed analysis of Josh. 24:25 or 2 Kgs 11:4, Valeton concluded that it was not possible to find here two-sided covenants but rather obligations being placed upon one party via Yahweh's representative.[61]

Valeton's contribution to the discussion of *bryt* was influential.[62] For the study of Josh. 24 his evaluation is particularly relevant in the following areas:

1) He provided an initial overview of various lexical, contextual and theological meanings of *bryt* in diverse categories of OT literature.
2) He stimulated discussion of the diversity of relationships extant between various parties engaged in covenants, e.g., two equal parties, unequal parties with initiative of the stronger party, or unequal parties with particular benefit for the weaker.
3) His employment of terms such as *Verpflichtungen*[63] and *Verfügung*[64] reflected his skepticism about the validity of considereing *bryt* to be essentially a *Bund* between Yahweh and Israel. In numerous contexts he denied that covenant was essentially a two-sided contract between God and man.[65] Nevertheless, he did not hesitate to speak of covenant as *Verheissung* for man and *Verbindung* for God.[66]

### 1.3.4 R.Kraetzschmar

R.Kraetzschmar's work[67] provides additional evidence of early discussion of an issue raised repeatedly regarding Josh. 24:25, namely, whether the covenant here described is between Yahweh and Israel with Joshua as mediator, or between Joshua and Israel. This question is indicative of the overarching concern prompting the division of Kraetzschmar's entire book into two sections, "Der Bund auf pro-

[61]Valeton, "Das Wort *bryt*," 1892, 231f.

[62]It is noteworthy that Wellhausen's *Geschichte Israels, I* (1878, 434) appeals to an article by Valeton of the same year in *Groninger Studien*, 143-164, with respect to the relationship of covenant and early prophets. The tribute to Valeton disappeared from later editions of Wellhausen's *Prolegomena* while his perspective remained constant.

[63]Valeton, "*bryt* im Priestercodex," 4f. These questions are taken up later by Begrich, Jepsen, and especially Kutsch, followed by Perlitt; see the discussion of these scholars in 1.6.

[64]Valeton, "*bryt* im Priestercodex," 6.

[65]Valeton, "*bryt* im Priestercodx," 13, 22; "Das Wort *bryt*," 1892, 227.

[66]Valeton, "*bryt* im Priestercodex," 6.

[67]R.Kraetzschmar, *Die Bundesvorstellung im Alten Testament in ihrer geschichtlichen Entwicklung untersucht und dargestellt* (Marburg, 1896).

fanem Gebiete" and "Die Bundesvorstellung auf religiosem Gebiete." He is careful, however, to stress that this is not an absolute distinction; so-called *secular* covenants are permeated with religious implications but they are typified primarily by a horizontal relationship between the agreeing parties rather than a covenant extended to man by Yahweh.[68]

Kraetzschmar noted that while previous consensus inclined to see a covenant between Yahweh and people recorded in Josh. 24,[69] current opinion tended to view it as a covenant between Joshua and the people in service of Yahweh.[70] In the light of present discussion regarding the meaning of *bryt*, Kraetzschmar's conclusions here are important. He too uses the term *bryt Verpflichtungen.*[71] These obligations are placed on the people by Joshua; they do not arise from him personally but from Yahweh. Consequently, it is not proper to speak of *either* a covenant beteen Yahweh and Israel *or* between Joshua and Israel.

> "Die Berith ist vielmehr die feierliche Form, durch die Josua das Volk auf ein Gelöbnis religiösen Inhaltes derart verpflichtet, dass es unter keinen Umständen wieder zurüch kann, ohne sich der schwersten Strafe auszusetzen."[72]

In agreement with Wellhausen and many others, Kraetzschmar stated, "Jos. 24 ist, abgesehen von redaktionellen Zuthaten, zweifellos aus dem elohistischen Kreise hervorgegangen."[73] But there is also an undeniable similarity between the ceremony narrated in Josh. 24 and that of 2 Kgs 23:3. Kraetzschmar argued, contra Wellhausen, that the Josianic covenant concept marked an unprecedented view of law in Israel and that it was not based upon a broader previous background of treaty relations.[74] In the time of Josiah law was first given its character of comprehensive, canonical validity in Israel.[75] Yet, with respect to the dating of Josh. 24 he concluded that this account could

[68]Kraetzschmar, *Die Bundesvorstellung*, 33ff.
[69]Kraetzschmar, *Die Bundesvorstellung*, 33.
[70]Kraetzschmar, *Die Bundesvorstellung*, 34.
[71]Kraetzschmar, *Die Bundesvorstellung*, 34.
[72]Kraetzschmar, *Die Bundesvorstellung*, 34.
[73]Kraetzschmar, *Die Bundesvorstellung*, 33.
[74]Kraetzschmar, *Die Bundesvorstellung*, 37.
[75]Kraetzschmar, *Die Bundesvorstellung*, 37.

hardly be viewed as a retrojection of the Josianic covenant.[76] Note too his conclusion regarding the relationship of 2 Kgs 11:17 to 23:3. "Sagt man sonst, dass grosse Ereignisse ihre Schatten vorauszuwerfen pflegen, so gilt hier wie so manches Mal im Alten Testamente das Umgekehrte; Beweis dafür ist 2 Kg. 11:17."[77]

### 1.3.5 P.Karge

P.Karge's discussion of covenant[78] betrays many points of agreement with the previous studies by Kraetzschmar and Valeton, and it is not our intention to repeat these aspects.[79] It is worthwhile, however, to note his summary of the general consensus which at that time was emerging with respect to the definition of *bryt*. Karge stated that two approaches were defended. The first and major position saw *bryt* as a treaty relationship (*Vertragsverhältnis*) between two parties of equal status, or in some cases with a superior party condescending to the level of the inferior, to establish a covenant (*Bund*) consisting of mutual responsiblities and rights (*Pflichten und Rechten*).[80] Secondarily, the covenant entails regulatory stipulations and laws (*regelnden Pflichten und Gesetze*) and accordingly it attained the meaning of legal stipulations (*Bestimmung, Gesetz*).[81]

The second, minority opinion reversed the order. The fundamental meaning of covenant was identifiable in the stipulations, which led only secondarily to the meaning of covenant (*Bund*) or treaty (*Vertrag*). Whatever the case, concluded Karge, the word *bryt* entailed

[76]Kraetzschmar, *Die Bundesvorstellung*, 37: "...bezüglich Jos. 24 sei bemerkt, dass der darin geschilderte Berithschluss wohl kaum als Zurückdatierung des josianischen aufzufassen ist."

[77]Kraetzschmar, *Die Bundesvorstellung*, 37.

[78]P.Karge, *Geschichte des Bundesgedankens im Alten Testament* (Münster, 1910).

[79]However, Karge went a step further than Kraetzschmar and Valeton when he asserted that Josh. 24 describes a covenant between Joshua and the people, not between Yahweh and the people. See his *Geschichte des Bundesgedankens*, 232, 252; cf. Kraetzschmar, *Die Bundesvorstellung*, 34, and Valeton, "Das Wort *bryt*," 1892, 231f.

[80]Karge, *Geschichte des Bundesgedankens*, 226. He emphasized repeatedly that such a *bryt* relationship was established via the media of various cultic rituals, e.g., blood ceremonies, sacrificial covenant meals, oath ceremonies, salt covenants (225, 235-246).

[81]Karge, *Geschichte des Bundesgedankens*, 226.

both the concept of *Bund* and *Bestimmung*.[82] The significance of the controversy summarized here in its seminal state cannot be fully appreciated until one views the recent works of Kutsch and Perlitt[83] where discussion of the meaning of *bryt* as "relationship" or "obligation" is once again tabled vigorously.

### 1.3.6 E.Sellin

A detailed theory of the relationship between Josh. 8:30-35 and 24 was presented by Sellin. Fundamental to his hypothesis are two basic considerations, namely, literary analysis of Josh. 1-11; 24 and the geographical location of Gilgal.[84] In accordance with the prevalent view, Josh. 1-11 and 24 were judged to be Elohistic.[85] Chs.1-11 in their present form have been shaped by Dtistic redaction. More important, however, is the fact that already previously in the Elohistic stage an older ($E^1$) and a younger ($E^2$) textual level may be identified.[86] Significantly, the older Elohistic level described the crossing of the Jordan not by Jericho but farther north, with Israel proceeding immediately to a Gilgal which was located near Shechem.[87] In $E^1$ this Gilgal was the setting of the circumcision and passover (Josh. 5:2-12), and the erection of an altar on Gerizim,[88] along with its accompanying covenantal ceremony (8:30ff.).[89] It was that Gilgal by Shechem which was the homebase for the conquest tradition;[90] Josh. 8:30-35 and 24 are descriptions of the same event,[91] which is an interesting conclusion in view of Sellin's contention that such a ceremony was held periodically at Shechem.

[82]Karge, *Geschichte des Bundesgedankens*, 227.

[83]See sections 1.6.4 and 1.6.5.

[84]See his *Gilgal: Ein Beitrag zur Geschichte der Einwanderung Israels in Palästina* (Leipzig, 1917), 1-60, and *Geschichte des Israelitisch-jüdischen Volkes*, 2 vols. (Leipzig, 1924–1932), 1:28, 96f.

[85]Sellin, *Gilgal*, 29.

[86]Sellin, *Gilgal*, 29f. Originally Sellin denied the presence of J, but in 1924 he reversed his opinion (*Geschichte*, 1:96). This did not affect the fundamental outline of his theory.

[87]Sellin, *Gilgal*, 32ff.

[88]Later changed to Ebal in anti-Samaritan interests (*Gilgal*, 26).

[89]Sellin, *Gilgal*, 38; *Geschichte*, 1:96f.: "Der kern von 8,30ff. schloss in der mündlichen Überlieferung einmal unmittelbar an 5,15 an."

[90]Sellin, *Gilgal*, 46.

[91]Sellin, *Gilgal*, 50-53; *Geschichte*, 1:98: Josh. 24 is "von Hause aus mit dem Kern von 8,30-35 eng zusammengehörend."

The cultic festival at Shechem was the avenue by which Yahweh, the covenant God experienced by only a small minority of Israelites in the wilderness, was identified with the local El gods of the land, and thus became the God of all Israel.[92] Undoubtedly, in the ensuing era a Shechem sanctuary was the site of a periodically held covenant festival fundamental to the coalition of the tribes.[93] In conclusion, with C.Steuernagel may be affirmed that the designation "Jahwe, der Gott Israels," later to become so important for Jerusalem, was first founded in Shechem.[94]

### 1.3.7 J.Pedersen

Pedersen's view of covenant is found in a couple of works which have since become classics.[95] In Pedersen's later writing the essence of covenant relations was explicitly attributed to inner psychic needs of the "soul" seeking *shalom*.[96] Covenant signifies primarily a striving for community, and it had a formative influence in the constitution

[92]Sellin, *Geschichte*, 1:98f.

[93]Sellin, *Geschichte*, 1:101: "Endlich hat zweifellos in der Folgezeit ein periodisch wiederkehrendes Bundesfest bei Sichem stattgefunden, in dem immer der Treuschwur der Stämmekoalition dem neuen Gotte und seinem Willen erneuert wurde, das auf eine Begründung in der Ära Josuas zurückweist vgl. Deut. 11,29f.; 27,12-26. Es is ganz ausgeschlossen, dass hier eine spätere deuteronomische Konstruktion vorliegt, denn die Väter dieser wären die letzten gewesen, die Sichem als ein Heiligtum von überragender Bedeutung anerkannt und den Altar auf dem Garizim auf Mose und Josua zurückgeführt hätten." See too his "Seit welcher Zeit verehrten die nordisraelitischen Stämme Jahwe?" in C.Adler–A.Ember, eds., *Oriental Studies Published in Commemoration of the Fortieth Anniversary (1883-1923) of Paul Haupt as Director of the Oriental Seminary of the Johns Hopkins University* (Baltimore, 1926), 124-134, esp. 126f.

[94]Sellin, *Geschichte*, 1:101. See too C.Steuernagel, *Jahwe und die Vätergötter* (Stuttgart, 1935).

[95]Best known is of course his *Israel: Its Life and Culture*, (London, I-II, 1926; III-IV, 1940). Also important for the particular question of covenant is his detailed comparative study of oath in his *Der Eid bei den Semiten in seinem Verhältnis zu verwandten Erscheinungen sowie die Stellung des Eides im Islam* (Strassburg, 1914). This technical analysis provided the groundwork for his subsequent observations regarding the role of covenant and oath in Israel's history and societal organization.

[96]See especially *Israel, I-II*, 263-310. He speaks of covenant as "union of souls," (287). And further, "The people with whom one made peace and covenant entered into a psychic community with the other party of the covenant" (291). And "once the covenant is made, no limit can be fixed for the exchange of the substance of souls" (291).

of the tribes of Israel.[97] Josh. 24 was interpreted by Pedersen as essentially a covenant between Joshua and the people.[98] Mainly on the grammatical structure of vs.25,[99] he concluded that Joshua's action in establishing the covenant was not that of a mediator but of a covenant partner.[100] Joshua's leadership position was adduced as proof of a previously existing covenant between him and the people; the ceremony in Josh. 24 constituted a reinforcement of that relationship.[101] However, Pedersen suggested elsewhere that the stone of 24:27 denoted a compact with God.[102]

Pedersen posited a possible connection between events at Shechem as related in Josh. 8:30-35; 24:1-28; Deut. 27, and pre-immigration cultic feasts later modified as common assemblies of local groups to renew covenant relations solidifying the idea of a united Israel.[103] He warned, however, that the importance attributed to Shechem in Josh. 24 may have stemmed from conditions which actually developed in the monarchical period.[104] His concern with the role of Shechem is indicative that Pedersen was not content to restrict questions of covenant to analysis of the meaning of *bryt*; equally significant in his estimation were questions pertaining to the traditio-historical transmission of narrative accounts, some of which were based on historical antecedents while other aspects were fictitious legend.[105] Of particular relevance is his repeated emphasis that *bryt* means a bond, compact, partnership, or the like, and that this concept is important for our understanding of Israel's early history, both with respect to relations among groups and regarding the relationship of Israel with Yahweh. Psychological and sociological aspects are given a central place in his attempt to reconstruct the period of Israel's early settlement. It is evident that Pedersen's view of unity among the tribes, as fostered by

[97]Pedersen, *Israel, I-II*, 31, 288.

[98]Pedersen, *Israel, I-II*, 360f.; *III-IV*, 76f.

[99]Especially *krt l* rather than *krt byn*.

[100]2 Kgs 11:17 was taken as the paradigm of a mediatorial designation (*Der Eid*, 61).

[101]Pedersen, *Israel, I-II*, 307.

[102]Pedersen, *Israel, I-II*, 169.

[103]Pedersen, *Israel, III-IV*, 85.

[104]Pedersen, *Israel, III-IV*, 85, 382. In Pedersen's opinion, a key factor in this respect was the question of whether the Ark of the Covenant was ever actually at Shechem.

[105]With respect to patriarchal traditions he speaks of legends "intermixed with fairy tales" (*Israel, I-II*, 14).

cultic, covenantal gatherings at local sanctuaries such as Shechem, has affinities to the views later elaborated in Noth's amphictyony thesis.

### 1.3.8 O.Eissfeldt

The source-critical analysis offered by Eissfeldt already in 1922[106] deserves careful attention for numerous reasons. As mentioned above, the initial views of Noth with respect to the literary composition of Josh. 24 were in fundamental agreement with the source-critical conclusions attained by Smend and Eissfeldt.[107] To the extent that Eissfeldt viewed the framework of Josh. 24 as part of E, his position typified the majority view at that time. More unique to his position, however, was his attribution of a significant percentage of the passage to L,[108] a source for which he found evidence in portions of vss.2,4,5,6,7,9,11,17,18,25,26,27. Comparison with similar terminology in the Pentateuch, along with an alleged duplicity of content in the present verses, constituted the most frequent rationale for these designations.[109] Josh. 24:22-27 was particularly important for his recognition of J, thereby distinguishing three sources for the passage.[110] He argued that mention of "witnesses" in vs.22 is clearly part of the E source narrated there. By contrast vs.27 has a stone as witness and must therefore belong to a different source. But the concept of "witness" is in fact mentioned twice in vs.27, which suggests that there must be parallel sources here. Accordingly, in vs.27a where the stone "hears" the words, Eissfeldt reasoned that this function of the stone betrays the antiquity of the narrative and provides good reason for attributing it to L. Repetition of the stone as witness (vs.27b) may then be attributed to J since vs.22 was already attributed to E, while P and D were not considered possible as candidates. And, since L seems to be prevalent as a source in vss.22-27, Eissfeldt thought it would be logical to see the same secondary source in parts of vss.2-19.

[106]Eissfeldt, *Hexateuch-Synopse*, esp. 72, 79-83, 219-220, 248-250, 281, 284.
[107]See section 1.2.
[108]Eissfeldt appealed to L (= "Laienquelle") as an older source containing certain material ordinarily treated by other scholars as simply part of the J document (*Hexateuch-Synopse*, xif.).
[109]Eissfeldt, *Hexateuch-Synopse*, 79-82.
[110]Eissfeldt, *Hexateuch-Synopse*, 80f.; "Deuteronomium und Hexateuch," *MIO* 12 (1966) 17-39, esp. 27 (= *Kleine Schriften*, vol. 4, edit. R.Sellheim und F.Maass [Tübingen, 1968], 238-258).

Consequently, the L source which had disappeared in Joshua after chs.6-7 makes a strong reappearance in the final chapter. Therefore, in Eissfeldt's opinion Josh. 24 provided some of the most compelling arguments for his proposal of an L source in Joshua, which in turn had crucial ramifications for his stance in the Pentateuch-Hexateuch debate. Another of Eissfeldt's recurring interests with respect to Josh. 24 was the bearing it has upon the question of the relationship of Yahweh to the patriarchal Gods.[111]

Eissfeldt also attributed great literary-critical significance to Josh. 8:30-35.[112] He repeatedly emphasized that this passage could only be understood in terms of a complex textual history. The presence of at least two layers of redaction in Josh. 8:30-35 betrays attempts to correlate extraneous material with the ancient traditions of the pre-Dtic Hexateuch narrative.[113] He argued that the initial account of the altar's construction is found in Josh. 8:30-31, and it may be attributed along with Deut. 27:4-7 to the hand of a mid-8th century redactor who wished to link the laws contained in the Book of the Covenant to the pre-Dtic Hexateuch.[114] A second redactor, about two hundred

[111]E.g., his "El and Yahweh" *JSS* 1 (1956) 25-37, esp. 31, 36; "Jahwe, der Gott der Väter," *ThLZ* 88 (1963) 481-490, esp. 484, 487; "Jakobs Begegnung mit El und Moses Begegnung mit Jahwe," *OLZ* 58 (1963) 325-331, esp. 330; "Der Kanaanäischen El als Geber der den Israelitischen Erzvätern Geltenden Nachkommenschaft- und Landbesitzverheissungen," *Studia Orientalia im memoriam Caroli Brockelmann. WZUH* 17 (1968) 45-53.

[112]Eissfeldt, *Hexateuch-Synopse*, 291: "Das Stück, mit dem Deut 27,1-8 zusammenhängt, gehört zu den umstrittensten Abschnitten des A.T. Mit Recht. Sellins 'Gilgal' von 1917 zeigt, welch weittragende Folgen für die Auffassung der ganzen Erzählung des Josua-Buches und des Hexateuch überhaupt ein bestimmtes Verständnis des Abschnittes nach sich zieht."

[113]Eissfeldt, *Hexateuch-Synopse*, 72, 281; "Die Älteste Erzählung vom Sinaibund," *ZAW* 73 (1961) 137; "Deuteronomium und Hexateuch," 24; *Einleitung in das Alte Testament*, 3rd ed. (Tübingen, 1964), 287-290 (= *The Old Testament: An Introduction*, 216-218); "Gilgal or Shechem?", in J.I.Durham–J.R.Porter, eds., *Proclamation and Presence: Old Testament Essays in Honour of G.H.Davies* (London, 1970), 90-101. Thus, the conclusions published already in 1922 are defended in writings by Eissfeldt spanning half a century!

[114]Eissfeldt, "Gilgal or Shechem?" 98. He suggested that the altar law in Ex. 20:24-26 was strategically placed at the beginning of the Book of the Covenant. Moreover, it is precisely via the connection between this opening law and the tradition of Deut. 27:4-7 and Josh. 8:30-31 that the Book of the Covenant is provided a place in the pre-Dtic narrative. Cf. 100 n.8: "Just as the Book of the Covenant is introduced by a statement concerning the altar, so also Deuteronomy (Deut. 12) and the Holiness Code (Lev. 17) begin with a similar injunction. The altar

years later,[115] reworked Josh. 8:30-35 and Deut. 27:5-7 in order to interpolate the present book of Deuteronomy into the Pentateuchal narrative.[116] Thus, while the first redactor was motivated by a desire to provide a place for the Book of the Covenant, the second redactor wished to accomodate the entire book of Deuteronomy into the pentateuchal tradition, which explains the expanded emphasis upon Mosaic law in Josh. 8:30-35, as well as the diversity of meaning with respect to the altar, the stone monument, the proclamation of law, and the curses and blessings.

A comparison of Eissfeldt's view of Josh. 8:30-35 with the opinion of Sellin shows notable similarity and disparity. Sellin attributed the passage to E, a judgement which Eissfeldt considered to be not without merit, but finally inferior to the redactor/interpolator theory of Smend.[117] In agreement with Sellin, he stated the impossibility of a full-fledged Dtist narrating an event of this nature in which an altar is built on Mt. Ebal.[118] And he too advanced a theory in which the events of Josh. 8:30-35 were originally connected with Gilgal, but he explained the connection as a mixing of traditions, thereby obviating the need to locate a Gilgal near Shechem.[119] In this view the emphasis upon Shechem is transferred from Deut. 11:29-32; 27:11-13, which demonstrates an ancient tradition of the proclamation of blessings and curses at Mt. Gerizim and Mt. Ebal.[120]

### 1.3.9 W.Rudolph

W.Rudolph's interpretation of Josh. 24:1-28 was consistent with his major premise regarding the entire Hexateuch; he denied the presence of E as an independent source and he concomittantly asserted the

command therefore sometimes represents the whole Law."

[115]Eissfeldt, "Gilgal or Shechem?" 98.

[116]Eissfeldt, *Einleitung*, 288f.; *An Introduction*, 217.

[117]Eissfeldt, *Hexateuch-Synopse*, 281. The main reason for rejecting Sellin's assertion that Josh. 8:30-35 belongs to E was based on a literary-critical analysis of the Book of the Covenant, which produced the conclusion that the corpus of laws now incorporated in Exodus was originally independent from E, or for that matter, from any of the other sources in the Pentateuch. The close literary connection noted between Josh. 8:30-35 and the Book of the Covenant led to the assumption that these verses could not be from E. Cf. 1.3.10 re Simpson's views.

[118]For Sellin's theory of a Gilgal in the neighborhood of Shechem see 1.3.6.

[119]Eissfeldt, "Gilgal or Shechem?" 90-101.

[120]Eissfeldt, *Einleitung*, 288; *An Introduction*, 217; "Gilgal or Shechem?" 96.

primacy of a Yahwistic narration supplemented by glosses, whether Dtistic or otherwise, accompanied by material from a later P source or redactor. This thesis was introduced previously in a work begun by P.Volz and completed in a less radical manner by Rudolph.[121] Accordingly, by the time he reached Josh. 24 Rudolph's arguments for seeing only J as a true source, supplemented by later glosses,[122] were based almost exclusively upon refuting the need to see E as an independent source. Since vs.26a was dropped as a gloss, he argued that with respect to divine names he had only to explain the presence of *h'lhym* in vs.1, which he dismissed as a stereotypical phrase irrelevant for source distinction.[123] As confirmation of this conclusion, Rudolph appealed to the fact that the same place mentioned in vs.1 as being *lpny h'lhym* is referred to later as *bmqdš yhwh*.

Advocates of E had appealed to the similarity of Josh. 24 to Gen. 33:18-20, 35:1ff., but these arguments were dismissed on the grounds that Gen. 33:20 had also been analyzed by Volz and Rudolph as belonging to J, and Gen. 35:1ff. was dependent upon Josh. 24 rather than vice versa.[124] The designation of the previous inhabitants of Canaan as Amorites was passed over without further comment.[125] For the rest, Rudolph asserted that the supposedly duplicate material could all be explained as glosses or explanatory expansions rather than as evidence for a parallel E source.

### 1.3.10 C.A.Simpson

Texts focusing on Shechem played a formative role in C.A.Simpson's traditio-historical analysis of the covenant concept in the OT. In his opinion it was possible to distinguish $J^1$, $J^2$ and E as distinct textual strands. $J^1$ was attributed to a southern, Kadesh tradition and focused upon Moses and Sinai,[126] but did not know of a covenant be-

[121]P.Volz–W.Rudolph, *Der Elohist als Erzähler. Ein Irrweg der Pentateuchkritik?* (Giessen, 1933).

[122]As glosses he identifies vss.1bA, 2aD, 5aA, 6aA,b, 7a (*wykshw*), 10a, 12b, 17a (*w't-'bwtynw* and *mbyt 'bdym*), 17bA, 18a *'l-kl-h'mym w*, 19-21, 22b, 26a, 27b (possibly), cf. his *Der "Elohist" von Exodus bis Josua* (Berlin, 1938), 245-248.

[123]Rudolph, *Der "Elohist"*, 249.

[124]Rudolph, *Der "Elohist"*, 249; Volz–Rudolph, *Der Elohist*, 122f., 130-134.

[125]Rudolph, *Der "Elohist"*, 249.

[126]C.A.Simpson, *Revelation and Response in the Old Testament* (New York, 1947), 95.

tween Israel and Yahweh.[127] $J^2$ represented a more northerly perspective and modified some of the stories, especially where predecessors were engaged in questionable behavior.[128] In this theory it was $J^2$ that initiated a syncretism between the $J^1$ perspective of the south and the Shechem tradition of the north.[129] Borrowing heavily from the work of E.Meyer,[130] Simpson argued that in pre-Israelite days an annual ceremony was performed at Shechem to renew a covenant between the city god *Baal-berith* and the inhabitants of Shechem.[131] $J^2$ viewed *Baal-berith* as a manifestation of Yahweh, and in syncretism with $J^1$ it localized the inauguration of the covenant at Sinai through Mosaic mediation immediately subsequent to the exodus.[132]

The E texts were attributed to yet another tradition underlying the earlier narratives.[133] Whereas the J tradition presented Hebron as the cultural and religious center of the south, E elevated Beersheba to prominence in the south and Shechem and Bethel in the north.[134] It was to E that he attributed Josh. 8:30-34; 24:1-25, texts which emphasize the fulfilment of requirements listed in Deut. 11:26-32; 27.[135] In his opinion, the original E narrative described the crossing of the Jordan at Adam, not Jericho. Immediately after the description of the crossing, the original E narrative of Josh. 8:30-34 and 24:1-25 would have presented the construction of the altar[136] at the beginning of the conquest.[137] The geographical description in Deut. 11:29f. was for Simpson a sure sign of E.[138] Subsequent redaction by a JE

[127]Simpson, *Revelation and Response*, 100.

[128]Simpson, *Revelation and Response*, 97.

[129]Simpson, *Revelation and Response*, 100f.

[130]Cf. E.Meyer, *Die Israeliten und ihre Nachbarstämme* (Halle, 1906), 542ff. See Simpson's praise of this work in his *The Early Traditions of Israel: A Critical Analysis of the Pre-deuteronomic Narrative of the Hexateuch* (Oxford, 1948), 31f.

[131]Simpson, *Revelation and Response*, 100; *Early Traditions*, 647.

[132]This syncretism was lauded by Simpson as an example of the daring way leaders kept religion related to daily life (*Revelation and Response*, 103f.).

[133]Simpson, *Early Traditions*, 34f. Simpson states that E attempted to correct what it deemed innacuracies of fact and emphasis in the J tradition, hence a plausible date would be soon after the fall of the northern kingdom, perhaps about 700 B.C.

[134]Simpson, *Early Traditions*, 35.

[135]Simpson suggests the altar was possibly made from stones removed from the bed of the Jordan, *Early Traditions*, 321, 645.

[136]Simpson, *Early Traditions*, 316-318, 645-647.

[137]Simpson, *Early Traditions*, 316, 318-319.

[138]Simpson, *Early Traditions*, 316.

redactor, in particular accomodation to J, would then account for Josh. 24's placement after the conquest.[139]

This entails for Simpson that Shechem in 24:1a is harmonizational; he suggests, "E would scarcely have had the tribes take their inheritance (cf. 18:2ff), and then be called to Shechem. 1a is a substitution for his statement that the people went up from the Jordan to Shechem."[140] In vss.2-7 multiple glosses and additions are indicated, many of which are attributed to the hand of a Dtistic redactor on the basis of terminology and the contention that they intend to make the speech a rehearsal of the mighty deeds of Yahweh.[141] Similarly, in the historical recapitulation of vss.8-13 numerous additions are credited to a JE redactor or a Dtistic redactor by virtue of comparison with accounts of the same events earlier in the Pentateuch.[142] The absence of foreign gods in the exodus and wilderness accounts convinced Simpson that Josh. 24:14f.'s emphasis to put away foreign was borrowed by E from Gen. 35:2-4.[143] The subsequent ceremony of renewal was colored by Yawhist influences; the Shechemite sanctuary and the associated practice of celebrating a covenant bond with the deity *Baal-berith* were appropriated and modified by Israel to a covenant to worship Yahweh alone.[144]

Josh. 8:30-34 in E would have originally followed upon 24:25a, but it was moved to its present position by a Dtistic redactor who associated the altar with the Gilgal stones, and thought it appropriate that the affair narrated in 8:30-34 be recorded when Joshua was in that area.[145] In the place of the material removed, which now stands at 8:30-34, the Dtistic redactor inserted 24:23, 24, 25b, 26a, thereby making the people witnesses instead of the for him inexplicable idea of a stone as witness, as originally described in E.[146]

This is only a sampling of Simpson's attempt to distinguish an original E account in Josh. 24. A similar textual analysis was made of Deut. 11:26-32; Deut. 27, and Josh. 8:30-35, always with the presup-

[139]Simpson, *Early Traditions*, 318.
[140]Simpson, *Early Traditions*, 318.
[141]Simpson, *Early Traditions*, 319.
[142]Simpson, *Early Traditions*, 319f.
[143]Simpson, *Early Traditions*, 646f.
[144]Simpson, *Early Traditions*, 647.
[145]Simpson, *Early Traditions*, 321, 400. Cf. more recently J.A.Soggin, *Joshua* (London, 1972), 220-244.
[146]Simpson, *Early Traditions*, 321.

position that this material was originally part of the same E tradition. What is striking, however, is how emaciated the E skeleton of Josh. 24 appears after the redactional flesh has been removed. Redactions are claimed in nearly every verse of 24:1-28.[147] That Simpson's extreme literary criticism was taken seriously by other scholars is attested by Eissfeldt's immediate response with an entire monograph.[148]

### 1.3.11 H.Mölle

It is appropriate to conclude this source-critical survey with a summary of the recent study by H.Mölle.[149] Advancement from the previous authors to Mölle involves a temporal jump of in most cases considerably more than fifty years.[150] This leap warrants an explanatory comment. It would be mistaken to give the impression that Mölle's approach fits generically with those works treated above, as if the intervening years were of little importance for his methodology. On the contrary, as even a survey of his index reveals, *literarkritische Analyse* is augmented by analysis of the text's form and structure (*formkritische Analyse* and *gattungkritische Analyse*), and finally by redaction criticism (*Kritik der Redaktionen*). Mölle's emphasis upon *formkritische Analyse* and *gattungskritische Analyse* produces a more systematic treatment than was previously the case when form criticism in its infantile stages was preoccupied with relating written texts to a presupposed oral tradition and a specific *Sitz im Leben*. Nevertheless, having made these qualifications regarding the influences brought upon Mölle's methodology by developments generally subsumed under the category of form-criticism, we may justifiably summarize his approach as remaining essentially source-critical.

However, while Mölle's method remains source-critical, his analysis ultimately does not produce a variety of literary sources. More

[147]Simpson's identification of redactional activity follows the German commentaries, e.g., C.Steuernagel, *Übersetzung und Erklärung der Bücher Deuteronomium und Josua, und allgemeine Einleitung in den Hexateuch* (HK; Göttingen, 1900); H.Holzinger, *Das Buch Josua* (KHC; Leipzig and Tübingen, 1901); and M.Noth, *Das Buch Josua* (HAT; Tübingen, 1938).

[148]O.Eissfeldt, *Die ältesten Traditionen Israels. Ein kritischer Bericht über C.A.Simpsons The Early Traditions of Israel* (Berlin, 1950); see esp. 87.

[149]H.Mölle, *Der sogennante Landtag zu Sichem* (Würzburg, 1980). For an earlier review, including numerous relevant criticisms, cf. R.G.Boling, *JBL* 102 (1983) 300f.

[150]A little more than thirty years in the case of Simpson.

precisely, he finds one initial source subsequently expanded in successive phases of textual redaction. He detects four phases (*Schichten*) in a supplementary hypothesis of textual development, which may be listed chronologically as follows:
**S** = original Shechem source
**E** = Elohistic redaction
**R**JE = Yahwist-Elohist redaction
**Dtr** = Dtistic redaction (with two subgroups)
The fourth phase is followed by **Z** = *Zusätze* (addenda) prior to canonization.[151] More important than this summary of his conclusions, however, is a description of his methodology in dissecting the text into strata.

The most important factors in Mölle's designation of diachronic elements may be broadly summarized under the category of alleged tensions, contradictions or unevenness in the text, which he seeks to expose via a detailed, verse by verse scrutiny.[152] A list of some of the major tensions he discerns will serve to illustrate this approach. Mölle finds clues, for example, in the appearance of various divine names.[153] Likewise, shifts of person, whether applying to God as subject, to Israel as audience, or in the designation of the speaker, provide evidence for diachronic composition in the oratory section (vss.2-15).[154] Crucial is the repeated emphasis that the progression of the discourse is frequently characterized by shifts in grammatical subject. At each successive indication of a break in the flow of the discourse he attempts to correlate the subject with a similar, preceeding line of thought, thereby allegedly producing strands of more homogeneously progressing narration, which may in turn be viewed with judicial precision as redactional phases.

Similar attention to detail is manifested in his appeal to expressions which range from synonymous, to similar, to quite disparate but related. So, for example, Mölle attempts to determine the most probable initial description of the group gathered at Shechem, whether as *kl šbty*, as *'t yśr'l*, or as *kl h'm*, and these various terms are suspected to reveal nuances which diverge sufficiently to warrant conclusions

[151]Mölle, *Der sogenannte Landtag*, 105-107, 208. The pertinent sections of the text in their respective phases are given in a German synopsis (283-289).
[152]This is the heart of the first section of his work (23-105).
[153]Mölle, *Der sogenannte Landtag*, 23.
[154]Mölle, *Der sogenannte Landtag*, 23, 27, 32, 35, 37, 39, etc.

regarding different redactional layers.[155] This methodology is applied to Josh 24:1-28 in its entirety, with the resulting strands collected under four phases or redactional stages.[156] To this point Mölle makes no overt attempt to identify authors/redactors, *Sitz im Leben*, or questions of that nature. These issues follow later as secondary steps, based upon the form-critical analysis. The impression is thus given that the various strands can be objectively determined and grouped on the basis of grammar, narrative progressions, thematic similarities, and connections amidst the diachronic disharmony of the text.

We have already listed Mölle's four resulting phases, to which may be added a summary of the major textual components in each phase. In essence it is not a simple matter to offer such a listing because Mölle's detailed dissections even segment individual words within a given subsection of a verse. For our purpose here we may ignore these finer distinctions, though the reader should be aware that the present list is not totally accurate but is meant rather to give an impression of the subsequent groupings:[157]

**Phase 1:** vss.1a, 2b,c,d, 3, 4d, 6a,c, 7c,d, 8a, 14c,d,e, 15a-h, 18b, 22, 26b,c
**Phase 2:** vss.1c, 3d, 4a-c, 12a,b, 16a-e, 17a,b,d,e, 18a,c, 19a,b, 20a-d,f, 21a-c, 23a-c, 24a,b, 25a,b, 27a,b,e,f, 28
**Phase 3:** vss.11c, 17f, 19c,e, 20e, 26d, 27c,d
**Phase 4:** vss. 1b, 4c, 5a-d, 6b, 7b,e-g, 8b-f, 9a,c-e, 10a-c, 11a,b,d, 13a-f, 14a,b, 17c, 19d, 24c, 26a

Noteworthy in this approach is an implicit confidence in one's ability to designate various textual layers on the basis of grammatical, stylistic, theological or thematic considerations as a preliminary step to the assignment of a *Sitz im Leben* for each phase of the redaction. The initial source analysis is conducted, in appearance at least, independent of the subsequent literary-critical and form-critical steps of assigning each redactional phase to a setting, possible author(s) and date.[158]

[155]Mölle, *Der sogenannte Landtag*, 24-27.
[156]Mölle, *Der sogenannte Landtag*, 105-107.
[157]Mölle, *Der sogenannte Landtag*, 105f.
[158]Mölle concludes that the Shechemite source originates from approximately 1200-1100 B.C., phase 2 (E) was from immediately prior to the overthrow of the Northern kingdom, and phase 3 (JE) was from soon after the demise of the North-

### 1.3.12 Summary

Our survey of source-critical analyses of Josh. 24:1-28 and previous investigations of its significance for the concept of covenant in the OT reveals the following points:

1. Wellhausen's opinion that Josh. 24:1-28 stemmed essentially from E, but that it underwent significant Dtistic redaction, especially of a "Jehovistic" flavor, was of considerable influence upon subsequent commentators. However, later commentators were determined to advance their research beyond the basic assertion of a JE combination. Compilation of terminology and ideology characteristic of J and E in the Pentateuch was thought to confirm the theory that the Book of Joshua showed dependence upon those sources, and that E in particular provided the framework for Josh. 24. In addition to terminological considerations, matters of grammar, e.g., changes of person and number, as well as the presence of parallel ideas, were appealed to as evidence for multiple sources within Josh. 24. By contrast, Rudolph's study purported that the evidence for E was inconclusive enough to allow one to assign Josh. 24:1-28 to J rather than E. Within the various source-critical treatments there was great diversity regarding the extent and identification of glosses.

2. Complementing the source-critical analyses, scholars naturally began to look for various nuances of the word *bryt* and the meaning of covenant in the individual textual strands. The works of Valeton, Kraetzschmar and Karge were foundational in this endeavor. While no unanimity was attained concerning the essence of the covenant related in Josh. 24, objections were raised against simply calling it a covenant between Yahweh and Israel. There opinions stand in stark contrast to Pedersen's emphasis upon the role of *bryt* in the formation of social bonds and relationships.

3. Wellhausen's discussion of covenant emphasized the importance of its connection with cultic practices and law. The correlation of covenant to cultus was also pursued by Sellin, with particular significance attributed to the role of Shechem in Israel's early history. Pedersen too argued that the concept of covenant was crucial in Israel's historical formation, but his appraisal tended to emphasize psychological and sociological aspects. When one compares these views

ern kingdom. Regarding phase 4 (Dtr), he suggest Dtr(a) was prior to the exile and Dtr(b) possibly somewhat later (cf. 280).

with the works of Kuenen, Eissfeldt, Simpson and Mölle, it is apparent that the role of the Shechem texts within the Dtistic history was investigated repeatedly, with little consensus attainable via the variant, often contradictory, source-critical methods.

## 1.4 Covenant and cult in Israel's history writing

### 1.4.1 M.Noth

In Noth's earliest treatment of Josh. 24 he observed that this passage had been attributed, virtually uncontestedly, to the E tradition –a basic premise which in his initial estimation needed no further defense.[159] Secondary glosses were usually assigned to a Dtistic hand.[160] The Elohist theory had been challenged, however, by Smend and, following him, by Eissfeldt, who attempted to discern distinct sources rather than simply Dtistic editing of E.[161] It was the position of Smend and Eissfeldt that Noth originally accepted and expanded; appealing to doublets and variations, he attempted to demonstrate the probability of a separate J account. He stressed the interchange of "you" and "your fathers" in vss.5-7,17;[162] material doublets in vss.5-7;[163] the switch to Yahweh in a 3rd person reference in vs.7;[164] possible doublets in vss.21-24;[165] and a variant understanding of the stone as witness in vs.27.[166] On the basis of this scrutiny he concluded that Josh. 24:1-28 was primarily an Elohistic text supplemented with a secondary Yahwistic source. To E he attributed most of vss.1-4,6a$\alpha$b,8-15,17b$\beta$,18,19,25,27b,28, while J was thought discernible in vss.5b,6a$\beta$,7,26b,27a.[167]

159Noth, *Das System*, 133.
160Noth, *Das System*, 133. As examples Noth cites Steuernagel, *Josua*; Holzinger, *Josua*; and O.Procksch, *Das nordhebräische Sagenbuch. Die Elohimquelle* (Leipzig, 1906).
161Noth, *Das System*, 133.
162Noth, *Das System*, 133; cf. *Josua* 1938, 106f.
163Noth, *Das System*, 134.
164Noth, *Das System*, 134f.
165Noth, *Das System*, 136.
166Noth, *Das System*, 137.
167Noth, *Das System*, 135-139. In vs.18 it is suggested that *'t-kl-h'mym* and *w't-h'mry* must be from two different sources; the latter is attributed specifically to E, so presumably the former belongs to J (cf. 136). Similarly, in vs.19 Noth argues that the parallel references *'lhym qdšym hw'* and *'l-qnw' hw'* are from different sources, but he does not say which belongs to E and which to J (cf. 136). In *Josua*

Noth also claimed to detect a series of Dtistic redactionary comments and glosses; he observed that vs.1bα is similar to 23:2[168] and comes from there; vs.2aβ is syntactically poor and a gloss; vs.9aβ mentions Israel in the 3rd person and is a gloss; in vs.11 the list of peoples is secondary; *l' bḥrbk wl' bqštk* is a gloss in vs.12, based on Gen. 48:22; in vs.14 *wbmṣrym* is not original as is evident from vs.15 –gods of Egypt were not originally part of the issue.[169] Furthermore, *wy'mrw 'dym* in vs.22b is suspect, and its connection with the context suggests that all of vss.22-23 should be considered secondary.[170] Removal of vss.22f. reveals that vs.21 and vs.24 are doublets, which means one of the two is also a later gloss added to anchor vss.22f. into the present text.[171] Finally, vs.26a is a late addition.[172] As noted above, Noth's initial analysis was an extension of the previous work by Smend and Eissfeldt.

In his later treatment of Josh. 24, more emphasis was placed upon Dtistic redaction, though Noth continued to maintain that there was undoubtedly a pre-Dtistic *Grundlage*.[173] In addition to the redactions and glosses detected in 1930, in 1953 Noth added *w't-'bwtynw* (vs.17), and *kl-h'mym w* (vs.18),[174] and emphasized the Dtistic character of vss.8b,9b,10 (except *w'ṣl 'tkm mydw*), parts of vss.13,17, and all of vss.19-24.[175]

The relationship between Josh. 23 and 24 was explained variously in Noth's works. In 1938 he viewed Josh. 1-12 and 24 together as evidence of a pre-Dtic tradition.[176] He asserted that the Deuteronomist used Josh. 24 as a model for ch.23.[177] In 1943 he soundly rejected this position.[178]

"Die allgemein und früher auch noch von mir geteilte An-

1938, 106, he prefers to view these titles as Dtistic formulations.

[168]Josh. 23:2 is considered Dtistic.

[169]Noth, *Das System*, 139; *Josua* 1938, 105.

[170]Noth, *Das System*, 136.

[171]Noth, *Das System*, 136.

[172]Noth, *Das System*, 136.

[173]Noth, *Josua* 1938, 105f., 108f.; 1953, 11-16, 135-140.

[174]Noth, *Josua* 1953, 140. One would also have to exclude a direct object marker, either preceding or following this phrase.

[175]Noth, *Josua* 1953, 10, 135.

[176]Noth, *Josua* 1938, xiii.

[177]Noth, *Josua* 1938, xiii, 101.

[178]Noth, *Überlieferungsgeschichtliche Studien. Die sammelnden und bearbeitenden Geschichtswerke im Alten Testament* (Halle, 1943), 9 n.1.

> nahme, dass Jos.23 von Dtr nach dem Vorbilde von Jos. 24 abgefasst worden sei, steht in Wirklichkeit auf überaus schwachen Füssen."

The main reason cited for reversing his opinion was that the connections between the two chapters were of such a general nature that literary dependence was not proven. At this time Noth also rejected the theory that Josh. 24 had belonged to the ***vordeuteronomistischen Landnahmeüberlieferungen*** but was replaced by the Deuteronomist with Josh. 23 because of elements theologically incompatible with his particular point of view. The real solution, Noth suggested, was that Josh. 24 derived from an independent and isolated tradition, was unknown by the *Landnahmeüberlieferung* of Josh. 2ff., and only at a stage subsequent to the groundwork of the Deuteronomists was redacted according to Dtistic style and added to the Book of Joshua because of its importance for the history of the period of Joshua.[179] In 1953 Noth reverted back to the theory that Josh. 24 was the model for ch.23, but he continued to argue that it came from an independent tradition, was added after most of the Dtistic shaping of Joshua was completed, and an original connection with the opening chapters of Joshua "lässt sich nichts Sicheres mehr ermitteln."[180]

Noth's conclusions regarding the relationship between Josh. 8:30-35 and ch.24 had a background in the studies of, inter alia, Sellin.[181] His conclusion that Josh. 8:30-35 represented ur-Dtistic material connected with Dt. 11:29f. and 27:1ff. as part of a Shechem cult

[179] Noth, *Überlieferungsgeschichtliche Studien*, 9 n.1

[180] Noth, *Josua* 1953, 139, and cf. 10f., 15f.

[181] Especially Sellin's *Gilgal*, 1917; "Seit welcher Zeit," 124-134; *Geschichte*, esp. 1:98-102, presenting Sellin's argument of a covenant amongst the tribes, important for Noth's subsequent delineation of an amphictyony; see further 1.3.6. Agreement was expressed by Noth's mentor, A.Alt, *Die Ursprünge des israelitischen Rechts* (Leipzig, 1934), 33, 62-67 (= "The Origins of Israelite Law," trans. R.A.Wilson, in A.Alt, *Essays on Old Testament History and Religion* [Oxford, 1966], 79-132). Here Alt suggested a cultic background and transmission for Israel's apodictic law. On the basis of Deut. 16:13ff; 27; 31:9-13 and Josh. 24 he thought it was perhaps possible to determine a setting for apodictic law in the celebration of the Feast of Booths, which might provide a setting for covenant renewal and tribal federation at Shechem. See too "Die Wallfahrt von Sichem nach Bethel," in *Kleine Schriften zur Geschichte des Volkes Israel*, vol. I (München, 1953), 85. Alt's essential agreement with Noth's theory of an amphictyony at Shechem is already expressed in *Die Staatenbildung der Israeliten in Palästina* (Leipzig, 1930), 10, 27f.

tradition[182] was not novel.[183] And Noth readily acknowledged[184] that his view of an Israelite amphictyony built particularly upon the work of H.Ewald.[185] Noth took Ewald's skeletal suggestion and brought it to life by adding the flesh and sinew of his own scholarship in such a realistic manner that for a number of decades his thesis was accepted as a discovery born and conceived naturally rather than created artificially. It is only in recent years that specialists studying the amphictyony thesis have begun to query whether their keen scalpels are dissecting prosthetic limbs in a post-mortem.[186]

Josh. 24:1-28 stole the *Ehrenplatz* in Noth's formulation of the amphictyonic hypothesis. In his opinion this passage constituted the most important single piece of textual evidence for a tribal confederation in central Palestine in the time of the judges.[187] In this view it was at Shechem that a union was reached between the Leah tribes and the house of Joseph, of which Joshua was a representative continuing the Mosaic tradition.[188] Shechem was thus thought to be the location of the first centralized sanctuary in Israel.[189]

Also significant is Noth's conclusion regarding which parties were involved in the covenant enactment described in Josh. 24. In his opin-

[182]Noth, *Das System*, 67, 71, 140ff.; *Josua* 1953, 51f.

[183]See the discussions of Kuenen, Sellin, and Eissfeldt above.

[184]Noth, *Das System*, 43, 46, 51, 86.

[185]H.Ewald, *Geschichte des Volkes Israel*, vol. I, 3rd ed. (Göttingen, 1864), esp. 528ff.

[186]G.Fohrer, "Altes Testament–'Amphiktyonie' und 'Bund'?" *ThLZ* 91 (1966) 801-816, 893-904; G.W.Anderson, "Israel: Amphictyony: *'AM; KĀHĀL; 'EDÂH,'* in H.T.Frank–W.L.Reed, eds., *Translating and Understanding the Old Testament: Essays in Honor of H.G.May* (Nashville, 1970), 135-151; R.Smend, "Zur Frage der altisraelitischen Amphiktyonie," *EvTh* 31 (1971) 623-630; Cross, *Canaanite Myth*, 77-144; C.H.J.de Geus, *The Tribes of Israel: An Investigation into Some of the Presuppositions of Martin Noth's Amphictyony Hypothesis* (Assen, 1976); O.Bächli, *Amphiktyonie im alten Testament: Forschungsgeschichtliche Studie zur Hypothese von Martin Noth* (Basel, 1977); H.Seebass, "Erwägungen zum altisraelitischen System der zwölf Stämme," *ZAW* 90 (1978) 196-219; "League of Tribes or Amphictyony," *JSOT* 15 (1980) 61-66; H.E.Chambers, "Ancient Amphictyonies, Sic et Non," in W.W.Hallo et al., eds., *Scripture in Context, II: More Essays on the Comparative Method* (Winona Lake, 1983), 39-59; B.Halpern, *The Emergence of Israel in Canaan* (Chico, 1983), 109ff.; N.P.Lemche, *Early Israel. Anthropological and Historical Studies on the Israelite Society Before the Monarchy* (Leiden, 1985).

[187]Noth, *Das System*, 66.

[188]Noth, *Das System*, 70ff. Cf. S.Mowinckel, "'Rahelstämme' und 'Leastämme'" in J.Hempel–L.Rost, eds., *Von Ugarit nach Qumran* (Berlin, 1958), 129-150.

[189]Noth, *Josua* 1953, 52.

ion this ceremony was not first of all an inter-tribal affair sanctioned by cultic actions. On the contrary, Noth placed primary stress upon the covenantal relationship between God and the people, as that took place at a central sanctuary. He stated,

> "Auch in Jos. 24 wird nicht gesagt, zwischen wem damals in Sichem der 'Bund' abgeschlossen wurde; und doch wird von niemand bezweifelt, dass es sich weder um einen Bund zwischen Josua und den israelitischen Stämmen noch um eine von Josua für das Volk erlassene Verfügung handelte, sondern um einen Bund zwischen Gott und Volk, und dass das von Josua dabei festgesetzte Recht als von Gott im Rahmen des Bundesverhältnisses gegeben galt."[190]

As is noted above, there were numerous scholars who had entertained precisely the doubts that Noth here so casually dismissed.[191] On the one hand he asserted that the covenant here made was between God and the people, not between the tribes as parties, and on the other hand he claimed that Josh. 24 constitutes the strongest textual evidence for a tribal confederation by means of which the Leah tribes and the house of Joseph—with allegedly totally different antecedent histories—were brought into confederation with each other under the religious arch of the central sanctuary. Not adequately addressed was the question whether Josh. 24's account of a joint *bryt* between the tribes and the deity could legitimately be employed as evidence for not only an amphictyony but for an inter-tribal confederation of such political and historical magnitude as well.

Various scholars prior to Noth had asserted that there was a conflict between the covenant tradition of Sinai and the covenant tradition of Shechem, and they argued that one was forced to choose for the historical authenticity and priority of one or the other.[192] Noth concurred with Sellin's assertion that it was not necessary to make a

[190]M.Noth, "Die Gesetze im Pentateuch," in *Gesammelte Studien zum Alten Testamentum* (München, 1957), 61; see too *Josua* 1953, 140; "Das alttestamentliche Bundschliessen im Lichte eines Mari-Textes," in: *Gesammelte Studien*, 152 (= "Old Testament Covenant-Making in the Light of a Text from Mari," in *The Laws in the Pentateuch and Other Studies*, trans. D.R.Ap-Thomas [London, 1966], 116).

[191]See already Valeton, "Das Wort *bryt*," 1892, 231; Kraetzschmar, *Die Bundesvorstellung*, 34; Karge, *Geschichte des Bundesgedankens*, 232, and many scholars since.

[192]Noth, *Das System*, 68; cf. Simpson, *Early Traditions*, 648.

choice between the two historical options; the covenant of Sinai and the covenant of Shechem represented the traditions of two originally separate groups, and it was only in the later stages of the historical narration that an attempt was made to include *all Israel* within these respective traditions.[193]

### 1.4.2 G.von Rad

The close interaction that existed between Noth and von Rad as contemporary figures[194] makes it appropriate to now present von Rad's contribution to the study of Josh. 24. One of the most challenging problems raised by von Rad's famous essay of 1938 entitled "Das formgeschichtliche Problem des Hexateuch"[195] focused upon the absence of the Sinai event in a number of texts which he classified as *historical credos*. The designation of "small historical creed" was applied first of all to Deut. 26:5b-9; Deut. 6:20-24; and Josh. 24:2b-13.[196] In these three passages von Rad purported to discern the clearest traces of an ancient[197] cultic creed. Numerous additional passages (1 Sam. 12:8; Ex. 15:4f.,8-10a,12-16; Ps. 78; 105; 106; 135; 136; Neh. 9:13-14) were determined by von Rad to contain less rigid remnants of the ancient creedal form.[198] He observed that, despite a flexibility of form and content in these passages, references to Sinai are conspicuously absent. "The earliest example of the interpolation of the Sinai story into the canonical story of redemption is found in the great prayer of Neh. 9:6ff.; there at last we find a passage of the kind which hitherto we have everywhere sought in vain."[199] Here the genre finally falls apart and the Sinai tradition is freely interwoven with the historical events of the exodus from Egypt and the entry into Canaan.[200] Ps. 106 represents a similar phenomenon, but the earlier "credo" texts

[193]Noth, *Das System*, 69.

[194]See von Rad's review of Noth in "Hexateuch oder Pentateuch?" *VuF* 1-2 (1947/48) 52-56, continued in his "Literarkritische und überlieferungsgeschichtliche Forschung im Alten Testament," *VuF* 3-4 (1949/50) 172-194. See too his *Old Testament Theology*, 2 vols., trans. D.M.G.Stalker (New York, 1962–1965), 1:13.

[195]See n.10 above.

[196]Von Rad, *Problem of the Hexateuch*, 3-8.

[197]G.von Rad, "Offene Fragen im Umkreis einer Theologie des Alten Testaments," *ThLZ* 88 (1963) 409.

[198]Von Rad, *Problem of the Hexateuch*, 8-13.

[199]Von Rad, *Problem of the Hexateuch*, 12.

[200]Von Rad, *Problem of the Hexateuch*, 13.

failed to make any mention of the Sinai events.

Von Rad's conclusions regarding these credo texts constituted a foundation stone for his theory of the literary composition of the Hexateuch. He concluded that "the canonical redemption story of the exodus and settlement in Canaan on the one hand, and the tradition of Israel's experiences at Sinai on the other, really stand over against each other as two originally independent traditions...."[201] Both the settlement and Sinai traditions were associated with particular cultic settings and backgrounds. The settlement tradition, to which the credo originally belonged, was celebrated at the Feast of Weeks[202] with its primary setting in Gilgal.[203] The Sinai tradition, on the other hand, was an independent sacral tradition and was "in fact the cult-legend of the ancient Yahwistic ceremony of the renewal of the covenants at the Feast of Booths."[204]

The literary composition of the Hexateuch was credited to the genius of the Yahwist who utilized the settlement tradition as his basic framework, supplemented in turn by subsequent incorporation of numerous originally independent traditions.[205] The incorporation of the Sinai tradition marks precisely such a fusion. Von Rad argued that a merging of the settlement and Sinai traditions could only have occurred at a relatively late date.[206] His argument was founded essentially upon the absence of the Sinai event in the credo texts which recount the history of redemption.[207] While settlement and Sinai motifs are interspersed in the final form of the Hexateuch, demonstrating that both traditions were known by the Yahwist, they are held conspicuously separate in the credos. It is only in Neh. 9 and Ps. 106 that the genre begins to disintegrate and Sinai events are brought *within* the credo. Incorporation of material from the patriarchal history,[208] and finally of primaeval history,[209] is also accredited

[201]Von Rad, *Problem of the Hexateuch*, 13; cf. *OT Theology*, 1:187ff.; *Deuteronomy*, trans. D.Barton (Philadelphia, 1966), 159.
[202]Von Rad, *Problem of the Hexateuch*, 42f.
[203]Von Rad, *Problem of the Hexateuch*, 46.
[204]Von Rad, *Problem of the Hexateuch*, 53.
[205]Von Rad, *Problem of the Hexateuch*, 51.
[206]This does *not* mean that he judged the Sinai tradition itself to be late; cf. *Deuteronomy*, 159.
[207]Von Rad, *Problem of the Hexateuch*, 53f.
[208]Von Rad, *Problem of the Hexateuch*, 54ff.
[209]Von Rad, *Problem of the Hexateuch*, 63ff.

to the Yahwist as supplementations of the basic settlement tradition within the Hexateuch.

Von Rad's suggestions regarding independent settlement and Sinai traditions received a sympathetic hearing from Noth. However, Noth rejected the idea of a Hexateuch, and he concluded that although the Sinai tradition was incorporated into the Pentateuch at a relatively late date, the fusion of settlement and Sinai traditions was accomplished "before the earliest literary form of the Pentateuch tradition known to us and therefore probably still in the period when the tribes were living on their own, before the beginning of the formation of the Kingdom."[210] In Noth's revised form, the credo theory received considerable initial support.[211] In subsequent years it was viewed more critically, and by a number of scholars was flatly rejected.[212] We will have occasion at a later point to enter into a more detailed evaluation of this hypothesis.[213] At present we wish primarily to highlight the role played by Josh. 24 in his far-reaching contentions.

Von Rad's credo theory assumes the validity of the historical reconstruction of Shechem's central role in the confederation of the Israelite tribes in Palestine as proposed by Noth and Sellin.[214] Regarding Noth's formulation, based on Josh. 24, of an amphictyony at

[210]M.Noth, *The History of Israel*, revised English ed. (New York, 1960), 127; cf. 128f., 133.

[211]J.P.Hyatt, "Were there an Ancient Historical Credo in Israel and an Independent Sinai Tradition?" in Frank–Reeds, eds., *Translating and Understanding the OT*, 152-170, esp. 155f.

[212]Cf. A.S.van der Woude, *Uittocht en Sinaï* (Nijkerk, 1960); J.A.Soggin, "Kultätiologische Sagen und Katechese im Hexateuch," *VT* 10 (1960) 341-347; Th.C.Vriezen, "The Credo in the Old Testament," in A.H.van Zyl, ed., *Papers read at the 6th meeting of OuTWP* (Potchefstrom, 1963), 5-17; C.H.W.Brekelmans, "Het 'historische credo' van Israel," *TvT* 3 (1963) 1-11; H.B.Huffmon, "The Exodus, Sinai and the Credo," *CBQ* 27 (1965) 101-113; L.Rost, *Das Kleine Credo und andere Studien zum Alten Testament* (Heidelberg, 1965), 11-25; J.Schreiner, "Die Entwicklung des israelitischen 'Credo'," *Concilium* 2 (1966) 757-762; W.Richter, "Beobachtungen zur theologischen Systembildung in der alttestamentlichen Literatur anhand des 'kleinen geschichtlichen Credo'," in *Wahrheit und Verkündigung* (Fs M.Schmaus; Paderborn, 1967), 175-212; J.A.Thompson, "The Cultic Credo and the Sinai Tradition," *RThR* 27 (1968) 53-64; D.J.McCarthy, "What Was Israel's Creed?" *LThQ* 4 (1969) 46-53; N.Lohfink, "Zum 'kleinen geschichtlichen Credo' Dtn. 26,5-9," *ThPh* 46 (1971) 19-39; E.F.Campbell, "Moses and the Foundations of Israel," *Interp* 29 (1975) 141-154.

[213]Cf. provisionally E.W.Nicholson, *Exodus and Sinai in History and Tradition* (Oxford, 1973).

[214]Von Rad, *OT Theology*, 1:16.

Shechem, von Rad suggested "the assumption ... is not a new one, but it has only recently been developed systematically and raised to such a degree of certainty as is attainable in this field."[215] Attempting to advance Mowinckel's search for the background to the decalogue,[216] he stated that the amphictyonic cultic festival at Shechem, which was celebrated liturgically as a covenant renewal ceremony, provides the setting for the literary deposit of the Sinai pericope in JE,[217] and it was in the district of Shechem that Yahweh became "the God of Israel."[218] Due to indigenous cultic ties within the clans, and pervasive interaction with Canaanite practices, the growth of religious uniformity in Israel was a long and gradual process.[219] From this cursory summary it is evident that Josh. 24 and the Shechem events occupied a linchpin position in von Rad's reconstruction of Israel's early history and faith.

### 1.4.3 H.-J.Kraus

Von Rad's view that the traditions of *Landnahme* and covenant were promulgated in the rubric of cultic festivals in Gilgal and Shechem respectively was advanced by H.-J. Kraus.[220] It is also apparent that the work of Alt was as foundational to Kraus's thesis as it was to von Rad's approach.[221] The same may be said regarding Mowinckel's influence. While Kraus rejected Mowinckel's postulation of mythic reenactment in an Israelite New Year enthronement festival, he accepted Mowinckel's stress upon the pervasive influence of the cult in the formation of Israel's religious traditions.[222] Noth's theory of an amphictyony at Shechem must be added to this list of previous

[215]Von Rad, *OT Theology*, 1:16f.

[216]S.Mowinckel, *Le décalogue* (Paris, 1927).

[217]Von Rad, *OT Theology*, 1:18 n.8, 192f.

[218]Von Rad, *OT Theology*, 1:19.

[219]Von Rad, *OT Theology*, 1:19f., 23ff. See too his "The Origin of Mosaic Monotheism," in *God at Work in Israel*, trans. J.H.Marks (Nashville, 1980), 128-138.

[220]In addition to his *Gottesdienst* (see n.11 above), consider his "Gilgal: Ein Beitrag zur Kultusgeschichte Israels," *VT* 1 (1951) 181-199. Note however, Kraus thought that Gilgal replaced Shechem as amphictyonic sanctuary at a relatively early point, and argued accordingly that *Landnahme* and Sinai stand closer together than von Rad had suggested ("Gilgal," 193f.).

[221]See above, 1.2.

[222]Kraus, *Gottesdienst*, 49-51.

studies particularly influential upon Kraus's thesis.[223] Building on the classic works of these scholars, Kraus constructed a theory of the relationship of covenant and cult which in its basic form at one time received approval from a majority of OT scholars.

According to Kraus, Josh. 24 describes a singular event typical of a very early tradition of recurring festivals at Shechem, in which the law was read to the people and they were given stipulations and obligations (cf. Ex. 24:13ff.; Deut. 26:16ff.; 27:1ff.; Josh. 8:30ff.).[224] Apodictic instruction to serve Yahweh alone was a constitutive part of the covenant renewal festival. The command in Deut. 31:9-13 to read the law every seven years is explainable in connection with the Feast of Booths indigenous to Israel's early history.[225] The cultic renewal of the covenant at Shechem demonstrates the importance of the mediatorial role of Joshua, a figure in the *Gestalt* of Moses,[226] which in turn had important implications for understanding the role of cultic mediators in the amphictyonic federation during the period of the judges,[227] in the Jerusalem sanctuary,[228] and in the cultic reforms of the southern kingdom.[229] Thus, covenant renewal ceremonies at the Feast of Booths –of which Josh. 24 and 8:30ff. provide concrete examples– constituted a most salient dimension of cultic influence in the shaping of Israel's religious and political expression.

### 1.4.4 E.Nielsen

A detailed attempt to analyze all OT traditions specifically related to Shechem was undertaken by E.Nielsen.[230] Along with patriarchal traditions from Genesis, and various references to Shechem in Judges-2 Kings, Josh. 24 and 8:30-35 were understandably given extensive

[223]Kraus, "Gilgal," 191f.; *Gottesdienst* 14, 17, 36f, 47, 56, 64, etc.

[224]Kraus, *Gottesdienst*, 47 (esp. n.83), 57; "Gilgal," 188, 191; "Gottesdienst im alten und im neuen Bund," *EvTh* 25 (1965) 172-174; "God's Covenant," *Reformed World* 35 (1978-79) 258f.

[225]Kraus, *Gottesdienst*, 48ff. In part with A.Alt, "Zelte und Hütten," *Alttestamentliche Studien* (Fs Nötscher; Bonn, 1950), 16-25 (esp. 23-25); contra Wellhausen's *Denaturierung* approach, cf. *Gottesdienst*, 23ff.; "Gottesdienst im alten und im neuen Bund," 182f.; "God's Covenant," 258.

[226]Kraus, *Gottesdienst*, 59.

[227]Kraus, *Gottesdienst*, 64f.

[228]Kraus, *Gottesdienst*, 69.

[229]Kraus, *Gottesdienst*, 80f.

[230]E.Nielsen, *Shechem: A Traditio-Historical Investigation* (Copenhagen, 1955).

attention, the latter especially in correlation with Deut. 11:26-32 and 27:1-26.

Nielsen's study of Josh. 24:1-28 divides the passage into three basic units (vss.2-13, vss.14-24, and vss.25-28), with vs.1 as an introduction to the entire passage.[231] In each section textual-critical questions are first discussed, with particular attention to a comparison of the MT, LXX A, LXX B and Pesh. It is not necessary here to enter into the details of these textual analyses, except to note that Nielsen's employment of the LXX traditions is *ad hoc* and eclectic. In every verse in which textual divergencies are detected between the MT and the LXX, an attempt is made to arbitrate between the options at the level of the verse, without an evident attempt to temper this judgment by trends detectable in LXX A and LXX B throughout the chapter as a whole, if not more extensively at the level of the Book of Joshua. For example, the presence in the LXX of Shiloh rather than Shechem in vs.1, and the absence of "Canaan" in vs.3, is judged to be theologically motivated,[232] but in vss.5-7, where there is a discrepancy with regard to the 1st or 3rd person singular subject, Nielsen chooses for the LXX as retaining the authentic reading.[233] Although he usually sees differences witnessed in the Syriac Peshitta as secondary, and vs.28 of the Syriac is judged to be a paraphrase rather than a translation,[234] in vs.17 it is deemed possible that the absence of *w't 'bwtynw* in the Peshitta "in this single instance may have preserved the original text."[235] These observations concerning methodology are not intended to minimize the insights brought by Nielsen's extensive textual comparisons, but it is imperative to note the eclectic nature of of his textual criticism.[236]

Subsequent to the textual-critical notes on each unit, Nielsen attempts to determine which parts of the text belong to a pre-Dtic tradition focusing on Shechem, and which elements are to be attributed to the final, Dtistic form of the text. This methodology has been self-consciously adopted;[237] Nielsen summarizes and rejects

[231]Nielsen, *Shechem*, 86-134.

[232]Nielsen, *Shechem*, 86f.

[233]Nielsen, *Shechem*, 88f.

[234]Nielsen, *Shechem*, 109.

[235]Nielsen, *Shechem*, 99.

[236]The matter of textual criticism in Josh. 24 is complex, and the problem is raised more extensively in sections 1.8, 2.2 and 3.6.

[237]Nielsen states at a later date that this work on the Shechem traditions was

a strictly source-critical approach, which he illustrates with recourse to K.Möhlenbrink, who "starts from the shift between 1st and 3rd sg. in the account of the acts of the Lord in the speech of Joshua, thus basing his analysis on the weakest foundation imaginable."[238] The approaches of Wellhausen, Meyer, Gressmann, Noth and von Rad are also briefly mentioned.[239] From Nielsen's ensuing analysis it is apparent that he wishes to incorporate von Rad's emphasis upon *kerygma* as having a powerful influence in the reshaping or retelling of a given tradition. But he does not accept the theory that Josh. 24:2-13 in its present form is an ancient credo. He states to the contrary, "The Old Testament symbols, such as Dt.26:5-9; 6:20-24, and Josh. 24:2-13 ... appear at a comparatively late stage of the literary development of the traditions."[240] This provides the underlying basis for his attempt to separate Dtistic kerygma from an antecedent Shechem tradition in Josh. 24:1-28.

Mention of the leaders in vs.1 is taken as evidence of "deuteronomizing,"[241] while the location at Shechem is viewed as proof of pre-Dtic tradition.[242] With regard to vss.2-13, Nielsen suggests, "On the whole we tend to hear the voice of the deut. school in v.2, vv.3-5 (esp. MT), as well as in vv.9-11."[243] Singled out as particularly Dtistic are the words *w'šlḥ 't-mšh w't-'hrn* (vs. 5),[244] *wylḥmw 'tkm* (vs.8) and *šny mlky h'mry* (vs.12).[245] Pre-Dtic tradition is detected

particularly influenced by I.Engnell, Noth, von Rad and Alt; see now his "The Traditio-historical Study of the Pentateuch since 1945, with Special Emphasis on Scandinavia," in *Law, History and Tradition: Selected Essays by Eduard Nielsen* (Copenhagen, 1983), 138-154, esp. 154 n.20.

[238]Nielsen, *Shechem* 90; cf. K.Möhlenbrink, "Die Landnahmesagen des Buches Josua," *ZAW* 56 (1938) 238-268, esp. 250-254. Nielsen's forceful rejection of the 1st/3rd person shift as a criterion for source division in Josh. 24:5-7 is prompted in part by his comparison of the LXX and the MT, in which he judges the LXX to be closer to the original reading. Elsewhere, with regard to Deut. 11:26-28, 31-32, he accepts the validity of source division upon the basis of a shift between 2nd sg. and 2nd pl., but here too he alludes to his view that a shift in *person* is not a legitimate basis for such divisions (43 n.2). For further discussion of shifts between 2nd. pl. and sg. see his *Die Zehn Gebote: Eine Traditionsgeschichtliche Skizze* (Copenhagen, 1965), 42f.

[239]Nielsen, *Shechem*, 91f.

[240]Nielsen, *Shechem*, 93.

[241]Nielsen, *Shechem*, 79, 87.

[242]Nielsen, *Shechem*, 87.

[243]Nielsen, *Shechem*, 95.

[244]Nielsen, *Shechem*, 94.

[245]Nielsen, *Shechem*, 98; cf. his "Historical Perspectives and Geographical Hori-

in the phrases *yhwh 'lhy yśr'l* and *b'br hnhr yšbw 'bwtykm m'wlm*, and likely in *wy'bdw 'lhym 'ḥrym* (vs.2), *wy'qb wbnyw yrdw mṣrym* (vs.4) as well as most of vss.6-8.[246]

With respect to vss.14-24, Nielsen suggests that the structure of the passage is determined by Joshua's fourfold actions. In vss.14-18 Joshua presents the choice of allegiance; in vss.19-21 he warns of the seriousness of the choice, and the people accept; in vs.22 he takes the people's oath; and in vss.23-24 he presents additional exhortations, to which the people declare their acceptance. "The present shape of the section thus exhibits a beautiful structure which at the same time evidently gives it its vivid character."[247] Here too it is Nielsen's goal to determine "whether or not the theory of a pre-Dtic nucleus worked over by the Deuteronomists, valid for vv.2-13, would also hold good for vv.14-24."[248] As evidence of a pre-Dtic tradition he cites *btmym wb'mt* and the putting away of foreign gods from beyond the river and from Egypt (vs.14-15, 23a),[249] the reference to a jealous God (vs.19), the presence of what appears to be a "faded oath" formula (vss.18, 21f.), and the dramatic character of the section.[250]

Similarly, vss.25-28 are thought to show clear evidence of a pre-Dtic tradition, e.g., in the stone of witness which *hears*, and in the reference *bmqdš yhwh*. On the other hand, writing in the book of the law (vs.26a) and the second reference to the stone as witness (vs.27b) are considered Dtic touches.[251] Thus, Josh. 24:1-28 is a Dtistic reworking of an ancient, pre-Dtic Shechem tradition. Nielsen's basic position is retained in a summary of "Judaean" and "northern, pre-Deuteronomic" elements published more than twenty years later, but it is noteworthy that at this time his identification of pre-Dtic elements becomes more meagre; in vss.2-13 he suggests, "Of pre-Deuteronomic, North-Israelite, elements there remains: the ancestors' dwelling on the other side of Euphrates, the immigration to Egypt,

zons," *ASThI* 11 (1977/1978) 86.

[246]Nielsen, *Shechem*, 98; "Historical Perspectives," 86.

[247]Nielsen, *Shechem*, 100.

[248]Nielsen, *Shechem*, 100.

[249]Nielsen, *Shechem*, 101-105; cf. his "The Burial of the Foreign Gods," *StTh* 8 (1955) 103-123, esp. 121f.

[250]Nielsen, *Shechem*, 105-108, esp. 108.

[251]Nielsen, *Shechem*, 108-134, esp. 109f, 133f.; cf. his *Oral Tradition* (London, 1954), 44-48, 56f.; "Moses and the Law," *VT* 32 (1982) 97, where Joshua is regarded as functioning in 24:25f. as one of the law-reciting judges.

the crossing of the Red Sea, and the war against the Amorites."[252] Regarding vss.14-24 he suggests, "a pre-Deuteronomic element may be inherent in v.17,"[253] and in vss.25-28 only the "sanctuary of the Lord" is referred to as betraying pre-Dtic phraseology.[254] In short, he continues to affirm a pre-Dtic tradition, but a considerably smaller portion of the text is designated as proof of this earliest layer.[255] Nielsen suggests that the historical background for the pre-Dtic tradition may reflect a political or tribal alliance within the house of Joseph, between Manasseh (originally from beyond the Euphrates) and Ephraim (the Moses tribe coming up from Egypt).[256] His historical conclusions thereby propose an alternative federation theory to the tribal union proposed by Noth.

Nielsen's literary conclusions regarding Josh. 8:30-35 differ considerably from those attained in Josh. 24:1-28. A comparison of these verses with Deut. 11:26-32, 27:1-26 convinces him that the Deuteronomy texts betray an ancient Shechem tradition, but Josh. 8:30-35 is a later, purely redactional creation based upon those earlier texts.[257]

### 1.4.5 S.Mowinckel

In the chronological overview offered at the outset of this chapter it has been suggested that Mowinckel's view of the cultus in Israel influenced Noth's methodology.[258] It might therefore seem anachronistic that the present section began with a presentation of Noth's position and now concludes with a survey of Mowinckel's contribution. Never-

[252] Nielsen, "Historical Perspectives," 86. Note that in 1955 he expressed some uncertainty as to whether or not the cult of "other gods" reflects a pre-Dtic tradition (*Shechem* 95-98). Later he concludes that it is "unmistakably Judaean" ("Historical Perspectives," 86)..

[253] Nielsen, "Historical Perspectives," 86.

[254] Nielsen, "Historical Perspectives," 86.

[255] This modification in Nielsen's conclusions is clearly influenced by Perlitt (for a summary of Perlitt's position see 1.6.5). Cf. Nielsen, "The Traditio-historical Study," 147f., 154 n.30, but he is unwilling to go as far as Perlitt does. In reference to Perlitt's study Nielsen states, "He denies, though in my opinion wrongly, the occurrence of any ancient element of tradition in Jos.24 and dates the chapter to the 7th century" ("Historical Perspectives," 89 n.39).

[256] Nielsen, *Shechem*, 126-132; "Historical Perspectives," 86.

[257] Nielsen, *Shechem*, 39-85, esp. 77-80, 85.

[258] See 1.2 above. Mowinckel's influence is also easily discernible in works by Weiser, von Rad, Kraus, and many other scholars investigating the role of the cultus in Israel's history.

theless, an analysis of Mowinckel's publications mentioning Josh. 24 demonstrates that treatment of Noth et al. prior to Mowinckel is neither anachronistic nor inappropriate. Whereas Mowinckel's emphasis upon the role of the cultus in Israel's history was already expressed in his earliest writings,[259] thereby exercising a formative influence upon Noth, his view of Josh. 24 was expressed most clearly in his latest publications in explicit dialogue with Noth's views which had by that time already become well-known.[260]

Unfortunately, however, Mowinckel's criticism of Noth's treatment of Josh. 24 does not give due regard to the various stages of his thought. Mowinckel asserted that Josh. 24 could not possibly have originally constituted the direct continuation of a pre-Dtic source in chs. 2-11 (12) as held by Noth.[261] However, a perusal of Noth's writings subsequent to the first edition of *Josua* (1938), shows that he had already modified his view of Josh. 24 considerably by the time of his *Überlieferungsgeschichtliche Studien* of 1943; there he argued that ch.24 came from an originally independent source, was later reworked by the Dtist, and finally was added to the book of Joshua in its present place.[262] The second edition of Noth's commentary (1953) maintains that the addition of this chapter was a secondary

[259]See especially his *Psalmenstudien*, 2 vols. (Amsterdam, 1961) (originally 6 vols. [Oslo 1921-1924]). His stress upon the cultus in Israel is further developed in subsequent publications such as *Zum Israelitischen Neujahr und zur Deutung der Thronbesteigungspsalmen* (Oslo, 1952); *Religion und Kultus*, trans. A.Schauer (Göttingen, 1953) (= *Religion og kultus*); *The Psalms in Israel's Worship*, 2 vols., trans. D.R.Ap-Thomas (Oxford, 1962) (= *Offersang og sangoffer* [Oslo, 1951]).

[260]Mowinckel's discussion of source-critical questions in the Pentateuch-Hexateuch debate are all undertaken in active dialogue with Noth. See his *Zur Frage nach dokumentarischen Quellen in Josua 13-19* (Oslo, 1946); *Erwägungen zur Pentateuch Quellenfrage* (Trondheim, 1964); *Tetrateuch-Pentateuch-Hexateuch. Die Berichte über die Landnahme in den drei altisraelitischen Geschichtswerken* (Berlin, 1964); "Israelite Historiography," *ASThI* 2 (1963) 4-26. For a summary of the debate between Noth and Mowinckel see conveniently A.G.Auld, *Joshua, Moses and the Land* (Edinburgh, 1980), 19-36.

[261]Mowinckel, *Tetrateuch-Pentateuch-Hexateuch*, 47. Mowinckel did not footnote which of Noth's publications he had in mind, but presumably he was referring to *Josua* 1938, xiii, where Noth thought that Josh. 24 was part of the traditional material utilized by the Dtist, providing the pattern for his authorship of ch.23. Mowinckel thought that 23:1 was the original beginning of ch.24.

[262]Noth, *Überlieferungsgeschichtliche Studien*, 9 n.1. Ironically, Mowinckel cites this work immediately after criticizing Noth for connecting ch.24 with chs.2-12; cf. Mowinckel, *Tetrateuch-Pentateuch-Hexateuch*, 47.

level of redaction after the Dtistic form was basically established.[263] In fact, Noth clearly stressed that, although there is a definite topical affiliation between ch.24 and 1-12, he detected no particular literary connection, and he concluded that it is unknown whether such a connection ever existed.[264]

Mowinckel stated that what remains of Josh. 24 after removal of the numerous Dtistic expansions "ist natürlich eine Sage."[265] Like all sagas it contains a kernel of historical value.[266] In expressed agreement with Sellin, Kittel and Noth, he sought the kernel of this tradition in a regularly held, ancient covenant ceremony at Shechem.[267] He also accepted Noth's claim that an amphictyony was established at Shechem,[268] but upon numerous occasions he argued that only ten tribes were involved; the twelve tribe amphictyony did not arise until the time of David at the earliest.[269]

Mowinckel's obvious interest in the role of the cultus makes it noteworthy, and at first surprising, that he never elaborated upon the significance of this allegedly regularly held cultic festival in Shechem.[270]

[263]Noth, *Josua* 1953, 10.

[264]Noth, *Josua* 1953, 15f.

[265]Mowinckel, *Tetrateuch-Pentateuch-Hexateuch*, 47, retaining the terminology popularized by Gunkel and Gressmann. He rejected Eissfeldt's assertion of a "Laienquelle" in Josh. 24, but he does not give his own opinion of the specific origin of the ancient tradition other than that it is a saga affiliated with Shechem (cf. 28, 33, 48, 74).

[266]Mowinckel, *Tetrateuch-Pentateuch-Hexateuch*, 48: "Die Sage wird aber, wie jede Sage, einen Kern von Tatsächlichkeit enthalten."

[267]Mowinckel, *Tetrateuch-Pentateuch-Hexateuch*, 48.

[268]Mowinckel, *Tetrateuch-Pentateuch-Hexateuch*, 48.

[269]Mowinckel, *Zur Frage nach dokumentarischen Quellen*, 18, 20-22; *Religion und Kultus*, 51, 144 n.107; "'Rahelstämme' und 'Leastämme'," 137f., 142, 150.

[270]In *The Psalms in Israel's Worship*, vol. 1, Mowinckel pays explicit attention to the topic of covenant renewal and cultic festivals, but Josh. 24 is never discussed in this connection, despite his claim that in Josh. 24 is found "der Kern der Überlieferung eine Erinnerung an eine in älterer Zeit in Sichem (regelmässig) gefeierte Bundesfeier" (*Tetrateuch-Pentateuch-Hexateuch*, 48). One might attempt to explain this peculiarity via the fact that the original *Offersang og sangoffer* was published in 1951 while the quotation just cited comes from a 1964 publication. But this solution is too simple. Mowinckel's *Tetrateuch-Pentateuch-Hexateuch*, despite its date of publication, was not likely written in his later years (cf. Auld, *Joshua, Moses*, 19). The assertion that Josh. 24 refers to a tradition of a regularly held cultic festival is defended by Mowinckel with reference to Sellin (1917), Kittel (1923) and Noth (1930, 1938). It is surely correct to conclude that Mowinckel, already at a very early stage of his career, accepted the conclusion of these scholars that Josh. 24 referred to a regularly occurring cultic festival, but he was not confident

In his *Psalmenstudien*, vol. 5, 1923, he brought Josh. 8:30-35 into his discussion of blessing and curse formulae in the cult, and in psalmic compositions,[271] but in later studies these texts did not play an explicit role in his view of the development of the cultus in Israel.[272] Finally, the most important reason why Mowinckel virtually ignored Shechem as a cultic center in Israel is the historical prominence he attributed to Jerusalem. Already in 1927 he concluded that the Sinai tradition received its form through cultic celebration in Jerusalem:

> "*Ce que J et E rapportent comme récit des événements du Sinaï n'est autre chose que la description d'une fête cultuelle célébrée à une époque plus récente, plus précisément dans le temple de Jérusalem, description présentée*

enough of this theory to elaborate possible implications for the role of the cultus in pre-monarchic Israel (cf. *Psalmenstudien*, 1923, 5:102, 105). In *Religion und Kultus* he states, "Der 'Bund' ist an die heilige Stätte, an Kadesch, Sinai, Sichem, Jerusalem gebunden" (57). The list of texts footnoted in support of this statement includes Josh. 24 and Judg. 9:4,46 (145 n.136), but Mowinckel does not discuss the significance of Josh. 24 with respect to a covenant festival at Shechem.

[271]See esp. 97-104. It is noteworthy that Mowinckel essentially agreed with Sellin that there was an Elohistic background to Josh. 8:30-35. Since Sellin's views have been dealt with above, it is not necessary to further delineate Mowinckel's opinion. For a summary of Mowinckel's various attempts to diagnose Deut. 27 see Nielsen, *Shechem*, 53-56.

[272]In contrast see A.Weiser, *The Psalms*, trans. H.Hartwell (Philadelphia, 1962). Weiser is much bolder in his claims for the role of Josh. 24 in the background of Israel's cultic festivals. He claims that in "the narrative of the assembly at Shechem in Josh. 24" we find "the *hieros logos* of the celebration of the constitution of the sacral confederacy of the Twelve Tribes in Canaan" (27). This idea is already expressed in his *Einleitung in Das Alte Testament* (Stuttgart, 1939), 73: "Eine ebenfalls alte, vielleicht die älteste, Nachricht über den nationalen kultischen Zusammenschluss der Stämme am Heiligtum von Sichem bietete Jos 24." Significantly, in this context Weiser appeals to Mowinckel: "Ferner hat Mowinckel (*Le décalogue* 1927, 114ff.) darauf hingewiesen, dass die Sinaierzählung von JE noch deutliche Merkmale enthält, die es wahrscheinlich machen, dass sie in ihrer jetzigen Gestalt aus der Liturgie des Bundesfestes herausgewachsen ist" (73f.). But Weiser employs Josh. 24 much more prominently than does Mowinckel's analysis of the cultus in Israel. When Weiser stresses that the cultic festival provides the background for various cultic elements in the Psalms, he frequently refers to Josh. 24 as proof, e.g., "Hence the *profession of loyalty* to Yahweh (Ex. 19.8; 24.3,7; Josh. 24.15ff.,24), the *renunciation of the foreign gods* (Josh.24.14f.,23; Gen. 35:2ff.; Judg. 10:16), the sanctification and self-purification of the Yahweh community have their place within the framework of the Covenant Festival and of its cultic tradition" (*The Psalms*, 33, and cf. 28, 31, 45, 47, 51, 76, 554). See too his "Das Deboralied," *ZAW* 71 (1959) 67-97, esp. 73, 76, 79n.50.

> *dans une forme historique et mythologique et adaptée au cadre historique et mythologique des récits de l'Exode.*"[273]

Throughout the duration of Mowinckel's career this *idée fixe* of Jerusalem as *pied-à-terre* of the cultus *ab initio* in Israel precludes a stress upon Shechem as a cultic center of major historical significance.[274]

### 1.4.6 Summary

It would be mistaken to suggest that Noth, von Rad, et al. had left behind the endeavors or methods of source criticism.[275] A survey of Noth's treatments of Josh. 24 reveals how important the question of sources remained for his position, whether in the earlier stage in which he accepted the basic view of an Elohistic document, or in his later position which placed more emphasis upon Dtistic redaction of a pre-Dtistic document. Accordingly, for him the source-critical questions shifted away from an attempt to distinguish between J and E, to a new attempt to more specifically discern between ancient tradition and later Dtic or Dtistic revision within the corpus of Dtistic history.

However, with Noth and von Rad a new stage in the study of Josh. 24 was opened. It was especially these two scholars who refocused questions raised by source-critical commentators on the one hand and the form-critical endeavors of Gunkel and Mowinckel on the other, in an attempt to draw major historical conclusions from Josh. 24. They thereby established the agenda for studies of this passage in the following decades.

Noth's view of amphictyony and von Rad's view of credo both placed unprecedented *historical* weight upon Josh. 24 and the hypothesis of an ancient, cultic, covenant ceremony at Shechem. It is significant in this regard that the earlier work by Mowinckel[276] attempted to find a background for the law collections of JE in relation to the cultic setting, but Mowinckel was extremely reluctant to sketch a concrete historical setting within the local cult traditions prior to

[273]Mowinckel, *Le décalogue*, 120 (original emphasis).

[274]See too his "Psalm Criticism between 1900 and 1935," *VT* 5 (1955) 13-33, esp. 16-17, 23, 27f. He suggests that the earliest Israelite cultic material was too Canaanite to be acceptable to later Yahwism and is therefore not represented in the canonical material.

[275]In the previous section we noted that scholars as recently as Mölle have undertaken major attempts to discern literary sources or levels in this chapter.

[276]Especially his *Le décalogue*.

Jerusalem. Von Rad, on the other hand, was eager to merge Noth's emphasis on amphictyony and Mowinckel's emphasis on the JE background of the law collection, attributing a special role to Shechem as the location of covenant festivals in the pre-monarchic period.[277]

The theories about a Shechem cult tradition, and possible associations with the festal calendar, were expanded by Kraus. And Nielsen's study provides an additional example of efforts to move beyond source analysis to a more detailed historical reconstruction of the Shechem tradition in Israel's history writing. However, in place of Noth's twelve-tribe amphictyony, he argued that there was a federation between the clans of Manasseh and Ephraim. When Mowinckel's ten-tribe federation is added to this picture, it becomes apparent that although Noth's basic thesis of a tribal federation at Shechem had gained almost unanimous support, the specific contention that it was a *twelve-tribe* amphictyony was sharply contested.

## 1.5 Covenant and treaty; new developments in form criticism

### 1.5.1 G.E.Mendenhall

The name Mendenhall stands in relation to covenant-treaty comparisons as the name Wellhausen to the documentary hypothesis, and Noth to the amphictyony thesis –not as inventor or originator but as primary stimulant.[278] In the last thirty years OT scholarship has been enriched by a wealth of material treating the concept of covenant and its broader *Sitz im Leben* in the ancient NE. The present interest in covenant certainly may not be attributed singularly to Mendenhall; his articles came at the right time to spark a flame in tinder which

[277]Von Rad, *OT Theology*, 1:17f., 192f. A similar emphasis is found in the works of Weiser, e.g., *Einleitung*, 73; "Das Deboralied," 73, 76, 79 n.50; *The Psalms*, 27, 33, etc.

[278]V.Korošec's observations in *Hethitische Staatsverträge. Ein Beitrag zu ihrer juristischen Wertung* (Leipziger rechtswissenschaftliche Studien 60; Leipzig, 1931), regarding the formal literary pattern of Hittite treaties, constituted a fundamental starting point for Mendenhall's groundbreaking essay, "Law and Covenant in Israel and the Ancient Near East," *BA* 17 (1954) 26-46, 50-76 (reprinted as a brief monograph, Pittsburgh, 1955; subsequent citations are from the latter edition). For expressed dependence upon Korošec cf. 29f., 32f.

for some time had been lying ready to burn.[279] Nevertheless, it is not without reason that *The Biblical Archaeologist* in 1979 published a précis of Mendenhall's views under the title "25 Years Ago,"[280] and most recent studies of the OT covenant concept pay justified tribute to Mendenhall's role in these discussions.[281]

Mendenhall argued that the Hittite treaty texts betray an "international form" which was "common property to many cultures,"[282] which entails that it is not far-fetched to draw comparisons between Hittite and biblical texts. Previously, V.Korošec had identified six elements usually appearing in the Hittite treaty texts:[283]

1. Preamble
2. Historical prologue
3. Stipulations
4. Deposition in the temple and periodic public reading
5. List of gods as witnesses
6. Curses and blessings formula

To those six elements Mendenhall added three additional characteristics:[284]

1. Formal oath by which the vassal pledged obedience
2. Solemn ceremony to accompany the oath
3. Form for initiating procedure against a rebellious vassal

In Mendenhall's opinion there were only two biblical traditions which closely fit the form here delineated, namely the Exodus decalogue and the narrative of Josh. 24,[285] and even in these two cases

[279]Consider for example the work done on Hittite texts by E.F.Weidner, *Politische Dokumente aus Kleinasien. Die Staatsverträge in akkadischer Sprache aus dem Archiv von Boghazköi* (Boghazköi Studien, 8-9; Leipzig, 1923); J.Friedrich, *Staatsverträge des Hatti-Reiches in hethitischer Sprache* (*MVÄG* 31/1, 34/1; Leipzig, 1926, 1930); Korošec (see previous footnote); E.Bickerman, "Couper une alliance," *Archives d'histoire du droit oriental* 5 (1950-51) 133-156, mentioned by Mendenhall (26 n.6, 36 n.6). And, see already Karge, *Geschichte des Bundesgedankens*, 235-254.

[280]*BA* 42 (1979) 189-190.

[281]E.g., McCarthy, *Treaty and Covenant*, 4. The work by Mölle (see 1.3.11) has ignored Mendenhall and virtually all of the related material to its own detriment.

[282]Mendenhall, *Law and Covenant*, 28, esp n.12.

[283]Korošec, *Hethitische Staatsverträge*, 12-14; cf. Mendenhall, *Law and Covenant*, 32ff.

[284]Mendenhall, *Law and Covenant*, 34f.

[285]Mendenhall, *Law and Covenant*, 36. See too P.Buis, "Les formulaires d'alliance," *VT* 16 (1966) 396-411; *La notion d'alliance dans l'ancien Testament* (Paris,

he noted that not all the elements are present.[286] A formal list of stipulations is not to be found in Josh. 24; the only stipulation is the imperative to put away foreign gods. Nor is a curse and blessing formula present.[287]

Mendenhall accepted Noth's amphictyonic setting for Josh. 24,[288] and he argued that only a federation covenant would explain the historical developments in Israel prior to the monarchy.[289] As to the origin of Josh. 24 he stated:

> "It is very difficult to escape the conclusion that this narrative rests upon traditions which go back to the period when the treaty form was still living, but that the later writer used the materials of the tradition which were of importance and value to him, and adapted them to his own contemporary situation."[290]

Mendenhall placed the classic treaty form in the second millenium B.C. He suggested that the covenant of Josh. 24 "is inserted into a narrative which obviously includes later material."[291] Nevertheless, comparison with the classic treaty form is employed as an argument for the "historical foundation of the narrative" which does not follow "the rigid pattern of the Deuteronomic historian."[292]

These observations are significant in comparison with subsequent assertions by Weinfeld and McCarthy that the form of covenant narrative found in Josh. 24:1-28 is moving in a direction *towards* the fuller form found in Dtic material, rather than *from* the classic form of the Late Bronze Age.[293]

1976).

[286]The decalogue misses the last three elements specified by Korošec, namely deposit in the sanctuary and periodic public reading, the list of gods as witnesses, and the curses and blessings, cf. *Law and Covenant*, 39f.

[287]*Law and Covenant*, 41. Mendenhall remarks that the "curses of Deut. 27 would fill in the gap of Joshua 24 beautifully" (42). Alt had previously suggested that the procedure described in Deut. 27 would fit the type of setting and ceremony found in Josh. 24, cf. his "Ursprünge des israelitischen Rechts." But such an observation asserts nothing regarding a *literary dependence* between the two accounts.

[288]Mendenhall, *Law and Covenant*, 36.

[289]Mendenhall, *Law and Covenant*, 25; "The Monarchy," *Interp* 29 (1975) 155-170, esp. 158.

[290]Mendenhall, *Law and Covenant*, 41.

[291]Mendenhall, *Law and Covenant*, 41.

[292]Mendenhall, *Law and Covenant*, 41 n.41.

[293]See the summaries of Weinfeld and McCarthy in 1.6.6 and 1.6.7. Menden-

### 1.5.2 K.Baltzer

Baltzer[294] offered a more detailed comparison of treaty texts and OT covenant narratives than was found in the earlier outline by Mendenhall. He insightfully refined certain terminology employed in the discussion of covenant and treaty. The key word in his title, "Bundesformular," is itself indicative that he avoided a mechanical correlation between treaty texts and OT texts. *Bundesformular*[295] is intended to designate a genre of OT covenant texts which are not per se treaty documents but which do bear an unmistakable affinity to the literary form and content of the extra-biblical treaties.[296]

Baltzer has been criticized for casting his net too widely, i.e., of including numerous elements and texts within his category of a covenant formulary which may not necessarily be part of a particular covenant "Gattung."[297] The validity of such criticism obviously depends upon how narrowly "covenant formulary" is defined. If the covenant formulary is defined too broadly it no longer deserves to be called a distinct genre. But Baltzer may be correct that the concept of covenant has had a more pervasive influence upon the shaping of OT texts than has often been recognized, in which case a broader categorization of the covenant genre would not be without merit. This is a prime example of the difficulty involved in form-critical comparisons of biblical and extra-biblical texts.

Baltzer identified a treaty element not listed by Korošec or Mendenhall, namely the "Grundsatzerklärung über das zukünftige Ver-

hall stayed with his original opinion that the covenant form in the OT did not originate in Israel with the Deuteronomist. This is evident from a recent essay in which he criticizes N.Gottwald; see his "Ancient Israel's Hyphenated History," in D.N.Freedman–D.F.Graf, eds., *Palestine in Transition: The Emergence of Ancient Israel* (Sheffield, 1983), 91-103: "The problem of Gottwald is that his liberated 'tribes' are liberated also from virtually any substance or cultural content, once 'egalitarianism' is disposed of. They evidently had a covenant, but there was no content to that either, until the Deuteronomist miraculously put himself into a time machine to resurrect faithfully the Late Bronze Age covenant structure that had been obsolete in the outside world for six centuries" (93, cf. 98-101).

294 K.Baltzer, *Das Bundesformular, sein Ursprung und seine Verwendung im Alten Testament* (Neukirchen, 1960).

295 The English equivalent, "covenant formulary," is employed in this study.

296 Baltzer, *Das Bundesformular*, 17ff.

297 See McCarthy, *Treaty and Covenant*, 6.

hältnis"[298] of respective parties[299] He suggested that this *Grundsatzerklärung* formed a close link between the preamble and historical prologue on the one side, and the particular stipulations[300] on the other. It constitutes a delineation of the purpose of the treaty, which is then reinforced with precise stipulations.[301] Josh. 24:14, according to Baltzer, constitutes a *Grundsatzerklärung* rather than the more precise *Einzelbestimmungen.*

It is surely not fortuitous that Josh. 24 is the first example Baltzer utilized to demonstrate an affinity between treaty texts and OT material, for he claims to find in this passage many similarities to the treaties. A summary of these claims serves to illustrate his approach.[302]

Josh. 24 is typified as a reworked treaty formulary (*erarbeitete Vertragsformular*), which may be divided into two major parts or acts:

1. vss.2-14: conditions of the covenant (*Bedingungen des Bundes*)
   a. preamble vs.2 *kh 'mr yhwh 'lhy yṣr'l*
   b. historical prologue vss.2-13
   c. *Grundsatzerklärung* vs.14
2. vss.15-27: swearing of the covenant (*Beschwörung des Bundes*)
   vs.15 transition; Joshua represents people rather than Yahweh
   vss.17-18a correspond with the historical prologue
   vss.16, 18b correspond with the *Grundsatzerklärung*
   vss.19-24 curse, blessing and witness
   vss.25-27 written documentation and depositing of document

Numerous scholars have disagreed with these conclusions, whether in finer details or in the broader analysis. It has not been our intention to enter into this debate, but rather to illustrate the manner in which Baltzer depicted Josh. 24 as an example of the covenant formulary.

[298]That is, fundamental statement of intentions regarding the future relationship.
[299]Baltzer, *Das Bundesformular*, 20. Baltzer noted (20 n.1) that A.Goetze, in his study of the treaty between Muršilliš II and Duppi-Teššub, identified a clause describing "future relations of the two countries," which followed the preamble and the historical prologue, cf. *ANET*, 2nd ed. (Princeton, 1955), 203f.
[300]Einzelbestimmungen der Verträge.
[301]Baltzer, *Das Bundesformular*, 22f.
[302]Baltzer, *Das Bundesformular*, 29-37.

### 1.5.3 W.Beyerlin

One of the most detailed responses to von Rad's hypothesis that the Exodus tradition was originally separate from the Sinai tradition was presented by W.Beyerlin.[303] The Sinai pericopes of the Book of Exodus provide the focal point for his work. He begins with textual analysis, and restricts his study to the Elohistic and Yahwistic material of Ex. 19; 20; 24; 32-34. A detailed analysis of Josh. 24 is not offered,[304] but the frequency with which it is appealed to in comparison with Exodus material demonstrates the significant role it played in his analysis of the Sinaitic complex and and subsequent narratives of covenant renewal festivals at a central sanctuary.

Beyerlin's observations regarding Josh. 24 and 8:30-35 are particularly interesting insofar as they demonstrate a self-conscious attempt to harmonize many of the historical conclusions of Alt, Noth, von Rad and Kraus with the newer trend of treaty-covenant comparisons. Beyerlin accepted the basic premise that Shechem was the location of a pre-monarchical amphictyonic covenant[305] enacted in a periodically repeated cultic festival at which the will of God was proclaimed in laws and statutes constituting covenantal obligations for the people.[306] The cultic covenant renewal festival of Shechem was judged to have had an enduring effect in Israel; the reading of the law and the covenantal response of the people is witnessed in connection with the Feast of Booths as late as Neh. 8.[307] Beyerlin concluded that throughout the period of the monarchy the Feast of Booths likely provided the setting for a cultic festival in which covenantal stipulations were established.[308] This ceremony was celebrated successively in various historical periods at sanctuaries in Shechem, Gilgal, and Jerusalem.[309]

Comparison of Josh. 24:1-28, 8:30-35 and Deut. 11:29f.; 27 with the Sinai account leads Beyerlin to qualified agreement with von Rad's theory that the Sinai traditions find their earliest *Sitz im Leben* in

[303]W.Beyerlin, *Herkunft und Geschichte der ältesten Sinaitraditionen* (Tubingen, 1961) (= *Origins and History of the Oldest Sinaitic Traditions* [Oxford, 1965]).
[304]Cf. Beyerlin, *Herkunft und Geschichte*, 172f. n.6.
[305]Beyerlin, *Herkunft und Geschichte*, 36, 54ff., 172ff.
[306]Beyerlin, *Herkunft und Geschichte*, 49, 173.
[307]Beyerlin, *Herkunft und Geschichte*, 49; see too Ezra 3:1-7.
[308]Beyerlin, *Herkunft und Geschichte*, 51.
[309]Beyerlin, *Herkunft und Geschichte*, 56f.

the Shechemite cult.[310] On the basis of the treaty pattern which he detected in the literary form of the Exodus narratives he disagreed, however, that Exodus and Sinai represent two originally separate traditions which were later merged in Israel's history writing.[311] Rather, in the wilderness period, under the mediatorial guidance of Moses at Kadesh, a covenant was enacted and duly documented according to the standard covenant form illustrated by Hittite texts;[312] that covenant tradition found immediate continuity in the cultic festival at Shechem,[313] and ultimately in Jerusalem during the time of the monarchy.

### 1.5.4 J.L'Hour

J.L'Hour speaks appreciatively of new methods of handling OT covenant texts in comparison with extra-biblical materials, especially as that method was promoted in the form-critical appraisal of Mendenhall–developments which in his opinion "infusé un sang nouveau aux recherches sur l'Alliance."[314] He places his study of Josh. 24 deliberately in the line of Mendenhall's work, but his initial focus is upon a literary-critical analysis of the text. As a second step he asks what sort of adjustments were necessary in the transformation of the covenant form from a political type of document to a liturgical text.[315] For our present purpose, it is not necessary to summarize L'Hour's observations concerning the form of extra-biblical treaties; we concentrate rather upon his particular claims concerning Josh. 24's alleged history of literary growth and its final, liturgical form.[316]

According to L'Hour, vss.1-13 reveal both ancient tradition and later redaction. In vs.1 the call to Shechem and the mention of *'lhym* is ancient, while the list of those who were gathered is a later at-

[310]Beyerlin, *Herkunft und Geschichte*, 58.

[311]Beyerlin, *Herkunft und Geschichte*, 165 n.1, 74ff., 168ff.; cf. F.C.Fensham, "Covenant, Promise and Expectation in the Bible," *ThZ* 23 (1967) 305-322.

[312]Beyerlin, *Herkunft und Geschichte*, 66, 168.

[313]Beyerlin accepts the MT rather than LXX in Josh. 24:1,25. This is mentioned not less than six times, with footnotes referring the reader to Muilenburg, "Form and Structure."

[314]J.L'Hour, "L'alliance de Sichem," *RB* 69 (1962) 6.

[315]L'Hour, "L'alliance de Sichem" 6: "Le transfert, à un plan religieux, d'un schéma culturel profane ne va pas sans laisser son empreinte sur la forme elle-même et, plus encore, sur la signification de la réalité sous-jacente."

[316]J.L'Hour, *La morale de l'alliance* (Paris, 1966), 9.

tempt to harmonize with 23:2b.[317] The introduction of speech in vs.2a is comparable to the introduction in ancient Hittite treaties.[318] Vss.2b-13 contain redactional retouching, e.g., vss.11b, 12b, 13, but for the rest, "le fond primitif demeure considérable et constitue une unité."[319] The choice presented by Joshua in vss.14-15, so vital to the historical reconstruction of a tribal confederation defended by Sellin and Noth, is also old.[320] Original and redactional material are considered difficult to distinguish in vss.16-24. Nevertheless, vss.16-18a are thought to be later additions, revealing similarity to Dtistic terminology, e.g., *'lhym 'ḥrym* and *yhwh 'lhynw*, as well as particular dependency upon prophetic material.[321] Vs.18b is sufficient as a response to vs.15.[322] Vss.19-24 are late.[323] "*En résumé*, le substrat ancien de cette section se limite aux vv.14-15 et 18b: invitation de Josué et choix du peuple."[324]

It is particularly in vss.25-27 that L'Hour misses certain details which might be expected in the treaty form, e.g., explicit mention of the stipulations, the curses and blessings, and inscription upon a stele as witness. The present state of the text is the product of considerable amelioration, finally by a post-exilic redactor influenced by the Dtistic movement but in fact working even later than this school. This conclusion hinges especially on the contention that *ḥq wmšpṭ, twrt 'lhym* and *bmqdš* are most closely paralleled in post-exilic texts.[325] Futhermore, L'Hour contends that the stipulations missing in vss.25-27 should be identified with an early form of the Book of the Covenant (Ex. 20:22-23:19).[326] He thereby reasserts a long-standing

[317] L'Hour, "L'alliance de Sichem," 23.

[318] L'Hour, "L'alliance de Sichem," 7, 22.

[319] L'Hour, "L'alliance de Sichem," 25.

[320] L'Hour, "L'alliance de Sichem," 25f.

[321] L'Hour, "L'alliance de Sichem," 27.

[322] L'Hour, "L'alliance de Sichem," 27f.

[323] L'Hour, "L'alliance de Sichem," 28: Vss.19-20 are considered scarcely comprehensible in light of vs.14. Furthermore, *qnw'* is considered late terminology on the basis of comparison with Nah. 1:2. Vs.21 is incomprehensible without vs.20. Vs.22 is thought to present a view of witness inconsistent with other covenant passages and with vs.27, "s'accorde mal tant avec le mode général des alliances qu'avec le v.27 qui présente les traits d'une antiquité manifeste," and *wy'mrw 'dym* in vs.22b, upon comparison with Ruth 4:10f. is taken as evidence of "un langage plus récent." Finally, vs.23a is a reduplication of vs.15, and vs.24 "est de style deutéronomiste."

[324] L'Hour, "L'alliance de Sichem," 28. Cf. *La morale de l'alliance*, 56.

[325] L'Hour, "L'alliance de Sichem," 29-34.

[326] L'Hour, "L'alliance de Sichem," esp. 18, 168, 182-184, 361, 364; *La morale de*

theory that an ancient Shechem covenant tradition was slowly replaced by a Sinaitic tradition, with the stipulations being transferred, under Dtistic influence, from Joshua to Moses as the legitimate lawgiver.[327] The new dimension to L'Hour's proposal is that his claim can be proven by the absence in Josh. 24:1-28 of certain elements crucial to the form of treaty texts, and secondly, that the final, postexilic redactor has attempted, via addition of material in vss.16-24 and amelioration of vss.25-27, to give the passage a character more predominantly liturgical than the legal emphasis which the ancient tradition once projected.

### 1.5.5 M.G.Kline / K.A.Kitchen

In the preceding paragraphs we have noted how Mendenhall, Baltzer, Beyerlin and L'Hour appealed to comparisons between a set treaty form and covenant texts in their analysis of Josh. 24:1-28 and the role of Shechem in Israel's history. Their conclusions were not unanimous, but a degree of solidarity was evident in their appraisal of the validity of drawing comparisons between Hittite treaty texts and Old Testament covenantal narratives. Josh. 24 was heralded as a prime text by which to demonstrate the validity of this approach.[328]

*l'alliance*, 53, 78.

[327]The first to suggest that the Book of the Covenant was originally the law given by Joshua in 24:25f. appears to have been H.Holzinger, *Einleitung in den Hexateuch* (Freiburg and Leipzig, 1893), 179f., 250. His proposal found a sympathetic reception in numerous works. See Steuernagel, *Josua*, 242; Sellin, *Gilgal*, 51f.; Rudolph, *Der "Elohist"*, 252; W.Staerk, *Das Deuteronomium* (Leipzig, 1894), 106. Holzinger's proposal was a modification of Kuenen's suggestion. Kuenen made no connection with Josh. 24, but he thought that the pre-Dtic Book of the Covenant originally may have been associated with a JE account of the covenant at Moab prior to the crossing of the Jordan, secondarily inserted into the Sinai account of Exodus (*Historisch-critisch onderzoek* 1885, 1:252-255; "Bijdragen tot de critiek van Pentateuch en Jozua. VIII, Israel bij den Sinai," *ThT* 15 (1881) 164-223). Holzinger's suggestion was an alternative to Kuenen's position, but he retained the idea that the present location of the Book of the Covenant is secondary. Skepticism concerning the proposals by Kuenen and Holzinger was expressed by O.Procksch, *Geschichtsbetrachtung und geschichtliche Überlieferung bei den vorexilischen Propheten* (Leipzig, 1902), 149 n.1. See also B.Luther and E.Meyer, in Meyer, *Die Israeliten*, 553; Mowinckel, *Le décalogue*, 35. L'Hour's judgment is strongly influenced by J.Morgenstern, "The Book of the Covenant, Part III–The Ḥuqqim," *HUCA* 8-9 (1931-1932) 65-68.

[328]See also Muilenburg, "Form and Structure" 351-365; W.Zimmerli, "Das Gesetz im Alten Testament," *ThLZ* 85 (1960) 481-498, esp. 492-494; von Rad, *OT Theol-*

Contemporaneous with the work of Baltzer and Beyerlin began a movement within more conservative OT circles to draw yet more consequential conclusions from such form-critical comparisons. The names of M.G.Kline[329] and K.A.Kitchen[330] may be mentioned as leaders. When the pendulum of scholarly opinion began to swing back from its initial inclination in the direction of Mendenhall et al.,[331] these scholars stood their ground, and throughout the last twenty-five years this position has retained a minority of advocates.[332]

Kitchen claims that Hittite treaties of the 14th and 13th centuries B.C. demonstrate a "remarkable consistency of form"[333] entirely distinct from Syrian and Mesopotamian treaties of the first millenium B.C.[334] Josh. 24 is not itself a covenant document, but a description of

*ogy*, 1:132; Huffmon, "The Exodus," 104; Hillers, *Covenant*, 46-71.

[329]M.G.Kline, "The Two Tables of the Covenant," *WTJ* 22 (1959-60) 133-146; "Dynastic Covenant," *WTJ* 23 (1960-61) 1-15 (these two articles are reproduced in *The Treaty of the Great King: The Covenant Structure of Deuteronomy: Studies and Commentary* [Grand Rapids, 1963]); "Law Covenant," *WTJ* 27 (1964-65) 1-20; "Oath and Ordeal Signs," *WTJ* 27 (1964-65) 115-139; "Oath and Ordeal Signs: Second Article," *WTJ* 28 (1965-66) 1-37 (these last three articles are reprinted with some updating in *By Oath Consigned* [Grand Rapids, 1968]); "Abram's Amen," *WTJ* 31 (1968-69) 1-11; *The Structure of Biblical Authority*, revised ed. (Grand Rapids, 1975).

[330]K.A.Kitchen, *Ancient Orient and Old Testament* (London, 1966), 89-111; "Ancient Orient, 'Deuteronism,' and the Old Testament," in J.B.Payne, ed., *New Perspectives on the Old Testament* (Waco, 1970), 1-24; *The Bible in its World* (Downers Grove, 1977), 75-85.

[331]Cf. also numerous studies by J.A.Thompson, e.g., "Non-Biblical Covenants in the Ancient Near East and Their Relevance for Understanding the Covenant Motif in the Old Testament," *ABR* 8 (1960) 38-45 (esp. 45, re Josh. 24); "The Significance of the Ancient Near Eastern Treaty Pattern," *THB* 13 (1963) 1-6 (esp. 3, 5); *The Ancient Near Eastern Treaties and the Old Testament* (London, 1964), esp. 34; "The Near Eastern Suzerain–Vassal Concept in the Religion of Israel," *JRH* 3 (1964) 1-19, esp. 9.

[332]E.g., S.R.Külling, *Zur Datierung der "Genesis-P-Stücke," namentlich des Kapitels Genesis XVII* (Kampen, 1964); J.B.Payne, "The B'rith of Yahweh," in Payne, ed., *New Perspectives*, 240-264; J.R.Vannoy, *Covenant Renewal at Gilgal: A Study of I Samuel 1:14-12:25* (Cherry Hill, NJ, 1977), esp. 132-159; E.C.Lucas, "Covenant, Treaty, and Prophecy," *Themelios* 8 (1982) 19-23; A.E.M.A.van Veen-Vrolijk, "Het Verbond in het Oude Nabije Oosten," in A.G.Knevel et al., eds., *Verkenningen in Genesis* (Kampen, 1986), 65; M.J.Paul, "De Verbondssluiting aan de Sinaï," in A.G.Knevel et al., eds., *Verkenningen in Exodus* (Kampen, 1986), 58-66.

[333]Kitchen, *Bible in its World*, 80.

[334]Kitchen, *Bible in its World*, 81.

covenant renewal;[335] nevertheless, it incorporates the elements of the earlier treaty pattern, which leads to the conclusion "Joshua 24 would necessarily stem from about 1200 BC or not long afterwards."[336]

Of particular significance in Kline's study is an emphasis upon the canonical importance of the treaty and covenant concept.[337] Kline argues that ancient NE treaty texts had an inherent canonical quality in their intentional binding of the receiving parties. The various legal documents are per se canonical.[338] In the OT decalogue, Deuteronomy, and passages such as Josh. 24 and 8:30-35 the classic international treaty-form of the Mosaic age was adopted along with its inherent literary implications regarding canonicity.[339] Kline asserts, "Canon is inherent in covenant, covenant of the kind attested in ancient international relations and the Mosaic covenants of the Bible."[340] It follows that canonicity does not stand at the end of the process of the OT's development but from the very beginning it is present in the covenantal character of the texts.[341] Text and covenant are thus inseparably related. Episodes of covenant making and of covenant renewal constitute "literary high points" in Israel's history writing,[342] of which Josh. 8:30-35 and 24 provide classic examples.

[335]Kitchen, *Bible in its World*, 81, 83.

[336]Kitchen, *Bible in its World*, 83.

[337]The canonical emphasis is especially dominant in *The Structure of Biblical Authority*, 1975, where numerous previous works are reissued under this overarching theme. Cf. his "The Correlation of the Concepts of Canon and Covenant," in Payne, ed., *New Perspectives*, 265-279.

[338]Kline, *The Structure*, 27-34; "The Correlation," 266-270.

[339]"The origin of the Old Testament canon coincided with the founding of the kingdom of Israel by covenant at Sinai" (*The Structure*, 43; cf. 35-37).

[340]Kline, *The Structure*, 43f.

[341]Kline, *The Structure*, 43-44, 66-68, 74-75. While there are significant parallels between Kline's emphasis on canonicity and that of Childs, the two may not be equated. A major differences is the respective emphasis upon divine initiative and community initiative in the instigation of canonical texts. Kline makes explicit, "Canonical authority is not derived from community, but covenantal canon connotes covenantal community." While this emphasis is not absent in Childs (cf. *Theology in Crisis*, 105), the main emphasis falls on the actualizing community (99-104); cf. his *Introduction to the Old Testament as Scripture* (Philadelphia, 1979), 51-106.

[342]Kline lists as covenantal climaxes, Josh. 8:30ff.; 23 and 24; I Sam. 12; 2 Sam. 7; 2 Kgs 11:17ff.; 22 and 23; 2 Chron. 15:8ff.; 34 and 35; Ezra 9 and 10; Neh. 9 and 10 (*The Structure*, 55).

### 1.5.6 P.Kalluveettil

Brief mention ought to also be made here of a recent work by P.Kalluveettil,[343] which is a study based upon his dissertation prepared under the direction of McCarthy.[344] Although this work restricts itself primarily to secular covenants,[345] and then specifically to the declaration formulae which constitute an important element of that particular category of covenant or treaty texts, Kalluveettil calls attention to numerous elements of significance for our study. He concludes that in texts such as Josh. 24:14 the word *w'th* serves as an *überleitungspartikel* in the covenant form to mark the transition from an historical section to a demand.[346] In his opinion, Josh. 24:15 concludes with a covenant oath.[347] Particular significance is attributed to the word *ywm* with the definite article (vs.15). Vs.18 is read as a *Bundesformel*, but here, as in 1 Kgs 18:39, it is the people rather than the superior party who enunciate the formula.[348] In vs.25, *bywm hhw'* is judged to be of special significance in the report of covenant making (cf. vs.15).[349] In agreement with W.L.Moran,[350] he sees the words *'t-hdbrym h'lh* in vs.26 as a reference to the covenantal stipulations, *ḥq wmšpṭ*, vs.25.[351]

Since Josh. 24 is classified as a religious covenant text, and Kalluveettil's focus is upon the declaration formula in secular covenants, the references to Josh. 24 are incidental. Nevertheless, these passing references indicate the similarities detected by Kalluveettil between Josh. 24 and secular covenant forms, both biblical and extra-biblical.

[343]P.Kalluveettil, *Declaration and Covenant: A Comprehensive Review of Covenant Formulae from the Old Testament and the Ancient Near East* (Rome, 1982).

[344]Kalluveettil, *Declaration and Covenant*, v; cf. section 1.6.7.

[345]"*Secular Covenants* designate those pacts to which Yahweh is not one of the parties involved, even though they are made effective by an oath which was usually an appeal to the deity" (*Declaration and Covenant*, 4).

[346]Kalluveettil, *Declaration and Covenant*, 115. See also Muilenburg, "Form and Structure," 353, 359; L'Hour, "L'alliance de Sichem," 25; Brekelmans, "Het 'historische Credo'," 7; A.Laurentin, "*We'attah–Kai nun*. Formule caractéristique des textes juridiques et liturgiques," *Bibl* 45 (1964) 168-197, 413-432; H.A.Brongers, "Bemerkungen zum Gebrauch des Adverbialen *We'attāh* im Alten Testament," *VT* 15 (1965) 289-299, esp. 290; McCarthy, *Treaty and Covenant*, 272.

[347]Kalluveettil, *Declaration and Covenant*, 184.

[348]Kalluveettil, *Declaration and Covenant*, 213.

[349]Kalluveettil, *Declaration and Covenant*, 184.

[350]W.L.Moran, "Review of K.Baltzer, *Das Bundesformular*," *Bibl* 43 (1962) 105.

[351]Kalluveettil, *Declaration and Covenant*, 33.

Furthermore, a careful study of the terms, expressions and formulas surveyed by Kalluveettil indicates numerous additional similarities between the vocabulary of Josh. 24 and terminology judged to be particularly characteristic of various covenant texts.[352] Consider, for example, the following possible candidates:

1) the root *'bd*, which frequently designates vassalship, occurs 16x in Josh. 24:1-28, i.e., vss.2, 14(3x), 15(4x), 16, 17, 18, 19, 20, 21, 22, 24.[353]

2) *wlḥṭ'wtykm* (vs.19); the Hebrew *ḥṭ'*, along with its Akkadian equivalent, *ḫaṭû*, can be a *terminus technicus* for treaty violation.[354] It is particularly interesting to note the connection with *pš'* here, which has been identified in other contexts as a treaty term.[355]

3) *whr'* and *hyṭyb* (vs.20).[356]

4) *šlḥ* at the conclusion of a covenant gathering (vs.28).[357]

5) *ntn* and granting of land (vss.4, 13).[358]

These examples demonstrate that Kalluveettil's analysis of declaration formulae in the covenant texts is potentially important for the study of Josh. 24:1-28.

### 1.5.7 Summary

Studies by especially Mendenhall, Baltzer, and Beyerlin stimulated a new phase in the study of Josh. 24. Typical of this movement was a search for literary correlations between biblical, covenantal texts and ancient treaty documents, which led to the assertion of a specific OT genre, a covenant formulary dependent upon the treaty form. Josh.

[352]Kalluveettil, *Declaration and Covenant*, 66f., 191-197.

[353]Kalluveettil, *Declaration and Covenant*, 71. See too Z.Zevit, "The Use of *'bd* as a Diplomatic Term in Jeremiah," *JBL* 88 (1969) 74-77; M.Fishbane, "The Treaty Background of Amos 1:11 and Related Matters," *JBL* 89 (1970) 315; F.C.Fensham, "Notes on Treaty Terminology in Ugaritic Epics," *UF* 11 (1979) 269, 272.

[354]Kalluveettil, *Declaration and Covenant*, 42-47, 176 (note the connection between *r'h* and *'zb* in Kalluveettil's discussion as well as in Josh. 24:20).

[355]See H.Wildberger, *Jesaja* (BKAT X,1; Neukirchen-Vluyn, 1965), 14; J.Limburg, "The Root *ryb* and the Prophetic Lawsuit Speeches," *JBL* 88 (1969) 303f.; Fishbane, "Treaty Background," 317; cf. Kalluveettil, *Declaration and Covenant*, 64 (re 1 Kgs 12:19).

[356]Kalluveettil, *Declaration and Covenant*, 200f.

[357]Kalluveettil, *Declaration and Covenant*, 200f.

[358]Kalluveettil, *Declaration and Covenant*, 178 n.225, 180 n.234.

24 and Ex. 24 were considered choice examples of literary dependence upon a Hittite treaty pattern, but there was no unanimity regarding the degree to which this literary correspondence could be drawn. Attempts to delineate specific correlations produced divergent results. Nevertheless, the fascination with ancient treaty texts eclipsed much of the previous effort to find various sources in Josh. 24.

What was not eclipsed in these studies, however, was the interest in Shechem as the setting for Josh. 24. The relationship between Sinai and Shechem remained as crucial for an evaluation of historical implications in this approach as it had been in the previous theories of Noth, von Rad and Kraus. This question is particularly critical for L'Hour, who argued that the standard treaty form which orginally provided the blueprint for Josh. 24 had already lost many of its indigenous features by the end of the complex redactional process which transformed Josh. 24:1-28 from a legal format to a heterogeneously constructed liturgical text.

Numerous scholars, including already Mendenhall,[359] argued that a close correspondence between the literary structure of Josh. 24 and treaty texts heightens the narrative's historical credibility. The emphasis on historicity was given greater attention in the studies of Kline, Kitchen et al., who used form-critical considerations to defend an early date for the literary composition of Josh. 24:1-28. The question of dating on the basis of form soon became a point of radical disagreement, as will be evident from the survey offered in the following section.

## 1.6 Covenant and Dtistic theology; writing history anew

### 1.6.1 Introduction

The preceding section surveyed the works of a number of scholars who attempted to explain Josh. 24 via recourse to form-critical comparisons with ancient treaty texts. Hittite sources played a predominant role in that endeavor. Unquestionably this was a desirable methodological advancement insofar as it broadened the field of comparison within which to discuss OT covenant texts. Earlier studies relied inordinately upon comparison with nomadic Arabic customs within

[359]Mendenhall, *Law and Covenant*, 41 n.41

clan and family structures, as is evident in comparisons drawn by Wellhausen,[360] Karge,[361] Pedersen,[362] and others.[363]

It is ordinarily not the *fact* that Hittite treaties were employed to attempt to clarify OT covenants, but rather the *manner* in which they were used that has been sharply criticized from various angles in the last two decades, and it is appropriate to now present the response of numerous scholars whose works can best be broadly subsumed under the theme of ***covenant and Dtistic theology.*** Within this grouping we collect numerous representatives whose methodology and conclusions are by no means homogeneous. The conclusions reached by McCarthy and Weinfeld, for example, contrast markedly with those of Perlitt and Kutsch. Nevertheless, what they have in common is a desire to re-evaluate the interpretation of Josh. 24 on the basis of recent theological developments in the area of Dtistic theology. These developments are accompanied by a new analysis of the meaning of *bryt* and its role in ancient Israel. Since the meaning of the word *bryt* has appropriated a central emphasis in various recent analyses of the covenant concept in Josh. 24, it is fitting to begin this section with a summary of studies by J.Begrich and A.Jepsen. Their essays provided a foundation for the assessment by Kutsch and, to a lesser extent, that of Perlitt.

In addition to questions arising directly from the semantic field of *bryt*, however, there is the broader question of Josh. 24's role in the entire corpus of historical writing from Deuteronomy–2 Kings. Currently it is in the area of Dtistic history that many contemporary scholars seek to answer the riddles of Josh. 24. In essence this marks a return, after an interlude in which studies focused primarily on covenant-treaty comparisons, to the agenda set by Noth and von Rad, albeit now tempered to varying degrees by insights gleaned from extensive comparison with ancient NE material of a wide diversity,

[360]J.Wellhausen, *Reste arabischen Heidentums*, 2nd ed. (Berlin and Leipzig, 1927), esp. 124-129, 186-195.

[361]Karge, *Geschichte des Bundesgedankens*, 235-246.

[362]Pedersen, *Der Eid*; the entire monograph focused upon Arabian practices, with much attention given to the study of inter-clan bonds established by various customs.

[363]E.g., W.R.Smith, *Lectures On the Religion of the Semites: The Fundamental Institutions*, 3rd ed. (London, 1927), esp. 312-352; *Kinship and Marriage in Early Arabia*, 2nd ed. (London, 1894), esp. 296ff.; H.C.Trumbull, *The Blood Covenant* (New York, 1885); cf. Mendenhall, *Law and Covenant*, 26 n.6.

not simply, or even primarily, Arabian or Hittite sources.

### 1.6.2 J.Begrich / A.Jepsen

Our review of Valeton, Kraetzschmar and Karge noted that in addition to source critical concerns these scholars display recurring efforts to define more precisely the OT meaning of *bryt* in the various literary genres. However, their conclusions concerning the meaning of *bryt* were presented as suggestive and tentative attempts at greater terminological precision, rather than definitive classifications. They questioned the propriety of treating *bryt* as a bilateral bond without due regard to the concomitant obligations placed upon Israel. Their analyses, although neither fully developed nor immediately integrated in broader OT circles of study, provided a stimulus for more recent appraisals by Begrich, Jepsen and Kutsch.

In Begrich's opinion, *bryt* originally denoted a unilateral relation between two people or groups,[364] by which the more powerful party was the initiator of the relationship.[365] Subsequent to the middle of the 9th cent. B.C., the meaning of *bryt* shifted to designate bilateral covenant relations in which both partners of the relationship have rights and obligations. Begrich claims that the bilateral dimension of human treaty relations was thereby imported into the description of the relationship between Yahweh and people. This shift from a unilateral to a bilateral meaning is recognizable in the terminology itself, and especially in the prepositions used in descriptions of the establishment of a *bryt*.

> "Die Umwandlung der Denkform wird nun aber daran erkennbar, dass statt der alten Formel *krt bryt l* sich nunmehr die Wendung bildet *krt bryt 't* oder *'m* oder auch *bn*, zumeist mit pluralischer Form des Verbs."[366]

Begrich suggests that this secondary meaning of *bryt* as bilateral treaty relation is evident in the redaction of covenant narratives describing the relationship between Israel and Yahweh, and it entailed a

[364] J.Begrich, "Berit. Ein Beitrag zur Erfassung einer alttestamentlichen Denkform," *ZAW* 60 (1944) 2.

[365] Begrich, "Berit. Ein Beitrag," 2-4. He notes that the weaker party could plea for protection, as in Josh. 9:6,11; 1 Sam. 11:1; 2 Sam. 3:12; 1 Kgs 20:34, but he argues that the stronger party is the founder of the relation and determines its character with the unilateral establishment of obligations.

[366] Begrich, "Berit. Ein Beitrag," 5.

shift to greater stress upon *obligatory law* as the essential element in Israel's relationship to Yahweh.[367] But there remained a hesitation, especially in P, to rigorously and consistently apply this new, bilateral understanding of the Yahweh-Israel relationship for fear that it would present Yahweh and people as two equal partners.[368]

Josh. 24:25-27 illustrates the secondary development in which the two-sided relationship is typified by both election and obligation.[369] Here the treaty relationship between Yahweh and people is visible in the merging of two aspects, *bryt* and law. The book of the covenant used in the covenant ceremony contains the law by which Israel obligates herself to obedience. This book becomes fundamental in the E tradition of covenant enactments.[370] Whereas the preposition *l* is retained here, the bilateralness of the relationship is made evident in the description of the ceremonial context within which the relationship is situated.[371] The new meaning of the relationship cannot yet be carried by the word *bryt* alone, so it must be clarified with a description of the accompanying legal ceremony. In this way the *bryt* relationship was made contingent upon observance of the law. It was no longer a free and unqualified donation by the superior party; by keeping the law Israel could insure her relationship with Yahweh, her covenant partner.

A.Jepsen went a step further than Begrich by questioning whether a *bryt* entailed a relationship between partners.[372] There remained in Begrich's position an ambivalence between *bryt* as "treaty" or as "relationship," as act or as consequence of the act.[373] Jepsen accepted the methodological procedure inherited from previous studies, using inter-human *bryt* texts in the OT as comparative material to explain the nature of a Yahweh–Israel *bryt*. But in his opinion the crux of

[367]See W.Eichrodt, "Bund und Gesetz. Erwägungen zur neueren Diskussion," in H.Graf Reventlow, ed., *Gottes Wort und Gottes Land* (Fs H.W.Hertzberg; Göttingen, 1965), 30-49 (= "Covenant and Law: Thoughts on Recent Discussion," *Interp* 20 [1966] 302-321).

[368]Begrich, "Berit. Ein Beitrag," 7-9.

[369]Begrich, "Berit. Ein Beitrag," 8.

[370]Begrich, "Berit. Ein Beitrag," 8. Begrich views Josh. 24 as an E tradition affiliated to Dtistic accounts of ceremonial covenant enactment.

[371]Begrich, "Berit. Ein Beitrag," 8.

[372]A.Jepsen, "Berith. Ein Beitrag zur Theologie der Exilseit," in A.Kuschke, ed., *Verbannung und Heimkehr. Beiträge zur Geschichte und Theologie Israels im 6. und 5. Jahrhundert v. Chr.* (Fs W.Rudolph; Tübingen, 1961), 161-179.

[373]Jepsen, "Berith. Ein Beitrag," 162.

the argument was not whether the *bryt* was unilateral or bilateral, or whether it involved equal or unequal parties, because examples of all these can be found.[374] The crux is the precise meaning of *bryt*, which Jepsen defined as the action or ceremony with which one takes obligations upon himself; "wenn sie eine Berith schneiden, eine feierliche Zusage geben, ein Versprechen ablegen, eine Verpflichtung übernehmen (nicht auferlegen!)".[375] This *self-obligation* is the heart of the matter in inter-human *bryt* forming.

But in a Yahweh-people *bryt* the emphasis is somewhat different. There it is always *God's bryt*; when Israel transgresses or breaks the *bryt* it is *God's* commandments, statutes, or stipulations that are broken, never Israel's *bryt*. This indicates the one-sided action of Yahweh in establishing the *bryt*.[376] The *bryt* concept as description of the relationship between Yahweh and Israel is primarily centered upon Yahweh's gracious approach to the people, whether to individuals such as Abraham or David, or to the nation, as at Sinai, in his declaration that he will be their God.[377] The essence of the "Gottes Berith" is thus placed in the rubric of what is generally termed the "*Bundesformel*."[378] The fact that God's gracious approach to man also entails subsequent demands of obedience does not alter the essential character of *bryt* as an act on the part of God. This leads Jepsen to raise his final question whether it isn't time to avoid the term *Bund* as translation of *bryt* in order to more correctly reflect the true nature of "Verheissung und Geheiss."[379]

[374]Jepsen, "Berith. Ein Beitrag," 165.

[375]Jepsen, "Berith. Ein Beitrag," 165. See 166: "So ergibt sich, dass eine menschliche Berith zuallermeist (Ausnahmen s. u.) den Akt einer feierlichen, vor Gott geschehenden Zusage, eines Versprechens, einer Selbstverpflichtung meint."

[376]Jepsen, "Berith. Ein Beitrag," 169f., 175.

[377]Jepsen, "Berith. Ein Beitrag," 174-178.

[378]For Jepsen this means that *bryt* has become *Theologumenon*. As to the origin of this *Gottes Berith* he says, "für die vorexilische Zeit finden sich nur wenige Belege," (178). Cf. R.Smend, *Die Bundesformel* (Zürich, 1963) (= *Die Mitte des Alten Testaments. Gesammelte Studien Band 1* [München, 1986], 11-39); N.Lohfink, "Beobachtungen zur Geschichte des Ausdrucks *'m yhwh*," in H.W.Wolff, ed., *Probleme biblischer Theologie* (Fs G.von Rad; München, 1971), 275-305. Smend and Lohfink agree that the *Bundesformel* was primarily used in exilic and post-exilic times, but they argue that it already existed in the time of the monarchy. Smend looks for a possible origin in the time of the Josianic reform "wo die Formel ja auch literarisch zu Hause ist" (16). Lohfink wishes to go back at least as far as Joash's coronation in 2 Kgs 11 (836 B.C.) (297-299).

[379]Jepsen, "Berith. Ein Beitrag," 179.

### 1.6.3 G.Schmitt

The agenda for Schmitt's monograph[380] is fourfold. Schmitt wishes to re-evaluate the literary-critical data pertinent to Josh. 24, the theological perspective of vss.2-24, the cultic background of the chapter, and finally, its historical reliability. His treatment of literary-critical questions is formulated essentially as a study of the extent to which Dtistic elements are discernible. He concurs with previous scholars that a series of glosses, whether Dtistic or otherwise, may be detected. In this category he lists *trḥ 'by 'brhm w'by nḥwr* (vs.2),[381] *w'šlḥ 't-mšh w't-'hrn*, and *hwṣ'ty 'tkm* (vs.5), *w'wṣy' 't-'bwtykm* (vs.6),[382] *w'šmydm mpnykm* (vs.8),[383] *l' bhrbk wl' bqštk* (vs.12),[384] *w't-'bwtynw* and *mbyt 'bdym* (vs.17),[385] *kl-h'mym w't* (vs.18),[386] *'lhynw* (vs.24),[387] and likely vss.26a, 27b.[388] Furthermore, an affinity to Dtistic terminology or ideology is detected in vss.1b,4b, the last part of 7b, in 10a,11 (*whgrgšy*), 12f.,17b,23b,24b.[389] Despite these affinities to Dtistic terminology, Schmitt argues that Josh. 24:2-24 finds its closest counterparts in portions of Exodus, Judg. 6:7-10; 10:10-16 and 1 Sam. 7-12, in material which cannot simply be classified as Dtistic.[390] The sermonic style must have been in use already prior to Deuteronomy. Considerable weight for Schmitt's denial that Josh. 24:2-24 is specifically Dtistic is also derived from comparison with Ps. 81,[391] and with Ex. 23:20ff.[392] In short, in Josh. 24:2-24 Schmitt sees striking similarities to Dtistic language, style and ideology, but he judges that there

[380] G.Schmitt, *Der Landtag von Sichem* (Stuttgart, 1964).
[381] Schmitt, *Der Landtag*, 10.
[382] Schmitt, *Der Landtag*, 8.
[383] Schmitt, *Der Landtag*, 10, 16.
[384] Schmitt, *Der Landtag*, 10, 16.
[385] Schmitt, *Der Landtag*, 9, 16.
[386] Schmitt, *Der Landtag*, 10.
[387] Schmitt, *Der Landtag*, 9.
[388] Schmitt, *Der Landtag*, 21.
[389] Schmitt, *Der Landtag*, esp. 16, 21, 57.
[390] Schmitt, *Der Landtag*, 17-21.
[391] Schmitt, *Der Landtag*, 22f.
[392] Schmitt, *Der Landtag*, 26-28. The list of nations (vs.11) is said to come from Exodus, not from Deuteronomy. Josh. 24:12 stands closer to Ex. 23:28 than to Deut. 7:20. Similarly, Josh. 24:17,18,19,24 all show affinity to Ex. 23. Schmitt conceeds that there is a close connection between Ex. 23:20ff. and Deut. 7, but he rejects Noth's conclusion that this makes the Exodus passage Dtistic. Cf. his *Du sollst keinen Frieden schliessen mit den Bewohnern des Landes* (Stuttgart, 1970), 13-21, esp. 18 n.5 regarding Josh. 24.

is sufficient evidence to demonstrate that the bulk of this material dates to a time previous to the Deuteronomist(s).[393] Furthermore, in vss.1a,25-28 he finds an older tradition to which vss.2-24 have later been added.[394] As a setting for the composition of the passage he suggests a time shortly after Elijah's opposition to the idolatry of the Omride dynasty.[395]

With respect to the passage's theology, Schmitt laments that in previous discussions it "ist von der Forschung etwas stiefmütterlich behandelt worden."[396] In his opinion the theology of vss.2-24 cannot be done justice in the tribal theories of Sellin and Noth, or in von Rad's credo theory. The dialogue between Joshua and the people is comprehensible only when one recognizes the original author's opinion that true worship of Yahweh is for the first possible when the people of Israel are in their own land.[397] It is in such a context that the affinities to the treaty texts are explicable. Basic agreement is expressed with the treaty analyses of Mendenhall, Baltzer and Beyerlin,[398] but the present form of the text derives from the cultic setting within which the covenant was periodically celebrated and renewed at Shechem, a location with an ancient covenant tradition.[399]

Schmitt posits that the question whether the passage describes a real event is not particularly relevant to vss.2-24, which are theologicaly motivated.[400] But vss.1,25-28, containing the older tradition, are another matter. The historical event attested here is misconstrued as the basis for a confederation of all the tribes (e.g., Noth), or Ephraim and Manasseh (Nielsen), and should rather be seen as the cultic establishment of laws and stipulations "in einer Gesetzgebung, die Israels Volksleben zu ordnen bestimmt ist."[401]

[393]Cf. Schmitt, *Frieden schliessen*, 39f.

[394]Schmitt, *Der Landtag*, 24. As an additional argument for a pre-Dtic date for Josh. 24, Schmitt appeals to the Hexateuch theory in which Josh. 24 is thought to be necessary as a conclusion to the *Landnahme* tradition(s) of JE (29f); cf. S.Tengström, *Die Hexateucherzählung. Ein literaturgeschichtliche Studie* (Uppsala, 1976), esp. 28, 33, 40-44, 117f., 154.

[395]Schmitt, *Der Landtag*, 32.

[396]Schmitt, *Der Landtag*, 7.

[397]Schmitt, *Der Landtag*, esp. 45-54, 80.

[398]Schmitt, *Der Landtag*, 60 n.10.

[399]Schmitt, *Der Landtag*, esp. 58-64, 77-79, 80; cf. his "El Berit–Mitra," *ZAW* 76 (1964) 325-327; *Frieden schliessen*, 108.

[400]Schmitt, *Der Landtag*, 80f.

[401]Schmitt, *Der Landtag*, 94.

### 1.6.4 E.Kutsch

During the last decades E.Kutsch has been one of the most prolific writers on the concept of covenant and the meaning of *bryt.*[402] He repeatedly emphasized that perennial claims regarding a *Bund* between Yahweh and Israel, alleged to be indigenous to the relation between Israel and Yahweh since Israel's earliest history, actually misconstrue the meaning of *bryt.* He expressed qualified agreement with Begrich. Kutsch viewed as helpful Begrich's emphasis upon *bryt* as obligation, but he refused to retain terminology such as "partners" and "relationship."[403] Following the lead of Jepsen, Kutsch denied that *bryt* originally meant relationship or partnership.[404]

Kutsch's argumentation is partially semantically based, but in the final analysis semantic questions are not axiomatic for his thesis.[405] His central argument is that that ***obligation***, with various nuances, is the most appropriate translation of *bryt* in the various OT contexts. From this perspective he seeks to clarify the nature of the obligation (*Verpflichtungsaktion*) involved in each case.

Accordingly, in Josh. 24:25 Kutsch asserts that it is not proper to speak of a *Bund* between God and Israel, but rather of the obligations (*Verpflichtungen*) placed by Joshua[406] upon the people in the presence

[402]E.Kutsch, "Der Begriff *bryt* in vordeuteronomischer Zeit," in F.Maass, ed., *Das Ferne und Nahe Wort* (Fs L.Rost; Berlin, 1967), 133-143; "Gesetz und Gnade: Probleme des alttestamentlichen Bundesbegriffs," *ZAW* 79 (1967) 18-35; "Von *bryt* zu 'Bund'," *KuD* 14 (1968) 159-182; "'Bund' und Fest. Zu Gegenstand und Terminologie einer Forschungsrichtung," *TheolQuart* 150 (1970) 299-320; "*Bryt* Verpflichtung," *THAT*, 339-352; "KARAT BERIT 'Eine Verpflichtung Festsetzen'," in H.Gese–H.P.Rüger, eds., *Wort und Geschichte* (Fs K.Elliger; Neukirchen-Vluyn, 1973), 121-127; *Verheissung und Gesetz. Untersuchungen zum sogenannten "Bund" im Alten Testament* (Berlin, 1973) (collects material from previous articles); "Gottes Zuspruch und Anspruch. *Bryt* in der alttestamentlichen Theologie," in C.H.W.Brekelmans, ed., *Questions disputées d'Ancien Testament. Méthode et Theologie* (23e session des Journées Bibliques de Louvain; Gembloux, 1974), 71-90.

[403]Kutsch, *Verheissung und Gesetz*, 5.

[404]Kutsch, "Gesetz und Gnade," 19-20, 34; "Sehen und Bestimmen: Die Etymologie von *bryt*," in A.Kuschke, ed., *Archäologie und Altes Testament* (Fs K.Galling; Tübingen, 1970), 169; "*Bryt* Verpflichtung," 340-352; *Verheissung und Gesetz*, 5.

[405]This is acknowledged by Kutsch, "Gesetz und Gnade," 20. It is also reflected in the order of his *Verheissung und Gesetz* in which the chapter on etymology follows his contextual survey of the meaning of *bryt* in the OT.

[406]Joshua's role here has generated much discussion and little consensus. Representative of the list of scholars arguing that Joshua represented Yahweh may be mentioned Valeton, "Das Wort *bryt*," 1892, 231f.; Schmitt, *Landtag*, 69: "Josua

of God.[407] Kutsch suggests that the phrase *krt bryt l* usually means obligating oneself (*Selbstverpflichtung*); Josh. 24:25 and 2 Kgs 11:4 are two exceptions in which this construction is used when obligations are placed upon another.[408] Josh. 24 does not describe a cultic festival of covenant renewal, and it emphatically is neither a treaty text nor an account of a treaty between Yahweh and Israel.[409] This assertion is consistent with his broader conclusion that prior to Jeremiah and Ezekiel, *bryt* does not mean *Bund* but *Verpflichtung*, and that there was not a covenant theology in early Israel.[410] It is not our intention here to evaluate Kutsch's position, but it must be noted that aspects of his method and conclusions alike have rightly been subjected to severe criticism by other scholars.[411]

### 1.6.5 L.Perlitt

The employment of covenant-treaty comparisons to defend an early date for Josh. 24 was challenged most severely by Perlitt.[412] Perlitt's major premise, which stands squarely in line with the thesis of Kutsch

handelt also als Vertreter Jahwes und in seinem Namen." For the view that Joshua was a third party mediator, but that he essentially represented the people, which is the meaning of *krt bryt l*, see Noth, "Old Testament Covenant-Making," 116f. H.W.Wolff responded to Noth with the contention that the Mari example of a mediator is not apropos to Josh. 24 because Joshua is not a "Höhergestellter" third party mediator ("Jahwe als Bundesvermittler," *VT* 6 [1956] 317). See also L'Hour, "L'alliance de Sichem," 29.

[407]Kutsch, "Der Begriff *bryt*," 140-141; "Von *bryt* zu 'Bund'" 161 n.11; "'Bund' und Fest," 307-308, 318.; *Neues Testament–Neuer Bund? Eine Fehlübersetzung wird korrigiert* (Neukirchen-Vluyn, 1978), 42.

[408]Kutsch, *Verheissung und Gesetz*, 22f.

[409]Kutsch, "'Bund' und Fest," 318f.; *Verheissung und Gesetz*, 64-66, 158-162, 167. Kutsch agrees with the complementary conclusions of Perlitt who dates Josh. 24 in the 7th cent. B.C. (see 1.6.5).

[410]Kutsch, "Der Begriff *bryt*," 142f.; *Verheissung und Gesetz*, 91f., 161.

[411]W.Eichrodt, "Darf man heute noch von einem Gottesbund mit Israel reden?" *ThZ* 30 (1974) 193-206, esp. 195 regarding Josh. 24:25; R.Martin-Achard, "Quelques remarques sur la nouvelle alliance chez Jérémie," in Brekelmans, ed., *Questions disputées*, 141-164, esp. 141f.; "Trois ouvrages sur l'alliance dans l'ancien testament," *RThPh* 110 (1978) 299-306, esp. 299-302; M.Weinfeld, "*Bryt*—Covenant vs. Obligation," *Bibl* 56 (1975) 120-128; J.Barr, "Some Semantic Notes on the Covenant," in H.Donner et al., eds., *Beiträge zur alttestamentlichen Theologie* (Fs W.Zimmerli; Göttingen, 1977), esp. 24f.; McCarthy, *Treaty and Covenant*, 16-22.

[412]L.Perlitt, *Bundestheologie im Alten Testament* (Neukirchen-Vluyn, 1969); this controversial study remains a standard work to be reckoned with by anyone who wishes to deal with the concept of covenant in the OT.

but works more with Dtistic theology than with the meaning of *bryt*, is that OT scholarship has long been guilty of reading into the Hebrew word *bryt* (and Greek $\delta\iota\alpha\theta\eta\kappa\eta$) a more global specification of the relationship between God and people than the meaning of the word in its OT usage merits. The term *bryt* does not provide a ready outline by which OT theology can be systematically structured.[413] The pervasive presence of the word *bryt* in the OT is credited to Dtistic influence in Israel's history writing, datable to the early exilic period.[414] This is not to say that the concept of *bryt* was invented by Israel's history writers, but that a true *Bundestheologie* first developed in the Dtistic concept of history.[415] In Dtistic history for the first, *twrh* and *bryt* come together to describe the relationship between Yahweh and Israel.[416] "Bundestheologie ... ist also die theologische Leistung der dtr Verfasser in einem Jahrhundert, in dem Israel genötigt war, Geschichte mehr zu erleiden als zu gestalten."[417]

The influence of this Dtistic "Bundestheologie" is judged to have been so pervasive that many covenant texts previously considered non-Dtistic are re-evaluated as evidence for redactional activity from a Dtistic perspective.[418]

It is hardly coincidental that whereas Baltzer began his study with Josh. 24,[419] that is precisely where Perlitt ends—but now with opposite conclusions. Baltzer utilized Josh. 24 as a springboard for his *Bundesformular* thesis. For Perlitt this passage crowns conclusions re-

[413]Perlitt, *Bundestheologie*, 2. Contra W.Eichrodt, *Theology of the Old Testament*, 2 vols., trans. J.A.Baker (Philadelphia, 1961-67).

[414]Perlitt, *Bundestheologie*, 30-32.

[415]See already Wellhausen, *Geschichte Israels, I*, 434f. n.1; Kraetzschmar, *Die Bundesvorstellung*, 37; R.H.Pfeiffer, "Facts and Faith in Biblical History," *JBL* 70 (1951) 2; Smend, "Die Bundesformel," 8f., 25-31; Whitley, "Covenant and Commandment," 42; Fohrer, "Altes Testament–'Amphiktyonie' und Bund," 901: "Aus alledem ergibt sich, dass eine wirkliche 'Bundes'-Theologie erst mit dem Deuteronomium beginnt...."; S.Herrmann, "Die konstruktive Restauration. Das Deuteronomium als Mitte biblischer Theologie," in Wolff, ed., *Probleme biblischer Theologie*, 155-170, esp. 162. See also H.-J.Hermisson, "Bund und Erwählung," in H.J.Boecker et al., eds., *Altes Testament* (Neukirchen-Vluyn, 1983), 222-243, esp. 223-229.

[416]Perlitt, *Bundestheologie*, 35.

[417]Perlitt, *Bundestheologie*, 30.

[418]See for example Hos. 6:7; 8:1; Gen. 15:18; Ex. 19:5; 24:7f.; 34:10, 27f.; 2 Sam. 23:5 discussed in McCarthy's review of Perlitt's study ("*Bᵉrît* in Old Testament," 110-121).

[419]Baltzer, *Das Bundesformular*, 29-37.

garding Dtistic theology drawn from his analysis of other texts. In his opinion Josh. 24:1-28 is not modelled upon a treaty form.[420] Its basic structure is divisible into two sections, a *Jahwerede* (vss.2-13) and a *Verpflichtungsszene* (vss.14-25).[421] The distinguishing characteristic and purpose of both sections is not narration of a covenant ceremony; the entire speech structure is kerygmatic. The stylistic *Gottesrede* and messenger formula placed in Joshua's mouth[422] in the first section, and the dialogical character of the second section, demonstrate that it is speech, not actions, that is the key to what is described here. The non-speech elements (vss.1,25f.,28) do not provide a narrative; they merely provide a minimal framework for the speech.[423] Furthermore, vs.19a proves that this can be neither treaty document nor cultic liturgy; vs.19a would be absurd in both cases.[424]

Theories of an ancient cultic festival or amphictyonic league at Shechem are rejected. Perlitt's work breaks as radically with the traditio-historical interpretations employing Josh. 24 as evidence for an early covenant tradition in Shechem as it does with the treaty-covenant comparisons. Josh. 24 does not provide a narrative tradition to support such conclusions.[425] Instead of proving a tradition of ancient covenant events at Shechem, Perlitt argues, Josh. 24 stands closer to Dtic texts such as Deut. 11:29; 27:12; Josh. 8:33.[426] A most plausible *Sitz im Leben* is provided by the reference to Assyrian gods beyond the river, which supports a 7th century date.[427] Perlitt's analysis thereby challenges fundamental and long-standing assumptions regarding the status of covenant as an essential component of the relationship between Yahweh and Israel from earliest times.[428]

[420]Perlitt's method and conclusions are enthusiastically received by L.Wächter, "Die Übertragung der Beritvorstellung auf Jahwe," *ThLZ* 99 (1974) 801-816.

[421]Perlitt, *Bundestheologie*, 242-243.

[422]Perlitt, *Bundestheologie*, 242.

[423]Perlitt, *Bundestheologie*, 241.

[424]"V.19a macht ein kultisches Gelübde absurd und ist als Vorbereitung eines Vertragsabschlusses so geeignet wie Öl zum Feuerlöschen" (*Bundestheologie*, 244).

[425]Perlitt, *Bundestheologie*, 248f. n.3, regarding Sellin's view of a periodically reccurring covenantal festival at Shechem he says, "Mit diesem Argument begann das ganze Unglück der Sichembund-Hypothesen; aber es ist grundfalsch ...."

[426]Perlitt, *Bundestheologie*, 248f.n3.

[427]Perlitt, *Bundestheologie*, 251f., 273. This makes Josh. 24 Dtic but prior to DtrH. Kutsch states his agreement with these conclusions, which complement his own position, cf. *Verheissung und Gesetz*, 65.

[428]Cf. the summary by Karge, *Geschichte des Bundesgedankens*, 255: "Der

### 1.6.6 M.Weinfeld

In the wake of Mendenall's studies, the validity of comparing OT covenant texts with extra-biblical documents has been vigorously disputed. Two important figures in this debate are Weinfeld and McCarthy, whose views are summarized in the present section and the next. Both stress the multiplicity of covenantal terminology and forms, and they emphasize the importance of both the similarities and differences which arise in a form-critical comparison of biblical covenants and extra-biblical treaties.

Weinfeld focuses particularly upon Deuteronomy, Dtistic theology, and history. And he has dedicated numerous studies to the covenant-treaty issue. In comparison with Perlitt's conclusion that Josh. 24 is Dtistic and is not patterned after a treaty form, it is instructive to now also present Weinfeld's opinion.

Weinfeld believes that the OT contains two conflicting traditions of when Israel became a nation in covenant under Yahweh, namely, the Sinai covenant cycle of Exodus, and the Moab-Shechem tradition preserved in certain texts in Deuteronomy and Joshua.[429] Deuteronomy betrays a compromise because it retains the leadership of Moses, while Josh. 24 attributes that leadership to Joshua.[430] Josh. 8:30-35 is from the Deuteronomist[431] while Josh. 24 is an older, Elohist document[432] which describes the enactment of a covenant loyalty oath.[433] Deuteronomy is thought to be a covenant document incorporating an ancient Shechem tradition; it was not transmitted via cultic ceremony and cultic clerics, but is an imitation of a covenant literary style which was prevalent in the 7th century.[434] Josh. 24, by contrast, only partially reflects a treaty pattern. Weinfeld asserts that

Bundesgedanke stand an der Wiege der israelitischen Religion und begann seine organisatorische Kraft im Augenblicke ihres Entstehens geltend zu machen. Unter der Form eines zwischen dem Bundesgott als Herrn des Bundes und dem von ihm erwählten Volke geschlossenen Berithverhältnisses trat die Jahwereligion ins Leben."

[429]M.Weinfeld, "The Emergence of the Deuteronomic Movement: The Historical Antecedents," in N.Lohfink, ed., *Das Deuteronomium: Entstehung, Gestalt und Botschaft* (*BETL* 68; Leuven, 1985), 76-79.

[430]Weinfeld, "Emergence," 78.

[431]M.Weinfeld, *Deuteronomy and the Deuteronomic School* (London, 1972), 65.

[432]Weinfeld, *Deuteronomy*, 165, 320.

[433]M.Weinfeld, "The Loyalty Oath in the Ancient Near East," *UF* 8 (1976) 405, 412; "*Bryt*-Covenant vs. Obligation," 123; "*Bryt*," *ThWAT*, 787.

[434]Weinfeld, *Deuteronomy*, 57, 59f.

standard treaty elements are lacking in Josh. 24, e.g., the curses and blessings,[435] invocation of cosmic witnesses,[436] oath-imprecation,[437] provision for deposit of the treaty text,[438] preparation of duplicate copies,[439] periodic reading of the treaty,[440] and delineation of the stipulations.[441] Deuteronomy, by virtue of its inclusion of all the standard elements, is much closer to the typical treaty form.[442] In short, in the OT, a covenant form comes to its fullest expression in the 7th century in Dtic literary imitation of an Assyrian form,[443] but the concept of covenant, and a vaguer literary covenant form, is already to be found in pre-Dtic material, for example Josh. 24.

Weinfeld carefully distinguishes royal land-grants from suzerain-

[435]Weinfeld, *Deuteronomy*, 61f.
[436]Weinfeld, *Deuteronomy*, 62.
[437]Weinfeld, *Deuteronomy*, 62f.
[438]Weinfeld, *Deuteronomy*, 63.
[439]Weinfeld, *Deuteronomy*, 63f.
[440]Weinfeld, *Deuteronomy*, 64f.
[441]Weinfeld, *Deuteronomy*, 65f.
[442]Weinfeld, *Deuteronomy*, 61, 66.
[443]The degree of continuity between the literary form of 2nd millenium treaty texts, especially Hittite documents, and the 7th century Assyrian treaty texts, and the implications for dating OT material, has been one of the most vigorously debated points in the entire field of covenant-treaty comparisons. The debate began with D.J. Wiseman, "The Vassal-Treaties of Esarhaddon," *Iraq* 20 (1958) 1-99. Regarding the Nimrud vassal-treaty, Wiseman observed, "In its form, language and spirit, however, it continues the tradition well-known from the Hittite treaties and Old Testament covenants (some of which may well have originated in the second millenium B.C.) and to be found in treaties made by both Neo-Assyrian and Neo-Babylonian kings" (28). Thompson asserted that there was a fairly consistent pattern of making covenants from about 1500–700 B.C. ("Non-Biblical Covenants," 39-45). See too his *Ancient Near Eastern Treaties*; here Thompson speculates that the absence of an historical prologue in some treaty documents "may be due merely to the accidents of transmission" (15). Kitchen, by contrast, maintained that structural differences between 2nd millenium and 7th century texts *prove* the antiquity of the covenant form in the OT (*Ancient Orient*, 92-102; *Bible in its World*, 84-85). On the other hand, R.Frankena ("The Vassal-Treaties of Esarhaddon and the Dating of Deuteronomy," *OTS* 14 [Leiden, 1965], 122-154) and M.Weinfeld ("Traces of Assyrian Treaty Formulae in Deuteronomy," *Bibl* 46 [1965] 417-427) both argued on the basis of the curse formulae that Deut. 28 is literarily dependent upon the vassal-treaties of Esarhaddon. Their employment of a comparison between Deut. 28 and the Assyrian treaty texts for purposes of dating was in turn rejected by numerous other scholars, cf. Payne, "The B'rith of Yahweh," 246f.; R.B.Dillard, review of M.Weinfeld, *Deuteronomy*, *WTJ* 36 (1973-74) 263-269; P.C.Craigie, *The Book of Deuteronomy* (Grand Rapids, 1976); Kitchen, *Ancient Orient*, 99f. n.49; *Bible in its World*, 85.

vassal treaties.[444] He argues that the form of the two was similar, but the function was different; the treaties specify the obligations of the vassal to the master, while the grants were bestowed on the vassal for loyal service.[445] The distinction is important for Weinfeld's analysis of OT covenants because he compares the Sinai and Shechem accounts of Exodus, Deuteronomy and Joshua with the treaties,[446] but the Abrahamic and Davidic covenants he compares with the land-grants.[447]

### 1.6.7 D.J.McCarthy

By virtue of numerous scholarly surveys and studies McCarthy has played a prominent role in recent covenant scholarship and has earned a reputation as one of the leading figures in this field.[448] His evaluation of the validity of using treaty and covenant comparisons is similar in many points to that of Weinfeld; Josh. 24 "does show elements from the form, but it is lacking a great number of important elements."[449] McCarthy and Weinfeld differ on some specific details of their appraisal of the covenant form. Contrary to Weinfeld's conclusion that a loyalty oath underlies Josh. 24, McCarthy concurred with G.M.Tucker[450] that Josh. 24:22 demonstrates a contract formula.[451] Nevertheless, they are in basic agreement that the present tendency by some scholars to deny the treaty analogy goes too far.[452] McCarthy argued that a more balanced comparison between

[444] M.Weinfeld, "The Covenant of Grant in the Old Testament and in the Ancient Near East," *JAOS* 90 (1970) 184-203; "Covenant Terminology in the Ancient Near East and its Influence on the West," *JAOS* 93 (1973) 194-196; "*Bryt*," *ThWAT*, 797-801.

[445] Weinfeld, "The Covenant of Grant," 184f.

[446] Weinfeld, *Deuteronomy*, 60ff.

[447] Weinfeld, "The Covenant of Grant," 185ff.; "Covenant Terminology," 194.

[448] See especially his *Treaty and Covenant: A Study in Form in the Ancient Oriental Documents and in the Old Testament*, 2nd ed. (Rome, 1978).

[449] D.J.McCarthy, *Old Testament Covenant: A Survey of Current Opinions* (Oxford, 1972), 29, cf. 74; "Covenant in the Old Testament: The Present State of Inquiry," *CBQ* 27 (1965) 230.

[450] G.M.Tucker, "Covenant Forms and Contract Forms," *VT* 15 (1965) 487-503; cf. his *Contracts in the Old Testament: A Form Critical Investigation* (Diss. Yale University, 1963), 179.

[451] McCarthy, *Old Testament Covenant*, 34.

[452] McCarthy, *Treaty and Covenant*, 14: "Simply ignoring an idea like the treaty parallel will not make it go away like the ghost at the head of the stairs, though,

biblical texts and ancient treaties is facilitated by a method less dominated by the Hittite texts, and by paying more attention to the treaty documents found at Alalakh, Sefire, and Nimrud, for example.[453] He asserted that the general uniformity of the treaty genre makes it an inadequate criterion for dating a document or an event,[454] but indispensable for understanding many aspects of the covenant texts in the OT.

McCarthy expressed grave doubts as to whether Shechem played the crucial role in transmitting a Mosaic covenant, via cultic ceremony, as proposed by Sellin, Alt, Noth, von Rad, Kraus et al.[455] On the other hand, he also was critical of Perlitt's attempt to attribute all covenant texts to Dtic and Dtistic influence.[456] Certain texts, Josh. 24:1-28 included, may be classified as pre-Dtic or proto-Dtic, as judged by linguistic and ideological characteristics.[457] Fundamental for McCarthy's analysis of Josh. 24 is the question of sources. That constitutes for him the first step of the analysis.[458] If earlier form-critical studies of Josh. 24 had eclipsed the questions of source criticism, the eclipse was as usual ephemeral, and the spotlight soon returned to the previous problems. But McCarthy's source analysis does not simply follow the track of earlier commentators who attempted to unravel E, JE redaction, or Dtistic redaction. Whereas for commentators it was always natural to begin with the historical section of vss.1-13, McCarthy's interest in the covenant ceremony brings him immediately to vss.25-28. He finds there a Shechem tradition which is not to be explained by any of the traditional sources.[459] The function of the stone in vs.26b and especially vs.27 constitutes decisive proof of a relatively ancient tradition; "the stone which not merely witnesses but actually hears *cannot be late*."[460] The logical setting for this local tradition is in Shechem,[461] and more precisely,

unfortunately, it can divert attention from important areas of study" (23).

[453]McCarthy, *Treaty and Covenant*, 7.

[454]McCarthy, *Treaty and Covenant*, 7.

[455]McCarthy, *Old Testament Covenant*, 74f.; *Treaty and Covenant*, 279-282.

[456]McCarthy, "*Bᵉrît* in Old Testament," 110-121; *Treaty and Covenant*, 23.

[457]McCarthy, *Treaty and Covenant*, 23, 283.

[458]McCarthy, *Treaty and Covenant*, 221.

[459]McCarthy, *Treaty and Covenant*, 222.

[460]McCarthy, *Treaty and Covenant*, 223 (original emphasis).

[461]McCarthy naturally appeals to additional texts such as Gen. 34f. and Judg. 9 to support his contention of local tradition at Shechem.

in some sort of affinity with a local divinity, Baal-berith or El-berith (Judg. 9:4,46).[462]

As a subsequent step to his analysis of vss.25-28, McCarthy proceeds to a textual appraisal of the prior verses, where there are numerous "almost Dtistic" phrases.[463] As a whole, the text of vss.1-28 shows some Dtistic interpolations and redactions, but a more satisfactory solution for most of the Dtistic sounding phrases is to see a stage in language development antecedent to the Dtic movement.[464] McCarthy is sympathetic to Schmitt's suggestion[465] that Josh. 24 could have its setting in the time of Elijah's revival of Yahwism.

### 1.6.8 J.Van Seters

J.Van Seters has taken a rather novel approach to Josh. 24. His perspective is already hinted in his work on the patriarchal narratives,[466] where he follows Childs[467] in questioning the antiquity of von Rad's credo. Especially important here is the observation that the Reed Sea episode is omitted in the credos of Deut. 26:5b-9; 6:20-24, which is consistent with its marked absence in Deuteronomy in general, while the Reed Sea plays an important role in the exodus descriptions found in the Tetrateuchal narration. In this context Van Seters raises the question whether the Tetrateuchal tradition is post-Dtic; the latest historical summaries (Ps. 136; Neh. 9:6ff. and Josh. 24:2b-13) do contain the Reed Sea episode.[468]

Van Seters' view that Josh. 24:1-27 must be credited to a post-

[462]McCarthy, *Treaty and Covenant*, 222, esp. n.20. Defense of related positions is found in F.Willesen, "Die Eselsöhne von Sichem als Bundesgenossen," *VT* 4 (1954) 216-217; Schmitt, "El-Berit–Mitra," 325-327; V.Maag, "Sichembund und Vätergötter, in *Hebräische Wortforschung* (Fs W.Baumgartner; Leiden, 1967), 205-218; E.Lipiński, "El-Berit," *Syria* 50 (1973) 50f. Cf. also R.E.Clements, "Baal-Berith of Shechem," *JSS* 13 (1968) 21-32.

[463]McCarthy, *Treaty and Covenant*, 233.

[464]McCarthy, *Treaty and Covenant*, 233f. "Thus we are compelled to treat the text as a block of pre-Dtic material" (234).

[465]McCarthy, *Treaty and Covenant*, 283; cf. Schmitt, *Landtag*, 32. Note McCarthy's rejection of Perlitt's proposed *Sitz im Leben* based on the reference to the gods from beyond the river.

[466]J.Van Seters, *Abraham in History and Tradition* (New Haven and London, 1975), 142f.

[467]B.S.Childs, "Deuteronomic Formulae of the Exodus Traditions," in *Hebräische Wortforschung* (Fs W.Baumgartner; Leiden, 1967), 30-39.

[468]Van Seters, *Abraham in History*, 143 n.54.

Dtic Yahwist, and that it stands as an addition to DtrH, is elaborated in a subsequent study devoted to Josh. 24:1-27.[469] His literary-critical analysis stresses similarities between Josh. 24 and Dtic style. Josh. 24 is modelled upon Dtic parenesis, makes similar use of divine speech and dialogue, and within the dialogue itself it contains shifts in subject and object, as is found also in Dtic material.[470]

Furthermore, the historical summary of vss.2-13 resembles Deut. 6:20-24, 26:5b-9, and various other passages held to be Dtic.[471] These details, accompanied by a further elaboration of the point made earlier regarding Yahwistic expansion upon Deuteronomy's exodus traditions,[472] leads to the conclusion that Josh. 24:1-27 derives from the Yahwist.[473] Regarding vss.25-27, so frequently considered to be conclusive proof of ancient tradition, Van Seters agrees with Perlitt[474] that "if one accepts the late date for the speeches then vv.25-27 cannot be otherwise."[475] He undergirds this assertion with a possible reconstruction of how the "statutes and ordinances" of vs.25b, paralleled in Ex. 15:25b, should be seen as a post-Dtic expression of the Yahwist.[476] Likewise, with regard to the stone in vss.26b,27, Van Seters acknowledges that the Dtic tradition took a dim view of such practices, but on the other hand they did continue even after the Josianic reform, and secondly, the precise function of the stone need not be interpreted animistically; the stone may have been inscribed with the events that took place, or it may be seen as a memorial of the event narrated in Josh. 24.[477] The emphasis in vss.14-18 upon

[469]J.Van Seters, "Joshua 24 and the Problem of Tradition in the Old Testament," in W.B.Barrick–J.R.Spencer, eds., *In the Shelter of Elyon: Essays on Ancient Palestinian Life and Literature in Honor of G.W.Ahlström* (Sheffield, 1984), 139-158.

[470]Van Seters, "Joshua 24," 147.

[471]Van Seters, "Joshua 24," 147f.

[472]See also J.Van Seters, *In Search of History: Historiography in the Ancient World and the Origins of Biblical History* (New Haven and London, 1983), 336.

[473]"From these observations the conclusion seems to me inescapable. The author of Joshua 24:1-27 is none other than the Yahwist of the Pentateuch. However, contrary to the views of earlier literary critics, it was not composed before the DtrH but comes later as an addition, just as the Tetrateuch was also an addition to Dtn and DtrH" ("Joshua 24," 149).

[474]Perlitt, *Bundestheologie*, 240-246.

[475]Van Seters, "Joshua 24," 150.

[476]Van Seters, "Joshua 24" 151. Van Seters posits an exilic date for this (154).

[477]Van Seters, "Joshua 24," 152.

maintaining the faith suggests an exilic *Sitz im Leben*,[478] a conclusion defended from a different angle in the views of Nicholson.

### 1.6.9 E.W.Nicholson

Nicholson's[479] recent survey of covenant passages in contemporary OT scholarship devotes a brief chapter to Josh. 24:1-28. He reviews the studies by Perlitt and McCarthy, rejects the background in an Aramean context suggested by McCarthy,[480] and accepts Perlitt's contention that the passage does not rest upon a more ancient historical nucleus. Nevertheless, he doubts Perlitt's proposed setting in conjunction with the Assyrian period, and he suggests instead that the emphasis upon sole worship of Yahweh is suggestive of a Dtistic composition in an exilic setting.[481] Matters of literary criticism are not addressed by Nicholson, which is crucial because Perlitt's literary-critical analysis led to the conclusion that Josh. 24:1-28 could not be dated later than the earliest stage of Dtic activity.

### 1.6.10 S.D.Sperling

Whereas Nicholson did not reconsider the literary-critical issues, these matters constitute the central focus of a significant recent article by Sperling.[482] His analysis is presented as a conscious alternative to the earlier studies by Perlitt and Van Seters. He contests the historical contexts proposed by both Perlitt and Van Seters, and he posits that his own analysis of "words, expressions and grammatical constructions in Josh. 24:1-28 leads to the conclusion that Perlitt's attempt to link Joshua 24 to Deuteronomy on linguistic grounds has virtually no basis."[483] Josh. 24 is determined by Sperling to be based upon early northern Israelite tradition focusing upon Shechem. It has access to some form of the JE material from the Pentateuch, but does

478 Van Seters, "Joshua 24," 152-154.

479 E.W.Nicholson, *God and His People: Covenant and Theology in the Old Testament* (Oxford, 1986).

480 Nicholson, *God and His People*, 158.

481 Nicholson, *God and His People*, 160-163. Contrary to the view of W.Zimmerli, *The Law and the Prophets: A Study of the Meaning of the Old Testament* (Oxford, 1968), 80, that Ezekiel was influenced by Josh. 24, Nicholson asserts that Josh. 24 was influenced by Ezekiel.

482 S.D.Sperling, "Joshua 24 Re-examined," *HUCA* 58 (1987) 119-136.

483 Sperling, "Joshua 24," 133.

not betray evidence of the P material. Yet, it "cannot be contemporary with the events it describes because it accepts the fall of Jericho to the Israelites as a real event and views Joshua as a full-fledged leader of all Israel."[484]

All these considerations lead Sperling to postulate an 8th century date of composition; he suggests the prosperous reign of Jeroboam II (c. 786-746) as a plausible setting. In terms of literary-critical evaluation and dating, therefore, Sperling's analysis exhibits notable parallels to the position advocated by McCarthy, but Sperling is even more reluctant than McCarthy to identify traces of Dtistic editing.

### 1.6.11 S.Kreuzer

As a final example of contemporary efforts to explain Josh. 24:1-28 in the rubric of Dtistic theology, reference may be made to the contribution by S.Kreuzer.[485] Kreuzer's treatment of Josh. 24:1-28 provides a clear illustration of the degree to which the thesis by Perlitt has been influential in shaping present research in this passage. Perlitt's textual analysis had been largely accepted by E.Blum,[486] but the latter rejected Perlitt's proposed setting, and argued instead for a post-exilic origin, basing his arguments essentially upon a theory of deliberate contact with the Samaritans, attempting thereby to clarify the setting of the narrative at Shechem. It is largely in dialogue with Blum and Perlitt that Kreuzer's analysis is conducted.

With respect to Blum's theory, Kreuzer concedes that the early post-exilic period was typified by attempts to revitalize an "all Israel" union of north and south, but he considers it inconceivable that an author in Judah would at this time choose Shechem as the location for a narrative intended as a call for such conciliation.[487] Having rejected a post-exilic setting for Josh. 24:1-28, Kreuzer returns to a few select matters of literary and textual criticism. He detects a major tension between vss.14f. and 19f. and he concludes that Josh. 24 contains two historical summaries; the first, from vss.2-15 contains older material, the second, from vs.16ff. is younger and strongly

[484]Sperling, "Joshua 24," 136.

[485]S.Kreuzer, *Die Frügeschichte Israels in Bekenntnis und Verkündigung des Alten Testaments* (Berlin, 1989), esp. 183-213.

[486]E.Blum, *Die Komposition der Vätergeschichte* (Neukirchen-Vluyn, 1984), esp. 45-61.

[487]Kreuzer, *Frühgeschichte*, 190.

influenced by Josh. 23. Especially influential in this judgement are the considerations that vs.17 is alleged to be strongly Dtistic, and vs.19 has been a constant enigma for commentators but may become explicable as an amplification of emphases discernible in Josh. 23.[488] These two historical summaries are now incorporated into a passage which also contains numerous ancient elements, whether cultic (tree and stone), or political (central location; significance of Shechem from LBA to the Israelite monarchy).[489]

Finally, Kreuzer's analysis of Josh. 24:1-28 places unprecedented emphasis upon the presence of the Amorites in this passage. He accepts the LXX's reading in vs.12 of the "twelve" kings of the Amorites as *lectio difficilior*. He then seeks to discern the most probable historical setting for a narrative designating the inhabitants of Canaan as Amorites in the manner attested in vss.8,12. He concludes that comparison with Assyrian employment of the term Amurru for Syria-Palestine demonstrates that an employment of Amorites in the manner attested in Josh. 24 was common in the 8th cent. but by the 7th cent. was archaic, which in his opinion supports a date of composition for Josh. 24 in the time of Josiah.[490] Accordingly, the reference to Amorites which on source-critical grounds was previously adduced as an argument for E is now employed historically as an argument for dating in comparison with Assyrian texts.

Consistent with our treatment of other positions above, a detailed evaluation of the merits of this analysis must wait until later. But a couple of preliminary remarks are warranted. The most original dimensions of Kreuzer's analysis are the assertion that the historical summary can be divided into two portions, with vss.16ff. serving as a deliberate amplification of Josh. 23, and secondly that the references to Amorites provide evidence dating the present form of the passage to the time of Josiah. However, it is doubtful that these assertions by Kreuzer can withstand a more detailed evaluation.[491]

[488]Kreuzer, *Frühgeschichte*, 193f.
[489]Kreuzer, *Frühgeschichte*, 212f.
[490]Kreuzer, *Frühgeschichte*, 196f., 208ff.
[491]There are formidable obstacles to Kreuzer's treatment of the historical summaries in two sections, with vss.2-15 older than vss.16ff. Structural arguments show that this material is more cohesive than he suggests. Furthermore, a thorough literary-critical analysis casts doubt upon the theory, e.g., use of *'lhym 'ḥrym* in vss.2,16 compared to *'lhy nkr* in vss.20,24 does not support the idea that vss.16ff. is later than vss.2-15. The same is true of the use of the verbs *yṣ'* (vs.5f.) compared

### 1.6.12 Summary

The dominance of the covenant and treaty comparison approach to Josh. 24 was ephemeral. Numerous scholars working with methodologies broadly subsumable under the classification of Dtistic theology criticized the manner in which previous form-critical approaches evaluated Josh. 24 in analogy to Hittite treaties. Put quite simply, the covenant-treaty debate since Mendenhall has revolved around two fundamental questions. First, do texts such as Josh. 24, Ex. 19-24, and Deuteronomy demonstrate unequivocally that they have been modelled in the literary form of extra-biblical treaty texts? Second, if there is a demonstrable resemblance between these two categories of texts, to what extent may it be used for dating the literary fixation of the biblical texts?

To both of these questions one could append a host of sub-questions. How closely must texts resemble each other in order to prove literary dependence? In form-critical studies such as these, by what criterion does one weigh the relative weight of similarities and differences between the respective textual genres? How many constant elements must be present in order to demonstrate a form, or to use the usual term in this case, a covenant formulary? How many ancient treaty texts are necessary in order to establish a control group to provide legitimate conclusions about standard forms and patterns? Is it methodologically acceptable to attempt to structure a time-line based upon extra-biblical texts, by which biblical texts can be plotted? The list could be multiplied considerably, but the point is that OT scholarship has produced a great variety of responses to these questions precisely because the establishment of an objective criterion by which to judge such comparative, form-critical studies, is an elusive endeavor.

These difficulties in attaining a consensus regarding a proper form-critical method for comparing covenant texts with ancient treaty documents, along with a concommitant renewed interest in pursuing more refined and detailed analysis of a Dtistic editing of Joshua-2 Kings,

to *'lh* (vs.17). Vs.17 is considered Dtistic, but precisely the terminology which supports this claim is absent in the LXX. The reading of the LXX in vs.12 is accepted as the more difficult reading, but in this case the more difficult reading is not likely the most original one. Finally, it is dubious that the references to Amorites can be used for purposes of dating in the manner attempted by Kreuzer; cf. Sperling, "Joshua 24," 126, and consult 6.3.7.

has led to more or less radical reappraisals of previously held conclusions regarding the origin and nature of Josh. 24:1-28. But it is equally clear that there is no single or accepted Dtistic approach to Josh. 24, as becomes evident at a glance when one considers the diversity of results attained by Schmitt, Perlitt, Weinfeld, McCarthy, Van Seters, Nicholson, Sperling[492] and Kreuzer. In some cases, as in the work of Kutsch, Perlitt, and Kreuzer the inclination has been to view Josh. 24 as a product of a Dtic movement from approximately the time of Josiah.

Weinfeld and McCarthy, by arguing a pre-Dtic *Sitz im Leben* for a text which resembles the treaty genre but does not employ it as fully as did the later Dtic movement, retain a more mediating position between the view of Perlitt and the previous assertion of an ancient cultic tradition at Shechem.[493] Sperling did not consider the form-critical questions but he argued primarily on the basis of literary criticism that Josh. 24:1-28 cannot be attributed to the hand of a Deuteronomist. Van Seters, on the other side of the debate, has argued for a post-Dtic theory in which Josh. 24 would have been written by the Yahwist, who in his view was dependent upon the Dtic movement. Nicholson rejects Van Seters' Yahwist theory, but he too argues on the basis of the emphasis upon service of Yahweh alone for an exilic origin. Finally, Blum attempts to defend an even later, post-exilic setting for Josh. 24:1-28 on the grounds that this passage sought to foster reconciliation with the Samaritans. The positions represented above, as well as additional studies which we have for the moment left beyond purview, dramatically demonstrate how variant methodologies have led to different, often contradictory, conclusions.

[492]Sperling goes so far as to deny the presence of significant Dtistic terminology in Josh. 24:1-28. His analysis has been included here because his agenda is entirely determined by the question of whether or not this passage is in fact Dtistic.

[493]Accepting much from previous covenant-treaty comparisons, and adding many new observations of their own, they argue that Josh. 24 represents a stage of literary development moving *towards* a fuller covenant form in Dtic literature, which finds its closest parallel in the later Assyrian treaties, rather than moving *from* the earlier Hittite treaty form. The latter thesis was central to L'Hour's diachronic hypothesis regarding transition from a treaty text to a liturgical text.

## 1.7 Josh. 24 and archaeology

### 1.7.1 Introduction

Archaeological activity at Shechem (*tell balâṭah*) in the 1950's and 60's renewed interest in an archaeological dimension to the study of Josh. 24. This is not to minimize the importance of the work conducted in approximately ten German campaigns from 1913-1933, primarily under the leadership of Sellin (replaced by G.Welter from the summer of 1928-1932). But improvements in archaeological techniques has made the results in recent decades much more precise than was possible at the beginning of this century. Therefore it is sufficient to concentrate primarily on the latest studies, though in a number of instances it is interesting to note that Sellin and F.M.Th.de Liagre Böhl already anticipated recent correlations between archaelogical data at Shechem and the biblical traditions.[494] While it would be incorrect to see these developments as constituting a new method of interpretation,[495] in a number of recent studies the archaeological factors have been weighed heavily, and our survey of this history of interpretation would be incomplete without a recognition of this dimension of the study of Josh. 24:1-28. It is neither possible nor necessary here to summarize all of the archaeological activity which

[494]For details on the earlier excavations cf. E.Sellin, "*Balâṭa*–Sichem," *AKAW* 51 (1914) 35-40, 204-207; *Wie wurde Sichem eine israelitische Stad?* (Leipzig, 1922); "Die Ausgrabung von Sichem," *ZDPV* 49 (1926) 229-236, 304-320; 50 (1927) 205-211, 265-274; "Die Masseben des El-Berit in Sichem," *ZDPV* 51 (1928) 119-123; "Der gegenwärtige Stand der Ausgrabungen von Sichem und ihre Zukunft," *ZAW* 50 (1932) 303-308; E.Sellin–H.Steckeweh, "*Balâṭa*," *QDAP* 5 (1936) 196; "Kurzer vorläufiger Bericht über die Ausgrabungen von *Balâṭa* (Sichem) im Herbst 1934," *ZDPV* 64 (1941), 1-20; G.Welter, "Stand der Ausgrabungen in Sichem," *AA* (1932) 289-316; F.M.Th.de Liagre Böhl, *De geschiedenis der stad Sichem en de opgravingen aldaar* (MAA 62, Serie B, No.1; Amsterdam, 1926); "Die bei den Ausgrabungen von Sichem gefundenen Keilschrifttafeln," *ZDPV* 49 (1926) 321-327; *De opgraving van Sichem. Bericht over de voorjaarscampagne en de zomercampagne in 1926* (Zeist, 1927); "Die Sichem-Plakette. Protoalphabetische Schriftzeichen der Mittelbronzezeit vom *tell balâṭa*," *ZDPV* 61 (1938) 1-25.

[495]Various scholars have called attention to the perils of a too easy identification of literary and archaeological data, cf. H.J.Franken, *Heilig-Land en heilige huisjes* (Leiden, 1962); E.Noort, *Biblisch-archäologische Hermeneutik und alttestamentliche Exegese* (Kampen, 1979); I.Finkelstein, *The Archaeology of the Israelite Settlement* (Jerusalem, 1988), 15-23, esp. 22.

has been conducted at Shechem.[496] The ensuing discussion will focus primarily on G.E.Wright and K.Jaroš, who explicitly draw from recent archaeological results in their studies of Josh. 24:1-28. Brief mention will also be made of A.Zertal's dramatic claims regarding Josh. 8:30-35, as well as the reservations expressed in studies by, inter alia, M.D.Fowler, L.Wächter, and I.Finkelstein.

### 1.7.2 G.E.Wright

Subsequent to four campaigns at *tell balâṭah* between 1956 and 1962 the veteran American archaeologist Wright[497] produced a monograph in which he undertook to sift the relevant data in an "attempt to understand the biblical traditions afresh in the light of the archaeological history."[498] In view of Wright's professed objective, it is instructive to summarize his employment of archaeological results to explain Josh. 24 and related textual traditions. Wright places extreme importance upon unearthed remains of temples on the western portion of the tell. Regarding the site of these temples, it is argued that sometime between circa 1800–1750 B.C. there was a massive filling and levelling of an area outside the fortified enclosure.[499] This area was later included within the fortification of the city and became the site of successive temple courtyard complexes.[500] In the MB II C period a fortress-temple was built on this location.[501] This temple underwent a period

[496]For an extensive bibliography see conveniently E.K.Vogel, "Bibliography of Holy Land Sites," *HUCA* 42 (1971) 76f. re Shechem and 62f. re Mt. Gerizim; E.K.Vogel–B.Holtzclaw, "Bibliography of Holy Land Sites, Part II," *HUCA* 52 (1981) 81 re Shechem and 30 re Mt. Gerizim; E.K.Vogel, "Bibliography of Holy Land Sites, Part III," *HUCA* 58 (1987) 57 re Shechem.

[497]Not to be confused with G.R.H.Wright who was also involved with the American expeditions at Shechem and has written on various aspects of this site.

[498]G.E.Wright, *Shechem: The Biography of A Biblical City* (New York, 1965); the citation is from xvi. Cf. his "Shechem," in D.W.Thomas, ed., *Archaeology and Old Testament Study: Jubilee Volume of the Society for Old Testament Study 1917-1967* (Oxford, 1967), 355-370. The Shechem expeditions continued through 1969. For a summary and additional literature see L.E.Toombs, "Shechem: Problems of the Early Israelite Era," in F.M.Cross, ed., *Symposia Celebrating the Seventy-fifth Anniversary of the Founding of the American Schools of Oriental Research (1900-1975)* (Cambridge, MA, 1979), 69-83.

[499]Wright, *Shechem: The Biography*, 110-112, 121f., 132; "Shechem," 357f.

[500]Wright, *Shechem: The Biography*, 112-120.

[501]Wright, *Shechem: The Biography*, 87-91, 122. Wright suggests a date of construction c. 1650–1600.

of reparation and was subsequently destroyed, probably by Egyptian conquest at about 1550–1540.[502] After a gap of about one hundred years a second fortress-temple was built upon the foundations of the previous temple, but with its axis now shifted five degrees south compared to the alignment of the former walls.[503] Wright suggests that this was the temple of *El-bryt* or *Baal-bryt* known from Judg. 9:4,46, destroyed by Abimelech (9:45-49) in the 12th century.[504] Furthermore, it is believed that a large cultic stone was erected in this second fortress-temple, along with two smaller ones which had already stood on either side of the entrance to the first fortress-temple.[505] Wright not only wishes to connect the fortress-temple with the Abimelech story of Judg. 9,[506] but he also affiliates the large upright stone with the stone mentioned in Josh. 24:26.[507] Wright notes that there are three different types of OT literature concerning Shechem, namely,

[502]Wright, *Shechem: The Biography*, 95, 101f.; "Shechem," 361f.

[503]Wright, *Shechem: The Biography*, 95-100; "Shechem" 362; Toombs, "Shechem: Problems," 73.

[504]Wright, *Shechem: The Biography*, 80-82, 101f., 123-128. Toombs, "Shechem: Problems," 73. See already de Liagre Böhl, *De opgraving*, 16, 20, 23, 28, 37; and also Sellin, "Die Masseben," 120, 122; "Der gegenwärtige Stand," 305f.

[505]These stones were suggested already by Sellin to have had a sacred, cultic function as upright stones, though Welter vigorously disagreed with this conclusion (Sellin, "Der gegenwärtige Stand," 304-307; Wright, *Shechem: The Biography*, 80-87, 93, 122).

[506]Wright admits that for this identification it is necessary to deny a a strict chronological sequence between vs.45 and vss.46-49; read sequentially it would appear as if the temple-fortress was not part of the city. He chooses to see vss.46-49 as a sort of appendix, describing what went on during the destruction of the city, in which case there is no conflict with the archaeological evidence which suggests that the temple which he desires to identify with Judg. 9 was inside the fortified city at this time (*Shechem: The Biography*, 124f.). However, the nature and location of the stronghold *ṣryḥ* has been widely debated, cf. J.Simons, *Geographical and Topographical Texts of the Old Testament* (Leiden, 1959), 297, par. 584; K.Jaroš, "Zur Bedeutung von *ṣryḥ* in Ri 9,46.49," *AUSS* 15 (1977) 57f.; J.A.Soggin, "Bemerkungen zur alttestamentlichen Topographie Sichems mit besonderem Bezug auf Jdc. 9," *ZDPV* 83 (1967) 183-198, esp. 197; *Judges* (London, 1981), 165-166; E.F.Campbell, "Judges 9 and Biblical Archaeology," in C.L.Meyers–M.O'Connor, eds., *The Word of the Lord Shall Go Forth: Essays in Honor of David Noel Freedman in Celebration of His Sixtieth Birthday* (Winona Lake, 1983), 263-271, esp. 268-270. Soggin argues for a location outside of the city, while Campbell sides with Wright and Jaroš.

[507]Wright, *Shechem: The Biography*, 136f.; "Shechem" 365. E.F.Campbell–J.F.Ross, "The Excavation of Shechem and the Biblical Tradition," *BA* 26 (1963) 11, 14. See already Sellin, "Die Masseben," 122.

"the Genesis stories (JE), an old covenant record (Joshua 24) and an old narrative about Abimelech (Judges 9),"[508] but they all share a number of constants, i.e., the emphasis upon covenant, a sacred precinct, and a tree within that precinct.[509] Josh. 24 is accepted as deriving from a very old tradition, "though in its transmission it has been touched up here and there by a 'Deuteronomic' editor, who included it as an appendix to the Book of Joshua."[510] Wright stressed repeatedly that Josh. 24 recounts a covenant ceremony initiating a tribal league in Palestine.[511] He believed that this covenant ceremony was repeated "annually, or at least periodically, at Shechem."[512] As proof for this assertion Wright appeals to Deut. 11:29; 27; Josh. 8:30-35, which are believed to stem from an old tradition utilized by the Dtic historian, along with Josh. 24, to explain the origin of a covenant ceremony still celebrated at later times at Shechem.[513] The detail that the texts in Deuteronomy and in Josh. 8:30-35 mention Mt. Ebal and Mt. Gerizim but not the city of Shechem might be attributed to the fact that, as archaeology has shown, the sacred area in Shechem was already destroyed in the 12th century.[514]

### 1.7.3 K.Jaroš

The subtitle of a recent monograph by Jaroš[515] is already indicative of the author's intention to re-evaluate Josh. 24 in the light of archaeological data from Shechem. The largest part of this volume is dedicated to a summary of both the German and American campaigns at Shechem, and an attempt to demonstrate the applicability of the ensuing results for clarification of biblical and extra-biblical texts.[516]

[508] Wright, *Shechem: The Biography*, 135.

[509] Wright, *Shechem: The Biography*, 135; "Shechem," 365.

[510] Wright, *Shechem: The Biography*, 134.

[511] Wright, *Shechem: The Biography*, 124, 132, 134f., 140f.; "Shechem," 364. Cf. his *The Old Testament against its Environment* (Chicago, 1950), 24 n.25, 61; *The Old Testament and Theology* (New York, 1969), 127f. n.12.

[512] Wright, *Shechem: The Biography*, 138.

[513] Wright, *Shechem: The Biography*, 137f.

[514] Wright, "Shechem," 370 n.27.

[515] K.Jaroš, *Sichem. Eine archäologische und religionsgeschichtliche Studie mit besonderer Berücksichtigung von Jos 24* (Göttingen, 1976).

[516] Jaroš, *Sichem*, 11-127. Jaroš reproduces many pictures and diagrams published previously by various authors in their preliminary reports, and he summarizes studies published in a variety of periodicals. Cf. also K.Jaroš–B.Deckert, *Studien zur Sichem-Aera* (Göttingen, 1977).

The final chapter concentrates on Josh. 24. Jaroš summarizes the "literarkritisch– formgeschichtliche und traditionsgeschichtliche Arbeit an Jos 24" with the conclusion that these methods are inadequate.[517]

The literary-critical attempts attain contradictory conclusions,[518] the covenant vassal-treaty theory of Mendenhall, Baltzer, Beyerlin, etc. cannot be sustained,[519] and the "traditionsgeschichtliche Forschungsrichtung" of Sellin, which led to Noth's amphictyony idea,[520] is refuted by growing criticisms of the whole amphictyony scheme in general,[521] and by the fact that "Das, was Jos 24 darstellt, ist nicht für eine Amphiktyonie spezifisch charakteristisch."[522] In a special section reviewing Perlitt's position, Jaroš says, "Grundsätzlich überzeugen seine Ausführungen: Jos 24 geprägt von D/Dtr Sprache ist eine Predigt aus dem 7.Jh.v.Chr."[523] But he indicates four matters not adequately accounted for by Perlitt:[524]
1) Perlitt fails to deal with the history of Shechem as that is now known via archaeological, biblical and extra-biblical sources.
2) The term "Predigt" need not exclude employment of ancient traditional material.
3) Perlitt does not adequately deal with the problem of divine names and the claim that the fathers served other gods.
4) He does not explain the presence of a tree and a stone in a Dtistic sermon.

Jaroš determines to integrate archaeological data to attain a more satisfactory answer to the questions left unanswered by Perlitt. He argues that in the early settlement period the names "Jacob" and "Israel" referred to distinct clans or groups, which joined in confed-

[517]Jaroš, *Sichem*, 131-136, esp. 131f. n.5. "Der Anfang der historisch-kritischen Forschung konzentrierte sich -neben der Textkritik- auf die literarkritische Erfassung von Jos 24. Doch gerade bei diesem Kapitel konnte, wie der Überblick zeigt, keine einheitliche Meinung erzielt werden" (131f.).
[518]Jaroš, *Sichem*, 132.
[519]Jaroš, *Sichem*, 132f., with appeal to McCarthy: "Der Text berichtet nach D.J.McCarthy nicht einfach einen Bund und die Aussage von V 19 'ihr könnt nicht Jahwe dienen' ist für einen aktuellen Bund unmöglich" (133).
[520]Jaroš, *Sichem*, 133.
[521]Jaroš, *Sichem*, 133-136.
[522]Jaroš, *Sichem*, 135.
[523]Jaroš, *Sichem*, 138.
[524]Jaroš, *Sichem*, 138.

eration at Shechem where they accepted as their God *'l 'lhy yśr'l.*[525] Joshua, on the other hand, is thought to have come from the Transjordan, and from the etymology of his name it is concluded that he worshipped Yahweh.[526] He was accompanied by Ephraim, or the ancestors of Ephraim, who brought the worship of Yahweh with them to Palestine. Jaroš accepts the Kenite-Midianite theory of the origin of Yahwism as being the most likely one,[527] and the location of the Sinai/Horeb encounter with the Midianites is thought to have taken place at the volcanic area of *Ḥala el Bedr.*[528] This group of newcomers joins the confederacy of the Jacob/Israel tribes at the fortress-temple which stood at Shechem, as is evident from historical memories preserved in the following portions of Josh. 24:25-27:[529]
vs. 25: "So Joshua made a covenant with the people that day";
vs. 26b: "and he took a great stone, and set it up under the oak in the sanctuary of Yahweh";
vs. 27 "And Joshua said to all the people, 'Behold, this stone shall be a witness against us; for it has heard all the words of Yahweh'."[530]

Jaroš believes that Joshua's entry into the land was accompanied by such awesome military success against enclaves of Canaanites that the Jacob/Israel group accepted Yahweh as being more powerful than the Canaanite god El with whom they had previously compared their patriarchal god *'l 'lhy yśr'l.*[531] Accordingly, in a covenant ceremony Joshua charges them to serve Yahweh alone, which in political-sociological terms amounts to a tribal confederation.[532] The upright

[525]Jaroš, *Sichem*, 144-146.

[526]Jaroš, *Sichem*, 146f.

[527]For objections to the Kenite-Midianite hypothesis see J.C.de Moor, *Uw God is mijn God. Over de oorsprong van het geloof in de ene God* (Kampen, 1983), 56-58.

[528]Jaroš *Sichem*, 147: "Es kann als ganz eindeutig angesehen werden, dass das Stammesgebiet Midians NIE auf der heutigen Sinaihalbinsel gewesen ist."

[529]Jaroš, *Sichem*, 148; cf. his *Die Stellung des Elohisten zur kanaanäischen Religion*, 2nd ed. (Göttingen, 1982), 146.

[530]This result is virtually the same as the $E^1$ source suggested in 1900 by Steuernagel (*Josua*, 242); cf. G.Hölscher, *Geschichtsschreibung in Israel. Untersuchungen zum Jahvisten und Elohisten* (Lund, 1952), 350. Jaroš does not mention these works.

[531]Jaroš, *Sichem*, 148.

[532]Jaroš, *Sichem*, 149. Jaroš argues extensively that the type of tribal confederation established in Josh. 24 is similar to Arabian, nomadic type covenants rather than Babylonian, Assyrian, Hittite or later Greek amphictyonic style treaties (cf. 139-144). This argument is heavily dependent upon Pedersen, *Der Eid* (cf. above, 1.3.7).

stone, which the archaeological reports show to have been affiliated with the Canaanite temple, is thought to have originally been viewed by the clans as representative of *'l 'lhy yśr'l*, but the Joshua clan now reidentifies it as representative of their God, Yahweh.[533] Jaroš dates this confederation towards the end of the 13th cent., or possibly in the 12th cent., but in any event, prior to the destruction of the temple at the end of the 12th century.[534]

### 1.7.4 A.Zertal

In 1980 a stone structure was discovered on Mt. Ebal, prompting a subsequent suggestion by archaeologist A.Zertal that this structure may be identified with the altar mentioned in Deut. 27:5-7, Josh. 8:30f.[535] The complex, built of "large, unhewn field stones"[536] is approximately 9 feet high, believed by Zertal to be nearly the original height. "The outside measurements are 24.5 feet by 29.5 feet. Its walls are 5 feet (1.4 meters) thick."[537] Zertal reports that the interior of the structure was filled with "deliberately laid strata or layers of field stones, earth and ashes, one layer on top of the other."[538] The layout is such that two corners point within a degree of north and south, the other two approximately east and west. Comparison with biblical and extra-biblical descriptions of altars convinces Zertal that the structure may be identified as an altar. On the basis of pottery finds as well as two "Egyptian-style" scarabs, the erection of the cultic site is dated to the 13th-12th cent. B.C.[539] Zertal's sensationally presented proposal understandably drew the curses and blessings of

[533] Jaroš, *Sichem*, 151.

[534] Cf. Jaroš–Deckert, *Studien zur Sichem-Aera*, 36f.

[535] A.Zertal, "Has Joshua's Altar Been Found on Mt. Ebal?" *BAR* 11 (1985) 26-43; "Mount Ebal," *IEJ* 34 (1984) 55. His position is expressed more cautiously in his "A Cultic Center with a Burnt-Offering from Early Iron Age I Period at Mt.Ebal," in M.Augustin–K.-D.Schunck, eds., *"Wünschet Jerusalem Frieden": Collected Communications to the XIIth Congress of IOSOT, Jerusalem 1986* (Frankfurt am Main, 1988), 137-153.

[536] Zertal, "Joshua's Altar," 30.

[537] Zertal, "Joshua's Altar," 30.

[538] Zertal, "Joshua's Altar," 31. He notes that bone tests show a close correspondence with the *kosher* animals of Lev. 1. The pottery in the fill is listed as all Iron Age I.

[539] Zertal, "Joshua's Altar," 42. He states that 70 percent of the pottery consisted of large collar-rim storage jars, 10 percent was jugs and chalices, with only a minor representation of "domestic pottery, such as cooking pots" (34f.).

opponents and advocates respectively in a vigorous debate regarding the true character and identification of this ancient site.[540]

### 1.7.5 Limitations of archaeology at Shechem

Archaeological studies are frequently appealed to as an objective criterion by which to evaluate the historical significance of biblical narratives. However, numerous archaeologists have raised serious warnings against claiming more for the archaeological data than is legitimate, and the studies focusing upon Shechem and surroundings must also be viewed in this light. H.J.Franken and C.A.Franken-Battershill expressed reservations about some of the reporting techniques used in the Shechem excavations.[541] Finklestein states, "It is, in fact, doubtful whether the results of the excavations have helped to clarify the history of Shechem during the period under discussion" (Iron I).[542]

Furthermore, Fowler[543] summarizes the evidence listed in Wright's attempt to identify the *migdal* temple of Judg. 9:46-49 and objects to Wright's assumption that "the *māqôm* of the Patriarchal period, and the temples of Joshua 24 and Judges 9 all point to the same sacred area which has been excavated."[544] Fowler's major contention is that it is rash to assume that the biblical traditions presuppose only one sacred precinct at Shechem.

Most recently Wright's equation of the sacred precinct of Josh. 24:26 with the temple of Judg. 9:46 has also been challenged by Wächter.[545] Wächter demonstrates that the affiliation of Abram and

[540]A.Kempinski, "Joshua's Altar–An Iron Age I Watchtower," *BAR* 12 (1986) 42, 44-49. Zertal responds in the same issue, "How Can Kempinski Be So Wrong?" *BAR* 12 (1986) 43, 49-53. M.Coogan argues that it was a cultic site but may originally have been Canaanite ("Of Cults and Cultures: Reflections on the Interpretation of Archaeological Evidence," *PEQ* 119 [1987] 1-8). Soggin attempts to associate it with the sanctuary of Judg. 9, cf. his "The Migdal Temple, Migdal Šᵉkem Judg 9 and the Artifact on Mount Ebal," in Augustin–Schunck, eds., *"Wünschet Jerusalem Frieden"*, 115-119. See too the summary by H.Shanks, "Two Early Israelite Cult Sites Now Questioned," *BAR* 14 (1988) 48-52.

[541]H.J.Franken–C.A.Franken-Battershill, *A Primer of Old Testament Archaeology* (Leiden, 1963), 12, 15, 17.

[542]Finkelstein, *Archaeology*, 82.

[543]M.D.Fowler, "A Closer Look at the 'Temple of El-Berith' at Shechem," *PEQ* 115 (1983) 49-53.

[544]Fowler, "A Closer Look," 52, quoting Wright (*Shechem: The Biography*, 137).

[545]L.Wächter, "Zur Lokalisierung des sichemitischen Baumheiligtums," *ZDPV* 103 (1987) 1-12.

Jacob with a sacred precinct presupposes a location outside of the city. The same would seem to be the case with the "Baumheiligtum" of Josh. 24:26 in contrast to the temple of Judg. 9:46.[546] Accordingly, both Fowler and Wächter have raised formidable objections to Wright's too facile identification of the sacred precinct of Josh. 24:26 with that of Judg. 9:46.

Similarly, Finkelstein raises a number of reservations about Zertal's evaluation of the findings at Mt. Ebal, concluding that it is too early for a definite stand on the matter.[547]

### 1.7.6 Summary

The archaeological considerations employed by Wright and Jaroš illustrate attempts to use extra-biblical evidence to provide an objective background against which to sketch the historical value of Josh. 24:1-28. Wright concludes that the temple unearthed at *tell balâṭah* can be associated with the temple of El-Berith (Judg. 9:4,46); and the upright stone is identified with that of Josh. 24:26. To these details Jaroš adds yet another version of the tribal confederation thesis. Wright and Jaroš do not provide a new understanding of Josh. 24:1-28, but they endeavor to bolster or modify existing interpretations. However, other scholars have raised serious objections concerning the degree to which the archaeological data can be applied to the biblical narratives.[548]

## 1.8 Textual criticism of Josh. 24:1-28

The question of the comparative value of the Greek and Hebrew texts of Josh. 24:1-28 has proven elusive. It is self-evident that text-critical questions in Josh. 24 cannot be isolated from similar concerns in Joshua as a whole. And in this chapter, as is usually the case in textual-critical debates, the central point of dissent has

[546] Wächter, "Zur Lokalisierung," 5-7.

[547] Finkelstein, *Archaeology*, 82-85, esp. 85.

[548] Since Wright and Jaroš employ archaeological arguments in conjunction with other methods of interpretation, an evaluation of their proposals must take into consideration the strengths and weaknesses of the other methods of handling Josh. 24:1-28 highlighted in the preceding sections. Our analysis in ch. 2 will return to these issues, including additional reservations about the claimed archaeological identification of the setting of Josh. 24:26.

focused upon the amount of weight to be placed upon the LXX and MT respectively in cases of pluses or minuses. Unfortunately, however, the complexity of the relationship between the Greek and Hebrew traditions has all too frequently led commentators to employ the various readings eclectically.[549] Specialists who have attempted to offer guidelines by which to assess the relationship between the various textual traditions have produced divergent results. Studies specifically addressing the relationship between the LXX and MT can basically be divided into two camps on the basis of whether they favour the Greek or the Hebrew text in cases of pluses and minuses. Studies by, e.g., A.Dillmann[550] and M.L.Margolis[551] revealed a frequent tendency to charge the translators of the LXX with curtailing various passages through omission of material found in the preserved Hebrew tradition.[552] Others have cautioned, however, that the matter is more complex. S.Holmes argued already in 1914 that in Joshua, the LXX gives a faithful translation of a Hebrew *Vorlage* which differed from the preserved MT.[553] His basic conclusions on this point have recently been reasserted by H.M.Orlinsky,[554] and supported by L.J.Greenspoon's exhaustive study of the Theodotionic recension of Joshua.[555] Greenspoon's study confirms the opinion that the careful attempt by Margolis to reconstruct the Original Greek (OG) translation is generally accurate, but Margolis' other conclusion that the LXX translator in some places took considerable liberty to curtail the Hebrew text must be rejected.[556] Greenspoon also concludes, "LXX B is far and away our surest guide to the OG, although

[549]See, e.g., the comments on Nielsen in 1.4.4. A survey of Joshua commentaries shows that Nielsen's approach is not exceptional.

[550]A.Dillmann, *Numeri, Deuteronomium und Josua*, 2nd ed. (Leipzig, 1886).

[551]M.L.Margolis, *The Book of Joshua in Greek* (Paris, 1931). It was generally thought that this work was completed only to Josh. 19:38, but E.Tov announces that he has found the fifth and final part, cf. his "The Discovery of the Missing Part of Margolis' Edition of Joshua," *BIOSCS* 14 (1981) 17-21.

[552]This tendency was not limited to studies of Joshua, but was characteristic of a frequently held approach to the relationship between the LXX and MT in general; see E.Tov, *The Text-Critical Use of the Septuagint in Biblical Research* (Jerusalem, 1981), 70f.

[553]S.Holmes, *Joshua: The Hebrew and Greek Texts* (Cambridge, 1914).

[554]H.M.Orlinsky, "The Hebrew *Vorlage* of the Septuagint of the Book of Joshua," in *Congress Volume, Rome 1968*, *SVT* 17 (Leiden, 1969), 187-195.

[555]L.J.Greenspoon, *Textual Studies in the Book of Joshua* (Chico, 1983).

[556]Greenspoon, *Textual Studies*, 1.

this manuscript is not immune to corruption through scribal error or hexaplaric influence."[557] The difficulty of distinguishing textual variants attributable to the LXX translators of Joshua from those which reflect a variant Hebrew *Vorlage* is underscored by Tov with examples from Josh. 24:1,25 (Shiloh rather than Shechem); 24:4 (cf. Deut. 26:5f.); 24:12 (twelve kings of the Amorites rather than two); 24:15 (LXX adds: for he is holy); and 24:32 (regarding burial of Joseph's bones).[558] An analysis by A.Rofé,[559] focusing specifically on Josh. 24:28ff., produced the conclusion that there is evidence for a different Hebrew *Vorlage* to the LXX.

A more radical appeal to give general priority to the LXX where there are pluses in the MT is made by Auld.[560] Auld suggests that if his conclusions regarding the LXX of Joshua can be sustained, "then the familiar Hebrew is disqualified from serving as the basis for a *close* examination of details of the literary structure and relationships of that book."[561]

Although it is impossible within the scope of this study to survey the general question of the relationship between the Greek and Hebrew texts of Joshua, the history of textual studies briefly summarized in the preceding paragraphs provides a framework within which to focus the textual questions which abound in Josh. 24:1-28. The net result of the studies by, inter alia, Holmes, Orlinsky, Greenspoon, Rofé, Tov and Auld caution against prematurely charging the translator(s) of the LXX with omitting material from a Hebrew textual tradition from which he was translating.[562] On the other hand, it would

[557]Greenspoon, *Textual Studies*, 7f. LXX A is thought to have been redacted in order to harmonize the Greek tradition with a text very close in virtually all respects to the present MT.

[558]E.Tov, "Midrash-Type Exegesis in the LXX of Joshua," *RB* 85 (1978) 50-61.

[559]A.Rofé, "The End of the Book of Joshua According to the Septuagint," *Henoch* 4 (1982) 17-36.

[560]A.G.Auld, "Textual and Literary Studies in the Book of Joshua," *ZAW* 90 (1978) 412-417; "Joshua: The Hebrew and Greek Texts," in J.A.Emerton, ed., *Studies in the Historical Books of the Old Testament*, *SVT* 30 (Leiden, 1979), 1-14; "Cities of Refuge in Israelite Traditions," *JSOT* 10 (1978) 29.

[561]Auld, "Textual and Literary Studies," 413. Cf. his "Joshua: The Hebrew," 7: "In short, it appears we should disqualify our familiar Hebrew text from serving as a sure base for a close examination of the literary structure and relationships of the book of Joshua."

[562]Cf. A.Rofé, "Joshua 20: Historico-Literary Criticism Illustrated," in J.H.Tigay, ed., *Empirical Models for Biblical Criticism* (Philadelphia, 1985), 131-147.

be premature to accept Auld's negative appraisal of the MT for a close reading of literary structure throughout the whole of Joshua.[563]

It should not be taken for granted that Auld's conclusions, based upon selected texts, especially those dealing with the acquisition and settlement of the land, are unequivocally valid for Josh. 24.[564] It is not self-evident that the entire translation of Joshua in the LXX is the work of one hand. Furthermore, if some of the differences between the Greek and the preserved Hebrew traditions actually go back as far as a Hebrew *Vorlage*, it remains necessary to entertain a variety of possible reasons for the differences at that stage of textual transmission. To assert a faithful translation simply pushes the question of divergent traditions one step further back. And it is far from proven that an alleged *Vorlage* of the LXX to Josh. 24 stands closer to the so-called "authentic" Hebrew text wherever the MT now has pluses. Therefore, the relative weight to be attributed to the LXX and the MT in instances of pluses, minuses, and other variants must continue to be a focal point in subsequent research in Josh. 24:1-28.

[563]In fairness to Auld it should be noted that he himself warns against applying his conclusions fanatically, and in Josh. 24:1 he prefers the MT's reading of Shechem rather than Shiloh of the LXX ("Joshua: The Hebrew," 14).

[564]Cf. Rofé, "Joshua 20," esp. 147.

# 2 An Analysis of Previous Research in Josh. 24:1-28

## 2.1 Introduction

The historical survey offered in the preceding chapter has revealed the disconcerting conclusion that not only have the various approaches to Josh. 24 produced a great diversity of incompatible data, but more surprising, none of the specific methods surveyed can claim an internal consensus amongst its adherents with respect to either procedure or results. We are confronted with competing and often contradictory methods, and within the various procedures themselves are irreconcilable differences of opinion. It is therefore imperative to compare and evaluate the textual, structural and theological arguments advocated in the various methods of interpretation. In doing so it is not our intention to simply illustrate the flatly contradictory results which have been previously defended. Our purpose, rather, is twofold. On the one hand we must look for possible trends towards consensus upon which additional study can build, and on the other hand we wish to re-evaluate the various methodologies in order to determine the extent to which approaches employed thus far are helpful for solving the literary questions of Josh. 24, and the extent to which new approaches ought to be developed in pursuit of a more convincing analysis of this important passage.

In order to facilitate a thorough appraisal of the relative strengths and weaknesses of the various analyses introduced above it is now advisable to abandon strict adherence to the divisions into the various categories we have employed for convenience up to this point. The classifications utilized in the first chapter were necessary in order to structure our survey of a history of interpretation which by virtue of its complexity and magnitude at first appears as a formidable maze of positions. Having traced the lines of development which are detectable in the various methods of interpretation, however, it is now preferable for the sake of precision to allow our discussion to be governed by comparison of various textual-critical, literary-critical, form-critical, structural, theological and historical considerations without attempting to fit advocates of various viewpoints into strictly defined methods of interpretation. Accordingly, the ensuing five major sections of the present chapter evaluate previous research in Josh. 24:1-

28 in the areas of textual criticism, literary criticism, form criticism, archaeology and structural analysis respectively.

## 2.2 Textual criticism of Josh. 24:1-28

We have called attention to various efforts to evaluate the relative weight to be attributed to the MT and the LXX with respect to textual pluses and minuses. It is evident that research into the relationship between the MT and the LXX has not yet provided definitive answers to these questions, and commentators in general continue to make eclectic use of the textual criticism. In addition to the observations offered above it is necessary to illustrate the need for further research into the relationship between the LXX and the MT with a few concrete examples of the inadequacy of previous treatments of Josh. 24.

R.G.Boling suggests not less than twelve haplographies in Josh. 24:1-27. He regularly resorts to this explanation to clarify the minuses in the LXX, thereby presupposing a most haphazard history of textual transmission.[1] However, his claimed haplographies are not all convincing.[2] On the other extreme, commentators have often appealed to the absence of material in the LXX, along with a certain duplicity of content, to substantiate their lists of alleged glosses in Josh. 24. But the identification of glosses here is more complex than such an employment of the LXX would imply, and it would be too simple to assume that pluses in the preserved MT are all glosses.[3] What now appears to the modern reader to be a redundant gloss may at one time have been a structurally significant synonym or repetition.[4]

[1]R.G.Boling, *Joshua: A New Translation with Notes and Commentary* (New York, 1982), 530-532.

[2]Boling uses the same approach in other chapters of Joshua; cf. also his "Some Conflate Readings in Joshua–Judges," *VT* 16 (1966) 293-298. But with respect to Josh. 23:7, for example, see W.T.Koopmans, "The Poetic Prose of Joshua 23," in W.van der Meer–J.C.de Moor, eds., *The Structural Analysis of Biblical and Canaanite Poetry* (Sheffield, 1988), 97f. n.42.

[3]See now the guidelines for identification suggested by G.R.Driver, "Glosses in the Hebrew Text of the Old Testament" in *L'Ancient Testament et l'orient. Étudees présentées aux VIes Journées Bibliques de Louvain (11-13 septembre 1954)* (Louvain, 1957), 123-161. Virtually all these characteristics are absent in the lengthy list of repeatedly alleged glosses in Josh. 24:1-28.

[4]J.Muilenburg, "A Study in Hebrew Rhetoric: Repetition and Style" in *Congress Volume Copenhagen 1953*, *SVT* 1 (Leiden, 1953), 100; Muilenburg correctly stresses

The absence of such a clause in the LXX does not necessarily disprove its authenticity in the passage. An example of this is found in vs.22. The clause *wy'mrw 'dym* is lacking in the LXX and has often been suspected of being a late gloss.[5] But the expression, within its context, should be compared with Ruth 4:9-11 and 1 Sam. 12:5, which demonstrates the unlikelihood that this cryptic response is a later gloss. Ruth 4:9ff. is part of a poetic narrative composition,[6] and for purpose of comparison we now reproduce Ruth 4:9-11; 1 Sam. 12:5; Josh. 24:22 all in similar format.

**Ruth 4:9-11**

| | |
|---|---|
| *wy'mr b'z lzqnym* | And Boaz said to the elders |
| *wkl h'm* | and to all the people, |
| *'dym 'tm hywm* | "You are witnesses today, |
| *ky qnyty 't kl 'šr l'lymlk* | that I bought all what was Elimelech's, |
| *w't kl 'šr lklywn wmḥlwn* | and all what was Kilion's and Mahlon's, |
| *myd n'my* | from the hand of Naomi. |
| | |
| *wgm 't rwt hm'byh* | And also Ruth the Moabitess, |
| *'št mḥlwn* | the wife of Mahlon, |
| *qnyty ly l'šh* | I bought as my wife, |
| *lhqym šm hmt 'l nḥltw* | to maintain the name of the dead on his property, |
| *wl' ykrt šm hmt m'm 'ḥyw* | so that his name will not be cut off from amongst his brothers, |
| *wmš'r mqwmw* | or from the gate of his place. |
| | |
| *'dym 'tm hywm* | You are witnesses today." |
| *wy'mrw kl h'm 'šr bš'r* | And all the people at the gate said, |
| *whzqnym* | as well as the elders, |
| *'dym* | "Witnesses!" |

that repetition in narrative "appears as a major stylistic feature."

[5]E.g., Steuernagel, *Josua*, 245; Rudolph, *Der "Elohist"*, 247; Noth, *Josua* 1938, 136; *Josua* 1953, 135.

[6]J.C.de Moor, "The Poetry of the Book of Ruth," *Or* 53 (1984) 262-283; "Part II," *Or* 55 (1986) 16-46, esp. 38.

**1 Sam. 12:5**

| | |
|---|---|
| *wy'mr 'lyhm* | And he said to them, |
| *'d yhwh bkm* | "Yahweh is witness against you, |
| *w'd mšyḥw hywm hzh* | and his anointed is witness this day, |
| *ky l' mṣ'tm bydy m'wmh* | that you have not found anything in my hand." |
| *wy'mr* | And they said, |
| *'d* | "Witness!" |

**Josh. 24:22**

| | |
|---|---|
| *wy'mr yhwš' 'l-h'm* | And Joshua said to the people, |
| *'dym 'tm bkm* | "You are witness against yourselves |
| *ky-'tm bḥrtm lkm 't yhwh* | that you have chosen for yourselves Yahweh, |
| *l'bd 'wtw* | to serve him." |
| *wy'mrw* | And they said, |
| *'dym* | "Witnesses!" |

When juxtaposed in this manner the similarity of form[7] and content becomes evident at a glance. Within the dialogical character of the legal setting the lead speaker calls the people to witness; he summarizes the rationale or charge for the witnessing with a *ky* clause, to which the cryptic response *'dym* is expected. The fact that the recital of the *ky* clause can be elaborated to varying lengths is in harmony with the principle of expansion and contraction,[8] and is apparently governed by the specific context and the amount of detail judged by the narrator to be necessary.[9] It is significant that Ruth 4:10 concludes with an exact repetition of the words *'dym 'tm hywm*, which

[7]Note that the Masoretic division of 1 Sam. 12:5 and Josh. 24:22 places the *'aṯnāḥ* in identical positions in the respective verses, in our opinion coinciding with a division between verses of poetic narrative.

[8]On the principle of expansion and contraction in Ugaritic and Hebrew poetry see J.C.de Moor, "The Art of Versification in Ugarit and Israel," in Y.Avishur–J.Blau, eds., *Studies in Bible and the Ancient Near East* (Fs S.E.Loewenstamm; Jerusalem, 1978), 127; *UF* 10 (1978) 187-217; *UF* 12 (1980) 311-315; M.C.A.Korpel–J.C.de Moor, "Fundamentals of Ugaritic and Hebrew Poetry," *UF* 18 (1986) 173-212, esp. 174, 178f., 187-189, 197f.

[9]A statement by Cross, though made in another context, is in principle equally valid here: "But singers of epic poetry also could expand or contract their songs to fit circumstance and occasion" ("The Epic Traditions of Early Israel," in R.E.Friedman, ed., *The Poet and the Historian: Essays in Literary and Historical Biblical Criticism* [Chico, 1983], 25).

refocuses the precise call to witness after the elaborated *ky* clause.

The close parallel detectable between the verses juxtaposed above makes it impossible to agree that Josh. 24:22b is simply a gloss in the MT. Failure to recognize the precise nature of the legal formulation leads many commentators to the conclusion that these words awkwardly interrupt the flow of Joshua's speech, and since the oath of the people already is present in vss.18,21,24, it is considered superfluous that they are called as witnesses to their own choice of allegiance.[10] However, the function of the witness to the oath of allegiance (vs.22) is not the same as the function of the oath of allegiance itself (vss.18,21,24). Ordinarily a 3rd party witness is called upon, but in Josh. 24:22,26f. this function is fulfilled by the people themselves and the stone of witness. The response of 22b can cogently be accepted as part of a legal formulation customary in ancient Israel, and the form of what Nielsen termed a "faded oath"[11] is actually clearer than his judgment would intimate. Nor is there any reason to conclude on the basis of comparison with Ruth 4:10f. that the language is late.[12] In this case the plus of the MT is probably preferable to the shorter reading of the LXX.[13]

The question of the relationship between the MT and the Greek traditions should be tempered by a study of all variant readings in the chapter, not simply the pluses and minuses. A comprehensive study of the variants cautions against assuming that the LXX is categorically more reliable than the MT. It is important to note, for example, that scholars almost unequivocally prefer the reading of Shechem in MT vss.1,25 to Shiloh of the LXX. And again, beginning at vs.4b the LXX tradition is influenced by Deut. 26:5ff.[14] Since it is possible to demonstrate that certain variants in the LXX tradition were influenced by other established biblical texts, whether at the time of translation or already prior to that in a Hebrew tradition divergent

[10]E.g., Dillmann, *Josua*, 587: "*wy'mrw 'dym* fehlt in LXX; nothwendig ist es nicht, u. Josua's Rede geht V.23 fort."

[11]Nielsen, *Shechem*, 108.

[12]Contra L'Hour, who argues in part on this basis for a post-exilic date ("L'alliance de Sichem," 28).

[13]It has previously been suggested that the LXX does not always provide a literal translation of dialogues, cf. J.W.Wevers, "Exegetical Principles Underlying the Septuagint Text of 1 Kings ii 12-xxi 43," *OTS* 8 (Leiden, 1950), 301.

[14]Dillmann, *Josua*, 584; H.Seebass, *Der Erzvater Israel und die Einführung der Jahweverehrung in Kanaan* (Berlin, 1966), 5; Tov, "Midrash-Type Exegesis," 59f.

from the preserved MT, one must be cautious about making generalizations concerning the priority of the alleged *Vorlage* of the LXX when compared to the MT where the latter has pluses.

Furthermore, claims that variations in the present Greek and Hebrew texts stem from differences already present in the Hebrew *Vorlage* of the Greek have not always been adequately substantiated.[15] For example, in Josh. 24:7 LXX B we find the reading *νεφελην και γνοφον* in place of the MT's *m'pl*. The LXX's rendering prompted Nielsen to suggest that the Greek is "certainly not a translation of MT's *m'pl* but more probably represents the *'nn wḥwšk* (sic) from Ex. 14:20."[16] Although at first glance Nielsen's proposal may seem appealing, further study of his suggestion casts serious doubt upon its validity. Nielsen's reading needs to explain why the translation gives *νεφελην και γνοφον* rather than *σκοτος και γνοφος* as found in the LXX of Ex. 14:20. If the translator's Hebrew text read *ḥšk*, it would most logically be translated with *σκοτος*.[17] The Hebrew word *m'pl* is a *hapax legomenon*, but the employment of *γνοφος* as a translation of *'pl* is attested in Ex. 10:22; Job 23:17; Prov. 7:9; Am. 5:10; Joel 2:2; Zech. 1:15; Jer. 23:12. Accordingly, the simplest solution is that the dual nouns in LXX B do not represent a translation of Ex. 14:20. Cases are known where the LXX adds a word or two to clarify a Hebrew reading.[18] It is possible that the decision here to translate *m'pl* with double nouns was influenced by the known parallel in Ex. 14:20.[19] But contrary to the opinion of Nielsen the evidence does not compel one to posit a Hebrew antecedent which differs from the present reading of the MT.

[15]Cf. S.Jellicoe, "Septuagint Studies in the Current Century," *JBL* 88 (1969) 191-199, esp. 192.

[16]Nielsen, *Shechem*, 89.

[17]See E.Hatch–H.A.Redpath, *A Concordance to the Septuagint* (Oxford, 1897; reprint ed. Grand Rapids, 1983), 1276. There is only one unequivocal example in the LXX of *γνοφος* as a translation of *ḥšk*, namely Job 17:13, where *γνοφος* is used instead of *σκοτος* because the latter is already employed for translation of *ḥšk* in the preceding verse and was therefore considered unavailable to the translator. Ex. 14:20 is ambiguous, but the most probable conclusion here is that *h'nn whḥšk* is translated by the LXX in reverse order, with *γνοφος* as a translation for *'nn*; cf. Deut. 4:11; Isa. 44:22; Job 3:5. Apparently Deut. 5:22 in the LXX is influenced by 4:11—which accounts for the addition of *σκοτος*, with *γνοφος* remaining a translation of *'nn*.

[18]Tov, *Text-Critical Use*, 83f.

[19]See also Ps. 97:2 (LXX 96:2).

Given the complexity of the relationship between the Greek and Hebrew traditions, rather than accept Auld's disqualification of the MT of Joshua as a valid basis for a structural analysis it is more desirable to study *both* the preserved Hebrew tradition and a hypothetically reconstructed *Vorlage* of the Greek texts in the hope that this might produce an objective basis for comparison of certain otherwise enigmatic pluses and minuses in the respective texts. If a convincing structure is discernible in either or both of the traditions, it may be expected in turn to be of benefit in answering some of the textual-critical questions which to this point have defied convincing resolution. The issues here raised are sufficient to demonstrate the necessity of paying renewed attention to the textual-critical problems of Josh. 24:1-28, especially pertaining to the numerous pluses in the MT as compared to the LXX.[20]

Our textual-critical comments thus far have been restricted to the relationship of the MT and LXX. While this is symptomatic of the interest which has dominated throughout the history of interpretation of Josh. 24, it is desirable to broaden the field of comparison. Holzinger[21] and Nielsen[22] provide helpful notations on places where the Peshitta and the MT differ, but a more systematic analysis of these variant readings remains to be conducted. The recently published translation of the Aramaic targums also facilitates a welcome addition to the textual study of this passage.[23] It is also desirable in the future to expand the study of the Hebrew tradition beyond the use of Leningrad Codex B 19[A], e.g., with the Aleppo Codex employed in the Hebrew University Bible Project.[24]

[20]See the detailed analysis of the LXX of Josh. 24:1-28 in ch.3 below.

[21]Holzinger, *Josua*, 93-95.

[22]Nielsen, *Shechem*, 86-90, 99f., 108f.

[23]D.J.Harrington–A.J.Saldarini, *Targum Jonathan of the Former Prophets: Introduction, Translation and Notes* (The Aramaic Bible, vol. 10; Edinburgh, 1987).

[24]Cf. the discussion of the various textual traditions in E.Würthwein, *Der Text des Alten Testament*, 4th ed. (Stuttgart, 1973) (= *The Text of the Old Testament*, trans. E.F.Rhodes [Grand Rapids, 1979], with updated bibliographical references); M.H.Goshen-Gottstein, "Hebrew Biblical Manuscripts. Their History and their Place in the HUBP Edition," *Bibl* 48 (1967) 243-290.

## 2.3 Literary-critical diversity and consensus

The difficulty in attaining a satisfactory literary-critical analysis of Josh. 24 has long been lamented. Möhlenbrink observed,

> "Genau besehen ist bei keinem grösseren Abschnitt des Hexateuchs die Frage der literarischen Vorgeschichte und der Quellenzusammenhänge so schwierig, wie bei den Sagen der ersten Hälfte und der Schlusskapitel des Josuabuches."[25]

Nielsen was forced to admit that his search for pre-Dtic elements in vss.2-13 was "fraught with some difficulty and much uncertainty."[26] McCarthy states that this is "problematic material."[27] Undaunted, all these scholars and a host of others besides have tried to clarify the literary composition of Josh. 24. As a result, the diversity of opinion with respect to the literary composition of Josh. 24 has frequently been noted by scholars who then proceeded to add one more "variation on a theme" to the already vast selection of options, without being able to adduce much new or convincing evidence in support of their novel or modified positions.

In order to bring the complexity of the literary-critical endeavor clearly into focus, it is helpful to present a concise summary or catalogue of the various positions which have been defended with regard to source or authorship of Josh. 24:1-28. Basically six major categories may be listed, each of which can potentially be sub-divided into a variety of related views.

1. A basic Elohist document, with later redactional glossing, whether Dtistic or otherwise.
2. A combination of Elohist and Yahwist sources, with later glossing and redacting, Dtistic or otherwise.
3. A Yawhist source, supplemented by additional material.
4. A Dtic or Dtistic composition.
5. An early covenant account or tradition, redacted to a degree.

[25] Möhlenbrink, "Landnahmesagen," 238.

[26] Nielsen, *Shechem*, 98.

[27] McCarthy, *Treaty and Covenant*, 231; cf. Muilenburg, who faults source critics for not having done justice to "this admittedly difficult text" ("Form and Structure," 357). Kreuzer, *Frühgeschichte*, 183: "Dieses Kapitel gehört zu den schwierigsten Texten des Alten Testaments und wird in der Forschung entsprechend divergierend beurteilt."

6. Authorship contemporaneous with or shortly after the event described.

A delineation of each of these positions, including a sample indication of its advocates and the major reasons cited for holding to the given theory, will serve to illustrate the major questions at hand.

### 2.3.1 An Elohist source

The predominant inclination in the end of the 19th cent. and the first half of the 20th was to assign Josh. 24:1-28 to an Elohist source. However, within this position there was always a great deal of diversity as to finer details in the subsequent history of redaction, e.g., Wellhausen's assertion of a JE combination and Dtistic glosses, Kuenen's P2 collector/redactor, and various other positions regarding Dtistic supplementing, glossing, or redacting—a matter of considerable disagreement amongst adherents to this position.

**Representatives:** Of the scholars whose positions are summarized in detail in the first chapter, Wellhausen, Kuenen, Valeton, Kraetzschmar, Karge, Sellin, Simpson, and von Rad all subscribed to the basic theory that Josh. 24:1-28 provides evidence of the continuation of the Elohistic source thought to be detected in the Pentateuch. To this list of representatives we can add a great number of other scholars, e.g., Dillmann,[28] Steuernagel,[29] Holzinger,[30] Luther and Meyer,[31]

[28]Dillmann, *Josua*, 583-588, 617 (Dillmann continued to designate the Elohist source as B).

[29]Steuernagel, *Josua*, 134, 241-245. Note that Steuernagel, building in part upon Kuenen's objections to the unity of E, thought it possible and necessary to distinguish $E^1$ and $E^2$. Steuernagel's discernment of $E^1$ and $E^2$ in Josh. 24 was followed closely by Hölscher, *Geschichtsschreibung*, 350. A more reserved opinion concerning discernment of $E^1$ and $E^2$ can be found in Holzinger's literary-critical treatment of this passage (*Josua*, 96f.).

[30]Holzinger, *Einleitung*. esp. 1:91, 97, 100, 173-175, 180, 181-191, 197f., 203f., 207, 209, 212, 213f., 226; *Josua*, 95-99.

[31]In Meyer, *Die Israeliten*, 542-561, esp. 549-553, 561. See already his "Kritik der Berichte über die Eroberung Palaestinas," *ZAW* 1 (1881) 121f.

Gressmann,[32] Morgenstern,[33] J.Garstang,[34] Weiser,[35] W.O.E.Oesterley and T.H.Robinson,[36] Pfeiffer,[37] Muilenburg,[38] M.L.Newman,[39] and Fohrer.[40] This selective list will suffice to demonstrate the substantial following which the Elohist theory of the origin of Josh. 24:1-28 was able to boast throughout the decades of the past century.

**Reasons:** Identification of Josh. 24:1-28 with E involved two related steps. The first step was to assume that the sources which had been detected in the Pentateuch would extend into Joshua as well. A statement by Pfeiffer is typical,

> "...the Book of Joshua is a compilation from separate sources. It is natural to assume that those are a continua-

[32]H.Gressmann, *Die Anfänge Israels. Die Schriften des Alten Testaments*, I/2 (Göttingen, 1922), 156-164. He considers Josh. 24 to be one of six heavily redacted parallel accounts of the gathering at Shechem. The other variant accounts are Deut. 11:26-32; 27:1-3; 27:4-8,12f.; Josh. 8:30-35; 23.

[33]J.Morgenstern, "The Book of the Covenant, I" *HUCA* 5 (1928) 8.

[34]J.Garstang, *Joshua, Judges: Foundations of Bible History* (London, 1931; reprint ed., Grand Rapids, 1978), 6f., 30f.

[35]Weiser *Einleitung*, 112-114.

[36]W.O.E.Oesterley–T.H.Robinson, *An Introduction to the Books of the Old Testament*, 3rd ed. (New York, 1958), 70. Here vss.11b,13 are assigned to D, vs.26b to P.

[37]R.H.Pfeiffer, *Introduction to the Old Testament*, 2nd ed. (London, 1948), 293-313. Pfeiffer does not doubt that the Pentateuchal E source underlies Josh. 24, but he asserts that Dtistic redaction and editing has been "so pervasive that its removal leaves only disconnected words and expressions belonging to E's language"(302). He believes that Deuteronomists working at about 550 B.C. replaced ch.24:1-27 with 23, but it was reinserted by later Deuteronomists, at about 400 B.C.

[38]Muilenburg, "Form and Structure," 355 n.2, 356.

[39]M.L.Newman, *The People of the Covenant: A Study of Israel from Moses to the Monarchy* (New York, 1962), 54, 108 n.18, 116. Ironically, Newman (108 n.18) basically accepts Noth's literary-critical analysis (as presented in *Josua* 1938), at a time when Noth had long previously modified his analysis. Newman's treatment of Josh. 24 is a popularization of Noth's amphictyony thesis.

[40]E.Sellin–G.Fohrer, *Introduction to the Old Testament*, trans. D.E.Green (Nashville, 1968) 155, 201-203 (with heavy stress on Dtistic recension). Fohrer argues elsewhere that Josh. 24 has its origin in the time and circumstances of Jehu's kingship treaty with the people ("Der Vertrag zwischen König und Volk in Israel," *ZAW* 71 [1959] 15). But this idea is absent in his later treatment of Josh. 24 when more emphasis is placed upon Dtistic redaction of "der alte Sagenkern, der Jos 24 zu grunde liegt." He continues, "Ob sich das tatsächlich in Sichem ereignet oder ob der Elohist, zu dessen Quellenschicht die Erzählung gehört hat, sie an diese Stätte, die er auch sonst bevorzugt, verlegt hat, lässt sich nicht mehr feststellen" ("Altes Testament –'Amphiktyonie' und 'Bund'?" 810).

tion of the Pentateuchal sources, that would scarcely end with the death of Moses."[41]

The second step was then to determine to which of the Pentateuchal sources Josh. 24 showed the closest terminological and ideological affinity. As characteristic of E, the advocates especially appealed to the role of Shechem (vss.1,25) as a holy place,[42] especially in comparison with Gen. 33:20, 35:2-5 (also putting away foreign gods),[43] the term *h'mry* as a general reference to the pre-Israelite inhabitants of Palestine,[44] the use of divine names in vss.1,19,26,[45] reference to foreign gods as *'lhy hnkr*,[46] *bḥrbk wbqštk* (cf. Gen. 48:22),[47] *śym ḥq wmšpṭ* (vs.25),[48] and the establishment of a covenant (esp. vss.25f.).[49]

### 2.3.2 An Elohist and a Yahwist source

**Representatives:** Closely related to the previous category is that which attempts to distinguish J and E sources. It should be recalled that numerous representatives of the Elohist theory spoke of E as a recognizable source in what has become a composite JE transmission, e.g., already Wellhausen's conclusion that "J und E zu JE verschmolzen sind."[50] While the majority of commentators thought it was only possible to extract E as a clearly distinguishable source in

[41]Pfeiffer, *Introduction*, 295.

[42]Dillmann, *Josua*, 583; Wellhausen, *Composition*, 134.

[43]Steuernagel, *Josua*, 241f.

[44]Wellhausen, *Composition*, 134; Meyer, "Kritik der Berichte," 121; Dillmann, *Josua*, 583, 617; K.Budde, "Die Gesetzgebung der mittleren Bücher des Pentateuchs, inbesondere der Quellen J und E," *ZAW* 11 (1891) 226; Steuernagel, *Josua*, 242; Holzinger, *Einleitung*, 182, 184; *Josua*, 95.

[45]Dillmann, *Josua*, 583; Wellhausen, *Composition*, 133f.; Holzinger, *Einleitung*, 180; *Josua*, 95.

[46]Dillmann, *Josua*, 583; Wellhausen, *Composition*, 133; Holzinger, *Josua*, 95; Hölscher, *Geschichtsschreibung*, 260.

[47]Dillmann, *Josua*, 503, 583; Wellhausen, *Composition*, 133; Holzinger, *Einleitung*, 180; *Josua*, 95.

[48]Dillmann, *Josua*, 583; Holzinger, *Josua*, 95; cf. his *Einleitung*, 188.

[49]Hölscher, *Geschichtsschreibung*, 141, 245.

[50]Wellhausen, *Geschichte Israels, I*, 370. Wellhausen was followed by many commentators who spoke of JE.

Josh. 24, Smend,[51] Eissfeldt,[52] and originally Noth[53] thought that *both* E and J could be identified in this passage as true sources. Subsequent to Noth, a position in some respects comparable was defended by Möhlenbrink, who thought that parallel traditions could be separated from each other into a "Josuarezension" and a "Jahwerezension,"[54] but he denied that the two parallel traditions could be equated with J and E.[55]

**Reasons:** Smend already offered a list of reasons why in his opinion it was necessary to resort to multiple sources rather than to the theory of a supplemented and glossed E source. He appealed especially to the interchange between 2nd person plural and "fathers" in vss.5-7,17-18, the list of nations in vs.11 as inconsistent with the "lords of Jericho," the doublet "and all the people through which we crossed over" stand-

[51]Smend, *Erzählung des Hexateuch*, 336.

[52]Regarding Eissfeldt see the summary in 1.3.8. Eissfeldt's L (*Laienquelle*) was postulated as a modification of the J theory. Smend, on the other hand, distinguished $J^1$ and $J^2$ in vss.25-27, thereby in essence also arriving at three sources.

[53]Noth's conclusion in 1930 was that it was possible, in addition to identification of glosses, to reconstruct two parallel traditions in Josh. 24:1-28. These he assigned to J and E. But he refused to concede a third source in vss.25-27 by sub-dividing J. *Das System*, 137f.; cf. 1.4.1).

[54]Möhlenbrink, "Landnahmesagen," 250-254. Möhlenbrink's position is comparable to Noth's insofar as it achieves two independent traditions which are able to stand parallel to each other. However, the verses assigned to each, and the criteria for separation of the sources differ, as do the alleged location and the historical significance of the covenants enacted in the respective ceremonies. Möhlenbrink's appeal to the LXX's localization at Shiloh is actually insignificant as evidence for two originally separate traditions. He argues that the two *Landnahme* traditions were already connected prior to their incorporation into J or E, at which time the tradition became more closely connected with Shiloh than Gilgal. Finally, E makes the shift from Shiloh to Shechem. Accordingly, the appeal to Shiloh in the LXX tradition as substantiation for his speculation regarding two sources is unfounded. If the change to Shechem was made already at an early stage by E, at the time of the compilation of the Pentateuch, as Möhlenbrink himself asserts, where did the LXX get knowledge of the Shiloh tradition so many centuries later? Furthermore, Möhlenbrink's evidence for two sources is *less* obvious in the syntax and grammar of the LXX than in the MT. And, even if the LXX had a Hebrew *Vorlage* which located this gathering at Shiloh rather than at Shechem, this would provide no evidence for Möhlenbrink's theory of two separate traditions, one at Shiloh and one at Gilgal. For reservations about the theory that a Hebrew *Vorlage* to the LXX read "Shiloh" see 3.6.3 (re 24:25).

[55]He posited two original sources, from Shiloh and Gilgal respectively, later combined and attributed primarily to Shiloh, with the location subsequently converted to Shechem by J or E, most likely the latter ("Landnahmesagen," 266-268).

ing parallel to the preceding clause (vs.17), and the double reference to God as "holy" and as "jealous" (vs.19).[56] Furthermore, he argued that vss.25-27 must be assigned to J1 and J2, not to E, whose hand was detected in the parallel reference to witnesses in vs.22.[57] Since the terminology of these "parallel accounts" is strikingly reminiscent of terminology employed elsewhere in Genesis and Exodus, Smend concluded that parallel sources are more likely than an extensive list of glosses.[58]

### 2.3.3 A Yahwist source

**Representatives:** Rudolph,[59] Van Seters[60]
**Reasons:** Rudolph's criterion for viewing Josh. 24:1-28 as essentially a Yahwistic document stood as part of his broader theory denying the existence of E as an independent source. He dropped vs.26a as a gloss, interpreted *h'lhym* in vs.1 as irrelevant for source distinction, attributed Gen. 33:18-20 to J, and posited the dependence of Gen. 35:1ff. upon Josh. 24 rather than vice versa.[61] Van Seters also argued that Josh. 24:1-27 was written by the Yahwist of the Pentateuch, but he dates this composition to the exilic age.[62] His article makes no mention of Rudolph's views, but this is less surprising when one considers that the most predominant characteristic shared in common by Rudolph's Yahwist and Van Seters' Yahwist is that they simply bear the same name. Van Seters' Yahwist theory differs radically from the previous ideas of Rudolph.[63]

### 2.3.4 A Dtic or Dtistic composition

**Representatives:** Perhaps this position has been stated most radically by E.Auerbach, "Es muss mit aller Schärfe gesagt werden, dass

[56]Smend, *Erzählung des Hexateuch*, 116, 310, 336-338.
[57]Smend, *Erzählung des Hexateuch*, 336-339.
[58]For some minor modifications see the sections on Eissfeldt and Noth above.
[59]Rudolph, *Der "Elohist"*, 244-252, 281 (cf. 1.3.9).
[60]Cf. 1.6.8.
[61]Cf. 1.3.9.
[62]For further details see the summary of Van Seters' position in 1.6.8.
[63]Rudolph worked within the classical framework of source-criticism, but denied the existence of E as a true source alongside J. On the other hand, Van Seters wishes to view the work of J in a post-Dtic setting in the time of the exile.

*hier von einer historischen Quelle gar keine Rede sein kann.*"[64] A similar position, however, is defended more elaborately in Perlitt's analysis, where it is argued that 24:1-28 is pre-exilic, Dtic, with the exception of vss.25b,26a, which are considered later Dtistic additions.[65] Nicholson accepts most of Perlitt's conclusions but he attributes authorship of the entire passage to an exilic, Dtistic setting.[66]
**Reasons:** Due to the significant implications and growing influence of Perlitt's position it is especially important to offer a detailed presentation of his literary-critical analysis.[67] Perlitt rejects as methodologically unsound any approach which recognizes abundant Dtic or Dtistic terminology but proceeds to account for it on the premise that the present text is a combination of an ancient source and later redaction.[68] He argues that Josh. 24:1-28 presents an independent literary unit which has only a meagre narrative connection with its immediate context. In fact, the entire passage is characterized essentially by dialogue (vss.2-24,27), rather than narration of events (vss.1,25f.,28)—which serve only to provide a skeletal setting for the dialogue.[69] The purpose of the passage is strictly apologetic; "Sowohl das Stilmittel des Dialogs als auch diese inhaltliche Offenheit für eine Entscheidung sogar gegen Jahwe schliessen den Kult als Sitz im Leben aus."[70]

As indications of Dtic terminology or ideas, Perlitt appeals to the following elements:[71] *kl-šbṭy yśr'l* (vs.1); the connection between the phrases *lpny h'lhym* and indiscriminate mention of *yhwh* (vss.2,26); similarity of vss.2-13 to the "credo" of Dtn. 26:5ff.; mention of the

[64]E.Auerbach, "Die grosse Überarbeitung der biblischen Bücher," in *Congress Volume, Copenhagen 1953, SVT* 1 (Leiden, 1953), 3 (original emphasis).
[65]See 1.6.5.
[66]Nicholson, *His People*, esp. 158-163. He states: "It is very probably a secondary addition to the Deuteronomistic history, possibly indeed a very late addition. In my opinion Perlitt is justified in rejecting the suggestion that it is based upon a more ancient nucleus" (158).
[67]The details listed in this section should be viewed in connection with the summary in 1.6.5.
[68]Perlitt, *Bundestheologie*, 240.
[69]Perlitt, *Bundestheologie*, 241. "Jos 24 gibt keinen Bericht von etwas Vergangenem, sondern stellt in der Verkleidung der historischen Begebenheit eine ebenso leidenschaftliche wie kunstvoll stilisierte Entscheidungsproklamation für gegenwärtige Hörer (und dann auch Leser) dar" (246).
[70]Perlitt, *Bundestheologie*, 244. Particular emphasis in this regard is placed upon comparison of form and detail with 1 Sam. 12 and Judg. 10:6-16.
[71]Perlitt, *Bundestheologie*, 249-270.

Amorites does not betray an interest in the people as such but only in the danger of their gods; contrary to Noth, vs.13 is Dtic and not a later Dtistic addition; the verb *grš* (vs.18) with Yahweh as subject is pre-Dtistic;[72] the vital position of *'bd* is recognized, and contra Noth it is argued that vss.19-24 cannot simply be extracted as a later gloss; the verb *swr* (Hiph.) is not to be read on the basis of Gen. 35:2 as a ceremonial ritual, but rather, in comparison with Judg. 10:10-16 and 1 Sam. 7:3; 12, it is more likely to have a political and theological emphasis, as is also the case with *bḥr* in vs.15; vs.20 must be dated after the fall of the Northern kingdom; finally, vss.25-27 are thought to be quite compatible with, and explainable by, a Dtic context. For these reasons Perlitt views Josh. 24:1-28 as Dtic but not yet Dtistic.

Auerbach justifies his assertion that Josh. 24 is a Dtistic compilation dating from the time of the exile on the grounds that Shechem never actually functioned as a central sanctuary in ancient Israel.[73] Furthermore, he argues that the reference to the tree in vs.26 and the suggestion in vs.23 that Israel would have worshipped foreign gods so soon after the death of Moses, betray the artificiality of the account.[74] Nicholson basically follows Perlitt's analysis[75] until it comes to a matter of dating, with respect to which he suggests an alternative in the time of the exile.[76]

[72]As is evident from its presence in Ex. 23:29f.; 33:2; 34:11, Judg. 6:9.

[73]Auerbach, "Überarbeitung," 3.

[74]Auerbach, "Überarbeitung" 3: "Die künstliche Konstruktion des Verfassers von Jos xxiv verrät sich durch die Erwähnung des Gottesbaumes in 26. Wann is diese Eich gewachsen? In den wenigen Jahren der Landeseroberung durch Josua? Die Idee, dass die Israeliten schon zur Zeit Josuas, wenige Jahre nach dem Tode Mose's, fremde Götterbilder besassen (xxiv 23), ist ebenso ungeheuerlich wie charakteristisch für die unhistorische Auffassung der Exilszeit." Auerbach's argumentation is weak. With respect to the tree it is obvious that the Israelites did not have to plant it first in order for it to function as a terebinth. Auerbach's assertion that it is improbable that idolatry already existed in the time of Joshua is equally superfluous, as is evident from the persistent disobedience of the Israelites throughout the duration of Moses' leadership, and the indictment in Deut. 32:15-18.

[75]But cf. Nicholson's objections to Perlitt (*His People*, 159f.).

[76]In support of this alternative to Perlitt's conclusion, he refers the reader to A.D.H.Mayes, *The Story of Israel between Settlement and Exile: A Redactional Study of the Deuteronomistic History* (London, 1983), 46-52; but Mayes too foregoes a literary-critical analysis.

### 2.3.5 Ancient tradition with later redaction

Within the general theory of an early covenant tradition at Shechem, later redacted from a given theological perspective, there is ample room for multiple approaches to Josh. 24:1-28. A seemingly endless list of scholars have creatively combined textual analysis with historical reconstructions of circumstances in which Shechem might have played a central role, to produce a virtually inexhaustible number of diverse explanations of the final composition and purpose of Josh. 24:1-28. The following subdivisions offer a representative range of these positions.

For many scholars who hold to the idea of ancient, traditional material employed in the final composition of Josh. 24, the distinction between their position and the earlier claims of an E source is only marginal;[77] the differences are usually related to the respective judgments pertaining to whether or not E continues as a written, documentary source from the Pentateuch through Josh. 24. In other words, the major differences coincide with the concerns of the Pentateuch/Hexateuch debate. While the advocates of the Elohist position assigned specific words, phrases or verses to E as a source, the more recent trend has been a more cautious discernment of terminological or conceptual affinity to earlier material found in E, J, etc. But it is not always clear in recent studies whether Josh. 24's connection to E or J material in the Pentateuch is thought to derive from a common local tradition in the form of a *written source*. Present studies are reluctant to accept the previous source-critical methodology which sought to identify specific terminology of E and tended to designate what remained as a parallel source, glosses or supplementation. On the contrary, present advocates of an ancient literary core or tradition argue that non-Dtic terminology indicates ancient tradition, while Dtic language may indicate later redaction. The net result is in many respects similar to the previous E position but there is considerable reservation about asserting a continuing source from the Pentateuch through Joshua. For the time being these remarks must suffice as a caveat that the boundary between the positions listed below and some of the most recent defenders of E above is a fluid one.[78] We list

[77]E.g., Weinfeld, *Deuteronomy*, 165.

[78]A good example of the ambiguity and uncertainty caused by the Hexateuch-Pentateuch debate when applied to the literary origin of Josh. 24 in comparison with the Pentateuchal traditions is found in the work of G.E.Wright. Pentateuchal

the following authors together in distinction from the Elohist position because of their common tendency to place more emphasis upon an older core of tradition as the basis of Josh. 24 than on the emphasis that this tradition is direct evidence of a Hexateuchal Elohist source.

**Pre-Dtic or proto-Dtic composition:** Of the positions summarized in the first chapter, the works of Schmitt, Weinfeld, McCarthy and Sperling can be included in this category. They do not deny the possibility of some secondary editing, but their main emphasis is that the basic contours of the present text are pre/proto-Dtic. Mölle too asserts an ancient Shechem tradition, but he goes a step further with his claim to distinguish later additions by RJE, E, Dtr1, Dtr2 and final glosses. To these positions we may also add the study of Seebass,[79] and the commentary by T.C.Butler.[80]

**Dtic editing:** The elements of Josh. 24:1-28 attributed by Nielsen to pre-Dtic tradition at Shechem have been listed above. In Nielsen's view the later employment of this tradition is to be localized in Jerusalem in connection with the Josianic reform, which accounts for the final form of the passage.[81] Since Jaroš accepts Perlitt's date for the final redaction,[82] but argues that it is based in part upon an older historical tradition, his name must also be added here. The same may be said of Kreuzer,[83] and this is also the position adopted in the recent commentary by E.J.Hamlin.[84]

narratives centered in Shechem are attributed to the "old epic account" of JE, but Josh. 24 is "a different type of literature" according to Wright. He asserts, "This chapter has generally been felt to derive from very old tradition, though in its transmission it has been touched up here and there by a 'Deuteronomic' editor, who included it as an appendix to the Book of Joshua" (*Shechem: The Biography*, 134, see too 135f.). See also his "Shechem," 364, where he terms it "strong northern tradition," and cf. his *God Who Acts* (London, 1952), 72-74. Clearly, the only reason that Wright hesitates to continue to call the tradition which he sees behind Josh. 24 as Elohistic is the fact that it stands at the end of Joshua rather than in the Pentateuch. Though he calls it "a different type of literature," he gives no justification for this claim.

[79]Seebass, *Der Erzvater*, esp. 5-8.

[80]T.C.Butler, *Joshua* (Waco, 1983), 265-269.

[81]Nielsen, *Shechem*, 323-357.

[82]Jaroš *Sichem*, 138. For details see 1.7.3.

[83]See 1.6.11.

[84]E.J.Hamlin, *Joshua: Inheriting the Land* (Grand Rapids, 1983), xvi, xxi, xxxiii, 191f.

**Dtistic editing during the exile or later:** Similar to the above mentioned position which focused upon Dtistic editing in the time of Josiah is that which sees an exilic or post-exilic setting as a logical clarification for the theological emphasis of Josh. 24:1-28.

**Representatives:**[85] Noth (1943 and later), Kraus,[86] Mowinckel,[87] L'Hour, H.W.Hertzberg,[88] J.Gray,[89] Mayes,[90] and R.D.Nelson.[91]

**Reasons:** Noth concludes, "Dtr verfasste sein Werk um die Mitte des 6.Jahrh.v.Chr., also in einer Zeit, als die Geschichte des Volkes Israel ihren Abschluss gefunden hatte."[92] Since he also believed Dtr used the core of the old tradition of Josh. 24 when composing ch.23, and that it was not until a later stage of Dtistic redaction that ch.24 was added, the final Dtistic redaction must be placed later than the main work of Dtr.[93] Hertzberg stresses similarly that Josh. 24 is characterized by Dtistic language and intention.[94] His conclusion relies heavily upon Noth's emphasis on Dtistic history writing and upon the increasing inclination to see local tradition behind narratives in

[85]For summaries of Noth, Kraus, Mowinckel and L'Hour, see the respective sections in ch.1.

[86]Kraus, *Worship in Israel*, 136: "In the first place the Deuteronomistic redaction on the basis of which we can attribute certain verses or parts of verses to the period of the Exile is unmistakable. The main part of the chapter, however, is pre-Deuteronomistic and, from the point of view of the history of tradition, points to the earliest period."

[87]Mowinckel argues that the final redaction of Joshua was post-exilic. As proof he appeals to an anti-Samaritan attitude in the treatment of Manasseh and Ephraim, part of which entailed a shift of emphasis to Shiloh as cultic center. The fact that Shechem is retained in Josh. 24 is evidence that as late as the Dtistic historians, Shechem was recognized as the center from which ancient covenant traditions derived (*Tetrateuch-Pentateuch-Hexateuch*, 73-75). The degree to which written sources would have survived the destruction of Jerusalem—a consideration which played an important role in his debate with Noth regarding boundary descriptions in Joshua—is not raised with regard to Josh. 24, and he is not specific in dating the present Dtistic redaction of Josh. 24. But, in any event, he is forced to claim that it is prior to the anti-Samaritan bias that he sees elsewhere in the final redaction of Joshua.

[88]H.W.Hertzberg, *Die Bücher Josua, Richter, Ruth* (Göttingen, 1953).

[89]J.Gray, *Joshua, Judges, Ruth* (Basingstoke and Grand Rapids, 1986), 52-55, 175-183. He claims to detect a "post-Exilic Deuteronomistic redactor" (52).

[90]Mayes, *Story of Israel*, 40-57, 134.

[91]R.D.Nelson, *The Double Redaction of the Deuteronomistic History* (Sheffield, 1981), 94-98.

[92]Noth, *Überlieferungsgeschichtliche Studien*, 91.

[93]Noth, *Josua* 1953, 10, 11, 15f., 133, 139.

[94]Hertzberg, *Josua*, esp. 8-12, 132-138.

this corpus of material. "Das Problem der 'Quellen' is von daher in den Hintergrund getreten."[95]

Mayes argues, in dialogue with Smend, that the book of Joshua along with the other material of the Dtistic history underwent two stages of consistent redaction, the first with an interest in history, the second with a particular emphasis upon covenant law, but Josh. 24:1-28 cannot be attributed to either of these layers because of the rough connection which it makes with Josh. 23. His conclusion is that along with Deut. 10:8-9; 11:29-30; 27:1-8,11-26; 31:9-13,24-29; Josh. 8:30-35, it must have been added at a later date.[96] "The lack of harmony with the context in which it now stands, the particular subjects with which it deals, the evidence that it is not just a matter of simple later composition but rather of late editing of older material, point in the direction of the preservation here of an ancient levitical tradition, associated with Shechem, and possibly reflective of long established covenant practice at the sanctuary there."[97] Recent attempts to place Josh. 24:1-28 within the corpus of Dtistic history stress the importance of determining its literary relationship to Josh. 23 and Judg. 1-2 in order to decide whether it is original to the Dtic history or is a later insertion. Opinions remain sharply divided on this point.[98]

**Ancient tradition, date of editing unspecified:** H.N.Rösel[99] disagrees with Perlitt that there is not an antecedent historical core to be recognized in the present text of Josh. 24. He appeals to Noth's contention that in the connection between Josh. 23 and 24 the latter employs older material while the former is purely a literary creation. Secondly, Perlitt has argued for a disguised polemic against the Assyrian state cultus of the 7th cent., but Rösel questions whether it is really plausible to force the references to the patriarchs into such a theory. He suggests that vss.11b-24 do not belong to the earliest level

[95]Hertzberg, *Josua*, 11.

[96]Mayes, *Story of Israel*, 49-52, 56, 134.

[97]Mayes, *Story of Israel*, 57; cf. 158f. See also his *Israel in the Period of the Judges* (London, 1974), 35-40. His statement, "Joshua 24 has certainly undergone deuteronomistic editing on an extensive scale, but the whole chapter cannot thereby be dismissed as little more than a pious sermon by someone steeped in covenant ideas and terminology" (35f.) is apparently intended as a rebuttal of Perlitt's view.

[98]Cf. Nelson, *Double Redaction*, 94-98; Auld, *Joshua, Moses*, 54f.

[99]H.N.Rösel, "Erwägungen zu Tradition und Geschichte in Jos 24," *BN* 22 (1983) 41-46.

of the text but were supplied by relatively early Dtistic redaction.

### 2.3.6 Authorship contemporaneous with or relatively soon after the events described

We complete this catalogue of positions regarding the authorship and/or source of Josh. 24:1-28 with reference to a number of authors who have argued that this passage was written by either a firsthand witness or by someone writing shortly after the occurrence of the events here narrated. Since the adherents to this position tend to base their arguments upon introductory questions regarding Joshua as a whole rather than literary-critical reconstructions of this chapter in particular, for our present discussion it will be sufficient to give only a brief indication of this view's advocates.

**Representatives:** The Talmud (Baba Bathra 14b, 15a) attributes basic authorship to Joshua, until his death (24:29), with the final verses subsequently added by Eleazar, until his death (24:33), and finally by Phinehas. This position is accepted by A.Cohen.[100] Y.Kaufmann, on the other hand, argues that while most of Joshua derives from an eye-witness author, 24:1-27 was added by the redactor in the time of the judges.[101]

Throughout the centuries a position comparable to the traditional Jewish view has at times been advocated by conservative Christian scholars, inter alia, C.J.Goslinga,[102] and E.J.Young.[103] On the other hand, most authors recognized the many difficulties involved in assigning most of the book to Joshua himself.[104] Accordingly, G.Ch.Aalders opted for authorship in the time of the judges by someone employing older written sources.[105] Harrison,[106] argues for a date somewhat later, probably at the beginning of the monarchy, perhaps

[100]A.Cohen, *Joshua, Judges: Hebrew Text and English Translations with Introductions and Commentary* (London, 1950), xiii-xv.

[101]Y.Kaufmann, *The Biblical Account of the Conquest of Palestine* (Jerusalem, 1953), 98.

[102]C.J.Goslinga, *Het boek Jozua* (Kampen, 1927), 13-22. Note that in the 3rd edition (Kampen, 1955, 20) Goslinga modified his view, suggesting authorship by one of Joshua's *šṭrym* mentioned in 1:10; 3:2; 8:33; 23:2; 24:1.

[103]E.J.Young *An Introduction to the Old Testament* (Grand Rapids, 1949), 162f.

[104]See already J.Calvin, *Commentaries on the Book of Joshua*, trans. H.Beveridge (Grand Rapids, 1949), xvii-xviii.

[105]G.Ch.Aalders *Oud-Testamentische kanoniek* (Kampen, 1952), 163-171.

[106]Harrison, *Introduction*, 673.

within the lifetime of Samuel.
**Reasons:** Despite the fact that others have long argued that the reference in Josh. 24:26 does not refer to the present Book of Joshua,[107] Young maintained that this verse is evidence that at least parts of Joshua were written by Joshua himself.[108] Harrison's suggested date for the authorship of Joshua in the early period of the monarchy appeals to the fact that the mandate for the expulsion of the Sidonians (13:6) does not mention Tyre, the inability to capture Jerusalem from the Jebusites indicates a pre-monarchic situation, as does certain tribal allotments from Shiloh.[109] His arguments are essentially a restatement of the opinion published by C.F.Keil.[110] Kline and Kitchen[111] argued upon the basis of form-critical considerations that Josh. 24 cannot be dated much later than the time of Joshua. As such their argument is a new apologetic for the ancient, orthodox view that Joshua was written either by the person whose name it bears, by a contemporary figure, or by someone writing shortly thereafter.

### 2.3.7 Inadequacy of the literary-critical approaches

Two things are clear when the various opinions regarding literary sources and authorship of Josh. 24:1-28 are collated as in the preceding paragraphs. First, while various trends towards a consensus challenging previous Elohistic theories in particular, and any documentary theory presupposing a Hexateuch in general, have emerged in studies of this passage in the last couple of decades, it is nevertheless impossible to discern a positive consensus with respect to the actual nature and composition of Josh. 24:1-28. Opinions remain radically disparate with respect to the date of authorship, the history of redaction, and even the fundamental purpose of the passage.

Secondly, it is also apparent that the traditional methods of employing literary or source criticism are inadequate for solving such

[107]Kuenen, *Historisch-critisch onderzoek*, 1:17; Gressmann, *Anfänge Israels*, 13; Aalders, *Oud-Testamentische kanoniek*, 164, 169.
[108]Young, *An Introduction*, 162f. Cf. the editorial footnote added to Calvin, *Joshua*, xviii.
[109]Harrison, *Introduction*, 672.
[110]C.F.Keil–F.Delitzsch, *Joshua, Judges, Ruth*, trans. J.Martin (Grand Rapids, 1950), 15-20. Cf. J.H.Kroeze, *Het boek Jozua* (Kampen, 1968), 6-8; M.H.Woudstra, *The Book of Joshua* (Grand Rapids, 1981), 5-13.
[111]See 1.5.5.

questions. The present disparity of opinion cannot be attributed to lack of rigour in applying present methods of critical interpretation. Rather, contemporary methods allow sufficient flexibility to facilitate reconstruction of the data in different ways. This entails that in order to make new advances in the study of Josh. 24:1-28 it will be necessary to sift the previous studies with a very fine screen. And it will be equally important to search for fresh ways of studying the passage. In keeping with the goal of the present section to evaluate previous literary-critical approaches, it is necessary to point out certain weakness of the previous studies.

#### 2.3.7.1 E and JE source criticism inadequate

The relationship of Josh. 24 to the Pentateuch demands further investigation. The Elohistic theory at one time seemed to provide a convenient means of explaining terminological and ideological affinity with Pentateuchal narratives by claiming common authorship or a common source. But recent studies of Joshua from the perspective of Dtistic history have been quick to indicate that there is little or no evidence for a direct continuation of literary sources from Genesis through Joshua. In essence this claim was already made long ago in the commentary by Keil, who argued that Joshua was always literarily independent from the Pentateuch.[112]

A growing consensus of opinion now rejects the assumption that Josh. 24:1-28 can be explained on the basis of an original connection with a source from the Pentateuch. A scrutiny of Josh. 24 reveals that the author's access to material from the Pentateuch cannot be restricted to an Elohistic tradition.[113]

The role of Shechem in the Patriarchal traditions (Gen. 12:6; 33:18; 35:4; 37:12-14) is presupposed in Josh. 24:1,25-26. The significance of Shechem in the history of Abraham and Jacob has often been discussed in connection with Joshua's covenant ceremony at Shechem, but Gen. 37:12-14 has been overlooked in this respect. Perhaps the reason for this is the fact that the prior texts are attributed to E, while the Joseph narratives are usually assigned to P. However, it can scarcely be coincidental that narration of Joseph's descent to Egypt

[112]Keil–Delitzsch, *Joshua*, 20f.

[113]M.H.Segal has in fact argued that the present Book of Joshua bears evidence of having access to the Pentateuch in basically its present form. See his *The Pentateuch, its Composition and its Authorship, and other Biblical Studies* (Jerusalem, 1967), 117-119.

is initiated by Jacob sending him from Hebron to Shechem, the city which functions so prominently in the life of Abraham and Jacob, and is the vicinity of Joseph's final burial place (Josh. 24:32). The role of Shechem cannot simply be relegated to an E strand, as is also suggested by the role of Shechem in Judg. 9 and in the inauguration narrative of 1 Kgs 12.

The historical summary in Josh. 24:2b-13 contains numerous allusions to, or terminological affiliations with, material from the Pentateuch. With respect to the selection of Abraham, compare Gen. 24:7 and Josh. 24:3, both using the term *lqḥ* in reference to Yahweh's action. Most of Gen. 24 was ordinarily attributed to J in the documentary theory.[114] Those who split the chapter into J and E material assign vs.7 to J.[115] Furthermore, a comparison of Josh. 24:5-7 with Ex: 13-15 suggests that the account of the delivery from Egypt borrows, paraphrases, or condenses freely from those chapters. In support of this suggestion the following elements in common can be adduced, some of which constitute closer parallels than others:

**Josh. 24:6b-7a**
*wyrdpw mṣrym 'ḥry 'bwtykm*, cf. *wyrdpw mṣrym 'ḥryhm* (Ex. 14:9)[116]
*brkb wbpršym*, cf. *kl-sws rkb pr'h wpršyw* (Ex. 14:9)[117]
*ym-swp*, cf. *ym-swp* (Ex. 13:18; 15:4)
*wyṣ'qw 'l-yhwh*, cf. *wyṣ'qw bny-yśr'l 'l-yhwh* (Ex. 14:10)
*wyśm m'pl bynykm wbyn hmṣrym*, cf. *byn ... wbyn* (Ex. 14:20)
*wyb' 'lyw 't-hym*, cf. *wyšb yhwh 'lhm 't-my hym* (Ex. 15:19)
*wykshw*, cf. *wyksw* (Ex. 14:28)[118]
*wtr'ynh 'ynykm*, cf. *wr'w* (Ex. 14:13)
*'t 'šr-'śyty bmṣrym*, (cf. Ex. 14:13,30f.)

Without at this point entering into further analysis of the respective passages, we may conclude that Josh. 24:6b-7a makes extensive use of Ex. 13-15. There is no evidence of direct copying, but Josh. 24:6-7 gives the impression of a free condensing of the Exodus account. Josh. 24:5 employs the verb *ngp*, which is characteristic of the Exodus narrative, e.g., Ex. 7:27; 12:23,27; 32:35, assigned by Dillmann to the

114 C.Westermann, *Genesis*, 3 vos. (Neukirchen, 1979), 1:469.
115 E.g., O.Procksch, *Die Genesis* (Leipzig, 1913), 143.
116 Note too Ex. 14:28, *hb'ym 'ḥryhm bym*.
117 Cf. Ex. 14:28, *hrkb w't-hpršym*.
118 Cf. also Ex. 15:5,10; Ps. 78:53; 106:11.

Yahwist.[119] Similarly, in Ex. 14:19 the cloud was usually attributed to J and the messenger of God to E.[120] Clearly, Josh. 24:7's description stands closer to the emphasis in Ex. 14 upon the cloud than it is does to the emphasis upon the messenger. Therefore, if one accepts the typical division of Ex. 14:19, Josh. 24:7 stands closer to J than to E.[121] According to most critical analyses the Exodus material is not homogeneous and is to be assigned to numerous sources. Yet we find Josh. 24:5-7 seems to know the entire corpus of material concerning the Reed Sea event. It is therefore difficult to accept the theory that Josh. 24:5-7 can simply be associated with an original E strand.[122]

Vss.8-10 can plausibly be seen as primarily a condensed summary of the events narrated in Num. 21-24. Vs.8 states that Israel came to the land of the Amorites who dwelt there, and inherited their land, which may be compared with Num. 21:31, *wyšb yśr'l b'rṣ h'mry*, (cf. 21:13,21,25f.,29,34 also designating this as territory of the Amorites). Num. 22:1 states that Israel was encamped *m'br lyrdn yrḥw*, cf. Josh. 24:8,11. The phrases *wylḥmw 'tkm*, *wylḥm byśr'l* and *wylḥmw bkm* (Josh. 24:8,9,11) find a counterpart in Num. 21:1, *wylḥm byśr'l*, cf. 22:11. Vs.8b may be compared with Num. 21:34f. *bydk ntty 'tw* and *wyyršw 't-'rṣw*, cf. 21:2f. The two verbs *wyšlḥ wyqr'* with respect to Balak son of Zippor summoning Balaam son of Beor[123] find a direct counterpart twice, in Num. 22:5 and 22:37. Josh. 24:10 can be read as a paraphrase of Num. 22:6,12; 23:12; 24:1,12f. With respect to the blessing expressed in the infinitive absolute construction, cf. Num. 22:6; 23:11,[124] 25; 24:10.

But an appeal to Num. 21-24 does not account for all the ter-

[119]Dillmann, *Josua*, 584.

[120]M.Weinfeld, "Divine Intervention in War in Ancient Israel and in the Ancient Near East," in H.Tadmor–M.Weinfeld, eds., *History, Historiography and Interpretation: Studies in Biblical and Cuneiform Literatures* (Jerusalem and Leiden, 1984), 143.

[121]Weinfeld, rightly rejects this division into J and E ("Divine Intervention," 143). The point we wish to stress here is that Josh. 24:7 cannot be simply equated with E.

[122]Cf. T.L.Thompson, "The Joseph and Moses Narratives," in J.H.Hayes–J.M.Miller, eds., *Israelite and Judaean History* (London, 1977), 164-166. However, the manner in which Thompson passes off Ex. 15 as a late passage dependent upon Ex. 14 is improbable, cf. Cross, *Canaanite Myth* 112-144.

[123]Cf. Josh. 24:9 and Num. 22:2,5.

[124]Cf. T.Muraoka, *Emphatic Words and Structures in Biblical Hebrew* (Leiden and Jerusalem, 1985), 87.

minology in vss.8-10. Noteworthy is the combination of the final two clauses, *wtyrš 't-'rṣm w'šmydm mpnykm*, which find their closest counterparts in Num. 33:52; Deut. 2:12,21f.; 4:26; 9:3; 28:63; 31:3; 2 Sam. 14:7. The last of these texts differs from the others in that *yrš* is used here as a noun substantive. In all the other cases the verbs *yrš* and *šmd* are combined in verses which are part of narrative descriptions localized in the setting of Israel's approach on "the other side of the Jordan," about to enter the land. The wording of vs.10 has at times been claimed to be directly dependent upon Deut. 23:6,[125] but this claim is of doubtful validity.[126] Nevertheless, in vss.8-10 it is possible to conclude that Josh. 24 makes free use of material from the Pentateuch, and it is improbable to restrict this dependence to an Elohist source.[127]

Examples of the sort listed here could be multiplied considerably.[128] The list of nations in vs.11, in close context to *hṣr'h* of vs.12, finds a counterpart in Ex. 23:23-28, cf. Deut.7:20.[129] Reference to *šny mlky h'mry* is similar to Deut. 3:8; 4:47; Josh. 2:10; 9:10, and appears to be part of a common tradition. The phrase *l' bḥrbk wl' bqštk* in vs.12b is an allusion to Gen. 48:22, usually assigned to E. On that basis Josh. 24:12b was also claimed as evidence for E.[130] But Gen. 48:22 gives no hint of authorial disapproval of Jacob's boast, whereas Josh. 24:12b seems to be a scarcely disguised critique of Jacob's words in the preceding text. How then can both verses simply be attributed to E? A host of subsequent commentators accordingly designate vs.12b as a later gloss,[131] despite lack of textual evidence for this claim other than the shift to singular suffixes.[132]

[125]H.Donner, "Balaam Pseudopropheta," in Donner, et al., eds., *Beiträge*, 121.

[126]Cf. the literary-critical observations in 4.3.3.2.

[127]To strike vs.10a as an editorial insertion on the basis of affinity to Deut. 23:6, as is done by, e.g., Steuernagel, *Josua*, 243 and Holzinger, *Josua*, 97, is methodologically unsound because it simply begs the question of sources.

[128]See also Richter, "Beobachtungen," 191-198; McCarthy, *Treaty and Covenant*, 234.

[129]Schmitt, *Landtag*, 26-28.

[130]See 2.3.1.

[131]See, e.g., Steuernagel, *Josua*, 244; Holzinger, *Josua*, xxi, 98; Noth, *Das System*, 139; *Josua* 1953, 135; Rudolph, *Der "Elohist"*, 247; Hölscher, *Geschichtsschreibung*, 350.

[132]Holzinger, *Josua*, 98. The possibility that the phrase is original deserves further consideration on the grounds that the emphasis found here is consistent with the central theme of Yahweh's beneficent assistance in all of the events constitutive of

Vs.13 is strikingly similar to Deut. 6:10f., which already prompted Wellhausen,[133] Kuenen,[134] Dillmann,[135] and a host of others to attribute it to a later hand.[136]

Such affinities to the Pentateuch or to other OT texts are not restricted to the historical summary in vss.2b-13. Vs.14 contains the pair *yr'* and *'bd*, found together elsewhere only in Deut. 6:13; 10:12,20; 13:5; 1 Sam. 12:14,20,24; 2 Kgs 17:33,35,41, as well as the pair *swr* and *'bd* found elsewhere only in Deut. 7:4; 11:16; 28:14; Judg. 10:16; 1 Sam. 7:3f.; 12:20. The tendency amongst advocates of the E position was always to attribute vs.14 to the Elohist on the basis of comparison with Gen. 35:2. A connection with the latter text is undeniable, but that does not yet prove a common E source. The texts listed above demonstrate that Josh. 24:14 is part of a series of texts which call Israel to put away the foreign gods.[137] The last two words of 14a, *btmym wb'mt*, find a direct counterpart in Judg. 9:16,19, but the various textual connections listed above argue against Nielsen's conclusion that Josh. 24:14 can simply be explained as representative of terminology indigenous to a local Shechemite tradition.[138] For vs.17, *wyšmrnw bkl-hdrk 'šr hlknw bh*, cf. Gen. 28:20, but Israel's confession is strikingly similar to 1 Kgs 18:39.[139] In vs.19, *'l-qnw' hw'* may be compared with Ex. 20:5; 34:14, the latter of which is usually assigned to J,[140] and *l' yś' lpš'km wlḥṭ'wtykm* is strikingly similar to Gen. 50:17.[141]

The examples listed above are sufficient to refute the claim that

the historical recital in vss.2b-13, and secondly, that the entire passage is characterized by allusions to material from the Pentateuch or other related passages in the OT. Regarding shifts in grammatical number cf. below in this section and in 4.3.3.2.

[133]Wellhausen, *Die Compositon*, 133.

[134]Kuenen, *Historisch-critisch onderzoek*, 1:129.

[135]Dillmann, *Josua*, 587.

[136]E.g., Holzinger, *Josua*, xxi, 98; Hölscher, *Geschichtsschreibung*, 350; Noth, *Josua* 1953, 10, 135; L'Hour, "L'alliance de Sichem," 25; Mölle, *Landtag*, 106, 243. But see Baltzer, *Das Bundesformular*, 30, followed by Perlitt, *Bundestheologie*, 256 n.2. In any event it is not evidence for E (cf. 4.3.3.4).

[137]Schmitt, *Landtag*, 48-50; Perlitt, *Bundestheologie*, 257-259.

[138]E.g., the connections with Mizpah (1 Sam. 7) and Gilgal (1 Sam. 12).

[139]Cf. von Rad, *OT Theology*, 2:17.

[140]Childs, *Exodus*, 604-609; F.-E.Wilms, *Das Jahwistische Bundesbuch in Exodus 34* (München, 1973), 156f.

[141]Schmitt, *Landtag*, 30; McCarthy, *Treaty and Covenant*, 229.

Josh. 24 is "offenbar eine Rekapitulation" of the E source.[142] The literary connections between the Pentateuch on the one hand, and the subsequent historical material on the other, are far more complex than the Elohist theory was able to accomodate. Significantly, Dillmann in 1886 already dutifully noted that vss.2f. seem dependent upon material from Genesis usually assigned to J, e.g., regarding the call of Abraham, his traversing the promised land, and the multiplication of progeny.[143] Holzinger's tabulation of terminology characteristic of J in the Hexateuch contains numerous entries where he is constrained to list references from Josh. 24:1-28 amongst the exceptions.[144]

The flip-side of the coin is the questionable status of some of the terms repeatedly listed in support of E. The appeal to divine names is mitigated by the fact that Yahweh and Elohim are both used in the passage.[145] Furthermore, contrary to the assertion of Wellhausen and Dillmann,[146] it is scarcely justifiable to attribute the plural adjective *qdšym* in vs.19 to a peculiarity of E.[147] This rare form is more likely found here because it is in parallelism with *'l-qnw' hw'*. The Elohist theory repeatedly appealed to the reference to the Amorites as evidence of E, but this too is debatable. In the first place, when the connection between Amorites and E was first alleged, it was on the grounds that E referred to the inhabitants of Palestine as Amorites. But as we have seen above, Josh. 24:8-10 is dependent upon Num. 21ff. which is localized beyond the Jordan, a fact which in itself would make the rule inapplicable to Josh. 24:8,12.[148]

Furthermore, Num. 21:27-30 claims to be an ancient ballad, a designation which there is little reason to doubt,[149] and this taunting

[142]Holzinger, *Einleitung*, 173f.

[143]Dillmann, *Josua*, 584, 622.

[144]Holzinger, *Einleitung*, 96-110: *ḥlylh* (97), *ḥytyb* (99), *kh-'mr yhwh* (100), in addition to numerous other words previously listed by Dillmann as characteristic of J but which upon closer analysis are unable to bear out such a conclusion, e.g., *'nky* (95; cf. Josh. 24:15, not listed by Holzinger), *grš* (96), *r' b'yny* (105), *qr' l* (107). Cf. also the discussion of *šm' bqwl* and *mṣrym* in the singular for the people of Egypt (108f.).

[145]It is not necessary to resort to F.Baumgärtel's suggestion that in vs.1 *h'lhym* is "ein Appellativum" in reference to a cultic place (*Elohim ausserhalb des Pentateuch* [Leipzig, 1914], 42).

[146]Dillmann, *Josua*, 618.

[147]Cf. Hos. 12:1 (ET 11:12), Prov. 9:10; 30:3.

[148]See R.de Vaux, *The Early History of Israel*, trans. D.Smith (Philadelphia, 1978), 564f.

[149]Cf. D.N.Freedman, "Archaic Forms in Early Hebrew Poetry," *ZAW* 72 (1960)

poem also uses the term Amorite (vs.29) in a manner consistent with its present narrative framework. If the narrator of Num. 21 is making recourse to an old tradition which uses the term Amorite in this manner,[150] it is scarcely credible to list the term Amorites in Josh. 24:8,12 as evidence of E. What other term could the author of Josh. 24:8 be expected to use as a designation of the local population in that particular area of the Transjordan? Should he be expected to substitute another term for the one used by the author of Num. 21, and found already in the poetic source employed there? His employment of the term Amorite is consistent with the usage in Numbers, as well as Deut. 3:8; 4:47; Josh. 2:10; 9:10. This also explains vs.12; the two kings of the Amorites can only be seen as a reference to Sihon and Og. It is not impossible to read vss.15,18 similarly as a reference to land inhabited east of the Jordan. More probable, however, is a reference to Amorites west of the Jordan, as in Gen. 15:16; 48:22; Num. 13:29; Deut. 1:7,20,27; Josh. 5:1; 7:7; 10:5f.; 1 Sam. 7:14. It is noteworthy that of these references the usage in Numbers, Deuteronomy, Joshua, and 1 Samuel applies the term Amorites to a restricted group in the hill country, in distinction from other groups in Palestine. It is not used as a collective term for the pre-Israelite inhabitants of Palestine in general. Perhaps it comes the closest to such a meaning in Josh. 24:15,18, where it could be a reference *pars pro toto*, but here too it can logically be taken as a reflection of what is narrated in 5:1; 7:7; and 10:5f. regarding the Amorites in the hill country.[151] As is in fact already conceded in part by Holzinger,[152] the term Amorites does not prove an E source.[153]

The E position was not only unable to account for numerous connections with the Pentateuch, but it was also unable to clarify certain terminology atypical of E. As a result, advocates of the Elohist position were coerced to resort to an extensive list of later redactional glosses in order to explain these obvious similarities with non-E ma-

101-107, esp. 106 where a date in the 13th cent. B.C. is posited.

[150] M.Weippert ("The Israelite 'Conquest' and the Evidence from Transjordan," in Cross, ed., *Symposia*, 22) and H.-Chr.Schmitt ("Das Hesbonlied Num.21, 27aBb-30 und die Geschichte der Stadt Hesbon," *ZDPV* 104 [1988] 31) regard vs.29bB as a later gloss, but Boling doubts this (*The Early Biblical Community in Transjordan* [Sheffield, 1988], 49).

[151] See 6.3.

[152] Holzinger, *Einleitung*, 182.

[153] See too H.W.Wolff, *Dodekapropheton. Amos* (Neukirchen–Vluyn, 1969), 204f.

terial.

Ultimately the same criticism is applicable to the JE position outlined above. While the JE theory obviously expands the potential to draw correlations with material from the Tetrateuch, it does not absolve the difficulties lodged above against a source-critical dissection of Josh. 24:1-28. Equally important, the criteria by which the JE position attempted to unravel different sources in Josh. 24 is highly suspect. The same may be said of all attempts to establish parallel sources in this passsage. The JE analyses of Smend and Noth, the JEL conclusions of Eissfeldt, the *Jahwerezension* and *Josuarezension* of Möhlenbrink, as well as Mölle's recent attempt to resurrect this type of literary criticism in Josh. 24, must ultimately be judged highly questionable. OT Hebrew constructs sentences by stringing together a series of relatively short clauses. It is often a simple matter to delete clauses and retain a grammatically acceptable sentence, which in turn facilitates dissection of a given sentence into what can appear to be independent units. The fact that the resulting dissection often produces simpler, grammatically acceptable sentences does not entail that the various clauses are to be attributed to different sources.

The appeal to shifts of grammatical number or person is also a dubious criterion for source criticism in Josh. 24.[154] This is of particular relevance with respect to vss.5-7,17. We recall that these verses were fundamental for the identification of J and E by Smend, Eissfeldt and Noth. And Möhlenbrink used similar arguments for his source division, though not equating his results with J and E. Nielsen was quite correct, however, when in response to Möhlenbrink's appeal to the shift between 1st and 3rd singular in the divine speech, he termed this "the weakest foundation imaginable" for source criticism.[155] The topic has been frequently raised in connection with texts in the Pentateuch, and especially in Deuteronomy.[156] Josh. 24 is specifically

[154]See already J.Sperber, "Der Personenwechsel in der Bibel," *ZA* 32 (1918-19) 23-33.

[155]Nielsen, *Shechem*, 89.

[156]J.H.Hospers, *De numeruswisseling in het boek Deuteronomium* (Utrecht, 1947); G.Minette de Tillesse, "Sections 'tu' et sections 'vous' dans le Deutéronome," *VT* 12 (1962) 29-87; N.Lohfink, *Das Hauptgebot. Eine Untersuchung literarischer Einleitungsfragen zu Dt. 5-11* (Rome, 1963), 239f.; "Credo," 23; J.G.McConville, *Law and Theology in Deuteronomy* (Sheffield, 1984), 5. C.J.Labuschagne, "Divine Speech in Deuteronomy," in Lohfink, ed., *Das Deuteronomium*, 112-114.

addressed by Baltzer[157] and by F.Nötscher[158] with examples of similar phenomena in extra-biblical ancient NE texts. In the light of the previous discussions it is difficult to understand why arguments of this sort continue to be adduced by J.Kühlewein[159] and Mölle as evidence for variant textual sources in these verses. Moran, in a review of Baltzer's monograph, stated, "The value of a change of person or number as a criterion is null."[160]

A caveat is also in order against use of repetition or synonyms, whether of single words or entire phrases and concepts, as a criterion for designating an alternate source or redactional gloss. This is a matter of utmost importance for a literary analysis of Josh. 24:1-28, where an extensive list of "doublets" has been alleged. The following words or phrases have been appealed to: *Elohim*, vs.1 and *Yahweh* vs.2;[161] *Israel*, *all the tribes* and *all the people* (vss.1f.);[162] *Joshua said to all the people*, and *thus says Yahweh the God of Israel* (vs.2);[163] *you*, and *your fathers*, etc. (vss.5-7, 17);[164] *all the peoples*, and *the Amorites* (vs.18);[165] *for he is a holy God*, and *he is a jealous God*

[157]Baltzer, *Bundesformular*, 29 n.4.

[158]F.Nötscher, "Bundesformular und 'Amtsschimmel'. Ein kritischer Überblick," *BZ* 9 (1965) 206f. See too Lohfink, "Credo," 38.

[159]J.Kühlewein, *Geschichte in den Psalmen* (Stuttgart, 1973), 155-158.

[160]W.L.Moran, *Bibl* 43 (1962) 103, cf. also S.Gevirtz, "On Canaanite Rhetoric: The Evidence of the Amarna Letters from Tyre," Or 42 (1973) 162-177, esp. 170f. The change of number may be explained as a peculiarity of Semitic style which originated in the awareness of being a corporate personality. See texts like Hos. 12:5 [4] and Is. 51:12f., with H.W.Robinson, *Corporate Personality in Ancient Israel*, revised ed. (Edinburgh, 1981).

[161]Mölle, *Landtag*, 23.

[162]Mölle, *Landtag*, 24-26. Note that Mölle follows a long line of commentators who judge the clause *wyqr' lzqny yśr'l wlr'šyw wlšpṭyw wlšṭryw* in vs.1b to be a later addition, partly on the grounds of duplicity and partly by virtue of comparison with 23:2.

[163]Möhlenbrink, "Landnahmesagen," 51. Surprising as it may be, Möhlenbrink even splits this formula into two sources, though it is generally recognized as a standard introduction to prophetic speech.

[164]Smend, *Erzählung*, 337f.; Eissfeldt, *Hexateuch-Synopse*, 79f., 248; Noth, *Das System*, 135f.; *Josua* 1953, 137, 150 (In 1953 Noth no longer dares to make an identification with J and E, but he continues to argue that there are two independent sources represented here). Rudolph excises the references to the fathers as later expansions (*Der "Elohist"*, 245-247). The same was already true of Dillmann (*Josua*, 585-587), Steuernagel (*Josua*, 243f.), and Holzinger (*Josua*, 97f.). Boling rightly rejects this approach: "The alternation here is stylistic, not a sign of mixed sources" (*Joshua*, 535).

[165]Eissfeldt, *Hexateuch-Synopse*, 80, 249; Noth, *Das System*, 136. In *Josua* 1953,

(vs.19);[166] *you are witnesses, this stone shall be a witness against* **us**, and *it shall be a witness against* **you** (vss.22,27).[167]

However, this initially impressive list of alleged doublets is based upon questionable methodological criteria. Increased knowledge of comparable ancient Semitic languages has demonstrated that repetition and employment of synonymous words or various types of parallelism is found similarly in texts for which the unity of authorship cannot be seriously questioned. This is particularly true of poetry,[168] but not exclusively so.[169] Many narrative texts also employ repetition or parallelism profusely and purposely.[170] This is already true of Hittite historiography.[171] Any methodology which does not accomodate at least the *possibility* that the type of repetitions listed above could be deliberate to the composition of the literary unit must finally be judged inadequate.

Our analysis thus far has focused upon the inability of the Elohist position to account for the complex connections of Josh. 24:1-28

140, Noth modifies his position by reading *kl-h'mym w* as a gloss rather than another source.

[166]Smend, *Erzählung*, 337f.; Eissfeldt, *Hexateuch-Synopse*, 80, 249; Noth, *Das System*, 136 (in *Josua* 1953, these phrases are viewed as Dtistic.); Mölle, *Landtag*, 71f., 112.

[167]Smend uses this as evidence of three sources, E, $J^1$ and $J^2$ respectively (*Erzählung*, 337-339). Eissfeldt also finds three sources, E, L, and J respectively (*Hexateuch-Synopse*, 80f., 249f.). Noth originally also derived three sources, Dtist, J and E respectively (*Das System*, 136f.). Mölle finally posits a fourth option for three sources, namely S, RJE and E respectively (*Landtag*, 102-104, 296, 298). Most other scholars were satisfied to solve the apparent problem of multiple references to witness with an appeal to only two sources, or one source plus redactional glossing, cf. Holzinger, *Josua* xxi, 99; Schmitt, *Landtag*, 21, 24.

[168]To list only a few choice examples of the recent literature studying parallelism, see S.A.Geller, *Parallelism in Early Biblical Poetry* (Missoula, 1979); J.L.Kugel, *The Idea of Biblical Poetry: Parallelism and Its History* (New Haven and London, 1981); W.G.E.Watson, *Classical Hebrew Poetry: A Guide to Its Techniques* (Sheffield, 1984); A.Berlin, *The Dynamics of Biblical Parallelism* (Bloomington, 1985); E.Zurro, *Procedimientos iterativos en la poesía ugarítica y hebrea* (Rome, 1987); L.Alonso-Schökel, *A Manual of Hebrew Poetics* (Rome, 1988); van der Meer–de Moor, eds., *Structural Analysis.*

[169]Cf. Kugel, *Idea*, esp. 59-95.

[170]Muilenburg, "Hebrew Rhetoric," 97-111; R.Alter, *The Art of Biblical Narrative* (New York, 1981), 88-113; A.Berlin, *Poetics and Interpretation of Biblical Narrative* (Sheffield, 1983), 73-79, 105, 136; M.Sternberg, *The Poetics of Biblical Narrative: Ideological Literature and the Drama of Reading* (Bloomington, 1987), 365-440.

[171]Cf. H.G.Güterbock, "Hittite Historiography: A Survey," in Tadmor-Weinfeld, eds., *History, Historiography*, 28f.

with other OT material, particularly in the Pentateuch. Secondly, the manner in which attempts were made to split this passage into various sources, or to identify later redactional expansions, has been rejected as inadequate. The latter concern was not restricted to the JE position, but is characteristic of a weakness in the source-critical methodologies in general.

It is noteworthy that the Elohist claim that Josh. 24 provides a summary of the E source finds a direct counterpart from defenders of a Yahwist theory. Van Seters asserts that the historical recitation "seems to correspond to a summary account of J's version of the Pentateuch." [172] In certain respects this claim is more difficult to refute because it is accompanied with a late date for J, which would accomodate possible influence from any other alleged source or tradition. However, here too it can be demonstrated that Josh. 24:1-28's connections with other material are so profuse that to suggest that a Yahwist would have produced a text with so many affinities to, or reminiscences of, E, and D would mean that when all is said and done there doesn't remain much which is particularly or exclusively "Yahwistic" in the whole passage.[173] Furthermore, Van Seters' assertion of a Yahwistic document is dependent upon an extremely late date for J, a presupposition which finally cannot be maintained in Josh. 24:1-28.[174] Since the question of the date of composition is also critical to the view of the advocates of a Dtistic composition, and Van Seters relies in many respects upon their conclusions, it is advisable to now proceed to an analysis of the various views which see Josh. 24 as either Dtic, Dtistic, or ancient tradition with later redaction.

#### 2.3.7.2 Dtic/Dtistic analyses

Removal of Josh. 24 from the framework of earlier source-critical theories facilitated the possibility of a broader comparison with a wide variety of other passages, both within the Pentateuch and in the following historical books. This new approach called for a total reappraisal of its composition and present position in Dtistic history. The results have diverged considerably, as may readily be ascertained

[172]Van Seters, *In Search of History*, 336. Cf. 1.6.8.

[173]Note that Van Seters' alternative to von Rad's theory of a credo in Josh. 24:2b-13 in essence replaces one *argumentum e silentio* (the absence of Sinai) with another *argumentum e silentio* (the absence of the Reed Sea in Deuteronomy).

[174]For additional difficulties in Van Seters' handling of Josh. 24:1-28 consult Sperling, "Joshua 24," 133-136.

from the surveys offered above. It is now necessary to evaluate the extent to which treatments of Josh. 24:1-28 as a Dtistic composition are adequate or convincing.

Perlitt's analysis of Josh. 24:1-28 has understandably been of considerable influence in recent years. Once one accepts the basic thesis of the pervasive influence of the Josianic reform of the 7th century for the moulding of the historical writings from Deut.-2 Kgs, it provides a logical basis for explaining a text such as Josh. 24 where great emphasis is placed upon exclusive worship of Yahweh. Nevertheless, multiple considerations in Josh. 24:1-28 suggest that even if one accepts the basic tenets of a Dtistic history as it is currently sketched in OT scholarship, Perlitt's view of Josh. 24 is untenable. A number of objections to Perlitt's position have been listed by Jaroš.[175] The weaknesses Jaroš singles out are crucial, but more must be said.

Perlitt correctly emphasizes that it is methodologically objectionable to separate vss.1,25-28 from vss.2-24, to claim a historical narrative for the former, and to reinterpret the intervening verses accordingly. The passage must be treated in the first place as a unity. However, Perlitt has in fact gone to excess in the opposite direction. His conclusions regarding a parenetic character and setting for vss.2-24 entail that he is unable to do justice to vss.1,25-28. The latter verses are treated as a fictitious framework provided by the Dtic author for the sermon. But this view is improbable. The presence of the stone which is said to "hear" the words of Yahweh (vs.27) can scarcely be the fictitious creation of a Dtic theologian attempting to convince Israel to maintain unequivocal allegiance to Yahweh, (cf. Deut. 12:2f.; 16:21f.). This difficulty is not absolved by appealing to the stone as an innocuous memorial. It is said to be raised *tḥt h'lh*. Whether this is translated as "terebinth" or simply as a pole,[176] it has a connection with the cultus, as is proven by the second clause, *'šr bmqdš yhwh*.

The term *mqdš yhwh* is reserved elsewhere for the temple in Jerusalem. It is therefore improbable that a Dtist would invent a fictitious *mqdš yhwh* at Shechem as a location for Joshua's reforms.[177] The same

[175]See section 1.7.2.

[176]Cf. J.C.L.Gibson, *Canaanite Myths and Legends* (Edinburgh, 1977), 141.

[177]The surveys in the opening chapter demonstrated that scholars such as Kuenen, Sellin, Eissfeldt, Noth, von Rad, Simpson, Nielsen, etc., all deemed it impossible to attribute the passages in Deuteronomy and Joshua which stress the role of Shechem

is true of the *'lh* in the sanctuary; the Dtists are generally believed to have opposed the asherah-poles and would not have invented this *'lh* themselves.[178] If a Dtic author in the 7th century was creating a fictitious setting in Josh. 24:1,25-28, as alleged by Perlitt, he could be expected to have done so in a less offensive manner.[179]

The function of the stone as a witness is described twice in vs.27 with precisely the same formulation, i.e., the verb *hyh* + prep. + pronominal suf. + prep. *l* + *'d*. The closest comparable formulation is found in Gen. 21:30.[180] To these cases may be added comparable references with the masculine form *'d* in Gen. 31:44; Deut. 31:19,21,26; Isa. 19:20; Mic. 1:2; and Job 16:8. Particularly significant are Gen. 21:30 and 31:44 because in both these cases the phrase *krt bryt* is also found. Furthermore, 31:44f. is also in the context of a stone monument. Perlitt unfortunately ignores these parallels entirely in his theory that *krt bryt l* is exclusive to texts in DtrG and later.[181] The fact that *krt bryt* is not followed by the preposition *l* in Gen. 21:32 or 31:44 is insufficient reason to exclude these texts from comparison with Josh. 24:25-27, as the other parallels mentioned above demonstrate. Perlitt has argued that any references to a *bryt* involving God and man in Genesis result from later Dtistic glosses or redaction, but this is a conclusion necessitated by his thesis rather than by conclusive exegesis.[182] Since Gen. 21:22-34 and 31:44 describe a *bryt* between two human parties, there can be little reason for later interpolation here from the hand of a Dtist. As such these passages provide confirmation of the authenticity of the covenantal action described in Josh.

to a Dtist. Perlitt does not adequately defend his reasoning for concluding the opposite with respect to Josh. 24. One can imagine that a later redactor would be reluctant to excise such accounts, but the idea that a Dtic author would create such a fiction goes contrary to what most scholars view to be essential to the Dtic movement.

178 See J.C.de Moor, "*'šrh*," *ThWAT*, 1:473-481; "Diviner's Oak," *IDBSup*, 243f.

179 Nielsen calls this the most un-Dtistic expression in the entire Dtic literature (*Shechem*, 133).

180 As is noted in the *Masora parva*, these are the only three references in the OT where the feminine form *'dh* is found with the preposition *l*.

181 Perlitt, *Bundestheologie*, 261f.

182 Cf. the comments on Gen. 15:18 by McCarthy, "*Berît* in OT," 115; Fensham, "Covenant," 310f.; Eichrodt, "Darf man heute," 196f.; G.F.Hasel, "The Meaning of the Animal Rite in Genesis 15," *JSOT* 19 (1981) 61-78. For a contrary opinion, accepting the conclusion of Perlitt, see J.A.Emerton, "The Origin of the Promises to the Patriarchs in the Older Sources of the Book of Genesis," *VT* 32 (1982) 17.

24:25-27. The role of the stone as "witness" finds its closest parallel in Genesis rather than in Dtic or Dtistic texts.[183] The three references in Deut. 31:19,21,26 are also instructive because of the obvious similarity between the role of Joshua and Moses in a final gathering before their impending deaths, summoning Israel to cultic obedience, and writing the words of the covenant law as a witness for Israel.[184] Perlitt rightly calls attention to Moses' connection with the writing of law for Israel.[185] But he does not do justice to the wording of *bspr twrt 'lhym.*[186] It is significant that Josh. 24:27 does not make an explicit correlation with the book of the law of Moses as is done in Josh. 8:31f. and 23:6, *spr twrt mšh.*[187]

Also noteworthy is the fact that Isa. 1:10 places the phrase *twrt 'lhym* parallel to *dbr-yhwh.* Josh. 24:26f. speaks similarly of *hdbrym h'lh* and *kl-'mry yhwh.* The fact that the latter phrase is usually a poetic term[188] is ignored by Perlitt. He dutifully footnotes a reference to Hos. 6:5,[189] but he neither accords the comparison the weight it deserves nor looks far enough. The noun *'mr* is found in Gen. 49:21; Num. 24:4,16; Deut. 32:1; Josh. 24:27; Judg. 5:29; Isa. 32:7; 41:26; Hos. 6:5; Job (11x); Ps. (7x); Prov. (22x) (cf. 3.4.10 re II.v.2 internal parallelism). This argues against the conclusion that vs.27 is a Dtic narrative fiction. The relationship between Josh.

[183]Cf. the reference in Isa. 19:20. The fact that scholars are divided with respect to source criticism in Gen. 21:22-34, or the date of its composition, is irrelevant for our main contention here, namely that it is not Dtistic. See D.J.McCarthy, "Three Covenants in Genesis," *CBQ* 26 (1964) 179-189; Westermann, *Genesis*, 1:422-428.

[184]Note that Weinfeld views Deut. 31:16-22 as Elohistic (*Deuteronomy*, 10).

[185]Cf. Ex. 24:4; 34:27f.; Deut. 9:10; 10:4; 30:10; 31:9,22.

[186]He lists *spr twrt (h)'lhym* as occurring only in Josh. 24:26; Neh. 8:8, 18 (270), and he contrasts this with *twrt 'lhym* in Isa. 1:10; Hos. 4:6; Ps. 37:31 (270 n.1), concluding that the transition to phrases including *bspr* is crucial for identifying a late character of the text. He fails to mention Neh. 10:30, where *spr* is not found, but more importantly, he does not justify his emphasis upon texts which have *bspr* in common, rather than upon texts which have *twrt 'lhym* in common. The latter emphasis would clearly argue ***against*** a Dtic conclusion. Although in his bibliography he lists Lohfink's study, "Die Bundesurkunde des Königs Josias," ***Bibl*** 44 (1963) 261-288, 461-498, no reference is made to it in this context, or to the fact that Lohfink's conclusions contradict his own, cf. esp. Lohfink, 286f.

[187]Cf. also Josh. 1:7f.; 2 Kgs 14:6; Neh. 8:1, where an allusion to Deut. 31:9 seems to be intended. See further R.E.Friedman, *The Exile and Biblical Narrative* (Chico, 1981), 8.

[188]Cf. Nielsen, *Shechem*, 108: "...apart from this passage occurs only in poetry"; L'Hour, "L'alliance de Sichem," 34.

[189]Perlitt, *Bundestheologie*, 267 n.1.

24:1-28 and Deut. 31 is in need of further study. But in light of the considerations raised above it is impossible to agree that Josh. 24:1,25-28 constitutes a Dtic fiction in order to provide a setting for the parenetic content of vss.2-24. Josh. 24:25-27 contains terminology out of place in Dtic lexicography, and the stone "hearing" and serving as a "witness" finds its closest parallels outside of the corpus of texts termed Dtic or Dtistic.[190]

Though Perlitt may be quite correct in concluding that comparisons with ancient NE treaty texts have sometimes been overdone in the past, it is surely unwarranted to ignore them in handling Josh. 24:25-27. It is one thing to argue that the treaty comparisons are inadequate to account for the final form of the entire chapter, and quite another to disregard their significance for illuminating certain of the customs which are presupposed as a background to Josh. 24:25-27.[191]

The deficiency of Perlitt's analysis of Josh. 24:1,25-27 necessarily prompts a re-evaluation of his treatment of vss.2-24 as well. It is not our intention to repeat all the observations made by other scholars. Particular mention should be made, however, of the fact that Perlitt's conclusions regarding Dtic language in vss.2-24 are contradicted on numerous points by Schmitt's earlier analysis,[192] and more strongly so in the subsequent analyses by McCarthy[193] and Sperling.[194] Perlitt's treatment of the patriarchs is highly questionable.[195] Another obstacle in his approach, which has not been adequately challenged, is the assumption that an alleged parenetic purpose in vss.2-24 should be associated with a religious-political goal rather than have any connection with a cultic or liturgical setting. His appeal to vs.19 in this regard is not convincing. To attribute the words "you are not able to serve Yahweh" to a Dtic/Dtistic hand hardly absolves their blunt character. In the first place, it does not sound much more probable

[190]The word *'amr* "speech" already belongs to the poetic vocabulary of Ugarit (cf. J.C.de Moor, *The Seasonal Pattern in the Ugaritic Myth of Ba'lu According to the Version of Ilimilku* [Neukirchen-Vluyn, 1971], 129), and a close parallel to the "listening" stones is found in the murmuring stones of the Ugaritic tablets (*Seasonal Pattern*, 108; "Diviner's Oak," 244).

[191]Baltzer, *Bundesformular*, 36f.; Brekelmans, "Credo," 7f.; Eichrodt, "Covenant and Law," 310; McCarthy, *OT Covenant*, 14; *Treaty and Covenant*, 222-224; Kline, *Structure*, 152.

[192]Schmitt, *Landtag*, 10-32.

[193]McCarthy, *Treaty and Covenant*, 221-234.

[194]Sperling, "Joshua 24," 123-133.

[195]Rösel, "Erwägungen," 42.

there than it would in a cultic setting.[196] Secondly, and this is crucial, Perlitt's analysis is unable to do justice to the remainder of the verse.

The parallel phrases *ky-'lhym qdšym hw'* and *'l-qnw' hw'* are of considerable importance for a literary analysis of Josh. 24. J.Alonso-Asenjo[197] and McCarthy[198] understand the parallelism as an element of ancient, liturgical poetry. The plural adjective *qdšym* is treated by Gesenius–Kautzsch as a *pluralis excellentiae* or *maiestatis*.[199] *Qdšym* without *'lhym* is found in Hos. 12:1; Prov. 9:10; 30:3 with an obvious singular meaning despite the plural form. Gesenius-Kautzsch entertains the possibility that the employment of formally plural references with respect to a numerically singular God could be explained in part as an acquiescence to a polytheistic form of expression, and secondly, a few related texts with a plural predicate for God may be in part a peculiarity of the E source in Genesis.[200] Gesenius-Kautzsch stress that in any event later texts tend to strictly avoid a plural predicate, as is demonstrated by a comparison of Neh. 9:18 with Ex. 32:4,8, and 1 Chron. 17:21 with 2 Sam. 7:23.[201] It is understandable that the preferred form for expressing the holiness of Yahweh was in the singular.[202] Segal, in an extensive study of the employment of divine names, concludes that the plural adjective with Elohim is an ancient feature.[203]

Though Seebass has argued that *'l qnw'* "kommt bis auf eine Ausnahme nur bei Dtr. vor,"[204] there is little reason to see the expression as a later Dtistic addition. It is probable that various of the divine epi-

[196]For similar emphases in the prophets see McCarthy, *Treaty and Covenant*, 240.

[197]J.Alonso-Asenjo, "Investigación crítica sobre Jos 24,19-20. Análisis de tres expressiones raras y significativas," *EstBib* 32 (1973) 257-270.

[198]McCarthy, *Treaty and Covenant*, 229.

[199]*GK*, §124 g-k, §132 h, §145 i.

[200]Cf. Gen. 20:13; 31:53; 35:7.

[201]The suggestion by M.Takahashi, to the effect that the plural forms are to be explained as an identification of God and the angels, is dubious ("An Oriental's Approach to the Problem of Angelology," *ZAW* 78 [1966] 345f.).

[202]Cf. Lev. 11:44f.; 19:2; 20:26; 21:7f.; 1 Sam. 6:20; Isa. 43:15; Ezek. 39:7; Ps. 99:5,9; Hab. 1:12.

[203]Segal, *Pentateuch*, 119; see too 104f.

[204]Seebass, *Der Erzvater*, 91; see also W.Berg, "Die Eifersucht Gottes—ein problematischer Zug des alttestamentlichen Gottesbildes?" *BZ* 23 (1979) 199. Note that already the early study by F.Küchler, "Der Gedanke des Eifers Jahwes im Alten Testament," *ZAW* 28 (1908) 42-52, singled out Ex. 20:5; 34:14; Josh. 24:19 as the oldest examples in the OT, but expressed some uncertainty as to the degree of Dtistic redaction present in Ex. 20 and Josh. 24.

thets in the OT derive from ancient cultic formulations. The antiquity of poetic formulae such as Ex. 34:6,14 is undeniable,[205] and it is significant that these designations are transmitted in cultic, covenantal material. It is also probable that Joshua's warning in vs.19 *ky-'lhym qdšym hw', 'l-qnw' hw'* represents an ancient cultic formula. It is noteworthy that as in Ex. 34:14 reference is made to God's jealousy.[206] The same adjective is used in Ex. 20:5; Deut. 4:24; 5:9; 6:15; Nah. 1:2. The oracular introduction in Nah. 1:2 makes a conscious appeal to the ancient decalogue; therefore, although the present context of Nah. 1:2 is late, this cannot be used as evidence that the poetic expression *'l-qnw'* is itself late or Dtic.[207] In short, the parallelism ought to be considered authentic,[208] and the evidence favors the probability of an early date for these formulations. A connection with the cultus is likely.

Perlitt is justified in noting that a cultic setting for vss.2-24 has been frequently alleged rather than adequately demonstrated. It is not difficult to amass a host of citations too simply asserting that Josh. 24:1-28 is a cultic or liturgical text.[209] The possibility of a cultic or liturgical background and character for Josh. 24:1-28 demands a more detailed investigation, especially since Perlitt's alternative is not

[205]D.N.Freedman, "The Name of the God of Moses," *JBL* 79 (1960) 151-156; B.Renaud, *Je suis un dieu jaloux. Étude d'un thème biblique* (Paris, 1963), 27-31; H.D.Preuss, *Die Verspottung fremder Religionen im Alten Testament* (Stuttgart, 1971), 22; Wilms, *Bundesbuch*, 157; J.Halbe, *Das Privilegrecht Jahwes. Ex 34,10-26 Gestalt und Wesen, Herkunft und Wirken in vordeuteronomischer Zeit* (Göttingen, 1975), 139; de Moor, *Uw God*, 54f.

[206]Regarding the vocalization see R.Meyer, "Bemerkungen zu den hebräischen Aussprachetraditionen von Chirbet Qumrān," *ZAW* 70 (1958) 40f.; F.Werner, *Die Wortbildung der Hebräischen Adjektiva* (Wiesbaden, 1983), 201f. For a discussion of the particular nuance and significance of *qn'* see A.Jepsen, "Beiträge zur Auslegung und Geschichte des Dekalogs," *ZAW* 79 (1967) 275-304, esp. 287-290, 300; Renaud, *Dieu jaloux*, 36-38.

[207]R.Sonsino, *Motive Clauses in Hebrew Law: Biblical Forms and Near Eastern Parallels* (Chico, 1980), 199. The impression created by L'Hour ("L'alliance de Sichem," 28) is therefore misleading. Cf. the literary-critical discussion in 4.4.3.

[208]Rudolph speaks of "die gehobene Sprache" (*Der "Elohist"*, 247); cf. Eichrodt, *Theology*, 1:272f.

[209]W.Harrelson, "Worship in Early Israel," *BR* 3 (1958) 1-14; Baltzer, *Das Bundesformular*, 73. L'Hour, "L'alliance de Sichem," 22, 168; *La morale*, 14; Kraus, "Gottesdienst," 172-176; H.Lubsczyk, "Einheit und heilsgeschichtliche Bedeutung von Ps 114/115 (113)," *BZ* 11 (1967) 163f. R.Polzin, *Moses and the Deuteronomist: A Literary Study of the Deuteronomic History* (New York, 1980) 141-144; Boling, *Joshua*, 526; Lucas, "Covenant," 19-23.

convincing.

It would be mistaken to assume that a cultic employment of a text (or parenetic for that matter) precludes an historical basis. Perlitt's attempt to provide a *Sitz im Leben* builds rather tenuously on the reference to the fathers and the gods from beyond the river. But the formulation of the reference to ancestors (vs.2) *b'br hnhr yšbw 'bwtykm m'wlm* is a perfectly natural way to introduce a historical reference. A comparison may be drawn with a similar phrase on the Mesha stele, *w'š gd yšb b'rṣ 'ṭrt m'lm.*[210] Here too, as in Josh. 24:2, the historical period of the ancestors is appealed to with a simple reference to the place where they dwelt *m'lm.* Mention may also be made of a comparable appeal to the time of the "fathers" in the historical prologue of a treaty text from Šuppiluliuma and Mattiwaza.[211] Josh. 24:2 is unable to bear the weight that Perlitt places upon it for purposes of dating.[212] Perlitt is guilty of circular reasoning when he dates the passage to the 7th cent. on the basis of the foreign gods, and then concludes that the gods of Egypt (vs.14b) do not fit the historical circumstances.[213] Nor does vs.20 prove a date after the fall of the Northern Kingdom. A *vaticinium ex eventu* interpretation is not new,[214] but it has also been shown to be precarious.[215]

The preceding observations call into question Perlitt's conclusions in Josh. 24 on the basis of evidence internal to the passage. It is also instructive to note briefly that his results are conditioned by the conclusion asserted repeatedly in the antecedent chapters of his study, viz., a true covenant theology begins with the Dtic school or movement. Josh. 24 is submitted as a final folder of evidence in a broader investigation which is already more or less complete, and it would be surprising if Josh. 24 should prove to be the one exception to the rule already established in the antecedent analyses. The degree of probability which Perlitt attributes to his conclusions in Josh. 24 is

[210] *KAI*, 181:10.

[211] Weidner, *Politische Dokumente*, 5.

[212] Perlitt, *Bundestheologie*, 251f. Cf. McCarthy, *Treaty and Covenant*, 225, 283.

[213] Perlitt, *Bundestheologie*, 257 n.1.

[214] See Rudolph, *Der "Elohist"*, 248.

[215] Baltzer, *Bundesformular*, 72 n.3; Moran, *Bibl* 43 (1962) 103; and especially Kitchen, "Ancient Orient, 'Deuteronism'," 5-7. Even H.-D.Hoffmann, though sympathetic to Perlitt's approach, cannot accept the *Sitz im Leben* he proposes (*Reform und Reformen. Untersuchungen zu einem Grundthema der deuteronomistischen Geschichtsschreibung* [Zürich, 1980], 305f.).

naturally contingent upon the measure of coalescence of these results with his study of other comparable OT passages. This is most evident in his treatment of the phrase *krt bryt l* in vs.25.[216]

Perlitt's hapless acceptance of Kutsch's too restricted definition of *bryt*, combined with his own conclusion regarding the date of a *Bundestheologie* in the OT, causes him to ahistoricize the entire *bryt* ritual of vs.25 into a theological and political polemic against other nations. He removes the concept of *bryt* from the ebb and flow of its natural environment and reintroduces it into the passage as a *theologumenon.* No comparison is made with the customs attested in passages such as Gen. 21:25-32 and 31:43-54 which can be neither coaxed nor coerced into a Dtic mold. Gen. 31:43-54 is redolent with archaic elements.[217] For example, in vs.44 *bryt* is paralleled with, and synonymous to, *l'd*, which looks here suspiciously like the use of Aramaic *'d*, Akkadian, *adû.*[218] The heap of stones as witness appears to be part of a widespread and ancient custom. Jacob swears *bpḥd 'byw yṣḥq* (vs.53, cf. vs.42). The term *pḥd* is debated, ordinarily translated "fear," but rendered by W.F.Albright[219] as "kinsman" on the basis of Arabic. His view was accepted by Eissfeldt.[220] But comparison with Arabic is unnecessary here.[221] It is not by the "kinsman" of Isaac that Jacob swears, nor *to* the kinsman—in which case we would expect the preposition *l*—but *pḥd* is rather a divine epithet, the archaic nature of which is generally recognized. These references in Genesis belie the theory that *bryt* entails a *Verpflichtungsszene* without specifically denoting a certain relationship between the respective parties.[222] It

[216]Perlitt, *Bundestheologie*, 260-263.

[217]Cf. R.Frankena, "Some Observations on the Semantic Background of Chapters XXIX-XXXI of the Book of Genesis," in *The Witness of Tradition*, *OTS* 17 (Leiden, 1972), 53-64.

[218]F.O.Garcia-Treto, "Genesis 31:44 and 'Gilead'," *ZAW* 79 (1967) 15; Cross, *Canaanite Myth*, 269; Kalluveettil, *Declaration*, 30.

[219]W.F.Albright, *From the Stone Age to Christianity* (Baltimore, 1946), 189.

[220]Eissfeldt, "El and Yahweh," 32 n.2; cf. F.M.Cross, "Yahweh and the God of the Patriarchs," *HTR* 55 (1962) 226.

[221]D.R.Hillers, "Paḥad Yiṣḥāq," *JBL* 91 (1972) 90-92; Cross, *Canaanite Myth*, 269 (revising his earlier opinion); K.Koch, "păḥăd jiṣḥaq – eine Gottesbezeichnung?" in R.Albertz, et al., eds., *Werden und Wirken des Alten Testaments* (Fs C.Westermann; Göttingen, 1980), 107-115.

[222]Note the parallels detected by Frankena between Gen. 31:46ff. and the treaty of Šuppiluliuma and Mattiwaza, where the treaty is not only of political significance but also provides for the well-being of the daughter given in marriage to the other party ("Some Observations," 63f.).

is illegitimate to ignore these parallels on the grounds that they describe a *bryt* between human parties and are therefore irrelevant for the study of *bryt* with respect to God and Israel.[223]

Furthermore, Perlitt's handling of numerous passages which do specify or imply a divine covenant with Israel fails to prove the point that he is attempting to demonstrate. It is not possible here to enter into an extensive analysis of Perlitt's work outside of Josh. 24, and a number of brief observations which counter the thesis that a covenant theology was first developed in the 7th century B.C. will need to suffice.

The paucity of references to *bryt* in the 8th cent. prophets does not necessarily warrant the conclusion that the covenant concept was unknown or unimportant at that time. The prophet Amos does not make explicit use of the term *bryt* in this manner, and it is difficult to draw conclusive evidence regarding the degree to which his prophecy was motivated by covenant theology. Amos knew the technicalities of international treaties[224] and he did employ related terminology to express the relationship between Israel and Yahweh. The word *pšʿ*, employed so prolifically by Amos,[225] is sometimes a technical term for treaty breaking or transgression,[226] as in 1:9 where the *pšʿy* of Tyre are explicated with the colon *wl' zkrw bryt 'ḥym.*[227] The same term *pšʿ* is applied directly to Judah and Israel for transgression of the law (2:4,6).[228] The use of *ydʿ* in Amos has been posited as technical usage in a covenantal sense,[229] and a covenant ceremony has been alleged

[223]J.C.L.Gibson, *Textbook of Syrian Semitic Inscriptions*, 3 vols. (Oxford, 1971-1982), 3:85.

[224]F.C.Fensham, "Clauses of Protection in Hittite Vassal-Treaties and the Old Testament" *VT* 13 (1963) 142f.

[225]Cf. 1:3,6,9,11,13; 2:1,4,6; 3:14; 4:4 (2x); 5:12.

[226]Fishbane, "Treaty Background," 317f. The etymology of *rḥymw* proposed by Fishbane is challenged by R.B.Coote ("Amos 1:11: RḤYMW," *JBL* 90 [1971] 206-208), and reasserted by Fishbane ("Additional Remarks on RḤYMW [Amos 1:11]," *JBL* 91 [1972] 391-393). Fishbane and Coote agree that the context is specifically covenantal.

[227]See A.S.Kapelrud, "The Prophets and the Covenant," in Barrick–Spencer, eds., *In the Shelter*, 180.

[228]It is unwarranted to conclude with M.L.Barré ("The Meaning of *l' 'šybnw* in Amos 1:3-2:6," *JBL* 105 [1986] 611-631) that this entails a covenant between Yahweh and the nations.

[229]H.B.Huffmon, "The Treaty Background of Hebrew *YĀDAʿ*," *BASOR* 181 (1966) 34.

as a background for the customs underlying chs.3-5.[230] The question remains whether the use of treaty terminology is sufficient to prove the presence of an explicit covenant theology.[231]

The evidence from Hosea is more conclusive than that from Amos. Hos. 8:1 presents the parallelism *y'n 'brw bryty* || *w'l-twrty pš'w.*[232] Perlitt's explanation of this passage by arguing for Dtistic editing of Hosea is improbable.[233] The parallel reference to *twrh* and *bryt* fits the context well.[234] Hos. 6:7 makes another reference to *bryt*, which should not be dismissed on the basis of the enigmatic preposition. Whether *b* or *k* is accepted with *'dm*, the reference *'brw bryt* stands in poetic parallelism with *bgdw by*. Breaking the covenant in Hos. 6:7, of whatever sort it was, was synonymous with dealing faithlessly with Yahweh.[235] The enigmatic nature of the parallelism is sooner an argument for the text's authenticity than a reason to dismiss it from the discussion.[236] The implications of the couplet *ky 'tm l' 'my, w'nky l'-'hyh lkm* in Hos. 1:9b is widely recognized as the reversal of the promise in Ex. 3:14; 6:7,[237] and it would be incomprehensible

[230]W.Brueggemann, "Amos iv 4-13 and Israel's Covenant Worship," *VT* 15 (1965) 1-15; M.O'Rourke Boyle, "The Covenant Lawsuit of the Prophet Amos: 3:1-4:13," *VT* 21 (1971) 338-362; J.Bright, *Covenant and Promise: The Prophetic Understanding of the Future in Pre-Exilic Israel* (Philadelphia, 1976), 84-87; M.J.Hauan, "The Background and Meaning of Amos 5:17b," *HTR* 79 (1986) 337-348.

[231]For a plausible explanation of the juxtaposition of the two oracles referring to treaty violation in Am. 1:3-2:3 see S.M.Paul, "Amos 1:3-2:3: A Concatenous Literary Pattern," *JBL* 90 (1971) 397-403.

[232]Cf. Am. 2:4,6.

[233]Perlitt, *Bundestheologie*, 146-149. His view is opposed by McCarthy ("*Berît* in OT," 113f.) and by D.R.Daniels (*Hosea and Salvation History: The Early Traditions of Israel in the Prophecy of Hosea* [Hamburg, 1987], 161-168).

[234]It is reinforced by additional covenant terms, *yd'* and *ṭwb* (vss.2-3); cf. Huffmon, "Treaty Background" 36; M.Fox, "ṬÔB as Covenant Terminology," *BASOR* 209 (1973) 41f.; I.Johag, "*twb*–Terminus Technicus in Vertrags- und Bundisformularen des Alten Orients und des Alten Testaments," in H.-J.Fabry, ed., *Bausteine Biblischer Theologie* (Fs G.J.Botterweck; Köln and Bonn, 1977), 3-23; D.J.McCarthy, "Ebla, *orkia temnein, ṭb, šlm*: Addenda to *Treaty and Covenant*," *Bibl* 60 (1979) 251.

[235]Note the conclusion drawn by B.Mazar that the references to Adam in Ps. 68:19; 78:60 and Hos. 6:7-8 are part of an ancient poetic and cultic tradition ("Biblical Archaeology Today: The Historical Aspect," in J.Amitai, ed., *Biblical Archaeology Today* [Jerusalem 1985], 17f.).

[236]Cf. Daniels, *Hosea*, 149-160.

[237]H.W.Wolff, *Hosea* (*BKAT* XIV/1; Neukirchen, 1961), 23; J.L.Mays, *Hosea* (Philadelphia, 1969), 29f.

apart from its implication of Israel's identity as a covenant people.[238] In addition, there are numerous texts in Hosea where a reference to a covenant relationship between Yahweh and Israel is implied. Hos. 4:1-3 knows the decalogue and interprets it as covenant law.[239] Hos. 9:11-14 may be similar,[240] especially so if *'hb* in 9:15 is a *terminus technicus* for covenant love.[241] Hosea did not hesitate to indict Israel for making a treaty with Assyria (*wbryt 'm-'šwr ykrtw*), and a covenant with Egypt (12:2).[242] Hosea suggests that in this context a treaty alliance with Assyria and with Egypt implied a rejection of the God who brought Israel out of Egypt (cf. 12:14f.; 13:4; 14:1-3) and it therefore constituted a breach of covenant faithfulness.[243] Kapelrud is surely correct when he demurs regarding Perlitt's treatment of covenant in Hosea, concluding instead, "Hosea did not merely mention the covenant in passing; he describes it as the basic foundation in the people's relationship with their God, a foundation which he considered as self-evident."[244] The marriage metaphor in Hosea is not

[238]Bright, *Covenant and Promise*, 90f.; de Moor, *Uw God*, 67; F.C.Fensham, "The Marriage Metaphor in Hosea for the Covenant Relationship between the Lord and His People (Hos. 1:2-9)," *JNSL* 12 (1984) 71-78.

[239]H.B.Huffmon, "The Covenant Lawsuit in the Prophets," *JBL* 78 (1959) 249f.; F.C.Fensham, "Malediction and Benediction in Ancient Near Eastern Vassal-Treaties and the Old Testament," *ZAW* 74 (1962) 9; A.Deissler, "Die wesentliche Bundesweisung in der Mosaischen und frühprophetischen Gottesbotschaft," in J.B.Metz et al., eds., *Gott in Welt*, vol. 1 (Fs K.Rahner; Freiburg, 1964), 456; A.S.Kapelrud, "The Spirit and the Word in the Prophets," *ASThI* 11 (1977-78) 44. With respect to 5:8-6:6 in a possible connection with a covenant renewal, see E.M.Good, "Hosea 5:8-6:6: An Alternative to Alt," *JBL* 85 (1966) 273-286.

[240]F.C.Fensham, "Psalm 21–A Covenant-Song?" *ZAW* 77 (1965) 193-202. Even if U.Cassuto overstated the evidence somewhat when he concluded that Hosea must have known the Torah in close to its final form, the knowledge of various covenantal passages now found in Exodus seems incontrovertible ("The Prophet Hosea and the Books of the Pentateuch" in *Biblical and Oriental Studies*, 2 vols. trans. I.Abrahams [Jerusalem, 1973-1975], 1:79-100); Fensham argues that Hos. 1:2-9 knows Ex. 34:15-16 ("The Marriage Metaphor," 76; cf. Halbe, *Privilegrecht*, 261-263).

[241]N.Lohfink, "Hate and Love in Osee 9,15," *CBQ* 25 (1963) 417; cf. W.L.Moran, "The Ancient Near Eastern Background of the Love of God in Deuteronomy," *CBQ* 25 (1963) 77-87.

[242]D.J.McCarthy, "Covenant by Oil," *VT* 14 (1964) 179-189; F.I.Andersen–D.N.Freedman, *Hosea* (Garden City, 1980), 605; M.Dahood, "The Minor Prophets and Ebla," in Meyers–O'Connor, eds., *Word of the Lord*, 50.

[243]This does not entail that for ancient Israel all international treaties meant a transgression of the covenant with Yahweh.

[244]Kapelrud, "Prophets," 178.

a forerunner of covenant theology but a vivid variant of an already present theme underlying the book of Hosea as a whole.[245]

Isaiah too employs treaty related terminology, including concepts which "implied covenant infidelity to the divine sovereign."[246] Covenant theology did not begin in the 7th century, nor is it simply the sudden spurt of a shoot developing from a seed starting to germinate in the 8th century. Whatever the reason for the relative paucity of employment of the word *bryt* itself, the 8th century prophets envisioned the relationship between Yahweh and Israel as covenantal.

The great diversity of references to covenant in literature from the 7th century is more of an argument favoring the complexity of its antecedent history than for the idea that it marks the beginning of a new development. The same is true of the variety of covenantal emphases and customs found in the historical writings. Even if a relatively late dating for the final editing of Kings is accepted, events are narrated there which become inexplicable apart from the presupposition of the covenant. For example, the ceremony described in 2 Kgs 11:4-17 is an enthronement ceremony in which the king was given the covenant law (vs.12),[247] kept in the Ark of the Covenant.[248] The fact that the cryptic synonymous parallelism of *bryt* and *'dwt* is presented without any further explication suggests that the identity of the two would have been comprehended and accepted without further ado as part of the understood ritual. There is no compelling reason to doubt the accuracy of vs.14, which states that the king stood by the pillar as stipulated (*kmšpṭ*, i.e., according to the protocol for such a ceremony). The entire scene was comprehensible to Athaliah at a glance. And comparison with other enthronement accounts suggests that it likely

[245]See K.Koch, *The Prophets*, 2 vols, trans. M.Kohl (Philadelphia, 1983), 1:90.

[246]Kalluveettil, *Declaration*, 28; cf. further 30-32, 127. See too W.Eichrodt, "Prophet and Covenant: Observations on the Exegesis of Isaiah," in Durham–Porter, eds., *Proclamation and Presence*, 167-188; Kapelrud, "Prophets," 179; Weinfeld, "Covenant Terminology," 197 n.99.

[247]Hebrew *'dwt* is synonymous with the Akkadian term for treaty, *adû*, pl. *adê*. See Wiseman, "Treaties of Esarhaddon," 81 n.1; J.A.Thompson, "Expansions of the *'d* Root," *JSS* 10 (1965) 239f.; Kalluveettil, *Declaration*, 31. The idea of a bracelet suggested by Z.W.Falk ("Forms of Testimony," *VT* 11 [1961] 88-91) may be rejected, as can the theory of an ornamented head cover proposed by S.Yeivin ("*'Ēdūth*," *IEJ* 24 [1974] 17-20).

[248]M.H.Woudstra, *The Ark of the Covenant from Conquest to Kingship* (Philadelphia, 1965), 79; T.E.Fretheim, "The Ark in Deuteronomy," *CBQ* 30 (1968) 12.

followed a ritual already attested in the united monarchy.[249] Vs.17, a summary statement of the foregoing events, states that the covenant was triangular, involving Yahweh, king and people. This evidence for the antiquity of the covenant concept in Israel cannot be dismissed on the grounds that it represents theological reinterpretation by a later historian or redactor. Whatever the final date of redaction of these materials, there is little reason to doubt that the covenant concept was indigenous to the events here described. Similar observations can be made with respect to the role of the covenant in the Sinai narratives of Exodus. Here too it is impossibe to attribute all covenantal references, whether explicit or implied, to the hand of a later Dtistic editor.[250]

### 2.3.7.3 Ancient tradition

Jaroš ascertained that Perlitt's view is unable to do justice to the uniqueness of Josh. 24:25-27, and he accordingly attempted to modify this position to accomodate the probability that these verses rest upon an older historical tradition.[251] But it is doubtful that Perlitt's position can be rescued in this manner. Jaroš asserts that a sub-stratum of historical memory is detectable in vss.25a,26b,27a.[252] But how reliable is this "echte historische Erinnerung"? In vs.26, for example, Jaroš concludes that only Joshua, the stone and the tree

[249]Z.Ben-Barak, "The Mizpah Covenant (I Sam 10:25)–The Source of the Israelite Monarchic Covenant," *ZAW* 91 (1979) 30-43.

[250]E.g., Ex. 24:3-8. Of extreme significance for the interpretation of this passage is a Hittite ritual text (ritual of Zarpiya), which according to O.R.Gurney "has been strangely neglected in the controversy over the significance of the West Semitic custom of killing an animal to sanctify a covenant or treaty" (*Some Aspects of Hittite Religion* [Oxford, 1977], 30). Gurney notes the similarity between the Hittite ritual and Ex. 24:5-8, both of which describe a covenant with the deity, established in a sacrificial meal. Significantly, the ancient custom of the sacrificial banquet as part of the ceremony accompanying a covenant between human parties is attested in Gen. 26:30 and 31:54 (cf. McCarthy, "Three Covenants in Genesis," 179-189; F.C.Fensham, "Die offer en maaltyd by die vorming van die verbond in Ou en Nuwe Testament," *Tydskrif vir geesteswetenskappe* 5 [1965] 77-85) and probably in Ex. 18:12 (cf. 4.2). On the debate regarding Ex. 24:3-8 see further E.W.Nicholson, "The Covenant Ritual in Exodus xxiv 3-8," *VT* 32 (1982) 74-86, and cf. 5.3.4 and 5.9.2.

[251]Smend is unnecessarily diffident about the matter when he concludes, "Ob und wieweit der dtr geprägten Erzählung von Landtag zu Sichem (Jos 24) ältere oder alte Tradition zugrundliegt, ist offen" (*Die Entstehung des Alten Testaments*, 3rd ed. [Stuttgart, 1984], 126).

[252]Jaroš *Sichem*, 148.

are historical.[253] But this raises a problem. His summary of the archaeological evidence at Shechem leads to the conclusion that the *grossen Kultmassebe* of the temple of El-berit must antedate Joshua. It was therefore part of the Canaanite sanctuary. How then is it possible to see the reference to Joshua raising the stone in the sanctuary as preserving a true historical memory? Jaroš avoids answering this ambivalence in his position by asserting that what actually happened was an appropriation of the stone by Joshua to represent Yahweh rather than *'l 'lhy yśr'l*. The earliest record of this event, according to Jaroš, portrayed the stone as "hearing," but since this was offensive a later interpretation (E?) makes it more innocuous as a "witness." But if Joshua did not raise the stone as the text asserts, is it credible to modify the "echte historische Erinnerung" to comport with a hypothetical theory of a clan confederation, and then claim that this conclusion is based upon the historical memory preserved in these verses?[254]

The attempt by Jaroš to construct a theory of tribal confederation on the basis of Josh. 24 is not more convincing than the amphictyony idea it intends to supplant. His inordinate reliance upon comparisons with nomadic Arabic customs[255] to explain the covenant in Josh. 24 is a step backwards in explaining OT covenant texts and the sedentarization of early Israel. The assertion that Joshua and the Ephraim clan came from the south via Transjordan, but that Manasseh came from an Aramaic background, via the Transjordan, and constituted part of the Jacob/Israel population living in Palestine when Joshua arrived,[256] makes it difficult to account for the repeated association of Ephraim and Manasseh, let alone their connection with Egypt. Finally, in accepting Perlitt's conclusions regarding the composition of vss.2-24, Jaroš' position incorporates the weaknesses indicated above with respect to Perlitt.

These observations suggest that the literary-critical analyses by Jaroš and Perlitt are inadequate to fill the hiatus created by rejection of the source-critical conclusions of the E, JE, or J theories. A more

[253]Jaroš, *Sichem*, 150: "Ausser der Nennung Josuas, des Steines und Baumes ist in diesem Vers nichts Historisches."

[254]Note that a similar reinterpretation has to be employed in order to account for the designation *mqdš yhwh*, also considered historical in vs.26.

[255]E.g., the studies by Pedersen and Smith, cf. 1.6.1.

[256]Jaroš, *Sichem*, 146f.

probable approach is found in theories of ancient tradition with later editing. But the problem here is that, as our survey above indicates, this has become a "catch-all" for a great variety of positions. In fact, even the positions summarized in section 2.3.6, to the extent that they at least allow for some later redaction, can be included here. The designation of Josh. 24 as ancient tradition with subsequent editing is so amorphous that our survey begins to look like a group photo of Noah's ark, with a few scholars grouped in pairs, perhaps the odd collection of seven, but surely every species is represented! Moreover, what is still necessary is a detailed, new literary analysis of the passage.[257]

It has become commonplace for commentators to assert the presence of an early tradition in Josh. 24, and then to assign the alleged expansions and editing to a subsequent date which rests on general conclusions regarding the editing of the Dtistic history as a whole, rather than on internal evidence of the chapter itself. The net result is that the various advocates in this position are more resolute in rejecting the previous approaches than they are in formulating a lucid and convincing literary analysis of Josh. 24. But even the question of a possible relationship to E remains a matter of considerable ambivalence. Thus, Weinfeld continues to speak of Josh. 24 as an "Elohist document" and an "Elohist Shechem tradition."[258] Boling accepts Wright's conclusions regarding the "independent antiquity of the Shechem account."[259] But as we have noted above, Wright's conclusions were fostered more by the fact that the present chapter stands in Joshua and not in the Pentateuch, than by a literary analysis of the text itself.[260] Nor has the list of alleged glosses and redactions

[257]Exceptions are provided by Schmitt and McCarthy, but here too an ambiguous relationship with an alleged E source remains problematic. McCarthy's conclusions will be dealt with more extensively in the following sections of this chapter regarding form criticism and structural analysis. In addition to the studies by Schmitt and McCarthy, the literary-critical analysis by Sperling ("Joshua 24," 119-136) is very important in questioning the literary-critical conclusions attained by Perlitt, but the question of Dtistic authorship or redaction must be treated more extensively than was possible in Sperling's article.

[258]Weinfeld, *Deuteronomy*, 165, cf. 327.

[259]Boling, *Joshua*, 526.

[260]The uncertain stance of Josh. 24's relationship to E is also reflected in a summary statement by Th.C.Vriezen–A.S.van der Woude, *De Literatuur van Oud-Israël*, 6th ed. (Katwijk, 1980), 199: "Ten slotte kan van cap. 24, hoewel met deuteronomistische toevoegingen, verondersteld worden, dat het een aan E verwant

inherited from previous generations of source critics been adequately re-evaluated in light of the rejection of the E or JE theories.[261] It has been shown above that one recurrent criterium by which phrases were designated as glosses or redactional expansions was the fact that they did not fit the style or terminology of E or JE. But once the strict dependence upon E or JE has been questioned, the criteria for distinguishing glosses must also be revised.

When Noth broke with the Hexateuch theory, he realized that this had paramount implications with respect to Josh. 24. He discontinued the reference to JE. To be sure, he continued to see some warrant for multiple sources, though the emphasis was shifted to focus upon later redaction. But perhaps the most important ramification of Noth's break with the Hexateuchal theory for this chapter was that it suddenly placed Josh. 24 in an enigmatic position. Did it have a relatively independent origin? What is its relationship to Josh. 23? What is its connection to the opening chapters of Judges? As noted above,[262] Noth was unable to answer these questions satisfactorily; he reversed or modified his previous opinions in each subsequent publication in which the matter was addressed.

A following generation of scholars, wrestling with the question of Dtistic history, has fared little better in attempting to find a definitive answer to these riddles of Josh. 24 bequeathed by their scholarly progenitor. Noth's ambivalence continues to be perpetuated in the current diversity of theories with respect to Josh. 24's place in Dtistic history. W.Richter[263] and Smend,[264] for example, contend that Josh. 24 was original to the Dtistic history. Josh. 23 is a later addition, and Judg. 2:6-10 is dependent upon Josh. 24:28ff. This conclusion is accepted by Auld.[265] Gray argues to the contrary that Josh. 24 was

verhaal is; de rol die Sichem hier speelt, het voorkomen van Elohim als Godsnaam (dat zo goed als hier alleen in het Jozuaboek voorkomt) wijzen daarop." The problem is precisely how are we to understand the term "verwant" in this conclusion?

[261]E.g., Nelson's typical conclusion, "The vast majority of commentators have recognized a pre-Deuteronomistic core in Josh. 24:1-27 overlaid by some Deuteronomistic additions" (*Double Redaction*, 95, 146 n.177).

[262]See the discussion at 1.4.1.

[263]W.Richter, *Die Bearbeitung des "Retterbuches" in der deuteronomischen Epoche* (Bonn, 1964), 45-47.

[264]R.Smend, "Das Gesetz und die Völker. Ein Beitrag zur deuteronomistischen Redaktionsgeschichte," in Wolff, ed., *Probleme biblischer Theologie*, 494-509.

[265]Auld, *Joshua, Moses*, 54f. The statement by Nelson (*Double Redaction*, 94), "The widespread acceptance of the hypothesis of the Deuteronomistic historian has

added by a post-exilic Dtistic redactor wishing to expand the account of Josh. 23, which in turn was based upon the event described in Josh. 24.[266] Nelson defended a similar position, asserting that Josh. 24:1-27 was inserted by an exilic editor, though he himself was not the actual author.[267] Mayes finds none of the preceding positions adequate. In his opinion the clash with Josh. 23 is of such a nature that Josh. 24:1-28 cannot even be attributed to the later Dtistic editor; it was introduced into Joshua at a final stage following the work of the second Dtistic editor, in other words, by a *third* Dtistic editor.[268]

Numerous major objections can be raised with respect to the views of Gray, Nelson and Mayes. In the first place, they are unable to do justice to the various references in Josh. 24 which refuse to be coerced into a late context. No plausible explanation is given for the manner in which an allegedly ancient tradition in Josh. 24 should be transmitted for so many centuries independent of Joshua and then inserted by an unknown redactor. Attempts to explain Josh. 24 in this manner ignore various connections which can be listed between this chapter and preceding portions of Joshua. Finally, and perhaps most incriminating, they do not account for the literary connection between Josh. 24:28-31 and Judg. 2:6-10.[269] Criticism of Gray, Nelson and Mayes does not entail that satisfactory answers were already provided by Richter and Smend. The variety of criticisms which ensued attest to the complexity of this matter, and the current diversity of attempts to place Josh. 24 in Dtistic history yields yet another convincing demonstration of the need for a new analysis.

created an almost equally widespread agreement that Josh. 24 is not part of the original work of this historian," obscures the diversity of opinion which exists on this point.

[266]Gray, *Joshua*, 52.

[267]Nelson, *Double Redaction*, 94-98.

[268]Mayes, *Story of Israel*, 49-57; cf. Nicholson, *His People*, 158.

[269]See now H.Rösel, "Die Überleitungen vom Josua– ins Richterbuch," *VT* 30 (1980) 342-350.

## 2.4 Form-critical approaches reconsidered

### 2.4.1 Inadequacy of previous form-critical approaches

Form-critical studies of Josh. 24:1-28 provide a telling example of a certain weakness in form criticism addressed by Muilenburg.[270] The analyses have been riveted so tightly to the question of whether Josh. 24 fits a certain pattern of treaty texts that they emphasize elements in common, or missing elements, but loose sight of the unique and unparalleled aspects of the text. This methodological limitation is understandable because the first step in a form-critical study is to show the validity of such a comparison by demonstrating that the given text belongs to a certain textual genre or form. If there is no agreement at this initial stage of the form-critical endeavor, it becomes virtually impossible to proceed to a more nuanced analysis of the particular emphases of the pericope, including dimensions which deviate from the form. This is exactly what has happened in form-critical studies of Josh. 24. Since scholars were not able to come to a consensus regarding whether or not it was valid in the first place to treat the text as part of a broader pattern of treaty texts or covenant formularies (the two categories are not to be simply equated), it was impossible to advance to a more refined analysis of the text's literary form, role and structure.[271]

Ambiguous undertaking of form-critical analysis of Josh. 24:1-28 has at times led to awkward formulation of results, as may be illustrated in the work of Weinfeld. He concludes that Josh. 24:2-14 contains a preamble (vs.2a), historical prologue (vss.2b-13), and basic stipulations of obedience (vs.14), but the remaining constitutive parts of the treaty form are lacking in the subsequent description of the covenant ceremony.[272] Weinfeld uses treaty terminology in vss.2-14 but he denies that a treaty is enacted in the second half of the chapter. He suggests that covenant clauses, invocation of witnesses, blessings and curses, oath-imprecation, deposit of the document, periodic reading, and provision for duplicate copies are all missing from the literary form of Josh. 24:1-28 compared to the classic treaty form[273] –but later he contradicts his conclusion regarding

[270] J.Muilenburg, "Form Criticism and Beyond," *JBL* 88 (1969) 4f.
[271] Cf. Nötscher, "Bundesformular," 197.
[272] Weinfeld, *Deuteronomy*, 66.
[273] Weinfeld, *Deuteronomy*, 66. He speaks of a preamble and a historical prologue,

deposit of the document.[274] Similarly, he asserts that the conditions (stipulations) of the treaty "are entirely lacking in Josh.24," but on the following page he lists 24:14 as evidence of stipulations.[275] His distinction between a covenant which receives its validity through a sworn imprecation and that which is ratified by a ritual ceremony[276] hardly does justice to Josh. 24. It is of questionable value to make a categorical distinction between the two types of covenant ratification in the OT. Gen. 21:27-32 describes the enactment of a *bryt* by ritual (seven sheep set aside as "witness") and sworn oath. Similarly, Gen. 31:43-54 shows a combination of ritual (stone pillar, sacrifice, covenant meal) and sworn oath (vs.54). In Josh. 24 the covenant is ratified by the people's verbal assent to it in the dialogue (vss.16-24) as well as the ritual (vss.25-27). One may also compare Ex. 24:3-8 where the ratification of the covenant contains verbal assent (vss.3,7) as well as ritual acts (writing of the words of the law, altar building, pillars, sacrifice, sprinkling of blood, reading of the words of the law).[277] To argue from the absence of the verb *nšbʿ* that the Exodus or Joshua covenants do not have a sworn agreement on the part of the people is not convincing.[278]

Weinfeld maintains that the covenants of Sinai and Shechem can be distinguished as a covenant of law and a covenant of vassalship respectively.[279] But here too the attempt to categorize does injustice to Josh. 24. While it is quite true that Ex. 24 places greater stress upon law than is found in Josh. 24, it is unfounded to state that

i.e., specific treaty terminology, in a text which is finally not a treaty text. The explanation for this is not that the prologue in Josh. 24 is a remnant of a text which previously coincided more closely with a treaty form; Weinfeld's entire argument regarding Josh. 24 is that the literary form is moving towards the treaty form, not away from it. Apparently he uses the term "historical prologue" loosely as a component of a covenant text, not necessarily only of a treaty text; but the important thing is that this ambiguity is already representative of his uncertain treatment of Josh. 24:15-28 in general.

[274]Weinfeld, *Deuteronomy*, 164, cf. 64.

[275]Weinfeld, *Deuteronomy*, 65f.

[276]Weinfeld, *Deuteronomy*, 63.

[277]These observations should also warn against the conclusions implied in McCarthy's vague claim that in the context of the cult a covenant was initially ratified by ritual and later by some sort of oath (*OT Covenant*, 88). On the combination of ritual and oath see already Fensham, "Offer en maaltyd," 78f.

[278]Contra Weinfeld, *Deuteronomy*, 62f. Cf. our ensuing comments with regard to McCarthy's discussion of vs.22.

[279]Weinfeld, *Deuteronomy*, 156, cf. 152.

"the law mentioned there (v. 25) has only secondary importance."[280] On the contrary, the repeated references in vss.25-27 to the law are essential for distinguishing the type of *bryt* here enacted.[281]

Unfortunately, Weinfeld's entire analysis of the literary character of Josh. 24 and its possible affinity to either a treaty form or a covenant form is hampered by his overriding attempt to demonstrate that a clearer affinity with the treaty genre is to be found in Deuteronomy than in Joshua. His list of elements lacking from the treaty pattern[282] fails to acknowledge the parallels suggested in previous works by other scholars. He offers a "list of covenant features in Deuteronomy and in other Biblical sources"[283] but he does not even include *krt bryt* for Josh. 24. His list for Josh. 24 implies that there is not a single covenant feature subsequent to vs.14, but this is misleading. With respect to invocation of witnesses, Weinfeld tacitly concedes that the people (vss.16-24) and stone (vss.27) can fill this role,[284] but he disqualifies these on the grounds that they are not cosmic witnesses.[285] Weinfeld obscures the study of Josh. 24 by disqualifying elements from comparison on the grounds that they

[280]Weinfeld, *Deuteronomy*, 152.

[281]Cf. *wyśm lw ḥq wmšpṭ bśkm* (vs.25), *wyktb yhwš' 't-hdbrym h'lh bspr twrt 'lhym* (vs.26), *kl-'mry yhwh 'šr dbr 'mnw* (vs.27). This repeated emphasis upon law can hardly be considered of secondary significance for delineating the nature of the *bryt* in Josh. 24; it provides the foundation for the ritual of covenant ratification. Cf. Kline, *By Oath Consigned*, 20. Note too that Weinfeld concedes that the first three commandments of the decalogue are of the vassal type (*Deuteronomy*, 156f.). Since the vassal type commandments provide the context for law in the Sinai covenant, and law is essential to the covenant at Shechem, it is hardly convincing to argue that the Sinai covenant and the Shechem covenant can be distinguished from each other as law covenant and vassal covenant respectively.

[282]Weinfeld, *Deuteronomy*, 66.

[283]Weinfeld, *Deuteronomy*, 66.

[284]Weinfeld, *Deuteronomy*, 62, 165.

[285]Weinfeld is quite correct in noting the diversity of opinion with respect to identification of the specific elements such as invocation of witnesses, oath, etc., but his conclusion that all elements giving binding judicial value are absent, misrepresents the nature of the solemn dialogue (vss.14-24) as well as the scene of law giving (vss.25-27). With respect to the invocation of witnesses in Josh. 24 see Muilenburg, "Form and Structure," 354; Baltzer, *Bundesformular*, 33-35; Beyerlin, *Herkunft und Geschichte*, 72f., 173 n.6; Kitchen, *Ancient Orient*, 97; *Bible in its World*, 82; Hillers, *Covenant*, 52; D.C.T.Sheriffs, "The Phrases *ina IGI DN* and *lipĕnēy Yhwh* in Treaty and Covenant Contexts," *JNSL* 7 (1979) 66f. Regarding a written document and its deposition in the sanctuary see Baltzer, *Bundesformular*, 36; Kitchen, *Ancient Orient*, 97; *Bible in its World*, 82; Hillers, *Covenant*, 64.

are not precisely identical to the *treaty* texts, and then on that basis eliminating them from his list of *covenant features*.[286] When he places the texts from Exodus, Joshua and Deuteronomy side by side, he uses *covenant features* as a criterion for *inclusion* of material from Deuteronomy, but *treaty features* as a criterion for *exclusion* of material from Ex. 19-24, Josh. 24. Since an invocation of witnesses, blessings and curses, oath-imprecation, deposit of written document, etc., in a form identical to the treaties is lacking in Josh. 24, he determines that there is no comparable covenant feature here. A more desirable approach to such matters as the presence of witnesses and the deposition of a written document would be to acknowledge that although the parallels found here do diverge in certain respects from the secular treaties, this does not disqualify them from comparison.[287] Once both the similarities and divergencies are acknowledged, it is possible to attempt a more refined analysis of how to explain the analogous and the contrasting features respectively.

McCarthy's similar assertion that Josh. 24:1-28 lacks vital elements of the treaty form also equivocates on certain crucial points. McCarthy accepts the conclusion that Josh. 24:22 is a contract form and not a covenant oath,[288] and he in fact places considerable importance upon this distinction for his final analysis of Josh. 24. McCarthy states, "This is *not* a form of oath, a fact which further complicates the already difficult problem of Josh. 24, for it deprives that key text for the reconstruction of Israelite religious history on the basis of the covenant form of another of the essentials of that form."[289] However, Tucker's conclusion regarding Josh. 24:22 is contingent upon a fatal oversight. He makes a salient distinction between contracts and treaty forms in ancient NE texts. However, in his application of this insight to OT texts, he compares Josh. 24:22 with Ruth 4:9-11, but

[286]This is the terminology that he himself uses (*Deuteronomy*, 66) and it is symptomatic of the inherent ambivalence in his methodology.

[287]This is true of the "preamble" and "prologue" as well.

[288]Following Tucker, "Covenant Forms," 487-503.

[289]McCarthy, *OT Covenant*, 34 n.47, original emphasis, cf. 75. See too *Treaty and Covenant*, 230, 236, 238. There is a reciprocal influence between McCarthy and Tucker. Tucker's article in 1965 accepts McCarthy's opinion as stated in *Treaty and Covenant* (1963), regarding the absence of some of the formal elements of the treaties in the OT covenant accounts. McCarthy in turn later views Tucker's article as a confirmation of his opinion, causing him to restate his view regarding absent elements more sharply.

somehow overlooks 1 Sam. 12:5 entirely.[290] Tucker works with the definition that "Contracts are private legal and economic agreements, such as conveyances, deeds, or work contracts."[291] Now it is apparent that 1 Sam. 12:5 does not fit this category any better than does Josh. 24:22. There is no question in either of these texts of a private transaction, an economic agreement, or the like. Are we to assume that in both 1 Sam. 12:5 and Josh. 24:22 a contract form was adapted to a context in which it is not appropriate? It is more credible to suggest that the witness scene of the type that we find in Ruth 4:9-11; 1 Sam. 12:5; Josh. 24:22, has a broader place in the OT than simply in a "contract form." McCarthy states elsewhere in the same monograph that contracts appeal to lists of human witnesses while treaties appeal to divine witnesses.[292] This distinction is deficient because treaties at times also appeal to human witnesses.[293] Moreover, 1 Sam. 12:5 appeals to Yahweh and his anointed (*'d yhwh bkm w'd mšyḥw hywm hzh*).[294] Is this then a contract form or a treaty form? If we are to follow the line of reasoning adopted by Tucker and McCarthy, comparison with Ruth 4:9-11 would suggest that it is a contract form adapted to another situation. But if we are to follow McCarthy's distinction based on the appeal to divine witnesses, it does not fit the contract form. And it obviously does not fit a contract context. There is in fact no evidence to suggest that Josh. 24:22 (or 1 Sam. 12:5) represents an adaptation of a form exclusively indigenous to a contract agreement.[295] In short, what McCarthy judges to be an "important precision contributed by G.Tucker"[296] is deluding when applied to Josh. 24:22.

This is not the only weakness in McCarthy's attempt to determine whether there is an oath in Josh. 24. As quoted above, he states that

[290]See 2.2. The parallels between Josh. 24 and 1 Sam. 12 had long been noted; cf., e.g., Eissfeldt, *Einleitung*, 349. In 1 Sam. 12:5 the *'d*-formula is undeniably an oath, cf. vs.3 *ngd yhwh wngd mšyḥw*, which emphasizes the legal setting of the witness scene, cf., e.g., Gen. 31:32,37, and passim.

[291]Tucker, "Covenant Forms," 487, cf. 503.

[292]McCarthy, *OT Covenant*, 65.

[293]Cf. 5.9.4.

[294]Note the external parallelism with *ngd yhwh wngd mšyḥw* (vs.3).

[295]Contra Tucker, "Covenant Forms," 502. Tucker posits that the reference *bkm* supports his conclusion of such an adaptation, because it supposedly is a deliberate attempt to bring it in line with the self-curse of the treaties. But 1 Sam. 12:5 has a similar reference *bkm*.

[296]McCarthy, *OT Covenant*, 34.

Josh. 24 is missing the covenant oath which he judges to be standard to the treaty form. But his treatment of oath as an essential element of the treaty pattern is ambiguous. He frequently appeals to the presence or absence of an oath to determine whether or not a text belongs to the treaty category.[297] But he argues in other contexts, such as 2 Sam. 3:21; 5:1-3, that "*krt bryt* by itself signifies an especially solemn oath."[298] If *krt bryt* at times already implies the oath, what is the point of arguing on the basis of the reinterpretation of vs.22 as a contract form that Josh. 24 is missing an oath? Furthermore, the study by Tucker upon which he bases the latter claim states, "The content of the *oath* in the covenant ceremony of Josh. xxiv is summarized when the people say: 'The Lord our God we will serve, and his voice we will obey' (vs.24, cf. vss.16ff.)."[299]

The upshot of McCarthy's discussion of oath in Josh. 24 appears to be an attempt to distinguish between a covenant *record* and covenant *report*. Josh. 24 is itself not a covenant text or record in the sense in which the original documentation of a treaty constitutes a treaty text. It is rather a report about a covenant event. As such McCarthy's observation regarding the explicit documentation of the oath in treaty texts in contrast to covenant accounts is significant. But his conclusion that the equivalent of an oath is absent in Josh. 24 cannot be substantiated. The witness declaration culminating in vs.24 can best be seen as a solemn oath ceremony, as can be deduced from the context and the legal formulation in which it is presented.[300]

[297]In *Treaty and Covenant* 1963, McCarthy concludes that the treaty always includes an oath, which is not always the case with *bryt*. "The very designation of the treaty implies an obligation assumed under oath. But *bryt* hardly does this. It may involve an oath or it may not. But the word itself does not imply oath the way the classic treaty terms, *māmītu* or *adē*, do" (169, cf. 47). A similar emphasis is found in *OT Covenant*, 26 n.29, 31, 38 n.7, 40, 41f., 44, 65f. 69, 80, and *Treaty and Covenant* 1978, 32-35, 77-81, 88f. 91 ("... mention of the oath which is the essential distinguishing element in the treaty..."), 118 ("... all ancient treaties are a kind of loyalty oath ..."), etc.

[298]D.J.McCarthy, "*Bryt* and Covenant in the Deuteronomistic History," in *Studies in the Religion of Ancient Israel*, *SVT* 23 (Leiden, 1972), 75 n.1.

[299]Tucker, "Covenant Forms," 496, emphasis added.

[300]The concept of witness (*'dym*) in vs.22 is not identical to the Akkadian *adē* and Aramaic *'dy*, terms which themselves imply a compact or treaty. See J.A.Fitzmeyer, *The Aramaic Inscriptions of Sefîre* (Rome, 1967), 23f. But the role of the witness ceremony here does place the people under legal oath. Cf. S.H.Blank, "The Curse, Blasphemy, the Spell, and the Oath," *HUCA* 23 (1950-51) 89 n.53. Blank's observation regarding 1 Sam. 12:5 is equally valid for Ruth 4:11; Josh. 24:22. Note

### 2.4.2 Importance of ancient NE parallels

The conclusions by McCarthy and Weinfeld concerning the absence of vital elements of a treaty form have been cited as conclusive evidence against reading Josh. 24 in comparison with treaty texts.[301] Numerous other scholars continued to assert that the basic structure of this chapter is that of a covenant formulary, which in turn is modeled directly upon the basic elements of the treaty texts.[302]

In short, discussion of the affinity between the literary structure of Josh. 24:1-28 and the structure of extra-biblical treaty texts has ground to a stalemate, which in turn has led to the present situation in which commentators arrange themselves somewhere on the spectrum of opinions without contributing significant new insights into the literary structure of this passage. On the one hand the similarities between Josh. 24 and the various treaty texts are undeniable. As McCarthy and Weinfeld have conceded, the numerous points of contact indicated by Mendenhall, Baltzer and Beyerlin, inter alia, are not simply coincidental,[303] but it is methodologically wrong to attempt to

Kalluveettil's conclusion regarding the oath of acclamation in Josh. 24:16-18,21-24 as well as the covenant oath in 24:15 (*Declaration*, 61 n.188, 184), and cf. Frankena, "Vassal-Treaties," 140.

[301]E.g., Nicholson "Covenant," 61-63; *His People*, 65; Perlitt, *Bundestheologie*, 246 n.3, appealing to McCarthy, *Treaty and Covenant* (1963). Perlitt calls McCarthy's work "die kundigste Auseinandersetzung" in this respect, and goes on to quote McCarthy to the effect that there are plenty of details which reflect the treaty tradition, but there remains an absence of the full covenant form. The "plenty of details" of comparison pointed out by McCarthy are not reflected in Perlitt's analysis. The only thing he has really accepted from McCarthy is the fact that Josh. 24 does not show the full treaty form, and that there are some parallels with 7th cent. Assyrian treaties.

[302]In addition to the extensive literature listed in 1.5, see Campbell, "Moses and the Foundations of Israel," 148, 150; J.D.Levenson, *Sinai and Zion: An Entry into the Jewish Bible* (Minneapolis, 1985), 32.

[303]Various scholars dismiss the comparisons with the Hittite texts on the grounds that the historical connection between the Hittites and the Israelites is uncertain, e.g., Hermisson, "Bund und Erwählung," 226. But such a dismissal appears to be based more upon an aversion to drawing conclusions which might in any way support an early dating of certain OT texts than upon a demonstration of the illegitimacy of making *textual comparisons*, as is evident from Hermisson's willingness to accept a comparison with late treaties on the basis of Perlitt's dating of covenant theology. Regarding contacts with the Hittites see Fensham, "Clauses of Protection," 134; A.Kempinski, "Hittites in the Bible–What Does Archaeology Say?" *BAR* 5 (1979) 20-45; J.C.Moyer, "Hittite and Israelite Cultic Practices: A Select Comparison," in Hallo et al., eds., *Scripture in Context*, 19-38. Two points

force the final literary form of Josh. 24 into an extra-biblical treaty mold, as is evident from the diversity of results attained by such attempts. If advancements are to be made beyond the present impasse in the covenant/treaty comparison debate, it will be necessary to allow both the similarities and the differences to play a legitimate role in the establishment of a method for comparing and contrasting the respective texts. This is already implicit in the realization that Josh. 24:1-28 itself does not purport to be a treaty text but is an account of a covenantal occurrence, a report of covenant making. This fact has been frequently noted[304] and then attributed insufficient methodological consideration in the subsequent form-critical studies. Greater restraint should also be excercised with respect to dating. Conservative scholars have overstated the evidence for an early date, as if comparison with extra-biblical treaties *proves* an early origin.[305] But such comparisons cannot prove a date of composition; at most they can be suggestive.

On the other side of the debate, attempts to minimize the number of elements shared in common between Josh. 24:1-28 and the Hittite texts are equally flawed by an agenda in which questions of dating, this time in the other direction, also played an inordinate role. This bias is detectable in the works of Weinfeld and McCarthy. It is more extreme in the approaches of Perlitt and Jaroš, who deem it possible to analyze this passage without any serious regard for the second millenium treaty comparisons. A defensible approach will employ the extra-biblical material to potentially illuminate and clarify terminology and context, without loosing sight of the uniqueness of the biblical text. If form criticism is to play a significant future role in advancing the study of Josh. 24:1-28, it will be necessary to adopt, adapt or develop a methodology which is able to facilitate an analysis at the level of individual words and phrases as well as a possible macrostructure. A number of possible affiliations with the ancient NE texts have been listed above in the summary of Kalluveettils's work, which can sup-

are easily overlooked by those who oppose comparison on the basis of time and/or nationality: 1) the necessarily international nature of the treaties, and 2) the traditionalism of the entire ancient NE in this respect was rooted in the desire to continue treaties forever if possible.

[304]E.g., Mendenhall, *Law and Covenant*, 41; McCarthy, *Treaty and Covenant*, 1963, 145-151; Nötscher, "Bundesformular," 197; Kitchen, *Bible in Its World*, 81.

[305]E.g., on the basis of the presence of a prologue, or the relationship of curses and blessings.

plement similarities detected in the previous form-critical analyses.

A new appraisal of the literary form in Josh. 24 must also attempt to move beyond the treaty comparisons in order to investigate the oft-repeated assertion that Josh. 24 is a cultic or a liturgical text. Recent definitions of form criticism as a method of interpretation are quick to remind that the goal or task of form critism should be set both more broadly and more inclusively than has often previously been the case; the ultimate goal is to attain a better understanding of a text's literary structure, and its subsequent implications for exegesis.[306] Form-critical categorization is but one step in that endeavor. This entails that questions generally labeled as form-critical must lead naturally to a search for possible internal literary structures, whether at sub-levels of the passage or spanning the pericope in its entirety. In this regard the form-critical studies of Josh. 24:1-28 have ultimately failed to progress much beyond an initial, equivocal attempt at categorization.

## 2.5 Archaeological approaches to Josh. 24:1-28

In our summary of the various approaches to Josh. 24, reference has been made to numerous studies which warned of the limitations which curtail the degree to which archaeological results can provide definitive answers to the literary questions arising from this passage.[307] We have noted in particular that Fowler and Wächter objected to Wright's attempt to identify the sacred precinct of Josh. 24:26 with the temple of Judg. 9:4,46 and secondly to argue that this temple has now been identified via archaeological excavation. Despite a number of similar earlier objections,[308] Campbell continued, albeit cautiously, to maintain that the sanctuary of Josh. 24:26 was to be equated with that of Judg. 9, and located within the city proper.[309]

A couple of additional observations cast doubt upon the validity of the attempts by Wright, Jaroš and Campbell to make an archaeological equation between Josh. 24:26 and the structures unearthed in Shechem itself. Wächter observed that Gen. 12:6f.; 33:18-20 appear

[306]R.Knierim, "Criticism of Literary Features, Form, Tradition and Redaction," in D.A.Knight–G.M.Tucker, eds., *The Hebrew Bible and Its Modern Interpreters* (Chico, 1985), 136-139.

[307]Cf. 1.7.5.

[308]Cf., e.g., Soggin, "Topographie Sichems," 197.

[309]Campbell, "Judges 9," 264f.

to refer to a sacred precinct outside of Shechem. Moreover, the preposition *b* in *bškm* does not disprove the possibility that Josh. 24:26 has a place in mind *outside* of the city walls. The reference *bškm* is used elsewhere to generally mean the area or vicinity of Shechem. Josh. 24:32 states that Joseph's bones were buried *bškm* in the purchased land, but from Gen. 33:18-20 it is clear that the land was outside of the city proper. It was there that Jacob built an altar which he called *'l 'lhy yśr'l.* The implication in Gen. 35:1-5 would seem to be that Jacob buried the false gods *tḥt h'lh* at the place of his first altar, near Shechem. These links with Josh. 24 would suggest that the reference *tḥt h'lh 'šr bmqdš yhwh* is a deliberate allusion to the place where Jacob buried the idols, outside the city. Furthermore, a city included the agricultural land outside of the protecting walls.[310]

A second and supporting observation is the fact that the gathering referred to in Josh. 24:1-28 would likely have taken place in open air.[311] This does not preclude the theoretical possibility that there could have been a procession from an open air gathering to a temple sanctuary,[312] but nothing in the text of Josh. 24:1-28 hints at such a movement.[313] Deuteronomy prescribes a covenant ceremony which was to take place in the neighborhood of Shechem, but the name of the city is not mentioned and the location is placed at Mt. Ebal and Mt. Gerizim, quite possibly having the same general location in mind as in Josh. 24. Whereas Zertal has thought to have found the location of the altar referred to in Josh. 8:30-35, scholarly reservations about his conclusions have been summarized above. In addition, Kreuzer has stressed the geographical difficulties involved in the theory of a mass gathering in that vicinity.[314] With respect to both Josh. 24:1-28 and 8:30-35 it is therefore necessary to conclude that archaeological evidence is insufficient to prove a precise location

[310]Cf. C.H.J.de Geus, *De Israëlitische stad* (Kampen, 1984), 135f.

[311]Cf. M.Haran, "Temples and Cultic Open Areas as Reflected in the Bible," in A.Biran, ed., *Temples and High Places in Biblical Times* ( Jerusalem, 1981), 36; *Temples and Temple Service in Ancient Israel* (Oxford, 1978), 49f. See too B.C.Crisler, "The Acoustics and Crowd Capacity of Natural Theaters in Palestine," *BA* 39 (1976) 128-141.

[312]Cf. R.D.Barnett, "Bringing the God into the Temple," in Biran, ed., *Temples*, 10-20.

[313]It is also noteworthy that in the Hittite festivals, e.g., there was often a ceremonial procession to a sacred, open air precinct (cf. 5.9.3).

[314]Kreuzer, *Frühgeschichte*, 202 n.46.

for the events described by the biblical narratives.

## 2.6 Structural analysis of Josh. 24

### 2.6.1 Diversity of claims regarding structure

The preceding sections of this chapter evaluated previous text-critical, literary-critical, form-critical and archaeological approaches to Josh. 24:1-28. Ample discussion of these dimensions of the text can be documented, but little consensus of opinion has been attained in any of these areas. Serious efforts to deal with the literary structure of this passage, by contrast, are scanty; the few existing analyses of literary structure in Josh. 24 are mainly of an incidental nature and methodologically unsubstantiated.[315] In short, incomplete and inadequate attention has been paid to questions of literary structure, as is evident from superficial comments by various scholars who in other areas attempt to be more rigorous in their research. Nielsen, for example, suggests that a significant structure is present in vss.14-24, but to substantiate this claim he merely appeals to Joshua's actions and the dialogical character of the text.[316] Muilenburg suggests that the present form of the text "is a precis or abridgement of what was once a more elaborate account," of which the form remains well preserved.[317] Jaroš attributes the final form of the text to Dtistic redaction, and finds the composition so artfully crafted that it is barbaric to tear it apart in source criticism;[318] nevertheless, his search for historical dimensions behind the diachronic evolution of the text is of such importance that it necessitates a dissection of the text anyway. He warns the reader from the outset[319] that present methods of structural analysis are not applicable to parenetic texts of this sort, which explains why he never advances beyond a passing tribute to its aesthetic quality. McCarthy too ventures that the text has a tight

[315]The form-critical studies summarized above are not considered here to be structural analyses because their concentration upon identification of elements in common with the treaty texts does not attempt to make a complete analysis of the structure of the passage.

[316]Nielsen, *Shechem*, 100.

[317]Muilenburg, "Form and Structure," 359. He calls attention to certain key words and phrases, but here too a more detailed examination is wanting.

[318]Jaroš, *Sichem*, 138f.

[319]Jaroš, *Sichem*, 7.

unity and structure.[320] He considers it to be a "sophisticated writing, a careful rhetorical and theological construction."[321] But in his opinion this does not entail a late dating. In fact he argues that the structure is pre-Dtistic, and that it is futile to try to identify a pre-Dtistic and a Dtistic stage. He accordingly denies that the present text was shaped by a Dtistic redactor working with ancient traditions. While McCarthy does recognize a number of Dtistic phrases, he is convinced that they can be explained as later intrusions which may have sharpened the text but have "no effect on the basic original structure."[322]

McCarthy's claim is a vital one and demands a much more detailed consideration than the comments he has offered. What precisely is the structure of Josh. 24? Are the affinities to material ordinarily classified as Dtic really inconsequential to the basic structure of the text? Perlitt appeals to the dialogical structure to argue virtually the opposite. Schmitt also places considerable significance upon form and structure. His argument purports that this chapter reveals close affinity to numerous texts in Judges and 1 Samuel, especially in its sermonic style and structure.[323] He conceeds that Deuteronomy too is known for its sermonic style, but Schmitt believes that this stylistic and structural affinity does not yet make Josh. 24 dependent upon Dtr. In fact, he states that Josh. 24 demonstrates a much simpler sermonic form.[324]

Not all scholars have been lavish in complimenting the final form of Josh. 24.[325] L'Hour's assertion of a disrupted structure becomes

[320]McCarthy, *Treaty and Covenant*, 232f., 284.

[321]McCarthy, *Treaty and Covenant*, 234. The intricacy of the passage is viewed as evidence of written rather than oral composition (284).

[322]McCarthy, *Treaty and Covenant*, 233. Rudolph argues similarly that later glosses have no significant bearing upon the basic structure of the present text (*Der "Elohist"*, 249).

[323]Schmitt, *Landtag*, 17-20.

[324]"Tatsächlich ist in Jos 24 und in den verwandten Abschnitten eine einfachere, noch nicht so entwickelte Form des Predigtstils festzustellen, der uns dann ausgeprägter im Deuteronomium begegnet" (*Landtag*, 20). This argument sounds suspiciously contradictory to what McCarthy asserts, though both Schmitt and McCarthy argue that the passage is essentially pre-Dtistic.

[325]E.g., L'Hour, "L'alliance de Sichem," 17: "Le texte principal se trouve en Jos. xxiv; malheuresement, sa forme actuelle laisse l'impression d'une citadelle démantelé et relevé vaille que vaille à l'aide de matériaux hétérogènes plus ou moins appropriès."

a major criterion for his diachronic attempt to disentangle various layers. Accordingly, as is also the case in the studies of McCarthy, Schmitt and Perlitt, structural considerations and conclusions are given a significance disproportionate to the initial effort expended in justifying the claims regarding literary structure. The only study which attempts to offer a detailed and somewhat systematic analysis is that of C.H.Giblin.[326] Since its appearance this article has been cited with varying degrees of approval,[327] but neither the methodology nor the conclusions found in Giblin's study have been adequately evaluated. Accordingly, before advancing our discussion of possible literary structures in Josh. 24 it is necessary to scrutinize Giblin's approach.

### 2.6.2 C.H.Giblin's structural analysis

Giblin attempts to discern numerical schematizations of key nouns and verbs as a means, along with other critical tools, of determining the unity and emphasis of a given passage,[328] which in turn can serve "in a modest way, as a check on the tendency to eliminate more and more of the text as secondary."[329] He emphasizes the need for careful delineation of a given pericope so as to determine the boundaries within which the numerical schematizations are to be sought. As such Giblin's method appears to be simple. One has only to determine the boundaries and then count key nouns and verbs in confidence that "when these elements are almost massive in character, when they cohere with one another and with the salient features of the literary form in which they appear, and when they support a good number of critical observations reached on other grounds, then they seem to form an integral part of the total literary production—at least in its final, definite stage."[330]

Giblin's study leads to the conclusion that the numbers seven and twelve are important in the structure of Joshua 24:1-25. For convenience we list his results here in point form.

[326]C.H.Giblin, "Structural Patterns in Jos 24:1-25," *CBQ* 26 (1964) 50-69.

[327]McCarthy, *Treaty and Covenant*, 229 n.30, 233 n.35, 284; Woudstra, *Joshua*, 20, 353 n.7; Boling, *Joshua*, 533; Sperling, "Joshua 24," 121f.

[328]Giblin, "Structural Patterns," 50f.

[329]Giblin, "Structural Patterns," 50.

[330]Giblin, "Structural Patterns," 50.

a. sevenfold dialogue marked by the *wyqtl* form of *'mr*
b. "Joshua" 7 times
c. "people" 7 times
d. 7 imperatives after *w'th* (5x in 14b-15b + 2x in 23)
e. in 14a-25b *yhwh* and *'bd* occur 14 times each
f. 7 pron. suf., pers. pron. etc. to refer to *yhwh* in 14a-25b
g. convergence in dialogue of 14th occurrence of *yhwh*, 12th of *'lhym*, 14th of *'bd*, and 7th pronominal reference to *yhwh*
h. 7 actions of Yahweh in vss. 5b-7 (5a eliminated as not original)
i. 7 times mention of "you" and "your fathers" in vss.5c-7
j. 7th occurrence of "father(s)," "Egypt," "cross" and "land" found in the profession of the people (vss. 17-18); ("and Egypt" in 14c is omitted as not original)
k. 7 verbs with Yahweh as subject (6x in 2-4, + 1x in 13a = 7x)
l. 7 verbs with Yahweh as subject in 8-12
m. 7 *wyqtl* verbs used of enemy in 8-12
n. 12x people as dir. obj. of vb., or as obj.-suf. of a prep. in 8-12

We have necessarily presented Giblin's results in some detail because without these specifics it is impossible to judge his approach. An evaluation is best conducted upon two levels, firstly regarding methodology and secondly pertaining to the credibility of the results. Since the second concern is contingent upon the former, we begin with an analysis of his methodology. Giblin acknowledges that his method depends upon a correct determination of the boundaries of the literary pericope within which to count the various elements. Giblin accepts Josh. 24:1-25 as a literary unit. He does so on the basis of a presupposed covenant-form reflected in the dialogue (vss.1-24), with a concluding covenantal act at Shechem (vs.25) forming an inclusion with vs.1.[331] In this delimitation he has simply followed the opinion of Muilenburg, who states, "It is not denied that vss.26-28 belong to the tradition, but they are not within the literary unit."[332] The only criterion upon which this judgment is defended is the alleged inclusions formed by Shechem (vss.1,25), and "Yahweh the God of Israel" (vss.2b,23b). Of course Giblin might argue that his results present *ad hoc* support for this delimitation, but to admit these results as evidence for the delineation of the pericope would entail circular rea-

[331]Giblin, "Structural Patterns," 51.
[332]Muilenburg, "Form and Structure," 358.

soning.

There are convincing reasons for rejecting Muilenburg's delimitation of the perimeters of the text. That a new pericope begins in 24:1 is indubitable. Separation upwards is universally recognized in the statement that Joshua gathered all the tribes of Israel together at Shechem. Further support can be adduced from the presence of the *petuchah* in the Masoretic text.[333]

Separation upwards is thus clear. Separation downwards, as most scholars have sensed, falls more convincingly after vs.28 than after vs.25. For this we adduce the following support: (1) Vs.28 is followed by a *petuchah.* (2) It is virtually impossible to see vss.26-28 as an independent literary unit because the content is dependent upon vs.25 specifically, and the preceding verses in general. (3) The phrase *wykrt yhwš'* in vs.25 is paralleled by Joshua's actions in the following verses, i.e., *wyktb yhwš', wyqḥ, wyqymh* (vs.26), *wy'mr yhwš'* (vs.27), and *wyšlḥ yhwš'* (vs.28). (4) A more satisfactory inclusion than the Shechem || Shechem correspondence is provided by vss.1a,28; cf. *wy'sp yhwš' 't-kl-šbṭy yśr'l škm* || *wyšlḥ yhwš' 't-h'm 'yš lnḥltw.* (5) An additional inclusion is present in the phrase *wy'mr yhwš' 'l-kl-h'm* found in identical form in vss.2,27. In all other similar phrases in the intervening verses of the MT, the *kl* is absent.[334] (6) Mention of Shechem in vs.25 is used deliberately to show how vss.25-28 bring to a conclusion the matters begun in vs.1. It therefore does have a literary purpose, but not that of inclusion in the sense intended by Muilenburg and Giblin. (7) There is a *setumah* after vs.26, which would make this a more probable candidate than vs.25 for separation downwards. But in this case the *setumah* is placed in accord with the final speech of Joshua in vs.27, thereby in all probability marking an internal division between sub-units of the text rather than the major literary division, which is marked by the *petuchah* after vs.28. In the light of these arguments the textual division presupposed by Giblin and Muilenburg is untenable.

[333]The *petuchah* and *setumah* are based upon an ancient, often reliable tradition. On their value as markers of separation cf. Korpel–de Moor, "Fundamentals," 201; van der Meer–de Moor, eds., *Structural Analysis*, vii. See also J.M.Oesch, *Petucha und Setuma. Untersuchungen zu einer Überlieferten Gliederung im hebräischen Text des Alten Testament* (Göttingen, 1979), esp. 4-17, 325-368; I.Yeivin, *Introduction to the Tiberian Masorah*, trans. I.J.Revell (Missoula, 1980), 40-42.

[334]Regarding the absence of *kl* in the LXX, and the relative weight to be placed on the textual differences in this verse, consult 3.6.3.

Rejection of vss.1-25 as a self-contained literary unit in Josh. 24 necessarily prompts a complete re-evaluation of Giblin's analysis, and the results are frankly devastating to his entire theory. Sevenfold dialogue expands to eight occurrences; the noun "Joshua" occurs three additional times, and the "people" twice more. Giblin's three prime examples are thereby invalidated. We need not consider all his examples; it will suffice to expose a couple of additional methodological weaknesses. Most of Giblin's numbers are based on smaller portions of the text without a rigorous and objective attempt to define structural units within the passage. The *petuchah* after vs.15 is ignored, and Giblin accordingly counts at times from vss.14-25, at other times within vss.8-12, vss.2-5, and even less credibly, counting at vss.14f. and 23 on the basis of the *w'th* while ignoring intervening material. Two of his cases are based upon textual emendation. The LXX is cited to support deletion of vs.5a but is ignored with regard to the counting of divine names and the "you" and "your fathers," where the LXX also differs from the MT. No justification is made for counting references to *'lhym* which refer either to God or to false gods as components of one category. In short, Giblin's study is methodologically unsound and its results are unconvincing.

Our criticism of Giblin's method is stringent, but a methodology which utilizes number counts must be able to pass the most rigorous requirements if it is to have any credibility. Numerical schematizations can easily be misleading. There are always various "key" nouns or verbal forms that can be counted, but only those yielding satisfactory results usually end up tabulated in the final presentation. Furthermore, almost any number can become a "key" number or part of a numerical combination. This is not to categorically deny the possibility of numerical totals playing a significant role in the final composition of a given text, but it is necessary to voice reservations about the measure of control which can be employed to objectively evaluate the results of such statistical studies.[335]

[335]Perhaps the most industrious advocate of numerical schematizations as a compositional and structural device, is the Dutch scholar C.J.Labuschagne. See his "The Pattern of the Divine Speech Fromulas in the Pentateuch," *VT* 32 (1982) 268-296; "Additional Remarks on the Pattern of the Divine Speech Formulas in the Pentateuch," *VT* 34 (1984) 91-95; "Pentateuchal Patterns: A Reply to P.R.Davies and D.M.Gunn," *VT* 34 (1984) 407-413; "On the Structural Use of Numbers as a Compositional Technique," *JNSL* 12 (1984) 87-99; "The Literary and Theological Function of Divine Speech in the Pentateuch," *SVT* 36 (Leiden, 1985), 154-173;

### 2.6.3 Need for a new analysis of structure

Our initial observations regarding the role played by structural analyses in various approaches to Josh. 24:1-28 demonstrate that conclusions regarding the final literary arrangement of the passage are critical for an understanding of its purpose and thematic development. Matters of structure have been weighed to varying degrees in respective attempts to ascertain the date and nature of its composition. Some have argued on the basis of structure for the internal unity of the passage; others, on the basis of structure, assert a complex history of textual expansion or supplementation. The form-critical studies border on structural analysis but fail to provide a complete analysis of the passage's literary arrangement. Little attention has been given within the form-critical approaches to the question of possible theological influence upon the final form of this passage in contrast to extra-biblical treaties. A structural analysis is an indispensable component of a methodology which attempts to understand a passage as complex and intricate as Josh. 24:1-28. Since previous attempts to clarify the literary structure are either incomplete or not convincing, it will be necessary to undertake a new analysis.

## 2.7 Conclusions

The conclusions attained in the preceding sections can be briefly summarized in order to focus the present state of research in Josh. 24. Recent tendencies to question the evidence for an E or JE source are justified. Various elements of the chapter remain inexplicable in attempts to strictly correlate Josh. 24 with a limited strand or strands within the Pentateuch. However, recent approaches which have rejected the previous E or JE positions have not been rigorous enough in reviewing the criteria by which previous source critics designated various words, phrases or entire verses as later glosses. Current studies reject the Hexateuchal theories with respect to source criticism, but all too frequently they retain the same criteria for distinguishing later redactional activity that were formulated in conjunction with

"Divine Speech," 111-126; "De literairkritische methode," in A.S.van der Woude, ed., *Inleiding tot de studie van het Oude Testament* (Kampen, 1986), 102-127; *Deuteronomium* (Kampen, 1988). Cf. also a recent example by the New Testament scholar J.Smit Sibinga, "Some Observations on the Composition of Psalm xlvii," *VT* 38 (1988) 474-480.

the Hexateuchal positions. Recent attempts to view Josh. 24:1-28 as a Dtic/Dtistic creation from the 7th century or later are not convincing. Similarly, recent form-critical attempts to either coax the passage into a treaty mould, or to disqualify certain elements from comparison with the extra-biblical texts, also exemplify serious methodological weaknesses. In view of the complexity of this situation, it is understandable that most recent studies have opted to assert that Josh. 24:1-28 contains an ancient tradition with subsequent redaction. But this conclusion, though probably correct, is too vague to be satisfying. Unfortunately, attempts to be more precise quickly part ways, producing an incredible variety of theories. The preceding discussion has posited certain weaknesses in all these approaches. In order to achieve a more convincing treatment, it will be necessary to seek new ways of analyzing the passage.

At present the most likely place to develop a new approach to Josh. 24:1-28 is in the area of structural analysis, broadly understood as the pursuit of a thorough, methodologically defensible analysis of the literary structure of this passage. Such an analysis, if attainable, may be expected to remedy some of the inadequacies of previous form-critical approaches. If a deliberate literary structure is discernible in Josh. 24:1-28, it should provide important clues with respect to the passage's original purpose and intention. It may also be hoped that such an analysis would yield added insight by which previous allegations regarding redactions and glosses may be tested. All the methods delineated above depend to some extent, whether explicitly or implicitly, upon conclusions regarding the literary structure of the passage. Yet, this has been the area most inadequately treated in previous research. Consequently, selection of the area of structural analysis as a starting point for new and intensive research is not an attempt to supplant the previous methods of analysis, but rather to remedy a most obvious weakness, in the hope that new insights with respect to literary structure may provide a means to supplement, correct, refine and advance previous analyses.

# 3 Structural Analysis of Josh. 24:1-28

## 3.1 The concept of poetic narrative

Our opening chapter began with a consideration of the work of Wellhausen. But one must go much further back in the history of interpretation to find evidence of positions which view Josh. 24:1-28 as a poetic composition. Moses ibn Ezra (c. 1055–after 1135),[1] a Spanish Jew who was himself an accomplished poet, argued in an Arabic treatise on rhetoric and poetry that Josh. 24:1 marks the beginning of a composition which is prose rather than poetry.[2] His treatment of this text, along with a few other passages which were thought to be borderline cases between poetry and prose, was prompted, at least in part, by a series of questions from a friend regarding the nature of Hebrew poetry.[3] Ibn Ezra compared Josh. 24:1 to the Arabic *ḫuṭba*. This in itself amounts to a concession that it is not ordinary prose. The *ḫuṭba* has been described as "a highly parallelistic Arabic style used in sermons, which in turn is distinguished from ordinary prose by its being 'constructed in [poetic] lines but unrhymed'."[4] What then is the deciding factor which prohibited Ibn Ezra from calling Josh. 24:1ff. and other *ḫuṭba*-like passages poetry? Ibn Ezra allowed for poetry in only three OT books, namely, Psalms, Job and Proverbs, and even here he was constrained to qualify his conclusion with the observation that this type of poetry is typified by neither rhyme nor meter in the sense of the Arabic *rajaz* poetry.[5] By this standard even the songs (*šyrwt*) in the OT outside of Psalms are not poetry.

It is our intention in the present chapter to reintroduce the question of whether Josh. 24:1-28 is actually a certain type of poetry, to be precise, narrative poetry. In the preceding chapter of this study the conclusion has been drawn that there is good reason for attempting a new analysis of literary structure. The present endeavor seeks to contribute towards that goal.

[1]*Encyclopaedia Judaica* (Jerusalem and New York, 1971), 8:1170 (this article is based on information from *Encyclopaedia Hebraica*).

[2]M.ibn Ezra, *Kitab al-Muḥāḍara wal Mudhākara*, ed. A.S.Halkin (Jerusalem, 1975), 21; Kugel, *Idea*, 133 n.90.

[3]*Encyclopaedia Judaica*, op. cit., 1171.

[4]Kugel, *Idea*, 131.

[5]Kugel, *Idea*, 132f.; R.Gordis, *Poets, Prophets, and Sages: Essays in Biblical Interpretation* (Bloomington and London, 1971), 63, 90.

Advancements in theories of OT poetics since the rediscovery of parallelism by R.Lowth[6] demonstrate that it is untenable to restrict OT poetry to the Psalms, Proverbs and Job. While the broader presence of poetry throughout the OT is now universally accepted, there is not yet a consensus on precisely how to differentiate between poetic and non-poetic texts. A comparison of various editions of the published text of the Hebrew Bible demonstrates that with respect to the question of identifying poetry or prose there is at times variance of opinion regarding large sections of text. Isa. 44:9-20 is written in BHS as poetry while previously in BHK it was printed as prose.[7] Ezek. 28 was presented as poetry in BHK but is treated as prose in BHS. Isa. 37:30-35 is repeated in 2 Kgs 19:29-34, but whereas the former text is printed as poetry, in the same edition of BHS the latter verses appear as prose.[8] It is especially in the area of the major prophets that recent scholarship has demonstrated a restlessness about accepting previously set boundaries for what is poetic.[9] But the problem is by no means restricted to the major prophets. In his commentaries on Genesis[10] and Exodus,[11] Cassuto frequently expressed his opinion that many verses in the Pentateuch are in fact poetic.[12] Numerous covenantal passages in the Pentateuch have in

[6]R.Lowth, *De Sacra Poesi Hebraeorum* (Oxonii, 1753) (ET: *Lectures on the Sacred Poetry of the Hebrews*, trans. G.Gregory [London, 1787; reprint ed., Hildesheim, 1969 and New York, 1971].

[7]See the conclusion by C.R.North, *The Second Isaiah* (Oxford, 1964), 139: "Parallelism is discernible throughout but it is not great poetry."

[8]For additional examples see J.Blenkinsopp, "Stylistics of Old Testament Poetry," *Bibl* 44 (1963) 32; Kugel, *Idea*, 77-84.

[9]An incomplete but telling list of articles which have attempted to demonstrate the presence of poetry in passages treated traditionally as prose may be found in Watson, *Classical Hebrew Poetry*, 59-62, 456. Many additional bibliographical references are listed in the footnotes below.

[10]U.Cassuto, *A Commentary on the Book of Genesis*, 2 vols., trans. I.Abrahams (Jerusalem, 1961-64).

[11]U.Cassuto, *A Commentary on the Book of Exodus*, trans. I.Abrahams (Jerusalem, 1967), esp. 2.

[12]See too his article "The Israelite Epic," in *Biblical and Oriental Studies*, 2:69-109 (= *Keneset* 8 [1943] 121-142 Hebrew); further, "Biblical and Canaanite Literature," ibid, 16-59. Cassuto is but one of many who seek an epic background for certain Pentateuchal narratives in order to explain their "poetry-like" character. The question of a possible epic and poetic background is widely disputed. See S.Mowinckel, "Hat es ein israelitisches Nationalepos gegeben?" *ZAW* 53 (1935) 130-152; Cross, *Canaanite Myth*, passim; F.I.Andersen, *The Sentence in Biblical Hebrew* (The Hague and Paris, 1974), 123-126.; S.Talmon, "The 'Comparative Method' in

particular spawned queries concerning a possible poetic format, e.g., Gen. 12:1-3;[13] 31:42ff.;[14] Ex. 19:3-6;[15] 33:12-17;[16] Lev. 26:3-45;[17] Deut. 27:15-26;[18] and the covenantal curses in Deut. 28, [19] along with many scattered verses.[20] These examples illustrate that a search for unidentified poetry in the OT is by no means far-fetched.[21] Numer-

Biblical Interpretation–Principles and Problems," in *Congress Volume, Göttingen 1977*, *SVT* 29 (Leiden, 1978), 320-356; "Did There Exist a Biblical National Epic?" in *Proceedings 7th World Congress of Jewish Studies, 1977* (Jerusalem, 1981), 41-62; C.Conroy, "Hebrew Epic: Historical Notes and Critical Reflections," *Bibl* 61 (1980) 1-30; Cross, "Epic Traditions," 13-39.

[13]Cassuto, *Genesis*, 2:309, 315; J.Gray, *The Legacy of Canaan*, 2nd ed. *VTS* 5 (Leiden, 1965), 308; Cross, "Epic Traditions," 21 n.25.

[14]Cf. the comments offered by Koch ("păḥăd jiṣḥaq," 109-115), where numerous poetic characteristics are noted.

[15]Cross, "Epic Traditions," 21-22.

[16]J.Muilenburg, "The Intercession of the Covenant Mediator (Exodus 33:1a, 12-17)," in P.R.Ackroyd–B.Lindars, eds., *Words and Meanings: Essays Presented to David Winton Thomas* (Cambridge, 1968), 164-166. Muilenburg appeals to J.A.Bruno, *Die Bücher Genesis-Exodus. Eine rhythmische Untersuchung* (Stockholm, 1953). Muilenburg is cognizant of the reservations most scholars would have of Bruno's methodology, but he states that at least Bruno's analysis demonstrates the rhythms which may have been behind the present text, and Muilenburg in turn presents the text in what he sees as a quasi-poetic format.

[17]Cf. H.Graf Reventlow, *Wächter über Israel. Ezechiel und seine Tradition* (Berlin, 1962), 4-42, 157f.; K.Elliger, *Leviticus* (Tübingen, 1966), 364-367; D.R.Hillers, *Treaty-Curses and the Old Testament Prophets* (Rome, 1964), 30-42; P.Buis, "Comment au septième siècle envisageait-on l'avenir de l'Alliance? Étude de Lv.26,3-45," in Brekelmans, ed., *Questions disputées*, 131-140.

[18]See already the comments by Mowinckel, in a chapter entitled "Die zweigliederige Segens- und Fluchformel in Kult und Psalmdichtung," in *Psalmenstudien*, 5:97-129.

[19]Cf. Hillers, *Treaty-Curses*, 30-42.

[20]Cf., e.g., W.F.Albright, *Yahweh and the Gods of Canaan* (London, 1968), 33 (re Ex. 14:3); F.I.Andersen, "A Lexicographical Note on Exodus xxxii 18," *VT* 16 (1966) 108 (re Ex. 32:18); B.Porten–U.Rappaport, "Poetic Structure in Genesis ix 7," *VT* 21 (1971) 363-369 (re Gen. 1:22; 9:7); Cross, *Canaanite Myth*, 167-168 (re Ex.40:34); J.S.Kselman, "Semantic-Sonant Chiasmus in Biblical Poetry," *Bibl* 58 (1977) 220 (re Gen. 27:36); "The Recovery of Poetic Fragments from the Pentateuchal Priestly Source," *JBL* 97 (1978) 161-173 (re Gen. 1:2,5,10,16,20,27; 5:1; 17:6,17; 35:11; Ex. 16:3,8,12; 40:38; Num. 14:2; 17:7; Deut. 34:7); R.Althann, "Unrecognized Poetic Fragments in Exodus," *JNSL* 11 (1983) 9-27 (Ex. 14:20; 16:8; 17:16; 18:10-12; 23:2; 32:35; 34:19); L.M.Barré, "The Poetic Structure of Genesis 9:5," *ZAW* 96 (1984) 101-104; cf. the reference by de Moor to "zeer oude poëtische fragmenten" with references to God as El in the patriarchal narratives, e.g., Gen. 12:2; 14:19f.; 16:11; 17:2,5; 35:11 (*Uw God*, 50-55).

[21]Cf. the conclusion by L.Alonso-Schökel, *Das Alte Testament als literarisches Kunstwerk* (Köln, 1971), e.g., 120: "Der Schritt von der Prosa zum Vers ist derart

ous attempts to demonstrate such poetry have appealed to possible covenantal and liturgical settings, perhaps stemming originally from Northern traditions.

However, the attempts here listed to identify poetry have generally been impeded by uncertainty with respect to whether or not meter is indigenous and indispensable to Hebrew poetry,[22] and until some consensus can be attained as to whether OT poetry is metrical, it will be most difficult to agree on how to formulate a basic definition of poetry, including *narrative poetry*. The problem of meter has been widely discussed from a great variety of perspectives but it would now appear that the conclusion is sluggishly being accepted that meter is not an indispensable hallmark of Northwest Semitic poetry.[23] Most important is the observation that poetic texts in parallel transmission have been proven to contain variant forms of the same cola. The

abgestuft, dass die Grenzen zwischen rhythmischer Prosa und freiem Vers fliessend sind." Cf. his observations regarding rhythm, e.g., in Lev. 24:1-5; Judg. 2:16-32; Deut. 34:1ff.; Num. 20:14-20 (ibid., 123). See too his *A Manual*, e.g., 42-44. Attempts to identify larger portions of poetry in Deuteronomy can be found in G.Braulik, *Die Mittel Deuteronomischer Rhetorik* (Rome, 1978) (re Deut. 4:1-40); D.L.Christensen, "Prose and Poetry in the Bible: The Narrative Poetics of Deuteronomy 1:9-18," *ZAW* 97 (1985) 179-189; C.Schedl, "Prosa und Dichtung in der Bibel. Logotechnische Analyse von Dtn 1,9-18," *ZAW* 98 (1986) 271-275.

[22]The question of meter was the fundamental norm employed in the effort to distinguish poetry and prose by E.König, "Poesie und Prosa in der althebräischen Literatur abgegrenzt," *ZAW* 37 (1917-18) 145-187, 245-250; *ZAW* 38 (1919-20) 23-53.

[23]The literature on meter is too vast to cite, but regarding a rejection of traditional metrical presuppositons consider, e.g., the conclusion by H.Kosmala, "Form and Structure in Ancient Hebrew Poetry," *VT* 14 (1964), 423-445; II, *VT* 16 (1966) 152-180. He states that "modern efforts in finding out the principles of Hebrew 'meter' were doomed to failure" because they scan verses according to the principles of Greek and Latin poetry (424). See especially de Moor, "Art of Versification, I," 119-139; M.O'Connor, *Hebrew Verse Structure* (Winona Lake, 1980), 138; W.S.LaSor, "Samples of Early Semitic Poetry," in G.Rendsburg et al., eds., *The Bible World: Essays in Honor of C.H.Gordon* (New York, 1980), 99, 120; Kugel, *Idea*, 70-76; R.Alter, *The Art of Biblical Poetry* (New York, 1985), 9; Korpel–de Moor, "Fundamentals," 174, 178-180; D.Pardee, *Ugaritic and Hebrew Poetic Parallelism: A Trial Cut ('nt I and Proverbs 2)* (Leiden, 1988), esp. 195f. Significantly, in recent study of Egyptian poetry the issue of meter is also strongly contested as a means of distinguishing poetry and prose, cf. I.Shirun-Grumach, "Bemerkungen zu Rhythmus, Form und Inhalt in der Weisheit," in E.Hornung–O.Keel, eds., *Studien zu altägyptischen Lebenslehren* (Göttingen and Freiburg, 1979), 318-322. The same is true in contemporary analysis of Sumerian poetry, cf. P.Michalowski, "Carminitive Magic: Towards an Understanding of Sumerian Poetics," *ZA* 71 (1981) 1-18.

present analysis therefore accepts as adequately demonstrated the tenet that metrical considerations do not provide an adequate criteria by which to determine what is or is not poetry in biblical Hebrew.

Similarly, differentiation theories based strictly upon either internal parallelism or prose particle counts offer inadequate criterion by which to distinguish between poetic and non-poetic compositions. This point has been argued previously by the present author,[24] but it is necessary to add a number of comments to the brief previous discussion. The method of the so-called prose particle counts works with a tabulation of the frequency of the direct object marker *'t*, the definite article *h*, and the relative particle *'šr*, within a given passage of biblical Hebrew.[25] The advocates of this theory have demonstrated that in what is generally considered to be ancient biblical poetry there is an absence or paucity of these particles. Their findings are therefore consistent with a known characteristic of other ancient Northwest Semitic literature.[26] But what has not yet been demonstrated is that the principle can be extrapolated to such a degree that it constitutes a valid basis upon which to differentiate poetic and non-poetic compositions in the present text of the Hebrew Bible. Freedman himself, when dealing with allegedly archaic poetry and when attempting to discern certain accentual patterns, has no reservations about ignoring as later accretions the presence of initial conjunctions,[27] or of seeing the presence of particles such as *'šr* to be the "prose adaptation of the original poetic formula."[28]

[24]See Koopmans, "Joshua 23," 83-90, 116.

[25]D.N.Freedman, "Pottery, Poetry and Prophecy: An Essay on Biblical Poetry," *JBL* 96 (1977) 6; "Another Look at Biblical Hebrew Poetry," in E.R.Follis, ed., *Directions in Biblical Hebrew Poetry* (Sheffield, 1987), 11-29; F.I.Andersen–A.D.Forbes, "'Prose Particle' Counts of the Hebrew Bible," in Meyers–O'Connor, eds., *Word of the Lord*, 165-183.

[26]S.Segert, *A Basic Grammar of the Ugaritic Language* (Berkeley, 1984), 15; F.M.Cross–D.N.Freedman, "Some Observations on Early Hebrew," *Bibl* 53 (1972) 418f.

[27]E.g., "Archaic Forms," 101-107; see also Geller, *Parellism*, 46.

[28]Freedman, "God of Moses," 154; F.M.Cross–D.N.Freedman, *Studies in Ancient Yahwistic Poetry* (Missoula, 1975) [orig. 1950], 19, 25, 28. See too Geller, *Parallelism*, 46 n.36. Similarly, when Cross attempts to demonstrate that Ex. 40:34 was originally poetic, he deletes the direct object marker (*Canaanite Myth*, 168). To say that the verse is prose with the markers and poetry without them would be reductionistic with respect to the essence of poetic composition, which in turn argues that the so-called prose particles provide inadequate criterion upon which to distinguish poetry.

The conclusion that the particle *'šr* could have been added in many poetic texts at a later date is highly probable. For example, comparison of Num. 24:4 with 24:16 suggests that the *'šr* in the former verse is a later insertion into archaic poetry. Along the same line, when Cross attempts to demonstrate the poetic nature of Ex. 19:3-6 he strips the text of its prose particles.[29] This already implies that greater caution is in order when asserting the utility of the presence of such particles in the present text for demonstrating the difference between poetic and non-poetic composition.[30] Furthermore, the extensive study by Andersen–Forbes demonstrates that a number of the Psalms have a score which, when judged against the standards adopted for this method of analysis, would call into question their identity as pure poetry.[31] Whereas the *absence* of such particles in certain OT poetry may in general be accepted as an archaic or archaizing feature, the *presence* of such particles could be due to later editing. Or again, in other poetic texts they may imply a date of composition at which time the older characteristic was already fading.[32] Watson is therefore justified in listing the absence of "prose particles" as a valuable indicator of poetic composition.[33] This is the lasting benefit of the studies by Freedman, Andersen and Forbes.

But this does not entail conversely that the presence of such par-

[29]Cross, "Epic Traditions," 21f.

[30]In its complex history of transmission, the OT texts must have been edited many times to comply with contemporary grammatical preferences, but such editing need not have been consistently applied to all of what is now in the OT canon, cf. F.M.Cross, "Biblical Archaeology Today: The Biblical Aspect," in Amitai, ed., *Biblical Archaeology Today*, 10. J.MacDonald has argued extensively that the employment of the particle *'t* underwent a long and complex history of development; it is not surprising that its presence in the OT is now diverse, that its redaction into older poetry took place in an incomplete manner, and that there must have been a gradual shift from the period in which it was absent to the time when it was employed profusely ("The Particle *'t* in Classical Hebrew: Some New Data on its Use with the Nominative," *VT* 14 [1964] 264-275). See also J.Hoftijzer, "Remarks Concerning the Use of the Particle *'t* in Classical Hebrew," *OTS* 14 (Leiden, 1965), 1-99, esp. 80-88.

[31]Andersen–Forbes, "'Prose Particle' Counts," 166.

[32]To provide another example, the construct form *'pr h'rṣ* in Isa. 40:12 differs from all other poetic occurrences which lack the article (Am. 2:7; 2 Sam. 22:43; Job 14:19), thereby agreeing formally with the construct form in all so-called prose occurrences; see Y.Avishur, *Stylistic Studies of Word-Pairs in Biblical and Ancient Semitic Literatures* (Neukirchen-Vluyn, 1984), 352. Yet this certainly does not call into question the poetic character of Isa. 40:12.

[33]Watson, *Classical Hebrew Poetry*, 54.

ticles can prove that a given text is *non-poetic*. In fact, upon occasion one even encounters poetic parallelisms such as *'šr* || *'šr*.[34] When all these considerations are taken together, one is forced to accept the conclusion that such "prose particles" do not provide adequate criterion for determining whether the present form of a text is poetic, let alone the possibility that a previous form of the text could have been poetic, but later during the history of transmission was redacted as prose.[35] Finally, in their evaluation of the statistical results, Freedman, Andersen and Forbes have not made any attempt to account for the possibility of poetic narrative, which if accepted as a genre of poetry considerably complicates the entire picture of the relationship between poetic and non-poetic textual identity.

Recent research in the area of biblical Hebrew poetry is suggestive that the most promising area in which to pursue the essence of poetic composition lies in a colometric approach with particular attention given to parallelism. However, the more research that is done in this area, in a sense the more complex the matter becomes. It is safe to conclude that the working categorizations proposed by Lowth have definitively been left behind for a more sophisticated appreciation of the multiple types of parallelism extant in biblical Hebrew poetry, as is evident from a survey of recent monographs[36] and articles[37]

[34]E.g., Lam. 1:12; 2:17; Ps. 89:52(51); Hos. 2:1(1:10); 2:14(12), etc., and for additional examples see below regarding int. par. at vs.15.

[35]Consult further Koopmans, "Joshua 23," 85-88.

[36]This starting point is shared by all major recent works on parallelism and need not be elaborated here. Cf. G.B.Gray, *The Forms of Hebrew Poetry* (Oxford, 1915; reprint ed. New York, 1972), 37-83; T.Collins, *Line-Forms in Hebrew Poetry: A Grammatical Approach to the Stylistic Study of the Hebrew Prophets* (Rome, 1978), 5-22; Geller, *Parallelism*, 375-385; P.van der Lugt, *Strofische structuren in de bijbels-hebreeuwse poëzie* (Kampen, 1980), 170-208; O'Connor, *Verse Structure*, 88-96; Kugel, *Idea*, 1-58; Watson, *Classical Hebrew Poetry*, 114-159; Berlin, *Dynamics*, 1-17; Zurro, *Procedimientos*, 7; Pardee, *Poetic Parallelism*, 168ff.

[37]E.g., M.Dahood, "Ugaritic-Hebrew Syntax and Style," *UF* 1 (1969) 15-36; P.B.Yoder, "A-B Pairs and Oral Composition in Hebrew Poetry," *VT* 21 (1971) 470-489; W.G.E.Watson, "The Pivot Pattern in Hebrew, Ugaritic and Akkadian Poetry," *ZAW* 88 (1976) 239-253; "Gender-Matched Synonymous Prallelism in the OT," *JBL* 99 (1980) 321-341; D.Grossberg, "Noun/Verb Parallelism: Syntactic or Ansyntactic?" *JBL* 99 (1980) 481-488; J.S.Kselman, "The ABCB Pattern: Further Examples," *VT* 32 (1982) 224-229; J.T.Willis, "Alternating (ABÁB́) Parallelism in the Old Testament Psalms and Prophetic Literature," in Follis, ed., *Directions*, 49-76; ibid., D.J.A.Clines, "The Parallelism of Greater Precision," 77-100. This is but a sampling of the more important works. For more complete bibliography consult the works listed here, the monographs in the previous footnote; A.Baker,

specifically treating parallelism. Contemporary research concentrates largely upon various aspects of semantic, grammatical and syntactical parallelism, all of which have been demonstrated to be of importance for postulating a complete picture of how parallelism operates in biblical Hebrew. Yet, one must be cautious about claiming these types of parallelism as constituting a dividing principle between poetry and prose because taken individually examples of all these types of parallelism are documented in the OT in passages traditionally treated as non-poetic.[38] Recognition of the multiplicity of parallelism operative in the OT on the one hand complicates the matter of poetry and prose, which has traditionally been too superficially treated, and on the other hand it provides new methods for a more systematic analysis of how respective cola can stand parallel to each other, thereby assisting in the recognition of poetry in passages previously not identified as such.

The present study assumes the working hypothesis that parallelism is essential to OT Hebrew poetry and any search for parallelism must recognize that it can manifest itself variously. For example, the phenomenon of parallelism is frequently operative as internal responsions created by paired words or phrases at the level of the poetic verse. This phenomenon has been widely studied in connection with comparable Northwest Semitic languages, especially Ugaritic[39] and Phoenician.[40] The history and relevance of this area of research is succinctly summarized in previous studies and need not be repeated here.[41] Recognition of internal parallelisms, many of which find a counterpart elsewhere in the OT or in extra-biblical poetry, is therefore one helpful avenue towards the demonstration of poetic structure.[42] Accordingly in the following analysis of parallelism

"Parallelism: England's Contribution to Biblical Studies," *CBQ* 35 (1973) 429-440; O.Loretz–I.Kottsieper, *Colometry in Ugaritic Poetry: Itroduction, Illustrations and Topical Bibliography* (Altenberge [1987]).

[38]This point is already stressed by Gray (*Forms*, 38-46).

[39]See especially M.Dahood–T.Penar, "Ugaritic-Hebrew Parallel Pairs," in L.R.Fisher, ed., *RSP, I* (Rome, 1972), 71-382; M.Dahood, "Ugaritic-Hebrew Parallel Pairs," *RSP, II* (Rome, 1975), 1-39; "Ugaritic-Hebrew Parallel Pairs," in S.Rummel, ed., *RSP, III* (Rome, 1981), 1-206.

[40]Y.Avishur, "Word Pairs Common to Phoenician and Biblical Hebrew," *UF* 7 (1975) 13-47; *Stylistic Studies* (with attention to biblical Hebrew, Ugaritic, Akkadian, Phoenician and Aramaic).

[41]See Dahood–Penar, "Parallel Pairs, I," 73-88; Avishur, *Stylistic Studies*, 1-49.

[42]Kselman, "Poetic Fragments," esp. 163, 172f., and the methodology assumed

in Josh. 24:1-28 references will be made where relevant to previous studies in which a given parallelism has been posited. Furthermore, the present author has made grateful employment of a computer concordance program by means of which it was possible to get an accurate list of all potentially parallel occurences of a given word-pair throughout the OT. Naturally, particular focus is directed to those pairs which occur in universally recognized poetry, but it would be a mistake to restrict a search for parallelistic use of words to these texts. As is evident in the lists published by Dahood and Avishur, classical word-pairs or fixed pairs are also found in passages which have not traditionally been treated as poetry. This is in keeping with the emphasis of the present study, and it would be an error in methodology to overlook the significance of such parallelisms. Verses cited in support of parallelism in passages which are printed in BHS as prose but are known to have been posited by other authors to be poetic, "quasi-poetic" or "rhythmic prose" are accompanied by the relevant bibliographical data. Upon occassion the present study identifies the presence of supporting poetic verses which have previously gone unrecognized, but the scope of this study has demanded that such examples be held to a minimum.

However, the presence of internal parallelism of corresponding words or phrases is but one dimension. That is to say, parallelism can also be created *between* rather than *within* poetic verses, thereby establishing *external parallelism.*[43] The presence of external parallelism has been noted previously to be of considerable importance for the identification of narrative poetry, and it seems to be a particular characteristic of this genre.[44] Accordingly the present study includes a detailed list of possible external as well as internal parallelism.

The fact that a given word-pair is used elsewhere in poetry does not yet prove that the contiguity of the same elements in the present passage is to be attributed to conscious parallelism. However, it is most instructive to evaluate the cumulative evidence derived from a tabulation of all such potential parallelisms.[45] This accordingly con-

throughout his article.

[43]Note that Pardee, for example, works with the same principle, which he calls "distant parallelism."

[44]De Moor, "Book of Ruth, I," 264; II, 46; Koopmans, "Joshua 23," 116.

[45]The term "potential parallelism" is employed here to reflect the consideration that whether a given combination indeed constituted a deliberate parallelism should be judged in part upon the cumulative evidence for the use of parallelism in the

stitutes a fundamental step in our colometric approach. Our list of potential parallelisms in Josh. 24:1-28 includes primarily word-pairs demonstrated elsewhere to be employed in deliberate poetic parallelism, whether in the OT or in extra-biblical ancient NE texts. Also included in our list are combinations which have a clearly synonymous or antithetical function in the present passage, as are repetitions of a given root[46] when they occur, for example, in more than one colon of a given verse (forming int. par.) or in more than one verse of a strophe (forming ext. par.). As is indicated above, detection of such internal and external connections does not yet exhaust the potential for researching various aspects of parallelism; recent research in OT poetry has demonstrated that parallelism can also be established via grammatical, syntactical and sonant connections. Therefore, upon occasion our lists also include examples of these types of parallelism. However, since additional research in the latter areas will be necessary before they can be employed with much confidence in an attempt to distinguish genres of poetry—especially narrative poetry—it would be hazardous at this stage to base major conclusions upon grammatical or syntactical aspects of parallelism.

In view of the foregoing discussion, it is possible to summarize the considerations which demonstrate the desirability of a new analysis of Josh. 24:1-28 as a composition possibly written in the genre of poetic narrative. As noted above, medieval Jewish scholars, though reluctant to admit the presence of poetry in the OT, concluded that Josh. 24:1ff. was not ordinary prose. Along a similar vein, in a recent study of the historical psalms, Kühlewein is inclined to speak of Ex. 15, Judg. 5, and Josh. 24 as "psalmähnliche Texte."[47] Many scholars have argued that Josh. 24:1-28 has a liturgical character,[48] a factor which if defensible is suggestive of a possible poetic composition.[49] The present author has attempted to demonstrate elsewhere that the farewell speeches in Josh. 23[50] and 1 Kgs 2:1-10[51] constitute poetic

passage in its entirety.

[46]On this phenomenon see especially Zurro, *Procidimientos*, passim; Pardee, *Poetic Parallelism*, 6f. and passim.

[47]Kühlewein, *Geschichte*, 10.

[48]See 2.3.7.2.

[49]Watson, *Classical Hebrew Poetry*, 79.

[50]Koopmans, "Joshua 23," 83-118.

[51]W.T.Koopmans, "The Testament of David in 1 Kings ii 1-10," (forthcoming in *VT*).

narratives. Significantly, both these texts are included along with Josh. 24:1ff. in Ibn Ezra's brief list of passages comparable to the Arabic *ḫuṭba*.[52] Although it is not ordinarily considered to be a poetic book,[53] there are sufficient indications to warrant a search for poetry throughout Joshua.[54]

Josh. 24:1-28 contains numerous parallel statements which were employed by previous literary-critical endeavors in a questionable effort to designate variant literary sources. Some of these clauses, such as *'lhym qdšym hw'* and *'l-qnw' hw'* can more justifiably be read as examples of poetic parallelism.[55] We have also noted how vs.22 is structurally similar to Ruth 4:9-11, which has been demonstrated elsewhere to be poetic narrative.[56] The presence in vs.27 of the noun *'mry*, which occurs elsewhere only in poetry, is an additional incentive to pursue the possibility of a poetic narrative. A promising method by which to conduct a structural analysis of Josh. 24:1-28 may be sought in the colometric delineation of poetic texts as advocated by the Kampen school, and which has in other cases proven helpful in the analysis of poetic narratives, both biblical[57] and extra-biblical.

[52]Also included are obviously poetic compositions such as 1 Sam. 2:1ff. and Isa. 5:1ff. For an analysis of the latter passage see M.C.A. Korpel, "The Literary Genre of the Song of the Vineyard (Isa. 5:1-7)," in van der Meer–de Moor, eds., *Structural Analysis* 119-155.

[53]Bruno's idiosyncratic attempt to read Joshua as poetry must be rejected; cf. his *Die Bücher Josua, Richter, Ruth: Eine Rhythmische Untersuchung* (Stockholm, 1955).

[54]BHS inevitably recognizes 10:12c,13a as poetry, but there is much more. Regarding 3:10 and 22:22 see Boling, *Joshua*, 164f., 503. Re 6:26 cf. J.Krašovec, "Merism–Polar Expression in Biblical Hebrew," *Bibl* 64 (1983) 233f. Gevirtz has called attention to the parallelism in Josh. 9:21 of *wyhyw ḥṭby 'ṣym* || *wš'by-mym lkl-h'dh* (cf. 9:23, 27a), which has parallels in the Amarna letters from Tyre as well as in Ugaritic poetry ("Canaanite Rhetoric," 162-177). On Josh. 11:6,9 consult E.Z.Melamed, "Break-up of Stereotype Phrases as an Artistic Device in Biblical Poetry," in Ch.Rabin, ed., *Studies in the Bible* (*ScH* 8; Jerusalem, 1961), 130. Regarding Josh. 15:18-19 consult Albright, *Yahweh and the Gods*, 42f. Along with the present author's article on Josh. 23, this amounts to considerable evidence for the presence of either poetic fragments or poetic narrative in Joshua.

[55]See the discussion in 2.3.7.2, including the conclusions reached by Alonso-Asenjo and McCarthy that the combination is an example of poetic parallelism.

[56]Cf. de Moor, "Book of Ruth, II," 38.

[57]De Moor, "Book of Ruth, I" 262-283; II, 16-46; R.de Hoop, "The Book of Jonah as Poetry: An Analysis of Jonah 1:1-16," in van der Meer–de Moor, eds., *Structural Analysis*, 156-171; Koopmans, "Joshua 23," 83-118; "Testament of David," (forthcoming).

With respect to the extra-biblical evidence for narrative poetry, the Mesha inscription is particularly relevant because the vertical strokes provide incontrovertible evidence that historical texts could be written as poetic narrative.[58] De Moor has also demonstrated the applicability of this method of analysis in a treatment of the Zakkur and Kilamuwa inscriptions.[59] It would now appear that such inscriptions were part of a widespread practice of writing various types of material in poetic format in the ancient NE.[60] When one adds to this the evidence for poetic composition in a wide variety of Ugaritic texts,[61] in the Amarna letters,[62] in the Egyptian narrative poetry of, to mention but one example, the Merenptah stele,[63] as well as additional evidence of narrative poetry,[64] it is clear that various types or genres of poetry were commonplace in the writings of Israel's neighbouring lands, and it should not come as a major surprise to find formal similarities in biblical Hebrew. The task of recognizing and analyzing the fundamental nature of Northwest Semitic poetry, both biblical and extra-biblical, has far to go before it will be possible to speak of reliable differentiation between poetic and non-poetic compositions, let alone classification of the various genres of poetry which now may be assumed to have existed.[65]

[58]J.C.de Moor, "Narrative Poetry in Canaan," *UF* 20 (1988) 149-171. Kugel calls attention to the similarity between the Mesha inscription and biblical poetry (*Idea*, 62f.), but his lack of a method to deal with *narrative poetry* hinders him from drawing maximum benefit from the comparison.

[59]De Moor, "Book of Ruth, I," 269-271; "Narrative Poetry," 160-171.

[60]With respect to ancient Hebrew writings, the Gezer Calendar bears witness to employment of a poetic format; cf. W.F.Albright, "A Catalogue of Early Hebrew Lyric Poems (Psalm LXVIII)," *HUCA* 33 (1950-51) 6f.n.14; Cross–Freedman, "Some Observations on Early Hebrew," 419.

[61]W.G.E.Watson, "The Character of Ugaritic Poetry," *JNSL* 11 (1983) 157-69. Note especially his category "narrative verse."

[62]Cf. Gevirtz, "Canaanite Rhetoric," 162-177; "Evidence of Conjugational Variation in the Parallelization of Selfsame Verbs in the Amarna Letters," *JNES* 32 (1973) 99-104; Avishur, "Word Pairs," 13: "From between the lines of the Akkadian El-Amarna letters peek fragments of poetry and proverbs...."

[63]J.A.Thompson, *The Bible and Archaeology*, 3rd ed. (Grand Rapids, 1982), 64.

[64]E.g., the poetic narrative relating the historical campaign of Shalmaneser, in which caesurae mark the division of the poetic lines. Cf. W.G.Lambert, "The Sultantepe Tablets VIII: Shalmaneser in Ararat," *AnSt* 11 (1961) 143-158; de Moor, "Book of Ruth, I," 271. See too A.Wolters, "Aspects of the Literary Structure of Combination I," (forthcoming in proceedings of the Deir 'Allah Symposium, Leiden 1989).

[65]Watson states, "Very little narrative—even 'heroic narrative'—is cast in poetic

## 3.2 Methodological considerations

The following method of poetic analysis in particular employs insights formulated by advocates of the Kampen school. This approach has been described in detail elsewhere,[66] and for our present purposes, in addition to the remarks offered above, it will be sufficient to briefly summarize the methodology and terminology employed. Josh. 24:1-28 is first presented in colometric format. This colometry is, however, the final product of a detailed and systematic analysis in which an attempt has been made to identify the constitutive elements of poetic composition at the level of cola, verses, strophes, canticles, and cantos as successive units or building-blocks.

1. The **cola**, and their arrangement in poetic **verses**, are distinguished on the basis of internal parallelism[67] and syntax, for which the Masoretic accentuation usually provides a helpful guideline.[68] As in other poetry in the OT, the Masoretic verse is in general longer than the poetic verse, but this does not negate the value of the disjunctive accents for determining the termination of the poetic verse. For example, in the colometry of Josh. 23 there are 34 poetic verses,

form" (*Classical Hebrew Poetry*, 55). This reflects the generally accepted starting point in OT circles. But the growing evidence for the widespread practice of poetic narrative calls for additional study of this matter. Alter denies the presence of narrative poetry in the OT (*Art of Biblical Poetry*, 27f.). He is surely correct that the content and purpose of OT materials differs significantly from the Ugaritic types of epic narrative. But it is not necessary for that reason to conclude that the biblical writers avoided all use of poetic narrative. Alter defines "narrative" such that even the historical psalms, the Song of the Sea, and the Song of Deborah are excluded from his category.

[66]Korpel–de Moor, "Fundamentals," 173-212.

[67]Internal parallelism (Int. || :) refers to that parallelism which is operative between cola of a given verse, while external parallelism (Ext. || :) is operative beyond the given poetic verse.

[68]In general, the higher the degree of internal parallelism the easier it is to determine the parameters of the cola. It therefore follows that in poetic narrative, where the parallelism is often external rather than internal, the determination of the extent of a colon can be difficult. However, this difficulty is by no means restricted to narrative poetry, as is well-known to anyone who has studied the quandary of scansion attempts in Isaiah and Jeremiah. In a recent article, M.DeRoche suggests, "A colon is a series of units in which there is little or no parallelism" ("Is Jeremiah 25:15-29 a Piece of Reworked Jeremianic Poetry?" *JSOT* 10 [1978] 59). DeRoche's definition is taken from Bright and Holladay, but it does not take into account the fact that many cola in Hebrew poetry contain syndetic or asyndetic parataxis, which is also a form of parallelism. For a more elaborate definition of the colon consult Korpel–de Moor, "Fundamentals," 175-181.

of which 16 terminate at a *sillûq*, 13 at an *'atnaḥ*, 3 at a *zāqēp̄ parvum*, 1 at a *s^eḡôltā*, and 1 at a *r^eḇî^a'*, all of which are *disjunctive accents*. The same principle can be extrapolated to the level of the colon. For this reason the transliterated colometric text in the present study includes a codification of the disjunctive accents which stand at the end of cola as presently divided. To indicate the relative weight of these accents a system has been adopted whereby a disjunctive accent at the end of a given colon is represented by a number corresponding to the order of the accents as published in the *tabula accentuum* of BHS. In other words a *sillûq* is marked by [1], an *'atnaḥ* by [2], *s^eḡôltā* [3], *šalšèleṯ* [4], *zāqēp̄ parvum* [5], *zāqēp̄ magnum* [6], *r^eḇî^a'* [7], *ṭip̄ḥā* [8], *zarqā* [9], *pašṭā* [10], *j^eṯîḇ* [11], *t^eḇîr* [12], *gèreš* [13], *garšájim* [14], *pāzēr* [15], *pāzēr magnum* [16], *t^elîšā* [17], *l^eḡarmēh* [18]. Only one colon has been terminated where there is not a disjunctive accent (17aB).[69] In such cases we include an exclamation mark with the conjunctive code.

This representation of the accents is not intended to give the impression that the Masoretic accentuation provides a facile method of colometric division. Such an impression would be patently false. The primary function of the accents does not appear to have been colometrical. Nevertheless, the accents provide one consideration amongst others, e.g., internal parallelism, in determining the extent of the cola. Since the accents attest to how the ancients syntactically divided the sentence, and since they indicate how the manuscript was read according to a certain tradition, they provide a clue as to which words are to be treated together as parts of a unit. Now it so happens that in the colometric division of Josh. 24:1-28 given below, virtually every colon terminates in harmony with a disjunctive accent, and only very seldom was it deemed necessary to break a colon off at an accent which is weaker than another disjunctive accent within the same colon.[70]

[69]This verse in the MT is textually problematic and will be dealt with extensively below.

[70]Cf., for example, the division made at 16aA with the *pašṭā* prior to *wy'mr* rather than following it with the *zāqēp̄ parvum*. The division opted for here is on the basis of the parallelism of *wy'n* and *wy'mr*. Similarly, in 23aA the sense of the colon, the internal parallelism, and the balance of the verse, demands that the *zāqēp̄ magnum* [6] on *w'th* at the beginning of the colon be ignored and a division made at *hnkr*, where there is a *ṭip̄ḥā* [8]. Such cases are surprisingly rare in this text, and it will be of interest to see whether future research confirms such patterns elsewhere.

2. Verses which cohere together in form and content, constitute the next structural unit, the **strophe**. Recognition of strophic division is usually facilitated by formal, literary markers of separation[71] It is at this level that external parallelism[72] within the strophe functions as a factor in determining strophic division.[73] In the colometric justification we employ the symbols Sep. ↑: and Sep. ↓: to indicate arguments of strophic division upwards and downwards respectively. Under these categories we pay particular attention to a listing of the formal markers of separation.
3. The strophes are usually arranged in subsequent groupings of **canticles**, which in longer compositions are in turn usually joined into **sub-cantos** and/or **cantos**, depending on the length of the composition. Determination of these groupings is based upon content and thematic shifts and patterns, as well as formal indications, such as external parallelism beyond the strophe to form responsion,[74] inclusion, concatenation,[75] or refrains.

These are the most important criteria upon which the colometry is based. Following the colometric presentation of the text, these criteria are listed systematically in a justification of the poetic structure. This leads to an investigation of whether the strophes, canticles, and cantos are arranged in a deliberate macrostructure, which in turn may help to confirm the poetic structure and elucidate textual and exegetical questions. The present study works with the assumption that the ultimate test for whether or not a particular composition is poetic narrative is to attempt to write it out colometrically in accordance

[71]See van der Lugt, *Strofische structuren*, esp. 508-527. It has been demonstrated that strophes are usually identifiable on the basis of content and formal markers of separation upwards and downwards, e.g., emphatic constructions, imperatives, vocatives, employment of certain particles, repetitive parallelism, tricolons, etc. (van der Meer–de Moor, eds., *Structural Analysis*, viii). For a previous study briefly hinting in this direction see Muilenburg, "Form Criticism," 10-18.

[72]As explained above, this refers to parallelism beyond rather than within a single verse.

[73]In this chapter, as in Josh. 23, the end of a poetic verse often coincides with an *'aṯnaḥ* [2], and the end of the strophe often falls in harmony with a *sillûq* [1], but here too we are making an *ad hoc* observation which is not suited to be used as a principle in determining the extent of the respective poetic units.

[74]Parallelism established by words in similar positions in the respective strophes or canticles e.g., a parallelism established between the opening verses of consecutive strophes.

[75]Parallelism formed between the end of one strophe and the beginning of the next, or the end of one canticle and the beginning of the next, etc.

with criteria for poetry established elsewhere for all the respective poetic units, i.e., foot,[76] colon, verse, strophe, canticle, and canto. If the colometry reveals a high degree of internal and external parallelisms at the respective poetic levels, and if the resulting verses, strophes and canticles produce the type of patterns found elsewhere typically in poetry, the evidence is cumulative that such phenomena can most cogently be accounted for on the basis of a poetic composition. This is especially true if the quantity of the parallelism is reinforced by considerations of quality, e.g., chiastic arrangements or elaborate patterns of parallelism in the larger units. An attempt is made below to demonstrate that Josh. 24:1-28 meets these criteria. The ensuing colometric presentation is based upon the Masoretic text—with a single rearrangement in 24:11-12 on grounds which are elaborated in the colometric justification.

## 3.3 Colometrical delineation of Josh. 24:1-28

### Canto I, canticle i

*petuchah* ______

**I.i**

| | |
|---|---|
| *wy'sp yhwš'* [*12*] | (1aA) And Joshua gathered |
| *'t-kl-šbṭy yśr'l škmh* [*2*] | (1aB) all the tribes of Israel at Shechem. |
| *wyqr' lzqny yśr'l wlr'šyw* [*7*] | (1bA) And he called the elders of Israel and his heads, |
| *wlšpṭyw wlšṭryw* [*5*] | (1bB) and his judges and his officers |
| *wytyṣbw lpny h'lhym* [*1*] | (1bC) and they stood before Elohim. |

.......................................................................

[76]It is debatable whether there are criteria which are indigenous to the poetic foot in distinction from a comparable unit in a non-poetic composition. Since certain diction is sometimes thought to be restricted to poetic texts, we include the foot here in our comprehensive list. The foot is usually insignificant for differentiating poetic and non-poetic texts, but in cases of unique diction it is potentially significant (cf. Watson, *Classical Hebrew Poetry*, 49, re *unusual vocabulary*).

## Canto I, canticle ii, strophes 1-3

### I.ii.1

| | |
|---|---|
| *wy'mr yhwš' 'l-kl-h'm* [*7*] | (2aA) And Joshua said to all the people, |
| *kh-'mr yhwh 'lhy yśr'l* [*3*] | (2aB) "Thus says Yahweh, God of Israel, |
| *b'br hnhr yšbw 'bwtykm m'wlm* [*5*] | (2bA) 'Across the river your fathers lived of old, |
| *trḥ 'by 'brhm w'by nḥr* [*2*] | (2bB) Terah, father of Abraham and of Nahor, |
| *wy'bdw 'lhym 'ḥrym* [*1*] | (2bC) but they served other gods. |

### I.ii.2

| | |
|---|---|
| *w'qḥ 't-'bykm* [*11*] | (3aA) And I took your father, |
| *'t-'brhm m'br hnhr* [*5*] | (3aB) Abraham, from across the river, |
| *w'wlk 'wtw bkl-'rṣ kn'n* [*2*] | (3aC) and I made him walk through all the land of Canaan. |
| *w'rb 't-zr'w* [*5*] | (3bA) And I multiplied his seed, |
| *w'tn-lw 't-yṣḥq* [*1*] | (3bB) and I gave to him Isaac. |

### I.ii.3

| | |
|---|---|
| *w'tn lyṣḥq* [*5*] | (4aA) And I gave to Isaac |
| *'t-y'qb w't-'św* [*2*] | (4aB) Jacob and Esau. |
| *w'tn l'św* [*13*] | (4bA) And I gave to Esau |
| *'t-hr ś'yr lršt 'wtw* [*5*] | (4bB) Mt. Seir, to inherit it. |
| *wy'qb wbnyw* [*8*] | (4cA) But as for Jacob and his sons, |
| *yrdw mṣrym* [*1*] | (4cB) they descended to Egypt. |

.........................................................................

## Canto I, canticle iii, strophes 1-4

### I.iii.1

| | |
|---|---|
| *w'šlḥ 't-mšh w't-'hrn [10]* | (5aA) And I sent Moses and Aaron, |
| *w'gp 't-mṣrym [5]* | (5aB) and I struck Egypt, |
| *k'šr 'śyty bqrbw [2]* | (5aC) with what I did in her midst. |
| *w'ḥr hwṣ'ty 'tkm [1]* | (5b) And afterwards I brought you out. |

### I.iii.2

| | |
|---|---|
| *w'wṣy' 't-'bwtykm mmṣrym [5]* | (6aA) When I had brought your fathers out of Egypt, |
| *wtb'w hymh [2]* | (6aB) and you came to the sea, |
| *wyrdpw mṣrym 'ḥry 'bwtykm [12]* | (6bA) the Egyptians pursued after your fathers |
| *brkb wbpršym ym-swp [1]* | (6bB) with chariots and horsemen, to the Reed Sea. |

### I.iii.3

| | |
|---|---|
| *wyṣ'qw 'l-yhwh [7]* | (7aA) And they cried out to Yahweh, |
| *wyśm m'pl bynykm [18]* | (7aB) and he set darkness between you |
| *wbyn hmṣrym [7]* | (7aC) and between the Egyptians. |
| *wyb' 'lyw 't-hym [10]* | (7bA) And he brought the sea upon them, |
| *wykshw [5]* | (7bB) and he covered them. |

### I.iii.4

| | |
|---|---|
| *wtr'ynh 'ynykm [5]* | (7bA) And your eyes saw |
| *'t 'šr-'śyty bmṣrym [2]* | (7bB) that which I did to Eygpt. |
| *wtšbw bmdbr [8]* | (7cA) And you dwelt in the desert, |
| *ymym rbym [1]* | (7cB) many days. |

.............................................................

## Canto I, canticle iv, strophes 1-3

### I.iv.1

| | |
|---|---|
| *w’b’h ’tkm ’l-’rṣ h’mry* [*10*] | (8aA) And I brought you to the land of the Amorites, |
| *hywšb b‘br hyrdn* [*5*] | (8aB) those living across the Jordan, |
| *wylḥmw ’tkm* [*2*] | (8aC) and they fought with you. |
| *w’tn ’wtm bydkm* [*10*] | (8bA) But I gave them into your hand, |
| *wtyršw ’t-’rṣm* [*5*] | (8bB) and you inherited their land, |
| *w’šmydm mpnykm* [*1*] | (8bC) and I destroyed them before you. |

### I.iv.2

| | |
|---|---|
| *wyqm blq bn-ṣpwr* [*10*] | (9aA) And there arose Balak son of Zippor, |
| *mlk mw’b* [*5*] | (9aB) king of Moab, |
| *wylḥm byśr’l* [*2*] | (9aC) and he fought against Israel. |
| *wyšlḥ wyqr’ lbl‘m bn-b‘wr* [*8*] | (9bA) He sent and called Balaam son of Beor, |
| *lqll ’tkm* [*1*] | (9bB) to curse you. |
| *wl’ ’byty lšm‘ lbl‘m* [*2*] | (10aA) But I would not listen to Balaam, |
| *wybrk brwk ’tkm* [*5*] | (10aB) and indeed he blessed you, |
| *w’ṣl ’tkm mydw* [*1*] | (10aC) and I delivered you out of his hand. |

### I.iv.3

| | |
|---|---|
| *wt‘brw ’t-hyrdn* [*9*] | (11aA) And you crossed the Jordan, |
| *wtb’w ’l-yryḥw* [*3*] | (11aB) and you came to Jericho, |
| *wylḥmw bkm b‘ly-yryḥw* [*17*] { } | (11aC) and the lords of Jericho fought you. |
| *w’tn ’wtm bydkm* [*1*] | (11c) But I gave them into your hand. |

.....................................................................

## Canto I, canticle v, strophes 1-3

### I.v.1

| | |
|---|---|
| *w'šlḥ lpnykm 't-hṣr'h* [5] | (12aA) And I sent before you the panic. |
| *wtgrš 'wtm mpnykm* [5] | (12aB) and it drove them out from before you, |
| <*h'mry whprzy whkn'ny* [7] | (<11bA>) the Amorites, and the Perizzites, and the Canaanites, |
| *whḥty whgrgšy* [5] | (<11bB>) the Hittites and Girgashites, |
| *hḥwy whybwsy* [2]> | (<11bC>) the Hivites and the Jebusites. |

### I.v.2

| | |
|---|---|
| <*wtgrš 'wtm mpnykm*> | (<12bA>) And it drove them out before you, |
| *šny mlky h'mry* [2] | (12bB) two kings of the Amorites. |
| *l' bḥrbk* [8] | (12cA) Not with your sword, |
| *wl' bqštk* [1] | (12cB) and not with your bow. |

### I.v.3

| | |
|---|---|
| *w'tn lkm* [13] | (13aA) And I gave to you |
| *'rṣ 'šr l'-yg't bh* [7] | (13aB) a land which you did not work in, |
| *w'rym 'šr l'-bnytm* [5] | (13bA) and cities which you did not build, |
| *wtšbw bhm* [2] | (13bB) and you dwell in them, |
| *krmym wzytym* [10] | (13cA) vineyards and olive groves |
| *'šr l'-nṭ't* [5] | (13cB) which you did not plant, |
| *'tm 'klym* [1] | (13cC) from them you are eating." |

## Canto II, canticle i, strophes 1-3

### II.i.1

| | |
|---|---|
| *w'th yr'w 't-yhwh [12]* | (14aA) "Now fear Yahweh, |
| *w'bdw 'tw btmym wb'mt [2]* | (14aB) and serve him completely and in truth. |
| *whsyrw 't-'lhym [7]* | (14bA) Put away the gods |
| *'šr 'bdw 'bwtykm [13]* | (14bB) which your fathers served, |
| *b'br hnhr wbmṣrym [5]* | (14bC) across the river and in Egypt, |
| *w'bdw 't-yhwh [1]* | (14bD) and serve Yahweh! |

### II.i.2

| | |
|---|---|
| *w'm r' b'ynykm [13]* | (15aA) But if it is evil in your eyes |
| *l'bd 't-yhwh [7]* | (15aB) to serve Yahweh, |
| *bḥrw lkm hywm [9]* | (15bA) choose for yourselves today |
| *'t-my t'bdwn [3]* | (15bB) whom you will serve. |

### II.i.3

| | |
|---|---|
| *'m 't-'lhym [14]* | (15cA) Whether the gods |
| *'šr-'bdw 'bwtykm [7]* | (15cB) which your fathers served, |
| *'šr b'br hnhr [5]* | (15cC) who were across the river, |
| *w'm 't-'lhy h'mry [5]* | (15dA) or the gods of the Amorites, |
| *'šr 'tm yšbym b'rṣm [2]* | (15dB) in whose land you are now living. |
| *w'nky wbyty [5]* | (15eA) But as for me and my house, |
| *n'bd 't-yhwh [1]* | (15eB) we will serve Yahweh." |

*petuchah* ..................................................

## Canto II, canticle ii, strophes 1-3

### II.ii.1

| | |
|---|---|
| *wy'n h'm [10]* | (16aA) And the people answered |
| *wy'mr ḥlylh lnw [5]* | (16aB) and they said, "Far be it from us, |
| *m'zb 't-yhwh [2]* | (16aC) abandoning Yahweh |
| *l'bd 'lhym 'ḥrym [1]* | (16aD) to serve other gods! |
| *ky yhwh 'lhynw [5]* | (17aA) For Yahweh is our God, |
| *hw' hm'lh 'tnw [23!]* | (17aB) he is the one who brought us up, |
| *w't-'bwtynw [12]* | (17aC) as well as our fathers, |
| *m'rṣ mṣrym [8]* | (17aD) from the land of Egypt, |
| *mbyt 'bdym [2]* | (17aE) from the house of bondage. |

### II.ii.2

| | |
|---|---|
| *w'šr 'śh l'ynynw [7]* | (17bA) and he did before our eyes |
| *'t-h'twt hgdlwt h'lh [5]* | (17bB) these great signs, |
| *wyšmrnw bkl-hdrk [10]* | (17cA) and he watched over us in every path |
| *'šr hlknw bh [5]* | (17cB) which we walked in, |
| *wbkl h'mym [5]* | (17dA) and in all the peoples |
| *'šr 'brnw bqrbm [1]* | (17dB) whom we crossed through. |

### II.ii.3

| | |
|---|---|
| *wygrš yhwh 't-kl-h'mym [7]* | (18aA) And Yahweh drove out all the peoples, |
| *w't-h'mry yšb h'rṣ mpnynw [2]* | (18aB) and the Amorites dwelling in the land from before us. |
| *gm-'nḥnw [10]* | (18bA) So as for us too, |
| *n'bd 't-yhwh [5]* | (18bB) we will serve Yahweh, |
| *ky-hw' 'lhynw [1]* | (18bC) for he is our God." |

*setumah* . . . . . . . . . . . . . . . . . . . . . . . . . . . . . . . . . . . . . . . . . . . . . . . .

## Canto II, canticle iii, strophes 1-3

### II.iii.1

| | |
|---|---|
| *wy'mr yhwš' 'l-h'm [7]* | (19aA) And Joshua said to the people, |
| *l' twklw l'bd 't-yhwh [5]* | (19aB) "You are not able to serve Yahweh, |
| *ky-'lhym qdšym hw' [2]* | (19bA) for he is a holy God, |
| *'l-qnw' hw' [5]* | (19bB) he is a jealous God. |

### II.iii.2

| | |
|---|---|
| *l'-yś' lpš'km [8]* | (19cA) He will not forgive your transgressions |
| *wlḥṭ'wtykm [1]* | (19cB) or your sins |
| *ky t'zbw 't-yhwh [5]* | (20aC) when you abandon Yahweh |
| *w'bdtm 'lhy nkr [2]* | (20aD) and you serve strange gods. |
| *wšb whr' lkm [10]* | (20bA) And he will turn and do evil to you, |
| *wklh 'tkm [5]* | (20bB) and he will consume you, |
| *'ḥry 'šr-hyṭyb lkm [1]* | (20bC) after having done good to you." |

### II.iii.3

| | |
|---|---|
| *wy'mr h'm 'l-yhwš' [2]* | (21aA) And the people said to Joshua, |
| *l' ky 't-yhwh n'bd [1]* | (21aB) "Nevertheless, Yahweh we will serve." |

. . . . . . . . . . . . . . . . . . . . . . . . . . . . . . . . . . . . . . . . . . . . . . . . . . . . . . . . . . .

## Canto II, canticle iv, strophes 1-3

### II.iv.1

| | |
|---|---|
| *wy'mr yhwš' 'l-h'm* [*7*] | (22aA) And Joshua said to the people, |
| *'dym 'tm bkm* [*5*] | (22aB) "You are witnesses against yourselves, |
| *ky-'tm bḥrtm lkm 't-yhwh* [*8*] | (22aC) that you have chosen for yourselves Yahweh, |
| *l'bd 'wtw* [*2*] | (22aD) to serve him." |
| *wy'mrw* [*8*] | (22bA) And they said, |
| *'dym* [*1*] | (22bB) "Witnesses!" |

### II.iv.2

| | |
|---|---|
| *w'th hsyrw 't-'lhy hnkr* [*8*] | (23aA) "And now, put away the strange gods |
| *'šr bqrbkm* [*2*] | (23aB) which are in your midst. |
| *whṭw 't-lbbkm* [*5*] | (23bA) And incline your hearts |
| *'l-yhwh 'lhy yśr'l* [*1*] | (23bB) to Yahweh, God of Israel." |

### II.iv.3

| | |
|---|---|
| *wy'mrw h'm 'l-yhwš'* [*2*] | (24aA) And the people said to Joshua, |
| *'t-yhwh 'lhynw n'bd* [*5*] | (24aB) "Yahweh our God we will serve, |
| *wbqwlw nšm'* [*1*] | (24aC) and to his voice we will listen." |

## Canto II, canticle v, strophes 1-3

### II.v.i

| | |
|---|---|
| *wykrt yhwš' bryt l'm bywm hhw'* [*2*] | (25A) And Joshua cut a covenant for the people in that day, |
| *wyśm lw ḥq wmšpṭ bškm* [*1*] | (25B) and he set for them a statute and judgment in Shechem, |
| *wyktb yhwš' 't-hdbrym h'lh* [*5*] | (26aC) and Joshua wrote these words |
| *bspr twrt 'lhym* [*2*] | (26aD) in a book of the law of God. |
| *wyqḥ 'bn gdwlh* [*5*] | (26bA) And he took a large stone, |
| *wyqymh šm* [*5*] | (26bB) and he raised it there |
| *tḥt h'lh* [*5*] | (26bC) under the terebinth |
| *'šr bmqdš yhwh* [*1*] | (26bD) which was in the sanctuary of Yahweh. |

*setumah*

### II.v.2

| | |
|---|---|
| *wy'mr yhwš' 'l-kl-h'm* [*7*] | (27aA) And Joshua said to all the people, |
| *hnh h'bn hz't* [*10*] | (27aB) "Behold, this stone |
| *thyh-bnw l'dh* [*5*] | (27aC) will be for us as a witness, |
| *ky-hy' šm'h* [*7*] | (27bA) for it has heard |
| *'t kl-'mry yhwh* [*5*] | (27bB) all the words of Yahweh |
| *'šr dbr 'mnw* [*2*] | (27bC) which he spoke to us. |

### II.v.3

| | |
|---|---|
| *whyth bkm l'dh* [*5*] | (27cA) And it will be to you as a witness, |
| *pn-tkḥšwn b'lhykm* [*1*] | (27cB) lest you deceive your God." |
| *wyšlḥ yhwš' 't-h'm* [*5*] | (28A) And Joshua sent the people away, |
| *'yš lnḥltw* [*1*] | (28B) every man to his inheritance. |

*petuchah*

## 3.4 Colometrical justification of Josh. 24:1-28

### 3.4.1 Canticle I.i (24:1)

Sep. ↑: *petuchah*[77]
Sep. ↓: tricolon; repetitive (rep.) *w* and *l*
Int. || : *yhwš'* || *yśr'l; wyqr'* || *wytyṣbw;*[78] *lzqny yśr'l wlr'šyw* || *wlšpṭyw wlšṭryw*[79]
Ext. || : *wy'sp* || *wyqr';*[80] *yśr'l* || *yśr'l;*[81] *škmh* || *lpny h'lhym;*[82]
Asson. : *šbṭy* || *špṭyw*

If our analysis is correct, the first canticle is comprised of a single,[83] compact strophe describing the setting for the historical speech and events which follow. The rationale for viewing Josh. 24:1 as an independent canticle is primarily derived from conclusions based upon the macrostructure of the entire composition, which is extensively governed by the dialogical patterns and shifts in discourse. This conclusion is reinforced by the strong formula in vs.2 introducing prophetic

[77]Compare a similar formula in Num. 11:16, also following a *petuchah.*

[78]Cf. Ex. 34:5; Deut. 31:14; 1 Sam. 3:10.

[79]The same combination of four groups of leaders is found in parallelism in Josh. 23:2; cf. Koopmans, "Joshua 23," 93 n.26. Especially significant for comparison is the chiastic enumeration in Isa. 3:2. The principle of enumeration of parallel terms for leaders is widely attested, e.g., *śr* || *špṭ*, discussed already by Cassuto (*Biblical and Oriental Studies*, 2:60-68) and Melamed ("Break-up," 131-133).

[80]For *'sp* and *qr'* in poetic parallelism compare Joel 1:14, which significantly is also in the context of the elders being gathered to the house of *yhwh 'lhykm*; cf. Joel 2:15f., which is an example of these words in external parallelism (W.van der Meer, *Oude woorden worden nieuw. De opbouw van het boek Joël* [Kampen, 1989], 54). In Ps. 50:4f. these verbs apparently form external parallelism since both are part of the same strophe (van der Lugt, *Strofische structuren*, 271). Cf. Gen. 49:1, printed in BHS as prose, and usually accepted as such (O'Connor, *Verse Structure*, 169), but identified as poetry by E.Lipiński, "*B'ḥryt hymym* dans les textes préexiliques," *VT* 20 (1970) 446f. See too W.G.E.Watson, "The Hebrew Word-pair *'sp* || *qbṣ*," *ZAW* 96 (1984) esp. 429 (poetic parallelism of Gen. 49:1), 428, 432 (re *'sp* || *qr'* in Joel 1:14; 2:16).

[81]Recognition of this parallelism obviates the need to conclude with Nielsen that repetition of Israel is bad style (*Shechem*, 87). This parallelism may actually be expanded to include *'t-kl-šbṭy* parallel to the list of leaders as representatives of the tribes.

[82]Parallelism as specification of place, with *locale he* and locative preposition. This parallelism already intimates that there was a *mqdš* at Shechem (26bD).

[83]Regarding the possibility of a canticle of one strophe consult Korpel–de Moor, "Fundamentals," 201.

speech. The macrostructure will be discussed more elaborately below.

### 3.4.2 Canticle I.ii (24:2-4)

**I.ii.1**

Sep. ↑: beginning of direct discourse; rep. *'mr*; messenger formula *kh-'mr yhwh 'lhy yśr'l*[84]

Sep. ↓: tricolon;[85] rep. *'b*; *'wlm*;[86] emphasized position of *b'br hnhr*

Int. || : *wy'mr yhwš'* || *kh-'mr yhwh*;[87] *'m* || *yśr'l*;[88] *yšbw* || *y'bdw*;[89] *'b* || *'b* (2x);[90]

Ext. || : *'m* || *'bwtykm*; *'lhy yśr'l* || *'lhym 'ḥrym*[91]

[84]"*Introductory formulae* such as *kh 'mr yhwh* ... can help show where major structural segments are demarcated" (Watson, *Classical Hebrew Poetry*, 164); Muilenburg, "Form and Structure," 359, with a comparison drawn with Ex. 19:3b. Furthermore, *'mr* is itself a marker of separation, cf. van der Lugt, *Strofische structuren*, 523f., and many examples in van der Meer–de Moor, eds., *Structural Analysis*.

[85]Research in a large corpus of OT poetry demonstrates that tricola are usually not found in the middle of a strophe (cf. van der Meer–de Moor, eds., Structural Analysis, viii). We therefore consistently include the presence of tricola as formal markers of separation.

[86]Cf. van der Lugt, *Strofische structuren*, 523f.

[87]Hebrew poetry often employs parallelism of variant forms of the same verb, either in the same or another stem (cf. Zurro, *Procedimientos*, 7, 240-283). The *yahwistic* personal name *yhwš'* stands in parallelism with *yhwh* here as well as in 19a,21,22a,24. For an elaboration of the significance of this parallelism cf. 6.2.2.

[88]Cf. R.G.Boling, "'Synonymous' Parallelism in the Psalms," *JSSt* 5 (1960) 236 (re Ps. 50:7; 81:9, 12, 14); W.R.Watters, *Formula Criticism and the Poetry of the Old Testament* (Berlin and New York, 1976), 155 no.6 (re Isa. 1:3; [10:22]; 11:16; 14:2; 19:25); O.Loretz, *Der Prolog des Jesaja Buches (1,1-2,5)* (Altenberge, 1984), 124; van der Meer, *Oude woorden*, 81f.

[89]There is a formal (i.e., grammatical) parallelism (for similar examples cf. Pardee, *Poetic Parallelism*, e.g., 9 n.15, and many times), and probably a semantic parallelism as well; to choose to live in a king's land entailed serving him (Jer. 40:9), and to live in Yahweh's land entailed serving him (Jer. 35:15); to live amongst other people entailed serving their gods (Ex. 23:33; Josh. 24:15).

[90]Cf. Dahood–Penar, "Parallel Pairs, I," 95, listing numerous examples of *'b* || *'b*. To these we may add the Moabite parallelism attested in the Mesha inscription (cf. de Moor, "Narrative Poetry," 152, 156).

[91]The antithetical parallelism of *yhwh* and *'lhym 'ḥrym* can be demonstrated in many texts, virtually exclusively in passages printed in BHS as prose. There are 22 verses in the MT where *yhwh* and *'lhym 'ḥrym* occur together, namely Deut. 7:4; 8:19; 11:28; 28:36; 28:64; Josh. 23:16; 24:2; Judg. 2:12; 2:17; 1 Sam. 26:19; 1 Kgs 9:9; 11:4; 11:10; 2 Kgs 5:17; 17:7; 17:35; Jer. 16:11; 22:9; Hos. 3:1; 2 Chron. 7:22; 28:25. At first glance this might be seen as an argument against reading the present passage as poetry. However, this list of texts does not exclude the possibility that

Asson. and allit.: *'by 'brhm*; *'lhym 'ḥrym*

**I.ii.2**

Sep. ↑: tricolon; change of subject
Sep. ↓: rep. *w ... 't*
Int. || : *w'qḥ* || *w'wlk*;[92] *'t-'bykm* || *'t-'brhm*[93] || *'wtw*; *m'br hnhr* || *bkl-'rṣ kn'n*;[94] *w'rb* || *w'tn-lw*;[95] *'t-zr'w* || *'t-yṣḥq*[96]
Ext. || : *w'qḥ* and *w'wlk* || *w'rb* and *w'tn*;[97] *'t-'bykm* || *'t-zr'w*; *'t-'brhm* || *'t-yṣḥq*;[98] *'wtw* || *lw*

Josh. 24 is *poetic narrative*, which is the precise focus of our argument. For the poetic structure of Josh. 23:16, e.g., see Koopmans, "Joshua 23," 92, 104.

[92]Formal parallelism, i.e., first sing. verbal forms referring to Yahweh's actions. In this context the actions are clearly synonymous.

[93]Note the association of "Abraham" and "father" in Gen. 26:24; 28:13; 32:10; Isa. 51:2. Note too the sonant parallelism.

[94]This parallelism contrasts two geographical areas on opposite sides of the river, cf. 1 Kgs 5:4 (M.Noth, *Könige* [Neukirchen-Vluyn, 1968], 75f.); 1 Chron. 19:16; Ezra 8:36; Neh. 2:7,9; 3:7.

[95]The parallel usage of *ntn* and *rbh* is reminiscent of a number of texts in Genesis, esp. 17:2,20; 26:4; 48:4. All these verses are written in BHS as prose but at least some can with profit be written colometrically. E.g., the blessing in 26:4 can be read as a strophe of 3 bicola verses:

| | |
|---|---|
| *whrbyty 't-zr'k* [10] | (4aA) And I will multiply your seed |
| *kkwkby hšmym* [5] | (4aB) as the stars of the heavens. |
| *wntty lzr'k* [5] | (4bA) And I will give to your seed |
| *'t kl-h'rṣt h'l* [2] | (4bB) all of this land. |
| *whtbrkw bzr'k* [5] | (4cA) And in your seed will be blessed |
| *kl gwyy h'rṣ* [1] | (4cB) all the nations of the land. |

This format reveals the threefold parallelism of the verbs, the threefold parallelism of "your seed" (*zr'k*) at the end of the A-colon in each verse, the merismus formed by *šmym* and *'rṣ*, and the repetitive employment of *kl* and *'rṣ*, producing three bicola in perfect alternating parallelism (regarding *šmym* || *'rṣ* cf., e.g., C.I.K.Story, "The Book of Proverbs and Northwest Semitic Literature," *JBL* 64 [1965] 328; Boling, "Synonymous Parallelsim," 239; Dahood–Penar, "Parallel Pairs, I," 356 no.554; Watters, *Formula Criticism*, 155 no.4; J.Krašovec, *Der Merismus im Biblisch-hebräischen und Nordwestsemitischen* [Rome, 1977], 11-39, 153 no.257; Loretz, *Der Prolog*, 128). The verbs *ntn* and *rbh* are employed in chiastic parallelism in 2 Sam. 22:36 (Ps. 18:36) and Isa. 40:29.

[96]For an additional example where *zr'* stands parallel to a proper noun see Isa. 41:8.

[97]All are 1st singular verb forms referring to the actions of Yahweh. There is also semantic parallelism to the extent that the reference to entry into the land and the multiplication of descendants both imply fulfilment of the covenantal promise to the patriarchs. Especially noteworthy is the inclusion *lqḥ* || *ntn*, cf. Dahood–Penar, "Parallel Pairs, I," 218 no.266.

[98]Cf. Ps. 105:9 (= 1 Chron. 16:16).

**I.ii.3**

Sep. ↑: *'t-y'qb w't-'św*[99]

Sep. ↓: emphasized position of the subjects *wy'qb wbnyw*

Int. || : *yṣḥq* || *y'qb* + *'św*; *ntn* || *yrš*;[100] *'św* || *ś'yr*;[101]
*y'qb* || *mṣrym*?[102]

Ext. || : *w'tn lyṣḥq* || *w'tn l'św*; *y'qb* || *y'qb*; *'św* || *'św*; *'t* || *'t*

In addition to the alternating parallelism of these verses, it is of interest to note the chiastic ordering of the names, Jacob, Esau, Esau, Jacob. Note too that *mṣrym* lacks a preposition or *locale he* (cf. our comment on I.iii.2).

**External parallelism in I.ii**

**I.ii.1 and I.ii.2**

*kl* || *kl* (2aA, 3aA);[103] *'m* || *'rṣ* (2aA, 3aC);[104] *b'br hnhr* || *m'br hnhr* (2bA, 3aA); *'bwtykm* || *'bykm* (2bA, 3aA); *'b* (2x) || *zr'* (2bB, 3bA; responsion); proper nouns, e.g., *'brhm* || *'brhm* (2bB, 3aB; concatenation)

[99]Demarcation of separation upwards is weak here, especially in light of the parallelism formed between *w'tn-lw 't-yṣḥq* and *w'tn lyṣḥq*, which can be seen as an argument against strophic division at this point. Nevertheless, the latter parallelism can also be viewed as a concatenation between strophes, which is supported by matters of theme and content; I.ii.2 deals with Abraham while I.ii.3 continues the history from Isaac to Esau and Jacob. Furthermore, when taken independently from vs.3, the three bicola in vs.4 produce a threefold alternating (ABÁB́) parallelism. The repetition of *ntn* is best viewed here as an example of the way strophes of poetic narrative can be closely linked via concatenation; cf. the similar phenomenon in the historical recital found in the Kilamuwa inscription (de Moor, "Narrative Poetry" 166ff.).

[100]For this parallelism see Ps. 105:44 (chiastic, cf. M.Dahood, *Psalms*, 3 vols. [Garden City, NY, 1966-70], 3:63); Neh. 9:15,22,24 cf. also Josh. 24:8. See further the parallelism in Ezek. 33:24, identified as poetry by W.H.Brownlee, "The Aftermath of the Fall of Judah According to Ezekiel," *JBL* 89 (1970) 393-404. The pair *ytn* || *yrṯ* is already attested in Ugaritic, KTU 1.2: I.18f.

[101]In Gen. 32:4 this parallelism would appear to be attested in the phrases *'l-'św 'ḥyw* || *'rṣh ś'yr* || *śdh 'dwm*; cf. Avishur, *Stylistic Studies*, 353. See too Gen. 36:8f.

[102]This parallelism is questionable because no synonymity or clear identification between the two is involved, but the association between Jacob and Egypt appears to stand in deliberate contrast to the inheritance implied in the *'św* || *ś'yr* parallelism, thereby creating dramatic tension. It is noteworthy that Jacob's descent to Egypt is remembered elsewhere in Israel's poetic tradition, e.g., Ps. 105:23, which is closely related to Josh. 24:4; cf. Ps. 114:1.

[103]Cf., de Moor, "Narrative Poetry," 152, 156.

[104]For *'m* || *'rṣ* cf. Boling, "'Synonymous' Parallelism," 236. The present claim for parallelism is reinforced by the presence of *kl* || *kl*.

**I.ii.2 and I.ii.3**

Yahweh's actions described with 1st sing. vbs; proper nouns (personal names and place names); *'rṣ kn'n* || *hr ś'yr* (3aC, 4bB; responsion);[105] *zr'w* || *bnyw* (3bA, 4cA; responsion)[106] *m'br hnhr* || *mṣrym* (3aB, 4cB; inclusion);[107] *w'tn-lw 't-yṣḥq* || *w'tn lyṣḥq* (3bB, 4aA; concatenation)

**I.ii.1 and I.ii.3**

Ext. || : *b'br hnhr* || *mṣrym* (2bA, 4cB; responsion); *'bwtykm* || *wbnyw* (2bA, 4cA; responsion);[108] proper nouns, especially *yśr'l* || *y'qb wbnyw* (2aB, 4cA; inclusion)[109]

The three strophes of canticle I.ii correspond with three stages of the fulfilment of the covenant promise pertaining to the acquisition of land and progeny. Transitions from beyond the river, to the land of Canaan, to the descent to Egypt accord with the strophic divisions. Characteristic of the canticle is the copious employment of verbs designating Yahweh's actions in the 1st singular form. Also noteworthy is the fact that I.ii.1 ends with emphasis upon service of other gods across the river, and I.ii.3 ends with the descent to Egypt, which essentially depicts the precariousness of the covenant relationship between Yahweh and Israel which is to be realized in the land of the promise.

[105]Regarding *hr* || *'rṣ* cf. W.G.E.Watson, "Fixed Pairs in Ugaritic and Isaiah," *VT* 22 (1972) 468; Avishur, *Stylistic Studies*, 278.

[106]Cf. Dahood, *Psalms*, 3:22 (re Ps. 102:29 and a similar parallelism in Phoenician; cf. Avishur, "Word Pairs," 2). See especially Ps. 105:6, *zr' 'brhm* || *bny y'qb* (= 1 Chron. 16:13 with "Israel" substituted for "Abraham"); see also Ps. 21:11; Avishur also lists Isa. 1:4; 57:3 (*Stylistic Studies*, 555—and also note the reference he makes to Jer. 16:15; 23:8 [657]); for ext. par. perhaps add Isa. 14:20f.; 43:5f.; Ps. 89:30f. The nouns *zr'* and *bn* are accepted as a word-pair in Isaiah by Watters, *Formula Criticism*, 155 no.11; Loretz, *Prolog*, 123.

[107]Parallelism is formed by these opposite geographical boundaries; also in Gen. 15:18; Isa. 11:15; 27:12; Jer. 2:18; 2 Chron. 9:26. The parallelism is heightened by the fact that Abraham is brought *to* the land of promise but Jacob descends *from* the land of promise.

[108]Numerous examples can be given of these nouns in parallelism, e.g. Isa. 14:21; Jer. 31:29; Mal. 3:24; Ps. 78:5. The pair occurs in ext. par. in Joel 1:2b,3a, as van der Meer shows (*Oude woorden*, 41, 43). For an extra-biblical example in the Mesha inscription consult de Moor, "Narrative Poetry," 152, 156.

[109]The parallelism of "Israel" and "Jacob" occurs too frequently to include a complete list, e.g., Gen. 49:2; Num. 23:7,10,21,23; 24:5,17,18; 2 Sam. 23:1; Ps. 14:7; 22:24; 53:7; 78:5,21,71; 81:5; 105:10, 23; 114:1; 135:4; 147:19 and many times in the Prophets.

### 3.4.3 Canticle I.iii (24:5-7)

**I.iii.1**

Sep. ↑: tricolon; rep. *'t*; Moses and Aaron[110]
Sep. ↓: unicolon;[111] emphasized position of *w'ḥr*
Int. ‖ : *w'šlḥ* ‖ *w'gp*;[112] *'t-mšh w't-'hrn* ‖ *'t-mṣrym*;[113]
Ext. ‖ : *šlḥ* ‖ *yṣ'*;[114] *'t-mšh w't-'hrn* ‖ *'tkm*

**I.iii.2**

Sep. ↑: temporal phrase introduced by *w*[115]
Sep. ↓: rep. *b*
Int. ‖ : *yṣ'* ‖ *bw'*;[116] *mmṣrym* ‖ *hymh*;[117]

[110]These arguments for strophic separation depend upon a colon in the MT not found in the LXX (see the discussion of the LXX offered below). Nevertheless, a consideration of the LXX reading tends to confirm rather than contest strophic division here.

[111]On the basis of the repetition of the verb *yṣ'* one might argue, contrary to the Masoretic accentuation, for reading 6a with 5b in a tricolon. However, in support of the Masoretic accentuation it will be shown below that vs.6 consists of two bicola verses with a clear alternating parallelism. The repetition of the variant forms of *yṣ'* can be explained as concatenation, and we therefore concur with the Masoretic accentuation by making a strophic division between vs.5 and vs.6.

[112]Formal parallelism is established by the corresponding verb forms designating Yahweh's action. See now also Ex. 7:27.

[113]Proper nouns employed grammatically as direct objects.

[114]Cf., e.g., Isa. 55:11, *'šr yṣ'* ‖ *'šr šlḥtyw*.

[115]Despite the absence of strong formal markers, alternating parallelism in vs.6a and 6b suggests the present strophic division. Due to the concatenation with the preceding strophe, the alternating parallelism becomes an important argument for strophic recognition here. Mention may also be made of the geographical movement and displacement characteristic of each colon of this strophe. Furthermore, it is questionable whether 6aA is a simple repetition of 5b. The *w'wṣy'* might introduce a temporal sentence, cf. *GK*, 501 §164; J.Williams, *Hebrew Syntax: An Outline*, 2nd ed. (Toronto, 1976), 83 §496. The Dutch Nieuwe Vertaling is probably correct in translating "Toen Ik uw vaderen uit Egypte geleid had" (When I had brought your fathers out of Egypt). For the apodosis starting with *w* see C.Brockelmann, *Hebräische Syntax* (Neukirchen, 1956), §176a.

[116]For the verbs *yṣ'* and *bw'* in poetic parallelism see especially Isa. 37:28; 48:3; Jer. 14:18; 51:10; Ezek. 7:10; Mic. 4:10; Zech. 5:4; Ps. 41:7 (as antithetical pair); 66:11f. (cf. van der Lugt, *Strofische structuren*, 296-298; Dahood, *Psalms*, 2:122); re Isaiah see Watters, *Formula Criticism*, 173, no.477. Consider also Judg. 9:15 (cf. W.G.E.Watson, "Chiastic Patterns in Biblical Hebrew Poetry," in J.W.Welch, ed., *Chiasmus in Antiquity* [Hildesheim, 1981], 137f.). For an attempt to designate this pair as meristic in a number of texts, see Krašovec, *Der Merismus*, 83 no.38; 109f. no. 113; "Merism–Polar Expression," 236.

[117]Note the parallel geographical transition implied in the preposition *mn* and

*mṣrym* || *brkb wbpršym;*[118] *'ḥry* || *b ... b*[119]
Ext. || : *'bwtykm* || *'bwtykm;*[120] *mmṣrym* || *mṣrym; hymh* || *ym-swp.*[121]

The external parallelisms here of "your fathers" (2x), "Egypt" (2x), and "*ym*" || "*ym-swp*" respectively show that the two bicola of this strophe are arranged in alternating (ABÁB́) parallelism; cf. above at vs.4.[122] Note too that *ym swp* lacks a preposition (cf. our comment on I.ii.3).

**I.iii.3**
Sep. ↑: tricolon; rep. *w*; rep. *byn*[123]
Sep. ↓: rep. *w*
Int. || : *byn* || *byn;*[124] *wyb' 'lyw* || *wykshw*[125]
Ext. || : *wyśm* || *wyb'* (formal); *m'pl* || *'t-hym;*[126] *bynykm* || *'lyw*[127]

the *locale he*. With respect to *mṣrym* || *ym-swp* consult Boling, "'Synonymous' Parallelism," 234; cf. Ps. 106:9; Neh. 9:9; Ps. 106:22 (*b'rṣ ḥm* || *ym-swp*, where "land of Ham" is Egypt, as in Ps.78:51).

[118]Regarding the parallelism of *mṣrym* and *rkb* see Watters, *Formula Criticism*, 171 no.425, based on Isa. 31:1 and 36:9. For *rkb* and *prš* see Krašovec, *Der Merismus*, 145 no.235; Watters, *Formula Criticim*, 168 no.331. It is significant that the asyndetic parataxis *lrkb* [*w*]*prš* occurs similarly in the poetic narrative of the Zakkur inscription (de Moor, "Narrative Poetry," 162). For a discussion of the poetic employment of the similar phrase *sws wrkb* see Melamed, "Break-up," 128-131.

[119]For employment of these prepositions in parallelism consult Dahood, "Parallel Pairs, III," 16 no.11.

[120]For this parallelism see I.ii.1 above.

[121]Cf. the poetic parallelism in Ex. 15:4. Cf. Watson, *Classical Hebrew Poetry*, 132; for *ym* || *ym* see too Dahood–Penar, "Parallel Pairs" 202.

[122]For additional examples of alternating parallelism in the OT see especially Willis, "(ABÁB́) Parallelism," 49-76.

[123]Perhaps mention can also be made of *wyṣ'qw*. This is by no means a strong marker of separation. Nevertheless, it would appear to begin a new strophe here because, if it was part of the preceding strophe, it would stand more directly in parallelism with *wyrdpw*, but since that verb refers to the Egyptians, such parallelism is syntactically certainly not intended.

[124]For the parallelism of *byn* || *b* consult Dahood–Penar, "Parallel Pairs, I," 136 no.95; Kselman, "Poetic Fragments," 169. Note the similarity between this verse and Ex. 14:20, which is identified as poetry by Althann ("Poetic Fragments," 14f.).

[125]See also Ps. 55:6; Eccl. 6:4.

[126]Both are objects used by Yahweh against the Egyptians. Comparison with Ex. 15 is instructive in this regard, cf. F.M.Cross–D.N.Freedman, "The Song of Miriam," *JNES* 14 (1955) 239; A.J.Hauser, "Two Songs of Victory: A Comparison of Exodus 15 and Judges 5," in Follis, ed., *Directions*, esp. 270-273.

[127]Prepositions with suffixes. Note that *byn* || *'l* is listed as a parallel pair by Dahood, "Parallel Pairs, III," 43 no.60.

**I.iii.4**
Sep. ↑: switch to 3rd fem. pl. verb form
Sep. ↓: *ymym rbym*[128]
Int. || : *r'h* || *'śh*[129]
Ext. || : *bmṣrym* || *bmdbr*[130]

## External parallelism in I.iii

### I.iii.1 and I.iii.2

*w'šlḥ* || *w'wṣy* (5aA, 6aA; responsion);[131] *w'ḥr* || *'ḥry* (5b, 6bA; responsion); *mṣrym* || *mṣrym* || *mṣrym* (5aB, 6aA, 6bA; responsion, inclusion); *'tkm* || *'bwtykm* (5b, 6bA; responsion);[132] *hwṣ'ty* || *w'wṣy'* (5b, 6aA; concatenation);[133] *'tkm* || *'t-'bwtykm* (5b, 6aA; concatenation); perhaps *w'šlḥ* || *wyrdpw* (5aA, 6bA)[134]

### I.iii.2 and I.iii.3

*mṣrym* || *mṣrym* || *mṣrym* (6aA, 6bA, 7aC; responsion / concatenation); *wtb'w* || *wyb'* (6aB, 7bA); *hymh* || *hym* (6aB, 7bA); *'ḥry* || *byn* (2x) (6bA, 7aB,C); *-km* || *-km* (6bA, 7aB); prepositions *b*... *wb*.. ||

[128]There are numerous OT texts where *ymym rbym* is followed immediately by a *petuchah* or a *setumah*, e.g., Gen. 21:34; Deut. 2:1; 1 Kgs 2:38; Jer. 32:14; 37:16, where the phrase clearly stands at the end of literary units. The same is true in Josh. 24:7 because in vs.8 the narrative shifts to the events which took place in the Transjordan as part of the acquisition of their land, not as part of the exodus itself or of the desert sojourn.

[129]E.g., Jer. 7:17; Ps. 86:17.

[130]Cf. Jer. 2:6 and Am. 2:10; see too Ezek. 20:10, which is written in BHS as prose but contains the additional parallelism formed by *w'wṣy'm* and *w'b'm*. For the parallelism of the prepositions *b* || *b* see Dahood–Penar, "Parallel Pairs, I," 134, no.90; Loretz, *Der Prolog*, 122.

[131]Cf. ext. par. in I.iii.1. Perhaps it is also possible to detect a parallelism between the verbs *šlḥ* and *bw'*; cf. the parallelisms in Jer. 14:3; 49:37; Joel 4:13; Obad. 1:13 and perhaps Ps. 43:3.

[132]Cf., e.g., Ps. 106:6f.

[133]For a discussion of parallelism formed by variant forms of the same consonantal root see especially M.Held, "YQTL–QTL (QTL–YQTL) Sequence of Identical Verbs in Biblical Hebrew and in Ugaritic," in M.Ben-Horin et al., eds., *Studies and Essays in Honor of A.A.Neuman* (Leiden, 1962), 281-290; Dahood, *Psalms*, 3:420-423; Gevirtz, "Conjugational Variation," 99-104; Watters, *Formula Criticism*, 106f.; Berlin, *Dynamics*, 35f.

[134]Cf. Am. 1:10-12. See too Jer. 29:17f., where *šlḥ* and *rdp* are used in external parallelism, as is proven by their combination with the list of three identical nouns in each case.

*bynykm wbyn* (6bB, 7aB,C);[135] *ym-swp* || *ym* (6bB, 7bA; responsion)

**I.iii.3 and I.iii.4**
*byn* (2x) || *b* (2x) (7a, 7b,c); *hmṣrym* || *bmṣrym* (7aB, 7bB; responsion); *ym* || *mdbr* (7bA, 7cA; responsion);[136] *bynykm* and *'ynykm* (7aB, 7bA; responsion and wordplay);[137]

**I.iii.1 and I.iii.3**
*mṣrym* || *hmṣrym* (5aB, 7aC; responsion); *-km* || *-km* (5b, 7aB)

**I.iii.1 and I.iii.4**
*mṣrym* || *mṣrym* (5aB, 7bB; responsion); *k'šr 'śyty bqrb* || *'t 'šr-'śyty b-* (5aC, 7bB; responsion);[138] *yṣ'* || *yšb* (5b, 7cA; responsion)[139]

**I.iii.2 and I.iii.4**
*-km* || *-km* (6aA, 7bA; responsion); *mmṣrym* || *bmṣrym* (6aA, 7bB; responsion); *ym-swp* || *bmṣrym* (6bB, 7bB; responsion);[140] *hym* and *ym-swp* || *bmdbr* (6aB, 6bB, 7cA; responsion)[141]

This analysis suggests that canticle I.iii is composed of four closely related strophes. As above, there are geographical and topical progressions correlating with the respective strophes; in this case the strophes proceed from Yahweh's actions in Egypt, to the arrival at the sea, the conflict at the sea, and finally a summary of Yahweh's actions

[135]Cf. I.iii.3, above.

[136]Cf. the references mentioned below in connection with *ym-swp* || *bmdbr* in ext. par. at I.iii.2 and I.iii.4.

[137]The wordplay is heightened by the mention of the fact that, despite *m'pl* set between them and Egypt, they ironically saw all that Yahweh did.

[138]For *bqrb* || *b* see U.Cassuto, *The Goddess Anath* (Jerusalem, 1971), 30; Dahood, *Psalms*, 3:447; Watson, "Fixed Pairs," 461. The identification of *b* and *bqrb* as a fixed pair is challenged by Avishur, *Stylistic Studies*, 10 n.6, 41f., 461 on the grounds that the elements are prepositional and therefore do not constitute a fixed pair. But the terminological objection to *fixed pair* as the proper designation does not challenge the parallelism of the prepositions as such. See further *bqrb* || *bbyth*, which can be added to the list of int. par. at VI.2 of the Mesha inscription as read by de Moor, "Narrative Poetry," 155, 158; cf. an Ugaritic parallelism evident in KTU 1.17: I 25-27, with *b bt* || *b qrb hklh* (O.Loretz, "Kolometrie ugaritischer und hebraischer Poesie," *ZAW* 98 [1986] 256).

[139]E.g., Isa. 37:28; Jer. 21:9; Ps. 68:7.

[140]For this parallelism cf. int. par. at I.iii.2 above.

[141]See especially Isa. 16:8; 42:10f. (cf. Watters, *Formula Criticism*, 166 no.286); Ps. 78:52f.; 136:15f. For further details on the structure of Ps. 78 see Korpel–de Moor, "Fundamentals" 208-212; W.T.Koopmans, "Psalm 78, Canto D – A Response," *UF* 20 (1988) 121-123.

in Egypt resulting in Israel's exodus and sojourn in the wilderness.[142] The outer two strophes make a very specific correlation in the references to "that which Yahweh did" in Egypt, i.e., external parallelism is made by the responsion *k'šr 'śyty bqrbw* || *'t-'šr 'śyty bmṣrym* (5aC, 7bB), which provides a literary frame for the climactic encounter between Yahweh and Egypt at the sea in the central two strophes.

### 3.4.4 Canticle I.iv (24:8-11)

#### I.iv.1

Sep. ↑: tricolon; change of subject, 1st sing. verb form;[143] cohortative; rep. *'tkm*
Sep. ↓: tricolon; rep. *w*; rep. *-km* forms[144]
Int. || : *'tkm* || *'tkm*; *'rṣ h'mry* || *hywšb*;[145] *ntn* || *yrš*;[146] *'wtm* || *'t-'rṣm*;[147] *w'tn 'wtm bydkm* || *w'šmydm mpnykm*[148]
Ext. || : *w'b'h* || *w'tn* (formal); *'tkm* || *'wtm*; *-km* (2x) || *-km* (2x); *'rṣ* || *'rṣm*; *yšb* || *yrš*;[149] *wylḥmw 'tkm* || *w'šmydm mpnykm*[150]

[142]Note how the use of *yṣ'* || *yšb* forms an inclusion at the level of the canticle, thereby marking the boundaries from the exodus out of Egypt to the wilderness dwelling. On the symbolism of sea and desert cf. N.Wyatt, "Sea and Desert: Symbolic Geography in West Semitic Religious Thought," *UF* 19 (1987) 375-389.

[143]The previous strophe ends with the 2nd pers. pl. verb.

[144]The following strophe begins with 2nd masc. pl. *wyqtl* forms.

[145]Watters, *Formula Criticism*, 168 no.346, lists *'rṣ* and *yšb* as a parallel pair in Isaiah, but a strict parallelism is not evident in all of the texts he appeals to. See too Dahood, "Parallel Pairs, III," 84 no.151. Perhaps the parallelism in the present context could be extended to include *'l-'rṣ* and *b'br hyrdn*, both of which refer to the same geographical area of the Amorites, cf. Judg. 10:8.

[146]The verbs *ntn* and *yrš* as parallels have been dealt with in I.ii.3 above. See especially Neh. 9:24.

[147]Parallel combination of direct object marker and 3rd masc. pl. suffix.

[148]There are multiple parallelisms here, namely the verbal forms, the synonymity of the action described, the 3rd masc. plural suffixes, the 2nd masc. pl. suffixes, and the prepositions (*b* and *mn*) plus body parts (*ydkm* and *pnykm*).

[149]See Isa. 54:3; Jer. 49:1; Mic. 1:15; Ps. 69:36 (contra Dahood, *Psalms*, 2:166, whose revocalizations of both terms does not take into consideration the external parallelisms formed by *yšb* || *škn* and *yrš* || *nḥl* in vs.37; see too his "Parallel Pairs, III," 175 no.338). Cf. Brownlee, "Aftermath," 399-404 (re Ezek. 33:24), and note Neh. 9:24. These two verbs are also attested in external parallelism in the Mesha inscription, though not listed by de Moor in his "Narrative Poetry," 152, 157 (at II.3).

[150]Semantic parallelism formed by war terms. Note also the dramatic reversal.

**I.iv.2**

Sep. ↑: tricolon; shift to 3rd masc. sing. verb forms
Sep. ↓: tricolon; *wl'*; emphatic infin. ab. cons. *wybrk brwk*;[151]
rep. *'tkm*
Int. || : *blq bn-ṣpwr* || *mlk mw'b*;[152] *mw'b* || *yśr'l*;[153] *šm'* || *brk*;[154]
*'tkm* || *'tkm*
Ext. || : *blq* || *bl'm*;[155] *bn-ṣpr* || *bn-b'wr*;[156] *lbl'm* || *lbl'm*; *qr'* || *šm'*;[157]
*lqll* || *wybrk brwk*;[158] *'tkm* || *'tkm* (2x)

[151]See Muraoka, *Emphatic Words*, 87.

[152]In our opinion the cola are to be divided here between the patronymic *bn-ṣpwr* and the title *mlk mw'b*. Cf. the poetic parallelism in Num. 23:7; Mic. 6:5. Mention must also be made of Judg. 11:25, which is likely also poetic though not ordinarily recognized as such. The use of the infinitive absolutes is especially striking, as is the wordplay *'th* || *'th*:

| | |
|---|---|
| *w'th hṭwb ṭwb 'th* [5] | (25aA) Now are you any better |
| *mblq bn ṣpwr* [8] | (25aB) than Balak son of Zippor |
| *mlk mw'b* [2] | (25aC) king of Moab? |
| *hrwb rb 'm-yśr'l* [5] | (25bA) Did he indeed contend with Israel, |
| *'m-nlḥm nlḥm bm* [1] | (25bB) did he indeed fight with them? |

Regarding the parallelism of Num. 23:7 consult O'Connor, *Hebrew Verse Structure*, 113, 185; Berlin, *Dynamics*, 77; Clines, "Parallelism of Greater Precision," 91. The parallelism of the patronymic and title *bn kmś*[*yt*] || *mlk m'b* is found in the opening verse of the Mesha inscription. Attention may also be called to the parallelism of the patronymics and the title *mlk bn 'mn* attested in a 7th cent. Ammonite poetic inscription, cf. H.O.Thompson–F.Zayadine, "The Tell Siran Inscription," *BASOR* 212 (1973) 5-11; F.M.Cross, "Notes on the Ammonite Inscription," *BASOR* 212 (1973) 12-15; C.Krahmalkov, "An Ammonite Lyric Poem," *BASOR* 223 (1976) 55-57.

[153]Cf. the poetic arrangement in Num. 23:7 and 24:17, where internal parallelism is formed by "Jacob" and "Israel" but external parallelism is formed between "Moab" and "Israel." See further Jer. 48:13 and 48:26f. (ext. par.). Internal parallelism of "Israel" and "Moab" has also been demonstrated in de Moor's handling of the Mesha inscription ("Narrative Poetry," 152, 156).

[154]This parallelism is found in Ps. 66:8, with "bless" also in the Piel form (Boling, "'Synonymous' Parallelism," 241). In the present context, Yahweh's unwillingness to listen to a curse is placed synonymous with resultant action in blessing.

[155]See Mic. 6:5.

[156]Two patronymics are placed parallel to each other here.

[157]Cf. 2 Sam. 22:7 (=Ps. 18:7); Jer. 4:5; Jon. 2:3; Mic. 6:9; Ps. 4:2,4; 17:6; 27:7; 34:7; Lam. 1:21; consider also the similar parallelisms in Isa. 48:1,8,12; 49:1; 60:18; 65:12,24; 66:4.

[158]The parallelism matches an infinitive construct with an infinitive absolute. These two verbs appear to occur together in the OT exclusively in poetry. See Ps. 37:22; 62:5; 109:28; Prov. 30:11; Gen. 12:2f. A poetic identity for Gen. 12:1-3 was suggested by Cassuto (*Genesis*, 2:309, 315), and accepted by E.Speiser (*Gene-*

**I.iv.3**

Prior to our treatment of strophe I.iv.3 it is necessary to comment upon our attempt to reconstruct the text of Josh. 24:11f. The list of nations stands in 11b without a verb and is grammatically suspect. Commentators have understandably tended to view it as a gloss.[159] It is also most improbable that the entire list of seven nations should stand in apposition to the citizens of Jericho. However, Schmitt's caveat against simply assuming that the list is a later gloss is warrranted.[160] Schmitt indicates many points of contact evident between Josh. 24:1-28 and Ex. 23:20-33, and a number of additional connections are mentioned in our analysis below.[161] Very important here is the fact that Ex. 23:23 also has a list of nations, beginning with Amorites. One of Schmitt's arguments is based upon the absence of the *waw* before the Hivites but is not convincing because he ignores similar cases in Deut. 20:17; Josh. 9:1; 12:8; 1 Kgs 9:20 (= 2 Chron. 8:7 with *waw*). Nevertheless, there are sufficient other reasons to emphasize the connection between Ex. 23:23,28 and 33:2 with Josh. 24:11. Note especially that the verbs *šlḥ* and *grš* are found together only in Ex. 6:1; 11:1; 23:28; 33:2 and Josh. 24:12. Ex. 23:28 appears to be the source of Josh. 24:12a, and it is therefore of extreme importance that here too the sending of the *ṣr'h* before Israel to drive out (*grš*) the enemy is followed by a list of nations. The list in Ex. 23:28 is shorter, but it might be significant that the reading of the LXX also includes the Amorites. Note the central emphasis in Josh. 24 upon the Amorites.[162] Comparison with Ex. 23:20-33 suggests that in Josh. 24:12 the sending of the *ṣr'h* originally was recorded in connection with driving out the nations. Further confirmation is found in Ex. 34:11 *hnny grš mpnyk*,[163] followed by a list of six nations, also beginning with the Amorites. Therefore, the list

*sis* [Garden City, 1964], 85), Gray (*Legacy*, 308), Watson (*Classical Hebrew Poetry*, 62), and Cross ("Epic Traditions," 21 n.25). For the parallelism of the verbs *qll* and *brk* see too Avishur, *Stylistic Studies*, 258. Attention may also be called to the similar parallelism of *'rr* || *brk*, cf. J.Krašovec, *Antithetic Structures in Biblical Hebrew Poetry*, *SVT* 35 (Leiden, 1984), 30-32, 108f., 129f.

[159]E.g., Dillmann, *Josua*, 586; S.Oettli, *Deuteronomium, Buch Josua und Buch der Richter* (München, 1893), 202; Wellhausen, *Composition*, 133.

[160]Schmitt, *Landtag*, 11, 26-28.

[161]Cf. 5.3.4.

[162]Also of importance, Gen. 48:22 speaks of taking Shechem from the Amorites, "with my sword and my bow" which may be compared to Josh. 24:12b.

[163]Cf. Josh. 24:12aB, *wtgrš 'wtm mpnykm*, and note the parallelism with *šlḥ*.

of nations in Josh. 24 originally would have stood as the object of *grš*. If this theory is correct, the list of nations has been displaced in the present order of the MT. This could easily have happened by an initial haplography, which was noted by a scribe, added to the margin, and then reinserted into the text at the wrong place.[164]

The colon *šny mlky h'mry* cannot be the beginning of a verse, and it must have been introduced by another colon. In our opinion a probable candidate would be *wtgrš 'wtm mpnykm.*[165] The presence of this colon would explain how a haplography could easily have occurred, with the eye skipping from the first presence of *wtgrš 'wtm mpnykm* to the second. Similar external parallelism of an entire colon is precisely the type of connection attested above, e.g., in *w'tn 'wtm bydkm* || *w'tn 'wtm bydkm* (8bA, 11c). Most importantly, in Josh. 24:16-18 the people's summary parallels the historical summary spoken by Joshua (see below). And in 18a we encounter a bicolon (*wygrš yhwh 't-kl-h'mym / w't-h'mry yšb h'rṣ mpnynw*). Here the people's parallel to Joshua's summary uses the verb *grš* in reference to driving out *both the nations and the Amorites* before them, in precisely the order we are suggesting here as the reconstructed form of two consecutive strophes. Anticipating observations elaborated below, we may also note that explaining vss.11f. as a displacement in the text rather than as a gloss is supported by the macrostructure of the entire passage, including the regular presence of three strophes per canticle.

Sep. ↑: tricolon; change of subject, shift to 2nd masc. pl. verbs;
  rep. *yryḥw*
Sep. ↓: unicolon; refrain;[166]
Int. || : *wt'brw* || *wtb'w*;[167]

[164]For an example of transposed verses in Ugaritic texts cf. J.C.de Moor, *An Anthology of Religious Texts from Ugarit* (Leiden, 1987), 230 n.43. For an example of the transposed order of cola—whether deliberate or accidental—in parallel passages, see Korpel–de Moor, "Fundamentals," 190, .

[165]As another possibility, in comparison with Josh. 2:10, one might also suggest *whḥrmtm 'wtm*. The parallelism of *hḥrm* and *ḥrb* is attested in Deut. 13:16; Josh. 6:21; 10:28, 35,37,39; 11:11; 1 Sam. 15:8, cf. Isa. 34:5. However, the emphasis upon *hḥrm* would contradict the statement that this was *not* by the sword of the Israelites, since the *ḥrm* was always said to be implemented "by the edge of the sword." The focus in canticle I.v is not upon Israel's fulfilment of the ban, but rather on Yahweh's driving out the nations to give them a land.

[166]Cf. 8bA and 10aC above.

[167]This parallelism is formal as well as semantic; cf. Isa. 10:28; 28:15; 41:3; Am.

*yrdn* || *yryḥw* (2x);[168]
Ext. || : *b'ly-yryḥw* || *'wtm*; *wylḥm bkm* || *w'tn 'wtm bydkm*[169]

Removal of the list of seven nations here produces a strophic structure identical to I.iii.1 above.[170] It produces a strophe in which the colon *w'tn 'wtm bydkm* (11c) now stands in the same position as its identical counterpart in 8bA. In both I.iv.1 and I.iv.3 the colon *w'tn 'wtm bydkm* now forms the conclusion to the phrases *wylḥmw 'tkm* (8aC), and *wylḥmw bkm* (11aC), which would hardly be the case if the latter strophe is interrupted by the list of nations.

**External parallelism in I.iv**

**I.iv.1 and I.iv.2**

*b'br hyrdn* || *mw'b* (8aB, 9aB; responsion); *wylḥmw 'tkm* || *wylḥm byśr'l* (8aC, 9aC; responsion); 1st sing. verbs referring to the actions of Yahweh (3x) || (2x); *w'tn 'wtm bydkm* || *w'ṣl 'tkm mydw* (8bA, 10aC); [171] *'tkm* (2x) || (3x) (also forming inclusion)

**I.iv.2 and I.iv.3**

*mlk mw'b* || *b'ly-yryḥw* (9aB, 11aC; responsion); *wylḥm byśr'l* || *wylḥmw bkm* (9aC, 11aC; responsion); *w'ṣl 'tkm mydw* || *w'tn 'wtm bydkm* (10aC, 11c; responsion)

**I.iv.1 and I.iv.3**

*w'b'h* || *wtb'w* (8aA, 11aB; responsion);[172] *b'br hyrdn* || *wt'brw 't-hyrdn* (8aB, 11aA; responsion); *wylḥmw 'tkm* || *wylḥmw bkm* (8aC, 11aC; responsion); *w'tn 'wtm bydkm* || *w'tn 'wtm bydkm* (8bA, 11c; responsion); *mpnykm* || *bydkm* (8bC, 11bD; responsion)

As in the preceding two canticles, it is possible to discern strophes which correspond to geographical and thematic progressions. Here

5:5; Cant. 3:4.

[168]In Num. 22:1; 26:3; 26:63; 31:12; 33:48; 33:50; 34:15; 35:1; 36:13; Josh. 13:32; 16:1; 20:8; 1 Chron. 6:63 we encounter the stereotypical expression *yrdn yrḥw*, which is suggestive that in Josh. 24:11 we may have an example of the break-up of a stereotyped phrase in order to establish internal parallelism in the respective cola.

[169]Cf. 8aC and 8bA above.

[170]Note too the same structure in the Mesha inscription at strophe V.1, also ending with a unicolon, cf. de Moor, "Narrative Poetry," 154.

[171]Cf. the inclusion formed by *ntn* and *nṣl* in Jer. 15:20.

[172]Cf., for example, the external parallelism in Jer. 2:7, where the colon *w'by' 'tkm 'l-'rṣ hkrml* finds a responsion in *wtb'w*.

the opposition to Israel is typified in the encounters with the Amorites, the Moabites, and finally the "lords" of Jericho. All three strophes are pressed from the same mold; the first poetic verse of each establishes the opposition through employment of *wylḥm(w)*. The conclusion is that the enemy is given into their hand or, as in the central strophe, that they are delivered out of the hand of the enemy. The similarity of these phrases adds to the cohesion of the entire canticle. The correspondence between the first and third strophe is the most precise,[173] thereby giving a concentric effect to the canticle. This is reinforced by the responsion *b'br hyrdn* || *wt'brw 't-hyrdn* as well as the use of *bw'* in both these strophes. While the central strophe has three poetic verses, the outer strophes both are composed of two verses.

### 3.4.5 Canticle I.v (24:12-13)

**I.v.1**

Sep. ↑: rep. *pnykm*; tautological *'wtm*[174]
Sep. ↓: tricolon; list of nations
Int. || : *w'šlḥ* || *wtgrš*;[175] *lpnykm* || *mpnykm*; list of seven nations
Ext. || : *'wtm* || list of nations

**I.v.2**

Sep. ↑: *'wtm*[176]
Sep. ↓: rep. *l'*; rep. *b*; rep. 2nd masc. sing. suffixes
Int. || : *'wtm* || *mlky h'mry*; *l' bḥrbk* || *wl' bqštk*[177]

[173]E.g., *wylḥmw* (plural) rather than *wylḥm* (singular), coupled with pronominal suffixes rather than the proper noun "Israel" as in I.iv.2. Furthermore, the phrase *w'tn 'wtm bydkm* is identical in I.iv.1 and I.iv.3 while the central strophe employs the related counterpart, *w'ṣl 'tkm mydw*.

[174]As it now stands, *'wtm* is a grammatically redundant indirect object paralleling the list of nations. It is therefore possible that this tautological presence of *'wtm* is to be accounted for as a marker of separation upwards; for a similar phenomenon see the employment of *lkm* in Josh. 23:5 (Koopmans, "Joshua 23," 95 n.31).

[175]There are only five verses in the OT where these two words are found together; for the other four see Ex. 6:1; 11:1; 23:28; 33:2.

[176]Cf. in I.v.1 above.

[177]The pairing of sword and bow occurs frequently in OT poetry, e.g., 2 Sam. 1:22 (W.H.Shea, "David's Lament," *BASOR* 221 [1976] 141-144, esp. 142); Isa. 21:15; 22:2f. (external parallelism); 41:2; Hos. 7:6; Zech. 9:13; Ps. 7:3; 37:14; 37:15 (cf. Dahood, *Psalms*, 1:228f.); 44:7; 76:4. For poetic syndetic parataxis see Hos. 1:7 and 2:20 (see too Gen. 48:22; 2 Kgs 6:22). Cf. Watters, *Formula Criticism*, 157 no.56, 174 no.513; Avishur, *Stylistic Studies*, 258. O.Keel, "Der Bogen als

Ext. || : *-km* || *-k* (2x)

**I.v.3**

Sep. ↑: shift to 1st person[178]
Sep. ↓: tricolon; emphatic *'tm 'klym*[179]
Int. || : *bnytm* || *wtšbw bhm*[180] *nṭ'tm* || *'tm 'klym*;[181] *krmym wzytym*[182] || *'tm 'klym*[183]
Ext. || : *'rṣ* || *'rym* || *krmym wzytym*;[184] *'šr l'* (3x); *yg't* || *bnytm* ||

Herrschaftssymbol," *ZDPV* 93 (1977) 141-177, esp. 175; Krašovec, *Der Merismus*, 101 no.93e,f. The phenomenon of paralleling weapons is widely attested in Ugaritic, cf. Dahood–Penar, "Parallel Pairs, I," 332-334. The phenomenon of negative *l'* || *l'* is too frequent to list, but see, e.g., Loretz, *Der Prolog*, 125.

[178]The previous strophe focused upon driving out the enemy; the present strophe highlights Yahweh's gracious gift of land.

[179]The final verse could have simply stated "And you eat from vineyards and olive groves which you did not plant." The present wording makes a parallelism with the preceding two verses, thereby establishing a cadence in the entire strophe.

[180]There are many poetic verses in which the verbs "build" and "dwell" are collocated, but see especially Am. 5:11; 9:14; Zeph. 1:13; Isa. 65:21f.; Jer. 29:5; 29:28. In Isa. 58:12 these verbs appear to constitute a deliberate inclusion. In Josh. 24:13 the parallelism is heightened by employment of the 3rd masc. pl. suffix parallel to the 2nd masc. pl ending, thereby also forming rhyme. The pair *bnh* and *yšb* is also employed in the Mesha inscription (V.1) and the Zakkur inscription (I'.3) (cf. de Moor, "Narrative Poetry," 154, 158, 162, 164).

[181]For this parallelism consult, e.g., Krašovec, *Der Merismus*, 123 no.158; Isa. 37:30 (= 2 Kgs 19:29 which is strangely presented in BHS as prose while Isa. 37:30 is presented as poetry); 65:21; 65:22; Am. 9:14. See also Jer. 25:5 and 29:28b, both of which are written as prose in BHS though their content and form is virtually identical to Isa. 65:21, which is presented as poetry. These observations illustrate the difficulty in distinguishing poetry and prose in portions of the prophetic books.

[182]For these two nouns as meristic pair see Krašovec, *Der Merismus*, 115 no.129; Loretz, *Der Prolog*, 125.

[183]Cf. Dahood–Penar, "Parallel Pairs, I," 108, with reference to Jer. 12:9f. Perhaps the parallelism with *krmym* should also include *nṭ'*, suggested as a word-pair by Watters, *Formula Criticism*, 159 no.96, on the basis of Isa. 5:7; 37:30; 65:21.

[184]The list proceeds from general to specific. For *'rṣ* and *'yr* paired as a poetic device see Isa. 1:7; 14:21; Jer. 2:15; 4:5, 7, 16; 8:16; 10:20; 14:18; 46:8; 47:2; 51:43; Ezek. 17:4; 19:7; Mic. 5:10; Ps. 72:16; 101:8; Lam. 2:15. On this pair see also Loretz, *Der Prolog*, 122; Avishur, *Stylistic Studies*, 278. It is also of interest to mention an internal parallelism in the Mesha inscription where *qrn* "cities" || *'rṣ* "land" is attested (de Moor, "Narrative Poetry," 155, 159). For an additional text in which *krmym wzytym* in syndetic parataxis is parallel to *'rym* see Neh. 9:25 (poetry). It is noteworthy that only in Josh. 24:13 and Neh. 9:25 do these three words occur in the OT within a single verse; extension to a span of two verses would also include Deut. 6:10f. Am. 4:8f.

*nṭ'tm;*[185] *wtšbw bhm* || *'tm 'klym*[186]
Rhyme: five of the seven cola end with *-m*

Willis demonstrates that alternating parallelism is a common phenomenon in the Prophets.[187] Included in his examples is a discussion of Am. 5:llc-f, which expresses the exact opposite of Josh. 24:13 and also employs *bnytm* || *tšbw bm*. Josh. 24:13 is therefore comparable to the poetry of Am. 5:11 with regard to both form and content.

## External Parallelism in I.v

### I.v.1 and I.v.2

*wtgrš 'wtm mpnykm* || <*wtgrš 'wtm mpnykm*> (12aB, <12bA>; responsion); *h'mry* || *šny mlky h'mry* (11bA, 12bB); *hṣr'h* || *ḥrbk* and *qštk* (12aA, 12cB; inclusion)[188]

### I.v.2 and I.v.3

negative *l'* (2x) || (3x)

### I.v.1 and I.v.3

*w'šlḥ lpnykm* || *w'tn lkm* (12aA, 13aA; responsion);[189] *'wtm* || *'tm* (12aB, 13cC; inclusion)

There is a thematic cohesion to this canticle, as is evident in the emphasis that Israel's acquisition of the land is facilitated by divine initiative. Vs.13 marks the end of the historical summary which began in vs.2b. Vs.14 shifts to injunctions based upon that historical

[185]For *bnh* || *nṭ'* consult Watters, *Formula Criticism*, 184 no.783.

[186]The verbs *'kl* and *yšb* are frequently used in parallelism, e.g., Isa. 24:6; 65:4; 65:21f. (2x) (cf. Watters, *Formula Criticism*, 184 no.785); Jer. 16:8 (cf. W.L.Holladay, "The Recovery of Poetic Passages of Jeremiah," *JBL* 85 [1966] 414f., 419); Hos. 9:3 (chiastic inclusion); Am. 9:14.

[187]Willis, "(ABÁB́) Parallelism," 49-76.

[188]Forming an antithetical pair and, as reconstructed here, standing as an inclusion of these two strophes.

[189]For verbal parallelism between *ntn* and *šlḥ* see Cassuto, *Biblical and Oriental Studies*, 2:64; Dahood, *Psalms*, 3:453; Dahood–Penar, "Parallel Pairs, I," 219; Avishur, *Stylistic Studies*, 542f.; van der Meer, *Oude woorden*, 78. On the one hand it must be conceded that the texts appealed to by Cassuto and Dahood are in the area of a messenger context, which raises reservations with respect to their utility to support parallelism here; but cf. Avishur's appeal to Job 5:10; Ps. 20:3-6; 78:24f.; 105:26-35; 106:15; 147:15f. Furthermore, parallelism in Josh. 24:12f. is heightened by the parallel prepositions with identical 3rd masc. pl. suffixes as well as the fact that the verbal forms are formally identical and both verbs refer to actions performed by Yahweh to actuate military victory for Israel.

summary. From this point the first person singular forms are no longer used in reference to Yahweh's actions. In the following section of our study it will be argued that at vs.14 a new canto begins. To this point Joshua has functioned as Yahweh's prophetic spokesman (cf. vs.2). With the *w'th* in vs.14, the dialogue shifts to Joshua's specific imperatives to the people.

### 3.4.6 Canticle II.i (24:14-15)

**II.i.1**

Sep. ↑: *w'th*;[190] imperatives *yr'w* and *'bdw*; rep. *'t*; rep. prep. *b*
Sep. ↓: quadrocolon;[191] imperatives *hsyrw* and *'bdw*; rep. *'t* and *'bd*
Int. ‖ : *yr'w* ‖ *w'bdw*;[192] *'t-yhwh* ‖ *'tw*; *whsyrw 't-'lhym* ‖ *w'bdw 't-yhwh*;[193] *'bdw* ‖ *w'bdw*
Ext. ‖ : imperatives *yr'w* and *w'bdw* ‖ *whsyrw* and *w'bdw*;[194] *'t-yhwh* ‖ *'t-'lhym*;[195] prepositions *b* (2x) ‖ *b* (2x)[196]

[190]This is a strong marker of separation. See van der Lugt, *Strofischen structuren*, 517. The function of *w'th* to mark strophes was already suggested by Muilenburg, "Form Criticism," 15. In addition consult his "Form and Structure," 353, 359; Laurentin, "*We'attāh-kai nun*," 168-195; 413-432; Brongers, "Adverbialen *We'ATTĀH*," 289-299.

[191]Regarding the existence of quadrocola see especially Korpel–de Moor, "Fundamentals," 190f.

[192]Both are imperatives, and there is a clear semantic parallelism between "fearing" and "serving," cf. Deut. 6:13; 10:12,20; 13:5; 1 Sam. 12:14,20,24; 2 Kgs 17:33, 35,41.

[193]The grammatical constructions are identical, with imperative + direct object marker + direct object. There is a semantic parallelism entailed in the respective imperatives to put away the gods and to serve Yahweh, cf. esp. Judg. 10:16; 1 Sam. 7:3f.; 12:20; 2 Chron. 34:33.

[194]For the possible parallelism of the verbs *yr'* and *swr* cf. 1 Sam. 12:20; Job 1:1,8; 2:3; Prov. 3:7; 14:16. It is noteworthy that in BHS only the latter two texts are printed as poetry, but the expression *yr' yhwh* ‖ *swr mr'* (Prov. 3:7) finds an exact counterpart in the three references in Job. Incidentally, this parallelism suggests that "Yahweh" or "Elohim" is to be read as the understood object in Prov. 14:16 (with Zürcher Bibel and NIV), contrary to the reading "A wise man is cautious" (RSV) and similarly, "Der Weise ist vorsichtig" (O.Plöger, *Spruche Salomos* [Neukirchen-Vluyn, 1984], 165.). This parallelism in Job is noted by Watters (*Formula Criticism*, 189 no.4) but he does not include the references in Proverbs in his discussion of whether or not Job 1:1ff. is poetic (cf. ibid., 122).

[195]Boling, "'Synonymous' Parallelism," esp. 242-251.

[196]Cf. the references at I.iii.4 above. The parallelism established by the prepositions with nouns in syndetic parataxis has the effect of contrasting the worship of false gods *b'br hnhr wbmṣrym* with the worship of Yahweh *btmym wb'mt*. For

Inclusion: *'t-yhwh* || *'t-yhwh*; *w'bdw* || *w'bdw*

**II.i.2**

Sep. ↑: conditional *w'm*[197]
Sep. ↓: imperative *bḥrw*[198]
Int. || : *bḥr* || *'bd*[199]
Ext. || : *-km* || *-km*; *l'bd* || *t'bdwn*; *'t-yhwh* || *'t-my*[200]

It is significant that the paucity of internal parallelism allows the emphasis to fall upon the alternating parallelism of the four cola in this strophe.

**II.i.3**

Sep. ↑: tricolon; *'m*; rep. *'šr*
Sep. ↓: *petuchah*; refrain;[201] emphatic hendiadys *w'nky wbyty*

additional examples of the syndetic parataxis of *btmym wb'mt* but in inverted order see Judg. 9:16,19; for poetic parallelism consult Ps. 15:2. In light of our attempt to read this passage as poetry, it is noteworthy that Butler concludes that *tmym* is basically cultic, listing numerous references in the Psalms, Proverbs and Job, and similarly, that *'mt* "finds its basic usage in the Psalms" (*Joshua*, 272f.).

[197]In this case the conditional conjunction *'m* is strengthened by an adversative or asseverative *waw*. For the conditional use of *'m* consult Williams, *Hebrew Syntax*, 74, §453. For *'m* as a marker of separation see van der Lugt, *Strofische structuren*, 522f.; cf. C.van Leeuwen, "Die Partikel *'m*," *OTS* 18 (Leiden, 1973), 15-48.

[198]Note that *t'bdwn* has the paragogic *nun*. It would be attractive to clarify this presence as creating a pausal effect or a particular emphasis at the end of the poetic strophe. Note that a major conclusion of the study by J.Hoftijzer, *The Function and Use of the Imperfect Forms with Nun Paragogicum in Classical Hebrew* (Assen, 1985), is that the *nun paragogicum* often conveys contrastivity or special emphasis (esp. 94); but Hoftijzer warns that the category in which Josh. 24:15 falls is not widely enough represented to allow for definite conclusions (55, 113 n.235). It is noteworthy that the next word begins with an *aleph*, cf. Ex. 3:12 (not pausal); on the other hand, the same form preceding an *aleph* in Jer. 5:19; 27:9, 14; Judg. 10:13 does *not* have the paragogic *nun*. In any event, separation downwards is relatively weak here. The apodosis of the conditional sentence is elaborated in 15c and 15d, with the double employment of *'m* expressing alternatives (cf. Williams, *Hebrew Syntax*, 74, §455). Nevertheless, 15c has a number of markers of separation, and, given the close relationship to 15d, these markers of separation in 15c can better be viewed as evidence for strophic division upwards between 15c and 15b than downwards between 15c and 15d. Taken together as a strophe, 15a and 15b provide another striking example of alternating paralllelism (cf. the list of external parallelisms).

[199]Cf. vs. 22 below. These are the only two verses in the MT where these two verbs occur together.

[200]Note that these external parallelisms suggest that once again we are dealing with a two bicolon strophe comprised of alternating parallelism.

[201]The employment of the verb *'bd* as a first person plural confession, *n'bd*, occurs

Int. || : *'šr* || *'šr*[202]
Ext. || : *'m 't-'lhym* || *w'm 't-'lhy*; *'šr* || *'šr*; *'bdw* || *n'bd*; *'bwtykm* || *'tm* || *'nky*; *b'br hnhr* || *b'rṣm*[203]
Inclusion: *'t-'lhym* || *'t-yhwh*; *'bdw* || *n'bd*[204]

### External parallelism in II.i

### II.i.1 and II.i.2

*'t-yhwh* || *'t-yhwh* (14aA, 15aB; responsion); *w'bdw* || *l'bd* (14aB, 15aB; responsion); *whsyrw* || *bḥrw* (14bA, 15bA; responsion);[205] *w'bdw* || *t'bdwn* (14bD, 15bB; responsion)

### II.i.2 and II.i.3

*w'm* || *'m* (15aA, 15cA; responsion) and *w'm* (15dD); *-km* || *-km* (15aA, 15cB; responsion); *lkm* || *'tm* (15bB, 15dB; responsion); *'t-my t'bdwn* || *n'bd 't-yhwh* (15bB; 15eB; responsion); *t'bdwn* || *'bdw* (15bB, 15cB; concatenation)

### II.i.1 and II.i.3

*'t-yhwh* || *'t-'lhym* (14aA, 15cA; responsion); *w'bdw* || *'bdw* (14aB, 15cB; responsion); *'t-'lhym* || *'t-'lhy* (14bA, 15dA, responsion); *'šr 'bdw 'bwtykm* (14bB, 15cB, inclusion); *b'br hnhr* (14bC, 15cC, responsion); *bmṣrym* || *b'rṣm* (14bC, 15dB); *w'bdw 't-yhwh* || *n'bd 't-yhwh* (14bd, 15eB, responsion)
Inclusion: *'t-yhwh* (14aA, 15eB); *w'bdw* || *n'bd* (14aB, 15eB)

four times in Josh. 24:14-24, and always at the end of a canticle, cf. 15eB, 18aA, 21B, 24B. This is especially significant in light of the fact that, although the verb *'bd* is employed nearly 300x in the OT (see C.Westermann, "*'bd*," *THAT*, 2:183), according to A.Even-Shoshan (*A New Concordance of the Bible* [Jerusalem, 1981], 818), the identical form *n'bd* is found only 3x in addition to Josh. 24, viz., Ex. 10:26; Judg. 10:10; 1 Sam. 12:10—the latter two with *waw*. (In addition there are instances in which it is accompanied by a suffix: Ex. 14:12; Deut. 12:7,14; 13:3; Judg. 9:28,38; 1 Sam. 11:1; 12:10; 1 Kgs 12:4; 2 Chron. 10:4; Job 21:15.) This suggests that the fourfold placement of the form *n'bd* in Josh. 24:14-24 is significant, especially when we note that all four times it is part of a refrain at the end of a canticle. These details are unfortunately overlooked by I.Riesener, who follows the analysis of Perlitt; cf. I.Riesener, *Der Stamm 'bd im Alten Testament* (Berlin and New York, 1979), 210f.

[202]In addition to the examples of this parallelism offered in the introduction to the present chapter, consider Isa. 1:29; 7:18; 50:1; 55:11, to list a few occurrences.

[203]Cf. *'rṣ* || *m'br lnhry-kwš*, attested in Isa. 18:1.

[204]This strong external parallelism is sufficient to neutralize the separating force of *w'm*, cf. de Moor, "Book of Ruth, I," 268 n.20, 277; Korpel–de Moor, "Fundamentals," 196.

[205]Imperative forms used antithetically, cf. also 2 Kgs 23:27.

In this canticle, as in numerous instances above, the strongest external parallelisms are formed between the first and last strophe, thereby on the one hand setting the canticle off from the surrounding material, and on the other hand forming a framework around a central strophe. The framing technique is especially evident in the formulaic employment of the colon *'šr ʿbdw 'bwtykm* (14bB, 15cB) as well as *bʿbr hnhr* (14bC, 15cC). It is worth noting that in this canticle, if all words joined by a *maqqeph* are counted as one poetic foot,[206] the central imperative *bḥrw* is both preceded and followed by 22 feet.[207] The colon in which *bḥrw* is found (15bA) is both preceded and followed by 8 cola, and the poetic verse in which it occurs is both preceded and followed by 3 poetic verses. These observations, along with the external parallelisms noted between II.i.1 and II.i.3 are indicative that the well-balanced literary construction serves to highlight the central imperative *bḥrw lkm hywm.*

### 3.4.7 Canticle II.ii (24:16-18)

**II.ii.1**

Sep. ↑: *petuchah*; quadrocolon;[208] *wyʿn hʿm wy'mr*;[209] emphatic *ḥlylh*
Sep. ↓: pentacolon;[210] *ky*;[211]

[206]Cf. Korpel–de Moor, "Fundamentals" 173f.

[207]Note that *'šr ʿbdw* in 14bB is not joined by a *maqqeph*, in contrast to 15cB.

[208]In support of the claim to read a quadrocolon here we note that *ḥlylh ly* does not need to stand in the opening colon of a strophe, cf. 1 Sam. 2:30.

[209]This marks a change of person and a shift in subject matter, corresponding with a new stage in the dialogue; to this point only Joshua has spoken. The response of the people stands at the beginning of a new canticle. The combination of *wyʿn* and *wy'mr* together makes a strong marker of separation. Cf. L.Delekat, "Zum hebräischen Wörterbuch," *VT* 14 (1964) 41, where Josh. 24:16 is included among a number of texts in which "*ʿnh* wird soviel wie 'feierlich sprechen,' bezeugen."

[210]A pentacolon is an admittedly rare occurrence, cf. Korpel–de Moor, "Fundamentals," 190f. In this respect a couple of observations are significant. The material found in 17aE-17bB is not present in the LXX. If 17aE is a later expansion, the original verse would have been a quadrocolon. Furthermore, *w't-'bwtynw* (17aC) is not present in the Peshitta, and it is theoretically possible that this too is a poetic expansion. The different readings of the LXX and MT are discussed more fully below.

[211]J.Muilenburg, "The Linguistic and Rhetorical Usages of the Particle *ky* in the Old Testament," *HUCA* 32 (1961) 135-160; "Form Criticism," 13f. See too Th.C.Vriezen, "Einige Notizen zur Übersetzung des Bindewortes *kī*," in Hempel–Rost eds., *Von Ugarit nach Qumran*, 266-273; A.Schoors, "The Particle *ky*," *OTS* 21 (Leiden, 1981) 240-276. The particle *ky* does not always function as a marker of sep-

*hw'*;[212] rep. *-nw*; rep. prep. *m*
Int. || : *wy'n* || *wy'mr*;[213] *'zb* || *'bd*;[214] *yhwh* || *'lhym 'ḥrym*;[215]
*yhwh* || *hw' hm'lh*;[216] *-nw* (3x);[217] *m'rṣ mṣrym* || *mbyt 'bdym*[218]

aration, but its emphatic nuance has long been posited with respect to Ugaritic as well as Hebrew poetry; cf. already R.Gordis, "The Asseverative Kaph in Ugaritic and Hebrew," *JAOS* 63 (1943) 176-178; J.H.Patton, *Canaanite Parallels in the Book of Psalms* (Baltimore, 1944), 12. Unavailable to the present writer was the study by B.Bandstra ("The Syntax of Particle ki in Biblical Hebrew and Ugaritic," [PhD diss, Yale University, 1982]), in which it is argued that *ky* rarely, if ever, has emphatic nuance.

212Van der Lugt, *Strofische structuren*, 521.

213It is difficult to determine whether *wy'n* and *wy'mr* should be viewed contrary to the Masoretic accentuation as a parallelism in successive cola, as we have chosen for here, or to view these verbs as part of the same colon. A survey of all such constructions in the OT shows that the Masoretic accentuation is not consistent on the matter of disjunctive or conjunctive accents in such cases. And in some instances where the Masoretic accentuation is disjunctive BHS reads the respective words as part of the same colon, e.g., at Joel 2:19, where van der Meer divides the cola more convincingly to include a parallelism between *'mr* and *'nh* (*Oude woorden*, 75, 78). Similarly, at Ruth 2:11 de Moor reads *wy'n* and *wy'mr* as parallels ("Book of Ruth, II," 20f.). Cf. Watters, *Formula Criticism*, 182 no.727. The same construction is prevalent in the poetic dialogue of the Book of Job.

214Cf. Josh. 24:20; Judg. 2:13; 10:6,10,13; 1 Sam. 8:8; 12:10; 1 Kgs 9:9; 2 Kgs 17:16; Jer. 5:19; 16:11; 22:9; 1 Chron. 28:9; 2 Chron. 7:19,22; 24:18. These are the only verses in which these two verbs are found together, and in every case they are part of a semantic parallelism. All these texts are prose in BHS.

215Cf. vs.2 in I.ii.1 above.

216For *yhwh* || to the participle *hm'lh* see Lev. 11:45; Deut. 20:1; 2 Kgs 17:7; Jer. 2:6 (in BHS as poetry—where *yhwh* is paralleled by the two participles *hm'lh* and *hmwlyk*); Ps. 81:11. See further Isa. 63:11, where *hm'lh* is an understood reference to Yahweh. There are many texts in the Psalms where *yhwh* is paralleled by *hw'* (Boling, "'Synonymous' Parallelism," 243). Consider also Deut. 32:4, where MT has *'l* || *hw'* but LXX represents *yhwh* || *hw'*.

217Note especially that *'tnw* || *'bwtynw* can be compared with the interchanges in vss.5-7 above.

218Cf. Melamed, "Break-up," 148. Additional support is gleaned from Mic. 6:4, where the phrase *m'rṣ mṣrym mbyt 'bdym*, although in syndetic parataxis, is distributed over two cola. Similarly, it is interesting to compare the distribution in Deut. 13:6, especially in light of the asyndetic parataxis attested in Ex. 20:2; Deut. 5:6; 6:12; 8:14; 13:11; Jer. 34:13. Of these verses Josh. 24:17 and Mic. 6:4 employ the verb *'lh* with reference to Yahweh, while the others employ *yṣ'* (see esp. J.Wijngaards, "*Hwṣy'* and *h'lh*: A Twofold Approach to the Exodus," *VT* 15 [1965] 91-102). In anticipation of the text-critical discussion of the LXX below we note that it is possible that there is an expansion here of the MT by means of the addition of *mbyt 'bdym* marking the completion of a stock phrase or parallelism, but most significantly, the various versions can be viewed as expanded or contracted forms of the very same poetic structure.

Ext. || : *yhwh* || *yhwh*; *'lhym 'ḥrym* || *yhwh 'lhynw*;
prep. *mn* || *mn* (2x); *l'bd* || *'bdym*;[219] *lnw* || *'tnw*
Rhyme: *-nw*

**II.ii.2**

Sep. ↑: *h'lh*[220]
Sep. ↓: rep. prep. *b*
Int. || : *-nw* || *-nw*; *bkl* || *bh*; *drk* || *hlk*;[221] *bkl* || *bqrbm*[222]
Ext. || : *bkl* || *bkl*;[223] *'šr hlknw bh* || *'šr 'brnw bqrbm*;[224]

Note the alternating (ABÁB́) parallelism of these six cola, and especially of the final two verses. It is instructive to compare the scansion of Isa. 1:29 as offered in BHS, i.e., *ky ybšw m'ylym / 'šr ḥmdtm* || *wtḥprw mhgnwt / 'šr bḥrtm*, where alternating parallelism is also formed with *'šr* in the B-cola.

**II.ii.3**

Sep. ↑: resumption of the subject *yhwh*;[225] rep. *'t*

[219]This external parallelism argues against seeing 17aE as simply a gloss.

[220]At first it is surprising to see a new strophe beginning with a relative clause, but a sentence running on through more than one strophe is by no means irregular, cf. Korpel–de Moor, "Fundamentals," 198f. The grammatical construction *w'šr 'śh* has been claimed in itself to be unusual, cf. B.Albrektson, "On the Syntax of *'hyh 'šr 'hyh* in Exodus 3:14," in Ackroyd–Lindars, eds., *Words and Meanings*, 22. Following a proposal by V.Baumann (*Hebräische Relativsätze* [Leipzig, 1894], 22), Albrektson treats the construction as a relative clause serving as predicate. It may be conceded on the one hand that the absence of 17b in the LXX makes it suspect, as will be more fully elaborated in the discussion of the LXX offered below. However, judgment in this case must be tempered among other considerations by the external parallelism formed with vs.7b. Note too that Josh. 24:31b uses *w'šr* in a comparable manner. For an additional example of a strophe beginning with *'šr* see van der Lugt, *Strofische structuren*, 292 (re Ps. 64:4f.).

[221]Cf. Dahood, "Parallel Pairs, III," 60f. no.98.

[222]For the parallelism of *b* || *bqrb* see the discussion above of ext. par. between 1.iii.1 and 1.iii.4.

[223]The parallelism formed by *bkl* would suggest that *hdrk* and *h'mym* could also be considered a parallelism here, but this is not attested as such elsewhere in the OT. For some examples of *bkl* || *bkl* see Isa. 7:19; Jer. 10:7; 15:13; Am. 5:16f. (3x). See too Koopmans, "Joshua 23," 102; "Testament of David," (forthcoming). For *mkl* || *bkl* in the Mesha inscription cf. de Moor, "Narrative Poetry," 152, 156.

[224]The verbs *hlk* and *'br* can be viewed as standing parallel in various OT verses. For examples consult Watters, *Formula Criticism*, 172 no.459 (re Isa. 33:21; 35:8; 43:2; 45:14 [chiastic]); de Moor, "Book of Ruth, II" 18f. (re Ruth 2:8). See also Am. 6:2; Cant. 2:11. The evidence for *b* || *bqrb* has been offered above at ext. par. in I.iii.1 and I.iii.4.

[225]Mention of Yahweh with the third pers. verb is significant here because of the

Sep. ↓: *setumah*; *gm*; independent *'nḥnw*; refrain with *n'bd*;[226] *ky-hw'*[227]
Int. || : *h'mym* || *w't-h'mry yšb h'rṣ*;[228] *-nw* || *-nw*;[229] *yhwh* || *'lhynw*[230]

### External parallelism in II.ii

### II.ii.1 and II.ii.2

*-nw* (4x) || (4x); *hm'lh 'tnw* || *hlknw* (17aB, 17cB);[231] *mṣrym* || *'mym* (17aD, 17dA; responsion)

### II.ii.2 and II.ii.3

*l'ynynw* || *mpnynw* (17bA, 18aB; responsion); *bkl-hdrk* || *kl-h'mym* (17cA, 18aA; responsion); *wbkl h'mym* || *kl-h'mym* (17dA, 18aA; concatenation); *bqrbm* || *mpnynw* (17dB, 18aB); *-nw* (4x) || (3x); *hlk* and *'br* || *yšb*[232]

### II.ii.1 and II.ii.3

*'t-yhwh* || *'t-yhwh* (16aC, 18bA; inclusion); *l'bd* || *n'bd* (16aD, 18bB, responsion); *'lhym 'ḥrym* || *'lhynw* (16aD, 18bC; responsion); *'tnw* || *'nḥnw* (17aB, 18bA); *hw'* || *hw'* (17aB, 18bB; responsion);[233] *ky yhwh 'lhynw* || *ky-hw' 'lhynw* (17aA, 18bB; responsion);[234] *'bdym* || *n'bd* (17aE, 18bB; responsion)

strong concatenation formed by *kl-h'mym*.

[226]It is noteworthy that the refrain is expanded with the colon *ky-hw' 'lhynw* in order to make a responsion with 17aA.

[227]Cf. the discussion at II.A.ii.1 above.

[228]Cf. D.W.Baker, "Further Examples of the *wāw explicativum*," *VT* 30 (1980) 132; for *'m* || *'rṣ* many times in Isaiah, see Watters, *Formula Criticism*, 162 no.190.

[229]This parallelism also occurs in the previous strophes of this canticle.

[230]Cf. Boling, "'Synonymous' Parallelism," 243 (re Ps. 18:32; 92:14; 116:5; 135:2; 147:7).

[231]This parallelism is debatable because it matches a participle in reference to Yahweh + 1st c. plural pronominal direct obj. with a 1st c. pl. verb form, but see, e.g., Jer. 2:6 with parallelism of the participles *hm'lh* and *hmwlyk* and the comparability of the following cola with Josh. 24:17; see too the external parallelism in Deut. 20:1,4 where *ky-yhwh 'lhyk 'mk / hm'lk m'rṣ mṣrym* || *ky yhwh 'lhykm / hhlk 'mkm*. This latter reference is part of a longer passage of poetic narrative.

[232]To pass through a land or place, and to inhabit it, are sometimes expressed as a parallelism in OT poetry, e.g., Jer. 2:6; 51:43; Zeph. 3:6. For the possible parallelism of *hlk* and *yšb* see Watters, *Formula Criticism*, 161 no.166. Regarding *yṣ'* and *yšb* see vss.5 and 7, I.iii.1 and I.iii.4.

[233]Cf., e.g., Ps. 33:9; 100:3.

[234]For similar expressions with *hw'* in the Psalms see, e.g., 45:12; 95:7; 100:3; 105:7.

Recognition of the poetic nature of the formulae *ky yhwh 'lhynw* and *ky-hw' 'lhynw* is of considerable importance for the interpretation of this passage and they therefore deserve extended comment here to justify the claim that they are poetic. The colon *ky yhwh 'lhynw*, where God is accompanied by the 1st pers. plural suffix, is found elsewhere in identical form only in Jer. 8:14 (poetry). Extension of our study to include slight variations on this confession serves to reinforce the conclusion that it is poetic, e.g., *whw' y'mr 'lhy* (Hos. 2:25, cf. Ps. 31:15); *ky 'th 'lhy* (Ps. 143:10); *ky 'th yhwh 'lhynw* (Jer. 3:22, cf. 31:18); *ky lyhwh 'lhynw ḥṭnw* (Jer. 3:25); *ky-qdwš yhwh 'lhynw* (Ps. 99:9); *ky-ṣdyq yhwh 'lhynw* (Dan. 9:14).[235] For the sake of completeness mention may also be made of Jer. 26:16, *ky bšm yhwh 'lhynw dbr 'lynw*, which is prose in BHS and is not part of a spoken confession; it narrates an event and is therefore not really comparable with the previously mentioned confessional texts.

The colon *ky hw' 'lhynw* (Josh. 24:18bC) is equally striking. The only exact parallel is Ps. 95:7, in a Psalm which exalts the kingship of Yahweh and contains a number of significant affinities with Josh. 24, which will be further elaborated below. These initial observations strongly suggest that the cola *ky yhwh 'lhynw* and *ky-hw' 'lhynw* have their most natural setting in confessional poetry.[236]

Our analysis of the present canticle would suggest that, like the preceding canticles, it is composed of three strophes.[237] The first verse introduces Israel's confession, which is further explicated in the ensuing verse and in the following two strophes. The first strophe deals with the delivery from Egypt, the second with the preservation of Israel during the entry into the land of the promise, and the third concentrates specifically on the theme of conquest, ending with a refrain.[238]

[235]Printed in BHS as prose but part of a confessional prayer with many poetic aspects, e.g., the vocative in vs.4, noted already in S.H.Blank, "Some Observations Concerning Biblical Prayer," *HUCA* 32 (1961) 80f., and see too Muilenburg, "Form Criticism," 16, regarding vocatives.

[236]For the parallelism of *yhwh* || *'lhynw* consult Boling, "'Synonymous' Parallelism," 243 (re Ps. 18:32; 92:14; 116:5; 135:2; 147:7); Loretz, *Der Prolog*, 124 (re Isa. 1:10).

[237]There are a number of highly significant responsions between II.i and II.ii. These responsions are elaborated below in the section dealing with macrostructure. For the present we note the structural similarity of the canticles, each consisting of three strophes and seven verses.

[238]The relationship of this confession to the historical summary (I.ii-v) and to

### 3.4.8 Canticle II.iii (24:19-21)

**II.iii.1**

Sep. ↑: *setumah*; *'mr*; change of subject
Sep. ↓: *ky*; rep. *'l* and *hw'*
Int. || : *yhwš'* || *yhwh*; *'lhym qdšym hw'* || *'l-qnw' hw'*;[239]
Ext. || : *yhwh* || *'lhym* and *'l*[240]

**II.iii.2**

Sep. ↑: quadrocolon;[241] rep. *l* and *-km*
Sep. ↓: tricolon; rep. *lkm*;[242]
Int. || : *lpš'km* || *wlḥṭ'wtykm*;[243]

Joshua's injunction (II.A.i) will be dealt with below.

[239]See the discussion in 2.3.7.2 above where the claims by McCarthy and Alonso-Asenjo concerning ancient cultic poetic formulations are summarized. In addition it should be noted that references to *El* are rare in Joshua, occurring only in 3:10; 22:22; 24:19. For the poetic identity of 3:10 and 22:22 consult Boling, *Joshua*, 164f., 503. Regarding 24:19 compare also the poetic descriptions of Yahweh in Isa. 43:3, 14f.; Ps. 99:8f. We have divided the verse contrary to the Masoretes, who apparently misplaced the *atnaḥ*, as is evident from the parallelism of *'lhym* || *'l*; *hw'* || *hw'*.

[240]For *yhwh* || *'l* in the Psalms see Boling, "'Synonymous' Parallelism," 228, 242f.; for *yhwh* || *'l* in Isaiah consult Watters, *Formula Criticism*, 159 no.109. For *'lhym* || *'l* in the Psalms see Boling, ibid., 228, 245; in Isaiah, Watters, ibid., 178 no.614, and in Job, ibid., 198 no.246.

[241]It is also possible that 19c should be treated as one colon rather than two, in which case we would have a tricolon rather than a quadrocolon here; but see the discussion of internal parallelism. Contrary to the Masoretic accents we take 19c and 20a together because the latter specifies the former. We translate *ky* here in a temporal sense. Knierim has shown that the *ky* should not be translated as a conditional but rather with a future indicative force (*Die Hauptbegriffe*, 138). He thereby recognizes the structural parallelism between vss.19 and 20. In fact, Knierim implicitly posits the poetic nature of these verses when he calls attention to their similarity in both "Stil und Inhalt" to Am. 3:2 (ibid., 140 n.78). Cf. Isa. 1:28.

[242]Reinforced by *'tkm* in the same verse, making a triple repetition of *-km*. Consider too the position of *'ḥry*, listed by W.J.P.Boyd as having a concessive function ("Notes on the Secondary Meanings of *'ḥr*," *JThSt* 12 [1961] 54). However, the other examples Boyd lists do not lend clear support for a function as a marker of separation.

[243]When these two nouns occur together they are usually in poetic parallelism, which is why we prefer to read a quadrocolon rather than a tricolon here, cf. Isa. 43:24f.; 44:22; 58:1; 59:12; Am. 5:12; Mi. 1:5, 13; 3:8; 6:7; Ps. 25:7; 32:5; 51:3-5; 59:4; Job 13:23; 14:16f.; 34:37; Dan. 9:24. For previous authors recognizing the parallelism of *pš'* and *ḥt'* see Dahood, "Parallel Pairs, III," 43 no.60h.; Boling, "'Synonymous' Parallelism," 231, 237; Watters, *Formula Criticism*, 157 no.43, 204

*lpš'km* || *'zb*;[244]
*wlḥṭ'wtykm* || *'zb*;[245]
*'zb* || *'bd*;[246]
*yhwh* || *'lhy nkr*;[247]
*lkm* || *'tkm* || *lkm*;
*r''* || *klh*;[248]
*r''* || *yṭb*[249]
Ext. || : *l'-yś' lpš'km wlḥṭykm* || *wšb whr' lkm*[250]
-*km* (2x) || -*km* (3x)[251] *'zb* || *šwb*[252]
Rhyme: -*km* (5x)

## II.iii.3

Sep. ↑: *'mr*[253]

no.380; Loretz, *Der Prolog*, 126; Avishur, *Stylistic Studies*, 221, 285, 659.

[244]Regarding the parallelism of the noun *pš'* and the verb *'zb* cf. esp. Prov. 28:13; Isa. 58:1f. (ext. par.); Jer. 5:6f. (ext. par.); for the verb *pš'* || *'zb* cf. Isa. 1:28.

[245]For the noun *ḥṭ'h* || *'zb* cf. Isa. 58:1f. (ext. par.); Jer. 16:10f. (ext. par.); and with the verb *ḥṭ'* see Isa. 1:4 (ext. par.); cf. Judg. 10:10; 1 Sam. 12:10. Recognition of the various forms of *pš'* and *ḥṭ'* with *'zb* justifies reading Josh. 24:19c-20a as a quadrocolon, or perhaps a tricolon. Regarding the parallelism of these three roots in Isaiah see Loretz, *Der Prolog*, 126.

[246]Cf. vs.16, above.

[247]Cf. the chiastic parallelism in Deut. 32:12; Ps. 81:10f. (Schmitt, *Landtag*, 22f.); cf. Jer. 8:19 (poetry); Jud. 10:16; 1 Sam. 7:3; 2 Chron. 33:15; Jer. 5:19 for similar parallelisms.

[248]This would appear to be a semantic parallelism in the sense of doing evil to someone, but supporting evidence is lacking.

[249]These two verbs occur within a single verse seven times in the OT, namely Lev. 5:4; Josh. 24:20; Isa. 41:23; Jer. 4:22; 10:5; 13:23; Zeph. 1:12. Significantly the last five of these references are all poetic. Regarding Lev. 5:4 see Avishur, *Stylistic Studies*, 122. See too Isa. 1:16f.; Zech. 8:14f. Since Josh. 24:20 refers to the actions of God, it stands closest to Isa. 41:23; Jer. 10:5; Zeph. 1:12, all of which are poetic. The parallelism of these verbs in the Hiph. form has been widely acknowledged, e.g., by Wildberger, *Jesaja*, 47; Watters, *Formula Criticism*, 156 no.30; Krašovec, *Der Merismus*, 106, no.107 and 146 no.237; *Antithectic Structure*, 81; Loretz, *Prolog*, 127; W.L.Holladay, *Jeremiah 1: A Commentary on the Book of the Prophet Jeremiah Chapters 1-25* (Philadelphia, 1986), 329. For a possible parallelism in one of the Lachish ostraca consult Gibson, *Semitic Inscriptions*, 1:44.

[250]The semantic synonymity is clear, and identification of this parallelism is reinforced by the observations by Dahood with respect to *pš'* and *šwb* ("Parallel Pairs, III," 172f. no.332).

[251]Forming rhyme at the end of five of the seven cola of the strophe.

[252]Compare Isa. 55:7; Neh. 9:17,28; Ruth 1:16 (de Moor, "Book of Ruth, I" 279).

[253]Cf. vs.24, where the same formulaic colon marking a shift in dialogue also

Sep. ↓: refrain with *n'bd*[254]
Int. || : *yhwš'* || *yhwh*

**External parallelism in II.iii**

**II.iii.1 and II.iii.2**

*l' twklw l'bd 't-yhwh* || *l'-yś' lpš'km wlḥṭ'wtykm* (19aB, 19cA; responsion); *l'bd 't-yhwh* || *w'bdtm 'lhy nkr* (19aB, 20aD; responsion);[255]

**II.iii.2 and II.iii.3**

*w'bdtm 'lhy nkr* || *'t-yhwh n'bd* (20aD, 21aB; responsion)[256]

**II.iii.1 and II.iii.3**

*wy'mr yhwš' 'l-h'm* || *wy'mr h'm 'l-yhwš'* (19aA, 21A; responsion and inclusion); *l' twklw l'bd 't-yhwh* || *l' ky 't-yhwh n'bd* (19aB, 21B; responsion and inclusion)[257]

Structurally and thematically the first two strophes are closely related. In both strophes Joshua warns the people of Yahweh's severe nature. The third strophe consists of a single bicolon verse which forms significant responsions and inclusion with the foregoing verses, especially with vs.19a, thereby marking the boundaries of the canticle as coinciding with the dialogical unit. An added degree of emphasis, in comparison with the preceding two canticles, is built into the refrain via the employment of *l' ky* along with *n'bd* in 21B.

## 3.4.9 Canticle II.iv (24:22-24)

**II.iv.1**

Sep. ↑: *'mr*;[258] quadrocolon; *ky*; rep. *'tm* and *-km*
Sep. ↓: *'mr*[259]

denotes the beginning of a new strophe.

[254]Cf. above. Mention may also be made of the emphatic and asseverative function of *l'-ky*, cf. Schoors, "Particle *ky*," 251. Already in 1944 Patton observed that at times in Ugaritic and Hebrew poetry *ky* causes the verb to fall at the end of the sentence (*Canaanite Parallels*, 12).

[255]Note that in essence the whole of 19b and 20b stand parallel as descriptions of Yahweh and the punishment which will ensue for disobeying him.

[256]Forming antithetical parallelism.

[257]Since the final strophe is only a single bicolon verse, these external parallelisms form responsion and inclusion at the same time.

[258]Cf. 19aA, where the contention that an identical colon stands at the beginning of a canticle is reinforced by the presence of a *setumah*.

[259]Regarding cola of single words see Korpel–de Moor, "Fundamentals," 177f. (including Isa. 49:6a, *wy'mr*; Ps. 78:19, *'mrw*). The context makes it clear that

Int. || : *'l-h'm* || *bkm* || *lkm*;[260] *yhwš'* || *yhwh*; *'tm* || *'tm*;[261]
*'t-yhwh* || *'wtw*
Ext. || : *wy'mr* || *wy'mrw*; *'dym* || *'dym*
Asson. and Rhyme: *h'm 'dym 'tm bkm ky-'tm bḥrtm lkm*[262]

**II.iv.2**
Sep. ↑: *w'th*;[263] imperative *hsyrw*
Sep. ↓: imperative *whṭw*; end of Joshua's speech
Ext. || : *hsyrw* || *hṭw*;[264] *'lhy hnkr* || *yhwh 'lhy yśr'l*;[265] *-km* || *-km*[266]
Inclusion: *'lhy* || *'lhy*

**II.iv.3**
Sep. ↑: *'mr*[267]
Sep. ↓: tricolon; refrain;[268] end of discourse

*'dym* is a single-word response by the people. The presence of *wy'mrw* is best read along with the preceding cola as part of a single strophe, not the indication of a new strophe. In this respect it is significant that the subject of the verb is left unstated in contrast to all other occasions here where the verb *'mr* plus the specified subject marks separation upwards. Furthermore, in contrast to the other places where *'mr* marks separation upward, the audience is left unspecified. In this strophe *wy'mrw 'dym* is part of a legal formulation which has been discussed above (see 2.2). The close correspondence with Ruth 4:9-11 supports the present strophic division. Cf. de Moor, "Book of Ruth, II," 38.

[260]The parallelism matches the prep. *'l* + people (indir. obj.) with the prep. *b* or *l* + suffix representing people pronominally as indir. obj.

[261]This parallelism, along with the preceding example of int. par., supports reading this verse as a quadrocolon.

[262]Taking *ky-'tm* as one poetic foot, we note that there are seven consecutive feet ending with *m*.

[263]Cf. the discussion at 14aA above.

[264]Both are imperatives, and there is moreover a semantic parallelism between the idea of putting away gods and inclining towards God. This parallelism is further attested in Isa. 30:11; Prov. 4:27. See too the parallel use of the imperatives in 2 Sam. 2:21f., *nṭh lk* || *swr lk*.

[265]Cf. 20a above, and the references given there.

[266]Perhaps this parallelism should be extended beyond the suffixes to include *qrb* || *lbb*; the former is a preposition denoting interior location, the second is an interior physical metaphor. The four cola of this strophe constitute a chiasm, i.e., A. gods, B. your midst, B́. your hearts, Á. God of Israel.

[267]Cf. at vs. 21 above.

[268]The idea that the refrain with *n'bd* is expanded for emphasis here with the extra colon *wbqwlw nšm'* is consistent with the principle of expansion noted above (see 2.2, with bibliographical references). A similar phenomenon is operative in the refrains employed in the poetic narrative of Josh. 23 (cf. Koopmans, "Joshua 23," 107-110).

Int. || : *'mr* || *šm'*;[269] *n'bd* || *bqwlw nšm'* [270]

## External parallelism in II.iv

### II.iv.1 and II.iv.2

*-km* (2x) || *-km* (2x) (22a, 23a-b); *'t-yhwh* || *'t-'lhy hnkr* (22aC, 23aA; responsion);[271] *bḥr* and *'bd* || *whṭw lbbkm*

### II.iv.2 and II.iv.3

*'t-'lhy hnkr* || *'t-yhwh 'lhynw* (23aA, 24B; responsion); *yhwh 'lhy yśr'l* || *yhwh 'lhynw* (23bB, 24B; concatenation); *yśr'l* || *h'm* (23bB, 24A; concatenation)[272]

### II.iv.1 and II.iv.3

*wy'mr yhwš' 'l-h'm* || *wy'mrw h'm 'l-yhwš'* (22aA, 24A; responsion);[273] *'mr* || *šm'* (22aA, 24C; inclusion);[274] *'t-yhwh* || *'t-yhwh* (22aC, 24B; responsion); *l'bd* || *n'bd* (22aD, 24B; responsion); *wy'mrw* || *wy'mrw* (22bA, 24A; responsion)

Compared to the previous canticles, internal and external parallelism is slightly less frequent here. The reason for this appears to be twofold. First, II.iv.1 conforms to the strictures of a certain legal formula. Second, the entire canticle mirrors the dialogical structure of the preceding canticle, thereby subordinating parallelism within the canticle to formal parallelism between the canticles. Canticles II.iii and II.iv have identical structures, with 3 strophes of 2+2+1 poetic verses in each, controlled by a single dialogical pattern.[275]

[269] Dahood, "Parallel Pairs, II," 32 no.64. Cf. II.v.2 below.

[270] For additional verses in which *'bd* and *šm'* have a similar meaning with regard to obedience, consult Deut. 11:13; 13:5; 30:17; 1 Sam. 12:14; Jer. 11:10; 13:10; 27:17; Job 36:11 (poetic, syndetic parataxis).

[271] Cf. the discussion of the responsion in 19aB, 20aB.

[272] Cf. the support for this parallelism at int. par. in I.ii.1.

[273] Cf. 19aA, 21A above.

[274] This pair stands as the first and last words of the canticle, thereby forming a perfect inclusion; for identification of the pair see int. par. at II.iv.3 above.

[275] See the more elaborate discussion of macrostructure below.

### 3.4.10 Canticle II.v (24:25-28)

#### II.v.1

Sep. ↑: quadrocolon;[276] change of subject;[277] *bywm hhw'*; *h'lh*;[278] rep. prep. *b* (3x); rep. *yhwš'*
Sep. ↓: *setumah*; quadrocolon[279]
Int. || : *wykrt* || *wyśm*;[280]
*bryt* || *ḥq*;[281]
*bryt* || *mšpṭ*;[282]

[276]The high frequency of strong internal parallelism between these four cola validates their treatment as a quadrocolon rather than two bicola.
[277]Joshua is now the acting subject following the people's concluding speech in the preceding dialogue.
[278]Cf. van der Lugt, *Strofische structuren*, 512.
[279]An alternative division of the verse, combining our 26bB and 26bC, would produce a tricolon. As presently divided the cola have 3, 2, 2, 3 stresses respectively, while a tricolon would have 3, 4, 3 stresses. On the basis of the parallelism of *śm* and *tḥt h'lh*, we have chosen for the former.
[280]Cf. G.E.Mendenhall, "Covenant," *IDB*, 1:716. While the most frequent term for establishing a covenant is *krt*, in 2 Sam. 23:5 a synonymous expression is found in the phrase *ky bryt 'wlm śm ly*. See further Isa. 28:15, Nah. 1:14 (parallelism questionable), and in treaty context, 1 Sam. 11:2. The parallelism of *krt* and *śym* in Josh. 24:25 is reinforced by the parallelism of the accompanying nouns.
[281]Regarding *bryt* || *ḥq* see Num. 18:19; 2 Kgs 17:15; 2 Chron. 34:31; Isa. 24:5; Ps. 50:16; 105:10 (= 1 Chron. 16:17); these are the only texts in the OT where these two words are found together in a single verse, and in every case they form a deliberate parallelism or parataxis. The first three of these references are in BHS as prose, the remainder are poetry. The parallelism of *bryt* and *ḥq* is recognized by G.Cooke, "The Israelite King as Son of God," *ZAW* 73 (1961) 202-225, esp. 214; Avishur, *Stylistic Studies*, 192. Cf. P.Victor, "A Note on *ḥq* in the Old Testament," *VT* 16 (1966) 359f.
[282]For *mšpṭ* || *bryt* cf. Lev. 26:15; Deut. 7:12; Isa. 61:8; Hos. 10:4. Along with Josh. 24:25 this is a complete listing of verses in which these two nouns occur together, and they are always in deliberate parallelism. The references from Isaiah and Hosea are poetic, and, if Lev. 26:15 and Deut. 7:12 are written out as poetry, they too form convincing parallelisms, e.g., Lev. 26:14f.:

| | |
|---|---|
| *w'm-l' tšmw ly* [2] | But if you do not listen to me, |
| *wl' t'św 't kl-hmṣwt h'lh* [1] | and you do not do all these commandments, |
| *w'm-bḥqty tm'sw* [5] | and if you despise my statutes, |
| *w'm 't-mšpṭy tg'l npškm* [2] | and if your soul abhors my judgments, |
| *lblty 'śwt 't-kl-mṣwty* [5] | so that you do not do my commandments |
| *lhprkm 't-bryty* [1] | but you transgress my covenant. |

What follows is a list of curses comparable to the poetic enumerations in ancient NE treaty listings, cf. Wiseman, "Vassal-Treaties of Esarhaddon," esp. 25, 60-80. Something of the poetic nature of the curses in Lev. 26 and Deut. 28 has been recognized by Hillers, *Treaty-Curses*, esp. 5, 28, 30-42, 78, 85. The similarities

*l'm* || *lw*;[283]
prep. *b* || *b* || *b*;
*dbrym* || *twrt 'lhym*;[284]
*wykrt yhwš'* || *wyktb yhwš'*;[285]

between Deut. 28 and the curses of Esarhaddon's treaty are further elaborated by Weinfeld, "Assyrian Treaty Formulae," 417-427; Frankena, "Vassal-Treaties," 123-154; but they do not attempt to analyze these texts as poetry. See too Fensham, "Malediction and Benediction," 1-9; "Common Trends in Curses of the Near Eastern Treaties and *Kudurru*-Inscriptions compared with Maledictions of Amos and Isaiah," *ZAW* 75 (1963) 155-175. Significantly, a number of additional studies have demonstrated the affinity of Lev. 26 with the poetry of Am. 4:3-13., e.g., H.Graf Reventlow, *Das Amt des Propheten bei Amos* (Göttingen, 1962), 83-85; Brueggemann, "Amos iv 4-13," 1-15. The question of whether Lev. 26:3-38 is poetry is entertained specifically by Elliger, *Leviticus*, 364-367. He notes that vss.3-13 are typified by a paucity of the prosaic *nota objecti* and contain a considerable number of cases of *parallismus membrorum*; in his opinion meter is also present. While most of vss.14-38 are considered "rhythmischer Prosa," he concludes that vs.15 is truly poetic. See further the comments by Reventlow, *Wächter*, 4-42, where comparisons are drawn between Lev. 26 and passages from Ezekiel, with particular attention to similar poetic aspects. His comparisons produce the conclusion "dass im Fluchteil von Lev 26,14ff. eine ganz ähnliche Gliederung zu bemerken ist" (39). In our opinion Deut. 7:12 can also be viewed as poetry:

| | |
|---|---|
| *whyh 'qb tšm'wn* [7] | And because you listen |
| *'t hmšpṭym h'lh* [5] | to these judgments, |
| *wšmrtm w'śytm 'tm* [2] | and you keep and you do them, |
| *wšmr yhwh 'lhyk lk* [7] | Yahweh your God will keep with you |
| *'t-hbryt whḥsd* [5] | the covenant and the kindness |
| *'šr nšb' l'btyk* [1] | which he swore to your fathers. |

Here follows a list of blessings in what appears to also be a poetic enumeration. Accordingly, if Lev. 26:15 and Deut. 7:12 are accepted as poetry, the parallelism of *mšpṭ* and *bryt* within a single verse is always poetic in the OT texts. Extension of the search to a span of two successive verses is equally revealing. External parallelism in poetry then appears to be present in Deut. 33:9f.; Isa. 28:17f.; Hos. 2:20f.; Mal. 2:17 and 3:1 (*'lhy hmšpṭ* || *ml'k hbryt*, external parallelism); Ps. 25:9f.; 105:7f. (= 1 Chron. 16:14f.). In addition to these poetic texts the combination occurs only in Lev. 26:42-46 (cf. above); Deut. 4:13f.; 5:1f.; 2 Kgs 17:34f., 37f.; Dan. 9:4f. (poetic prayer, cf. already König, "Poesie und Prosa," [1919-20], 26). Regarding the recognized parallelism of *ḥq* and *mšpṭ* in other texts see, e.g., Reventlow, *Wächter*, 7-10; Schmitt, *Landtag*, 23; Koopmans, "Testament of David," (re 1 Kgs 2:3).

[283]Sperling, "Joshua 24," 131 n.68.

[284]Watters, *Formula Criticism*, 156 no.19; Loretz, *Der Prolog*, 123, 128. The most relevant texts in recognized poetic parallelism are Isa. 1:10; 2:3; Mic. 4:2; Jer. 6:19; 8:8f.; Ps. 119:17f., 28f., 43f., 113f., Prov. 13:13f. See too Deut. 17:11; 32:46 and the syndetic parataxis of Zech. 7:12.

[285]Cf. Ex.34:27, where *ktb-lk 't-hdbrym h'lh* is paralleled by *krty 'tk bryt w't-yśr'l*.

*wyśm* || *wyktb*[286]
*bryt* || *dbrym*;[287]
*bryt* || *twrh*;[288]
*ḥq wmšpṭ* || *dbrym*;[289]
*ḥq wmšpṭ* || *twrh*;[290]
*ktb* || *spr?*;[291]
*wyqḥ* || *wyqymh*;[292]
*'bn* || *h'lh?*[293]

[286]Cf. Ex. 17:14; Deut. 31:19.

[287]The parallelism of ***bryt*** with the noun ***dbr*** is asserted by Mendenhall, "Covenant," 716, with the suggestion that ***dbr*** may have been the original term for covenant. His proposal is followed by Dahood, ***Psalms***, 3:53 (re Ps. 105:8, with an appeal as well to vs.42 and Deut. 9:5). Mention should also be made of the parallelism in Ex. 24:8; 34:27f.; Deut. 4:13 (all prose in BHS), as well as Hos. 10:4; Neh. 9:8; Ps. 50:16f.; 1 Chron. 16:15 (= Ps. 105:8).

[288]In numerous texts ***bryt*** || ***twrh*** constitutes a fixed pair, e.g., Isa. 24:5; Hos. 8:1; Mal. 2:8; Ps. 78:10, see also Deut. 29:20; 31:9, 26; Jer. 31:33.

[289]See esp. Ps. 147:19, ***mgyd dbrw ly'qb / ḥqyw wmšpṭyw lyśr'l***, which places the syndetic combination of ***ḥq*** and ***mšpṭ*** in parallelism with ***dbr*** in a manner analogous to the internal parallelism we are defending here. For the parallelism of ***ḥq*** and ***dbr*** (noun), cf. esp. Ps. 119:16; Ex. 12:24; Deut. 17:19. In ext. par. cf. Ps. 50:16f.; 119:25f.; Neh. 1:7f.; and in concatenation cf. Ps. 119:8f.,16f.,48f.,64f.,80f. And for ***mšpṭ*** || ***dbr***, in addition to Ps. 147:19 see Ps. 119:160; Hos. 10:4; and cf. Ps. 33:4-6; 105:7f.; 112:5; 119:42f.,74f.,101f.,105f.,107f.,160f. The synonymity here of ***ḥq wmšpṭ*** with ***dbrym*** is made explicit by the author's use of ***h'lh***. On the basis of this parallelism, as well as the additional parallelisms in 25-26a, we read a quadrocolon here rather than two bicola. To read vss.25-26a as two bicola would leave the strophic indicator ***h'lh*** standing in the central verse of the strophe.

[290]For verses containing both ***ḥq*** and ***twrh*** see Ex. 18:16,18; Lev. 26:46; Deut. 4:8; 17:19; 2 Kgs 17:37; Isa. 24:5; Am. 2:4; Mal. 3:22; Ps. 105:45; Ezra 7:10; 9:13,14; 10:30; 2 Chron. 19:10; 33:8 (complete list); for ***mšpṭ*** and ***twrh*** see Lev. 26:46; Num. 15:16; Deut. 4:8; 17:11; Deut. 33:10; 1 Kgs 2:3; 2 Kgs 17:34, 37; Isa. 42:4; 51:4; Ezek. 44:24; Hab. 1:4; Mal. 3:22; Ps. 89:31 (Yoder, "A–B Pairs," 476); Ezra 7:10; Neh. 8:18; 9:13, 29; 10:30; 2 Chron. 19:10; 30:16; 33:8 (complete list). Cf. Watters, ***Formula Criticism***, 175 no.546 (re Isaiah); Koopmans, "Testament of David" (forthcoming). From these lists it is apparent that the parallelism of ***ḥq*** and/or ***mšpṭ*** with ***twrh*** is well attested in both prose and poetry in the OT and therefore these parallelisms by themselves do not prove an identity as poetry or prose. For further discussion of synonyms for law and covenant consult B.Lindars, "Torah in Deuteronomy," in Ackroyd–Lindars, eds., ***Words and Meanings***, 117-136.

[291]Cf. Dahood–Penar, "Parallel Pairs, I," 86, 238f. no.308; also listed as a parallelism by Watters, ***Formula Criticism***, 198 no.229, re Job 19:23; Mal. 3:16 and a number of more questionable possible parallelisms such as Job 31:35; Jer. 3:8; 32:10; 45:1; 51:60.

[292]Parallel actions of Joshua expressed with ***wyqtl*** verbs.

[293]Since the noun ***h'lh*** with this vocalization is found only here in the OT, the

prep. *šm* and *tḥt* || *b*[294]
Ext. || : *wyśm* || *wyqḥ* and *wyqymh*;[295]
prep. *b* (3x) || *b*;[296] *yhwš'* (2x) || *yhwh*

**II.v.2**

Sep. ↑: *setumah*; tricolon; *'mr*; *hnh*;[297]
Sep. ↓: tricolon; *ky*
Int. || : *'l-kl-h'm* || *bnw*; *šm'* || *'mry* || *dbr*[298]

parallelism of this combination must be considered uncertain. Nevertheless, both appear to have a cultic function or identity here. Furthermore, *'bn* is at times paralleled by *'ṣ* "wood," and more importantly, also *'ṣ* "tree" (M.Dahood, "The Phoenician background of Qoheleth," *Bibl* 47 [1966] 279; Dahood–Penar, "Parallel Pairs, I," 100 no.9 [re Eccl. 10:9; Jer. 3:9; Ezek. 26:12; 1 Chron. 22:15; 2 Chron. 2:13 plus Ug. 52:66 (CTA 22:66)]; Avishur, *Stylistic Studies*, 594). On the parallelism of *'ṣ* and *'bn* in Jer. 2:27a consult S.M.Olyan, "The Cultic Confessions of Jer. 2,27a," *ZAW* 99 (1987) 254f. The combination of the stone and the "terebinth" in Josh. 24:26 may be viewed against the background of a variety of OT texts which associate worship, altar building, sacrificing, theophany, etc. with a location near or under a sacred tree, e.g., Gen.12:7f.; 35:2; Judg. 6:11, 19-24, 25-28; Hos. 4:13. Perhaps *mqdš* can therefore also be added to form a triple parallelism.

[294]Cf. J.C.Greenfield, "The Prepositions B... Taḥat... in Jes 57,5," *ZAW* 73 (1961) 226-228; Watson, "Fixed Pairs," 461; *Classical Hebrew Poetry*, 345; Dahood, "Parallel Pairs, III," 186 no.23

[295]For *śym* || *qwm* consult the internal parallelism of Ps. 78:5, *wyqwm 'dwt by'qb* || *wtwrh śm byśr'l*. Significantly, in Josh. 24:25f. we have the related idea of setting covenant laws, and of a witness to these laws. See too Isa. 27:9. There are many verses where the verbs *lqḥ* and *śym* are parallel, e.g., Gen. 28:11,18; Ex. 17:12; 1 Sam. 7:12 (all these are with setting up stones); for poetic parallelism see esp. Ezek. 17:5; 19:5; Hag. 3:23; Job 22:22.

[296]Note especially the locative parallelism *bškm* and *bmqdš yhwh*.

[297]For *hnh* as a marker of separation see Muilenburg, "Form Criticism," 15; van der Lugt, *Strofische structuren*, 514. See as well C.J.Labuschagne, "The particles *hn* and *hnh*," *OTS* 18 (1973) 1-14; Andersen, *Sentence*, 94-96; D.J.McCarthy, "The Uses of *wᵉhinnēh* in Biblical Hebrew," *Bibl* 61 (1980) 330-342, esp. 334; A.Berlin, *Poetics and Interpretation of Biblical Narrative* (Sheffield, 1983), 62f., 91-95; S.Kogut, "On the Meaning and Syntactical Status of *hnh* in Biblical Hebrew," in S.Japhet, ed., *Studies in Bible* (*ScH 31*; Jerusalem, 1986), 133-154; H.-P.Müller, "Die Konstructionen mit *hinnē* 'siehe' und ihr sprachgeschichtlichen Hintergrund," *ZfA* 2 (1989) 45-76.

[298]If our analysis is correct, vs.27 places in parallelism the verb "to hear," the noun "words," and the verb "to speak." It must be admitted that this parallelism is not very precise, but it is instructive in this respect to note the presence of these same three words in the bicolon verse of Deut. 32:1, *h'zynw hšmym w'dbrh* || *wtšm' h'rṣ 'mry-py*. Josh. 24:27 and Deut. 32:1 are the only verses in the OT where these three words occur together. Deut. 32:1 is listed by Dahood, "Parallel Pairs, III," 163 no.312, as an example of the collocation of the pair *šm'* and *'mr(h)*. We have already noted that the noun *'mr* occurs elsewhere in the OT only in poetry (cf.

Ext. || : *kl* || *kl*;[299] *h'bn* || *hy'*; *bnw* || *'mnw*;
*wy'mr yhwš'* || *'mry-yhwh 'šr dbr*[300]

**II.v.3**

Sep. ↑: *whyth*; *pn*; rep. *km*; rep. *b*[301]
Sep. ↓: *petuchah*
Int. || : *bkm* || *b'lhykm*;[302] *h'm* || *'yš*[303]

On the basis of formal strophic indicators we have made a division between 27b and 27c. On the basis of content one might also consider reading 27c with 27a-b. This would keep Joshua's speech together in a single strophe,[304] and the final strophe would be restricted to Joshua action in dispersing the people (vs.28). However, in addition to the formal indicators listed above, it is noteworthy that the tradition behind the LXX contains an additional colon *b'ḥryt hymym*, which makes 27c a tricolon and supports the present division.[305]

2.3.7.2). The related masc. noun vocalized *'ōmer* and the fem. noun *'mrh* are also found only in poetry. These various nouns occur in the Pentateuch and Former Prophets typically in what is usually thought to be archaic poetry, e.g., Gen. 4:23; 49:21; Num. 24:4,16; Deut. 32:1,2; 33:9; Judg. 5:29; 2 Sam. 22:31.

[299]Cf. at II.ii.2, above.

[300]This parallelism is supported by the instances noted above of *yhwš'* || *yhwh*. The verbs *'mr* and *dbr* form a parallel pair too frequently to list; for Isaiah cf. Watters, *Formula Critcism*, 170 no.403.

[301]These markers of separation are important because of the strong concatenation between 27aC and 27cA.

[302]The parallelism of *b* || *b* has been noted frequently above, where the prepositions have the meaning "in." Here they have the meaning "against"; cf. the ext. par. of *bnw* || *bkm* and *b'lhykm*. For additional examples of *b* || *b* meaning "against", see Dahood–Penar, "Parallel Pairs, I," 133 no.88 (they list Gen. 16:12; Mic. 7:6; Hab. 3:8; Mal. 3:5; Ps. 50:20; 149:7; Ug. 1001:9-10).

[303]A similar construction in which *'yš*, *i.e.* "each person," is employed as an explication of *'m* can be found in BHS in prose (Ex. 33:20; Num. 11:10; Josh. 6:20; Judg. 2:6 [= Josh. 24:28]; 9:49; 1 Sam. 10:11, 25; 13:2; 14:34; 30:6; 2 Sam. 2:27; 6:19 [cf. 1 Chron. 16:43]; 15:30; Neh. 8:16; 2 Chron. 23:10) as well as poetry (Isa. 3:5; 6:5; Jer. 51:45; Mic. 4:5). A similar construction is found in the Mesha inscription, where *h'm* || *'š* constitutes internal parallelism, cf. de Moor, "Narrative Poetry," 155, 158.

[304]A responsion would also be produced with "Joshua" and "people" standing in the first cola of all three strophes in this canticle.

[305]Cf. the discussion of LXX vs.27 below.

## External parallelism in II.v

### II.v.1 and II.v.2

*wykrt yhwš‘ bryt l‘m* || *wy'mr yhwš‘ 'l-kl-h‘m* (25A, 27aA; responsion); *wyktb yhwš‘* || *wy'mr yhwš‘* (26aC, 27aA; responsion);[306] *hhw'* and *h'lh* || *hz't* (25A, 26aC, 27aB; responsion); *dbrym* and *twrh* || *'mry yhwh* and *dbr* (26a, 27b; inclusion);[307] *'bn gdwlh* || *h'bn hz't* (26bA, 27aB; concatenation); *yhwh* || *yhwš‘* (26bD, 27aA; concatenation)

### II.v.2 and II.v.3

*wy'mr yhwš‘ 'l-kl-h‘m* || *wyšlḥ yhwš‘ 't-h‘m* (27aA, 28A; inclusion); *thyh-bnw l‘dh* || *whyth bkm l‘dh* (27aC, 27cA; responsion);[308] *mqdš* || *nḥlh* (26bD, 28B; responsion)[309] *yhwh* || *'lhykm* (27bB, 27cB; concatenation); *yhwh* || *yhwš‘* (27bB, 28A; responsion)

### II.v.1 and II.v.3

*'lhym* || *'lhykm* (25B, 27cB; responsion); *wykrt yhwš‘ bryt l‘m* || *wyšlḥ yhwš‘ 't-h‘m* (25A, 28A; inclusion); *lw* || *bkm* (25B, 27cA; responsion); prep. *b* (3x) || (2) (25, 26aD, 27c; responsion); *yhwh* || *'lhykm* (26bC, 27cB)

Canticle II.v, like the previous four canticles of canto II, is composed of three strophes. This canticle is typified by a strong emphasis upon covenant, law, and witnessing. Repetition of Joshua as subject adds cohesion to the three strophes of the canticle. The legal actions described here provide a fitting conclusion for the entire poetic composition of Josh. 24:1-28.

[306]For *ktb* || *'mr* see Watters, *Formula Criticism*, 177 no.591.

[307]Regarding *dbr* (noun) || *'mrh* see already Cassuto, *Biblical and Oriental Studies*, 2:65, cf. Prov. 4:20 (int. par.); Job 32:11f. (ext. par.); Prov. 4:4f. (ext. par.). See too Kselman, "Semantic-Sonant Chiasmus," 219-223. The parallelism of *twrh* and *'mry-ph* is recognized in Watson, *Classical Hebrew Poetry*, 134, 137 (re Ps.78:1; Job 22:22); see too Prov. 7:1f. (ext. par.).

[308]For *bnw* || *bkm* and *b'lhykm* see the comments on int. par. above.

[309]It may be questionable whether this is a deliberate parallelism. However, the parallelism of Ug. *qdš* "sanctuary" and *nḥlt* is identified by Dahood–Penar, "Parallel Pairs, I," 324 no. 484, in comparison with Ps. 78:54f.; 79:1; Isa. 57:15; 63:17f. Cf. Ex. 15:17 (Cross–Freedman, "Song of Miriam," 250; Avishur, *Stylistic Studies*, 428f.). See below regarding the LXX variant at Josh. 24:28.

## 3.5 The macrostructure of Josh. 24:1-28

### 3.5.1 Introduction

In the preceding structural analysis Josh. 24:1-28 was divided colometrically into strophes. Our argumentation relied especially upon formal markers of strophic division, as well as internal parallelism operative at the level of the verse and external parallelism connecting verses within the strophes. The resulting strophic divisions are not always equally clear. Nevertheless, by honouring both formal markers attested elsewhere as strophic indicators and content,[310] it is possible to analyze the present text as narrative poetry. Thematic and formal considerations also coalesced to facilitate division of the strophes into canticles.

By reading this passage as narrative poetry, significant responsions which otherwise go unnoticed are brought into focus. For example, within the historical recital of vss.2-13 the strophic divisions correspond with historical progressions, and various canticles are marked by responsions or repetitions such as the use of *'šr 'śyty* (5aC, 7bB; inclusion of I.iii) and *w'tn 'wtm bydkm* (8bA, 11c; responsion in I.iv). Similarly, the first four canticles of canto II all end with a refrain employing *n'bd*. In canto II, as in canto I, at times entire cola are repeated to establish external parallelism. In our discussion of the macrostructure of this pericope we will first present a statistical survey of all the poetic units represented at the various poetic levels. Following this, a detailed analysis of the macrostructure will be conducted in order to demonstrate the external parallelisms operative between the canticles and the cantos respectively.

### 3.5.2 Overview of structural totals

The following tables provide an overview of the structural statistics which result from the foregoing analysis. Totals which are affected by our reconstruction of canticles I.iv-I.v are marked with an asterisk.

310 It is only in vs.27c that we noted a possible conflict between the strophic division which is suggested by formal markers and that which might be preferred on the basis of content without regard to formal indicators.

| canto | canticle | strophe | verses |
|---|---|---|---|
| I | i | | 2 (2+3) |
| | ii | 1 | 2 (2+3) |
| | | 2 | 2 (3+2) |
| | | 3 | 3 (2+2+2) |
| | iii | 1 | 2 (3+1) |
| | | 2 | 2 (2+2) |
| | | 3 | 2 (3+2) |
| | | 4 | 2 (2+2) |
| | iv | 1 | 2 (3+3) |
| | | 2 | 3 (3+2+3) |
| | | 3 | 2 (3+1)* |
| | v | 1 | 2 (2+3)* |
| | | 2 | 2 (2+2)* |
| | | 3 | 3 (2+2+3) |
| canto | canticle | strophe | verses |
| II | i | 1 | 2 (2+4) |
| | | 2 | 2 (2+2) |
| | | 3 | 3 (3+2+2) |
| | ii | 1 | 2 (4+5) |
| | | 2 | 3 (2+2+2) |
| | | 3 | 2 (2+3) |
| | iii | 1 | 2 (2+2) |
| | | 2 | 2 (4+3) |
| | | 3 | 1 (2) |
| | iv | 1 | 2 (4+2) |
| | | 2 | 2 (2+2) |
| | | 3 | 1 (3) |
| | v | 1 | 2 (4+4) |
| | | 2 | 2 (3+3) |
| | | 3 | 2 (2+2) |

Summarizing these totals statistically we note the following results:

| *Canto I* | *Canto II* |
|---|---|
| canticles: 5 | canticles: 5 |
| strophes: 1+3+4+3+3 | strophes: 3+3+3+3+3 |
| verses: 2+7+8+7+7 | verses: 7+7+5+5+6 |

It is significant that canto I and canto II, despite the diversity of their respective contents, attain a close uniformity of total canticles, strophes and verses, and even cola:

| *canto* | *totals* | | | |
|---|---|---|---|---|
| **Canto I** | 5 canticles | 14 strophes | 31 verses | 72 cola |
| **Canto II** | 5 canticles | 15 strophes | 30 verses | 81 cola |

It is noteworthy that in both cantos there is a tendency to include 3 strophes per canticle. This is true of 8 of the 10 canticles.[311] It is also noteworthy that, as divided above, the number of cola per canticle is also fairly uniform, cf. 5/16/17/18/16/ || 17/20/13/13/18. The regularity of all these structural statistics at the respective levels of the poetic composition provides an important confirmation of our divisions into strophes, canticles and cantos,[312] and it provides additional evidence for the validity of treating this passage as poetry.

### 3.5.3 The macrostructure of canto I

It has been suggested above that the first strophe (= I.i, Josh. 24:1) sketches the setting for the historical summary which follows. This opening strophe, while standing alone as a canticle, is linked to Joshua's ensuing recital via a number of significant external parallelisms.

**Ext. par. between I.i and I.ii**

*wy'sp yhwš'* || *wy'mr yhwš'* (1aA, 2aA; responsion);[313] *kl-šbṭy yśr'l* ||

[311]Including our reconstruction of canticle I.v to produce 3 strophes and seven verses. Moreover, I.iii, which we have divided into 4 strophes, does not contain very strong markers of separation between the strophes. We have in general followed the divisions suggested by the Masoretic accentuation. However, a possible alternative division would in fact produce 3 strophes, namely 5aA-6aB (with our 5b-6aB rearranged as a tricolon), 6bA-7aC, 7bA-7cB. Therefore, if I.iii was originally a canticle of 3 strophes, the only exception would be I.i.

[312]The research of van der Lugt (*Strofische structuren*, passim) demonstrates that a characteristic of the Psalms is that they usually tend to be composed with a general uniformity at the level of the higher structural units. The same principle is demonstrated in Lamentations by J.Renkema ("The Literary Structure of Lamentations," in van der Meer–de Moor, eds., *Structural Analysis*, 294-396). Examples in narrative poetry are found in de Moor, "Book of Ruth, II," 42-46; Koopmans, "Joshua 23," 114f.

[313]Compare esp. Gen. 49:1; Ex. 3:16 (and more remotely 32:26); Num. 11:16; 21:16; 1 Sam. 5:8; Mic. 4:11. Also significant is the parallelism of the imperative

*kl-h'm* (1aB, 2aA; responsion);[314] *wytyṣbw lpny h'lhym* || *wy'bdw 'lhym 'ḥrym* (1bC, 2bC; responsion);[315] *'lhym* || *'lhym 'ḥrym*[316]

**Ext. par. in I.ii-I.v, Joshua's historical recital**

These four canticles of Joshua's historical recital have a number of structural characteristics in common. The transitions from one to the next correspond with geographical progressions, and the strophes of the respective canticles are generally shown to belong together by employment of key literary responsions. In the following analysis particular attention will be focused upon the inter-relationship of these four canticles to see whether a similar principle is valid for the macrostructure of the entire historical recital. In other words, we now look for responsions which occur in the corresponding strophes of the three respective canticles, as well as concatenations which tend to link the canticles together, or inclusions which serve to frame the larger unit.

### I.ii and I.iii

*nhr* (2x) || *ym* (3x) (2bA, 3aB, 6aB, 6bB, 7bA);[317] *'b* (4x) || *'b* (2x) (2b, 3aA, 6aA, 6bA; responsion); *yrš* || *yšb* (4bB, 7dA; responsion);[318] *hr* ||

*'sp* with *'mr* regarding the national assembly in Joel 2:16f. Cf. van der Meer, *Oude woorden*, 75—though he does not list *'sp* and *'mr* as a parallelism. These texts demonstrate that to gather people into an assembly and to address them formally constituted two actions which could naturally be placed parallel to each other.

[314]Compare Gen. 49:16 (Geller, *Parallelism*, 36); Deut. 33:5 (*wyhy byšrwn mlk* || *bht'sp r'šy 'm* || *yḥd šbṭy yśr'l*); Judg. 20:2 (in BHS as prose, but shows clear parallelism [*wytyṣbw pnwt kl-h'm* || *kl šbṭy yśr'l bqhl 'm h'lhym*—BHS omits the space between the last two words, cf. R.Wonneberger, *Leitfaden zur Biblia Hebraica* (Göttingen, 1984), 100]). Comparison with Gen. 49:16; Deut. 33:5 and Judg. 20:2 is particularly interesting because of the gatherings narrated in these texts. For *'m* || *yśr'l* see further the references given under int. par. at I.ii.1 above.

[315]The parallelism is antithetical and already serves to set the tone for the choice being made in the entire passage, whether to serve Yahweh or other gods. In light of this parallelism, perhaps a responsion should also be noted between the list of leaders in 1b and the fathers in 2b.

[316]Antithetical parallelism. See too the discussion above regarding the antithetical parallelism of *yhwh* with *'lhym 'ḥrym* (vs.2) and *yhwh ('lhy yśr'l)* with *'lhy nkr* (vss.20,23).

[317]The parallelism of *nhr* and *ym* occurs frequently and has been widely discussed as a parallel pair (cf. Boling, "'Synonymous' Parallelism," 232f., 234; Dahood, *Psalms*, 3:450; Yoder, "A-B Pairs," 486 n.1; Watson, "Fixed Pairs," 461f.; Watters, *Formula Criticism*, 164 no.230, 196 no.175; Krašovec, *Merismus*, 107f. no.109; Watson, *Classical Hebrew Poetry*, 131; Avishur, *Stylistic Studies*, 305, 369f., 439.

[318]The parallelism of *yrš* and *yšb* has been dealt with at I.iv.1.

*mdbr* (4bB, 7dA; responsion);[319] *yrd* || *yšb* (4cB, 7cB; responsion);[320] *mṣrym* || *mdbr*;[321] *mṣrym* || *mṣrym* (5x) (4bC, 5aB, 6aA, 6bA, 7aC, 7cB; esp. forming concatenation [4bC, 5aB] and responsion [4cB, 7bB]); *yšb* || *yšb* (2bA, 7cA; inclusion); *'wlm* || *ymym rbym* (2bA, 7cB; inclusion);[322] *b'br hnhr* || *bmdbr* (2bA, 7cA; inclusion)[323]

The temporal parallelism established by *yšb ... m'wlm* || *tšbw ... ymym rbym* constitutes an inclusion from the first colon of direct discourse to the last colon of the canticle dealing with the exodus from Egypt, thereby providing a temporal framework from the earliest patriarchal period and the sojourn *b'br hnhr* to the more recent sojourn *bmdbr*. Canticle I.ii consists of 16 cola, while Canticle I.iii is composed of 17, which illustrates a close balance at this level.

[319]Compare int. par. in Lam. 4:19; Isa. 16:1; Jer. 9:9 (*hrym* || *n'wt mdbr*) (cf. Krašovec, "Merism–Polar Expression," 234). The parallelism in Lam. 4:19 is deliberate because the author uses both *hr* and *mdbr* again in ext. par. (cf. Renkema, "Literary Structure of Lamentations," 386). Regarding the collocation of Mt. Seir and wilderness see esp. Gen. 14:6, and cf. Mal. 1:3. In addition, *hr* || *mdbr* occurs in many texts not ordinarily recognized as poetry, e.g., Ex. 3:1; 4:27; 18:5; 19:2; Lev. 7:38 (*bhr syny* || *bmdbr syny*).

[320]The parallelism of *yrd* || *yšb* was noted by Cassuto, *Biblical and Oriental Studies*, 2:55f., and further examples were demonstrated by Avishur, "Word Pairs," 25f.; *Stylistic Studies*, 541f.

[321]Cf. ext. par. in I.iii.4.

[322]Cf. Watters, *Formula Criticism*, 173 no. 484 (re *ywm* || *'wlm* in Isa. 34:10 and perhaps in 51:9; 63:11). Of particular importance, note the inclusion formed by *ymn rbn* || *'lm* in strophes II.1 and II.2 of the Mesha inscription, cf. de Moor, "Narrative Poetry," 152. Comparison with the Mesha inscription is the more remarkable because there *ymn rbn* is placed in inclusionary ext. par. with *'rb'n št* "forty years" (cf. strophe II.3, ibid., 152). This may be compared to the *ymym rbym* of Josh. 24:7, which in comparison with other OT references must also be assumed to correspond with forty years (cf. Sperling, "Joshua 24," 125).

[323]It is interesting to compare the boundary descriptions in Ex. 23:31; Deut. 11:24; Josh. 1:4; 1 Chron. 5:9, which all record borders marked by *mdbr* and *nhr*. Note the collocation of these terms in poetry in Isa. 41:18f.; 43:19; 43:20; 50:2; Ps. 78:15f.; 107:33, where an antithetical meaning is evident. Cf. also the parallelism of *nhrym* || *tbl* noted by Watson, "Fixed Pairs," 468, n.9, along with a reference to an equivalent Akkadian pair. Also relevant for comparison is the pair *mdbr* || *thmwt* attested in recitals remembering the exodus in Ps. 106:9; 78:15; Isa. 63:13 (cf. Avishur, *Stylistic Studies*, 244). Furthermore, note *ym* || *mdbr* (Watters, *Formula Criticism*, 166 no.286; Wyatt, "Sea and Desert," 375ff.), and cf. the discussion of ext. par. at I.iii.2 and I.iii.4, as well as I.iii.3 and I.iii.4 above.

## I.iii and I.iv

*w'šlḥ* || *w'b'h* (5aA, 8aA; responsion);[324] *w'gp* || *w'šmydm* (5aB, 8bC);[325] *yṣ'* (2x) || *bw'* (2x) (5b, 6aA, 8aA, 11aB; responsion and inclusion);[326] *mṣrym* || *'rṣ h'mry* (5aB, 8aA; responsion); *mṣrym* || *mw'b* (6aA, 9aB; responsion); *mṣrym* || *yryḥw* (5aB, 7bB, 11a; inclusion and responsion); *bw'* (2x) || *bw'* (2x) (6aB, 7bA, 8aA, 11aA);[327] *ym* (3x) || *yrdn* (2x) (6aB, 6bB, 7bA, 8aB, 11aA);[328] *wyrdp* || *wyqm ... wylḥm* (6bA, 9a; responsion);[329] *ṣ'q* || *šm'* (7aA, 10aA; responsion);[330] *yṣ'* (Hiph.) || *nṣl* (Hiph.) (5bA, 6aA, 10aC);[331] *yšb* || *yšb* (7dA, 8aA; concatena-

[324]Regarding *šlḥ* || *bw'* cf. ext. par. between I.iii.1 and I.iii.2 above.

[325]An external parallelism of these verbs may perhaps be intended in the curses of Deut. 28:24f.

[326]The parallelism of *yṣ'* and *bw'* has been dealt with above at I.iii.2 in connection with int. par. of 6a. Note that the responsion in 5bA, 8aA of *hwṣ'ty 'tkm* || *w'b'h 'tkm* is heightened by the identical subject and object. The verbs *yṣ'* and *bw'* are used only in these two canticles. Subsequently *'lh* (17aB) and *hlk* (17cB) are used.

[327]Note that in Josh. 24:1-28 the verb *bw'* is used only in these two canticles.

[328]These words occur only in these two canticles.

[329]There are actually multiple parallelisms in these verses signifying opposition against Israel, e.g., *mṣrym* || *blq* and *mw'b*; *'bwtykm* || *yśr'l*, as well as the specific terms of opposition, i.e., *wyrdpw ... brkb wbpršym* || *wyqwm ... wylḥm*. Mention should also be made of *šmd* in 8bC, which may be compared with the parallelism of *rdp* || *šmd* in 2 Sam. 22:38 (differently in Ps. 18:38), and note the use of *qwm* in the following verse there.

[330]This external parallelism as a responsion at the climax of the respective canticles employs the frequent parallelism of *ṣ'q* and *šm'*; cf. esp. Ex. 22:22 (note the infin. absolutes *'m-'nh t'nh 'tw* || *ky 'm-ṣ'q yṣ'q 'ly* || *šm' 'šm' ṣ'qtw*). See further Isa. 42:2; Jer. 22:20f. (ext. par. 2x); 49:2f. (ext. par. as supported by *'l-rbt* || *bnwt rbh*); Ps. 34:18; Job 35:12f. (ext. par.); Neh. 9:28. Similar documentation could be adduced for *z'q* || *šm'*, e.g., Isa. 15:4; 30:19; Ezek. 27:30; Hab. 1:2; Neh. 9:27-29 (ext. and int. par.); 2 Chron. 20:9 (Jehoshaphat's prayer).

[331]This word-pair is clearly illustrated by Avishur (*Stylistic Studies*, 88). Note especially the connection with *wyṣ'qw 'l yhwh*, demonstrated by Avishur in refrains in Ps. 107:6,13,19,28, which may be compared with the same phrase in Josh. 24:7aA. Significantly, Avishur also notes the parallelism of *hwṣy'* and *hṣyl* in Ex. 6:6, in the context of the exodus. In I.iii-iv of the present text we therefore have strong external parallelism formed by the distribution of word-pairs and use of formulaic language. Note the additional references in I.iii and I.iv to terms of deliverance by Yahweh, e.g., *wyb' 'lyw 't-hym wykshw* (7aC) and *w'ṣl 'tkm mydw* (10aC). It is also noteworthy that in the poetic description of Ex. 15 the words of the enemy *twryšmw ydy* (vs.9) form external parallelism with the reference to Yahweh *nṭyt ymynk* (vs.12), while the dramatical reversal between these two references is enacted by Yahweh, who uses the sea to cover the Egyptians, *ksmw ym* (vs.10). This may be compared to the reference to the sea covering the Egyptians in Josh. 24:7, and the threefold use of "hand" in terms of deliverance in canticle I.iv.

tion); *mdbr* || *'rṣ* (7cA, 8aA; concatenation)[332]

### I.ii and I.iv

*'br hnhr* (2x) || *'br hyrdn* (2x) (2bA, 3aB, 8aB, 11aA; responsion and inclusion);[333] *yšbw* || *hyšb* (2bA, 8aB; responsion); *w'rb 't-zr'w* || *wybrk brwk 'tkm* (3cA, 10aB; responsion);[334] *ntn* (3x) || *ntn* (3bB, 4aA, 4bA, 8bA, 11cA; responsion); *yrš* || *yrš* (4bB, 8bB; concatenation)[335]

The various parallelisms listed here suggest that a very deliberate progression is sketched by the narrator. In I.ii Abraham is brought into the land from "across the river." Covenant blessing is partially fulfilled via the multiplication of progeny. But the full blessing of the land is not yet Israel's to enjoy. In fact, as noted in the parallelism of I.ii.3 above it is only "Esau" who has land to possess, while Jacob and his sons descend to Egypt. But in I.iv Israel's situation is reversed. When Jacob descends to Egypt the lack of a land of inheritance stands out prominently. Now, in approaching the land "across the Jordan" it is explicitly stated that Israel is given a land to inherit, *wtyršw 't-'rṣm* (vs.8), but, as in canticle I.iii, Yahweh must deliver Israel from the enemy. Finally, in I.iv.3 Israel has once again crossed a river, *wt'brw 't-hyrdn* (11aA) to enter the land.

### Macrostructural connections with I.v

Since the present treatment of this canticle is based upon a hypothet-

[332]Cf. Ex. 14:3, asserted to be poetry by Albright (*Yahweh and the Gods*, 33; cf. Avishur, *Stylistic Studies*, 278).

[333]It is significant that "the river" and "the Jordan" are used twice in the respective canticles, the latter forming inclusion at the level of the canticle. For *nhr* || *yrdn* see Job 40:23, though some commentators view *yrdn* here as a gloss (cf. A.de Wilde, *Das Buch Hiob*, *OTS* 22 [Leiden, 1981], 384). It is of interest to note that C.H.Gordon, *Before the Bible: The Common Background of Greek and Hebrew Civilisation* (London, 1962), 284f. proposed to view *yrdn* as originally a common noun meaning "river."

[334]The Pentateuchal narration of the covenant blessing often plays on the parallelism established between "blessing" and "multiplication" of seed; cf. esp. Gen. 1:22,28f.; 8:22; 9:1; 17:19f.; 22:17f.; 26:3f.; 26:24; 28:3f.; 48:3f.; Deut. 7:13; 30:16; Isa. 51:2; Ps. 107:38. With respect to the poetic nature of Gen. 1:22 see specifically Porten–Rappaport, "Poetic Structure," 363-369; Kselman, "Poetic Fragments," 162; cf. the parallism suggested in our division of Gen. 26:4 in the discussion of int. par. at I.ii.2 above.

[335]Occurring in the final strophe of I.ii and the first strophe of I.iv but no additional times in Josh. 24:1-28.

ical reconstruction, we refrain from making a detailed comparison of I.v with all the previous canticles. We restrict the present analysis to a number of the most significant literary links, especially those not affected by our reconstruction. Important connections between this canticle and the preceding canticles include *w'šlḥ* || *w'šlḥ* (5aA, 12aA, responsion at the beginning of the canticles). A clear responsion is formed as well by the military terminology which links I.iv.1 with I.v.1. In particular, notice can be taken of *wylḥmw 'tkm* || *wtgrš 'wtm mpnykm* (8aC, 12aB; responsion).[336] Similarly, *w'šmydm mpnykm* || *wtgrš 'wtm mpnykm* (8bC, 12aB, <12bA>),[337] and *'wtm* || *'wtm* (11cA, 12aB; concatenation). Via these connections vs.12 fulfills an important role in summarizing the element of Yahweh's assistance and deliverance in the face of military conflict. Similarly, the words *ntn* (13aA), *'rṣ* (13aB), and *yšb* (13bB), all help to emphasize that vs.13 constitutes a summary of the concept of land inherited as a free gift from Yahweh.[338] Canticle I.v thereby provides a twofold emphasis, on military deliverance and the gift of the land, as a fitting conclusion to the historical summary.

### 3.5.4 The macrostructure of canto II

It has been indicated above that the four occurrences of the form *n'bd* all fall in the refrain verses of the first four canticles of canto II. It will be demonstrated here that numerous literary markers help to reinforce the connections between the five canticles of canto II. It is especially noteworthy that in II.i-II.ii and in II.iii-II.iv, the three

[336]For this parallelism there is a striking analogy in the Mesha inscription, in the conflict between Omri and Mesha as narrated by the latter. The colon *wyšb bh bhlthmh by* stands in the same strophe as the following colon, *wyršh kmš mpny*. The respective contexts of Josh. 24:8,12 and Mesha V.1 have in common the verbs *yšb*, *lḥm*, *grš* and the prep. *mpny* (cf. de Moor, "Narrative Poetry," 154). Note that this strophe of the Mesha inscription also speaks of building a city and dwelling in it, which may be compared with the final strophe of I.v (cf. esp. *bnh* and *bh* in both). These observations are not affected in any way by our reconstruction in this canticle.

[337]Significantly, both statements are in context of the Amorites.

[338]For *ntn* cf. 3bB,4aA,4bA,8bA,11c; for *'rṣ* cf. 3aB,8aA,8bB, and for *yšb* see 2bA,7cA,8aB. The connection with 2bA forms inclusion, with 7cA responsion, and with 8aB inclusion between successive canticles, thereby linking I.ii-I.v via the strategic use of *yšb* one time in each canticle.

strophes of the corresponding canticles stand parallel to each other to produce an A.B.C || Á.B́.Ć pattern at the level of the strophes within the canticles. Accordingly, in the following analysis particular attention is given first to the connections evident between (*a*) II.i and II.ii, and (*b*) II.iii and II.iv. Secondly, we note the external parallelism between II.i-ii taken together and II.iii-iv taken together. Finally, we note the various connections linking canticle II.v to the preceding four canticles. The cumulative evidence of these external parallelisms at the level of the macrostructure demonstrate clearly that a new canto begins with the *w'th* of vs.14.

**Canticles II.i and II.ii**

With respect to the first strophes of the respective canticles, mention may be made of the following parallelisms:
*yhwh* (2x) || *yhwh* (2x) (14aA, 14bD, 16aC, 17aA; responsion); *'bwtykm* || *'bwtynw* (14bB, 17aC; responsion); *whsyrw 't-'lhym* || *l'bd 'lhym 'ḥrym* (14bA, 16aD)[339] *wbmṣrym* || *m'rṣ mṣrym* (14bC, 17aD; responsion).

In the central strophes, i.e., II.i.2 and II.ii.2, we encounter a striking parallelism, *b'ynykm* || *l'ynynw* (15aA, 17bA; responsion). It is also noteworthy that both these strophes are composed of bicola verses arranged in alternating parallelism.

Also the third strophes of the respective canticles are clearly linked via numerous parallels:
*'lhym* and *'lhy* || *hw' 'lhynw* (15cA and 15dA, 18bC; responsion); *h'mry* || *h'mry* (15dA, 18aB; responsion); *yšbym b'rṣm* || *yšb h'rṣ* (15dB, 18aB; responsion); *w'nky wbyty* || *gm-'nḥnw* (15eA, 18bA; responsion); *n'bd 't-yhwh* || *n'bd 't-yhwh* (15eB, 18bB; responsion)

These responsions demonstrate that the three strophes of II.i are intended to stand parallel to the three strophes of II.ii. As additional evidence we note that inclusion between the canticles is formed by *yhwh* || *yhwh* (14aA, 18bB), and *'bd* || *'bd* (14aB, 18bB). The use of *yhwh* and *'bd* also forms concatenation, (15eB, 16aC-D). The three strophes of II.i constitute the exhortation of Joshua, ending with the

[339]Forming antithetic parallelism (cf. the discussion of int. par. at II.i.1 above). Note that this responsion is intensified in the edition presupposed by the LXX (cf. the discussion of the LXX at vs.14, below).

refrain *n'bd.* The parallel declaration by the people in II.ii ends with the same refrain, and significantly it at the same time recapitulates the basic steps of the exodus and conquest as delineated by Joshua in the historical summary.

**Canticles II.iii and II.iv**

Once again, the two canticles are written with an A.B.C || Á.B́.Ć pattern of strophic parallelism. The evidence for this is conclusive in the various responsions. In the first strophes (II.iii.1 and II.iv.1) we note the following details:
*wy'mr yhwš' 'l h'm* || *wy'mr yhwš' 'l h'm* (19aA, 22aA; responsion); *l'bd* || *l'bd* (19aB, 22aD; responsion); *'t-yhwh* || *'t-yhwh* (19aB, 22aC; responsion)

The central strophes (II.iii.2 and II.iv.2) are also clearly linked:
*'lhy nkr* || *'lhy nkr* (20aD, 23aA; responsion)[340] *yhwh* || *yhwh 'lhy yśr'l* (20aC, 23bB); *-km* (5x) || *-km* (2x) (19c, 20b, 23).
In addition to these formal parallelisms, the responsion between the two entire strophes is built around an antithetical parallelism of the concepts of abandoning Yahweh to serve strange gods, or putting away the strange gods to serve Yahweh—both spoken as parts of direct discourse by Joshua.[341]

Finally, for II.iii.3 and II.iv.3 the following responsions are important:
*wy'mr h'm 'l-yhwš'* || *wy'mr h'm 'l-yhwš'* (21A, 24A; responsion); *'t-yhwh n'bd* || *'t-yhwh 'lhynw n'bd* (21B, 24B; responsion)

The exactness of the formulas marking speech transitions in 19aA, 21A, 22aA, 24A provided evidence for strophic divisions. The present list of external responsions corroborates the previous observations. The six strophes of these two canticles contain significant verbal parallels. As was the case above, these canticles employ the terms *yhwh* and *'bd* to form inclusion and concatenation. The same is true of the cola marking changes in dialogue, cf. *wy'mr yhwšw' 'l-h'm* || *wy'mr h'm 'l-yhwš'* (19aA, 24A; inclusion), as well as *wy'mr h'm 'l-yhwš'* ||

[340]These are the only two occurrences of the phrase *'lhy nkr* in the whole of Joshua. The precise responsion made here is certainly not coincidental. A similar external parallelism is found in Gen. 35:2,4 (cf. 5.3.1).

[341]Note especially the antithetical parallelism established between *t'zbw 't-yhwh w'bdtm 'lhy nkr* (20aD) and *hsyrw 't-'lhy hnkr 'šr bqrbkm whṭw 't-lbbkm 'l-yhwh 'lhy yśr'l* (23bB).

*wy'mr yhwšw' 'l-h'm* (21A, 22aA; concatenation). Here again we are confronted with the repetition of entire cola to form external parallelism. A few formal details are pertinent as well. These canticles demonstrate a 2+2+1 || 2+2+1 structure of poetic verses per strophe. Both canticles total precisely 13 cola. In each of the six strophes Yahweh is mentioned once. Joshua is mentioned in the 1st and 3rd strophe of each canticle.

**The relationship of II.i-ii and II.iii-iv**

Numerous formal and literary factors demonstrate the interconnection of these four canticles. Each canticle is composed of 3 strophes and ends with a refrain employing *n'bd.* And each canticle employs the infinitive construct *l'bd* one time. Three of the four canticles employ this form of *'bd* in the opening strophe, thereby forming inclusion with *n'bd* in the refrain. In II.i *l'bd* is found in the central strophe, but inclusion with *n'bd* is formed via the threefold employment of *'bd* in the opening strophe, twice in imperatives. These observations demonstrate that the structure of all four canticles is completely dominated by the placement of the verb *'bd.*

The four canticles of the dialogue in vss.14-24 are also linked via numerous external parallelisms. Joshua's exhortation in the first canticle begins with *w'th* (14aA), which finds an inclusionary responsion with *w'th* (23aA) in his final unit of speech in the fourth canticle. Similarly, the imperative *whsyrw 't-'lhym* (14bA) makes an inclusion with *hsyrw 't-'lhy hnkr* (23aA). In the first canticle Joshua commands "*bḥrw lkm,*" and in the fourth canticle he echoes "*bḥrtm lkm.*" These inclusions formed via Joshua's speech in the first and fourth canticle employ the key words *w'th, swr*, and *bḥr*, found only here in the whole of Josh. 24:1-28. This confirms that their placement here is deliberate.

The responsions forming inclusion between the first and fourth canticles (II.i and II.iv) prompt an investigation into whether the same is true of the second and third canticles (II.ii and II.iii), thereby in fact making a chiastic correlation of these four canticles. Clearly, II.ii (vss.16-18) is the people's summary of Yahweh's identity as their historic deliverer, which functions as a motivation for their present pledge of allegiance. Joshua's response in II.iii also concentrates entirely upon Yahweh's identity, but it stresses that he is a vengeful and punishing God. The basic content of these respective canticles thereby already indicates a somewhat antithetical parallelism in their descriptions of Yahweh's identity and character.

This initial observation is reinforced by a close scrutiny of detail. Israel's emphatic opening declaration *ḥlylh lnw m'zb 't-yhwh l'bd 'lhym 'ḥrym* (16a) is countered by Joshua's antithetical claim *ky-t'zbw 't-yhwh w'bdtm 'lhy nkr* (20aA). Again, the key word *'zb* is used only these two times in the entire chapter. The people appeal to formulaic, confessional expressions which are at home in the cultus; *ky yhwh 'lhynw* (17aA), and *ky-hw' 'lhynw* (18bC). Joshua again counters similarly with cultic formulae, *ky- 'lhym qdšym hw'* (19bA), and *'l-qnw' hw'* (19bB). The people's response in vss.16-18 parallels Joshua's previous historical recital, summarizing the stages of deliverance from Egypt to the entrance amongst the nations, to the occupation of the land. Their description of God employs the designation *hw' hm'lh* (17aB); they confess that he is the one who preserved them (*wyšmrnw*) (17cA), and drove out the inhabitants of the land before them (*grš*) (18aA).[342] Joshua does not deny any of this. But he is quick to warn that there is another side to Yahweh's identity. In the event of disobedience he will turn and consume them (20bB), after having done good to them (20bC). From these multiple correlations it is clear that II.ii and II.iii are intended to be read in literary responsion with each other.

In summary of the preceding analysis of II.i-II.iv, we note that the three strophes of II.i and II.ii as well as of II.iii and II.iv respectively are all arranged in two sets of A.B.C || Á.B́.Ć parallelism, but the four canticles are in turn arranged chiastically in an A.B || B́.Á pattern. These structural observations do much to alleviate the uneasiness expressed by many previous scholars with respect to the redundancy of the dialogical material in vss.14-24.[343] The present form of the text is meticulously structured. The dialogical character of vss.14-24, with its precise strophic responsions and its formulations reminiscent of confessional language in the Psalms, would be appropriate to a cultic and liturgical setting and function.[344]

## The relationship of II.v to II.i-iv

In the preceding analysis we have shown how the four canticles of

[342]Joshua's speech in 12a employs the same verb.

[343]E.g., L'Hour's suggestion that the original stratum could be restricted to Joshua's injunction in vss.14-15 and the people's adequate response in 18b. See the summary offered in 1.5.4.

[344]Contra Perlitt, *Bundestheologie*, 242f.

II.i-iv on the one hand can be divided into two groups of two (i.e., II.i-ii and II.iii-iv) on the basis of external parallelism between the strophes. On the other hand, there are sufficient literary clues to show that these four canticles are arranged chiastically and therefore they belong together. For this reason it is not necessary to separate II.i-ii and II.iii-iv into two sub-cantos. The literary connections joining these four canticles with II.v are less predominant. Nevertheless, there are sufficient reasons to treat II.v as the final canticle of canto II rather than as an independent canto. Of particular significance here is the emphasis upon a witness, cf. *'dh* in 27aC, 27cA in comparison with *'dym* in the preceding canticle (22aA, 22bB). Furthermore, there is a significant connection of *šm'* || *šm'* (24C, 27bA).[345] Finally, in both preceding canticles (II.iii and II.iv) inclusions are formed by the words *yhwš'* and *h'm* (cf. 19aA, 21A, 22aA, 24A). The same is true of canticle II.v (cf. 25aA, 28aA).

### 3.5.5 Canto I and canto II

Also deserving brief comment are the literary connections which link the two cantos of Josh. 24:1-28 into one unified poetic composition. A clear correlation is made between Joshua's speech in canto I.ii-v and his speech in canto II. Consider especially the responsions formed in the first strophes of his actual speech, notably by *b'br hnhr* || *b'br hnhr* (2bA, 14bC; responsion);[346] *'bwtykm* || *'bwtykm* (2bA, 14bB; responsion); *'bdw* || *'bdw* (2bC, 14bB, 15cB; responsion);[347] These connections show that deliberate responsions are made between I.ii.1 and II.i.1.

Furthermore, the reference *wbmṣrym* (14bC) forms a link with 4bC and all four strophes of I.iii. Similarly, the bicolon of 15d *h'mry 'šr 'tm yšbym b'rṣm* forms a parallelism with *h'mry hywšb* (8a), of I.iv,[348] and with *h'mry* (12bB), *'rṣ* (13aB), and *wtšbw bhm* (13bB) of I.v, thereby effectively linking Joshua's exhortation to every canticle

[345]This responsion is reinforced by an association in both instances with the speech of Yahweh (cf. *bqwlw* [24C] and *'mry yhwh* [27bB]).

[346]See further 3aB and 15cC for a repetition of this parallelism.

[347]A precise responsion is made with 14bB; in both cases the reference is to the fathers' worship of other gods. The LXX of vs.14 makes the correlation even stronger with its added reference to *'ḥrym*.

[348]It has been observed above that *h'mry* forms inclusion at the level of this canticle.

of the historical recital. In addition, Muilenburg is surely correct when he concludes that the identical reference to *yhwh 'lhy yśr'l* in vss.2,23 fulfills a deliberate literary function of inclusion linking Joshua's first and last words.[349]

It is not only Joshua's speech which harks back, for this phenomenon is equally clear in the people's response. The first verse of their reply makes an explicit allusion to Joshua's opening strophe and canticle, i.e., *wy'bdw 'lhym 'ḥrym* || *l'bd 'lhym 'ḥrym* (2bC, 16aD; responsion). Significantly, the second verse of their response makes an explicit responsion with the second canticle of Joshua's speech via *mṣrym* || *mṣrym* (5aB, 17bD; responsion); *yṣ'* || *'lh* (5bA and 6aA, 17aB).[350] And this pattern of responsions continues. The people's next strophe (II.ii.2) parallels Joshua's next canticle (I.iv) in the reference to all the nations through which they safely crossed. The term *'br*, which forms inclusion via a responsion established between the first and last strophe in canticle I.iv,[351] is now employed in 17dB to make this connection explicit. This link is strengthened by another word-pair, *bw'* || *drk* (8aA and 11aB, 17cA).[352] In I.iv the twofold usage of *bw'* and *'br* respectively forms inclusion of the canticle, so it is evident that the people's speech makes responsions with key words in the previous dialogue.

Finally, the last strophe of the people's response (II.ii.3) makes a deliberate correlation with the final canticle of Joshua's speech in canto I, e.g., *wtgrš* || *wygrš* (12aB, <12bA>, 18aA);[353] list of nations || *kl-h'mym* (11b, 18aA); *h'mry* || *h'mry* (12bB, 18aB); *mpnynkm* || *mpnynw* (12aB, <12bA>, 18aB); *'rṣ* || *'rṣ* (13aB, 18aB).

[349]Muilenburg, "Form and Structure," 358; unfortunately, Muilenburg concludes from this that vss.26-28 are not part of the literary unit. See also 2.6.2.

[350]As terms of exodus, cf. Wijngaards, "*Hwṣy'* and *h'lh*," 91-102. It is instructive to compare a parallelism from prophetic discourse in Judg. 6:8, *'nky h'lyty 'tkm mmṣrym* || *w'ṣy' 'tkm mbyt 'bdym*. For additional evidence of these verbs in mainly external parallelism consult, e.g., Ps. 135:7; Jer. 2:3; 4:7; 10:13; 46:9; 51:16. Note too the additional connection between Joshua's speech and the people's speech via *yrd* || *m'lh* (4cB,17aB) (cf. Avishur, *Stylistic Studies*, 510), which demonstrates that Yahweh's deliverance of Israel from Egypt is the reversal of Jacob's descent to Egypt.

[351]See 8aB,11aA,17dB.

[352]Avishur, *Stylistic Studies*, 444, 458, 460f. (re Mic. 5:4f. and a Phoenician parallelism in an incantation text from Arslan Tash).

[353]The verb *grš* is used only here in this passage.

These lists of external parallelisms demonstrates that the speech of the people summarizes the speech of Joshua in the same order presented in canto I. It is to be readily conceded that some such repetitions and parallelisms could occur in any narration where a given portion alludes back to previously mentioned events. However, it is of interest here that the responsions are made in the same order as the divisions into strophes and canticles outlined above. Furthermore, the degree of precision in these external parallelisms suggests that this arrangement is deliberate. The connections are reinforced by employment of word-pairs attested elsewhere in poetry. The cumulative weight of these responsions shows that the people's speech in Josh. 24:16-18 was intended not only to parallel Joshua's exhortation (vss.14-15) but also to provide a précis of the four canticles of Joshua's historical summary (vss.2-13).

**The relationship of II.v to canto I**

It is readily apparent that a number of connections serve to link canticle II.v to the opening strophes of canto I. In the first place, vs.25 makes a deliberate correlation with the setting established in vs.1 via *škmh* || *bškm* (1aB, 25aB). The ensuing ceremony involves raising a stone *bmqdš yhwh* (26bD), which makes a literary link with the gathering *lpny h'lhym* (1bC). Furthermore, Joshua's final speech in vs.27 is introduced by the colon *wy'mr yhwš' 'l-kl-h'm* (27aA), which is an exact repetition of 2aA and is distinguished from 19aA and 22aA by the presence of *kl*. Joshua's final action in sending the people away (vs.28) forms an inclusion with the initial action in gathering the people (vs.1).[354] By means of these literary connections an explicit correlation is made with the setting established in the opening strophe (I.i) and with the beginning of the historical summary (I.ii.1). Joshua's final action in sending the people to their *nḥlh* forms a parallel with Yahweh's gift of the land, thereby establishing a responsion in the last strophes of the two cantos (I.v.3 and II.v.3).[355] On the basis of the foregoing observations the conclusion is warranted that Josh.

[354]On *'sp* || *šlḥ* see esp. Ps. 104:29f. (*tsp rwḥm* || *šlḥ rwḥk*) and cf. Lev. 26:25; 1 Sam. 5:8, 11; 2 Sam. 11:27; 2 Kgs 23:1 (2 Chron. 34:29). From these texts it is apparent that *šlḥ* can either be synonymous with *'sp* in the sense of summon together, or it can be the opposite, to disperse, as in Josh. 24:28.

[355]Note too that canticle I.v employs the same verb, *šlḥ* (12aA) as is used of Joshua (28A), cf. also 5aA. Accepting an alternate reading of the LXX in 28a instead of *nḥlh* does not weaken the connection with I.v.3 (see below).

24:1-28 demonstrates a deliberate poetic composition, with significant degrees of parallelism operative at every structural level, from the internal parallelism of the cola to the macrostructural arrangement of the cantos themselves.

The foregoing discussion has in numerous instances alluded to textual differences between the MT and the LXX. This entails that it is necessary to pay detailed attention to the witness of the LXX. A theory regarding the literary structure of a given passage cannot afford to ignore textual evidence which might either counter or confirm the clues present in the MT. This is especially true in view of the conclusion expressed recently by Auld that the LXX provides a more reliable basis for a detailed analysis of structure than does the MT.[356] For this reason the following section offers a detailed analysis of the differences between the MT and the LXX, with a specific view towards implications for the theory of a poetic narrative as outlined above.

## 3.6 Comparison of the MT and LXX of Josh. 24:1-28

### 3.6.1 Introduction

Our main intention in this section is to study those differences which are of possible significance for a structural analysis. Variants have been divided into two categories. In the first category are included the differences in vs.4f. and vs.17, where the disagreements are of such a nature that they give evidence that an originally shorter text has been expanded. Furthermore, a careful analysis suggests that the differences in these two places are probably related. It is especially important here to ask how the differences would affect the structure of the respective strophes or canticles. The presence of an "expansion" or "contraction" in a given unit of Hebrew poetry is not necessarily evidence of a redaction which disregards the poetic structure of the original composition. In fact, it has been demonstrated that one of the essential characteristics of Hebrew and Canaanite Poetry is the flexibility to lengthen or shorten cola, verses, strophes, canticles, etc., in a self-conscious manner which honours the basic format of the

[356]For a summary of Auld's position see 1.8.

original composition.[357]

In the second category are included the remaining variants. However, these entries are not all of the same weight. For example, where MT reads Shechem, LXX reads Shiloh (vss.1,25). This variation is of significance for the history of the respective textual traditions, it may be symptomatic of theological predilection, but it is by itself of little structural significance.[358] There are, however, many other points of minor disagreement between the two texts which, although not major enough to affect the structure of an entire strophe or canticle, have ramifications for a discernment of internal or external parallelism. A tabulation and analysis of all these differences and their implications for parallelism and structure may possibly provide clues with respect to the separate textual histories of the LXX and MT traditions. A structural analysis cannot by itself hope to solve a problem as complex as the relationship between the LXX and MT. It may be hoped, however, that it would make a worthwhile contribution to the broader endeavor.

The question of internal and external parallelism is more appropriate to a Hebrew *Vorlage* than to a Greek translation, which entails the necessity of trying to separate those variants which derive from a *Vorlage* from those which could result from translation or transmission. On the other hand it is of considerable interest for our present analysis to ask whether the variations between the MT and the LXX give any indication that there was an awareness of a deliberate literary structure in this text. This entails that for each entry it is important to judge whether the variant derives from a different Hebrew *Vorlage* or is to be attributed to the hand of the translator. In this respect we concur with recent research in the LXX of Joshua that a different Hebrew *Vorlage* seems probable, but that the safest procedure is first to attempt to account for variants on the basis of factors in translation or transmission.[359] Secondly, as is noted recently by Butler, the fact that a given clause can easily be retroverted into Hebrew does not prove a Hebrew original.[360] Postulation of a Hebrew *Vorlage* rests on

[357]Cf. the references listed in 2.2, and esp. ch.2 n.8, above.

[358]However, the LXX plus in vs.25 is significant (see below).

[359]Tov, *Text-Critical Use*, 81.

[360]Butler, *Joshua*, 263. Butler's comment is made with respect to 24:4b. The observation is valid, though in this context it is superfluous since there probably is a Hebrew original, namely Deut. 26:5.

surest grounds when it is possible to indicate Hebraisms, Hellenized Semitic words,[361] or matters of grammar which reveal a Hebrew antecedent not attested in the present MT. But in such a case it is also necessary to demonstrate that the minus in the MT does not derive from textual corruption. When these criteria are met one has virtual proof of a Hebrew *Vorlage* which differs from the MT.[362] Such certain examples for Joshua are rare.[363] But there are other means of adducing the probability of a *Vorlage* which differed from the present MT., e.g., by the degree of literalness with which a translator ordinarily renders his text.[364] With these preliminary comments in mind, we can turn to a more detailed analysis of differences in the LXX and MT of Josh. 24:1-28.[365]

### 3.6.2 Textual differences in Josh. 24:4f.,17

**Josh. 24:4f.**

The first major difference which affects the structure of the passage is the plus which is found in the LXX at the end of vs.4. We have noted above that this passage is related to Deut. 26:5f.; this connection warrants further study.

MT Deut. 26:5b *wyhy-šm lgwy gdwl ʻṣwm wrb*

LXX Deut. 26:5b *και ʾεγενετο ʾεκει ʿεις ʾεθνος μεγα και πληθος πολυ και μεγα*

LXX Josh. 24:4d *και ʾεγενοντο ʾεκει ʾεις ʾεθνος μεγα και πολυ και κραταιον*

The following observations are important:

[361]P.Walters [formerly Katz], *The Text of the Septuagint: Its Corruptions and the Their Emendation*, edit. D.W.Gooding (Cambridge, 1973), 141-196.

[362]Cf. Rofé, "End of the Book of Joshua," esp. 19f.

[363]A list of major LXX pluses in Joshua is offered by Tov ("The Growth of the Book of Joshua in the Light of the Evidence of the LXX Translation," in Japhet, ed., *Studies in the Bible*, 321-339, esp. 336). But for most of these texts Tov is able to indicate verses elsewhere in the OT which may have influenced the variant reading. A somewhat unique situation is the LXX plus at the end of Josh. 24:33. Tov appeals to Rofé ("The End of the Book of Joshua") and accepts the conclusion that it reflects a Hebrew addition (Tov, ibid., 324), and he also suggests reasons why such texts may have been deleted from the MT.

[364]Tov, "Growth," 327-329.

[365]In the absence of a more reliable edition of the LXX text of Josh. 24, we used *Septuaginta, Id est Vetus Testamentum graece iuxta Lxx interpretes*, ed. A.Rahlfs, vol. 1, 9th ed. (Stuttgart, 1935), 402-405.

1. The style of this LXX plus is more typical of language in Deuteronomy than in Josh. 24. Deuteronomy is known to collect strings of adjectives in the manner of the three adjectives in parataxis here.
2. LXX Josh. 24:4d is closer to the Hebrew text of Deut. 26:5b than the LXX translation of that verse. In fact, LXX Josh. 24:4d is in certain respects a more literal translation of Deut. 26:5b than is offered by the LXX there. The Hebrew combination *'ṣwm wrb* is simply translated in inverted order.[366] This demonstrates that the LXX plus in Josh. 24:4d is not based on the LXX of Deut. 26:5b but rather on a Hebrew text. If the insertion was made by the translator of Josh. 24, it was taken from a Hebrew manuscript of Deuteronomy. Otherwise the LXX translator was working with a different Hebrew text of Josh. 24 in which the addition was already present. In the light of other studies on the differences between the LXX and MT traditions of Joshua, it is possible that the plus was already made in a Hebrew *Vorlage*. In either event, the plus here is an expansion in the LXX, not a deletion in the MT.[367] Accordingly, it cannot be taken as evidence for an orginal poetic structure other than that which we have determined on the basis of the MT. Nevertheless, it is significant that retroversion to the Hebrew suggested above would add the external parallelism of *rb* || *rb* ([4dB], 7cB).[368]
3. It may be of some significance that the expansion witnessed in the LXX falls between two canticles. If the expansion was already present in a Hebrew *Vorlage*, it was inserted at a place where it would essentially leave the structure of the canticles intact. Accordingly, it is of interest to ask whether the idea that this expansion was made at a time when the poetic composition of Josh. 24 was still recognized would offer an explanation for the absence of *w'šlḥ 't-mšh w't-'hrn* in the present text of the LXX. In this respect there are actually a couple of possibilities. Either *a*) this phrase could have been deleted from the tradition of the LXX when the expansion was made on the

[366]This is a frequent phenomenon in the translation of the LXX. See Tov, *Text-Critical Use*, 58.

[367]Contrary to Holmes (*Joshua*, 78), who unfortunately was either unaware of the connection with Deut. 26:5f. or failed to accord it the necessary weight, recognition of which also renders moot the differences of opinion between Hollenberg and Driver regarding the Hebrew "original."

[368]Forming responsion in the final cola at the end of the canticles (cf. below). Moreover, emphasis upon increasing to a great nation would fit thematically with I.ii.

basis of Deut. 26:5f., or *b*) the phrase could be an independent expansion in the textual tradition of the MT. Both possibilities deserve consideration.

*a*) LXX expands on the basis of Deut. 26:5f. but deletes 5aA:
In this theory the final verse of canticle I.ii becomes expanded as follows.

| | |
|---|---|
| *wy'qb wbnyw* | But as for Jacob and his sons, |
| *yrdw mṣrym* | they descended to Egypt, |
| *wyhyw šm lgwy gdwl* | and they became there a great nation, |
| *'ṣwm wrb* | mighty and numerous. |

And the first colon of the following canticle is replaced:

| | |
|---|---|
| *wyr'w 'tm hmṣrym* | But the Egyptians did evil to them. |
| *wngp yhwh 't-mṣrym* | so Yahweh struck the Egyptians |
| *b'šr 'śh bqrbm* | in that which he did in their midst. |

In this way the first verse of canticle I.iii remains a tricolon. The second colon shifts from 1st person discourse (MT) to a 3rd pers. subject. The third person references are maintained throughout the rest of the historical recital, whereas in the MT the shift is only found in vs.7.

This is a plausible option but it does not give an entirely satisfactory explanation for why the colon *w'šlḥ 't-mšh w't-'hrn* would have been dropped. It could as easily have been converted to *wyšlḥ yhwh 't-mšh w't-'hrn*[369] and retained as part of a quadrocolon at the beginning of the strophe. If the preceding cola are indeed expansions, the motivation for this might be based on a desire to attain historical completeness. In that case, someone missed certain details about the sojourn in Egypt which were provided elsewhere in Deut. 26:5f. and judged them important enough to insert here. It is unlikely that the same person would delete the reference to Moses and Aaron. Nor can any clear reason be seen for the deletion of this clause at a subsequent point. This entails that it is necessary to consider option *b*) The MT is independently expanded:
It is possible that the tradition behind the MT and the *Vorlage* of the LXX at one time originally contained the bicolon:

[369]Cf. 1 Sam. 12:8.

| | |
|---|---|
| *w'gp 't-mṣrym* | And I struck Egypt, |
| *k'šr 'śyty bqrbw* | with what I did in her midst. |

This edition could have been expanded independently from the *Vorlage* of the LXX. The addition could have been made on the basis of a couple of other references. Especially revealing here is a comparison with 1 Sam. 12:8 which in the same context of the descent of Jacob to Egypt narrates:

| | |
|---|---|
| *wyšlḥ yhwh 't-mšh w't-'hrn* | And Yahweh sent Moses and Aaron. |

Furthermore, the text in 1 Sam. 12:8 also contains the colon:

| | |
|---|---|
| *wywṣy'w 't-'bwtykm mmṣrym* | and he brought your fathers out of Egypt |

This colon is virtually identical to Josh. 24:6aB in our structural analysis. Furthermore, in 1 Sam. 12:8 the colon *wyz'qw 'bwtykm 'l-yhwh* can be compared with *wyṣ'qw 'l-yhwh* in Josh. 24:7. These similarities show the close correspondence of the respective historical recitals,[370] and it is possible that Josh. 24:5aA is an expansion based upon 1 Sam. 12:8. However, also instructive is Mic. 6:4:

| | |
|---|---|
| *ky h'ltyk m'rṣ mṣrym* | For I brought you up from the land of Egypt, |
| *wmbyt 'bdym pdytyk* | and from the house of slavery I redeemed you. |
| *w'šlḥ lpnyk* | And I sent before you |
| *'t-mšh 'hrn wmrym* | Moses, Aaron and Miriam. |

This verse is followed in Mic. 6:5 with a reference to Balak and Balaam. Accordingly, here too we have an historical recital which includes a reference about the sending of Moses and Aaron, and has other points of contact with Josh. 24:1-28. In other words, there are other comparable verses and contexts which could provide the specific incentive for an expansion in Josh. 24:5aA.[371] In our opinion this possibility is more probable than the idea that it was excised from the LXX or the *Vorlage* of the LXX. If this conclusion can be sustained it would confirm the conclusion by Tov on other grounds that the differences between the present LXX and MT texts need not always be explained on the basis of textual corruptions, but that

[370] A more detailed comparison of these passages is offered in 5.5.3.

[371] Cf. Ps. 105:26 (*šlḥ mšh 'bdw || 'hrn 'šr bḥr-bw*).

they at times derive from different *editions*.[372] In general the MT may reflect more expansions upon the original, shorter text which underlies the LXX and the MT editions than does the LXX; however, at times, as in Josh. 24:4f., it is possible that *both* the LXX and the MT underwent expansions. The interesting fact in Josh. 24:4f. is that both editions would expand here in the same place between the respective canticles. Furthermore, both editions would base the expansions upon cola found elsewhere in the OT in parallel accounts of the same event. What is also extremely significant is that in the poetic tradition of Ps. 105 one finds material which parallels *both the expansion in the LXX and in the MT*. The reference to Moses and Aaron in 5aA with *šlḥ* is paralleled by 105:26. The expansion in LXX dealing with the multiplication of the descendants of Jacob and the cruel treatment at the hands of the Egyptians is paralleled in the two poetic verses of Ps. 105:24f. It is hardly likely that pure coincidence would account for the coalescence of independent expansions in the tradition of the LXX and MT with material found together in the parallel account of Ps. 105:24-26. It is more likely that the present differences in the LXX and the MT attest to a state in which at least two Hebrew editions were extant with minor variations.

These variations do not entail a major change in the poetic structure of the text itself. The expansion in the LXX adds a responsion of *wrb* || *rbym* (4dB, 7cB).[373] The responsion would significantly be between the final words of the respective canticles, I.iii and I.iv. This may plausibly explain why the expansion in the LXX chooses to follow Deut. 26:5 rather than the parallel material in Ps. 105:24. And the expansion in the MT of Josh. 24:5aA adds the responsion *w'šlḥ 't-mšh w't-'hrn* || *w'šlḥ lpnykm 't-hṣr'h* (5aA, 12aA). Significantly, here the responsion is between the first words of the respective canticles, I.iii and I.v. In other words, the differences now witnessed between the MT and the LXX can plausibly be accounted for as slightly different poetic editions which do not alter the structure of the composition. Since our analysis of macrostructure demonstrated the employment of deliberate responsions between the canticles, it is striking that both the presence of *rb* at the end of I.ii and *šlḥ* at the beginning of II.iii

[372]Tov, "Growth," 337-339. Note that Tov uses the term "editions" advisedly. His employment of this word is felicitous and is confirmed by our research in this chapter.

[373]For the retroversion *wrb* see above.

would form perfect responsions with other canticles of the same canto.

### Josh. 24:17

The second major difference between the LXX and the MT is in vs.17 where the MT has a plus, *mbyt ʿbdym wʾšr ʿśh lʿnynw ʾt-hʾtwt hgdlwt hʾlh*. The present diversity can be explained on the basis of one of three possible solutions.
*a*) The LXX has a minus via textual corruption.
*b*) The LXX has a minus via deliberate deletion.
*c*) The MT has a plus via deliberate expansion.
For possibility *a*) no logical explanation for an error in transmission presents itself. In fact, for such an error to begin in the midst of the formula *mʾrṣ mṣrym mbyt ʿbdym* is improbable. Nor is there a ready reason why the LXX would have a deliberate deletion. Secondly, there is an observed tendency elsewhere to expand *mmṣrym* to the fuller formula *mʾrṣ mṣrym*[374] and by comparison it is more logical to assume that the formula was deliberately expanded in Josh. 24:17 than that it was contracted in the LXX. In the light of the foregoing discussion of vs.5, and in view of the conclusions that the MT of Joshua shows a tendency to expand an earlier and shorter edition,[375] it is logical to approach the present divergence as a deliberate expansion in the MT.

Syntactically it is in fact neccessary to view the present divergence as two pluses. The first is the clause *mbyt ʿbdym* (17bC), the second is *wʾšr ʿśh lʿynynw ʾt-hʾtwt hgdlwt hʾlh* (17cA-B). Both expansions could have been added at the same time, but it is also conceivable that they were added independently. With respect to 17aE, it is noteworthy that the same clause occurs in Mic.6:4. This is most striking because of the possible connection which we saw above with respect to the expansion in 24:5aA. According to Weinfeld, the origin of the phrase is perhaps Elohistic.[376] But it is significant that Weinfeld's list also shows that it is a common phrase in Deuteronomy, i.e., 5:6; 6:12; 7:8; 8:14; 13:6,11. This might not seem important until it is recognized that one of the characteristics of pluses in the MT of Joshua is a trend of influence by Deuteronomy.[377] It is probably not nec-

[374]Wijngaards, "*Hwṣy* and *hʿlh*," 93.
[375]Tov, "Growth," 321-339.
[376]Weinfeld, *Deuteronomy*, 326f.
[377]This is suggested by Tov as an area which demands further study ("Growth,"

essary to choose between influence from Mic. 6:4 or Deuteronomy; concomittant influence of both is possible. If there is a general trend of expansions in Joshua with terminology at home in Deuteronomy, this could coalesce with the similar text in Mic. 6:4 to explain the formula in vs.17 as an expansion to *m'rṣ mṣrym mbyt 'bdym*. If the longer formula became a more or less stock phrase, it is not surprising that such an expansion could be incorporated into the text. The net result is a very long verse, but it produces both internal parallelism (with 17aD) as well as external parallelism at the levels of the strophe (with *'bd* in 16aD) and canticle (with *'bd* in 18bB).

The plus in 17b is more substantial since it entails more than the completion of a stock phrase attested frequently elsewhere. The syntax of *'t-h'twt hgdlwt h'lh* is in itself not unusual, but in the present context it is nevertheless noteworthy. There are no other examples in Josh. 24:1-28 of a demonstrative used together with an adjective in this manner.[378] Moreover, the employment of *gdl* to modify *'wt* is itself revealing. There are only seven verses in the OT where these two words occur together, namely Deut. 4:34; 6:22; 7:19; 26:8; 29:2; Josh. 24:17; Jer. 32:21. However, in all six of the other verses the adjective *gdl* is not simply used with *'wt* or *'wtt*; it is used either with a combination, such as *h'tt whmptym* (Deut. 6:22; 7:19; 29:2), or of the synonym *mwr'ym* (4:34; 26:8; Jer. 32:21). Furthermore, in each of the six occurrences in Deuteronomy and Jeremiah, *'wt* is accompanied by *mwptym*. In Deuteronomy the two nouns are virtually an inseparable pair, occurring together nine times. The only exception when used of wonders performed by Yahweh is in 11:3 where there are other synonyms. For the combination outside of Deuteronomy cf. Ex. 7:3; Isa. 8:18; 20:3; Ps. 78:43; 135:9; Neh. 9:10; Jer. 32:20f. This would suggest that the combination did not necessarily originate in Deuteronomy; but when *'wt* is used there in the sense of signs performed by Yahweh, it is always accompanied by *mwpt* or a synonym. In other words, an expansion in Josh. 24:17 could have been influenced by traditional language from Deuteronomy,[379] but the language and style stops short of the stereotyped collocation of nouns found in Deuteronomy.

335f., 338).

[378]Cf. Josh. 23 in contrast, where this type of construction is prevalent.

[379]Cf. Butler, *Joshua*, 264; Tov, "Growth," 336. It is striking that this is the only place in Joshua where explicit mention is made of the signs performed in Egypt.

This plus in the MT is also structurally significant. In the colometric division offered above, it constitutes two cola. We have noted that 17bA forms a responsion with 15aA. It also makes a more distant link with I.ii, esp. 5aC,7b. In the macrostructure, the response of the people traces the same historical progressions as Joshua's historical recital. The plus in 17b elaborates the otherwise terse reference by the people to the Egyptian sojourn, and it strengthens the connection between the words of Joshua and the words of the people.

Since the Masoretic pluses in Josh. 24:5aA and 17aE *both* show a striking parallel to Mic. 6:4, it is more probable that these places represent expansions in the MT than deletions in the LXX tradition.[380] What is crucial, however, is that, if 17aE and 17b are poetic expansions, they are sensitive to the structure which we have defended in Josh. 24:1-28, as is evident from the parallelisms listed above. And their deletion would still leave a canticle of 3 strophes. The result in II.ii would be 6 verses rather than 7 (cf. II.i, 3 strophes, 7 verses), and 17 cola (cf. II.i, 17 cola), and 17a would be reduced to a quadrocolon.[381] Accordingly, these textual variations between the LXX and the MT can be explained in terms of subsequent poetic expansion which is either conscious of the literary structure outlined above, or minimally, if it was unconscious of the entire structure, it happened to produce a high number of additional external parallelisms without disturbing the overall structure. Once again the LXX and the MT can be evaluated as having various editions of the same poetic text, the latter containing a slightly expanded version.[382]

### 3.6.3 Minor differences possibly affecting structure

#### Josh. 24:1

1. MT Shechem, LXX Shiloh, see below at vs.25.

[380]This agrees with the general conclusions drawn by Tov and Auld that the MT of Joshua is often expanded. Regarding Josh. 24:17aE comparison must also be made with Judg. 6:8; 1 Sam. 10:18; 12:8 all of which are literarily connected with Josh. 24:1-18 (see below).

[381]If a variant reading in the Peshitta is accepted, one could also view 17aC as a poetic expansion along the same lines as is argued here regarding the LXX, in which case the original verse may have been a tricolon.

[382]If 17b is viewed as a later expansion of II.ii.2, the original strophe would have been marked with separation upwards by rep. prep. *b*. It would have contained two bicola verses in alternating parallelism, precisely as in the corresponding strophe of II.i.2, for which see the ext. par. between II.i and II.ii listed above.

2. List of leaders: LXX A agrees with MT. LXX B has τους πρεσβυτερους as translation of *zqny yśr'l*, and a translation of *r'šyw* is lacking. A different Hebrew *Vorlage* is doubtful. In 23:2 LXX B freely translates *zqnyw* with γερουσια in order to distinguish it from the reference to Joshua in 23:1.[383] In 23:2 the Hebrew *wlšpṭyw wlšṭryw* is also translated in inverted order. The sequence in LXX B of Josh. 23:2 and 24:1 thereby agrees with the list in LXX 9:2d (= MT 8:33). The LXX does not always give a literal translation of such lists of leaders (cf. Deut. 29:9 and 31:28, and note how LXX A in Ex. 18:21, 25 appears to accommodate its translation to Deut. 1:15). It is safest to conclude that LXX B gives no proof of a different Hebrew *Vorlage*.[384]

3. LXX ἱστανaι as translation of *yṣb* Hithp. is acceptable; cf. Ex. 9:13; 14:13; Deut. 31:14; 2 Sam. 18:13; 21:5; Judg. 20:2, etc.[385]

**Josh. 24:2**

The LXX translates *m'wlm* as an adjective modifying "fathers" rather than as an adverb modifying "dwelt."

**Josh. 24:3**

LXX lacks "Canaan." The expression "land of Canaan" is frequent in the patriarchal narratives of Genesis, cf. esp. 17:8 and Ps. 105:11. Significantly, in Josh. 5:12 the LXX also lacks "Canaan." MT would appear to be the most original since a retroversion to *bkl-h'rṣ* would be an unlikely Hebrew reading here.

**Josh. 24:4**

LXX lacks *w'tn*, which can be accounted for stylistically as an attempt to get rid of the redundant verb. Cf. the absence of "Israel" above. Its function in the MT is important with respect to the alternating parallelism of the verse.

**Josh. 24:5**

From here on the actions of Yahweh are consistently described in the

[383]It is difficult to say whether this was motivated by the LXX's desire for a categorical distinction between Joshua and the other elders, or simply for stylistic variety. For examples of the latter consult Wevers, "Exegetical Principles," 301 n.2. In either event, the difference between the MT and the LXX can be attributed to the translator rather than to variant *Vorlages*.

[384]Contra Nielsen, *Shechem*, 87.

[385]One must therefore be cautious about concluding on this basis that there is "an increasing hierarchy" in the actions of Joshua (Nielsen, *Shechem*, 87), but Nielsen is correct to the extent that LXX A has the same verb but with the people as subject.

third person rather than 1st person. The matter is complicated by the fact that LXX A and LXX B frequently disagree with each other in their references to the people, e.g., LXX A "and afterwards he brought you out of Egypt"; LXX B "and afterwards he brought our fathers out of Egypt." The eclectic edition of Rahlfs accepts LXX A, apparently on grounds of harmonization with the following aorist 2nd. pl. verb in vs.6a. A second complicating factor is to be noted in the fact that the MT and LXX do not agree as to which actions are attributed to Yahweh and which are attributed to the people, cf. vs.8. The differences in vss.5-13 with respect to grammatical person cannot be solved individually. It is therefore necessary to list all the differences in the hope that a pattern or trend will become visible.

**Josh. 24:6**
LXX B plus *την 'ερυθραν* = *ym-swp*, apparently anticipating the translation of the second reference in the same verse. LXX B reads "our fathers."

**Josh. 24:7**
LXX has "we cried" (1 pl.). Retroverted to Hebrew = *wnṣ'q*, which is identical to Deut. 26:7.[386] This is significant because of the demonstrated dependence of the LXX upon Deut. 26:5f. for the expansion at vs.4 (see above). Another possible clarification may be sought in a desire by the translator to avoid any possible misunderstanding that it was the Egyptians who cried out to Yahweh, which might be implied in the grammatically ambiguous 3rd pl. form. For the translation of *m'pl* as *νεφελην και γνοφον* see 2.2 above. LXX B reads "between us" rather than "you" of MT and LXX A, but in the reference "your eyes saw" LXX B agrees with MT and LXX A. A final difference between the LXX and MT is the fact that *wtšbw* is translated less than literally by *'ητε*. Elsewhere the latter is virtually always a translation of *hyytm*.[387] The difference may seem minor, but it is of significance for two reasons. First, the translator perhaps thought that the verb "dwell" was too strong to accurately describe the wilderness sojourn and wanderings, and therefore opted for a less than literal translation which in his opinion was truer to the historical circumstances. If this phenomenon is paralleled in other similar cases, it gives us an idea of

[386]The only other occurrence of the identical form is significantly in the parallel historical recital in Num. 20:16. For the synonymous form *wnz'q* see 2 Chron. 20:9.
[387]Cf. Hatch–Redpath, *Septuagint*, 383a.

the degree of literalness in the translator's approach. Secondly, the verb *yšb* may have been employed deliberately in the Hebrew for reasons of structure, cf. 2ba, 8aB, 13bB, 15dB, 18aB and the discussion of macrostructure above.

**Josh. 24:8**

1. LXX B does not contain a translation of *wylḥmw 'tkm*. A helpful discussion is offered by Greenspoon, who demonstrates that there are two possibilities.[388] The first explanation is that an inner Greek corruption per homoioarchton caused the deletion of *και παρεταξαντο 'υμιν* from between *περαν* and *παραδεδωκεν*. The support for this explanation is strong. A second possibility is that the MT has an expansion in order to facilitate the parallelism with 24:11. In our opinion the former explanation is more probable.[389] However, if the latter case is accepted, this would imply that at a relatively late date the external parallelism of the Hebrew tradition witnessed in the MT continued to be strengthened by means of such responsions.

2. LXX continues 3rd per. ref. to Yahweh, and 1st c. pl. references to the people until the final two action verbs, which are in the 2nd pl. forms. Since the LXX is proceeding with Joshua speaking as representative of the people rather than in the direct form of the *Jahwerede* as in the MT, this has two consequences. The verb *yrš* would seem to exclude Joshua. Secondly, the people rather than Yahweh stand as the acting subject of the verb *šmd*. The difference in the latter case is one between the "ban" and "heilige Krieg."[390] The predominant theme in the present form of the historical recital in both the MT and the LXX is that of Yahweh's deliverance, not of the people's valiant fulfillment of the ban. The reference in LXX, if based on a Hebrew antecedent, would have to be either *wtšmydm* or *tšmyd 'wtm*. The

[388]Greenspoon, *Textual Studies*, 326f.

[389]A telling argument against the latter explanation, which posits an expansion in MT, is one from purely historical considerations; of the three cola in 8bA,10aC, and 11bD, the first stands most naturally as a summary statement based upon Num. 21:21ff. Without the phrase *wylḥmw* there would be no expression of opposition in this narration (cf. Num. 21:1f., where *wylḥm byšr'l* is followed by the same expression *ntn byd*). Josh. 24:8 therefore follows the standard paradigm. To facilitate the poetic external parallelism the paradigm is maintained even in 9aC *wylḥm byšr'l* with respect to Balak, even though this seems to be a very free representation of the historical account given in Num. 22-24. This would suggest that the reference in 8bA is original and not a later expansion.

[390]D.Vetter, "*Šmd*," *THAT*, 2:963-965.

reading is plausible if it is an alternative reading in distinction from the MT, which emphasizes Yahweh's deliverance. More likely is a tendency in the LXX translation to attain consistency of form in the verbs *yrš* and *šmd*.

**Josh. 24:9**

The choice in LXX B to render *lqll* with the infinitive ἀρασασθαι is informative with respect to the method of translation. By far the preferred form is καταρασθαι. Furthermore, ἀρασθαι, though rarely used, is employed for two different verbs in Num. 22:6(LXX B),11; 23:7,8. The translator in Numbers likely employed the form for variety in the multiple references there to cursing. The usage in Josh. 24:9 is in turn influenced by the parallel LXX texts in Numbers.[391] This conclusion is consistent with a tendency observed throughout our study; the translation in LXX B is frequently influenced by parallel texts.

**Josh. 24:10**

If there is any doubt after vs.9 that LXX B, whether at the level of the translator or antecedent tradition, is strongly influenced by parallel texts, the case is clinched in vs.10. The comments by Butler[392] call attention to Deut. 23:6, and the correctness of this conclusion is demonstrated by the fact that the LXX witnesses the 2nd singular references found in Deuteronomy. But this does not yet account for all the differences. Butler may be correct that there is a theological reason for altering *lšm' lbl'm*, to avoid the impression that God could be manipulated by the voice of man.[393] For our purposes it is also of interest to note that the presence of Greek ἀπολεσαι instead of Hebrew *šm'* could also be taken as a translation of *šmd*,[394] thereby forming parallelism with 8bC. And παρεδωκεν could be the equivalent of *wytn*. While a literally retroverted Hebrew *wytn 'wtm* would stand

[391]According to Hatch–Redpath (*Septuagint*, 152), it is used elsewhere only in Judg. 17:2 (LXX B); 1 Sam. 14:24; 1 Kgs 8:31 (= 2 Chron. 6:22).

[392]Butler, *Joshua*, 264.

[393]For some examples of antianthropomorphisms and antianthropopathisms underlying the translation of the LXX consult Wevers, "Exegetical Principles," 318-320, esp. 319f. and the discussion of 1 Kgs 17:22, where the LXX fastidiously avoids translation of the MT reference to Yahweh listening to Elijah (*wyšm' yhwh bqwl 'lyhw*).

[394]Cf. Deut. 2:12(LXX A),21; 33:27; Josh. 11:14; Est. 4:8. Greenspoon correctly objects to Hollenberg's explanation that *lbl'm* could have been misread as an infinitive of *bl'* (*Textual Studies*, 157).

awkwardly at the end of this verse, an original *wytn 'wtm bydkm* would stand well as a final colon here. It would establish internal parallelism at the level of the verse, as well as heightening the responsion with *w'tn 'wtm bydkm* (8bA, 11bD).[395] Actual proof for a retroversion to a differing Hebrew *Vorlage* is tenuous here, but it is indeed striking that the key words *šmd* and *ntn* would heighten the parallelism with the corresponding strophes in the same canticle, and the witness of the different Greek text tends to strengthen rather than refute the allegation of external parallelism here.[396]

**Josh. 24:11**

LXX "citizens" of Jericho is a free equivalent of *b'ly-yryḥw*. Butler's implication[397] that the LXX variant is due to an aversion to Baal is quite possible.[398] It is also possible that specific mention of "lords" of Jericho appeared to be unwarranted by the account in Josh. 6, in which case the change could have occurred either in a *Vorlage* or by the translator, but in either case the contextually more difficult reading of MT would seem to be original. If a change was made in a Hebrew *Vorlage* of the LXX, it could have been intended to make a responsion with *yšb h'rṣ* in the parallel recital of the people (18aB). As above, the people are referred to in 1st pl., and Yahweh in 3rd rather than 1st sing. As elsewhere, the list of nations in LXX B differs from MT and LXX A, cf. Josh. 3:10; 9:1; 11:3; 12:8. The reason for the different order is a mystery, and there is no logical reason for attributing it to the translator.[399]

**Josh. 24:12**

LXX (A and B) continues in 3rd sing. and 1st pl.[400] references. LXX

[395]The absence of a translation for the second occurrence of *yd* could be explained as a stylistic simplification and avoidance of redundancy similar to the phenomenon operative above where "Israel" (vs.1) and "*ntn*" (vs.4) are left untranslated in repeated occurrences (cf. below re *'bd* in vs.15, where the third occurrence of the verb is left untranslated).

[396]Cf. the discussion above of the external parallelism of I.iv.

[397]Butler, *Joshua*, 264.

[398]Cf. the LXX translation of *b'ly bryt* in Gen. 14:13, the less than literal translation in 1 Sam. 23:11f., and the preferred translation of simply 'οι 'ανδρες in the multiple references in Judg. 9.

[399]In light of the predominent role played Amorites in the chapter, it may be significant that both the MT and the LXX prominently place the Amorites at the head of the list.

[400]Rahlfs chooses against LXX A and B to read "you" in these verses.

B "twelve kings," LXX A "twelve cities,"[401] is of little apparent structural significance. Nevertheless, the reading of the LXX presupposes that vs.12 must continue the account of the conquest in chronological order. Our analysis of structure in the MT, by contrast, suggests that a new canticle begins in vs.12. Furthermore, this is the final canticle of the historical recital, and as a summary of the conquest it need not follow chronologically upon the reference to the nations in vs.11. Hence, the two kings in MT can refer to the Transjordanian experiences; the reference only becomes problematic when one attempts to read it in a strictly chronological fashion.

**Josh. 24:13**

LXX B has "you" plural where MT and LXX A have the singular. The reading of LXX B appears to be stylistic streamlining.[402]

**Josh. 24:14**

If the reading *τους θεους τους ἀλλοτριους* is accepted as a translation of *'lhym 'ḥrym* or *'lhy nkr*, the structure of the verse is not affected and additional external parallelism is established in responsion with 16aD. It has been demonstrated above that in II.i and II.ii the initial strophes of the respective canticles are clearly linked via a number of responsions. The presence of *'ḥrym* here would add to that connection. It would also make a significant responsion with 2bC, linking the beginning of the historical recital with the beginning of the dialogue in canto II. A different *Vorlage* is not proven here, but if accepted it would strengthen rather than weaken our determined macrostructure.[403]

**Josh. 24:15**

For the LXX's translation of *w'm r' b'ynykm* consult Prov. 24:18; Isa. 59:15 (both poetic). The LXX chooses, apparently for stylistic reasons, to omit translation of the third occurrence of the verb *'bd*. The translation flows more smoothly than if the verb were rendered a third time, but the resulting "whether the gods of your fathers, those beyond the river..." is not an accurate translation of the Hebrew *'šr-'bdw 'bwtykm 'šr b'br hnhr*. This is another example of non-literal

[401]Perhaps confusing *mlky* for *mlkwt*.

[402]Tov, *Text-Critical Use*, 224.

[403]For a similar plus in the LXX consult Deut. 4:28, and note the comments by Walters (*Septuagint*, 252, 344f.).

translation for stylistic reasons.[404] In 15c, LXX has a final plus, ὅτι ἅγιος ἐστιν, which can be retroverted as *ky qdwš hw'*. If accepted in a *Vorlage*, it expands the final bicolon of this strophe and canticle to a tricolon, thereby strengthening separation downwards. Furthermore, it forms an excellent responsion with the corresponding colon in 18bB (*ky-hw' 'lhynw*) in the matching refrain.[405] Acceptance of *ky qdwš hw'* strengthens the connection between the refrains via the parallel *ky*-clause motivating *n'bd*. Moreover, this colon would make a connection with *ky-'lhym qdwšym hw'* in 19bA where Joshua's speech resumes, thereby bracketing the answer of the people with a twofold assertion of Yahweh's holiness. This is another example of the desirability of speaking of different *editions* of the passage rather than simply textual variations where one is coerced to choose for one reading or the other as the "better" text.

**Josh. 24:17a**

Here LXX apparently misunderstands the syntax of *ky yhwh 'lhynw, hw'....*[406] The disjunctive accent (*zāqēp̄ parvum*) ought to be accepted. This suggests that the translator of the LXX did not regard the poetic structure here. The Peshitta lacks *w't-'bwtynw*, and on this basis some argue to omit it as secondary in the MT.[407] The Peshitta in many instances tends to paraphrase, and it is questionable how much weight it deserves to receive, but cf. the discussion of vs.17a above (3.6.2).

**Josh. 24:18**

LXX reverses the order of "all the nations" and "Amorites." Holmes thinks that *'t-kl-h'mym* is a post-LXX addition to the MT, later inserted into the LXX itself.[408] BHS and many commentators concur that it is a gloss.[409] Unfortunately they have missed the significance of the alternating (ABÁB́) poetic parallelism which totally dominates

[404]Cf. Schmitt, *Landtag*, 9; contra Holmes (*Joshua*, 79), who ambivalently postulates either an abbreviation by LXX or a theological revision by MT.

[405]We have noted that the 3 strophes of II.i and the 3 strophes of II.ii are structurally and thematically parallel, both ending with a refrain employing *n'bd*.

[406]Holmes, *Joshua*, 79; Butler, *Joshua*, 264.

[407]Cf. Holmes, *Joshua*, 79; Nielsen, *Shechem*, 99.

[408]Holmes, *Joshua*, 79.

[409]E.g., Dillmann, *Josua*, 587. Dillmann stated in 1886 that it is "ohne Zweifel Zusatz des R," and few commentators have demurred. Agreement is stated by Steuernagel (*Josua*, 245); Rudolph (*Der "Elohist,"* 247); Hölscher (*Geschichtsschreibung*, 350); Noth, (*Josua* 1953, 140); Schmitt (*Landtag*, 10).

the preceding strophe, and which in turn leads to a concatenation and alternating parallelism between 17d and 18a, i.e., *wbkl h'mym* || *wygrš yhwh 't-kl-h'mym* (A || Á) and *'šr 'brnw bqrbm* || *w't-h'mry yšb h'rṣ mpnynw* (B || B́); see above regarding this parallelism. The LXX, not recognizing the alternating poetic parallelism, inverts the order for a syntactically and stylistically smoother reading. Holmes' speculation of complicated double redaction is thereby rendered improbable, and the reasons cited by other commentators for viewing it as a gloss are no longer compelling.

**Josh. 24:19**
LXX deletion of *'l* is perhaps due to syntactical simplification[410] because the LXX generally translates both *'lhym* and *'l* with θεος.[411]

**Josh. 24:20**
LXX B's translation of *'lhy nkr* with θεοις ἑτεροις can perhaps be explained as a translation informed by vss.2,16. However, ἑτερος is virtually always a translation of *'ḥr*, and nowhere else is it a translation of *nkr*.[412] It is accordingly interesting that *'ḥrym* rather than *nkr* in 20aB would add an external sonant parallelism with *'ḥry* in 20bC without removing the responsion with *'t-'lhy hnkr* in 23aA. Note too the presence of τους θεους τους ἀλλοτριους in the LXX at vs.14. The cumulative evidence of these differences posits the possibility of slightly different responsions established in various editions or stages of the Hebrew text; we are faced with a choice of crediting the variant to either an improbable and non-literal translation of *nkr*, or a *Vorlage* with a different but equally convincing external parallelism formed by the presence of *'lhym 'ḥrym* rather than *'lhy nkr*. The presence of comparable phenomena throughout the passage makes the latter explanation a viable possibility.

**Josh. 24:22**
The words *wy'mr 'dym* should be retained with MT against LXX as part of a legal formula.[413]

**Josh. 24:24**
Absence of *'lhynw* in LXX weakens ext. par. with 23bB but con-

[410]With Holmes, *Joshua*, 79; Butler, *Joshua*, 265.
[411]Cf. Greenspoon, *Textual Studies*, 287.
[412]Hatch–Redpath, *Septuagint*, 560; cf. Walters, *Septuagint*, 344f. n.4.
[413]Cf. the detailed discussion in 2.2.

comittantly strengthens the link with 22b.

**Josh. 24:25**

The LXX variations in this verse are universally recognized to be related to those of vs.1 where LXX also reads Shiloh rather than Shechem. Recognition of the poetic nature of Josh. 24 opens a new possibility with respect to understanding the extra phrase at the end of the verse, ἐνωπιον της σκηνης του θεου Ισραηλ. Holmes attributes the addition to influence from Ps. 78:60.[414] Butler looks in the direction of Josh. 18:1.[415] The differences have usually been attributed to the Greek translator.[416]

Before one is willing to accept the conclusion that the LXX plus is due to a translator, it is necessary to at least entertain the possibility that such an expansion could have been incorporated already in a Hebrew text. The LXX plus is retroverted by Boling as *lpny mškn 'lhy yśr'l*.[417] This provides a literal translation of the Greek, but it renders a Hebrew construct chain not attested elsewhere in the OT.[418] Substitution of *'hl* for *mškn* is equally difficult since this noun in construct with *'lhy yśr'l* is also unattested.[419] Admittedly, these are arguments from silence, but they do raise reservations about postulating a Hebrew *Vorlage* with a reading of *lpny mškn 'lhy yśr'l*.[420] A more probable Hebrew combination would be *mškn yhwh*.[421] But this becomes so distant from a literal rendering of the Greek that it is hardly convincing as an original Hebrew equivalent. One might

[414]Holmes, *Joshua*, 79.

[415]Butler, *Joshua*, 265. D.G.Schley (*Shiloh: A Biblical City in Tradition and History* [Sheffield, 1989], 225 n.1) thinks of "scribal alteration, to bring Joshua 24 into conformity with the emphasis placed on Shiloh in Joshua 18-22."

[416]Nielsen, *Shechem*, 86: "The Greek variant is only of interest in so far as it reveals that the ancient translators felt that there was a problem in the prominence held by Shechem in this tradition."

[417]Boling, *Joshua*, 532.

[418]The closest equivalent would be *mškn byt h'lhym* attested only in 1 Chron. 6:33.

[419]There is only one form which comes close to this, namely *'hl mw'd h'lhym* in 2 Chron. 1:3.

[420]The improbability of a *Vorlage* for this clause is reinforced by the use of ἐνωπιον. Elsewhere the Hebrew term *lpny* with respect to a position before the *mškn yhwh* is rendered with ἐναντι (cf. Lev. 17:4; Num. 7:3; 16:9; 1 Chron. 16:39; 2 Chron. 1:5). Accordingly, Boling's retroversion has little to support it.

[421]In addition to the texts in the preceding note, consult Num. 19:13; 31:30; 31:47; Josh. 22:19; (Ps. 84:2); (132:5); 2 Chron. 29:6. Less likely would be *'hl yhwh* attested uniquely in three occurrences in 1 Kgs 2:29-30.

also consider *byt 'lhy yśr'l*, but this too is impossible because the LXX never translates *byt* with *σκηνη*; it consistently uses *'οικος*. The conclusion of most commentators that the phrase is to be attributed to a translator into Greek is thereby vindicated. It is therefore of considerable interest that the LXX plus brings vss.1 and 25f. into clear correlation with each other via a number of words and phrases. To be specific, *και 'εστησεν 'αυτους 'απεναντι του θεου* (vs.1) finds a close responsion in *και 'εστησεν 'αυτον...'απεναντι κυριου* (vs.26) and *'ενωπιον της σκηνης του θεου Ισραηλ* (vs.25). Similarly, *κυριος ὁ θεος Ισραηλ* finds a responsion in *του θεου Ισραηλ* (vss.2,25). The setting for the gathering is thereby altered into a regular meeting in the congregation before the tabernacle rather than the more enigmatic *mqdš yhwh* of the MT. Furthermore, in the LXX the *τερεμινθον* is no longer explicitly in the sanctuary, but simply "before Yahweh." The net theological result of all these changes is a more innocuous edition in the LXX.[422] Since the clause *'ενωπιον της σκηνης του θεου Ισραηλ* has been demonstrated to be out of place in a Hebrew text, we may tentatively conclude that the affiliated changes, including the shift from Shechem to Shiloh, were probably made by the same translator.[423]

Is it possible to discover more about the rationale by which the alternate reading of the LXX may have been justified? Mention has been made of Shiloh in Josh. 18:1, but equally deserving of our attention is the information gleaned from Josh. 22:12,29, where the Hebrew text speaks of the altar of Yahweh which was before the sanctuary. Shiloh is specifically mentioned as the place of assembly in 22:12, while 22:29 speaks of the *mzbḥ yhwh 'lhynw 'šr lpny mšknw*, cf. the LXX translation, *'εναντιον της σκηνης αυτου*, and note that the Syriac here has an equivalent for *'lhy yśr'l*, which corresponds to the LXX in Josh. 24:25. The translator of the LXX may have been suspicious about the presence of Shechem in Josh. 24:1,25, and the details of Josh. 22:12,29 would have provided just the details necessary to "clarify" the objectionable elements of Josh. 24:25f. If this is correct, the translator does not fabricate an alternative account, but

[422]Significantly, it is known from other contexts that translators of the LXX were squeamish about cultic improprieties (Wevers, "Exegetical Principles," 313-317).

[423]This raises reservations concerning the cautious proposal by other scholars that the change from Shechem to Shiloh was already made in a Hebrew *Vorlage* (cf. Greenspoon, *Textual Studies*, 80f.).

rather he makes some adjustments based upon comparable texts.

**Josh. 24:26**

In conjunction with the previous verse, it is significant that *šm* of the MT is represented by a recension in Theodotion not in OG. Greenspoon evidently is convinced that *šm* is a later amplification in the Hebrew tradition behind the MT,[424] but his analysis gives no indication of taking into consideration the related differences in LXX 24:1,25-27, which have a bearing on the question of where the gathering and ceremony took place, and cast some doubt on the reliability of the Greek translations to reconstruct the "original" reading. However, if *šm* were to be taken as secondary and the quadrocolon in 26b would be reduced accordingly to a tricolon, this would not weaken separation downward and it would be of little apparent structural significance.

**Josh. 24:27**

This verse has a number of variations between the LXX and MT; some are inconsequential but others are very revealing. The reading of ὑμιν for *bnw* appears to harmonize with the following reference and is probably to be attributed to the stylistic preference of the translator. Similarly, the LXX absence of *kl* with *h'm* could be an accommodation to the previous parallel references. However, compared to the MT it weakens the connection with vs.2, whereas we have noted in vs.25f. that the LXX makes a deliberate correlation with vs.2. It would therefore be surprising if the LXX would arbitrarily drop the *kl* here for stylistic reasons. The presence of *kl* in the MT makes a deliberate inclusion with the beginning of dialogue in vs.2, and it was likely included in the MT tradition for precisely this purpose.[425]

An additional LXX plus in vs.27 also warrants consideration, namely ἐπ' ἐσχατων των ἡμερων, which makes a loose parallelism with ἀπ' ἀρχης (24:2). Most important, however, is a parallelism with σημερον (24:27 LXX). The phrase ἐπ' ἐσχατων των ἡμερων is virtually always a translation of *b'ḥryt hymym*.[426] Many of these ref-

[424]Greenspoon, *Textual Studies*, 157.

[425]However, it is also possible that the LXX translation is influenced by the similar formulations in vss.16,19,21.

[426]Cf. Gen. 49:1; Num. 24:14; Deut. 4:30; 31:29; Jer. 23:20; 30:24 (LXX 37:24); 49:39 (LXX 25:18); Ezek. 38:16; Dan. 10:14; Hos. 3:5; Mic. 4:1; cf. Deut. 8:16 (*b'ḥrytk*); 32:20 (*'ḥrytm*); Dan.2:45 (Aramaic *'ḥry dnh*).

erences are in poetry,[427] in which case the phrase either stands alone or with *hyh* as a complete colon. The Greek σημερον (vs.27b) can be seen as a translation of *hywm*, as in vs.15, and would fit very well as a final word on 27bC, producing the colon *'šr dbr 'mnw hywm*. Accordingly, when these two Greek pluses are retroverted to Hebrew, we get the striking parallelism of *hywm* || *b'ḥryt hymym*. The latter colon would expand 27c to a tricolon, thereby helping to mark separation upwards. The ext. parallelism with *hywm* is one of concatenation. The parallelism is more obvious in Hebrew than in Greek, and it is placed so strategically that it can hardly be attributed to coincidence produced by arbitrary expansions in the Greek text. First, it makes an explicit correlation with 15bA as well as with *bywm hhw'* in vs.25, producing *ywm* || *ywm* (25aA, 27bC LXX; inclusion). Secondly, Hebrew *ywm* in 27bC would strengthen the legal emphasis in vs.27 in a most appropriate manner.[428] Thirdly, *b'ḥryt hymym* adds a nuance of a "testament" to the final words of Joshua. This is most striking in light of the poetic usage in Gen. 49:1, where we have noted the parallelism of *qr'* || *'sp*, which is also found in Josh. 24:1.[429] Moreover, *b'ḥryt hymym* is used in a similar setting in Deut. 31:29 with respect to the farewell instructions of Moses. Accepting the retroversion *b'ḥryt hymym*, we would be confronted in 27c with a tricolon:

| | |
|---|---|
| *whyth bkm l'dh* | And it will be to you as a witness |
| *b'ḥryt hymym* | in the days to come, |
| *pn-tkḥšwn b'lhykm* | lest you deceive your God. |

This produces a threefold repetition of the preposition *b*, it makes concatenation with 27bC (LXX), and responsion with *bywm hhw'* in 25aA as well as with the threefold usage of the preposition *b* in 25a. The LXX pluses therefore occur at structurally strategic places.

In the light of all these factors it is virtually certain that the LXX pluses are deliberate, and they probably can be traced to a poetic Hebrew text differing slightly from the present MT. It is improbable that both pluses in the LXX would be omitted by accident of transmission in the MT. The only way to do justice to the complexity of this issue is to conclude that once again we have evidence of different editions

[427]E.g., Gen. 49:1; Mic. 4:1; Jer. 23:20; 30:24; 49:39; cf. Deut. 32:20.
[428]Cf. the discussion of *ywm* offered by Kalluveettil (*Declaration*, 184).
[429]Cf. Lipiński, "*B'ḥryt hymym*," 446f.

of this passage as represented in the present texts. Both show the same basic structure but with different emphases. These variations provide confirmation of the colometric nature of the passage because the rationale for the pluses becomes explicable when they are viewed as reinforcements of external parallelisms and responsions in a poetic Hebrew text.

**Josh. 24:28**

The relationship of Josh. 24:28-31 to Judg. 2:6-10 is dealt with extensively below.[430] For the present discussion of structure it is necessary to note that the LXX translation indicates a Hebrew text differing from the present MT. This is not per se true of *και ̓επορευθησαν*, which must be dealt with in conjunction with *wylkw* in Judg. 2:6. But, as noted by Rofé,[431] *̓εις τον τοπον* can hardly be a translation of *lnḥltw*. In addition to the observations by Rofé, we note that *nḥlh* is virtually always translated by *κληρονομια*;[432] nowhere else is *nḥlh* rendered by *τοπον*. But the LXX is not necessarily translating *mqwm*. It is advisable to also consider a possible reading of *byt*. To be sure, Greek *τοπος* is usually a rendering of Hebrew *mqwm*.[433] But the matter is complicated by the translation of LXX A at Judg. 2:6. Here LXX A has the clause *̓εις τον ̓οικον ̓αυτου*, which is absent in LXX B. It stands parallel to *̓εις την κληρονομιαν ̓αυτου*, which represents the reading of LXX B and MT *lnḥltw*. The unnecessary and mysterious plus in Judg. 2:6 LXX A has every indication of being a harmonization with a Hebrew *Vorlage* of Josh. 24:28 where, as we have seen with Rofé, there must have been a reading other than *nḥlh*. In support of this we note that LXX A of Judg. 2:6 is not dependent upon LXX of Josh. 24:28, *τον τοπον*. In Ex. 16:29 and Ezek. 12:3, where LXX B translates *mqwm* with *τοπος*, LXX A chooses for an exceptional rendering with *̓οικος*. This makes Rofé's postulation of *mqwm* at least possible. On the other hand, *̓οικος* is usually a translation of *byt*. And, significantly, Greek *τοπος* is used elsewhere to translate *byt*, namely 1 Sam. 10:25; 24:23; 1 Kgs 8:42, 43 (LXX A = *̓οικος*); Ps. 119 [118]:54; Jer. 7:14 (LXX B *̓οικος*). The *context and grammatical construction* in 1 Sam. 10:25 is parallel to Josh. 24:28; the suggestion in BHS to read *mqwm* is not convincing because the

[430]See 5.4.1.
[431]Rofé, "End of the Book of Joshua," 21f.
[432]Cf. Hatch–Redpath, *Septuagint*, 769.
[433]Cf. Hatch–Redpath, *Septuagint*, 1364-1366.

choice of the translators here is probably motivated by a desire for variety from the use of *'οικος* as a translation for *byt* in the following verse (1 Sam. 10:26). All things considered, it is more likely that both *τοπου* (Josh. 24:28 LXX) and *'οικου* (Judg. 2:6 LXX A) are a translation of *byt* than of *mqwm*, and we conclude that the Hebrew *Vorlage* in Josh. 24:28 likely read *lbytw*. Alteration to *lnḥltw* in the MT would have been motivated by a Hebrew text of Judg. 2:6 on the grounds specified by Rofé. Acceptance of an original reading *lbytw* in 28B would produce a possible responsion with *mqdš yhwh* in II.v.1 (26bD).[434]

### 3.6.4 Conclusions regarding the LXX and MT

On the basis of the variations between the MT and the LXX it is possible to draw a number of significant conclusions. Different textual readings are found in nearly every verse of this passage. Nevertheless, an analysis of these differences tends to strengthen rather than weaken our conclusions regarding poetic structure. It has been noted that many of the minor differences can convincingly be accounted for on the basis of stylistic or grammatical simplification or harmonization by a translator. Secondly, numerous of the differences can be attributed to attempted harmonization with other canonical passages. In such cases it is difficult to discern whether the harmonization occurred at the time of translation or already prior. But there is another category of variations which cannot be explained by recourse to either errors in transmission, stylistic considerations, or textual harmonization. In such instances it is not always possible to determine whether the variant reading arises at the time of the translation, or whether there was a different Hebrew *Vorlage* for the LXX.

The cumulative evidence, however, has in numerous cases pointed to different Hebrew editions. Often a retroversion of the LXX plus into Hebrew produces words or cola which fit the structure well and establish significant external parallelisms within the poetic structure, e.g., vs.4f., vs.10 *šmd* and *ntn*; vs.14 *'lhym 'ḥrym* or *'lhy nkr*; vs.15 *ky*

[434]For the parallelism of *mqdš* and *byt (yhwh)* see esp. Jer. 51:51; Ezek. 9:6; 23:39; 43:21; 44:5,7,11; 45:4; 48:21; Am. 7:9,13; Lam. 2:7. Neither *nḥlh* nor *byt* makes an unequivocal responsion because neither one is intended in a sense synonymous with *mqdš yhwh*, but it is of interest that both the reading of the LXX and the MT perhaps establish remote responsions here.

*qdwš hw'*; vs.27 *hywm* and *b'ḥryt hymym*.[435] To this may be added *lbytw* or *lmqwm* in vs.28, which, although not a LXX plus, does attest to a different *Vorlage*. Likewise, LXX's θεοις 'ετεροις in vs.20 may plausibly reflect a Hebrew text with *'lhym 'ḥrym* rather than *'lhy nkr*. Moreover, the MT pluses of vss.5,17 warrant similar conclusions because the material now attested in the MT is integrally incorporated into the poetic composition. In all these cases it is advisable to speak of different editions rather than of a "better reading" or a "poorer reading." These conclusions contradict the verdict by Auld that the MT cannot serve as the basis for a detailed structural analysis in Joshua.[436] Rather than choose for one of the traditions, it is advisable to compare both. It will be of interest in subsequent analyses in Joshua to see whether the theory of variant editions can be sustained in other chapters as well.

The idea that there could be variant editions of the same passage, with essentially the same poetic structure but incorportating different external parallelisms and responsions and thereby establishing alternative nuances, is illuminating with respect to the history of transmission of such a poetic text. On the one hand, the structure remains essentially unaffected. On the other hand, there was enough fexibility in the transmitted form of the text to allow for various actualizations. This seems to be true of the LXX plus in vs.27, which brings out the nuance of Josh. 24:1-28 as a testament of Joshua. Perhaps the theory of editions with a slightly different actualization can also account for the variations of grammatical person in the LXX and MT in the historical summary in vss.5-13. Recognition of the poetic form supports the conclusion that we are dealing with a liturgical text. A slightly different liturgical actualization in the respective editions is one way of explaining these differences of grammatical person. It is of significance that the poetic narrative of Josh. 23 also witnesses a discrepancy between 1st and 2nd person forms, with "your God" of the MT becoming "our God" in the LXX. Greenspoon thinks that the differences can be traced back to different Hebrew readings behind the OG and MT traditions.[437] At present it is difficult to determine

[435]The suggestion of *lpny mškn 'lhy yśr'l* in vs.25 may be similar but, because of the unattested form of the Hebrew retroversion, we hesitate to put any weight on it for a possible alternative Hebrew reading.
[436]Cf. the summary of Auld's conclusions in 1.8.
[437]Greenspoon, *Textual Studies*, 153-155.

whether these differences are to be explained as variant actualizations of a liturgical text, or as stylistic or literary preferences in the Hebrew textual traditions.[438] Either way, the differences do not alter the basic structure of the passage. The poetic nature of these two final chapters of Joshua provides a plausible explanation for why the text could undergo these minor expansions or alterations and yet remain structurally intact.

## 3.7 Summary observations

Our analysis of Josh. 24:1-28 as a form of narrative poetry suggests that Watson is correctly cautious with respect to the complicated matter of distinguishing between poetic and non-poetic composition in the OT.[439] Watson stresses that there is no single and facile way to distinguish the two. He chooses instead to list a number of typical poetic phenomena, the cumulative evidence of which is for him suggestive of whether the composition is in reality poetry.[440] Our methodology has much in common with this approach, especially with respect to the characteristics Watson lists under the category of *structural* indicators,[441] for example, the significance of parallelism, word-pairs, chiastic patterns, envelope figure,[442] break-up of stereotyped phrases,[443] and repetition. The preceding analyis of Josh. 24:1-28

[438]The present author has suggested previously that the MT of Josh. 23 repeatedly employs *'lhykm* as part of an elaborate system of rhyme at the end of the cola (cf. "Joshua 23," esp. 118). The effect of this form stresses the emphasis of testament in the final words of Joshua. On the other hand, employment of *'lhynw* gives the text an explicitly confessional character appropriate to a liturgical setting. This provides yet another example of the desirability of speaking of different *editions* of the text, rather than "better" or "worse" textual witnesses.

[439]Watson, *Classical Hebrew Poetry*, 44-65.

[440]To identify poetry, Kselman also works with the concept of cumulative evidence derived from multiple poetic devices (cf. "Poetic Fragments," esp. 163).

[441]Watson, *Classical Hebrew Poetry*, 46f. Watson's method, like that of the Kampen approach employed in this study, works from the principle of smallest to largest poetic units (cf. ibid., 11).

[442]The comparable term applied in the analysis above is *inclusion* at the various levels of poetic units, e.g., strophe, canticle, canto, etc.

[443]In practice this often is the same thing as external parallelism beyond the strophe, formed by the distribution of a common word-pair. In fact, the designation of external parallelism formed by such words facilitates greater precision because it not only identifies the pair which has been broken up, but it signals the strategic structural placement of the components as well.

has accepted as valid the conclusion that when present the cumulative evidence of such phenomena provides vital confirmation of the poetic character of the composition.

The significance of such phenomena or characteristics for positing a poetic structure is already indicative that it is necessary to pursue a systematic and methodological analysis of the text, rather than a somewhat haphazard search for such structural indicators. To facilitate a controlled analysis the passage has been written out colometrically, with divisions into cola, verses, strophes, canticles, and cantos as successive levels of poetic units. This colometric division has been conducted with careful attention to parallelism, formal indicators of strophic division, content, and the Masoretic accentuation, the latter not as a factor of *metrical* significance, but rather as one consideration whereby the disjunctive accents occurring at the termination of cola provide clues to the syntactic units envisioned by the ancients, who in turn were informed by the antecedent traditions concerning how the text was to be read or sung. These disjunctive accents have not always been honoured in the colometry above, but when tempered by considerations of parallelism and strophic divisions they have proven to provide a helpful guideline.

A colometric format is essential for discerning the type of structural indicators listed by Watson as criteria for poetic identification, indicators which without a colometric presentation would often go unnoticed. It is therefore significant that the text of Josh. 24:1-28 can be divided not only into cola, but into successive units of strophes, canticles, and cantos as well.[444] Our method of reading the text brings to light a sufficient degree of poetic characteristics to demonstrate that Josh. 24:1-28 is carefully composed poetic narrative.

Internal parallelism functions less prominently in poetic narrative than in other genres of poetry, e.g., psalmic composition or prophetic, oracular discourse. Nevertheless, analysis of internal parallelism in Josh. 24:1-28 is revealing. An exhaustive list of all possible internal parallelisms produces a surprisingly high frequency of word-pairs identified previously by scholars analyzing other passages of poetry. Moreover, a computer search for occurrences of similar components in parallelism in other passages has frequently rendered supporting

[444]The present search for parallelism at all the successive poetic levels is also consistent with the emphasis of Pardee (*Poetic Parallelism*), upon what he calls *distant parallelism* as an essential element for poetic analysis.

examples of poetic parallelism. It is not necessary at this point to enter into a debate regarding the propriety of terming all such parallelisms a word-pair. Throughout the analysis above the more neutral designation of *parallelism* has been employed. Whatever one's position on the question of word-pairs, it should be evident that the employment of words or phrases functioning in parallelism is a broader phenomenon than the use of categorically recognized word-pairs or stock phrases.[445]

One might object that *any* narrative would automatically produce repetitions and parallelisms, so this does not yet prove that the text is poetic. This objection is to a certain degree valid despite the fact that many of the parallelisms listed above have been attested elsewhere in the OT, and secondly many are also attested in other ancient NE languages. Nevertheless, the objection that such parallelisms could simply be due to the unavoidable occurrence of repetition and parallelism in any text, or that they could have been deliberately employed in a prose text which is not poetic, is dispelled when one notices the intricacy of parallelisms documented for external parallelism at the level of the strophe and beyond, which produces literary connections and patterns which cannot be attributed to coincidence and are only truly apparent once the text is accepted as being colometric. In our search for external parallelism not every repetition in the entire passage was listed; entries were restricted to responsions, inclusions or concatenations at the respective levels of poetic units. It is therefore significant that many of these noted responsions consist of words found nowhere else in the passage. This suggests that where they do occur their presence is deliberately intended to form the noted literary connection. Numerous of the entries are whole phrases or entire cola. Their function here can be compared in certain respects to formulaic responsions present in other poetic material.[446]

The parallelisms listed above, when judged individually, are not all of the same quality. Some are more specific than others. Some are widely attested in other OT literature while others appear to be unique to the present passage—which is in itself by no means surprising. Watters concludes that, of the word-pairs discerned in his

[445]Cf. Zurro, *Procedimientos.*

[446]Cf. R.C.Culley, *Oral Formulaic Language in the Biblical Psalms* (Toronto, 1967).

study of Job, 3/5 of the pairs repeat elsewhere.[447] A broader analysis of OT poetry leads him to the conclusion that non-repeating pairs outnumber those which recur by a ratio of 2:1.[448]

One of the clearest illustrations that the macrostructure of Josh. 24:1-28 betrays a poetic nature can be seen in the refrain verses of II.i-II.iv. The refrains of these four canticles are the following:

| | |
|---|---|
| Canticle II.i | |
| *w'nky wbyty* | But as for me and my house |
| *n'bd 't-yhwh* | we will serve Yahweh. |
| Canticle II.ii | |
| *gm-'nhnw* | And so we too |
| *n'bd 't-yhwh* | we will serve Yahweh |
| *ky-hw' 'lhynw* | for he is our God. |
| Canticle II.iii | |
| *wy'mr h'm 'l-yhwš'* | And the people said to Joshua, |
| *l' ky 't-yhwh n'bd* | 'Nevertheless, Yahweh we will serve.' |
| Canticle II.iv | |
| *wy'mr h'm 'l-yhwš'* | And the people said to Joshua, |
| *'t-yhwh 'lhynw n'bd* | 'Yahweh our God we will serve, |
| *wbqwlw nšm'* | and to his voice we will listen,' |

We have noted that in Josh. 24:1-28 the form *n'bd* occurs only these four times, and it is relatively rare in the OT as a whole. In the last two refrains "Yahweh" is placed before *n'bd*, thereby inverting the order of the preceding two refrains. In the discussion of macrostructure we have noted many additional factors which link II.i-ii and II.iii-iv respectively. The fourfold use of these refrains, the A.B.C || Á.B́.Ć pattern of the strophes and the A.B || B́.Á concentric arrangement of the canticles leaves no doubt that this is poetry.

In summary, the foregoing discussion has argued that the present

[447] Watters, *Formula Criticism*, 89.

[448] Watter's ratio might need to be modified somewhat if the corpus of comparative material were broadened via a computer search of the entire OT, including passages not ordinarily recognized as poetry, but the claim that a substantial percentage of parallelisms in a given passage can be unique is certainly valid.

form of Josh. 24:1-28, when written out colometrically, provides a sufficient degree and quality of internal and external parallelism to warrant the conclusion that the passage is narrative poetry. Division of the passage into strophes produces generally positive results. Identification of the canticles is usually clear on the basis of both formal markers and content, especially in canto II where refrains are employed in four of the five canticles. The analysis proposed above is supported by the uniformity of structural totals attained. It is also supported by a comparison of the MT and the LXX, where many of the differences between the two traditions can be attributed to minor harmonizations of various sorts from the hand of the translator, but numerous other variations argue for the existence of a Hebrew *Vorlage* of the LXX which differed in some respects from that of the MT. On the basis of these hypothetically retroverted differences the suggestion has been made that it is necessary to speak of different *editions* of the Hebrew text, not simply of a better or poorer witness to the original. In both editions the basic poetic structure of the passage remains constant. The final poetic compositon is one of considerable complexity and literary skill, carefully fashioning a network of parallelisms and external responsions. Observations regarding both structure and diction are suggestive that this passage may have had a liturgical function in ancient Israel. This question remains to be further explored in the following chapter where we will return to the issues raised in previous literary-critical approaches to the passage, focusing on diachronic textual questions of sources, redactions and their connection with Dtistic history.

# 4 Textual Analysis of Josh. 24:1-28

## 4.1 Introduction

Recognition of the poetic character of Josh. 24 facilitates an evaluation of the passage's literary character and quality from a new dimension. This entails that the previously used criteria for judging the text's literary unity and integrity will have to be reassessed. For example, the many repetitions which have been noted in the progression of the dialogical unit in vss.14-24, instead of constituting evidence for later redaction provide valuable clues for the deliberate structuring of the composition. And the phenomenonon of poetic repetition in these verses can now be compared to the widespread employment of this stylistic device in ancient NE literature. A few examples will demonstrate the point.

For many scholars the composition of the Sumerian poetic narrative *Dumuzi's Dream* lacked literary quality because of the presence of many redundancies, but a recent study by W.R.Millar illustrates that the use of repetition as a stylistic device is very skillfully employed for rhetorical effect in this poetry.[1] The employment of repetition for emphasis is also found in many Neo-Assyrian texts. In the Zakutu treaty, for example, there is a fourfold repetition that the bound party must swear to report to Zakutu and Ashurbanipal anyone overheard scheming insurrection.[2] This fourfold repetition is in certain respects like the fourfold use of *n'bd* in the refrains of Josh. 24:14-24.

Closer in language to the Hebrew texts, it has been recently demonstrated that the recurrence of whole verses within the Ugaritic epic narrative of Kirtu also serves a structural function.[3] Such examples in ancient NE literature could be multiplied considerably, and the number will continue to grow with the increased attention presently being devoted to a study of literary stylistics in these genres. The net implication for biblical studies is that scholars will need to be more

[1]W.R.Millar, "Oral Poetry and *Dumuzi's Dream*," in C.D.Evans et al, eds., *Scripture in Context: Essays on the Comparative Method* (Pittsburgh, 1980), 27-57.

[2]Cf. S.Parpola, "Neo-Assyrian Treaties from the Royal Archives of Nineveh," JCS 39 (1987) 161-189, esp. 165-167.

[3]K.Spronk, "The Legend of Kirtu (KTU 1.14-16): A Study of the Structure and its Consequence for Interpretation," in van der Meer–de Moor, eds., *Structural Analysis*, 62-82.

cautious about using repetition as a criterion for source distinction.

But it would be false to conclude from these observations that a given OT text ought to be evaluated only as a synchronic entity, the structure of which was set from the beginning and never altered. Numerous studies have proven that there was a certain degree of flexibility in the transmission of ancient NE texts, by means of which the essential message was retained without the need for a meticulous or slavishly verbatim reproduction.[4] Our analysis of the variations between the MT and the LXX of Josh. 24:1-28 has suggested the likelihood that even as late as the *Vorlage* of these traditions there was sufficient freedom in the transmission of the text to allow for a flexibility of nuance or of actualization. Presumably a text such as Josh. 24 could have gone through various minor transitions prior to attaining its final form. This is completely in harmony with principles which can be ascertained in a comparison of parallel OT sources, e.g., 2 Sam. 22 and Ps. 18, or "duplicate" material in the books of Kings and Chronicles, where it is evident that the author employing older traditions does not hesitate to substitute words and phrases for theological or stylistic reasons, or simply to employ more contemporary language. Minor modifications of this sort are also attested in the portion of Josh. 24:28ff. reproduced in Judg. 2:6ff. It was only relatively late in the history of transmission that the text began to be treated as a static entity to be preserved and transmitted unaltered.

These observations are not entirely new, but they need to be stressed because of their methodological implications for literary-critical analyses. It has been demonstrated in the first two chapters of the present study that literary-critical endeavors on Josh. 24 focused initially upon attempts to link Josh. 24 with Pentateuchal sources, especially E or JE. But upon closer inspection these approaches were not acceptable, and most recent scholars, rather than look over their shoulders towards the Pentateuch, have opted to look ahead within the framework of Dtistic history. The lasting value of this shift in emphasis was the demonstration that Josh. 24:1-28 is inextricably linked with a series of texts in the historical framework of Deuteronomy–2 Kings in which the matter of sole allegiance to Yahweh is emphasized. At the same time it was argued above, in criticism of the more

[4]For various examples of this principle consult G.D.Young, "The Significance of the Karatepe Inscriptions for Near Eastern Textual Criticism," *OTS* 8 (Leiden, 1950), 291-299. See too Tigay, ed., *Empirical Models*, passim.

radical assertions of Dtistic influence, that the present chapter is not likely a Dtistic creation. From these observations it becomes evident that Josh. 24:1-28 cannot be treated in connection with *either* the Pentateuch *or* Dtistic history at the exclusion of the other without doing grave injustice to the complexity of the passage. Previous lexicographical studies, whether consciously or not, have tended to opt for one approach or the other, always producing ambiguous results. Moreover, in our analysis of parallelism it has become evident that various portions of Josh. 24:1-28 bear a striking correlation to material found elsewhere, primarily in the Prophets or in the Psalms. Prior to the recognition of the poetic character of the passage there was little incentive to pursue such correlations in detail.

In short, the importance of the literary-critical issues raised in previous approaches and the lack of ensuing consensus prohibit acceptance of Schmitt's opinion that "was zur Literarkritik von Josua 24 zu sagen ist, ist schon gesagt."[5] If this opinion were correct, we would be doomed to admit that lexicographical studies have little to contribute definitively with respect to an understanding of the provenance and present form of the text. Fortunately, however, a more detailed analysis than has previously been attempted produces more certain results than the diversity of previous positions would presuppose. The ensuing analysis treats Josh. 24:1-28 in three units: the first is the setting in vss.1,25-28, the second is the historical summary in vss.2-13, and the third is the dialogue in vss.14-24.

## 4.2 The Assembly in Josh. 24:1,25-28

The analysis of macrostructure offered in the preceding chapter demonstrated that Josh. 24:1 sets the stage for the entire scene which follows in vss.2-28. It is therefore of considerable importance to conduct a detailed investigation of this verse with respect to its content and possible provenance. The deliberate links which join the gathering of the assembly in vs.1 to the ceremony in vss.25-28 suggest that a literary analysis of vs.1 ought not to be isolated from the latter verses, as has typically been done in previous literary-critical analyses.[6]

[5]Schmitt, *Landtag*, 8.

[6]Important exceptions may be found in McCarthy, *Covenant and Treaty*, 221-242; Floss, *Jahwe dienen*, 334-348.

### 4.2.1 The setting in Josh. 24:1

The emphasis upon the gathering at Shechem places Josh. 24 in the realm of a formal assembly. Gordis is inclined to view this gathering from a strongly judicial or democratic perspective, rather than liturgical.[7] While he is no doubt correct in emphasizing the legal nature of the assembly, this need not exclude a liturgical setting, as will become more evident from the ensuing analysis. The present form of Josh. 24:1-28 integrates history, law and liturgy in an inextricable combination, and there is finally little reason to believe that this connection is either secondary or artificial.

From the perspective of comparison with analogous OT texts, the introduction of the assembly proceeds ordinarily. However, a possible clue to Dtistic redaction has often been identified in the correspondence between the list of leaders in 24:1 and 23:2.[8] McCarthy, on the other hand, thinks that only *wlšpṭyw wlšṭryw* is a later addition to bring the reference in line with the Dtistic terminology of 23:2.[9]

It is evident that a very close correlation does exists between Josh. 23:2 and 24:1. An exact correspondence of the same four categories of leaders is not found elsewhere in the OT,[10] which suggests a literary dependence between the two passages. The close correspondence of the present listings is amplified by the presence of the 3rd masc. sing. suffixes referring to Israel, as well as the verb *qr'* in both contexts.[11] Whether these correlations stem from the time of original composition or later harmonization is difficult to determine on the basis of the similarities alone, and this question can best be assessed on the total evidence gleaned from the two passages. The same holds true with respect to the direction of dependence; on the basis of a comparison of these verses in isolation from the implications of the contexts it is

[7]Gordis, *Poets*, 55.

[8]Wellhausen, *Composition*, 133; Dillmann, *Josua*, 584 ("Der Satz *wyqr'*—*wlšṭryw*, wie 23,2; ohne Zweifel erst von R$^{d}$ eingefügt, um zu verstehen zu geben, dass unter der Versammlung der Stämme die ihrer Vertreter u. Beamten gemeint sei."); Steuernagel, *Josua*, 242; Holzinger, *Josua*, 95; Noth, *Das System*, 139; *Josua* 1953, 135; Rudolph, *Der "Elohist"*, 245; Hölscher, *Geschichtsschreibung*, 350; Nielsen, *Shechem*, 79, 87; L'Hour, "L'alliance de Sichem," 23; Giblin, "Structural Patterns," 56; Mölle, *Landtag*, 109.

[9]McCarthy, *Treaty and Covenant*, 224, 233; see too Schmitt, *Landtag*, 57.

[10]As is noted already in the *Masora parva*.

[11]For *qr'* in the Qal form with "elders of Israel" as object cf. Ex. 12:21; Lev. 9:1; see too Ex. 19:7 *wyqr' lzqny h'm*; 1 Kgs 20:7 *wyqr' mlk-yśr'l lkl-zqny h'rṣ*.

impossible to determine the direction of influence.

It is imperative to take a close look at the list of leaders, both individually and collectively, since it is primarily in this regard that evidence of later redaction has been posited in 24:1. Weinfeld has shown that mention of the entire populace being present or represented at a covenant ceremony finds significant parallels in Hittite and Assyrian contexts.[12] In the present text the reference to "all the tribes of Israel" is explicated with a list of leaders representing the people, and a detailed examination of the four categories of leaders demonstrates their appropriateness to the type of setting here narrated, which cautions against ascribing the entire list of leaders to a Dtistic predilection.

The elders (*zqny yśr'l*) are frequently mentioned as playing a prominent role in the leadership of Israel already in the narration of the exodus.[13] They function along with Moses and Aaron in Ex. 18:12 in what appears to be a covenant setting.[14] In the equally archaic Ex. 24:9[15] they have an important function in the covenant between Israel and Yahweh. Deut. 27:1 and 31:9 attribute to the elders a particular responsibility with respect to the recitation of the law. Their prominence is also evident in the period of the judges, as well as the time of the monarchy,[16] especially in connection with the question of kingship in Israel. Various scholars have argued for the authenticity of such references to the role of the elders in the earliest periods of Israel's history.[17] This significant role of the "el-

[12]Weinfeld, "The Loyalty Oath," 392f.

[13]Cf. Ex. 3:16; 4:29; 12:21; 16:6.

[14]C.H.W.Brekelmans, "Exodus xviii and the Origins of Yahwism in Israel," *OTS* 10 (Leiden, 1954), 215-224; F.C.Fensham, "Did a Treaty between the Israelites and Kenites Exist?" *BASOR* 175 (1964) 51-54; A.Cody, "Exodus 18:12: Jethro Accepts a Covenant with the Israelites," *Bibl* 49 (1968) 153-166; McCarthy, "*Bᵉrît* in OT," 112; Sheriffs, "The Phrases *ina IGI DN*," 57f.; Kalluveettil, *Declaration and Covenant*, 13, 28, 61, 89; Y.Avishur, "Treaty Terminology in the Moses–Jethro Story (Exod. 18:1-12)," *Aula Orientalis* 6 (1988) 139-147.

[15]Cf the opinion of Th.C.Vriezen ("The Exegesis of Exodus xxiv 9-11," *OTS* 17 [Leiden, 1972], 100-133), contrary to the often repeated allegation that Ex. 24:9-11 is late, e.g., E.Ruprecht, "Exodus 24, 9-11 als Beispiel lebendiger Erzähltradition aus der Zeit des babylonischen Exils," in Albertz et al, eds., *Werden und Wirken*, 138-173. See also our comments on Ex. 24:3-8 in 2.3.7.2 and 5.3.3.

[16]Cf. 1 Sam. 4:3; 8:4; 2 Sam. 3:17; 5:3; 17:4,15.

[17]E.g., J.Lindblom, "Zur Frage des kanaanäischen Ursprungs des altisraelitischen Prophetismus," in Hempel–Rost, eds., *Von Ugarit*, 100; Noth, *History of Israel*, 108f.; cf. G.H.Davies, "Elder in the OT," *IDB*, 2:73; G.Bettenzoli, "Gli 'Anziani

ders" is in accord with the patriarchal societal structure of ancient Israel,[18] and the designation *zqny yśr'l*, with the elders in construct form with "Israel," demonstrates their prominent position.[19] It is significant that the verb *qr'* with *zqny yšr'l* is found in Ex. 12:21, with *zqny h'm* in Ex. 19:7 in the context of law-giving,[20] and in Lev. 9:1 with "Aaron, his sons and the elders of Israel." These references are the closest parallels to *wyqr' lzqny yśr'l* in 24:1bA,[21] and they argue against the conclusion that the combination of *qr'* with *zqny yśr'l* is Dtistic. A survey of the distribution of the construct form *zqny yśr'l* makes the conclusion that it is not Dtistic even clearer. In addition to Ex. 12:21 and 19:7, this construct is found in Ex. 3:16 (with *'sp*); 3:18; 4:29; 17:5f.; 18:12 (with *lpny h'lhym*); 24:1,9 (Sinaitic law and covenant); Num. 11:16 (with *'sp*);[22] 11:30 (with *'sp*); 16:25; Deut. 27:1; 31:9;[23] Josh. 7:6 (*lpny 'rwn yhwh*); 8:10; 1 Sam. 4:3; 8:4 (*wytqbṣw kl zqny yśr'l*); 2 Sam. 3:17;[24] 5:3 (making *bryt* with David as king) (= 1 Chron. 11:3); 17:4,15 (Absalom's attempt to gain kingship); 1 Kgs 8:1,3 (=2 Chron. 5:2,4);[25] 1 Chron. 15:25[26] Ezek. 14:1;

di Israele'," *Bibl* 64 (1983) 47-73; "Gli 'Anziani' in Giuda," *Bibl* 64 (1983) 211-224; H.Reviv, *The Elders in Ancient Israel* (Jerusalem, 1983).

[18]For an excellent survey of the comparable function of the elders in political, juridical, and cultic or religious capacities in the ancient NE, where they are often mentioned in conjunction with other groups of leaders, e.g., the *Fürsten, Befehlshaber, Statthalter*, or *Ratgeber*, cf. H.Klengel, "Die Rolle der 'Ältesten' (LÚ MES ŠU. GI) im Kleinasien der Hethiterzeit," *ZA* 57 (1965) 223-236.

[19]M.Weinfeld, "Elder," *Encyclopaedia Juduaica*, 6:578-580. Weinfeld calls attention to the fact that there were elders of different levels, e.g., area, city, country, etc. This fact has been overlooked by Nielsen, who suggested that "the repetition of 'Israel' in MT ... is at any rate bad style" (*Shechem*, 87); we have noted above that recognition of the internal parallelism of *yšr'l* || *yšr'l* ought to temper that judgment, and the present observation that *zqny yšr'l* is a technical term designating a specific category of elders, i.e. *national* elders, adds to the conclusion that Nielsen's stylistic observation is not convincing.

[20]Compare *wyśm lpnyhm 't kl-hdbrym h'lh 'šr ṣwhw yhwh* (Ex. 19:7b) with *wyšm lw ḥq wmšpṭ* (Josh. 24:25b) and *wyktb yhwš' 't-hdbrym h'lh* (24:26aA).

[21]Cf. Ex. 4:29 *wy'spw't-kl-zqny bny yśr'l.*

[22]Cf. 11:24 with *zqny h'm.*

[23]It is significant that the two references in Deuteronomy are both in connection with the giving of law in a legal ceremony.

[24]In treaty context (cf. Kalluveettil, *Declaration and Covenant*, 47).

[25]Solomon's ceremonial procession to bring up the Ark of the Covenant; note parallelism with *'t-kl-r'šy hmṭwt.*

[26]David's ceremonial procession to bring up the ark; the reference to *zqny yśr'l* is not found in the parallel account of 2 Sam. 6:12.

20:1,3. From these texts it is clear that *zqny yśr'l* refers to those elders who functioned in assemblies where matters of collective importance were handled.[27] The distribution of the phrase in the OT refutes the idea that it is Dtistic. Furthermore, the fact that the patriarchal elders continued to play a significant role in the leadership of Israel during the period of the monarchy is essentially in agreement with the presence of elders alongside the king as attested in other ancient NE contexts.[28]

The reference to the "elders" is accompanied by the "heads" of the people. Ex. 18:25 provides an account of how the *r'šym* were set as *śr* of the respective groups of thousands, hundreds, fifties and tens in hierarchical fashion. Their local role is illustrated, for example, in Judg. 10:18; 11:8,9,11. It is therefore quite appropriate that Josh. 24:1 places the *r'šym* second after the *zqny yśr'l*. Once again we must conclude that there is nothing particularly Dtistic about this category of leaders. The term is employed prolifically throughout the OT, and already in the ancient poetry of Deut. 33:5 we read of an assembly of the heads of the people.[29] Examples can be found in the Hittite texts as well where the elders and the heads of the people are mentioned as two categories in simultaneous but not synonymous representation of the people.[30] These observations lend considerable support to McCarthy's conclusion, contra many previous commentators, that *wyqr' lzqnyw yśr'l wlr'šyw* cannot simply be dismissed as Dtistic.[31]

While defending the authenticity of the reference to the elders and heads, McCarthy concedes that the "judges and officers" constitutes a later addition.[32] In fact, the collocation here of judges and officers

[27]Cf. Klengel, "Rolle der 'Ältesten'," esp. 232, regarding extra-biblical evidence where "... der Ältesten auf religiös–kultischen Gebiet werden noch in einer ganzen Reihe von Texten belegt. Es handelt sich dabei um die Beschreibungen von Festen, bei denen die Ältesten als vertreter ihrer Gemeinden eine gewisse Rolle spielten."

[28]Cf. M.Weinfeld, "Judge and Officer in Ancient Israel and in the Ancient Near East," in *Israel Oriental Studies*, 7 (Annual Publication of the Faculty of Humanities, Tel-Aviv University, 1977), 81f. Consider too a reference from Ebla where the king and the elders are mentioned in one breath (Dahood, "Minor Prophets and Ebla," 60f.). Cf. Kalluveettil, *Declaration and Covenant*, 150f.

[29]Note *bht'sp r'šy 'm || yḥd šbṭy yśr'l*; cf. I.L.Seeligmann, "A Psalm from Pre-Regal Times," *VT* 14 (1964) 82f.; de Vaux, *Early History*, 459.

[30]Cf. Klengel, "Rolle der 'Ältesten'," 225.

[31]McCarthy, *Treaty and Covenant*, 224.

[32]On the grounds of harmonization with 23:2, cf. his *Treaty and Covenant*, 224, 233.

has frequently been viewed as a late combination[33] which could not have preceded the reform of Jehoshaphat. However, an investigation of the role of the *špṭ* in OT texts, as well as in other ancient NE texts, suggests that their presence in such contexts as Josh. 24:1 is appropriate and not per se due to a Dtistic penchant for piling up synonyms. Contrary to the suggestion of Z.Falk that the semantic background for *špṭ* is to be explained as a development from *šbṭ* in the time of the monarchy when expert judges where appointed in a specialized judicial position,[34] S.E.Loewenstamm has argued that *špṭ* is proto-Semitic, attested in Ugaritic, Qatabanian and Minean.[35] He notes that "the judges mentioned in the Ugaritic texts were the heads of the people and their kings,"[36] which in turn suggests a close analogy with the role of the "judges" in Josh. 24:1 and comparable situations in which they are not designated in a specialized legal position as professional jurists but in a more general capacity as leaders and representatives of the people.[37] Recent research in this area indicates that the amphictyonic framework for the judges proposed by Alt[38] and Noth[39] ought to be abandoned, and the function of the judges should be viewed in light of the *špṭ* attested in Akkadian, Ugaritic and Phoenician contexts.[40]

[33]This view is clearly expressed by G.Liedke, "*špṭ*," *THAT*, 2:1004: "Die dtr. Aufzählungen Jos 8,33; 23,2; 24:1 sind von den vieldiskutierten Bestimmungen Dtn 16,18; 17,9ff.; 19,16ff.; 21,1ff.; 25,2 abhängig, in denen vor allem das Nebeneinander von Priestern und Richtern, bzw. von Richtern und *šṭrym* schwierig ist ...."

[34]Z.Falk, "*Šopeṭ* and *Šebäṭ*," *Lěšonénu* 30 (1966) 243-247.

[35]S.E.Loewenstamm, "*Šopeṭ* and *Šebäṭ*," in *Comparative Studies in Biblical and Ancient Oriental Literatures* (Neukirchen-Vluyn, 1980), 270-272 (= *Lěšonénu* 32 [1968] 172-174 [Hebrew]).

[36]Loewenstamm, "*Šopeṭ* and *Šebäṭ*," 271.

[37]Cf. Weinfeld, "Judge and Officer," esp. 67, concerning the overlapping of *špṭ* and *śr*.

[38]Alt, *Ursprünge*, 31-33 (= *KS*, 1:300-302).

[39]M.Noth, "Das Amt des 'Richters Israels'," in *Festschrift für Alfred Bertholet* (Tübingen, 1950), 404-417.

[40]See now especially F.C.Fensham, "The Judges and Ancient Israelite Jurisprudence," *OTWSA* 2 (Potchefstrom, 1959), 15-22; W.Richter, "Zu den 'Richtern Israels'," *ZAW* 77 (1965) 40-72; C.H.J.de Geus, "De richteren van Israël," *NThT* 20 (1965-66) 81-100, e.g., 82f.: "En wat de ugaritische teksten duidelijk maakten, werd steeds meer bevestigd door de nog steeds groeiende hoeveelheid phoenische en punische inscripties: *špṭ* betekent het uitoefenen van gezag, heerschappij." Similarly, A.Malamat, "Mari," *BA* 34 (1971) 2-22, esp. 19: "The *šapiṭum* and his counterpart in Judges, the *shopeṭ*, were actually prominent tribesmen who had acquired an authority far exceeding that of a mere 'justice'." Cf. A.Marzal, "The

The fourth category in the list of leaders is the *šṭrym*. Here too some scholars have previously attempted to argue that the role of the *šṭr* likely did not develop in Israel until the time of the monarchy.[41] Nevertheless, there are significant factors which cast doubt upon the validity of this argument. The root *šṭr* is related to the Akkadian word "to write."[42] Weinfeld has demonstrated that the subordinate task of the *šṭr*, who assisted other officers such as the judges in administrative or scribal activities, has a broader background in the ancient NE.[43] Against this background the references to the role of the *šṭrym* in a premonarchical setting is perfectly plausible[44] if one is willing to grant that the Israelites possessed the ability to write at this time, for which there is growing evidence.[45]

It is instructive to assess the reference to the *šṭrym* from yet an-

Provincial Governor at Mari: His Title and Appointment," *JNES* 30 (1971) 186-217; M.Stol, "Akkadisches šāpiṭum, šapāṭum und westsemitisches špṭ," *BiOr* 29 (1972) 276f.; J.D.Safren, "New Evidence for the Title of the Provincial Governor at Mari," *HUCA* 50 (1979) 1-15; H.Niehr, *Herrschen und Richten. Die Wurzel špt im Alten Orient und im Alten Testament* (Würzburg, 1986); T.J.Mafico, "The Term Šāpiṭum in Akkadian Documents," *JNSL* 13 (1987) 69-87.

[41] J.van der Ploeg, "Les *šṭrym* d'Israël," *OTS* 10 (Leiden, 1954), 185-196.

[42] Weinfeld, "Judge and Officer," 83. Cf. M.Ellebogen, *Foreign Words in the Old Testament: Their Origin and Etymology* (London, 1962), 161; H.Cazelles, "Institutions et terminologie en Deut. I 6-17," in *Volume du congrès Genève 1965, SVT* 15 (Leiden, 1966), 97-112, esp. 104f.

[43] Weinfeld, "Judge and Officer," 83-86, with references from Egyptian and Old Babylonian literature.

[44] Cf. Ex. 5:6,10,14f.,19; Num. 11:16; Deut. 1:15; 16:18; 20:5,8,9; 29:9; 31:28; Josh. 1:10; 3:2; 8:33; 23:2; 24:1.

[45] J.Naveh, "A Paleographic Note on the Distribution of the Hebrew Script," *HTR* 61 (1968) 68-74; A.R.Millard, "The Practice of Writing in Ancient Israel," *BA* 35 (1972) 98-111; "An Assessment of the Evidence for Writing in Ancient Israel," in Amitai, ed., *Biblical Archaeology Today*, 301-312; A.Demsky, "A Proto-Canaanite Abecedary Dating from the Period of the Judges," *Tel Aviv* 4 (1977) 14-25; "The 'Izbet Ṣarṭah Ostracon Ten Years Later," in I.Finkelstein, ed., *'Izbet Sartah: An Early Iron Age Site near Rosh Ha'ayin in Israel* (Oxford, 1986), 186-197; E.M.Yamauchi, "Documents from Old Testament Times: A Survey of Recent Discoveries," *WTJ* 41 (1978-79) 1-32. It has been demonstrated that the cuneiform alphabets of the LBA were all derived from earlier linear alphabets, which means that the linear alphabets were widely known in Canaan by the middle of the 2nd millenium, cf. M.Dietrich–O.Loretz, *Die phönizisch-kanaanäischen und altarabischen Alphabete in Ugarit* (Münster, 1988). In addition to the *šṭrym*, in Judg. 8:14, the term *n'r* may perhaps imply someone with a clerical function in the city administration, cf. J.MacDonald, "The Status and Role of the Na'ar in Israelite Society," *JNES* 35 (1976) 158.

other angle, namely the appropriateness of a written record or documentation being made in the immediate context of such a gathering. Throughout the history of interpretation of Josh. 24:1-28 the opinion has repeatedly been voiced that we are confronted here with an event which was part of a covenant festival. While the matter of a festival setting in general—and a more specific categorization in particular—needs further study, we may at this point anticipate conclusions elaborated more fully below which suggest that the events here described do indeed point to an origin in a festival of some sort. By comparison it is then of significance to note that a written description of the whole procedure constituted a vital element of the Hittite festivals dating from around the middle of the 2nd millenium B.C. and following. A high percentage of the texts found in Boğazköy-Hattuša belong to the category of the festivals.[46] The situation is comparable in Mari,[47] Emar,[48] and Ugarit.[49]

The importance of the written record of the festival is implicitly demonstrated by the high percentage of texts documenting a great variety of festivals and rituals.[50] In addition there is explicit evidence from the colophons which demonstrate the propriety of a series of tablets recording the events of the various days of the festivals.[51] Furthermore, it is now well documented that legal stipulations in the

[46]I.Singer, *The Hittite KI.LAM Festival. Part One* (Wiesbaden, 1983), 1 (Singer notes "the festival texts ... constitute the largest group of tablets found in Boğazköy-Hattuša, the Hittite capital. The proportion of festival texts is on the rise as more and more texts are published." Cf. Gurney, *Hittite Religion*, 25.

[47]G.Dossin, "Un rituel du culte d'Ištar provenant de Mari," *RA* 35 (1938) 1-13.

[48]D.Arnaud, *Recherches au pays d'Aštata, Emar VI.3* (Paris, 1986), 326ff.

[49]J.-M.de Tarragon, *Le culte à Ugarit* (Paris, 1980); P.Xella, *I Testi Rituali di Ugarit-I* (Rome, 1981). Of special importance is a *descriptive* ritual like KTU 1.161 (de Moor, *Anthology*, 165ff.).

[50]For a scattered selection of the festival and ritual texts published, consider the following examples from the series *Studien zu den Boğazköy-Texten*: H.M.Kümmel, *Ersatzrituale für den hethitischen König* (Wiesbaden, 1967); E.Neu, *Ein althethitisches Gewitterritual* (Wiesbaden, 1970); H.Otten, *Ein hethithisches Festritual, (KBo XIX 128)* (Wiesbaden, 1971); N.Oettinger, *Die Militärischen Eide der Hethiter* (Wiesbaden, 1976); Singer, *The Hittite KI.LAM Festival*.

[51]E.g., the significance of the expression ANA GIŠ.ḪUR-*kan ḫandan*, which suggests that clay tablets were written on the basis of original documents prepared on wooden tablets covered with wax (Singer, *The Hittite KI.LAM Festival*, 40-43). For an additional example of written records of the days of the festival, cf. V.Haas, "Betrachtungen zur Rekonstruktion des hethitischen Frühjarsfestes (EZEN *purulliyaš*)," *ZA* 78 (1988) 284-298.

ancient NE context were regularly committed to writing to give them lasting and binding value, which helps to illuminate the background of Josh. 24:26.[52] It may therefore be not coincidental that so many of the earliest references to writing in Israel's history focus upon the documentation of laws established in formal gatherings, as in the Sinai complex of Exodus, in Deut. 31, and in Josh. 24.

The preceding considerations suggest that it is necessary to reassess the assertion that *wlšpṭyw wlšṭryw* in Josh. 24:1 is Dtistic. It is helpful to distinguish three arguments. The first is the matter of correlation to Josh. 8:33; 23:2. Since these two texts are ordinarily treated as Dtistic, Josh. 24:1 is placed in the same category. The vulnerability of this argument is, however, self-evident because it assumes that Josh. 24:1 is dependent upon 23:2, and not vice versa. Although this assumption has often been posited, it has never been demonstrated in a convincing fashion. We have noted above that Noth was ambiguous on the matter. Nevertheless, certain scholars[53] have appealed to Noth's proposal and accepted his conclusion as if it were the definitive answer, even though he himself repeatedly demonstrated his uncertainty about the relationship between the two passages.[54] There are in fact stronger reasons for seeing 23:2 as dependent upon 24:1.[55] Furthermore, Noth concludes that the *šṭrym* in 8:33, where the suffix is conspicuously absent, represents a late gloss.[56] It is indeed possible that *šṭrym* in 8:33 is a deliberate harmonization with 23:2 and 24:1.[57] In that case it is unwarranted to employ 8:33 to argue for a Dtistic origin of the latter texts.

The second argument is that the combination of "judge and officer" is relatively late, and Josh. 24:1 must be dependent upon the references in Deuteronomy. But here too, although the matter is difficult to decide with certainty, the conclusion that the combination of

[52]Baltzer, *Bundesformular*, 36; Brekelmans, "Credo," 7; Weinfeld, *Deuteronomy*, 164; McCarthy, *Covenant and Treaty*, 30, 64-66, etc.

[53]Cf., e.g., de Geus, "Richteren," 88 n.2.

[54]Cf. the summary in 1.4.1.

[55]Cf. the more extensive discussion in 5.7.

[56]Noth, *Josua* 1953, 50.

[57]Cf. the manner in which the *šṭrym* are added to the Samaritan edition of Ex. 18:24 on the basis of Deut. 1:15 MT, as is demonstrated by J.H.Tigay, "Conflation as a Redactional Technique," in Tigay, ed., *Empirical Models*, 67, 91.

"judge and officer" is per se late is unfounded.[58] Weinfeld's article[59] has demonstrated that considerable caution is in order, which in fact was also recognized previously by de Geus who concluded that the reference to the leaders in Ex. 17; 18; 24; Num. 11; Deut. 19; 21 and 22 are found in very old texts.[60] The references to *šṭrym* in Ex. 5:6,10,14f.,19 and Num. 11:16 cannot be dismissed as Dtistic, and on this basis there is finally no convincing reason to see the combination with *špṭ* in Josh. 24:1 as Dtistic.

Finally, a third argument implicitly functioning in the conclusion of previous commentators that the fourfold list of leaders in 24:1 is Dtistic is related to the stylistic consideration that conspicuous collocations of synonymous terms is a particular hallmark of the Dtist. But the foregoing discussion shows that the list of leaders does not really present synonymous terms; each leader had a specific role and function.[61] Furthermore, not all texts which have a stylistic or even theological affinity to Deuteronomy can be considered dependent upon Deuteronomy.[62] A similar caveat is asserted by Weinfeld.[63] If Josh. 24 and much of Deuteronomy both trace their origins back to material transmitted in Northern cultic traditions, as has often been asserted,[64] one must leave open the possibility that a certain degree

[58]It is noteworthy that the LXX reading of Deut. 29:9 is perhaps influenced by Josh. 23:2; 24:1. The list in Deut. 29:9 demonstrates the appropriateness of these various categories of leaders at a legal ceremony such as is described in Deut. 29 and Josh. 24. It does not prove exclusive Dtistic terminology. Note the absence of *špṭym* in 29:9.

[59]Weinfeld, "Judge and Officer," 65-88.

[60]De Geus, "Richteren," 90: "zeer oude teksten."

[61]Cf. the many examples given by Klengel, "Die Rolle der 'Ältesten'," 223-236, where the Hittite texts mention multiple categories of leaders represented at the official gatherings.

[62]C.H.W.Brekelmans, "Die sogenannten deuteronomischen Elemente in Gen.–Num. Ein Beitrag zur Vorgeschichte des Deuteronomiums," in *Volume du congrès Genève 1965*, *SVT* 15 (Leiden, 1966), 90-96: "Bis jetz hat man vielfach ohne weiteres angenommen, dass Texte mit deuteronomischem Gepräge von Deuteronomium abhängig sind. Dies wird erstens nicht bewiesen, und hat, zweitens, mindestens den Nachteil, dass der Stil und die Theologie des Deuteronomiums in der Überlieferungsgeschichte plötzlich und unvorbereitet als eine vollendete Grösse vor uns stehen" (92).

[63]Weinfeld, *Deuteronomy*, 1.

[64]E.g., N.W.Porteous, "Actualization and the Prophetic Criticism of the Cult," in W.Würthwein–O.Kaiser, eds., *Tradition und Situation. Studien zur alttestamentliche Prophetie* (Fs A.Weiser; Göttingen, 1963), 99; R.E.Clements, "Deuteronomy and the Jerusalem Cult Tradition," *VT* 15 (1965) 300-312 (with bibliography).

of stylistic similarity between the two does not yet indicate that Josh. 24:1-28 is significantly shaped by Dtistic redaction. The matter can finally only be judged on the total evidence from the entire unit of 24:1-28.

A number of comparable OT texts illuminate the rubric within which the present gathering must be understood. The verb *'sp* is often found in contexts of major assemblies, e.g., Ex. 3:16; 4:29; Num. 11:24; Deut. 33:5; Judg. 9:6; 2 Kgs 23:1; Neh. 8:13; 9:1, etc. Similarly, the verb *nṣb* (here in Hithp.) is used of the assembly at the foot of the mountain to receive the law in Ex. 19:17 (*wytyṣbw btḥtyt hhr*). In Num. 11:16 the seventy elders are assembled before the Tent of Meeting to be consecrated for special service. Similarly, in Deut. 31:14 Moses and Joshua are gathered to the Tent of Meeting for Joshua's commissioning in connection with Moses's impending death. In Judg. 20:2 the chiefs and the tribes of Israel are assembled *bqhl 'm h'lhym* to settle matters of national and tribal concern. Also highly significant are two texts in the context of an enthronement ritual, namely 1 Sam. 10:19 and 12:7, where the people are ordered to present themselves before Yahweh (*htyṣbw lpny yhwh*). These references reinforce the legal character of the setting, but such events can be clothed in a process of ritual and ceremonial action appropriate to the specific occasion of law-giving, appointment to office, or settlement of affairs relevant to the future of the tribes or nation of Israel.

The present gathering is said to take place *lpny h'lhym.* Segal has argued that the historical narratives in the OT demonstrate an unequivocal preference for *lpny yhwh* rather than *lpny 'lhym.*[65] As exceptions he lists *lpny 'lhym* in Josh. 24:1; Judg. 21:2; Gen. 6:11; Ex. 18:12; 1 Chron. 13:8. The last of these texts is a parallel to 2 Sam. 6:5, where Yahweh is used, and it illustrates Segal's assertion published in another study, where he posits that at the time of the writing of Chronicles there was a tendency to shift back to the premonarchical use of Elohim.[66] If Segal's observations are valid, they

In ch.2 above we have criticized the theory that Josh. 24:1-28 can be strictly connected in a literary fashion with an alleged E strand in the Pentateuch (cf. 2.3.1 and 2.3.7), but this does not disqualify the possibility that the chapter was at one time at home in a Northern setting.

[65]Segal, *The Pentateuch*, 118.

[66]M.H.Segal, "The Composition of the Pentateuch: A Fresh Approach," in Rabin, ed., *Studies in the Bible*, 83 with additional examples of texts in which Chronicles

are of considerable significance for the origin and dating of this verse, and the matter accordingly deserves more detailed analysis.

The *Masora parva* notes that the combination *lpny h'lhym* occurs 6x plus always in Ecclesiastes. This total is intended to differentiate those references including the article before *'lhym* from those in which the article is absent. The former category includes the texts listed by Segal above, plus 1 Chron. 16:1; Eccl. 2:26; 5:1; 7:26. Of these texts, 1 Chron. 16:1 replaces *yhwh* of 2 Sam. 6:17 with *h'lhym*, thereby providing another example of the phenomenon noted by Segal in 1 Chron. 13:8. In addition, there is a number of references without the article, namely Num. 10:10; 1 Chron. 13:10; 2 Chron. 33:12; 34:27; Ezra 8:21; Job 15:4; Ps. 56:14; 61:8; 68:4.[67] These references demonstrate that the phrase in question is attested in post-exilic writings, in a few instances in early traditions, and in a few cases in select texts of the Writings.[68] The expression *lpny 'lhym* never occurs in Deuteronomy or so-called Dtistic texts. The significance of this is already suggested by Segal, who states that *lpny yhwh* occurs hundreds of times.[69] It is not necessary to list all the times in Deuteronomy–2 Kings where *lpny yhwh* occurs, but a few examples are highly significant, e.g., the analogous gathering of Deut. 29:9:

| | |
|---|---|
| *'tm nṣbym hywm klkm* [*5*] | All of you are standing this day |
| *lpny yhwh 'lhykm* [*2*] | before Yahweh your God; |
| *r'šykm šbṭykm* [*7*] | your heads of your tribes, |
| *zqnykm wšṭrykm* [*5*] | your elders and your officers |
| *kl 'yš yśr'l* [*1*] | all the men of Israel. |

substitutes Elohim for Yahweh.

[67]Cf. *pny 'lhym* in Ps. 42:3; *mpny 'lhym 'lhy yśr'l* in Ps. 68:9, and see further Ps. 114:7, *mlpny 'lwh y'qb*; more remote are Dan. 10:12; Mal. 1:9.

[68]The occurrences in Psalms are of interest. Ps. 68 is generally held to be archaic, e.g., in the classic thesis of Albright, "Catalogue (Psalm LXVIII)," 1-39; Dahood, *Psalms*, 2:130-152. Weiser posits that Pss. 56 and 61 derive from the cultic festival (*The Psalms*, 69-76, 84, 422, 443, etc.). However, Pss. 56; 61 and 68 are all part of the so-called Elohistic psalter, and the possibility that the presence of Elohim rather than Yahweh is due to a later editor cannot be discounted, though Kraus's policy of simply substituting Yahweh for Elohim may be a premature reaction to the supposed activity of an editor.

[69]Segal, *The Pentateuch*, 118. A more precise counting is suggested by M.D.Fowler ("The Meaning of *lip̄nê* YHWH in the Old Testament," *ZAW* 99 [1987] 384-390), who notes that the expression *lpny yhwh* occurs 236 times in the OT.

Here Deut. employs *lpny yhwh 'lhykm*, and the examples could be multiplied many times.[70] Perlitt called attention to the similarity with 1 Sam. 12:7a,[71] but he did not pursue the difference between *lpny h'lhym* and *lpny yhwh*. He concludes:

> "V.1a and 1bA benutzen Formeln, die im dt Bereich gewachsen, also nicht erst einer dtr Spätschicht zu zutrauen sind. Der Pleonasmus verfolgt hier das Ziel, eine auch ständisch gegliederte, also legitimierte Gesamtheit Israels *lpny h'lhym* zu bringen. Aus *h'lhym* is quellenkritisch nichts zu folgern ...."[72]

To be sure, Perlitt is quite correct that the mention of *h'lhym* cannot be employed in the manner of previous source-critical attempts to separate J and E. However, the evidence amassed by Segal and supported in the observations above is of considerable significance in response to Perlitt's too easy association with Dtr. We have noted that the phrase *lpny h'lhym* or *lpny 'lhym* is foreign to Deuteronomy.[73] A straightforward analysis of the evidence suggests either a *later* date, or possibly an older one.[74]

In the light of the foregoing study concerning the list of leaders in 24:1, and in view of the observations which demonstrate that *wytyṣbw lpny h'lhym* is not Dtistic, it is necessary to reasses the claim that 24:1 is to be attributed in part or as a whole to a Dtic/Dtistic origin. Considerable weight in Perlitt's approach was placed upon the assertion that the phrase *kl-šbṭy yśr'l* is restricted to both earlier and later layers of DtrG.[75] He lists a number of exceptions,[76] but he doesn't elaborate the claim further.

[70]For *lpny yhwh* in Deuteronomy consult 1:45; 4:10; 6:25; 9:18,25; 10:8; 12:7,12,18(2x); 14:23,26; 15:20; 16:11,16(2x); 18:7; 19:17; 24:4; 24:13; 26:5,10,13; 27:7; 29:9,14; 31:11. Numerous of these 27 references are *lpny yhwh 'lhykm*, but significantly not once do we find a reference to *lpny 'lhym* or *lpny h'lhym*.

[71]Perlitt, *Bundestheologie*, 243.

[72]Perlitt, *Bundestheologie*, 249f.

[73]Cf. the distribution of *lpny yhwh* in Deuteronomy, as listed above.

[74]E.g., on the basis of Ex. 18:12, cf. our comments above on the role of the elders, and below regarding *'t-ḥqy h'lhym w't-twrtyw* (Ex. 18:16) in comparison with Josh. 24:26.

[75]Perlitt, *Bundestheologie*, 249: "*kl-šbṭy yśr'l* ist ein auf frühere und spätere Schichten des DtrG beschränkter Ausdruck für die grossisraelitische Idee."

[76]Perlitt, *Bundestheologie*, 249 n.1: "Ausserhalb des DtrG nur Ex. 18,19; Sach 9,1; und in der Chronik." Apparently his reference to Ex. 18:19 must be an error for Ezek. 48:19. The references in Chronicles are 2 Chron. 6:5 (= 1 Kgs 8:16);

A number of considerations must be raised in response. First, Perlitt offers no justification for restricting his study to *kl-šbṭy yśr'l* at the exclusion of *šbṭy yśr'l* without *kl*. Examples of the latter are found in the archaic poetry of Gen. 49:16, parallel to *'mw*,[77] and Deut. 33:5.[78] In a number of cases *kl-šbṭy yśr'l* and *šbṭy yśr'l* are used together in close context, e.g., Judg. 21:5 (with *kl*) compared to 21:8,15 (without *kl*), and 2 Sam. 15:10 (with *kl*) compared to 15:2 (without *kl*). It is noteworthy that in Josh. 24:1f. we find the external parallelism of *kl-šbṭy yśr'l* || *kl-h'm*, which not only has a striking correlation to the poetry of Gen. 49:16 and Deut. 33:5, but in light of the *kl* || *kl* correlation may explain why the author did not simply say *šbṭy yśr'l*. Nevertheless, it is instructive to follow Perlitt's lead and assume for the sake of the investigation that, where the fuller formula with *kl* does occur, it may be of some theological significance, and it may provide a clue to the relationship of the various passages.

The authorship of numerous of these references is enigmatic, e.g., 2 Sam. 24:2, where David tells Joab and his officers to number all the tribes of Israel (*šwṭ-n' bkl-šbṭy yśr'l mdn w'd-b'r šb'*). With respect to the last half of this statement, "from Dan to Beersheba," de Vaux calls attention to the poetic formula in Am. 8:14 and suggests that it is possible that the formula was abandoned when the sanctuaries were condemned.[79] However, 2 Sam. 24 was treated by Wellhausen as part of an appendix to Samuel.[80] Noth concurs,[81] followed by Mayes,[82] and all these scholars posit a compilation based upon older source material, which leaves unanswered the question of whether *bkl-šbṭy yśr'l* was part of an older source or is to be attributed to the later editor. The same question may be asked of Judg. 20:2,10; 21:5 as part of the appendices to Judges. The appendices have long been thought to derive from a source relatively independent from the main body of the book, and this conclusion is reinforced by recent statistical analyses.[83] The events of Judg. 19-21 appear to have been

11:16 (not in Kings); 12:13 (1 Kgs 14:21); 33:7 (2 Kgs 21:7), which cannot really be considered exceptions to his thesis because they parallel material from Kings.

[77]Cf. vs.28, *kl-'lh šbṭy yśr'l*.

[78]As noted above we have the parallelism *bht'sp r'šy 'm* || *yḥd šbṭy-yśr'l*.

[79]De Vaux, *Early History*, 7.

[80]Wellhausen, *Composition*, 258, 260-263.

[81]Noth, *Uberlieferungsgeschichtliche Studien*, 62 n.3, 137.

[82]Mayes, *Story of Israel*, 83.

[83]Y.T.Radday, et al, "The Book of Judges Examined by Statistical Linguistics,"

well-known to both the prophet Hosea and his 8th. cent. audience since he is able to allude to the scandal of Gibeah without further elaboration.[84] This does not preclude the possibility that the present formulation in 20:2,10; 21:5 is owing to a redactor, but the reference to the assembly of all the tribes constitutes an indigenous part of the story,[85] and these three references in Judges can hardly be admitted as evidence that the formula belongs to a Dtistic hand in DtrG.

Similarly, the references in 2 Sam. 15:10 and 19:10 form a natural link in the Absalom narrative cycle; they are indigenous and indispensable to the narration and give no clue that they should be attributed to a Dtistic hand. Nor is there any reason to call 20:14 Dtistic; it has every appearance of being an authentic tradition regarding the insurrection of someone named Sheba. Perlitt does not defend the statement that, where the formula with *kl* appears, the references come from Dtistic influence in DtrG. Judg. 20:2,10; 21:5; 2 Sam. 15:10; 19:10; 20:14 cast doubt upon his conclusion unless with DtrG he simply means that these texts fall in Deuteronomy–2 Kings, in which case the term becomes rather meaningless. Nevertheless, setting aside for a moment the supposition that all of these occurrences are from DtrG, it would appear that the observation that these texts are linked by a common thread may be significant. A complete list of references from Deuteronomy–2 Kings includes Deut. 12:5; 18:5; 29:20; Josh. 24:1; Judg. 20:2,10; 21:5; 1 Sam. 2:28; 10:20; 2 Sam. 5:1; 15:10; 2 Sam. 19:10; 20:14; 24:2; 1 Kgs 8:16; 11:32; 14:21; 2 Kgs 21:7.

What is especially striking is that these texts, with the possible exceptions of Deut. 29:20 and 2 Sam. 24:2, fall into two basic categories: (a) texts with respect to an assembly of all the tribes, and/or the establishment of a king in Israel, and (b) references with respect to the place Yahweh chooses from all the tribes. In the first group we may include Josh. 24:1; Judg. 20:2,10; 21:5; 1 Sam. 10:20; 2 Sam. 5:1; 15:10; 19:10; (20:14).[86] The remainder of the texts, in-

*Bibl* 58 (1977) 469-499; Y.T.Radday–H.Shore, "An Inquiry into the Homogoneity of the Book of Judges by Means of Discriminant Analysis," *Linguistica Biblica* 41/42 (1977) 21-34.

[84]Hos. 10:9. For the most recent attempt to deal with this reference see P.M.Arnold, "Hosea and the Sin of Gibeah," *CBQ* 51 (1989) 447-460.

[85]E.g., while 20:3 may be owing to a redactor, that is less probable with 20:2.

[86]This latter text is related to the others to the extent that it is concerned with David's pride in numbering the tribes to demonstrate the extent of his kingship.

cluding the references from 2 Chronicles, deal with the election of the place out of all the tribes of Israel where Yahweh has chosen to put his name.[87] The latter expression is evidently a stereotyped formula in Kings and Chronicles. But these references do not prove a Dtiscic origin for references in the previous category. The assertion of a Dtistic authorship is improbable for 2 Sam. 15:10; 19:10; 20:14. The status of the three references to tribal assemblies in the appendix of Judges is also questionable as proof of Dtistic origin. Regarding 1 Sam. 10:20, Noth[88] again follows the opinion of Wellhausen that 1 Sam. 10:17-27a is Dtistic, but Schmitt correctly notes that it is important to differentiate between "der deuteronomistischen Literature und dem bezeichneten Komplex in Jdc 2–1 Sam 12."[89] The account of this enthronement ritual[90] cannot simply be ascribed to DtrG. The same is true of David's treaty[91] with all the tribes in 2 Sam. 5:1-5.

In this whole group of texts revolving around national assemblies, enthronement festivals, establishment of the king, or insurrection against the kingdom, it is understandable that the adjective *kl* is used to demonstrate the national character of the event.[92] In such cases the presence or absence of *kl* is of questionable validity to determine date or authorship.[93] This observation is in harmony with the technical usage of *zqny yśr'l*, outlined above, where the latter phrase also has a national character. It is noteworthy that *kl-šbṭy yśr'l* is found in 24:1 with the verb *'sp*. The only place in Deuteronomy where the verb *'sp* is used in reference to an assembly is in the archaic poetry of 33:5, where it appears also in the context of the "heads of the people" and the "tribes of Israel." Finally, the reference to Shechem as the location of the covenant ceremony can scarcely be attributed to a

[87] Deut. 18:5 refers to the chosen priest and appears therefore to be related, as is 1 Sam. 2:28. Note that the latter text refers to Shiloh, not Jerusalem, which argues against presupposing that Deut. 12:5 necessarily has Jerusalem in mind.

[88] Noth, *Uberlieferungsgeschichtliche Studien*, 54f.

[89] Schmitt, *Landtag*, 16-21; cf. McCarthy, *Treaty and Covenant*, 206.

[90] Cf. Ben-Barak, "Mizpah Covenant," 30-43; Kalluveettil, *Declaration and Covenant*, 61.

[91] Cf. Kalluveettil, *Declaration and Covenant*, 60, 209f.

[92] Cf. the treatment of *kl-yśr'l* in T.Ishida, "Royal Succession in the Kingdoms of Israel and Judah with Special Reference to the People under Arms as a Determining Factor in the Struggle for the Throne," in J.A.Emerton, ed., *Congress Volume Jerusalem 1986*, *SVT* 40 (Leiden, 1988), 96-106, esp. 98-100, 105f.

[93] K.A.Kitchen, "Historical Method and Early Hebrew Tradition," *TB* 17 (1966) 85-88.

Dtistic redaction, even less to a Dtistic fiction. Hence, there is little support for Perlitt's theory regarding the origin of this part of vs.1 (our 1aA-B).

### 4.2.2 The ceremony in Josh. 24:25-28

Of all the verses in Josh. 24:1-28, it is probably vss.25-27 which have commanded the greatest amount of attention throughout the history of interpretation.[94] However, the enactment of the covenant and the prescription of laws for the people have been explained in radically divergent manners, and the conclusions which have been drawn with respect to the origin of Josh. 24:25-28 are extremely disparate. A lexical study of the most important terms and combinations found here is of great significance. However, as is demonstrated in the different conclusions attained by, e.g., McCarthy and Perlitt, the evidence has unfortunately been mustered to defend incompatible theories, which in turn necessitates a rigorous reanalysis of the data. In 2.3.7.2, numerous arguments were advanced to show that Perlitt's attempt to view the present account as a Dtic fiction is not convincing. A number of technical points were left undeveloped, and it is necessary at this point to raise additional questions regarding Perlitt's approach. The matter is of significance because Perlitt's view has drawn a following[95] and is clearly the most serious attempt thus far to argue for a Dtic origin for the present passage.

Criticism of Perlitt's perspective does not entail, however, that other previous treatments were sufficient, and in the present analysis we are not satisfied to simply arbitrate between the opinions of previous scholars. As noted in 2.4.1 above, McCarthy's treatment of the relationship between the covenant in Josh. 24 and the form of extra-biblical treaty documents suffered from serious methodological weaknesses. The same has been asserted with respect to the conclusions of Weinfeld, who attempted without proper justification to make a sharp distinction between a covenant validated by oath and

[94]Cf. Nielsen, *Shechem*, 109.

[95]E.g., the degree to which Van Seters has accepted Perlitt's analysis. He states, "Yet, as Perlitt has pointed out, no elements in the narrative can stand as independent from the previous speech units. If one accepts the late date for the speeches then vv.25-27 cannot be otherwise" ("Joshua 24" 150). Consider too the influence of Perlitt upon Wächter, "Berîtvorstellung," 801-816; Jaroš, *Sichem*, 138; Nicholson, "Covenant," 54-69; *His People*, 151-163; Blum, *Komposition*, 45-61.

a covenant ratified by ritual ceremony. Multiple sources in vss.26f. have been almost unanimously asserted in all critical analyses of these verses, but in the opinion of the present author the claims have never been demonstrated in a convincing manner.[96]

Certain weaknesses of the previous assertions become especially clear when one recognizes the poetic character of these verses, which helps in part to explain why the present text suffered literary injustice at the pen of endless modern scholars. However, the problem goes deeper. At the heart of the matter are fundamental differences with respect to the degree of evidence which is necessary, upon a source-critical basis, to assign a given text the designation "Dtistic." A survey of previous analyses indicates that the lexical studies were generally so influenced by attempts to demonstrate affinity to an alleged source (e.g., at first E, J or JE) and date (e.g., ancient tradition or post-exilic redaction) that many significant dimensions of the text have gone unnoticed. By now it has become common for scholars to reiterate the theory that Josh. 24 is heavily redacted without critically evaluating the previous claims, many of which upon closer scrutiny prove untenable. These comments will suffice as an introduction to the analysis which follows.

#### 4.2.2.1 Josh. 24:25

It has been a common procedure to appeal to the formulation *krt bryt l* as a clue to not only the nature of the covenant enacted but also to the "literary strand" of the OT to which the present text belongs.[97] However, just how precarious it is to place a great deal of weight upon the preposition *l* rather than *'m* or *'t* is evident from an analogous extra-biblical example. In a 7th cent. B.C. Arslan Tash inscription one finds the expression *krt 'lt l*[98] instead of the typical *krt 'lt 'm* or

[96]Typical is the claim by Morgenstern ("Book of the Covenant, Part III," 67): "These considerations make it clear that we no longer have the original narrative of Josh. 24 in its primary form. We have only a composite and confused narrative resulting from very far-reaching re-editing of the original narrative."

[97]Cf. Valeton, "Das Wort *bryt*," 225; Begrich, "Berit," 8; L.Köhler, "Problems in the Study of the Language of the Old Testament," *JSS* 1 (1956) 4; Perlitt, *Bundestheologie*, 261f.

[98]The Phoenician term *'lh*, literally "curse," by metonymy at times takes on a meaning virtually synonymous with *bryt*, as does Hebrew *'lh*; cf. Hillers, *Treaty-Curses*, 184 n.23; W.Schottroff, *Der altisraelitische Fluchspruch* (Neukirchen, 1969), 29; Weinfeld, "Covenant Terminology," 196; C.A.Keller, "*'lh* Verfluchung," *THAT*, 1:149-152; H.Tadmor, "Treaty and Oath in the Ancient Near East: A Histo-

*'t*.[99] Furthermore, Perlitt is forced to concede that the expression *krt bryt l* is also found in Ex. 23:32; 34:12,15. And to describe the relationship of these texts to DtrG as "verwandten Texten,"[100] ultimately is of questionable value because Perlitt does not give adequate attention to the possibility that the direction of influence could be from Exodus to Deuteronomy rather than vice versa.[101] Perlitt's list of texts where the formula occurs omits reference to Isa. 55:3; 61:8; Jer. 32:40; Ezek. 34:25; 37:26; Hos. 2:20; Ps. 89:4, presumably because in these cases the subject is God and not a human. But there is little reason for omitting these references from comparison with Josh. 24:25, especially because the question of Joshua's mediatorial role as representative of God, which has been debated time and again,[102] is supported by the recurring poetic parallelism between *yhwš'* and *yhwh*.[103]

As with Perlitt's discussion of "all the tribes of Israel," the term DtrG again becomes of little significance when, for example, the covenant with the Gibeonites (Josh. 9:6,7,11,15,16) is included in this category without further explanation. The authorship of this fascinating passage has been the subject of a great deal of discussion, with a majority of scholars concluding both that the text must contain an an-

rian's Approach," in G.M.Tucker–D.A.Knight, eds., *Humanizing America's Iconic Book: SBL Centennial Addresses 1980* (Chico, 1982), 136; Kalluveettill, *Declaration and Covenant*, 14, 19; J.C.de Moor, "Demons in Canaan," *JEOL* 27 (1983) 108. In Ugarit *'alt* is attested in the meaning of "sworn agreement," cf. de Moor, "Contributions to the Ugaritic Lexicon," *UF* 11 (1979) 650.

[99]Gibson, *Semitic Inscriptions*, 3:85.

[100]Perlitt, *Bundestheologie*, 261.

[101]To be sure, many scholars have been willing to concede that Ex. 23:32 is either related to or even influenced by Dtr. This text will be handled more extensively in the following chapter and for the time being we note that the reverse, e.g., the dependence of Deut. 7:13ff. upon Exod. 23:20ff. has been argued numerous times (cf. Schmitt, *Landtag*, 26-28; Weinfeld, *Deuteronomy*, 46-48; "Emergence," 81; cf. Brekelmans, "Deuteronomistischen Elemente," 90-96). The matter of 34:12,15 is related, and these texts ought not to be dismissed so easily from the picture. Ex. 34 is generally considered to rely upon ancient tradition (cf. Wilms, *Bundesbuch*, 157), which is supported by the old poetic formulae it contains (de Moor, *Uw God*, 54f.). According to Cross, Ex. 34:10-27 contains expansion and reworking but the account of a J covenant tradition in vs.10 is authentic (*Canaanite Myth*, 86, 261). For additional reservations about Perlitt's handling of Ex. 34:10 as Dtistic cf. McCarthy, "*Berît* in OT," 110-121; for the most extensive attempt thus far to argue that Ex. 34:10-26 is pre-Dtic consult Halbe, *Privilegrecht*.

[102]Noth, "Covenant Making," 116f.

[103]Cf. above in int. par. at 2a,19a,21,22a,24a, as well as in ext. par.

cient tradition and that the present text shows the influence of P and of Dtistic redaction.[104] Arguments have been advanced for comparing this passage with other ancient NE treaty texts,[105] and in the opinion of some scholars the extra-biblical treaties cast sober doubt upon the validity of the documentary splitting of the present chapter.[106] It is not necessary here to enter into a detailed debate regarding different sources in Josh. 9[107] for the simple reason that when the chapter is divided into different sources the verses in which *krt bryt l* is found are attributed to ancient tradition and not to Dtic redaction.[108] Consequently, the expression *krt bryt l* in Josh. 9:6,7,11,15,16 lends no support to the theory that Josh. 24:25 is Dtic.[109]

A similar observation can be made with respect to 1 Sam. 11:1. In attempts to divide the material in Samuel, this verse is ordinarily viewed as part of a pre-Dtic tradition.[110] In short, Perlitt's list of the frequency of *krt bryt l* in so-called DtrG texts says little about the matter of authorship or date. It does not prove anything with respect to Dtistic redaction, and, if anything, it suggests the opposite

[104]According to M.Haran, it is a "hotchpotch of Deuteronomistic and Priestly redactions" ("The Gibeonites, the Nethinim and the Sons of Solomon's Servants," *VT* 11 [1961], 161); Soggin suggests that Deuteronomic redaction is found in vss.1-2,9-10,24-25,27b (*Joshua*, 111).

[105]F.C.Fensham, "The Treaty between Israel and the Gibeonites," *BA* 27 (1964) 96-100.

[106]E.g., J.M.Grintz, "The Treaty of Joshua with the Gibeonites," *JAOS* 86 (1966) 113-126.

[107]One of the arguments often appealed to is the fact that "hewers of wood" and "drawers of water" (9:21,23,27a) is priestly, but this detail must be used with caution since the same parallelism is also attested in Ugaritic and in the Amarna Letters, cf. Gevirtz, "Canaanite Rhetoric," 167—overlooked, e.g., in A.D.H.Mayes, "Deuteronomy 29, Joshua 9, and the Place of the Gibeonites in Israel," in Lohfink, ed., *Deuteronomium*, 321-325; M.Rose, *Deuteronomist und Jahwist. Untersuchungen zu de Berührungspunkten beider Literaturwerke* (Zürich, 1981), 171-220. See further Fensham, "Treaty Terminology," esp. 269, 273.

[108]Cf. J.Halbe, "Gibeon und Israel," *VT* 25 (1975) 613-641, esp. 629: "Die Grundüberlieferung liegt in v.3-7, 9ab*A* 11-15a." See further his *Das Privilegrecht*, 341-346; J.Liver, "The Literary History of Joshua IX," *JSS* 8 (1963) 227-243; Noth, *Josua* 1953, 53; Rose, *Deuteronomist*, 192 n.22.

[109]Floss is quite correct in rejecting Perlitt's characterization of the term *krt bryt l* in Joshua (*Jahwe dienen*, 346 n.76).

[110]Cf. Wellhausen, *Composition*, 241f.; L.Rost, *Die Überlieferung von der Thronnachfolge Davids* (Stuttgart, 1926), 74-80; Noth, *Überlieferungsgeschichtliche Studien*, 54-57; A.F.Campbell, *Of Prophets and Kings: A Late Ninth-Century Document (1 Samuel 1–2 Kings 10)* (Washington, 1986), 127f.

in the light of *krt bryt* in Deuteronomy, where the phrase *krt bryt l* is found only in 7:2 in a chapter often claimed to be influenced by material from Exodus. By contrast, *krt bryt ʿm* is attested in 4:23; 5:2; 9:9; 29:11,24. Similarly, the preposition *ʾt* is used in 5:3; 28:69; 29:13; 31:16. And again, in Jeremiah the construction *krt bryt l* is found only in 32:40, while *krt bryt ʾt* is employed in 11:10; 31:31,32,33; 34:8,13. Jeremiah is universally recognized to be influenced by the language of Deuteronomy. The construction of the various *krt bryt* formulae in both Deuteronomy and in Jeremiah lends no support to the implication that *krt bryt l* is Dtic/Dtistic.[111] In 24:25aA the formula is completed with the designation *bywm hhwʾ*, which has been recognized as an indigenous element of specific legal contexts, including covenant or treaty ratification.[112]

Having reviewed the evidence for 25aA we may now turn to the colon "and he set for them a statute and judgment in Shechem" (25aB). Previous opinions have differed radically with respect to the combination *śym ḥq wmšpṭ*. Early commentators had a tendency to attribute the expression to E.[113] Eissfeldt thought it was from L.[114] Rudolph quite naturally voted for J.[115] Others thought that it is a later Dtistic expression.[116] Möhlenbrink wished to attribute it to the literary source of the *Josuarede*.[117] Some viewed it as a post-exilic

[111]Note that Begrich ("Berit," 5), in line with previous studies, viewed *krt bryt l* as the oldest of the various formulations.

[112]Kalluveettil, *Declaration and Covenant*, 184, with reference to Josh.24:15,25, along with Gen. 31:48. Recognition of the legal formulaic character of this expression invalidates the argument proposed by Weinfeld for viewing Deut. 26:16-18; 27:9 as standing in conflict with Ex. 6:7; 19:4-8; 34:10-11 with respect to the day when Israel became God's nation, cf. Weinfeld, "Emergence," 78f.

[113]Dillmann, *Exodus und Leviticus* (Leipzig, 1880), 163 (Note that Dillmann's B = E); *Josua*, 583, 587, 618. According to Holzinger (*Einleitung*, 188), Ex. 15:25 is E but in Gen. 47:18-26 *śym lḥq* is J. In his *Josua*, xxi, Josh. 24:25 is assigned to E. Steuernagel attributes Josh. 24:25 to $E^1$ (*Josua*, 242, 245). Apparently Noth also attributed it to E (*Das System*, 137), but he viewed Shechem as a possible sign of J (cf. ibid., 92 139).

[114]Eissfeldt, *Hexateuch-Synopse*, 81.

[115]Rudolph, *Der "Elohist"*, 248, 281.

[116]Hölscher, *Geschichtsschreibung*, 350 (Rp); Fohrer, "'Amphiktyonie' und 'Bund'?" 897; Perlitt, *Bundestheologie*, 269.

[117]We recall that Möhlenbrink attempted to distinguish here between two sources on the basis of *Jahwerede* and *Josuarede* ("Landnahmesagen," 251f.).

redaction,[118] while others attributed it to ancient tradition.[119]

The diversity of opinion witnessed here does little to bolster confidence in the ability of traditional literary-critical methods to explain the provenance of Josh. 24:25. Most of the previous approaches have isolated Ex. 15:25; Josh. 24:25; 1 Sam. 30:25 and Ezra 7:10 and then attempted to work from there to the question of dating and authorship. Arguments in favour of J, E, or ancient tradition are based upon comparison of Ex. 15:25 and Josh. 24:25 with similar emphases of law-giving in the Pentateuch, as well as supporting evidence within the immediate context itself. Arguments for a late date are based upon attempts to see the work of a redactor in these passages or, as in the case of Van Seters, a late composition for the entire passage.

On the one hand, the observation by Nielsen that Ex. 15:25 and Josh. 24:25 are deliberately correlated by the fact that they fall at crucial stages of Israel's history at first glance appears attractive.[120] But Nielsen has not taken into consideration 1 Sam. 30:25, a reference which mitigates the force of his argument. Perlitt thinks that 1 Sam. 30:25 is the oldest of the four similar references; he attributes Ex. 15:25 and Josh. 24:25 to Dtic influence, and finally sees the combination in Ezra 7:10 as the latest of the four references.[121]

However, in addition to the fact that 1 Sam. 30:25 bears no indication of being Dtisitc, the expression *śym lḥq wmšpṭ* can hardly be used by itself as a criterion for judging either authorship or date. The similarity of this expression to references from Mari has been noted by Malamat.[122] While the concept of law is central to Deuteronomy,

[118]Morgenstern, "Book of the Covenant," 65-68; L'Hour, "L'alliance de Sichem," 30; cf. the opinion of Van Seters that the entire composition is a post-Dtr work ("Josh. 24," 151, 154).

[119]Schmitt, *Landtag*, 24; McCarthy, *Treaty and Covenant*, 221-224.

[120]Cf. Nielsen, *Shechem*, 121f. Nielsen argues that Ex. 15:25 borrows from Josh. 24:25. He attempts to bolster his argument with an appeal to 1 Sam. 10:25, a verse to which we will return in the next chapter below.

[121]Perlitt, *Bundestheologie*, 268f.

[122]Malamat, "Mari," 19: "The expression *šipṭam nadānum/šakānum*, met with in the Mari documents, corresponds to the biblical *sim mishpaṭ* 'to lay down a ruling' (by duly authorized person) employed in connection with the authoritative acts of a Moses, a Joshua or a David (Exod. 15:25; Josh. 24:25; I Sam. 30:25)." Cf. his "The Ban in Mari and in the Bible," *OTWSA* 9 (1966) 45; A.Marzal, "Mari Clauses in 'Casuistic' and 'Apodictic' Styles (Part I)," *CBQ* 33 (1971) 333-364, esp. 335-339; "... (Part II)," *CBQ* 33 (1971) 492-509, 492-495; Niehr, *Herrschen und Richten*, 25-41.

there is nothing particularly Dtistic about the concept of law—a fact which is too often forgotten in contemporary allegations of Dtistic redaction throughout the OT. As is emphasized by P.A.H.de Boer,[123] the combination of *śym* + *l* + *dbrym*, *mšpṭym*, *twrh* or *ḥq* is a natural construction.[124] Furthermore, a study of the distribution of these combinations offers little support for the idea that the expression in Josh. 24:25b is Dtistic. The combination of *śym* and *ḥq* is found in Gen. 47:26; Ex. 15:25,26; Josh. 24:25; 1 Sam. 30:25; Prov. 8:29 (cf. Jer. 5:22; 38:10). Cf. also the similar use of *ḥqh* in 2 Kgs 17:34; Jer. 33:23; Ezek. 44:5; Job 38:33. The combination of *śym* and *mšpṭ* is attested in Ex. 15:25; 21:1; Josh. 24:25; 1 Sam. 30:25; 2 Kgs 17:34; Isa. 28:17; 42:4; Hab. 1:12; (cf. 2 Sam. 15:4; 1 Kgs 10:9).

The combination of *ḥq* and *mšpṭ* is found nowhere as prolifically as in Deuteronomy.[125] But this does not make the phrase Dtistic. In Deut. 4:8, Weinfeld thinks "there may be an echo of the Code of Hammurabi."[126] More importantly, the stylistic characteristics typical of the employment of the phrase in Deuteronomy are absent in the terse references in Ex. 15:25 and Josh. 24:25.[127] Furthermore, Schmitt has already called attention to the fact that Ps. 81:5 contains the singular terms in parallelism, which is especially significant because of a number of additional elements which closely correlate Josh. 24:1-28 with this Psalm, e.g., *'l nkr* (vs.10), the Hiph. part. *'lh* in reference to Yahweh as deliverer from Egypt (vs.11), and the expression *šm' lqwl* (vs.12).[128] It is perhaps not coincidental that Ps. 81 is thought to be "a composite liturgy of North Israelite origin."[129]

[123]P.A.H.de Boer, "Numbers vi 27," *VT* 32 (1982) 8f.

[124]Cf. Weinfeld, "Covenant Terminology," 196f.

[125]Cf. 4:1,5,8,14,45; 5:1,31; 6:1,20; 7:11; 11:32; 12:1; 26:16.

[126]Weinfeld, *Deuteronomy*, 150.

[127]E.g., in Deuteronomy the terms are always plural, the references are usually accompanied by a combination of the verbs *šmr*, *'śh*, *ṣwh* as well as an *'šr*–clause following the mention of the "ordinances and judgments." The difference between Josh. 24:25b in the singular and the references from Deuteronomy in the plural was conceded by Perlitt (*Bundestheologie*, 261) but played little role in his final evaluation of vs.25; cf. also Floss, *Jahwe dienen*, 346 n.76; Lohfink, "Die *ḥuqqîm ûmišpāṭîm* im Buch Deuteronomium und ihre Neubegrenzung durch Dtn 12,1," *Bibl* 70 (1989) 1-29. Re Ezra 7:10 cf. Sperling, "Joshua 24," 131f. n.69.

[128]Schmitt, *Landtag*, 23.

[129]Dahood, *Psalms*, 2:263. Other origins and dates have been proposed recently, however, e.g., Th.Booij, "The Background of the Oracle in Psalm 81," *Bibl* 65 (1984) 465-475 (late pre-exilic); P.Schelling, *De Asafspsalmen, hun samenhang en achtergrond* (Kampen, 1985), esp. 246 (post-exilic circles related to the Chronicler).

Weiser summarizes the evidence which connects Ps. 81 to the autumn festival of the New Year,[130] and, in any event, a background in a cultic festival is without doubt.[131] The parallelism in the present context of *krt bryt l* || *śym lw ḥq wmšpṭ* is composed of two sequences which are atypical of the covenantal language of Deuteronomy.

Mention of Shechem in 24:25b also ought to be recognized as an obstacle against assigning it to a Dtistic hand.[132] Whereas Deuteronomy narrates events which took place in the area of Shechem, it makes no mention of the name of the city itself.[133] These observations nullify the assertion that Josh. 24:25b is either directly dependent upon Deuteronomy or is shaped by the hand of a Dtist. Josh. 24:25 in fact bears no concrete evidence of later editing or redacting.

#### 4.2.2.2 Josh. 24:26

Most scholars have accepted the assertion of Wellhausen[134] that vs.26a is a Dtistic addition.[135] Apparently the strongest motivation for this assignment is an alleged dependence upon texts such as Deut. 31:9; Josh. 8:31f.; 23:6.[136] However, the question of Dtistic influence upon 24:26 is not as simple as has often been implied. In the discussion of Josh. 24:1 above it has been argued that it is precarious to presuppose that Josh. 24 is dependent upon Josh. 8:30-35 or ch.23, and an appeal to these texts in an attempt to demonstrate that ch.24 is Dtistic is unfounded. Furthermore, while Josh. 23:6 speaks of *spr twrt mšh*, and 8:31f. makes an explicit correlation with the role of Moses as law-giver in Deuteronomy, such an emphasis is entirely lacking in Josh. 24.[137] For this reason it even seems unlikely that a

It would take too much room to refute the latter thesis on the basis of the archaic elements in Ps. 81. In any case, it is unlikely that such a late author would diverge from the decalogue as in the wording of vs.10.

[130]Weiser, *The Psalms*, 553; cf. J.C.de Moor, *New Year with Canaanites and Israelites*, 2 vols. (Kampen, 1972), 1:28.

[131]Cf. J.Ridderbos, *De Psalmen*, 2 vols. (Kampen, 1955-58), 2:316-324; H.-J.Kraus, *Psalmen* (Neukirchen, 1960-79), 2:561-568; Eichrodt, "Darf man heute," 200.

[132]Nielsen, *Shechem*, 87.

[133]Cf. Deut. 11:29-32; 27; and cf. Josh. 8:30-35.

[134]Wellhausen, *Composition*, 133.

[135]Cf. Holzinger, *Josua*, xxi, 99; Noth, *Das System*, 136; Rudolph, *Der "Elohist"*, 248; Hölscher, *Geschichtsschreibung*, 350; Hertzberg, *Josua*, 137f.; Nielsen, *Shechem*, 110; Schmitt, *Landtag*, 21.

[136]Cf. Eissfeldt, who despite these references opts to attribute the present reference to his ancient L source (*Hexateuch-Synopse*, 81).

[137]In fact the only reference to Moses in the entire passage is in 24:5aA, which on

Dtic author would accord Joshua the same status in Josh. 24:26 as Moses. Sperling has argued that in Deuteronomy the corpus of the law is treated as already complete.[138] Objections have been raised above concerning Perlitt's treatment of *spr twrt 'lhym*.[139] As noted in the internal parallelism of the structural analysis, the parallelism of *dbrym* || *twrt 'lhym* finds a close counterpart in Isa. 1:10 (cf. 2:3; Mic. 4:2; Ps. 37:30f., etc.) which also casts doubt upon the simple manner in which Josh. 24:26a has been viewed by a century of commentators as a late Dtistic insertion.[140] Considerable evidence has also been adduced above to support the parallelism of *bryt* || *twrt*, as well as additional parallelisms between 25 and 26a. Josh. 24:26a certainly does not demonstrate a *textual* dependence upon Deut. 31:9. Furthermore, the antiquity of the festival tradition presupposed by Deut. 31:9-13 is misconstrued in the view which attempts to see these verses as late redactional material.[141]

To this discussion we may add the observation that the word *spr* in 26a does not itself support a late dating for the passage. The root *spr* is attested already in Ugaritic. What is more, in some cases *spr* is a technical term for a legal document.[142] What exactly is envisioned with respect to the "book" in Josh. 24:26 is not clear from the context.[143] In Ex. 18:16 we encounter *'t-ḥqy h'lhym w't-twrtyw*, cf.

the basis of the LXX is textually questionable and probably is a poetic expansion of the original composition.

[138]Sperling, "Joshua 24," 132.

[139]Cf. the discussion in 2.3.7.2. As a result of his lengthy treatment of this topic, Lohfink concludes with respect to *spr twrt 'lhym*, "Diese Formulierung ist vor Neh 8,18 einmalig und sicher nicht auf die deuteronomistische Überarbeitung zurückzuführen, falls in diesem Kapitel eine solche vorliegt. Sie kann damit vorexilisch, ja sogar sehr alt sein. Die Ausdruck *spr htwrh* taucht hier in gleichem Kontext auf wie *spr hbryt* in Ex. 24 und 2 Kö 23" ("Bundesurkunde," 287). It is regrettable that the discussion by Nelson seems to be unaware of Josh. 24:26 ("Josiah in the Book of Joshua," *JBL* 100 [1981] 531-540).

[140]In addition to the references in the previous footnotes, consider the manner in which it is dismissed by Butler, *Joshua*, 277.

[141]Halbe is rightly critical of the manner in which the evidence from the Psalms is ignored by Perlitt in his attempt to maintain Alt's position (Halbe, *Privilegrecht*, 336-338).

[142]Cf. B.Kienast, "Rechtsurkunden in ugaritischer Sprache," *UF* 11 (1979) 445.

[143]It has been suggested that the words of the law were written on the stone in a manner similar to what was prescribed in Deut. 27:2-8 (cf. L'Hour, "L'alliance de Sichem," 30). However, the text itself gives little support to this theory, cf. Soggin, *Joshua*, 240. See too Boling, *Joshua*, 540.

vs.20 LXX. The issue here is the *špṭ* on the *dbrym*. Therefore, it is by no means excluded that we have to read *twrt* in Josh. 24:26 as a *plural*, and that the *spr* was an existing scroll with legal decisions on religious matters. Accordingly, we note the similarity of Josh. 24:25 with Ex. 15:25, and Josh. 24:26 with Ex. 18:16,20. This is of considerable importance because already von Rad argued, essentially upon the basis of Ex. 15:25; 18:16,20, for a Kadesh tradition of sacral law independent from the Sinaitic law.[144]

However, it is impossible to associate Josh. 24:25f. with a Kadesh tradition at the exclusion of the Sinaitic law. For example, another important parallel for the present discussion is found in Ex. 34:27, which also appears to be narrative poetry.

| | |
|---|---|
| *wy'mr yhwh 'l-mšh* [*5*] | And Yahweh said to Moses, |
| *ktb-lk 't-hdbrym h'lh* [*2*] | "Write for yourself these words. |
| *ky 'l-py hdbrym h'lh* [*7*] | For in accord with these words |
| *krty 'tk bryt* [*8*] | I cut a covenant with you |
| *w't-yśr'l* [*1*] | and with Israel." |

Here, as in Josh. 24:25f., the actions of writing and of "cutting a covenant" are placed parallel to each other, adding one more piece of evidence for the close affinity of Josh. 24:25f. to the Sinaitic covenant as described in Ex. 34.[145] Contrary to the opinion of Floss,[146] there is nothing awkward or out of place in the manner in which vs.26a connects with vs.25. The technical use of *dbrym* as covenant stipulations has been amply documented.[147] In the present structure of the passage, *dbrym* progresses very naturally from the *ḥq wmšpṭ* of the preceding colon.[148] There remains no reason to perpetuate the theory which arose from 19th century presuppositions concerning the establishment of law in Israel that 24:26a is a late redaction.[149]

The idea that 24:26b is "a verse marked by antique and un-Dtistic

[144]Von Rad, *Problem of the Hexateuch*, 15.

[145]Cf. the discussion of *krt bryt l* above and cf. 5.3.4.

[146]Floss, *Jahwe dienen*, 346f.

[147]Cf. Kalluveettil, *Declaration and Covenant*, 32-34.

[148]W.L.Moran, "Review of K.Baltzer, *Bundesformular*," *Bibl* 43 (1962) 105.

[149]E.g., the opinion of Holzinger (*Josua*, 99), that the present reference could not be correct and must be a mechanical copying of Deut. 31:9 because the book of the law could not have been written so quickly: "Das Gesetzbuch kann er nicht so geschwind niederschreiben."

ideas"[150] has been alluded to above,[151] and it is not our intention to reiterate the previous discussion. It is not likely to be fortuitous that the present verse places *bspr twrt 'lhym* and *bmqdš yhwh* in external parallelism.[152] Both actions, namely the writing of the law and the setting of the stone, are appropriate to the ratification of the legal ceremony,[153] as has been demonstrated in comparison with ancient NE treaty documents.[154] The reference in 26b is generally acknowledged to fit the circumstance of vs.25 very well,[155] so there is finally no significant evidence for treating either 24:26a or 26b as a Dtistic redaction.[156]

### 4.2.2.3 Josh. 24:27

As in vs.26, scholars have long been inclined to attribute the present verse to at least two different hands. But once again the variety of combinations conceived of in the various detailed analyses is instructive, because it may provide a clue to the reason why recent scholars are satisfied merely to assert that the text must be heavily redacted and leave the matter at that. Holzinger suggested that 27a from *wy'mr* through *thyh-* was from E, *bnw* through *whyth* was from $JE^S$ (not $R^D$), and the final portion was again from E.[157] Steuernagel thought to divide the verse between $E^1$ and $E^2$, with *ky-hy' šm'* ... *'mnw* as a probable gloss.[158] According to Smend, 27a could be at-

[150] McCarthy, *Treaty and Covenant*, 223.

[151] Cf. the discussion in 2.3.7.2.

[152] The whole of Josh. 24:1-28 revolves around acceptance of Yahweh as the God of Israel. Within the liturgical dialogue this is brought to a climax in the confessions *ky yhwh 'lhynw* (17aA) and *ky-hw' 'lhynw* (18bC). Similarly, 24:1f. collocates the reference to Israel gathering *lpny h'lhym* and the message on behalf of *yhwh 'lhy yśr'l*.

[153] A comparison with Ex. 24:4 is correctly stressed by A.González ("El Rito de la Alianza," *EstBib* 24 [1965] 217-238, esp. 219, 226, 232, 233).

[154] Cf. Baltzer, *Bundesformular*, 36.

[155] "Daher spricht nichts dagegen, auch v 26b zum Kontext vv 1ab*B*. 25 zu rechnen" (Floss, *Jahwe dienen*, 347).

[156] Additional evidence that the ceremony ending in the *mqdš yhwh* cannot be considered Dtistic is offered in our discussion of Deut. 11:29-31 and ch.27 (see 5.3.2).

[157] Holzinger, *Josua*, xxi, 99. Apparently Mölle is inclined to agree with this division of the verse, cf. his *Landtag*, 102-105, 113, 298.

[158] Steuernagel, *Josua*, 242, 245. He does not bother to explain why someone would later add that the stone "heard" the words of Yahweh, an element which most commentators agree must be archaic.

tributed to J[1] and 27b to J[2].[159] Eissfeldt appealed to 27a as evidence for L, and attributed 27b to E.[160] In 1930 Noth was content to attribute 27a to J and 27b to E.[161] For Möhlenbrink the duplicity of the verse was sufficient reason to divide it between his "Jahwerede" and "Josuarede."[162] Rudolph assigned 27a to J and left the origin of 27b open.[163] Hölscher attributes 27a to E[1] and 27b to a Dtistic addition by Rp.[164] Nielsen attributes 27a to ancient tradition and 27b to Dtic redaction.[165] Perlitt finally attributes the entire verse to the Dtic fiction of vss.25-28,[166] while McCarthy designates the verse in its entirety as ancient tradition.[167] We need not belabor the matter by adding to this caleidoscopic picture with other possible combinations. The fact is that previous literary-critical approaches have not known what to do with the present verse.

A defensible analysis of vs.27 must meet two related criteria. First, it must determine whether the verse is to be treated as a unity or a compilation from sources. Second, it must ask whether the relationship to the context argues for an original cohesion with the surrounding verses. In other words, does the diction and content posit convincing reasons to attribute the verse in whole or in part to a hand other than that of the preceding and following verses?

With respect to the unity of the verse, the preceding documentation of source-critical approaches demonstrates the 27a and 27b have most often been attributed to different sources. The uncritical criterion for this was the presupposition that parallel expressions must derive from parallel sources. But the preceding analysis of poetic structure suggests that this is false. The expressions *thyh-bnw l'dh* and *whyth bkm l'dh* may be accepted as external poetic parallelism, which offers no support for the theory of variant traditions now spliced together.[168] This eliminates the most important criterion

[159]Smend, *Erzählung des Hexateuch*, 336, 339.

[160]Eissfeldt, *Hexateuch-Synopse*, 80.

[161]Noth, *Das System*, 137.

[162]Möhlenbrink, "Landnahmesagen," 252.

[163]Rudolph, *Der "Elohist"*, 248.

[164]Hölscher, *Geschichtsschreibung*, 350.

[165]Nielsen, *Shechem*, 109f.; cf. L'Hour, "L'alliance de Sichem," 33f. (27b *pn-tkḥšwn* is post-exilic); Schmitt, *Landtag*, 21.

[166]Perlitt, *Bundestheologie*, 241f., 263, 266f., 273.

[167]McCarthy, *Treaty and Covenant*, 221, 223.

[168]For a comparison of the grammatical construction with references in Genesis cf. 2.3.7.2..

for previous source-critical divisions of vs.27. However, this does not yet entirely eliminate the hypothetical possibility that in the colometric structure delineated above the bicolon of 27cA-B *whyth bkm l'dh / pn-tkḥšwn b'lhykm* could be a deliberate expansion of the previous emphasis upon the stone as witness. In such a case, it would not be simply a later gloss but rather a deliberate expansion in conscious poetic parallelism for the purpose of an added nuance with respect to the role of the stone as witness; but this theory is not very likely.[169]

If L'Hour is correct, the phrase *pn-tkḥšwn* is post-exilic and is intended to take emphasis away from the stone as a witness.[170] But L'Hour's analysis of the expression is inadequate. He correctly notes that the expression is neither Dtic nor Dtistic.[171] But to stress the correlation with *'lhym* in Isa. 59:13; Job 31:28; Prov. 30:9 (as texts which are "certainment postexiliques") and Jer. 5:12 ("date indécise"),[172] while ignoring the rest of the references where the verb is found, is methodologically unsound.[173] It is not justifiable to ignore the use of the root *kḥš* in the Pentateuch, the Psalms and other prophetic material for the present analysis.[174]

The expression *pn-tkḥšwn* is not an afterthought added to modify the previous emphasis. The verb form is a Piel imperfect indicative with a *nun paragogicum*, and grammatically there is little to com-

[169]Cf. D.R.Daniels, "Is There a 'Prophetic Lawsuit' Genre," *ZAW* 99 (1987) 339-360, esp. 357-360, where it is argued that the use of stones and pillars for witnesses, as found in Josh. 24:25-27; Ex. 24:3-8, is un-Dtistic.

[170]L'Hour, "L'alliance de Sichem," 34. Cf. Jaroš, *Sichem*, 148, 151.

[171]Neither the verb *kḥs* nor the noun of the same root occurs in Deuteronomy other than in the poetic reference of 33:29. In Joshua–2 Kings the root is attested in Josh. 7:11; 24:27; 2 Sam. 22:45 (poetry); 1 Kgs 13:18.

[172]L'Hour, "L'alliance de Sichem," 34 n.157.

[173]Schmitt (*Landtag*, 21f.) is rightly skeptical.

[174]It is significant that Hos. 4:2 uses the verb in the context of a covenant lawsuit. The two bicola verses of Isa. 30:9, *ky-'m mry hw' / bnym kḥšym*, and *bnym l'-'bw šmw' / twrt yhwh*, also provide an example of the connection of *kḥš* with Yahweh's law. (Cf. the usage in Gen. 18:15, and esp. Josh. 7:11; and note a possible parallelism in Ps. 81:16 *mśn'y yhwh || ykḥšw-lw*.) See further Lipiński's discussion of the verb *kḥš* in the Niphal and Hithpael forms followed by the preposition *l*, "Dans l'usage de la langue, cette expression évoquait l'attitude des vassaux et des courtisans s'efforçant de s'attirer la bienveillance du prince par leurs paroles louangeuses" (*La royauté de Yahwé dans la poésie et le culte de l'ancien Israël*, 2nd ed. [Brussels, 1968], 237 n.3). In Josh. 24:27 the attitude of the people against their God is described similarly in an active form with a Piel and the preposition *b*.

mend the opinion that it is a gloss, as is evident from the study of Hoftijzer.[175] As is seen from Hos. 4:2, the use of *kḥš* within a prophetic lawsuit is appropriate. In Hos. 4:1 the *ryb* begins with the injunction *šmʿ dbr-yhwh*, which may be compared to the emphasis in Josh. 24:27 that the stone is a witness to the covenant because it heard[176] all the words of Yahweh.[177] And, as Gibson has indicated,[178] the verb *kḥš* in the Piel may be compared with *yšqr* in biblical and extra-biblical covenants or treaties. There are therefore no grounds for considering *pn-tkḥšwn* to be a secondary modification of the role of the stone as a witness to the covenant. If anything, it calls extra attention and emphasis to the stone rather than rendering it innocuous, as L'Hour and Jaroš have attempted to argue. Since *pn-tkḥšwn* cannot be considered Dtic or Dtistic, and since the present verse is both internally coherent and fits its entire context well, there is no reason to allege that Josh. 24:27 bears marks of later redaction. The entire verse may be accepted as part of the original composition.

### 4.2.2.4 Josh. 24:28

Josh. 24:28 contains little terminology of particular importance for a literary-critical analysis.[179] The noun *nḥlh* is often considered to be primarily found in Dtistic texts, but the analysis of the LXX demonstrates that the present reference in the MT is not original. Its presence here seems to indicate a substitution in terminology based upon the parallel in Judges.[180] As such it is evidence for later redaction

[175]Cf. Hoftijzer, *Function and Use*, 29f., 108 n.153. Note that Hoftijzer's study shows that the use of the *nun paragogicum* often entails an element of contrastivity, which might be important with respect to the identification of strophic division here, cf. vs.15b.

[176]Cf. Judg. 11:10f., where Yahweh is witness to the contract between Jephthah and the elders, and the words are spoken "*lpny yhwh bmzph.*" See also Sheriffs, "Phrases *ina IGI DN*," 58f.

[177]*ky-hy' šmʿh 't kl-'mry yhwh 'šr dbr ʿmnw.* Cf. the discussion of *'mr* in 2.3.7.2, and note in particular the distribution of *'ēmêr* and *'imᵉrāh* in archaic poetry, namely Gen. 4:23; 49:21; Num. 24:4,16; Deut. 32:1,2; 33:9; Judg. 5:29; 2 Sam. 22:31, and nowhere else in Genesis–2 Kings.

[178]Gibson, *Semitic Inscriptions*, 2:38.

[179]Regarding the use of *'yš* in apposition to *hʿm* cf. the notes on internal parallelism in the structural analysis above.

[180]See the discussion of the LXX above, as well as the comparison of Josh. 24:28 with Judg. 2:6 and 1 Sam. 10:25 below.

and *not* Dtistic composition.[181] In our opinion it does not belong to the original poem. Use of the verb *šlḥ* at the dispersal of the covenant gathering is attested similarly elsewhere in the OT.[182]

## 4.3 The historical summary in Josh. 24:2-13

In the preceding discussion, it has been demonstrated that in the narrative setting sketched in 24:1,25-28 there is, contrary to the claims of many previous literary-critical analyses, little evidence of Dtic editing or redacting. While there is a certain congruence of emphasis upon covenant and law as found here and in Deuteronomy, a close analysis of terminology suggests that the present account was written independent from significant influence from so-called Dtistic vocabulary. Furthermore, the content of vs.27 argues against Dtic influence in these verses. This is reinforced by the fact that the present form of the text is a well-formed poetic unit which makes it virtually impossible to divide the present text into ancient tradition and later redaction.

It now remains to investigate whether the same holds true for the dialogical interaction spanning vss.2-24. It has been shown in the structural analysis above that II.i-iv (vss.14-24) was likely influenced by liturgical considerations. This is a plausible explanation of the precise strophic delineation employing the confessional refrain built on the verb *n'bd* in four successive canticles. We may presuppose that a liturgical text to some extent was a dynamic and living text. However, the degree to which such a passage could be modified, expanded, contracted or redacted is open to question. Our analysis of the variations between the LXX and the MT brought the conclusion that until a very late date minor changes in emphasis and nuance could be "actualized" in the text without changing the basic structure or content of its message. It is likely that in the earlier stages of transmission there also was some flexibility with respect to diction, establishment of parallelisms, and updating of older language by replacement with more modern diction.

[181]Contra Perlitt, ***Bundestheologie***, 266, esp. n.2.

[182]Kalluveettil, *Declaration and Covenant*, 200f. (re Gen. 26:29, 31; 2 Sam. 3:21-23; 1 Kgs 20:34b). Cf. already Brekelmans, "Exodus xviii," 223: "The stories of the covenant-making in the Book of Genesis all conclude in generally the same way, saying that each of the partners went home."

On the other hand, it would be premature to suggest that the entire dialogue is a liturgical creation inserted into the historical setting at a later point in time. For example, vs.22 has been seen to have the same legal format as Ruth 4:9-11 and 1 Sam. 12:5. A comparison with 1 Sam. 12:5 shows how well it fits the covenant context and setting, and there can be little doubt that this verse was original to the narrative.[183] Opinions have differed radically with respect to whether vss.2-24 are liturgical. Evidence has been adduced above to suggest that there can be little doubt about an affirmative answer in vss.14-24. It is more difficult to provide a definitive answer in vss.2-13. Is the so-called "credo" liturgical? Many scholars have asserted that it is. Weiser appeals to Josh. 24:2ff. as an example of "die liturgische Rekapitulation der heilsgeschichtlichen Tradition im Rahmen des Jahwefestes...."[184] Others have categorically denied this claim.[185]

For the present purpose it is primarily important to refocus the matter of methodology. Perlitt argued that it was incorrect to assert that vss.1,25-28 are ancient and upon that basis to date vss.2-24 accordingly. In this respect we agree entirely. However, this does not entail that one can reverse the issue, suggest that the dialogue of vss.2-24 is parenesis, that the setting in vss.1,25-28 is fictional and therefore cannot be earlier than the parenesis for which it was created.[186] Perlitt's basic argument is that the narrative elements in vss.1,25-28 cannot stand alone; therefore the setting cannot be older than the speeches. The argument suffers from a number of weaknesses. Though this was not likely ever the case, the material in the setting of vss.1,25-28 *could* conceivably have stood alone. To be sure, it would then be a rather terse account of covenant making. A second possibility, however, which has been ignored by Perlitt, Van Seters and Nicholson, is that the original account did contain a dialogue, which during its history of transmission may have been edited and redacted upon occasion.[187]

[183]Further evidence is provided in our comparison with 1 Sam. 10:24 (see 5.5.1).

[184]Weiser, "Das Deboralied," 79. For additional examples consult 2.3.7.2.

[185]Perlitt, *Bundestheologie*, 244; T.L.Thompson, "Joseph and Moses," 164-166.

[186]Perlitt, *Bundestheologie*, 241; accepted by Van Seters ("Joshua 24," 150) and Nicholson (*His People*, 151-163).

[187]Various versions of this basic position were defended, for example, by Nielsen, Schmitt and McCarthy (see the summaries in ch.1).

## 4.3.1 The patriarchal period (24:2-4)

### 4.3.1.1 Josh. 24:2

The tone for Joshua's discourse is set by the phrase *kh-'mr yhwh 'lhy yśr'l*. Since this formula is of considerable importance for a correct interpretation of the passage, it warrants a detailed investigation. The OT messenger formulae have been treated in some detail in previous research,[188] and for the present purpose it will be necessary to supplement the implications of the previous studies in two areas. First, it is necessary to indicate the significance of the distribution of the exact formula *kh 'mr yhwh 'lhy yśr'l* throughout the OT.[189] Secondly, it is necessary to briefly note the relationship of the present usage in comparison to similar expressions in other ancient NE documents. In light of these two areas of study, and in view of certain clues produced by the specific context at hand, it is possible to ivestigate the implications deriving from the presence of this formula in Josh. 24:2.

The exact formula *kh-'mr yhwh 'lhy yśr'l* is found a total of thirty-two times.[190] It is reserved in the Pentateuch for Moses and Aaron,[191] and in Joshua for Joshua himself. The single occurrence in Judges is with an unknown prophet.[192] Thereafter in Samuel–Kings it is used in connection with Samuel, Nathan, Ahijah, Elijah, a young prophet sent by Elisha to anoint Jehu, Isaiah, "Yahweh's servants the prophets" and the prophetess Huldah. In the Prophets it is used only in connection with Isaiah and Jeremiah.[193] It is also instructive to focus upon the shorter phrase, *kh-'mr yhwh*. In the Pentateuch this is

[188]See especially the classic study of the "Botenspruch" by L.Köhler, *Deuterojesaja (Jesaja 40-55) stilkritisch untersucht* (Giessen, 1923), esp. 102-109; C.Westermann, *Grundformen prophetischer Rede*, 5th ed. (München, 1978) (does not treat Josh. 24:2); R.Rendtorff, "Botenformel und Botenspruch," *ZAW* 74 (1962) 165-177.

[189]For a previous study partially treating this concern see D.U.Rottzoll, "Die *KH 'MR*...–Legitimationsformel," *VT* 39 (1989) 323-340.

[190]It occurs in the following texts: Ex. 5:1; 32:27; Josh. 7:13; 24:2; Judg. 6:8; 1 Sam. 10:18; 2 Sam. 12:7; 1 Kgs 11:31; 14:7; 17:14; 2 Kgs 9:6; 19:20; 21:12; 22:15, 18 (= 2 Chron. 34:23,26); Isa. 37:21; Jer. 11:3; 13:12; 21:4; 23:2; 24:5; 25:15; 30:2; 32:36; 33:4; 34:2, 13; 37:7; 42:9; 45:2.

[191]In Ex. 9:1,13; 10:3 the variant formula *kh-'mr yhwh 'lhy h'brym* is found.

[192]See our discussion of Judg. 6:7-10 in 5.4.2.

[193]Note that in addition to the fourteen occurrences listed above there are thirty-four cases of *kh-'mr yhwh ṣb'wt 'lhy yśr'l* in Jeremiah, a combination not found elsewhere in the OT.

found exclusively in Exodus.[194] It does not occur in Joshua–Judges.[195]

On the basis of these statistics, it is possible to draw a number of significant conclusions. In the Pentateuch the formula is employed only in relationship to Moses (and Aaron, cf. Ex. 5:1) and only so in Exodus. In Joshua–Judges it occurs only in Josh. 7:13; 24:2 and Judg. 6:8. In the light of Perlitt's thesis that Josh. 24:2ff. is Dtic parenesis, it is important to investigate the connection between these texts and the other occurrences in both the Pentateuch and in 1 Samuel–2 Kings. From the outset it would appear that Perlitt's methodology is inadequate. He concludes that the messenger formula is simply a stylistic device;[196] without mentioning that it is used in Exodus with respect to Moses, and also in Josh. 7:13 in conjunction with Joshua, he classifies it as Dtistic on the basis of Judg. 6:8; 2 Kgs 22:15,18.[197] One could question the propriety of calling an expression Dtistic when it is not once found in Deuteronomy, though hypothetically it is of course possible that a "Dtistic school" might employ an expression not attested in the book which supposedly inspired it. But Perlitt has not demonstrated this to be the case in the present text, and the references in Exodus suggest otherwise.

A study of the present reference should begin with the parallel in Josh. 7:13. According to Noth, Dtr does not seem to have touched the Ai story of Josh. 7-8,[198] but this text is ignored by Perlitt even though it stands in the same book as Josh. 24:2 and should therefore be the first candidate for comparison.

As is demonstrated below,[199] Judg. 6:8 cannot legitimately be appealed to as evidence for a Dtic creation of this formula in Judges because Judg. 6:7-10 is dependent upon Josh. 24:2-24. This entails that, the only time the formula is found in Judges, it is borrowed from a previous source. 1 Sam. 10:18 must be seen in the same light

[194]Cf. Ex. 4:2; 7:17,26; 8:16; 9:1,13; 10:3; 11:4.

[195]In Samuel it is found in 1 Sam. 2:27; 15:2; 2 Sam. 7:5,8; 12:11,24; in Kings: 1 Kgs 12:24; 13:2, 21; 20:13,14,28,42; 21:19; 22:11,20; 2 Kgs 1:4,6,16; 2:21; 3:16, 17; 4:43; 7:1; 9:3,6,12; 19:6; 20:1,5; 22:16.

[196]Cf. Perlitt, *Bundestheologie*, 242.

[197]Perlitt, *Bundestheologie*, 250.

[198]Noth, *Überlieferungsgeschichtliche Studien*, 42: "In die Ai-Geschichte Jos.7.8 hat Dtr anscheinend so gut wie gar nicht eingegriffen;" Cf. more recently C.Begg, "The Function of Josh. 7, 1-8, 29 in the Deuteronomistic History," *Bibl* 67 (1986) 320-334.

[199]See 5.4.2.

since it in turn is literarily dependent upon Judg. 6:8.[200] 2 Sam. 12:7 has traditionally not been considered to be Dtistic,[201] though in more recent studies some voices are going in this direction.[202] Nevertheless, the study by J.Harvey, which demonstrates the close affinities of the present passage to the prophetic *ryb* pattern, cautions against the assertion that 2 Sam. 12:7-12 is a later insertion into the so-called succession narrative.[203]

The next occurrence of the formula *kh-'mr yhwh 'lhy yśr'l* is in 1 Kgs 11:31, which according to recent research is an original part of the Jeroboam narrative and is untouched by Dtic redaction.[204] This is followed by the reference in 14:7, again in a speech by the prophet Ahijah, concerning which opinions about Dtic redaction are divided. Noth originally argued that 14:1-18 continues a pre-Dtic Ahijah story,[205] but in his commentary[206] he views this part of vs.7 as a later redactional intrusion into the Ahijah narrative. Campbell disagrees and concludes, "The specifically dtr elements begin with v.8b, and no earlier."[207] In the literary-critical analysis of this passage by Seebass,[208] vs.7 is considered to be part of an ancient source. And if the conclusions by H.N.Wallace[209] can be sustained, the Hebrew *Vorlage* presupposed by the LXX in 3 Reg. 12:24g-n presents an older

[200]See 5.5.1.

[201]Cf. Rost, *Überlieferung von der Thronnachfolge*, 96.

[202]W.Dietrich argues for the hand of a Priestly redactor (DtrP) in 2 Sam. 12:1-14 (*Prophetie und Geschichte. Eine redaktionsgeschichtliche Untersuchung zum deuteronomistischen Geschichtswerk* [Göttingen, 1972], 127ff.). Apparently T.N.D.Mettinger agrees with this analysis (*King and Messiah: The Civil and Sacral Legitimation of the Israelite Kings* [Lund, 1976], 19f., 204).

[203]J.Harvey, *Le plaidoyer prophétique contre Israël après la rupture de l'alliance* (Montreal, 1967), 74f.

[204]H.Weippert, "Die Ätiologie des Nordreiches und seines Königshauses (1 Reg 11:29-40)," *ZAW* 95 (1983) 344-375, esp. 346-355. For extensive bibliography of previous studies recognizing that 11:31 is non-Dtistic see ibid, 344 n.3; Campbell, *Prophets and Kings*, 25. Cf. also Nelson, *Double Redaction*, 111f., 147 n.42.

[205]Noth, *Überlieferungsgeschichtliche Studien*, 81, 82.

[206]Noth, *Könige*, 311, 315.

[207]Campbell, *Prophets and Kings*, 33. Cf. Mettinger, *King and Messiah*, 165, 168; he interprets this portion as an original, prophetic oracle from Ahijah, who was from Northern extraction. Similarly, Mayes, *The Story of Israel*, 115.

[208]H.Seebass, "Tradition und Interpretation bei Jehu ben Chanani und Ahia von Silo," *VT* 25 (1975) 175-190, esp. 189.

[209]H.N.Wallace, "The Oracles against the Israelite Dynasties in 1 and 2 Kings," *Bibl* 67 (1986) 21-40.

account untouched by the Dtic historians.[210] This would agree with the explicit evidence suggested by 2 Chron. 9:29 that Ahijah left behind written accounts of his prophecy. Since the author of Chronicles was aware of the prophecy of Ahijah the Shilonite in a written source, presumably this material could also have been availabe to the author of 1 Kgs 14:1-18.[211] The reference in 1 Kgs 17:14 in connection with a prophetic utterance from Elijah is ordinarily accepted as original and not Dtistic,[212] so it is not necessary to pursue this reference further.

The formula *kh-'mr yhwh 'lhy yśr'l* occurs five times in 2 Kings. The first, in 9:6 at the anointing of Jehu, is thought by Noth to have originally been part of a prophetic cycle.[213] According to him, the narrative is only slightly altered by Dtr, and 9:6 is not listed among these minor hints of a later redactor. 2 Kgs 19:20 is parallel to Isa. 37:21 and cannot be considered the work of Dtr. This text provides us with another unambiguous example of the manner in which the compilers of Samuel and Kings employed prophetic oracles found in their sources; they did not themselves supply the formula *kh-'mr yhwh 'lhy yśr'l*.[214]

Also to be considered is 21:12, which is usually viewed as part of a late indictment of Manasseh.[215] This passage does indeed read like a late summary depicting the entire reign of Manasseh in retrospect, and it may have been compiled at the final stage of redaction of 1-2 Kgs. But that makes it all the more striking that in contrast to the preceding passages where *kh-'mr yhwh 'lhy yśr'l* is employed, here the summary message is recalled as the words of anonymous prophets.[216] And here too there are some clues that the prophetic indictment is based upon prophetic sources. The message of the measuring line is

[210]Wallace, "The Oracles," 28.

[211]Cf. 1 Chron. 29:29f.; 2 Chron. 12:15; 20:34; 24:27; 26:22; 27:7; 32:32, etc. There is little reason to doubt the accuracy of the claim that the writer used older prophetic sources which were contemporary with the actions described.

[212]Cf. H.Schmoldt, "Zwei 'Wiederaufnahmen' in I Reg 17," *ZAW* 97 (1985) 423-426 (includes bibliographical references).

[213]Noth, *Überlieferungsgeschichtliche Studien*, 80, 84.

[214]Note that 2 Kgs 18:9-20:19 is basically parallel to Isa. 36:1-39:8 (minus 38:9-20). In 2 Kgs 20:20 explicit reference is made to a source in which the deeds of Hezekiah were recorded, and 2 Chron. 32:32 claims a direct connection with the writing of these chronicles by Isaiah son of Amos.

[215]Nelson, *Double Redaction*, 43, 65f.; Mayes, *Story of Israel*, 11, 111.

[216]Cf. vs.10, *wydbr yhwh byd-'bdyw hnby'ym*.

reminiscent of prophecies in Isaiah[217] and Lamentations.[218] The diction in vss.12-15 is typical of a prophetic oracle and it contains poetic parallelism, which suggests that these verses, including the introductory formula, may have been borrowed from a prophetic source.[219]

The last two references are in 2 Kgs 22:15,18 in pronouncements by the prophetess Huldah. Opinions about the redaction history of 2 Kgs 22 vary immensely,[220] and it is impossible in the present context to enter the debate as to whether or not the Huldah oracles derive from a previous source or are a later fiction created to serve the flow of the Josiah narrative. It will suffice to note that the entire trend to this point has been that the *kh-'mr yhwh 'lhy yśr'l* formulas are not the creation of a Dtistic redactor. The opinions on 2 Kgs 22:15,18 are so diversified that it is precarious on the basis of these references to decide that Josh. 24:2 is a Dtistic, stylistic creation. A thorough analysis of the *kh-'mr yhwh 'lhy yśr'l* formula in Exodus–2 Kings suggests that Perlitt's appeal to 2 Kgs 22:15,18 to imply that Josh. 24:2 is Dtistic, is premature and unfounded. A cautious tabulation of the evidence suggests exactly the opposite.

It is also necessary to comment briefly upon the title *yhwh 'lhy yśr'l*, which is often thought to trace its earliest origins to an iden-

[217]Cf. Isa. 18:2,7; 28:10,13,17; 34:11,17.

[218]Cf. Lam. 2:8. The image of the measuring line is also used as a symbol of restoration and rebuilding in Jer. 31:39; Ezek. 47:3; Zech. 1:16. Other than 1 Kgs 7:23 (= 2 Chron. 4:2) and Job 38:5, the noun *qw* is found only in the Prophets.

[219]Weinfeld, on the basis of Jer. 19:3, considers "at which the two ears of him who hears of it shall tingle" (2 Kgs 21:12) to be phraseology of Dtr (*Deuteronomy*, 351). However, most important, a dependence upon Jer. 19:3 seems likely, cf. *hnny mby' r' h 'l-yrwšlm wyhwdh*, which could be a modification of *hnny mby' r' h 'l-hmqwm hzh*. Since the preceding part of Jer. 19:3 mentions Jerusalem and Judah, it was not repeated in 19:3b, but in 2 Kgs 21:12 the two places are substitued for *hmqwm hzh*. If this wording is borrowed from Jer. 19:3, we may have a ready explanation for why the prophetic source is kept anonymous in its application to the time of Manasseh. But 1 Sam. 3:11 suggests that it may have been a prophetic formula which did not belong to any particular school. If 2 Kgs 21:12 is taken from Jer. 19:3 or from another prophetic source, this would agree with what we have observed elsewhere in 1 Samuel–2 Kings. The compiler does not simply create a *kh-'mr yhwh 'lhy yśr'l* formula; where present it is either part of an original oracle intact in its present place in the historical narrative or is borrowed from prophetic tradition.

[220]Cf. E.Würthwein, "Die Josianische Reform und das Deuteronomium," *ZThK* 73 (1976) 395-423; W.Dietrich, "Josiah und das Gesetzbuch (2 Reg xxii)," *VT* 27 (1977) 13-35; M.Rose, "Bemerkungen zum historischen Fundament des Josia-Bildes in II Reg 22f.," *ZAW* 89 (1977) 50-63; N.Lohfink, "Zur neueren Diskussion uber 2 Kon 22-23," in Lohfink, ed., *Das Deuteronomium*, 24-48.

tification of the proper name *yhwh* with the archaic title *'l 'lhy yśr'l* found in Gen. 33:20.[221] It is of significance that this passage describes Jacob's altar-building precisely at Shechem,[222] in a passage which has deliberate literary connections with Josh. 24:1-28.[223] The designation *yhwh 'lhy yśr'l* is found in the archaic poetry of Judg. 5:3,5.[224] In the Pentateuch it is attested only in Exodus,[225] but in Joshua–2 Kings there are many examples of the combination. It occurs fourteen thimes in Joshua,[226] but not once is the combination *yhwh 'lhy yśr'l* found in the Deuteronomy.[227] This adds another argument against reading the formula *kh-'mr yhwh 'lhy yśr'l* in Josh. 24:2 as a Dtistic opening for the following speech.[228] Our study indicates that the use of the messenger formula in connection with a prophetic discourse is not employed indiscriminately.[229] Clearly, the use in Josh. 24:2 stands closer to terminology in Exodus than in Deuteronomy.

The covenant ceremony of Ex. 19:3ff. is similarly introduced by the poetic parallelism *kh t'mr lbyt y'qwb || wtgyd lbny yśr'l*.[230] After the opening lines, this passage introduces the main demand with *w'th*,

[221]On this title see Cross, *Canaanite Myth*, 11, 46. Baltzer considers *yhwh 'lhy yśr'l* to be a "feierlicher Titel" (*Bundesformular*, 29).

[222]A particular connection between *yhwh 'lhy yśr'l* and Shechem was suggested already by Steuernagel ("Jahwe, der Gott Israel," in *Fs J. Wellhausen* [Giessen, 1914], 331-349; *Jahwe und die Vätergotter*). The connection of *yhwh 'lhy yśr'l* with the title *'l 'lhy yśr'l* in Gen. 33:20 has been accepted by many OT scholars, cf. R.Rendtorff, "Der Kultus im Alten Israel," *JHL* 2 (1956) 1-21 (= *Gesammelte Studien zum Alten Testament* [München, 1975], 89-109); Beyerlin, *Herkunft und Geschichte*, 34f.; Seebass, *Der Erzvater*, 7, 11; Jaroš, *Sichem*, 146. The association receives support from the connection between Josh. 24:1-28 and Gen. 35:1-4.

[223]Cf. 5.3.1.

[224]Cf. *'lhym 'lhy yśr'l* in the Elohistic psalter in Ps. 68:9(8); 72:18; cf. 41:14; 106:48.

[225]Cf. Ex. 5:1; 32:27; 34:23.

[226]Josh. 7:13, 19, 20; 8:30; 9:18,19; 10:40, 42; 13:14, 33; 14:14; 22:24; 24:2,23.

[227]This makes it all the more significant that in Josh. 8:30 this identification is used at the covenant ceremony at Mt. Ebal and Mt. Gerizim in fulfilment of the prescription of Deut. 11:29; 27:1-8.

[228]The title *yhwh 'lhy yśr'l* is used frequently in Joshua, and its presence is not restricted to the messenger formula. By contrast, in Jeremiah, for example, the title *yhwh 'lhy yśr'l* is never used outside of a *kh-'mr* formula.

[229]This is also true of other slight variations. E.g., in Egypt Yahweh is identified three times in a *kh-'mr* formula as *'lhy h'brym*, cf. Ex. 9:1,13; 10:3; this full formula is found only in these three texts, but cf. 3:18; 5:3; 7:16 (*'lhy h'brym*).

[230]Freedman, "Epic Traditions," 21f. For a comparison of Ex. 19:3-8 and Josh. 24:2ff. see Muilenburg, "Form and Structure," 351-365; Buis, "Les formulaires d'alliance," 396-411; McCarthy, *Covenant and Treaty*, 272. See also 5.3.4.

thereby providing a clear example from Exodus of the use of the messenger formula in the context of law and covenant in a manner directly parallel to Josh. 24:2.[231] The provenience of the formula in Josh. 24:2 finds a more probable explanation in connection with a covenant ritual, as attested already in Exodus, than in an alleged stylistic device by an author or redactor with a Dtistic predilection for parenesis.

It may be helpful to also recall the connection of the OT prophetic messenger formulae to various examples in extra-biblical contexts.[232] For an analysis of Josh. 24:2 the most important comparison is with the style of the treaties, which reveal a set pattern:

1) **Opening formula**: *umma* PN + titles "Thus (speaks king) PN + titles"[233]
2) **Historical prologue**
3) **Stipulations** introduced by *anumma* or *inanna* "now"

Examples of this pattern are found in the treaties between Hittite and Ugaritic kings.[234] Moreover, the same pattern is present in the speeches of Ramses II in the Literary Record of the Battle of Kadesh. These speeches clearly presuppose vassal treaties between Egyptian kings and their Canaanite subjects. Several elements are of particular interest, e.g., the loyalty oath, the recognition of the king as personal suzerain, the obligations of the vassal, and the permission to live on property of the Pharaoh. Also interesting are the explicit references to the past which serve to demonstrate the disloyalty of the vassals.[235]

In the light of this treaty pattern, it is significant that our structural analysis revealed that Josh. 24:1 provides the narrative setting

[231]Kalluveetill, *Declaration and Covenant*, 115.

[232]Cf. already Korošec, *Hethitische Staatserträge*, 12; Muilenburg, "Form and Structure," 354; Baltzer, *Bundesformular*, 29 n.3.; S.E.Loewenstamm, "On Stylistic Patterns in Biblical and Ugaritic Literatures: Mission and Letter Formulae in Ugaritic Literature," in *Comparative Studies* 256-261 (= *Lĕšonénu* 32 [1968] 27-35 [Hebrew]).

[233]See on this formula E.von Schuler, "Die Einleitung der 'Autobiographie' Ḫattušilis," in J.Tischler, ed., *Serta Indogermanica* (Fs G.Neumann; Innsbruck, 1982), 392ff.

[234]J.Nougayrol, *Le palais royal d'Ugarit IV* (Mission de Ras Shamra, IX) (Paris, 1956), 29ff.; E.von Schuler, "Vertrag zwischen Suppiluliuma I. und Niqmaddu II. von Ugarit," *TUAT*, I/2, 131-134; G.F.del Monte, *Il trattato fra Muršili II di Ḫattuša e Niqmepa' di Ugarit* (Roma, 1986).

[235]See the discussion by S.Morschauser, in H.Goedicke, ed., *Perspectives on the Battle of Kadesh* (Baltimore, 1985), 123-206.

for the gathering. This is followed by four canticles (vss.2-13), introduced by the opening formula *kh 'mr* + DN + title, followed by the historical prologue, leading to *w'th* "now" in vs.14, which introduces the demands of the speaker. The wording of vs.2a is therefore essential not only as a standard formula, but as part of the treaty pattern reflected in vss.2-13 and continuing with the imperatives in vss.14ff. as well. This shows that the assertion by Perlitt that the formula does not have a proper ending is incorrect. He states "aber sie endet ohne förmliche Ausleitung und auch inhaltliche so unvermittelt, dass die Botenformel am Anfang als ein blosses Stilmittel erscheint."[236] Perlitt thinks that the *w'th* of vs.14 comes too late for a messenger formula,[237] but this argument is hardly convincing in light of the treaty pattern as well as other extra-biblical evidence. McCarthy has already called attention to a parallel from c. 18th cent. B.C. Mari, where "a prophet opens with *umma* and continues with an 'historical prologue' and conditional blessing and curse, for all the world like a treaty."[238] McCarthy notes that the opening formula is at home in prophetic usage as well as royal decrees, including treaties.[239] It is therefore probably not necessary to ask whether the present formula is a prophetic messenger formula *or* a "treaty" proclamation.[240] To posit an either/or distinction places an unnatural form-critical restriction upon the present text. It is better to see the present example as a formula comparable to the prophetic formulae in the OT, which is at the same time analogous here to the introduction of the suzerain in a treaty context. Josh. 24:1-28 borrows heavily from the treaty form, but the author is free to structure the entire canto II in accordance with the specific emphasis of Israel's choice to serve Yahweh alone. Kalluveettil lists a number of OT texts which revolve around the concept of a loyalty oath and the recognition of kingship.[241] There are persistent clues in Josh. 24:1-28 to suggest that these concerns are also central to the present passage.

[236]Perlitt, *Bundestheologie*, 242.
[237]Perlitt, *Bundestheologie*, 242.
[238]McCarthy, *Treaty and Covenant*, 224 n.23. See too Kalluveettil, *Declaration and Covenant*, 145.
[239]His conclusion is therefore in line with a thought expressed earlier by L'Hour ("L'alliance de Sichem," 7): "Il serait intéressant d'étudier dans quelle mesure cette ouverture reflète ou non la fonction du héraut royal."
[240]Cf. Moran, *Bibl* 43 (1962) 105.
[241]Kalluveettil, *Declaration and Covenant*, 147-152.

As is stressed in previous studies comparing Josh. 24:2-13 with treaty prologues, the historical summary begins in vs.2b in a manner typical of the ancient NE documents where it is usual to sketch the antecedent relationship between two parties. It is not exclusively in the context of a treaty that antecedent history was recounted. It was typical in ancient NE documents to identify the speaker by means of a short introduction to his previous history.[242]

In comparison with Josh. 24:2b, however, it is significant that in several treaties from the LBA the historical prologue starts with a reference to the fathers.[243] In ch.2 we noted that a close parallel to the present text is found in the Mesha inscription, *w'š gd yšb b'rṣ 'ṭrt m'lm*. This citation from Mesha, along with the realization that *'br hnhr*[244] was a relative geographical designation employed not only in Hebrew texts but Akkadian as well[245] is sufficient to cast doubt upon the correctness of Perlitt's understanding of the opening words in the historical summary.[246] The enigma of the reference *b'br hnhr* disappears once it is recognized that the threefold use of this expression in vss.2,3,15 is motivated in part by the structural responsion that it forms with *b'br hyrdn* (vss.8,14).

The term *m'wlm* has at times been treated artificially in both Josh. 24:2 and the Mesha inscription. A statement by Weippert with respect to Israel's claims about the settlement of Canaan is a prime example.[247] The term *m'wlm* sometimes only means "from

[242]Cf., e.g., the introductions in the Mesha and Kilamuwa inscriptions. Many other examples could be added.

[243]Nougayrol, *Le palais royal, IV*, 35 (RS 17.132:8), 88 (RS 17.353:2); Statue of Idrimi, lines 45-53, cf. M.Dietrich–O.Loretz, "Die Inschrift der Statue des Königs Idrimi von Alalaḫ," *UF* 13 (1981) 199-269, esp. 205, 217.

[244]Cf. J.P.U.Lilley, "By the River-Side," *VT* 28 (1978) 165-171.

[245]E.g., M.Weippert, "Menahem von Israel und seine Zeitgenossen in einer Steleninschrift des assyrischen Königs Tiglathpileser III. aus dem Iran," *ZDPV* 89 (1973) 29f.

[246]The interpretation of Nicholson (*His People*, 160), that the reference to gods "beyond the river" is an allusion to gods in the period of the exile, is virtually an allegorical reading of the passage and does not commend itself any more than does Perlitt's theory of veiled allusions from a Yahwistic movement during the time of Assyrian rule (his possibility 1, *Bundestheologie*, 274-276)—concerning which Nicholson thinks "reserve is surely justified" (160)—or McCarthy's theory of Aramean gods in the time of the Omride dynasty (*Treaty and Covenant*, 283)—which Nicholson judges to be "untenable" (158).

[247]He cites the reference from Mesha and concludes, "For the Israelite with even a little knowledge of history, this piece of information must have been quite surprising.

long ago."[248] The prophet Amos can refer to the days of David from a couple of centuries earlier as "the days of old," *kymy 'wlm.*[249] The present reference has the intention of summarizing the relationship between Yahweh and Israel as that traces back in ancient memory.[250] It is significant to note in this connection that the historical prologue of several treaties found in Ugarit contain the phrase *ultu labirti* "since times long past."[251]

It has been repeatedly noted that "Terah, father of Abraham and father of Nahor" does not agree grammatically with the plural verb *yšbw.*[252] This construction is sometimes explained as a gloss which attempts to exculpate Abram from such worship, showing that it was actually his father Terah that was intended.[253] This is indeed possible, but the assertion of a gloss may in fact not be necessary. The colon *trḥ 'by 'brhm w'by nḥr* reads like an excerpt from a geneaology. For example, in Gen. 11:29 we read *mlkh bt-hrn 'by mlkh w'by yskh.* It is striking that this too is in the genealogy of Terah.[254] Similarly, in 1 Chron. 2:49 is found *'t-šw' 'by mkbnh w'by gb'.* In short, it is possible that at the time of composition the excerpt *trḥ 'by 'brhm w'by nḥr* was intended to place the reference to the *'bwtykm* within its proper chronological period. In that case, the fact that the verb *yšbw* agrees with "fathers" and not with Terah is of minor relevance. The authenticity of this colon finds additional support from the poetic parallelism of *'bwtykm* || *'by* (2x). Finally, it is possible that the

If the Bible may be considered indicative, the Israelites never claimed that they had resided in their land *m'wlm*, from time immemorial. Instead, they were convinced that they had take possession of it at a certain point in history via difficult struggles with the previous inhabitants and through the assistance of their God" (Weippert, "The Israelite 'Conquest'," 15.

[248]Cf. E.Jenni, *Das Wort 'ōlām im Alten Testament* (Berlin, 1953), 29: "Auch hier wie sonst immer ist *'wlm* ein Grenzbegriff. *m'wlm* bezeichnet den äussersten denkbaren terminus a quo. ... Bei einem Verbum ist ein rein adverbieller Ausdruck vorzuziehen: 'seit jeher' (Mesa 10, Jos 24,2)."

[249]Cf. also in poetry Deut. 32:7; Ps. 25:6; Isa. 42:14; 57:11, etc.

[250]Cf. J.Barr, *Biblical Words for Time* (London, 1962), 70.

[251]Nougayrol, *Le palais royal, IV*, 64 (RS 17.237:12), 71 (RS 17.335:3), 77 (RS 17.368:8), 80 (RS 17. 382:3). Cf. M.Tawil, "Some Literary Elements in the Opening Sections of the Hadad, Zākir, and the Nērab II Inscriptions in the Light of East and West Semitic Royal Inscriptions," *Or* 43 (1974) 40-65, esp. 42 n.10.

[252]E.g., Steuernagel, *Josua*, 242 ("ist wohl Zusatz nach Gen 11.27ff."); Noth, *Das System*, 139.

[253]Cf. Giblin, "Structural Patterns," 56.

[254]Cf. Gen. 11:27.

etymology of the name "Terah" was recognized as illustrative of the assertion in the same context that the fathers served other gods,[255] and the name Nahor might make an association with a place "*b'br hnhr*."[256] It is significant that when Jacob made a treaty with Laban he appealed to the "God of Abraham and the God of Nahor" as judges in the role of witnesses.[257] Eissfeldt is justified in asserting that this verse originally referred to more than one god.[258] The narrator of this entire account plays very deliberately upon the Aramaic background of the patriarchs.[259] By comparison, it would certainly not be too subtle for the author of Josh. 24:2 to include an excerpt from a genealogy including Terah, Abraham and Nahor in order to make a connection with the reminiscence of worship of other gods beyond the river in the time of the patriarchs.[260]

The final clause of vs.2, *wy'bdw 'lhym 'ḥrym*, has sometimes been thought to be Dtic, but a couple of factors caution against such a conclusion. Weinfeld argues that *'lhym 'ḥrym* is a neutral phrase which "cannot be considered specifically deuteronomic."[261] Nielsen notes that the term "other gods" occurs in the decalogue (Ex. 20:3; Deut. 5:7) and otherwise primarily in Northern traditions.[262] Close paral-

[255]The name Terah is thought to be a theophoric representation of the moon god Waraḫ; cf. J.B.Segal, "The Hebrew Festival and the Calendar," *JSS* 6 (1961) 76; J.C.L.Gibson, "Light from Mari on the Patriarchs," *JSS* 7 (1962) 58; E.M.Yamauchi, *The Stones and the Scriptures* (Philadelphia, 1972), 37; de Vaux, *Early History*, 191. Others, however, are inclined to posit a connection with Akkad. *turaḫu* "ibex" (L.Hicks, *IDB*, 4:574).

[256]The name Nahor has often connected by with the town *Naḫur* of the Mari letters; cf. Gibson, "Light from Mari," 54 n.1.

[257]Cf. Gen. 31:53.

[258]Eissfeldt, "El and Yahweh," 32. He correctly calls attention to the plural form of the verb *yšpṭw*, obscured in the LXX.

[259]E.g., in the respective terms used by Laban and Jacob to refer to the stone-heap of witness, *ygr śhdwt'* and *gl'd*; cf. Garcia-Treto, "Genesis 31:44," 13-17; Cross, *Canaanite Myth*, 269; Kalluveettil, *Declaration and Covenant*, 30.

[260]In light of the present emphasis upon the fathers, it is worth noting that one of the main ingredients of Canaanite religion was the worship of forefathers as gods, cf. de Moor, "The Ancestral Cult in KTU 1.17:I.26-28," *UF* 17 (1986) 407-409. It is possible that Terah himself became the object of such veneration, cf. K.Spronk, *Beatific Afterlife in Ancient Israel and in the Ancient Near East* (Neukirchen-Vluyn, 1986), 193 n.3.

[261]Weinfeld, *Deuteronomy*, 2.

[262]Nielsen, *Shechem*, 46f. For an extensive discussion of this phrase see, with reservations, A.Alghisi, "L'espressione 'altri dèi' nella fraseologia deuteronomistica," *RivBiblIt* 33 (1985) 135-163, 263-290.

lels to the present colon are found in Deut. 29:25 (26)[263] and 1 Sam. 8:8.[264] But it is hardly possible on this basis to argue that the presence of *'lhym 'ḥrym* in Josh. 24:2 shows Dtic influence. The essence of Deut. 29:25-26 is presupposed already in Ex. 34:10,14f., references which are of considerable importance for our present analysis. With respect to 34:14a Halbe notes,"Die Altertümlichkeit des Singulars *'l 'ḥr* is nicht zu bezweifeln."[265] Halbe also notes that the plural form is especially prevalent in Dtic–Dtistic texts, but as exceptions he lists Ex. 20:3; 23:13; Josh. 24:2,16; Judg. 10:13; 1 Sam. 8:8; 26:19; 2 Kgs 22:17; Hos. 3:1.[266] It is not possible to discuss all these texts, but a few observations are imperative. Halbe has correctly recognized that the concept of worshipping foreign gods as a primary theme in Joshua–2 Kings cannot be simply attributed to Dtic influence. And in Hos. 3:1 the parallelism formed by the expressions "turn to other gods" and "love cakes of raisins" seems to imply a festival in which the Israelites were worshipping other gods.[267] It is generally acknowledged that Hosea knew the decalogue,[268] which is significant because of the prohibition in Ex. 20:2. Hosea is composed to a large degree around the theme of true worship of Yahweh. Presupposed is the possibility of true worship within the prescribed cultic festivals. And 3:1 indicts Israel for worship of false gods, presumably also in their festivals. Comparison with Am. 5:25f. is also instructive, for there too Israel is condemned for the ritual worship of other gods.

[263]This connection is all the more significant because of the similar list of leaders mentioned in 29:10, the reference to the exodus in 29:16, etc.

[264]Note that here, as in Josh. 24:20, the worship of false gods is synonymous with abandoning (*'zb*) Yahweh.

[265]Halbe, *Privilegrecht*, 119.

[266]Halbe, *Privilegrecht*, 119 n.65.

[267]The connection with a cultic feast is noted by Mays, (*Hosea*, 57), with reference to 2 Sam. 6:19. Here the whole procession with the ark does indeed bear many resemblances to the cultic festivals of other peoples; e.g., in the Hittite KI.LAM festival there is a description of a procession strikingly similar to that in 2 Sam. 6, including ox-drawn carts accompanied by musicians, naked dancers, sacrifice and distribution of food (cf. Singer, *The Hittite KI.LAM Festival*, 1:56-80). Various types of bread or cakes played a prominent role in the Hittite rituals (cf. Otten, *Ein hethitisches Festritual*, 2-17, 30, 39). The same was true in Ugaritic (cf. de Moor, *The Seasonal Pattern*, 61; *New Year*, 1:9f., 14). See further Jer. 7:18; 44:19; Isa. 16:7 (cf. Wildberger, *Jesaja*, 625). Mention may also be made in this respect of the covenantal and sacrificial meal in the OT as well as other ancient NE contexts, cf. McCarthy, "Three Covenants in Genesis," 184f.

[268]Wolff, *Hosea*, 74 (calling attention to 12:10; 13:4; 4:2).

Finally, the connection between *'l 'ḥr* in Ex. 34:14 and the liturgical reference to *'l nkr* in Ps. 81:10 is of considerable importance[269] because of the numerous parallels between Josh. 24:1-28, Ps. 81,[270] and passages such as Judg. 10:6-16 and 1 Sam. 7:3-17. The expression *'lhy nkr* is atypical of Deuteronomy,[271] but in the macrostructure of Josh. 24 it is employed in vss.20,23 in the same manner as *'lhym 'ḥrym* in vss.2,16. Similarly, Judg. 10:13,16 uses both phrases. In the light of all these considerations, it is quite plausible that both expressions, *'lhym 'ḥrym* and *'lhy nkr*, date back to usage in the cultic liturgies in which Israel was enjoined to avoid worship of foreign deities.

### 4.3.1.2 Josh. 24:3

Previous analyses have generally treated vs.3 as an original unity. It was ordinarily assigned to E, though numerous scholars working with other presuppositions argued for a different source.[272] Some scholars suggest that the specific mention of Abraham in apposition to "your father" is an intrusion.[273] Seebass argues that in vs.2 "Terah, the father of Abraham and the father of Nahor," is a later insertion along with the present reference to Abraham in vs.3, which demonstrates that in the original account the patriarchs were anonymous.[274] However, for a number of reasons this theory is hardly credible. The use of the verb *lqḥ* to denote the selection of Abraham must be compared with Gen. 24:7.[275] Furthermore, in Josh. 24:3 the pronoun *'wtw* as well as the 3rd masc. sing. suf. in *zr'w* and *lw* presupposes that Abraham has already been mentioned. The gift of Isaac as his progeny would not have been mentioned without a specific reference

[269]Halbe, *Privilegrecht*, 119; and see the discussion of Josh. 24:25 above.

[270]Cf. Schmitt, *Landtag*, 22f.; and note the discussion of *ḥq wmšpṭ* above.

[271]According to Dillmann it is a sign of B (= E) (*Josua*, 583, 618). Cf. Nielsen, *Zehn Gebote*, 69f. It is found in Deut. 31:16, which Weinfeld judges to be Elohistic (*Deuteronomy*, 10 n.2); cf. already Eissfeldt, "Die Umrahmung des Mose-Liedes Dtn 32,1-43 und des Mose-Gesetzes Dtn 1-30 in Dtn 31,9-32,47," *WZUH* 4 (1954-55) 411-417.

[272]E.g., Rudolph's assertion of J (*Der "Elohist"*, 245); Möhlenbrink assigned it to the "Jahwerede" ("Landnahmesagen" 251).

[273]Seebass, *Der Erzvater*, 10, 94 n.40; Mölle, *Landtag*, 29.

[274]Seebass, *Der Erzvater*, 10.

[275]Cf. Segal, *The Pentateuch*, 127f. Note the reference in Gen. 24:7 to the sending of an angel to guarantee success, and cf. Ex. 23:20,23 at the beginning of a passage demonstrated below (5.3.4) to have many striking correlations with Josh. 24:1-28.

to Abraham. Nor is it possible to argue that *'t-'bykm* is a later gloss and that the original reading was simply *'t-'brhm*. As is noted in the structural analysis, *'t-'bykm* forms an external parallelism with *'bwtykm* in the preceding verse. And it is once again instructive to realize against the background of the patriarchal worship of multiple gods[276] that the continuation of the narrative with Abraham at the exclusion of Nahor is a deliberate, dramatic progression.[277] Therefore the three cola of 3a should be accepted as an original unity.

The tricolon of 24:3a may be viewed as a concise summary of what is narrated in Gen. 11:31-12:9; 13:14-17. For example, in Gen. 13:17 we find *qwm hthlk b'rṣ*, to which may be compared the colon *w'wlk 'wtw bkl-'rṣ kn'n*. It is significant that "land of Canaan" is used prolifically in Genesis–Numbers. but only occurs once in Deuteronomy.[278] The phrase occurs eight times in Joshua, and it cannot be considered Dtistic.[279] The fact that Yahweh brought Abraham throughout the entire land is surely an explicit allusion to an initial fulfilment of the covenantal promise of the gift of land which runs as an easily traced thread throughout Genesis.[280] The appropriateness of the land-grant as a covenantal gift has been well documented in previous research and need not be elaborated here.[281] Similarly, the multiplication of progeny is clearly mentioned in Josh. 24:3b as a fulfilment of the covenantal blessing delineated in Genesis.[282] The verb *ntn* in the sense

[276]E.g., Gen. 31:53a, *'lhy 'brhm w'lhy nḥwr yšpṭw bynynw*.

[277]Compare the manner in which the narrator raises literary tension in the following verse via mention of Esau's inheritance and Jacob's descent into Egypt.

[278]This single occurrence is in 32:49, assigned by Weinfeld to P, not D, (*Deuteronomy*, 342).

[279]If anything it tends to be found in material often attributed to P. Note that the only place outside of Josh. 24:3 that *kl-'rṣ kn'n* occurs is in Gen. 17:8, which is also attributed to P. With respect to dating of this passage, see especially Külling, *Zur Datierung*, 250-283.

[280]The suggestion by Hoftijzer (*Die Verheissungen an die drei Erzväter* [Leiden, 1956], 14), that Josh. 24:2f. is not connected with a promise misses the fact that the present description clearly presupposes the fulfilment of an earlier promise. See Eissfeldt, "El als Geber," 46, 52 n.16; D.J.A.Clines, *The Theme of the Pentateuch* (Sheffield, 1978), 29-43.

[281]See conveniently Weinfeld, "Covenant of Grant," 184-203. On the concept of blessing and covenantal gift see too Kalluveettil, *Declaration and Covenant*, 28f.

[282]Conversely, the destruction of the "seed" is a common element in treaty maledictions, cf. Fensham, "Psalm 21," 199f. The idea that God blesses with progeny is found already in poetic format in Gen. 49:25. See further Gen. 13:16; 15:5,13,18; 16:10; 17:20; 22:17, etc. Note how this ancient tradition is also remembered in the

of God giving children is found in the Pentateuch in Gen. 15:3 (to Abram); 17:16 (to Sarah); 30:6 (to Rachel); 48:9 (to Joseph).

**4.3.1.3 Josh. 24:4**

Josh. 24:4 is a concise and carefully structured unit. The genealogical announcement of Esau and Jacob is presented in a manner which creates a clear contrast. Esau has a land to inherit, but every Israelite would recognize that it was outside of the true land of the promise. Jacob has sons, but they descend to Egypt. Since the narrator has specifically mentioned in the preceding verse that Yahweh brought Abraham throughout the entire land of Canaan, the present geographical references and their covenantal significance is surely deliberate. It is therefore impossible to agree that mention of Esau is a late gloss by someone who missed his name beside his twin brother.[283]

On the other hand, many scholars have argued that *lršt 'wtw* is a Dtistic gloss.[284] In this respect two considerations are important. First, Josh. 24:4 bears a close similarity to Deut. 2:5.[285] Second, it must be asked whether the verb *yrš* is particularly Dtistic. With respect to Deut. 2:5, it may be of some signifcance that Weinfeld compares this verse to the Hittite vassal treaties of land-grant.[286] The contexts of Deut. 2:5 and Josh. 24:4 are from this respect similar insofar as in both instances it is Yahweh who is speaking in an historical recital comparable to the treaty prologues. The respective passages have a number of interesting details in common.[287] The fate of Esau is not generally a major concern throughout the OT, but Deut. 2:22 repeats the fact that Esau was given an inheritance.[288] But in this respect the archaic poetry of Num. 24:18 is also important. Here it is stated that Edom and Seir (poetic parallelism) will be dispossessed.

This brings us to the second point, namely that the root *yrš*,

poetry of Isa. 51:2 with the collocation *w'brkhw w'rbhw*.

[283]Contra Mölenbrink, "Landnahmesagen," 251.

[284]Steuernagel, *Josua*, 242f.; Holzinger, *Josua*, xxi, 95; Noth, *Josua* 1953, 10, 135; Schmitt, *Landtag*, 16.

[285]Cf. Deut. 2:5b, *ky-yršh l'św ntty 't-hr ś'yr*, and Josh. 24:4bA-B, *w'tn l'św 't-hr ś'yr lršt 'wtw*.

[286]Weinfeld, *Deuteronomy*, 72.

[287]E.g., Deut. 2:26-3:22 provides an elaborate summary of the conflict with the two kings of the Amorites, a theme also surfacing in Josh. 24:8,12. In addition to the comments offered here, see the discussion of the relationship between Josh. 24:1-28 and Deuteronomy (5.3.3).

[288]See too Deut. 2:8,29.

though it is "dtn.-dtr. besonders beliebt,"[289] is by no means exclusively Dtic or Dtistic.[290] The form of the root *yrš* in Deut. 2:5,9,12,19; 3:20 is the rather rare feminine noun vocalized *yᵉruššāh*; it is found elsewhere in Josh. 1:15; 12:6,7; Judg. 21:17; 2 Chron. 20:11; Ps. 61:6; Jer. 32:8. It is striking that this form in Deuteronomy is restricted to the opening chapters.[291] It is not possible to demonstrate that Josh. 24:4 is directly dependent upon Deut. 2:5,[292] nor is the terminology per se Dtistic,[293] but the similarities are certainly striking.

A descent to Egypt is attested elsewhere in the OT where the verb *yrd* is employed. Most instances occur in Genesis.[294] In Gen. 46:3,4 Jacob is given divine permission to "go down" to Egypt,[295] with the assurance of Yahweh's blessing, and he is accompanied by his sons (46:6f.). Josh. 24:4 may recall this passage in abbreviated form, but the formula chosen is unique in the OT and points to the originality of the present compositon. The descent of the patriarchs is also recalled with the same verb in the historical summaries of Num. 20:15; Deut. 10:22; 26:5. The expansion in the LXX in Josh. 24:4 has already

[289]H.H.Schmid, "*yrš*," *THAT*, 1:780.

[290]In addition to Num. 24:18 it occurs in archaic poetry in Deut. 33:23 (cf. Ex. 15:9; Cross–Freedman, *Ancient Yahwistic Poetry*, 60.). The verb is from a common NW Semitic root, attested, e.g., in Ugaritic (C.H.Gordon, *Ugaritic Textbook* [Rome, 1965], 415 no.1161; Schmid, "*yrš*," 778f.) and Moabite (in the Mesha inscription). Cf. J.Huehnergard, "Northwest Semitic Vocabulary in Akkadian Texts," *JAOS* 107 (1987) 725.

[291]Von Rad suggests that this "prologue" in Deuteronomy preserves a collection of memories which may have been kept alive as part of a more extensive Mosaic literature (*Deuteronomy*, 21). Cf. W.A.Sumner, "Israel's Encounters with Edom, Moab, Ammon, Sihon and Og According to the Deuteronomist," *VT* 18 (1968) 216-228.

[292]Sperling concludes, "The closest linguistic parallels, however, are Lev. 20:24 and Num. 33:53" ("Joshua 24," 124).

[293]A comparable use of the infinitive is found in Gen. 15:7 (*lršth*, with suffix marking indirect object), but this text is as hotly debated as the present one (cf. Westermann, *Genesis*, 2:256, 266; Richter, "Beobachtungen," 203-205) and many recent scholars are inclined to see 15:7 as Dtistic. For a defense of the antiquity of the description of the *bryt* ritual in Gen. 15 see McCarthy, "*Bᵉrît* in OT," 115f.; for an extensive discussion of *yrš* in this context see L.A.Snijders, "Genesis XV. The Covenant with Abram," *OTS* 12 (Leiden, 1958), 261-279, esp. 265-271. Auld suggests that the common Dtic usage is *lršth* while references such as Lev. 20:24; Num. 33:53 have *ršt 'th* (*Joshua, Moses*, 74). Cf. here, *lršt 'wtw*.

[294]Cf. Gen. 12:10; 26:2; 37:25; 39:1; 42:2,38; 43:4f.,15,20,22; 44:26; 45:13; 46:3f.; Num. 20:15; Deut. 10:22; 26:5; Josh. 24:4; Isa. 30:2; 31:1.

[295]Contrast 26:2 and Isa. 30:2; 31:1.

been mentioned above with reference to Deut. 26:5b. The promise of blessing in Gen. 46:3 (*ky-lgwy gdwl 'śymk šm*) finds explicit fulfilment in this LXX expansion. It is noteworthy that in both Josh. 24:4 and 1 Sam. 12:5 Egypt lacks a *locale-h*.

### 4.3.2 The Egyptian period (24:5-7)

#### 4.3.2.1 Josh. 24:5

The first colon of this verse, "And I sent Moses and Aaron," has been discussed above with respect to the LXX. Similar phrases are found in Deut. 26:8; 1 Sam. 12:8; Mic. 6:4; Ps. 105:26. These passages have been dealt with variously as ancient cultic formulations[296] or late Dtistic parenesis.[297] However, an attempt to date the origin of these texts primarily on the basis of terminology is a questionable endeavor. As Schreiner correctly observes, material transmitted as part of the cultic traditions in Israel can have an ancient origin and yet in the final form in which they are found in the MT bear the marks of late formulation.[298] A study of the similarities and differences of these respective historical summaries suggests the possibility that throughout the centuries of transmission there was a certain process of equalization of language and content. It is therefore a matter of extreme difficulty to determine which elements in common are to be attributed to ancient cultic traditions, which are the result of specific periods of editing, and which are simply part of the "leveling process" which parallel texts can undergo throughout the history of transmission.

The difficulties involved in such an attempt to "unravel" traditons can scarcely be illustrated more effectively and clearly than in Josh. 24:5. Thanks to the witness of the LXX and the parallel traditions of Deut. 26:5-8; Mic. 6:4; 1 Sam. 12:8, it appears to be possible to determine late redactional influence in the opening colon. But this hardly dates the passage itself. The following colon, "and I struck Egypt," employs terminology reminiscent of that which is used in

[296]Von Rad (see the summary in 1.4.2).

[297]For Mic. 6:4 see H.W.Wolff, *Micha* (Neukirchen, 1982), 143. For more extensive studies questioning the antiquity of the so-called credo consult Rost, *Credo*, 11-25; Richter, "Beobachtungen," 175-212. Cf. A.Deissler, "Micha 6,1-8: Israel um das rechte Bundesverhältnis," *TThZ* 68 (1959) 233: "Die Erwähnung von Moses, Aaron und Mirjam ist um 700 mindestens so plausibel wie später."

[298]Cf. Schreiner, "Die Entwicklung," 757-762.

Exodus.[299] The parallel account of Deut. 26:7f. does not refer to Yahweh's striking of Egypt, and Josh. 24:5 of the MT is not based upon these verses from Deuteronomy.

The phrase "with what I did in her midst" finds a direct parallel in Ps. 78:4 in the same context of the exodus from Egypt and the wonderous acts of deliverance. The closest parallel, however, is offered already in the prediction of Ex. 3:20, *'šr "śh bqrbw*, which forms the background for the fulfilment described by both Josh. 24:5 and Ps. 78:4 in their own ways. The same thought is found in Ex. 10:1 and especially Num. 14:11, which is identical to *k'šr 'śyty bqrbw* in Josh. 24:5 except for the absence of the *k*. These texts make clear that Josh. 24:5aC is a reference to the signs and wonders performed by Yahweh in Egypt. This is of considerable significance for the present analysis because the sobrietry and restraint of this formulation stands in marked contrast to the extravagant lauding of Yahweh's signs, wonders and miracles in the wording of Deuteronomy.[300] This observation is strengthened by the fact that, as demonstrated above in the structural analysis, an inclusion is formed by the responsion of this phrase with *'t-'šr-'śyty bmṣrym* (7bB). The narrator has thereby afforded a significant structural position to the signs and wonders performed in Egypt, but he has done so in a reserved manner[301] atypical of the sublime expressions characterizing Deuteronomy.[302]

[299]Cf. the use of the verb *ngp* in Ex. 7:27 (ET 8:2); 12:23,27 with Egypt as object. See too Isa. 19:22 (2x); Zech. 14:18f. The verb *ngp* in Deuteronomy is found in 1:42 in a summary of an older source (cf. Num. 14:42); other than this it occurs only in 28:7,25, in two verses forming literary inclusion (cf. Weinfeld, *Deuteronomy*, 119 n.1). The formulation in Josh. 24:5 is atypical of Deuteronomy (cf. Sperling, "Joshua 24," 124f.).

[300]Cf. Deut. 26:8, and see further Deut. 4:34; 6:22f.; 7:19; 11:3; 29:2; 34:11f.

[301]Cf. the similarly frugal description in Ex. 19:4, which obviates the proposal by Noth to add *b'twt* in the present verse (cf. *Josua* 1953, 136).

[302]Note too that the precise expression *k'šr 'śyty* spoken by Yahweh as subject is found only in Gen. 8:21; Josh. 24:5; Isa. 10:11; Jer. 7:14. See further Ezek. 12:11; 24:22, where Ezekiel is instructed by Yahweh to say these words. The same expression is found with human subject in Judg. 1:7; Zech. 7:3 and in slight variation in Judg. 15:11. There are a number of *k'šr*-clauses occurring frequently in Deuteronomy, but *k'šr 'śh* is not one of these, cf. A.R.Hulst, "Opmerkingen over de *ka'ašer*-zinnen in Deuteronomium," *NThT* 18 (1963-64) 337-361. The only time that Josh. 24:1-28 comes to an explicit mention of the signs performed in Egypt is in vs.17, in what appears to be a late poetic expansion in the MT approximating Dtistic language, but even there having certain significant differences from the stereotyped expressions found in Deuteronomy (see 3.6.2).

Vs.5 ends with the cryptic colon, "And afterwards I brought you out," the significance of which is elaborated in the following strophe. The verb *yṣ'* has frequently been studied as a possible clue to Dtistic authorship or redaction of various OT passages, especially in comparison and contrast with *'lh.*[303] The analysis by Richter leads to the conclusion that both expressions as a reference to the exodus from Egypt are ancient.[304] According to Wijngaards the use of *yṣ'* with respect to the exodus events may originally have had a particular connection with the delivery at the Reed Sea, which is precisely the context in which it is used in Josh. 24:5f.[305] but the connection with the deliverance at the Reed Sea is a matter of ongoing debate.[306]

#### 4.3.2.2 Josh. 24:6

It has been argued above that a change of grammatical person, or as in this verse the switch between "you" and "your fathers," does not provide evidence of various sources.[307] What needs to be investigated further is the more recently asserted idea that it demonstrates a liturgical character.[308] It is true that numerous OT passages can be listed to support this assumption. For example, the similar recital in Deut. 26:5-9 is asserted to be a summary spoken in the festival of the first-fruits, and here too there is an equation made between the fathers and the present generation via an interchanging of 1st and 3rd person.[309] Ps. 106:6f.,46f. provide similar examples, as does Dan. 9:5-19, esp. vs.16. These texts may plausibly be understood as containing liturgical formulations. However, the matter becomes somewhat more involved in a number of other texts. Mic. 6:2-5 begins with 3rd person references to Israel and then shifts to 2nd person in the direct accusation. This can conceivably be explained form-critically on the

[303]Cf. especially Wijngaards, "*Hwṣy'* and *h'lh*," 91-102; Richter, "Beobachtungen," esp. 178-202.

[304]Richter, "Beobachtungen," 185. The conclusion is accepted by Lohfink, who with additional considerations summarizes, "So kann *jṣ'* hif. für die Befreiung aus Ägypten trotz der vielen Belege im Dtn nicht als Zeugnis deuteronomischer Sprache angeführt werden" ("Credo," 28).

[305]Wijngaards, "*Hwṣy'* and *h'lh*," 94. It is clear that the formulation in Josh. 24:5f. is not influenced by Deut. 26:8.

[306]Cf. G.W.Coats, "The Traditio-Historical Character of the Reed Sea Motif," *VT* 17 (1967) 253-265, esp. 258f. n.6; and see further at vs.6 below.

[307]Cf. section 2.3.7.1.

[308]E.g., Newman, *People of the Covenant*, 114; Butler, *Joshua*, 271.

[309]Lohfink, "Credo," 22f.

basis of the lawsuit pattern.[310] But this does not detract from the obvious treatment of Israel as having had a collective presence in the exodus of the fathers from Egypt.

Similar observations can be made in various poetic parallelisms of Deut. 32, a passage also often viewed as containing a formal lawsuit.[311] Here the poet has no qualms about switching from 3rd sing. to 2nd sing. and back to 3rd. sing. within the span of three cola (vs.15), though this grammatical inconsistency was apparently offensive to the translator of the LXX. The poet proceeds to indict the previous generations for their unfaithfulness, for sacrificing to gods "your fathers never worshipped" (vs.17), but he abruptly shifts to a 2nd pers. charge with the words "you did not know the rock that bore you" (vs.18). The historical summary of Num. 20:14-16 demonstrates precisely the same phenomenon as found in Josh. 24:5-7. One might suggest that in Num. 20:15 the identification with the fathers was made possible because the generation delivered from Egypt was still alive, but this is hardly convincing due to the fact that the expression *wnšb bmṣrym ymym rbym* refers to the duration of the entire Egyptian sojourn, not simply the lifetime of the present generation.

The historical summary in 1 Sam. 12:7 also makes an explicit equation between Yahweh's actions on behalf of "you and your fathers." It is possible that a text such as Num. 20:14-16 or 1 Sam. 12:7 may have been employed in cultic recitals of Yahweh's actions in Israel's antecedent history, but it is not self-evident that this was the case. Similar exchanges between 3rd and 2nd person forms are found in Am. 2:4-16 and Hos. 12-13. It has been suggested previously that the historical summaries introducing a treaty relationship often contain shifts in grammatical person,[312] which is another possible explanation for the grammatical shift in vss.5-7 from Yahweh speaking via Joshua in the 1st sing. to a 3rd sing. reference in vs.7. On the other hand, similar changes are found in the Psalms as well. To explain a similar shift in Ps. 61, Dahood appeals to "court style" writing.[313] Most importantly for the present study, in the decalogue

[310]Cf. Harvey, *Le plaidoyer prophétique*, 42-45.

[311]Cf. G.E.Wright, "The Lawsuit of God: A Form-Critical Study of Deuteronomy 32," in B.W.Anderson–W.Harrelson, eds., *Israel's Prophetic Heritage: Essays in Honor of James Muilenburg* (London, 1962), 26-67; Harvey, *Le plaidoyer prophétique*, 31-36.

[312]Baltzer, *Bundesformular*, 29 n.4; Nötscher, "Bundesformular," 206f.

[313]Dahood, *Psalms*, 2:83f., 87f. See too his discussion in *Psalms*, 1:142f.

of Ex. 20, Yahweh begins in the 1st sing. (vs.2), but by vs.7 the actions of Yahweh have shifted to a 3rd singular reference in a manner entirely analogous to Josh. 24:7. This shift can be explained form-critically on the grounds that these passages begin with a proclamation or identification of divine self-revelation, but in the course of the passage shift to 3rd sing. references.[314] Such changes in person do not indicate different sources, they can hardly be used as evidence for dating,[315] and it is finally difficult to say whether they are per se due to liturgical influence upon the present texts.

It is also necessary to comment briefly upon the theory that the association between the exodus and the crossing of the Reed Sea is a late and secondary affiliation. The proposals by Coats[316] and Childs[317] suffer from a number of weaknesses. They assume the validity of Noth's source-critical analysis of Josh. 24:5-7,[318] but their present emphasis upon Dtic redaction does not adequately reflect Noth's conclusions in these verses.[319] Furthermore, the criterion upon

[314]This is of considerable importance because of Josh. 24:1-28's correlation with the first commandment.

[315]Cf. in archaic poetry, e.g., Judg. 5:15f.: Reuben is referred to first in a 3rd person observation, then directly addressed in a 2nd person question, and finally again in a repetition of the 3rd person observation as a refrain. A citation from Gevirtz is relevant here: "Another peculiarity of West Semitic rhetoric is the alteration of grammatical person (3d to 2d and 2d to 3d) within one sentence or unit of thought while the reference remains to the same individual. It is a well-documented though often overlooked feature of biblical Hebrew literary style" ("Canaanite Rhetoric," 170, with examples following in Hebrew, Phoenician, Aramaic and Ugaritic). See also M.Dijkstra, *Gods voorstelling. Predikatieve expressie van zelfopenbaring in oudoosterse teksten en Deutero-Jesaja* (Kampen, 1980), esp. 128f., 240ff. The phenomenon is also attested in Akkadian poetry; see, e.g., K.Hecker, *Untersuchungen zur akkadischen Epik* (Neukirchen, 1974), 70ff.

[316]Coats, "Traditio-Historical Character," 253-265.

[317]Childs, "Deuteronomic Formulae," 30-39; "A Tradition-historical Study of the Reed Sea Tradition," *VT* 20 (1970) 406-418; *Exodus*, 221-224.

[318]Coats states that Josh. 24:5f. shows "a rather marked Deuteronomistic reworking" ("Traditio-Historical Character," 261), but he offers no evidence to support the claim. Similarly, Childs appeals to Noth to support his assertion that Josh. 24:2ff. "with its strong Deuteronomic flavor shows several layers of expansion" ("Deuteronomic Formulae," 36 n.1). R.Schmid makes a similar assertion on the basis of the shifts in grammatical person ("Meerwunder- und Landnahme-Traditionen," *ThZ* 21 [1965] 260-268, esp. 267).

[319]Noth's focus in the second edition (*Josua* 1953) placed greater stress upon Dtistic redaction in Josh. 24:1-28 than was the case in the first edition (1938), but his treatment of vss.5-7 does not give specific examples of major Dtic redaction as would seem to be implied by both Childs and Coats (cf. Noth, *Josua*, 136f.).

which Noth based his source-critcism in these verses has been demonstrated above to be invalid for proving separate traditions.[320] In contrast to the opinion of Coats and Childs, Cross concludes that the account of the conflict at the sea in Josh. 24:5-7 is an archaic tradition from the ninth century or earlier "only slightly reworked by the Deuteronomistic editor."[321] But even he fails to give any examples of the alleged Dtistic influence. Coats argues that the use of the *waw-consecutive* imperfects suggests a later ordering of a number of incidental events. His argument ignores the fact that the phrase *k'šr 'śyty* (5aC) and *'šr-'śyty* (7bB) form a deliberate inclusion around the events of the exodus, of which the deliverance at the Reed Sea stands central.[322] Also ignored is the fact that *k'šr 'śyty bqrbw* is clearly intended to show the fulfilment of the promise in Ex. 3:20. Childs is willing to concede that Josh. 24:5 follows the account of the Tetrateuch,[323] but he too ignores the repetition of the *'šr 'śyty* formula in vs.7.

Furthermore, the body of evidence which does present the Reed Sea event as an early and indigenous element of the exodus is not given adequate representation in these studies. Coats states, "The Reed Sea motif rarely appears in pre-Exilic texts."[324] But his support for this argument is weak. He appeals to Noth's dating of Ex. 15:1-19 without mentioning that orthographic and philological studies by students of the Albright school have raised formidable arguments favouring an earlier date.[325] Coats ignores or downplays the evidence from the Psalms, such as Ps. 78:40-55;[326] 114; and cf. Isa. 10:26; 11:15.

[320]Cf. R.E.Clements, *Prophecy and Covenant* (London, 1965), 47f.

[321]Cross, *Canaanite Myth*, 133.

[322]The inclusion is most obvious in the structural analysis offered above, but even without a colometric layout it can hardly be missed.

[323]Childs, "Deuteronomic Formulae," 37.

[324]Coats, "Traditio-Historical Character," 262.

[325]See especially Cross–Freedman, *Ancient Yahwistic Poetry*, 45-65; "Song of Miriam," 237-250. See too Cross, *Canaanite Myth*, 112-133. Childs admits the weight of these arguments but does not allow them adequate influence upon his methodology (*Exodus*, 245f.) Nor are these arguments taken seriously enough by Van Seters ("Joshua 24," 148).

[326]The Psalm has been dated very early by Eissfeldt ("Das Lied Moses Deuteronomium 32:1-43 und das Lehrgedicht Asaphs Psalm 78 samt einer Analyse der Umgebung des Mose-Liedes," in *Ver. Sächs. Acad. Wiss. Leipzig*, Phil.-hist. Kl. 104, 5 [Berlin, 1958], 26-41. See also Albright, *Yahweh and the Gods*, 15 n.41; Wright, "Lawsuit of God," 36-41. Cross argues for a later date "in any case pre-Exilic" (*Canaanite Myth*, 134). The argument by Childs that the plagues and the

There is finally little evidence to support the claim by Coats that the mention of the Reed Sea in Josh. 24:6 does "not seem to be well integrated into either the Exodus theme or the wilderness theme."[327]

**4.3.2.3 Josh. 24:7**

A glance in a concordance demonstrates that the verb *ṣ'q* as an appeal to Yahweh for help cannot be considered Dtistic. The only time that the verb is used in this sense in Deuteronomy is in 26:7 in a context parallel to Josh. 24:7, and it is evident that both these references summarize the account of the deliverance from Egypt as presented in Exodus.[328] The non-Dtistic character of the opening tricolon in 7a is confirmed by the employment of *m'pl*. It is possible that the *m* here is to be attributed to dittography,[329] but this does not change the fact that we have a unique description of the encounter at the Reed Sea, which may suggest an ancient formulation.[330] The similarity with *ḥšk-'plh* in Ex. 10:22[331] suggests that Josh. 24:7aB forms an external responsion with *w'gp 't-mṣrym* in 5aB. Also of interest are the singular suffixes employed in *'lyw* and *wyksw*. It has long been thought to be a peculiarity of Genesis and Exodus that the Egyptians are referred to in the singular. As in vs.6, it is of importance to note the cryptic manner in which the crossing through the Reed Sea is described.[332] It is doubtful whether these verses can be posited as

sea event are temporally distinct in this psalm ("Deuteronomic Formulae," 36) as in Josh. 24:5f. is irrelevant as evidence that they come from originally independent traditions or that the encounter at the Reed Sea was not initially part of the Exodus account. In the present text they are interwoven in a carefully constructed poetic canto (cf. Korpel–de Moor, "Fundamentals," 208-212; Koopmans, "Psalm 78, Canto D," 121-123.

[327]Coats, "Traditio-Historical Character," 265.

[328]Cf. W.Beyerlin, "Gattung und Herkunft des Rahmens im Richterbuch," in Würthwein–Kaiser, eds., *Tradition und Situation*, 10f. It is not necessary to follow Beyerlin in accepting von Rad's date for Deut. 26:7 to argue for the antiquity of the phrase *ṣ'q 'l-yhwh*, but it is evident that Josh. 24:7 is not dependent upon the parallel summary in Deuteronomy. See already Holzinger (*Einleitung*, 187) for an attempt to identify *ṣ'q 'l* with J.

[329]Noth, *Josua* 1953, 136, but cf. Jer. 2:31.

[330]It is for this reason that Eissfeldt attributed the verse to L (*Hexateuch-Synopse*, 80). Steuernagel suggests, "gemeint ist die dunkle Wolkensäule Ex 14.19b" (*Josua*, 243); this is no doubt correct and makes it all the more significant that the narrator here employs a unique description.

[331]Usually attributed to J, cf. Childs, *Exodus*, 131.

[332]Cross notes that the closest parallel is found in Ex. 15:1-18, which plays an important role in his dating of the account in Josh. 24:5-7 (*Canaanite Myth*, 133).

standing entirely independent from the narrative in Ex. 14,[333] but the present account is not Dtistic.

It is also worth noting that divine military intervention employing a dark cloud or enveloping mist is attested in a Hittite parallel in the Annals of Muršili where the Storm-god uses a cloud to protect his troops from the enemy.[334]

Even a phrase such as "your eyes have seen," while common in Deuteronomy,[335] does not per se prove Dtistic influence upon the present text.[336] It is difficult to determine whether particular significance is to be attributed to the reference "and you dwelt in the wilderness many days." It is possible that a comparison is intended with Ishmael,[337] or with Abraham.[338] But it can also simply be a reference to the period Israel dwelt at Kadesh,[339] or at Mt. Seir,[340] without any allusion to the patriarchal period. If an allusion is intended to the sojourn at Mt. Seir as described in Deut. 2:1,[341] a subtle external responsion may be intended with *'t-hr ś'yr* in Josh. 24:4.

### 4.3.3 Conflict with the nations (24:8-13)

#### 4.3.3.1 Josh. 24:8

Josh. 24:8 is essentially a concise summary of the events narrated in Num. 21:21-35.[342] We have already listed the connections between

[333]See the summary of correspondences listed in 2.3.7.1.

[334]Cf. Weinfeld, "Divine Intervention," 143-145, with additional examples.

[335]See Weinfeld, *Deuteronomy*, 357.

[336]The closest parallels are in Deuteronomy, but cf. already Ex. 14:13,30,31 to which the present reference alludes, and consider the similar allusion in Ex. 19:4; (see too 1 Sam. 24:11; 1 Kgs 10:7). The phrase "to see with your own eyes" is attested already in the Amarna Letters (*CAD* 1:2, 8f.). Nothing precludes the conclusion that such phrases were quite common, and they cannot be attributed to any particular time or genre.

[337]Cf. Gen. 21:20f.

[338]Gen. 21:34.

[339]Deut. 1:46; note the comparison above of Ex. 15:25 and Josh. 24:25, law-giving at Kadesh and Shechem

[340]Deut. 2:1.

[341]Note the designation here of the wilderness as *hmdbrh drk ym-swp*. They were at Mt. Seir *ymym rbym*, but note that the verb for dwelling is different than in Josh. 24:7. However, it may be significant that Deut. 2 proceeds to narrate an encounter with all the various nations, as does Josh. 24:8ff. in its own way.

[342]Cf. as well Num. 33:52-55. The conclusion by Auld (*Joshua, Moses*, 74-75) that these verses are a "blend of Deuteronomistic and Priestly terminology" is

these passages.[343] Numerous of the phrases and expressions are also paralleled elsewhere in the OT in historical summaries. The colon "I brought you to the land of the Amorites" has a parallel in the historical summaries of Judg. 2:1; Jer. 2:7 in the context of *Jahwerede*.[344] We have already stressed that the pair *yrš* || *šmd* is found only in Num. 33:52; Deut. 2:12,21f.; 4:26; 9:3; 28:63; 31:3 and 2 Sam. 14:7, which at first glance suggests that Josh. 24:8 betrays Dtic influence in the employment of this pair.[345] The poetic account in Am. 2:9-10 is of considerable significance as proof that the encounter with the Amorites was remembered within Israel's early prophetic traditions.[346]

The phrase "and I gave them into your hand" (Josh. 24:8bA) has often been treated as part of a Dtistic redaction,[347] but this assertion is not convincing. This stereotypical phrase describing the actions of a deity giving the enemy into the hands of his people was part

not totally convincing; Auld also lists a high frequency of unique expressions and terminology. The passage could also be an original summary.

[343]See 2.3.7.1, which calls into question the conclusion by Richter ("Beobachtungen," 192-194) that Josh. 24:8 is literarily independent from the account in Num. 21.

[344]Cf. also Ex. 19:4. For the vocalization of *w'b'h* in Josh. 24:8 consult E.J.Revell, "First Person Imperfect Forms with *Waw* Consecutive," *VT* 38 (1988) 419. The phrase *hywšb b'br hyrdn* differentiates these Amorites from those dwelling in the hill country west of the Jordan. For a variant textual reading *'rṣ hkrml* see F.Diaz Esteban, "The Sefer Oklah w'Oklah as a Source of Not Registered Bible Textual Variants," *ZAW* 70 (1958) 253.

[345]One must, however, be cautious here. We have quoted the conclusion by Sperling that the closest linguistic parallels to Josh. 24:4 are found in Num. 33:53 and Lev. 20:24. This suggests that Num. 33:52f. is a crucial text for determining whether the present formulation of Josh. 24:8 is Dtistic. Significantly, Deut. 2:12,21f. summarizes the original Transjordanian accounts from Numbers. Deut. 9:3 (*wh'bdtm* Hiph.) may be reminiscent of Num. 33:52 (*w'bdtm* Piel), and all the additional references in Deuteronomy are in the context of the Transjordanian setting. We have noted that Num. 33:50-55 contains many similarities to both Dtic formulation and P but it also contains a high frequency of unique expressions. For all these reasons the statistical listing of the pair *yrš* || *šmd* does not yet prove that Josh. 24:8 is later than the employment in Deuteronomy, especially since Josh. 24:8 shows no literary dependence upon the verses listed in Deuteronomy and it is demonstrated below that Josh. 24:13 influenced the formulation of Deut. 6:10f.

[346]Cf. especially the external parallelism formed in Am. 2:9f. between *w'nky hšmdty 't-h'mry mpnym* and *w'nky h'lyty 'tkm m'rṣ mṣrym*. The first of these may be compared with Josh. 24:8, the second with 24:17a. See too Ps. 135:11f.; 136:17-22.

[347]E.g., Steuernagel, *Josua*, 243; Noth, *Josua* 1953, 135; Seebass, *Der Erzvater*, 96; Mölle, *Landtag*, 39f., 240, 289.

of the common vocabulary of the ancient NE. Identical expressions are found, e.g., in texts from Mesopotamia, Anatolia and Amarna.[348] The attestation in the Amarna correspondence is revealing; Tušratta of Mittani writes to Amenophis III of Egypt: "Tešub, my Lord, gave them (him) into my hand and I destroyed them (him)."[349] Significantly, this reference contains the combination "*DN* gave into hand" and "destroy them."[350] A similar correlation is made in the Apology of Ḫattušiliš III, where it is claimed that Ishtar gave the enemy into his hand and he utterly destroyed them.[351] This combination is similar to Josh. 24:8b, "But I gave them into your hand, and you inherited their land, and I destroyed them before you."[352] The expression "*ntn byd*" as divine military deliverance in the OT is found frequently in material ordinarily assigned to DtrG. But Kang is correct in asserting that the OT usage can scarcely be thought to have originated with a Dtic school.[353] Scholars have also thought that the colon *w'šmydm mpnykm* falls too late grammatically.[354] However, we have noted similar combinations in Akkadian (EA 17:33) and Hittite (Apology of Ḫattušiliš III).[355] There is finally little reason to view either 8bB or 8bC as a later addition. Also significant in this regard is the function of the poetic tricolon to mark separation downwards at the end of the strophe.

#### 4.3.3.2 Josh. 24:9-10

Since vss.9-10 focus upon the encounter with the Moabites, these verses can be treated together. For the present concern two aspects must briefly be considered, first the matter of the literary connection with Num. 22-24 and Deut. 23:3-5, second the question of whether

[348]S.-M.Kang, *Divine War in the Old Testament and in the Ancient Near East* (Berlin and New York, 1989), 43f., 67.

[349]*EA* 17:32f.: $^{d}$*Tešub bēlī ana qātīya iddinšuma u addukšu*; cf. S.A.B.Mercer, *The Tell El-Amarna Tablets*, 2 vols. (Toronto, 1093), 64f.

[350]On the translation of *addakšu* cf. H.Tadmor, "Historical Implications of the Correct Rendering of Akkadian *dâku*," *JNES* 17 (1958) 129-141.

[351]Kang, *Divine War*, 67.

[352]Note that the Hittite idiom "*piran huwāi-*" denotes assistance from the gods and literally means "to go before one" (cf. E.H.Sturtevant, *A Hittite Glossary*, 2nd ed. [Philadelphia, 1936], 53). It therefore makes a close parallel with *mpnykm* in the sense attested in Josh. 24:8bC.

[353]Kang, *Divine War*, 130.

[354]Holzinger, *Josua*, 97; Schmitt, *Landtag*, 10; Floss, *Jawhe dienen*, 350.

[355]See too A.Goetze, *Die Annalen des Muršiliš* (*MVÄG* 38; Leipzig, 1933), 158, lines 26, 29-31.

vss.9f. is an original unity or displays evidence of later redaction. Josh. 24:9f. is primarily dependent upon material from Num. 22-24.[356] It is as easy to assert that Deut. 23:6 is based upon a combination of Num. 22:5 and Josh. 24:10 as it is to suggest that Josh. 24:10 is dependent upon Deut. 23:6.[357] In any case, the theory defended by Noth,[358] and especially Donner,[359] that Josh. 24:9b,10abA is an insertion which is again secondarily influenced by Num. 22-24 is possible but neither proven nor probable.[360] Here too it is significant that the encounter with Balak and Balaam was known in the early prophetic traditions of Israel.[361]

### 4.3.3.3 Josh. 24:11-12

The present discussion of Josh. 24:11f. presupposes our previous proposal to rearrange this material somewhat.[362] Vs.11a states that the lords of Jericho "fought" against Israel, thereby maintaining the external parallelism with 8aC and 9aC. It has been demonstrated that the present formulation in Josh. 24:11a does not follow the account of Josh. 6.[363] The designation of the citizens of Jericho as

[356]See the discussion in 2.3.7.1.

[357]It is evident that Neh. 13:2 is dependent upon Deut. 23:6, but the same is not true of Josh. 24:10.

[358]M.Noth, "Israelitische Stämme zwischen Ammon und Moab," in *Aufsätze zur biblischen Landes- und Altertumskunde*, 2 vols., (Neukirchen, 1971), 1:404 n.53.

[359]Donner, "Balaam," 117, 121.

[360]Josh. 24:9f. places the verbs *šmʿ* and *brk* in parallelism (cf. the structural analysis above), while such a parallelism with the noun *brkh* in Deut. 23:6 is more remote. Furthermore, Deut. 23:6 contains the motivation *ky 'hbk yhwh 'lhyk*. If Josh. 24:10 were based upon this verse, it would not have been necessary to drop this clause. Josh. 24:10 does not appear to be based upon the present form of Deut. 23:6, and there is no indication that it depends upon an older form. On the other hand, it is plausible that the law about the Moabites in Deut. 23:5f. is based upon historical recollections in Num. 22-24 as well as Josh. 24:9f. It is also possible that the closeness of terminology in Deut. 23:6 and Josh. 24:10 is due to late harmonization, which is evident to an even stronger degree in the reading of the LXX. On the uniqueness of the infinitive *brwk* consult P.Humbert, "Review of Koehler-Baumgartner," *ThZ* 6 (1950) 60.

[361]Cf. Mic. 6:5, and also Judg. 11:25 (discussed above under structural analysis). Note that some scholars see the regulations in Deut. 23:1-8 as part of ancient laws preserved in Deuteronomy, cf. von Rad, *Deuteronomy*, 145f. (positing a connection with the cultic assembly).

[362]Cf. the discussion in 3.4.4 in connection with the structural analysis.

[363]Cf. McCarthy, *Treaty and Covenant*, 226; J.A.Soggin, "The Conquest of Jericho through Battle. Note on a Lost Biblical Tradition (Josh. 24:11; 5:13ff.; 2:18 LXX)," *ErIs* 16 (1982) 215-217; Sperling, "Joshua 24," 127.

*b'ly* in construct form with the place name argues against Dtistic influence.[364] Evidence for the dependence of Josh. 24:11b-12 upon Ex. 23:20-33 has been listed above, especially in light of the use of *grš* regarding expulsion of the nations and *šlḥ* in reference to Yahweh's sending of *hṣr'h*[365] before them. In the opinion of the present writer the connection with the angel of Ex. 23:20f. and the parallelism with *'ymty* (Ex. 23:27), makes a translation of "hornet" unlikely, and that of "panic" more probable.[366] Since Schmitt[367] is correct that Josh. 24:12a stands closer to Ex. 23:28 than to Deut. 7:20, as is evident from the verb *grš*,[368] we have valuable evidence that Josh. 24:12a follows material from Exodus rather than the parallel account in Deuteronomy.[369] Vss.11b-12a is apparently intended to stress that the promise of Ex. 23:23,27f. is fulfilled.

[364]Cf. Num. 21:28; Judg. 20:5; 1 Sam. 23:11f.; 2 Sam. 21:12; Neh. 6:18; and prolifically in the ancient narrative of Judg. 9. Earlier commentators were inclined to see *b'ly* as proof of E, cf. Holzinger, *Einleitung*, 91, 183. The usage of *bêl ālīm* denoting the military rulers of a vassal city-state is attested in the Amarna correspondence and has been adduced as a parallel to Josh. 24:11, cf. G.E.Mendenhall, *The Tenth Generation: The Origins of Biblical Tradition* (Baltimore, 1973), 128 n.31; Boling, *Joshua*, 536.

[365]The meaning is widely debated. It is thought by some to be an allusion to Egypt, cf. Garstang, *Joshua*, 258-260; Y.Yadin, "The Transition from a Semi-Nomadic to a Sedentary Society in the Twelfth Century B.C.E.," in Cross, ed., *Symposia*, 57-68. A theory of insects as warfare agents was proposed by E.Neufeld ("Insects as Warfare Agents in the Ancient Near East," *Or* 49 [1980] 30-57), but his theory was justly criticized by Emerton ("Review of Koehler–Baumgartner," *VT* 34 [1984] 504f). The choice can be narrowed to a translation as "hornet" or a secondary meaning of "panic" (cf. L.Koehler–W.Baumgartner, *Hebräisches und aramäisches Lexikon zum Alten Testament*. 3rd ed. [Leiden, 1983], 989). Emerton is correct in emphasizing the importance of the Samaritan reading supporting the latter translation, as well as reminding the editors of Koehler-Baumgartner that the parallelism with *'ymty* (Ex. 23:27) supports rather than refutes this position (cf. *'t-'ymty 'šlḥ lpnyk* || *wšlḥty 't-hṣr'h lpnyk*). The wordplay established in Ex. 23:27 as well as in Deut. 7:21 is noted by O.Borowski ("The Identity of the Biblical *ṣir'â*," in Meyers–O'Connor, eds., *Word of the Lord*, 315-319: with bibliography).

[366]The significance of panic in warfare is attested in other ancient NE literature, cf., e.g., Weinfeld, "Divine Intervention," 135, 137. Cf. Josh. 2:11; 5:1; 10:10, etc. Note too our discussion of Josh. 24:7 above.

[367]Schmitt, *Landtag*, 26.

[368]The verb *grš* is found in Deuteronomy only in the poetry of 33:27. See by contrast in Exodus in reference to the conquest 23:28,29,30,31; 33:2; 34:11. Cf. Halbe, *Privilegrecht*, 140-142; Weinfeld, *Deuteronomy*, 47, 342.

[369]Confirmed by use of *šlḥ* || *grš* found elsewhere only in Ex. 6:1; 11:1; 23:28; 33:2. In both Ex. 23:28 and 33:2 the verbs are used in conjunction with the displacement of the various groups of Canaanites.

Employment of the verb *grš* argues against Dtic influence[370] while *šny mlky h'mry* might favour it.[371]

The bicolon of 12b, "Not with your sword, and not with your bow," makes an intriguing correspondence with Gen. 48:22 in Jacob's promise to Joseph. In Gen. 48:21f. one finds two details which may both be secondary to their context.[372] The significance of these references in the context of a testament of Jacob is widely debated,[373] but for the present analysis it is significant that *both* the statement that Joseph would return to the land of his fathers (Gen. 48:21), and the reference to the taking of *škm* from the Amorites with his sword and bow (48:22) make explicit connections with Josh. 24.[374] It is not possible to enter into the seeming discrepancy of whether this land was purchased or taken by force; for the present analysis the significant point is that both aspects which are judged by commentators to stand somewhat out of place in Gen. 48:21f. make a strong literary connection with Josh. 24 in deliberate literary allusions by means of which Josh. 24 summarizes the period of the patriarchs.[375]

#### 4.3.3.4 Josh. 24:13

Josh. 24:13 provides another classic example of literary-critical disagreement. Many scholars have thought to detect the hand of a glossator,[376] and some argued specifically that the verse owes its origin

[370]Weinfeld observes that "*grš* 'drive out', which is very common in JE in the context of conquest, never occurs in D" (*Deuteronomy*, 342).

[371]McCarthy goes so far as to posit that the "two kings of the Amorites" argues *against* Dtic influence because it places the Amorite kings in Palestine rather than in the Transjordan (*Treaty and Covenant*, 226f.). But this argument should not be weighed too heavily because of the inclusionary function of this reference to the kings of the Amorites, which is not likely intended to be geographically specific. Sperling ("Joshua 24," 126) notes that, in contrast to Josh. 2:10; 9:10; 12:2,4,5; 13:10,12,21,27 the two kings are not named; but cf. Deut. 3:8, where the names occur in the context but not in the formulation of the verse itself, which makes it close to Josh. 24:12a. The evidence is finally too inconclusive to demonstrate literary dependence one way or another.

[372]According to Westermann (*Genesis*, 1:216), "Es folgen zwei Nachträge, die weder miteinander noch mit dem Vorangehenden zusammenhängen, V.21-22."

[373]Cf. de Vaux, *Early History*, 637-640.

[374]In addition to 24:12b, consider the fact that Joseph's bones are buried at Shechem (24:32).

[375]This reinforces what has been observed throughout the analysis of vss.2ff. The historical summary in Josh. 24 attempts to show the completion of themes introduced in the Pentateuch. This point is elaborated in 5.3.

[376]Dillmann, *Josua*, 586; Steuernagel, *Josua*, 244; Möhlenbrink, "Landnahmesagen," 251 ("vielleicht sekundär").

to a Deuteronomist.[377] Others attribute it to J,[378] or to E,[379] while some are content with a more general designation as late redaction[380] or ancient tradition.[381]

Scholars appealing to Dtistic redaction ordinarily have based their claim upon comparison with Deut. 6:10-13. Baltzer has demonstrated that this connection is to be viewed against a broader background of such lists in ancient NE material.[382] The parallelisms noted in the structural analysis above demonstrate a close connection with recurring similarities in the prophetic books of the OT.[383] Nevertheless, the closest connection can be identified with the wording of Deut. 6:10f. because both these verses include *cities* and the *vineyards and olive groves*. But there are a few differences in detail which are telling. Deut. 6:10 speaks of *'rym gdlt wṭbt 'šr l'-bnyt*, while Josh. 24:13 is devoid of the adjectives, reading simply *w'rym 'šr l'-bnytm*. The use of the double adjectives in Deut. 6:10 is typical of the style of Deuteronomy. Similarly, Deut. 6:11 reads "you eat and are satisfied" (*w'klt wśb't*), employing the word *śb'*, which is very common in Deuteronomy (cf. 8:10,12; 11:15; 14:29; 26:12; 31:20), while Josh. 24:13 simply reads *'tm 'klym* and makes no mention of *śb'*. On the basis of this comparison, it is not at all likely that Josh. 24:13 is dependent upon Deut. 6:10-11. An alleged Deuteronomist composing, expanding or redacting Josh. 24:13b on the basis of Deut. 6:10f. could hardly be expected to delete specifically that terminology which is most characteristic of Deuteronomy. If there is a direct literary connection between the two texts, which is hardly to be doubted, one must conclude that Deut. 6:10f. is an expanded version of Josh. 24:13, adding

377 Holzinger, *Josua*, xxi, 98; Hölscher, *Geschichtsschreibung*, 350; cf. Schmitt, *Landtag*, 16.

378 Rudolph, *Der "Elohist"*, 247.

379 Smend, *Erzahlung des Hexateuch*, 337; Eissfeldt, *Hexateuch-Synopse*, 249; Noth, *Das System*, 139; but note that in *Josua* 1953, 10, 135, Noth sees Dtistic redaction starting at *wtšbw bhm*.

380 L'Hour, "L'alliance de Sichem," 25.

381 McCarthy, *Treaty and Covenant*, 227.

382 Baltzer, *Bundesformular*, 29f.

383 Cf. esp. Am. 4:8f.; 5:11; 9:14; Isa. 37:30; 65:21f.; Jer. 29:5,28; Ezek. 28:26; Zeph. 1:13; Neh. 9:25. Cf. the evidence for *bnh* || *nṭ'* (structural analysis of I.v.3 above). The present wording reads like the reversal of well-known curses, cf. Deut. 28:30,33 as well as the Ugaritic references collected by Baltzer (*Bundesformular*, 30). In Hittite treaties cf. Weidner, *Politische Dokumente*, 68:48ff.

the adjectives *gdlt wṭbt*, as well as the verb *śb'*.[384]

## 4.4 The dialogue in Josh. 24:14-24

Numerous factors facilitate a somewhat briefer treatment of these verses than was the case with the preceding historical summary. The dialogue in vss.14-24 contains many cola paralleling the historical material of vss.2-13.[385] In combination with the high degree of external parallelism at the level of the canticles and canto, this results in relatively little new and significant diction in the present unit. It is therefore expedient to handle the literary-critical issues canticle by canticle. Our analysis of macrostructure demonstrated that the present form of the text constitutes a carefully structured unit, and for that reason it will not be necessary to elaborate extensive criticism of previous literary-critical dissections of the text based upon the criterion that repetitions or parallelisms betray variant sources. Given the demonstrated unity of the present text, it is more helpful to ask whether the present structure betrays signs of significant Dtistic influence or, conversely, whether it portrays fundamental independence from terminology usually held to be Dtistic.

### 4.4.1 Canticle II.i Josh. 24:14-15

The parallel use of the verbs *yr'* and *'bd* is found elsewhere in Deut. 6:13; 10:12,20; 13:5; 1 Sam. 12:14,20,24; 2 Kgs 17:33,35,41.[386] Upon first glance this would suggest that the combination is Dtistic. However, such a conclusion may be premature. It is striking that the reference in Deut. 6:13, as in Josh. 24:14, comes immediately after the parallel references to the gift of the land. It has been argued above that Josh. 24:13 is not dependent upon Deut. 6:10f. Furthermore, Deut. 6:14-25 contains numerous additional points of thematic contact with Josh. 24:1-28, but it is not possible to demonstrate any places where Josh. 24:1-28 is directly dependent. And Deut. 7 follows with an account which is literarily dependent upon Ex. 23.[387]

[384]These observations reinforce the conclusion by Sperling that Josh. 24:13 "is obviously primary" ("Joshua 24," 128).

[385]See the discussion of macrostructure in the structural analysis above.

[386]Cf. Jer. 40:9 = (2 Kgs. 25:24).

[387]Cf. Schmitt, *Landtag*, 27; Weinfeld, *Deuteronomy*, 46ff. See too A.Phillips, "A Fresh Look at the Sinai Pericope: Part 1," *VT* 34 (1984) 49.

The references in Deut. 10:12,20; 13:5 are all accompanied by other synomymous expressions in the style of Deuteronomy, which is not the case in Josh. 24:14f. In fact it is noteworthy that, just as the Sinai event is ignored in the historical summary, the present verses say nothing about laws or commandments which must be obeyed, as is so predominantly the case in Deuteronomy.[388]

The use of the Hiph. imperative of *swr* makes a clear connection with Gen. 35:2, on the one hand, and with texts such as Judg. 10:16; 1 Sam. 7:3f. on the other hand.[389] It has been pointed out by A.van Selms[390] that the manner of putting away foreign gods as described in Gen. 35:2-4 and Josh. 24:14,23 is remarkably different from the violent destruction and iconoclasm prescribed in Deut. 12:3; 7:5,25f. Nor can these ceremonies be compared with the violent destructions attributed to Hezekiah (2 Kgs. 18:4) or Josiah (2 Kgs. 23:4-24),[391] which are fully in the spirit of Deuteronomy. Although in the opinion of the present writer the evidence does not warrant the conclusion that the ceremonies described in Josh. 24:14,23 or Gen. 35:2-4 betray only temporary henotheism with the option to retrieve the gods at a later time, it is evident that these descriptions do not follow either the legislation of Deuteronomy[392] or the reform accounts of Hezekiah or Josiah, which are narrated with a view to fulfilment of the Deuteronomic law. This is itself already an important argument against a Dtic or Dtistic provenance of Gen. 35:2-4; Josh. 24:14,23.

The combination *btmym wb'mt* finds a direct parallel in Ps. 15:2 and in inverted order in Judg. 9:16,19.[393] These terms are generally

[388]Cf. in connection with the verses listed above Deut. 10:13; 11:1; 13:5. The style of Josh. 24:14 is significantly different in this respect.

[389]Cf. also Ex. 23:25 and 1 Sam. 12:20.

[390]A.van Selms, "Temporary Henotheism," in M.A.Beek et al, eds., *Symbolae Biblicae et Mesopotamicae Fransisco Mario Theodoro de Liagre Böhl Dedicatae* (Leiden, 1973), 341-348.

[391]Van Selms, "Temporary Henotheism," 344f.

[392]The burial of the gods under a terebinth in Gen. 35:4 is balanced in 35:8 by the burial of Rebekah under a terebinth, which itself might imply that farewell was said to the gods in the same reverent manner as to the deceased nurse of the tribal anacestress.

[393]While the degree of later editing or redacting is debated, Judg. 9 is often thought to belong to the earlier stages of Judges, e.g., W.Harrelson, *Interpreting the Old Testament* (New York, 1964), 143 ("Yet this story is told with such power, directness, and faithfulness to topography, to customs and practices known to characterize the people and region of central Palestine, that it seems safe to consider the story to be a report either by an eyewitness or one who lived very near to

explained in the context of treaty or covenant terminology.[394] The use of the verb *'bd* and related expressions for serving Yahweh places the analysis of Josh. 24:14-24 in the midst of one of the most complex literary-critical debates, namely the relationship of texts such as Ex. 23 and 34 to Deuteronomy, and the concomittant question of the degree to which it is necessary and legitimate to speak of Dtistic language in the framework of Judges and throughout 1 Samuel. Since the relationship of Josh. 24 to these other chapters is dealt with extensively below, it is not necessary here to pursue the matter further. It is worth mentioning, however, that the term *'bd* is already used as a description of the service of a deity in Ugarit and goes back to ancient NE tradition.[395] In Ugarit, as in Hebrew, it has sometimes been viewed as a technical term denoting vassalage.[396] In the Amarna Letters, where various terms are employed to designate vassal servitude under the Pharaoh, there are two examples of the root *'bd*,[397] i.e., *ú-bu-dì* and *ú-bu-ud*, present in the texts as West Semitic glosses[398] on the term MI-*ru*-TI "service." Numerous of the Amarna Letters contain explicit declarations of service,[399] often as a 1st person dec-

the period described."); cf. R.G.Boling, *Judges* (Garden City, 1975), 29ff.; Mayes, *Story of Israel*, 162 n.12. According to V.Fritz ("Abimelech und Sichem in Jdc. IX," *VT* 32 [1982] 129-144), vs.16a is to be attributed to a Dtistic historian, and vs.19a to an even later Dtistic redactor. His analysis is countered by T.A.Boogaart ("Stone for Stone: Retribution in the Story of Abimelech and Shechem," *JSOT* 32 [1985] 45-56).

[394]See Frankena, "Vassal-Treaties," 136f., 141; Kline, "Abram's Amen," 6-8; Weinfeld, "Covenant of Grant," 186; *Deuteronomy*, 84; Kalluveettil, *Declaration and Covenant*, 50f.; Mettinger, *King and Messiah*, 141. Dahood has argued that in the Psalms too the term *'mt* can function as an emphatic substantive ("Hebrew-Ugaritic Lexicography III," *Bibl* 46 [1965] 317). Butler notes that both *'mt* and *tmym* find a predominantly liturgical usage in the Psalms (*Joshua*, 272f). The similarity between employment of these terms in an oath of allegiance (treaty context) and to demonstrate loyalty to Yahweh (e.g., cultic use in the Psalms) need not be further elaborated here.

[395]For references cf. J.C.de Moor, "Knechten van goden en de knecht van Jhwh," in *De Knecht. Studies rondom Deutero-Jesaja* (Fs J.L.Koole; Kampen, 1978), 131.

[396]J.C.Greenfield, "Some Treaty Terminology in the Bible," in *Fourth World Congress of Jewish Studies: Papers Vol. 1* (Jerusalem, 1967), 117-119.

[397]EA 151:19-20 and EA 152:55-56.

[398]C.Grave, "Northwest Semitic *ṣapānu* in a Break-up of an Egyptian Stereotype Phrase in EA 147," *Or* 51 (1982) 166 n.30; W.L.Moran, *Les Lettres d'el-Amarna: Correspondence diplomatique du pharaon* (Paris, 1987), 385.

[399]Cf. EA 89:17; 118:39-40; 119:43-44; 253:26-28; 254:10-11; 266:16. Cf. D.Lorton, *The Juridical Terminology of International Relations in Egyptian Texts*

laration, and it sometimes is repeated more than once within a single letter.[400]

We have noted above that Josh. 24:1-14 generally follows the literary pattern of the treaties. It is now also possible to view the confessional declarations of service employing the root *'bd* in 24:15e,18b,21,24 in comparison with the widely attested ancient NE declarations of allegiance to the suzerain.[401] Akkadian terminology already employs social terms such as "master" and "slave" to express the covenantal relationship between sovereign kings and their minor dependents.[402]

In vs.15 the expression *r' b'yny* was sometimes thought to be a sign of J, but in 1893 Holzinger argued that it was found in all the Pentateuchal sources.[403] The combination *bḥr* with the root *'bd* is found in Josh. 24:15,22 and nowhere else in a given verse in the OT, which reinforces the conclusion that the external parallelism here is deliberate. The phrase "gods of the Amorites" is found elsewhere in Judg. 6:10 and is not Dtistic.[404] Use of *'nky* rather than *'ny* was at one time thought to be characteristic of J, but this identification could not withstand a more critical analysis.[405] The occurrences of the form *n'bd*, with or without a suffix, have been listed above.[406] The closest parallels are in Ex. 10:28; Judg. 10:10; 1 Sam. 12:10.

*through Dyn. XVIII* (Baltimore, 1974), 132, 176-179.

[400]Also interesting, in comparison to our thesis that Josh. 24:14-24 employs *n'bd* as a 1st person declaration of service in poetic refrains, is the detail that when Lab'ayu of Shechem declares his servitude to the Pharaoh (EA 254:10-15) he emphasizes it with what can be read as two poetic bicola in which he denies that he is guilty of insurrection. Cf. EA 254:11-15, following the translation by Moran, *Lettres d'el-Amarna*, 481 but rearranged colometrically:

*Je ne suis pas un rebelle,*
*et je ne manque pas à mon devoir;*
*je n'ais pas refusé de payer mon tribut,*
*je n'ai rien refusé de ce que mon Commissaire avait demandé.*

[401]Cf. Tadmor, "Treaty and Oath," 140, plus the literature he lists in n.71.; Weinfeld, "Loyalty Oath," 392-413.

[402]Tadmor, "Treaty and Oath," 131 (including references).

[403]Holzinger, *Einleitung*, 105.

[404]Early source-critical analyses posited a connection with E (cf. Meyer, "Eroberung Palestinas," esp. 144f.), but the employment of the term "Amorites" as proof of a specific source has since been proven doubtful (see 2.3.7.1).

[405]Cf. F.Giesbrecht, "Zur Hexateuchkritik, der Sprachgebrauch des hexateuchischen Elohisten," *ZAW* 1 (1881) 177-276, esp. 249-258; Holzinger, *Einleitung*, 95.

[406]Cf. the discussion of the refrain forming separation downwards in II.A.i.3.

### 4.4.2 Canticle II.ii Josh. 24:16-18

The expression *ḥlylh*, whether written *plene* or *defective*, is found 21x in the OT,[407] and always in heightened discourse. The combination of *'zb* (Yahweh) and *'bd* (other gods) is found in Josh. 24:16,20, establishing an external parallelism. The combination functions similarly in Judges (2:6; 10:6,13) as well as 1 Samuel (8:8; 12:10), but is absent in Deuteronomy.[408]

The use of *'lh* in the Hiph. participle in reference to Yahweh as deliverer from Egypt is attested elsewhere in Lev. 11:45; Deut. 20:1; 1 Sam. 7:10; 2 Kgs. 17:7; Jer. 2:6; Ps. 81:11. Previous studies have suggested that the use of *'lh* rather than *yṣ'* in general argues against the theory of a Dtistic hand.[409] Vs.17b is often considered evidence of Dtistic redaction. We have noted in the comparison with the LXX that vs.17b constitutes a deliberate poetic expansion of the original composition. The language may be classified as Dtistic but it differs in minor details from similar stereotyped terminology in Deuteronomy.[410] Since it is a poetic expansion incorporated into the text independent from the *Vorlage* of the LXX, it may be attributed to fairly late amplification. The use of the verb *šmr* for Yahweh guarding Israel is found already in Gen. 28:15,20, which is particularly important because of the additional connections linking Josh. 24:1-28 to the Jacob cycle in Genesis. Note too Ex. 23:20; Ps. 91:11. It is used in this sense in particular in the Psalms.[411] The non-Dtistic character of the verb *grš* has been treated in vs.12 above. The acclamations *ky yhwh 'lhynw* and *ky-hw' 'lhynw* have been dealt with in connection with the structural analysis, where it was demonstrated that they have close parallels in the poetry of Jeremiah and the Psalms. Since

[407]Gen. 18:25 (2x); 44:7,17; Josh. 22:29; 24:16; 1 Sam. 2:30; 12:23; 14:45; 20:2,9; 22:15; 24:7; 26:11; 2 Sam. 20:20 (2x); 23:17 (= 1 Chron. 11:19); 1 Kgs. 21:3; Job 27:5; 34:10.

[408]Numerous of the texts where the combination occurs have often been treated as Dtistic, cf. esp. 1 Kgs. 9:9; 2 Kgs. 17:16; Jer. 5:19; 16:11; 22:9. Regarding the correlation of Josh. 24 with Judges and Samuel see 5.4 and 5.5, and see provisionally Weinfeld, *Deuteronomy*, 320.

[409]Cf. the discussion of vss.5-7 above and the sources listed there.

[410]See 3.6.2; McCarthy, *Treaty and Covenant*, 228; Weinfeld, *Deuteronomy*, 330.

[411]G.Sauer, *šmr*, *THAT*, 2:982-987, esp. 985. In Ugaritic it is already attested in the form *ḏmr* as a specific term for divine protection, cf. M.Dykstra–J.C.de Moor, "Problematical Passages in the Legend of Aqhatu," *UF* 7 (1975) 175f.; P.Bordreuil–D.Pardee, "Le sceau nominal de 'Ammīyiḏtamrou, roi d'Ugarit," *Syria* 61 (1984) 13; J.C.de Moor, "The Ancestral Cult," *UF* 17 (1986) 409.

they play upon the self-revelation of Yahweh (cf. Ex. 6:7, *ky 'ny yhwh 'lhykm*),[412] the confessional response can hardly be dated[413] or assigned to a source.[414]

### 4.4.3 Canticle II.iii Josh. 24:19-21

As was the case in the preceding canticle, an analysis of terminology in vss.19-21 demonstrates that a Dtistic provenance for these verses is unlikely. Weinfeld is justified in stressing that the phrase *l' twkl* cannot be admitted as evidence of Dtic influence or origin.[415] The parallelism of *'lhym qdšym hw'* and *'l-qnw' hw'* may be taken as ancient cultic formulations.[416] The combination of *pš'* and *ḥṭ'* is definitely not Dtistic.[417]

Whereas Deuteronomy ordinarily speaks of *'lhym 'ḥrym*,[418] Josh.

[412]Cf. Ex. 8:6; 16:12; 20:5; 29:46 etc.

[413]The liturgical confession can be as old as the worship of Yahweh. See Eissfeldt, "'Mein Gott' im Alten Testament," *ZAW* 61 (1945-48) 3-16.

[414]Note that Kalluveettil (*Declaration and Covenant*, 61 n.188) compares Josh. 24:16-18,21-24 and Ex. 24:3,7 as covenantal acclamation formulae.

[415]Weinfeld, *Deuteronomy*, 2f.

[416]Cf. at 2.3.7.2. It is noteworthy that in the decalogue, Ex. 20:5 states *ky 'nky yhwh 'lhyk*, which is followed by the designation *'l qn'*. Similarly, in Lev. 11:44 the statement *ky 'ny yhwh 'lhykm* is followed with a demand for holiness, "because I am holy," *ky qdwš 'ny*. On *'lhym qdwšym* and possible correlation with extra-biblical epithets cf. A.Cooper, "Divine Names and Epithets in the Ugaritic Texts," in Rummel, ed, *RSP*, 3:431f. On Ex. 34:14b consult Halbe, *Privilegrecht*, 134-140. On the basis of the orthography of *qnw'* in Nah. 1:2 and Josh. 24:19, L'Hour argued for a post-exilic date, thereby ignoring the parallels in Ex. 20:5; 34:14b. The precariousness of his argument based upon orthographic presence of the *matres lectionis waw* is readily evident from the fact that the Nash Papyrus in Ex. 20:5 has the same form as Josh. 24:19; Nah. 1:2, cf. BHS crit. app.; Nielsen, *Zehn Gebote*, 34f.; see too Meyer, "Ausprachetraditionen," 40f. The orthography of *qnw'* in Josh. 24:19 could be due to preference at a late stage in the transmission of the text and proves nothing with respect to the date post quem of the original composition.

[417]Cf. the complete listing offered in connection with the structural analysis above. The root *pš'* never occurs in Deuteronomy as either a noun or a verb. Contrast its presence in Ex. 22:8; 23:21; 34:7 and prolifically in 8th cent. prophecy. In his analysis of *nś' 'wn wpš' wḥṭ'h* in Ex. 34:7, R.C.Dentan is lead to the conclusion that the use of *nś'* in the sense "to forgive" finds a fairly broad distribution in the OT but "most striking is *the absence of any occurrence in the Deuteronomic literature*" (original emphasis) ("The Literary Affinities of Exodus xxxiv 6f.," *VT* 13 [1963] 45).

[418]Except 31:16 (considered by Weinfeld to be from E [*Deuteronomy*, 10 n.2, 83 n.2]) and 32:12 (song of Moses).

24:20,23 employs *'lhy nkr*, which constitutes a strong argument against a Dtistic origin.[419] The parallelism of *r''* (Hiph.), *klh* (Piel) and *yṭb* (Hiph.) has been defended in the structural analysis. For the present concern it remains to be asked whether the combination of these terms is Dtistic. The Hiph. of *r''* with Yahweh as subject is found elsewhere in Ex. 5:22; Num. 11:11; Ruth 1:21; 1 Kgs. 17:20; Mic. 4:6; Jer. 25:6, 29; 31:28; Zeph. 1:12; Zech. 8:14; Ps. 44:3.[420] This distribution, and the absence of such usage in Deuteronomy, casts serious doubt upon the assertion that *wšb whr' lkm* can be considered Dtistic.[421] A similar trend is found with *klh* (Piel).[422] The Hiph. of *yṭb* with Yahweh as subject is found in Deuteronomy,[423] but this is by no means a unique usage of this book.[424] In short, Josh. 24:20 can scarcely be considered Dtistic.

As was the case with *ḥlylh* in vs.16, *l' ky* is an emphatic form indigenous to heightened dialogue.[425] It should be considered a characteristic of Hebrew dialogue, and it does not provide criterion for source distinction.

### 4.4.4 Canticle II.iv Josh. 24:22-24

Since Josh. 24:22 is demonstrated via a form-critical comparison with Ruth 4:9-11 and 1 Sam. 12:5[426] to be built upon a legal oath, previous

[419] Schmitt, *Landtag*, 22f. Nielsen, *Zehn Gebote*, 69f.; and see already Dillmann, *Josua*, 583, 587, 618.

[420] Cf. Is. 41:23 regarding false gods.

[421] Contra E.Noort, "JHWH und das Böse. Bemerkungen zu einer Verhältnisbestimmung," *OTS* 23 (Leiden, 1984), 126.

[422] With Yahweh as subject in the sense of "destroy" or "consume" see Ex. 32:10,12; 33:3,5; Lev. 26:44; Deut. 28:21; Num. 16:21; 17:10 (ET 16:45); 25:11 (with *qn'*); Is. 10:18; Jer. 5:3; 9:15; 14:12; 49:37; Ezek. 20:13; 22:31; 43:8 (with *qdš*); Ezra 9:14; Ps. 59:14; 78:33. For further discussion and comparison with cognate and synonymous readings in Ugaritic see Cassuto, *Biblical and Oriental Studies*, 2:41f.

[423] Cf. Deut. 8:16; 28:63; 30:5.

[424] Cf. Gen. 32:10,13 (with Hiph. inf. abs. const.); Ex. 1:20; Num. 10:32; Judg. 17:13; 1 Sam. 2:32; 25:31; 1 Kgs. 1:47; Jer. 18:10; 32:40; Mic. 2:7; Zeph. 1:12; Zech. 8:15; Ps. 51:20 (cf. Is. 41:23). See too Johag, "*ṭwb*–Terminus Technicus," 3-23.

[425] Cf. Gen. 18:15; 19:2; 42:12; Josh. 5:14; Judg. 15:13; 1 Sam. 12:12; 2 Sam. 24:24 (= 1 Chron. 21:24); 1 Kgs. 2:30; 3:22 (2x),23; 2 Kgs. 20:10; Isa. 30:16; Jer. 2:25; 42:14. Cf. Z.Zevit, "Expressing Denial in Biblical Hebrew and Mishnaic Hebrew, and in Amos," *VT* 29 (1979) 506.

[426] See 2.2.

attempts to declare the entire verse to be a late insertion[427] are not convincing.[428]

According to Weinfeld the expression *hṭh lb* belongs to the didactic vocabulary common to the wisdom literature and Deuteronomy,[429] but a reference such as Judg. 9:3[430] cautions against putting much weight upon the claim.[431] To be quite precise, contrary to Weinfeld's implication, the verb *nṭh* with "heart" as direct object is never found in Deuteronomy, and *nṭh* itself is used only stereotypically there.[432] An imperative similar to Josh. 24:23 is found in Ps. 119:36. The combination *nṭh* plus "heart" is found elsewhere in 2 Sam. 19:15; 1 Kgs. 8:58; 11:2,3,4,9; Ps. 119:112; 141:4; Prov. 2:2 (cf. Isa. 44:20). The combination is therefore hardly evidence for Dtistic authorship.[433] The imperatives of Josh. 24:23 are widely recognized to form a parallel with Gen. 35:2.

The refrain in vs.24 is composed of a tricolon. The third colon, *wbqwl nšm'*, is of particular interest for an analysis of this canticle because the phrase *šm' bqwl* has at times been asserted to be a Dtistic expression.[434] The claim is countered by two factors. First, the combination *šm' bqwl* or *šm' lqwl* is found in many non-Dtistic texts.[435]

[427]Contra Holzinger, *Josua*, 99; Noth, *Das System*, 136; *Josua* 1953, 10, 135; Möhlenbrink, "Landnahmesagen," 252; L'Hour, "L'alliance," 28. The main reason why Noth strikes vs.22 as a gloss appears to be an attempt to avoid postulating a third source in addition to the two of vss.26-27. Eissfeldt did not hesitate to opt for three sources (*Hexateuch-Synopse*, 80).

[428]See too the comparison with 1 Sam. 10:24 (5.5.1).

[429]Weinfeld, *Deuteronomy*, 304.

[430]With the verb in the Qal form.

[431]The connection between *btmym wb'mt* (24:14) and Judg. 9:16,19 has been referred to above. Additional parallels between these passages with their settings at Shechem are delineated in 5.4.3.

[432]It is found in only two clichés, "an outstretched arm" (4:34; 5:15; 7:19; 9:29; 11:2; 26:8) and "pervert justice" (16:19; 24:17; 27:19), both of which find counterparts already in the Tetrateuch.

[433]This point is not mitigated by a survey of the distribution of the similar phrase "to incline one's ear."

[434]Perlitt, *Bundestheologie*, 259 n.4.; McCarthy, *Treaty and Covenant*, 231. McCarthy bases his judgment upon the combination of *'bd* and *šm' bqwl*. The argument has some merit cf. Deut. 13:5; but there the combination is embedded in other synonyms in the style of Deuteronomy, which is not the case in Josh. 24:24; 1 Sam. 12:14. Furthermore, ignored is the fact that the form *n'bd* in Josh. 24:14 places this usage in a class of its own.

[435]Cf. Gen. 3:17; 26:5; 30:6; Ex. 5:2; 23:21f.; Num. 14:22, etc. See further Schmitt, *Landtag*, 23. Already in 1893 Holzinger argued that the expression *šm'*

Secondly, the expression is attested in both biblical and extra-biblical texts in terms of obedience to treaty regulations.[436]

## 4.5 Conclusions regarding textual analysis

The preceding analysis has subjected Josh. 24:1-28 to an extensive examination of terminology. This study has been conducted both at the level of individual words and with respect to verbal combinations and phrases. The conclusions contradict the previous theories that this passage can be dissected into various sources represented in the Pentateuch. A strict correlation with an alleged J, E, or P document is excluded. Similarly, claims of a substantial presence of Dtic/Dtistic editing or redacting in this passage find little support from the text itself. There is only evidence for minor Dtistic influence. For example, in the plus in the MT of vs.17b the terminology can be viewed as Dtistic. But it is significant that this plus has been demonstrated to be poetic expansion of the original composition. One can also mention in this respect the wording of vs.5a and the presence of *nḥlh* in vs.28, both of which have at times been referred to as evidence of Dtistic language. Both these cases also reflect late modifications, albeit probably still with a view to the poetic character of the text. A few additional minor examples of terminology generally held to be Dtistic are present, but the unambiguous result of our analysis firmly supports the opinion expressed by Sperling that "the language of the chapter is not Deuteronomic or Deuteronomistic."[437]

At numerous points there is a conceptual affinity to material presented in Deuteronomy, but Josh. 24:1-28 employs a high percentage of terminology clearly atypical of Deuteronomy. Moreover, various details such as the "listening stone," the role of Shechem, the focus upon putting away the gods rather than upon their violent destruction, the emphasis upon choosing (*bḥr*) Yahweh, and the role of Joshua as lawgiver, all reinforce the conclusion based on vocabulary that previous allegations of either a Dtic/Dtistic composition or extensive redaction are unfounded. Moreover, since it is possible to demonstrate that Josh. 24:13 influenced the wording of Deut. 6:10f. one cannot exclude

*bqwl* is found in J, E, and D (*Einleitung*, 107, 190).

[436]Weinfeld, "Covenant of Grant," 186; Kalluveettil, *Declaration and Covenant*, 135, 157.

[437]Sperling, "Joshua 24," 133.

the possibility that Josh. 24:1-28 also had a broader influence upon the content and vocabulary of Deuteronomy. Previous claims that Josh. 24:1-28 is Dtic or Dtistic were especially influenced by general theories regarding a Dtistic history extending from Deuteronomy–2 Kings and are not able to withstand a more detailed lexicographical analysis. Contrary to the opinion of numerous previous scholars,[438] it is scarcely plausible to view Josh. 24 as a secondary addition to an earlier Dtic version of Joshua. Our research also reveals that the present structure of Josh. 24:1-28 is not the product of a long series of patching and editing but more likely, with the exception of some minor details, reflects an original composition.

While there is a degree of conceptual and thematic affinity between Josh. 24:1-28 and Deuteronomy, there is an even closer correlation with numerous passages in Ex. 23:20-33; 24; 34; Judg. 2:6–1 Sam. 12. It has been noted that these texts too have often been considered Dtistic, but the designation is not entirely felicitous because much of the significant terminology employed is actually un-Dtistic. The historical summary in 24:2-13 paraphrases the original accounts in Genesis, Exodus and Numbers, and in general it is literarily dependent upon those parallel passages. This fact, combined with the absence of Dtistic terminology, makes it necessary to raise reservations concerning the conclusion that Josh. 24 was specifically composed in order to function literarily in a Dtistic history running from Deuteronomy–2 Kings. Since Josh. 24:1-28 demonstrates a clear and purposeful correlation with select texts in the Pentateuch as well as bearing numerous linguistic and conceptual affinities with a number of passages in Judges–2 Kings, it is advisable to turn to a more detailed analysis of these specific connections prior to drawing more extensive conclusions regarding the preceding textual analysis. This will be the focus of the following chapter of our study.

[438] Cf. G.J.Wenham, "The Deuteronomistic Theology of the Book of Joshua," *JBL* 90 (1971) 140-148; M.A.O'Brien, *The Deuteronomistic History Hypothesis: A Reassessment* (Freiburg and Göttingen, 1989), 79.

# 5 The Literary and Historical Setting of Josh. 24

## 5.1 Introduction

The preceding textual analysis of Josh. 24:1-28 demonstrated that an acceptable evaluation of its literary provenance and its present placement in the OT canon must analyze connections established between it and select passages in the Pentateuch on the one hand and in Judges–2 Kings on the other. An analysis of these connections brings to light important considerations regarding Josh. 24's function in the OT canon. It also serves to highlight numerous factors which must be taken into consideration in any attempt to determine the date of this passage's literary composition.

It is necessary at the outset to limit the boundaries of our study. A discussion of Josh. 24:1-28's literary placement inevitably lodges one in the midst of a complex Pentateuch-Hexateuch debate.[1] Our analysis of terminology and content in Josh. 24:1-28 underscored the correspondence between this chapter and numerous passages in Genesis, the Sinai complex of Exodus, Transjordanian accounts from Numbers, certain legal and covenantal passages in Deuteronomy, and select passages from Judges and 1 Samuel. The latter texts have in turn been vigorously debated with respect to whether they are Dtistic. It is necessary to recognize that an analysis of Josh. 24:1-28 can neither entertain nor answer all these related questions. Nevertheless, a detailed evaluation of the connections between Josh. 24:1-28 and a selection of important related passages may be expected to contribute to the broader study of the literary and thematic arrangement of the historical writings spanning from Genesis through 2 Kings.

Since a study of Josh. 24:1-28's literary placement in the canon cannot be divorced from a consideration of its theological purpose and function, it is also beneficial to make certain comparisons with a number of extra-biblical ancient NE texts. This has been explicitly

[1]E.g., the significance of Josh. 24 constitutes one of the most fundamental arguments for the Hexateuch theory of Tengström, *Hexateucherzählung*, esp. 24 n.38, 28, 33, 40-44, 67f., 118, 127, 132, 154. Although considerable reserve is warranted regarding Tengström's theory of a Hexateuch, his discussion does demonstrate the significant role that Josh. 24:1-28 must have in any such discussion. For a different approach, also highlighting the significance of Josh. 24, see Brekelmans, "Joshua XXIV" (forthcoming).

recognized previously in the various form-critical correlations drawn with treaty texts. The structural analysis offered above provides an avenue for a reassessment of the degree to which Josh. 24:1-28 fits the patterns recognized elsewhere. Furthermore, the attention paid to the treaty texts has eclipsed another field of comparison which may prove of some interest, namely the festival and ritual texts widely represented in the Hittite archives but also amply documented in the Ugaritic and Akkadian material.

Finally, comparison with other texts should not exclude the concomitant element of contrast. Josh. 24:1-28 is in various respects a unique passage, and as a methodological principle it is ordinarily helpful to ascertain precisely the exceptional elements of a passage as clues to its specific purpose and intention. It is for this reason that the following analysis commences with a brief summary of those aspects which are *sui generis*.

## 5.2 Material unique to Josh. 24:1-28

Designation of the gathering as taking place "before Elohim" (*lpny h'lhym*, vs.1) rather than "before Yahweh" (*lpny yhwh*) is not entirely unique, but it is certainly rare. The same is true of the employment of the formula *kh 'mr yhwh 'lhy yśr'l* in the mouth of someone not designated specifically as a prophet or prophetess. Explicit reference to patriarchal service of other gods is both unique and highly significant in Josh. 24:1-28. While the historical material of vss.2b-13 generally summarizes more detailed narrative accounts found in Genesis, Exodus and Numbers, there are numerous unique features in the present descriptions, e.g., the formulation *wy'qb wbnyw yrdw mṣrym*,[2] the presence of *m'pl* in vs.7, and the employment of the verb *lḥm* in vss.9,11 to typify the opposition of the Moabites and the citizens of Jericho. Perhaps the use of the verb *lḥm* is to be attributed in part to a desire to establish external parallelism.[3] Nevertheless, it is significant that the present account does not follow the outline of the conquest as delineated in the earlier chapters of Joshua.

The presentation of the choice to serve Yahweh, the gods whom the fathers served, or the gods of the land in which they are now living, is a unique combination. This is not to say that Israel nowhere else

[2]See 4.3.1.3.
[3]Cf. 8aC, 9aC, 11aC (3.4.4 re parallelism in I.iv).

is told to make a choice. In Deut. 30:19, with a similar imperative, they are told to choose life, *wbḥrt bḥyym*. While these texts are in certain respects comparable, the frank wording of Josh. 24:14f.,22 is markedly different from the choice between life and death presented in Deut. 30:19 and its context. A comparison with the ancient poetry of Judg. 5:8aA[4] is both inevitable and instructive, as is the reference in Judg. 10:14 to Israel's being condemned for having chosen false gods. Elsewhere it is always Yahweh who chooses Israel,[5] and never vice versa. The significance of this emphasis upon choosing Yahweh is reinforced by the fact that the parallelism of *bḥr* and *'bd* occurs twice here and nowhere else in the OT within a single verse. A possible explanation for the present use may be sought in the underlying theme of Yahweh as king.[6]

Similar observations may be raised with respect to the frank warning in 24:19, "You are not able to serve the LORD." Analogies have been drawn with statements in the prophetic literature.[7] Comparison with the role of the curses in treaty texts is also relevant. But these observations do not take away from the uniqueness of the present warning precisely in a passage intended to motivate Israel to serve Yahweh.

The refrain built upon the repetitive verbal form *n'bd* has been demonstrated above to be both unique and central to the present passage. It is also unique to find acclamation formulae such as *ky yhwh 'lhynw* and *ky-hw' 'lhynw* within the corpus of material from Genesis through 2 Kings. The call for the people to witness against themselves in vs.22 has been claimed by McCarthy to be highly anomalous.[8] Although McCarthy's analysis of this verse is untenable,[9] the present formulation is indeed rare, and it provides significant clues for comparison with a couple of other passages.[10]

[4] "They chose new gods."

[5] Cf. Deut. 7:6f.; 10:15; 14:2, plus many times. To the bibliography listed by H.Wildberger ("*bḥr* erwählen," *THAT*, 1:275-299), add G.Fohrer, "Action of God and Decision of Man in the Old Testament," in *Biblical Essays 1966, Proceedings of the Ninth Meeting of 'OTWSA'* (Potchefstrom, 1967), 31-39; Th.C.Vriezen, *De verkiezing van Israel* (Amsterdam, 1974).

[6] Evidence is presented below; see especially the comparison with 1 Sam. 10:24. Note too the use of *n'bd* in 1 Kgs 12:4.

[7] E.g., Amos 3:2; Isa. 1:28; cf. 3.4.8.

[8] McCarthy, *Treaty and Covenant*, 230.

[9] See 2.4.1.

[10] Cf. Deut. 31:19; 1 Sam. 10:24 and 12:5, discussed below.

Erecting a stone under a "terebinth" in a *temenos* designated as a *mqdš yhwh* provides a combination which finds no exact parallel in the OT. The closest comparisons in the OT involve the altars built to the patriarchal deity in the narratives of Genesis. Analogous extra-biblical texts can be introduced for comparison, e.g., Ugaritic and Hittite references,[11] but understandably none of these refer to the sanctuary as belonging to *Yahweh.* This suggests that the ceremony described in 24:26f. ought to be accorded considerable significance in comparison and contrast to both biblical and extra-biblical references. The attribution of the role of witness to a stone in the sanctuary—because it heard the words of Yahweh—is singular within the OT material.[12] Also unique is the precise designation of the law book as a *spr twrt 'lhym.*

In short, it is especially within the dialogue of vss.14-24 and the description of the ceremony in vss.26f. that a number of highly unusual features are identifiable. These details are not peripheral to the passage; they are indigenous to the central choice to pledge sole allegiance to Yahweh. Against this background it is possible to explore the specific lines of connection with other OT passages.

## 5.3 Connections with the Pentateuch

Rejection of source-critical endeavors to unravel Hexateuchal strands in Josh. 24:1-28 in the manner long practiced by previous generations of scholars should not obscure the validity of tracing literary and conceptual themes progressing from the Pentateuch into Joshua and beyond into the description of the historical period post-settlement. Numerous of these connections have been alluded to above. The present section elaborates the affinities with a number of the more significant Pentateuchal parallels.

### 5.3.1 Shechem and the period of the patriarchs

Foregoing an attempt to provide an exhaustive account, Genesis narrates select events which typify the period and importance of the pa-

[11]See 4.2.2, and cf. below regarding relationships with ancient NE material.

[12]The ability to function as a witness to a covenant entails having heard the details of the covenant instituted (cf. Deut. 31:28; Jer. 6:18; Am. 3:13). Ordinarily in the OT it is heaven and earth that are called to witness (cf. Deut. 4:26ff.; 33:19; Ps. 50:4; Is. 1:2; 34:1; Mic. 6:2.) and not a stone in the sanctuary.

triarchs. Numerous of the patriarchal narratives are summarized or alluded to in Josh. 24, e.g., the fulfilment of the Abrahamic promise regarding the multiplication of progeny and the inheritance of the land. It is noteworthy, however, that although the main theme of the first canticle in the historical summary focuses upon this fulfilment, it does so against the background of the unique reference to the patriarchal service of foreign gods (24:2bC). Given the theme of allegiance to Yahweh, which stands at the core of Josh. 24:1-28, the explicit mention of the foreign gods already in 2bC cannot be coincidental. The author of Josh. 24 recognizes Yahweh as the God who called Abram from the land of his fathers. He describes him as *yhwh 'lhy yśr'l* (vss.2,23), a term which we have seen is never used in Deuteronomy.[13] It is now necessary to pursue the possibility that Josh. 24:1-28 wishes to make a deliberate correlation between *yhwh 'lhy yśr'l* and *'l 'lhy yśr'l* of Gen. 33:20.[14]

When Abram first traversed the land of Canaan, he traveled to Shechem by the great terebinth; there he received a promise to inherit the land, and there he built an altar to Yahweh (Gen. 12:6-8).[15] But the narrator suggests that he could not stay there because the Canaanites were in the land.[16] The Jacob cycle deliberately follows the pattern set down by the Abram cycle. Jacob too builds an altar at Shechem (33:20). And he too is unable to dwell there because of the Canaanite inhabitants (Gen. 34).

The similarity of Gen. 35:2-5 with Judg. 10:16; 1 Sam. 7:3f., and Josh. 24:14ff. has long been noted,[17] and the relationship between Gen. 35:2-5 and Josh. 24:14ff. may be treated briefly here. Both

[13]Cf. 4.3.1.1. Note that although Josh. 24:1-28 makes frequent allusion to the period of the fathers, it does not employ the designation *yhwh 'lhy 'bwtyk(m)* as found, for example, in Deut. 6:3.

[14]Cf. 4.3.1.1.

[15]Cf. G.T.Manley, "The God of Abraham," *THB* 14 (1964) 3-7.

[16]Gen. 12:6. On the early history of Shechem see W.Harrelson, "Shechem in Extra-Biblical References," *BA* 20 (1957) 2-10; W.F.Albright, "The Amarna Letters from Palestine," in *CAH*[3], II/2 (Cambridge, 1975), 98-116. esp. 115f.; E.F.Campbell, "Shechem in the Amarna Archive," in Wright, *Shechem: The Biography*, 191-207; "Two Amarna Notes: The Shechem City State and Amarna Administrative Terminology," in F.M.Cross et al, eds., *Magnalia Dei: The Mighty Acts of God* (New York, 1976), 39-54; G.W.Ahlström, *Who Were the Israelites?* (Winona, 1986), 65ff.

[17]Alt, "Die Wallfahrt," 218-230; Nielsen, "Burial," 103-123; *Shechem*, 108; Van Selms, "Temporary Henotheism," 344-346; Blum, *Komposition*, 38-61.

employ the imperative of *swr* (Hiph.) with *'t-'lhy hnkr* as direct object (cf. Gen. 35:2; Josh. 24:23). When written colometrically the similarity of the passages can be investigated from a new angle.[18]

| Gen. 35:2 | Josh. 24:23 |
|---|---|
| *wy'mr y'qwb 'l-bytw* | |
| *w'l kl-'šr 'mw* | |
| *hsrw 't-'lhy hnkr* | *w'th hsyrw 't-'lhy hnkr* |
| *'šr btkkm* | *'šr bqrbkm* |
| *whṭhrw* | *whṭw 't-lbbkm* |
| *whḥlypw śmltykm* | *'l-yhwh 'lhy yśr'l* |

The first colon of Gen. 35:2 (*wy'mr y'qwb 'l-bytw*) may be compared with Josh. 24:22aA (*wy'mr yhwš' 'l-h'm*). The second colon (*w'l kl-'šr 'mw*) adds nothing new and appears to be present primarily for the purpose of the *parallelismus membrorum* of the bicolon. As is evident from the colometric delineation above, the following two bicola are structurally parallel in Gen. 35:2b-c and Josh. 24:23a-b. In addition there is an affinity of content; *'šr btkkm* is synonymous with *'šr bqrbkm.*[19] A degree of correspondence can also be detected in *whṭhrw* (purify yourselves) and *whṭw 't-lbbkm* (incline your hearts); both are imperatives and both are actions appropriate to preparation for true cultic worship.

An additional similarity between these passages is identifiable in the references to the presence of Elohim/Yahweh in previous travel (cf. Gen. 35:3b, *wyhy 'mdy bdrk 'šr hlkty*, and Josh. 24:17c, *wyšmrnw*

[18]Previous studies have debated the criteria which validate a comparison of Gen. 35:2-5 with other texts, e.g., Nielsen, "Burial," 104; O.Keel, "Das Vergraben der 'Fremden Götter,' in Genesis XXXV 4b," *VT* 23 (1973) 305-336, esp. 306-315. Unfortunately, Keel's treatment of the literary placement of Gen. 35:2-5 and Josh. 24:14f.,23 is too receptive of the date suggested by Perlitt (cf. Keel, 328f. n.4). Note van Selms' emphasis on the non-violent, non-iconoclastic nature of the reform, atypical of Deuteronomy ("Temporary Henotheism," 344-346). For an attempt to distinguish between an original tradition and expansions in 35:1b$\beta$, 3b$\beta$, 7b, (14a$\beta$) influenced by Gen. 28:11ff. cf. E.Otto, *Jakob in Sichem* (Stuttgart, 1979), 82-88, 245.

[19]On *btk* || *b* in Ugaritic and Hebrew consult Dahood–Penar, "Parallel Pairs, I," 158 no.138; for *b* || *btk* see 138 no.97; for *b* || *bqrb* consult 137 no.96. These parallels lead one to expect to also find the combination *btk* || *bqrb*, which is indeed attested in Isa. 24:13 *bqrb h'rṣ* || *btwk h'mym*; Am. 9:3 *btwkh* || *bqrbh*; Job 20:13f. ext. par.; cf. Ezek. 22:26f.

*bkl-hdrk 'šr hlknw bh*). Gen. 35 proceeds with the burial of the gods under the oak at Shechem[20] and subsequent altar-building to Elohim at Bethel. Josh. 24 proceeds with establishment of covenantal law at Shechem and the erection of a stone in the sanctuary of Yahweh. A contrast and progression is apparently built into these passages. The land around Shechem, which the patriarchs could not settle in, has in Josh. 24 finally become the claimed possession of Israel. Purification for service of Elohim in the time of Jacob progresses to purification for service of Yahweh in the time of Joshua.

A question inevitably raised by a comparison of such clearly linked passages is that of literary priority. There have been supporters for the priority of either Gen. 35:2-5 or Josh. 24:14-27 respectively.[21] However, it is hardly possible to accept the view that Gen. 35:1ff. is primarily dependent upon Josh. 24.[22] The statement "and he was with me in the way in which I walked" (*wyhy 'mdy bdrk 'šr hlkty*, Gen. 35:3b) makes an unmistakable link with Jacob's initial vow in 28:20f.[23] Jacob's vow is central to the Jacob cycle, and it forms an indispensable element not only of the relationship between Gen. 28 and 35,[24] but also of the narration of Yahweh's providential presence in the intervening period. It is precisely the presence of Yahweh with Jacob that is cited as the motivation for accepting him as God (cf. Gen. 28:21b, *whyh yhwh ly l'lhym*). The parallel established in Josh. 24:17 is apparent, for there too the acclamation of Yahweh as Israel's God is based upon his previous providential presence in the way that they traveled. Jacob's vow is concretized with erection of a stone as a *massebah* which he calls *byt 'lhym*. The people's vow of service in Josh. 24:16-22 leads to the erection of a stone *bmqdš yhwh*.

Since Jacob's vow to serve Yahweh as his God stands central to

[20]For possibly comparable ancient NE customs cf. J.A.Soggin, *Old Testament and Oriental Studies* (Rome, 1975), 112-119; D.Ussishkin, "The Syro-Hittite Ritual Burial of Monuments," *JNES* 29 (1970) 124-128.

[21]Prevalent is the theory of the priority of Gen. 35. For the opposite view cf. Volz-Rudolph, *Der Elohist*, 130-134; Rudolph, *Der "Elohist"*, 245-248.

[22]Note that in Gen. 35:2 the expression *wṭhrw whḥlypw śmltykm* is unique, whereas Josh. 24:23b employs the more common *hṭh lb(b)*.

[23]Cf. J.P.Fokkelman, *Narrative Art in Genesis* (Assen, 1975), 231-235; *Oog in oog met Jakob* (Assen, 1981) 129.

[24]This is true whether or not one accepts a source division of these chapters, e.g., into J and E (A.de Pury, *Promesse divine et légende cultuelle dans le cycle de Jacob. Genèse 28 et les traditions patriarcales* [Paris, 1975], 503-585), or the theory of redaction proposed by Otto (*Jakob in Sichem*, 82-88).

the Jacob cycle, it is virtually impossible to abstract Gen. 35:1-5 from its context on the grounds that it is a late composition built upon the pattern of the Shechem ceremony in Josh. 24:1-28. Nevertheless, this does not preclude the possibility that at the time of the composition of the entire corpus of patriarchal narratives dealing with the promise of the land, Joshua's ceremony at Shechem was known and had an influence upon the compilation of the Genesis narratives. Already in Gen. 12:6f. it is apparent that the narrator's interest in Abram's sojourn at Shechem cannot be extricated from the theme of Canaanite habitation there. Literarily it is narrated with a proleptic vision to the period of the later settlement. This is also true of the Jacob cycle and of Joseph's wandering to Shechem at the outset of his descent to Egypt.[25]

Jacob's final prediction that Joseph will return to the land of the promise, and his gift of Shechem to the house of Joseph (Gen. 48:21f.), literarily anticipates Josh. 24:32.[26] The focus upon Shechem in Gen. 48:22 and Josh. 24:32 is reinforced by an additional detail. When Jacob gives Shechem to the house of Joseph, he claims to have taken it from the Amorites "with my sword and my bow." Josh. 24:12 contains a contrasting counterpart; while gathered at Shechem, prior to Joseph's burial, Israel's leader from the house of Joseph reminds them that the Amorites were driven out "not by your sword or your bow."[27]

All these considerations suggest that the narrator of Genesis knows the central position of Shechem in the time of the settlement.[28] Therefore, a reciprocal influence in the shaping of the present texts is possible.[29]

[25]Cf. Gen. 37:12-14. Note, with reservations, the discussion by Tengström (*Hexateucherzählung*, 40-47).

[26]Thematic connections with Shechem are undeniable. Gressmann attempted to prove from this that the original setting for Gen. 48 was in Shechem ("Ursprung und Entwicklung der Joseph-Sage," in H.Schmidt, ed., *Eucharisterion I* [Fs H.Gunkel; Göttingen, 1923], 1-55).

[27]Note that Jacob is said to be able to travel from Shechem to Bethel because the terror (*ḥth*) of God fell upon the surrounding cities so that they did not pursue Jacob (Gen. 35:5), while in Joshua 24 it is suggested that the Israelites are able to gain access to the land—and ultimately gather at Shechem—because Yahweh sent panic (*ṣr'h*) before them to drive out the inhabitants of the land (Josh. 24:12).

[28]De Vaux, *Early History*, 171-174.

[29]Cf., e.g., the comments by Blum, especially regarding the sudden presence of *'lhy hnkr* in Gen. 35:2,4, and the emphasis upon crossing the river in Gen. 31:21,

Josh. 24 is as indispensable for completion of literary themes treating the identification of Yahweh as the God of the patriarchs as it is for the narration of the patriarchal relationship to the land of the promise. It is not coincidental that the pledge of allegiance to serve Yahweh alone (esp. Josh. 24:17c) and the imperative to put away the other gods (24:23) make precise literary connections with Gen. 28:20f. and 35:2f. respectively.[30] The details of Josh. 24 complete both the theme of the occupation of the promised land in the area of Shechem,[31] as well as the worship of *yhwh 'lhy yśr'l* in the place previously identified with *'l 'lhy yśr'l*.[32]

### 5.3.2 Josh. 24:1-28 and the Mt.Ebal–Mt.Gerizim tradition of Deut. 11:29-32; 27

In the light of the close connection detectable between Josh. 24 and the role of Shechem in Genesis, and the important consideration that the term *Israel* is first used in the area of Shechem,[33] it is noteworthy that the description of conquest in Joshua never mentions the capture of Shechem. Equally significant is the altar-building near Shechem, as narrated in Deuteronomy. However, here references are made to Mt. Ebal and Mt. Gerizim rather than specifically to Shechem itself. Erection of altars by Abram and Jacob in the vicinity of Shechem anticipates the later inheritance of the land. The description in Deut. 11:29ff. includes a reference to the trees by Moreh, thereby making a clear link with Gen. 12:6f. The prescribed ceremony, including the building of an altar, shows the realized attainment of the land

*wy'br 't-hnhr* (*Komposition*, 40f., 43); cf. Josh. 24:2,3,14,15 and the discussion of macrostructure above.

[30]Unacceptable is the modified view of a "Hexateuch" proposed by Blum. He builds upon the analysis by Perlitt, adding a novel but untenable theory of Samaritans as the original audience of Josh. 24:1-28 (*Komposition*, 60). Blum's theory must be rejected because it cannot withstand a more detailed literary-critical analyses, and it is unable to do justice to the place of Shechem in the worship of *yhwh 'lhy yśr'l*; cf. the discussions of Ex. 24:9-11 and Judg. 9 below.

[31]Without Josh. 24 the emphasis in Genesis upon Shechem would stand open-ended and incomplete. This is unfortunately left out of purview by Clines (*Theme of the Pentateuch*).

[32]It may be of significance that Josh. 24:14,15 twice lacks the article *h* where it would be expected in reference to *'t-'lhym*. Does the wording betray an attempt to persuade Israel to worship their God as *Yahweh* rather than as *Elohim*?

[33]Cf. provisionally de Vaux, *Early History*, 172.

anticipated proleptically in the Abram and Jacob cycles.[34] This is of considerable importance for a comparison with Josh. 24:1-28, where the ceremony at Shechem is described without any reference to the parallel emphasis in Deut. 11:29ff.; 27, passages which are themselves ordinarily treated as pre-Dtic.[35]

The description of the altar is most detailed in ch.27. Scholars have long noted that the literary composition of this passage is problematic.[36] One of the important conclusions stated already by Kuenen and Steuernagel was that the altar law of 27:5-7 appears to be taken up from an independent account. This conclusion has been repeated many times, most recently by M.Anbar.[37] Indeed, as Anbar demonstrates, a comparison with Ex. 20:24f. leaves little doubt that the altar law is a standard description incorporated by the author of Deut. 27:1-8. However, the repetition of vs.3a in vs.8 is not necessarily evidence of two different sources. It is more probably a literary device necessary to incorporate the external material of vss.5-7 into the present account. The altar description in vss.5-7 is a coherent unit of four poetic verses:

| | |
|---|---|
| *wbnyt šm mzbḥ* [*5*] | (5aA) And build there an altar |
| *lyhwh 'lhyk* [*2*] | (5aB) to Yahweh your God, |
| *mzbḥ 'bnym* [*5*] | (5aC) an altar of stones. |
| *l'-tnyp 'lyhm brzl* [*1*] | (5bA) Do not let iron pass over them; |
| *'bnym šlmwt tbnh* [*5*] | (6aB) with whole stones you shall build |
| *'t-mzbḥ yhwh 'lhyk* [*2*] | (6aC) an altar to Yahweh your God. |

| | |
|---|---|
| *wh'lyt 'lyw 'wlt* [*5*] | (6bA) Offer on it burnt-offerings |
| *lyhwh 'lhyk* [*1*] | (6bB) to Yahweh your God. |
| *wzbḥth šlmym* [*8*] | (7A) Sacrifice peace offerings, |
| *w'klt šm* [*2*] | (7B) and eat there, |
| *wśmḥt lpny yhwh 'lhyk* [*1*] | (7C) and rejoice before Yahweh your God |

[34] Kuenen, "Bijdragen tot de critiek, V," 312.

[35] Weinfeld, "Emergence," 78-80. Cf. G.J.Wenham, "Deuteronomy and the Central Sanctuary," *TB* 22 (1971) 117f.

[36] Kuenen, "Bijdragen, V," 297-323; Steuernagel, *Josua*, 96-98; von Rad, *Deuteronomy*, 164-169; Eissfeldt, "Gilgal or Shechem," 90-101.

[37] M.Anbar, "The Story about the Building of an Altar on Mount Ebal," in Lohfink, ed., *Das Deuteronomium*, 304-309.

These two strophes[38] may be accepted as a relatively ancient poetic composition. The description does not contain a single article *h* or relative *'šr*, and the lone object marker *'t* (6aC) is possibly a later editorial accretion. Inclusion is formed by twofold use of *šm* (5aA, 7B) and the root *zbḥ* (5a [2x], 7A). There are multiple external parallelisms, e.g., *bnh* || *bnh* (5aA, 6aB); *'bnym* || *'bnym* (5aC, 6aB), as well as the strategic repetition of the root *zbḥ* (5aA, 5aC, 6aC, 7A). Wordplays are established by *šlmwt* || *šlmym* and *l'-tnyp 'lyhm* || *wh'lyt 'lyw 'wlt*. The fourfold repetition of *yhwh 'lhyk*, which occurs once in each verse, functions as a mini refrain. Note too that *zbḥ* || *'kl* is attested in poetic parallelism in Hos. 8:13. These words are also found together in many passages not generally considered poetic, i.e., Gen. 31:54; Ex. 34:15; Deut. 12:15,21; 1 Kgs 1:25; 19:21; Ezek. 16:20; 34:3; 39:17,19; 2 Chron. 30:22. This once again demonstrates that internal parallelism by itself is insufficient to prove poetic composition.[39] The parallelism of *zbḥ* and *śmḥ* is also attested elsewhere in the OT.[40] The total structure is a 3+3 || 2+3 arrangement.[41] It is not our purpose here to elaborate comparisons with Ex. 20:24f.[42] For the present discussion, the primary consideration is that the author(s) of Deut. 11:29ff.; 27 makes a correlation with the altar of Abram in the neighborhood of Shechem, likely to show that the attainment of the land in the time of Joshua is a fulfilment of the Abrahamic promise. The significance attributed to these references in 11:29ff.; 27 is also evident in the structural framework or inclusion they provide for the Dtic-code in chs.12-26.[43] Significantly, the altar must now be built according to the precise prescription in the Torah, an emphasis which

[38]Despite the thematic and terminological coherence, a division into two strophes is warranted by the ponderous threefold repetition of the root *'lh* in 6bA. This is supported by consideration of content; the first strophe focuses upon building the altar, the second upon sacrificial actions.

[39]As was the case in our evaluation of Josh. 24:1-28, the conclusion that the passage is in fact poetic is based upon the cumulative evidence of a colometric analysis of the text.

[40]See ext. par. in Deut. 33:18f.; Hab. 1:15f.; note the twofold use of *zbḥ* and fivefold use of *śmḥ* in Neh. 12:43. Employment of this parallelism was enduring, as is attested by its employment in part of the Musaf Service recited at the beginning of the new month (Kugel, *Idea*, 307f.). Cf. Vannoy, *Covenant Renewal*, 90f.

[41]Cf. the close similarity with 1 Sam. 11:14f. delineated below.

[42]Cf. the synopsis offered by Anbar, "The Story," 306.

[43]J.Blenkinsopp, "Are There Traces of the Gibeonite Covenant in Deuteronomy?" *CBQ* 28 (1966) 208 n.3.

is reinforced by the explicit command to write upon the stones all the words of the law.

Josh. 8:30-35 demonstrates that the mandate of Deut. 11:29ff.; 27 is fulfilled. However, despite the fact that Josh. 24:1-28 too makes an unequivocal connection with the patriarchal altar-building at Shechem, it makes no effort to show that the activities are now conducted in accordance with the prescriptions of the Torah. In fact, Josh. 24:26f. raises a stone in the sanctuary of Yahweh, under a terebinth, in a manner which would appear to conflict with the law of Deuteronomy.[44] Moreover, the law in Deuteronomy is treated as a completed corpus which must be transmitted as prescribed by Moses, as is stated repeatedly in Josh. 8:30-35, whereas in Josh. 24:25f., Joshua establishes new laws for Israel.[45]

The differences between the account in Deut. 11:29ff.; 27 and Josh. 8:30 on the one hand and Josh. 24:1-28 on the other are telling. Since the Dtic prescription was known to the final editor of Joshua, and since it was weighed heavily enough to cause explicit narration of its fulfilment in 8:30-35, one might suppose that if 24:1-28 was a relatively late composition from the time of the final redaction of Joshua, as has at times been suggested, it would have been most natural to treat the gathering at Shechem in conjunction with the mandate delineated in Deuteronomy. This argument coalesces with what has been observed above with respect to a relatively low incidence of Dtistic terminology in 24:1-28 and the presence of a high number of characteristics which are undeniably atypical of Deuteronomy. It therefore provides confirmation regarding the thesis that Josh. 24:1-28 was written basically independent from major Dtistic influence.

### 5.3.3 Additional connections with Deuteronomy

In addition to similarities between Josh. 24:1-28 and Deut. 11:29ff.; 27, it is important to note connections with Deuteronomy in two additional areas, i.e., (a) in the respective summations of antecedent history and (b) in their common emphasis upon absolute fidelity to

[44]Cf. Deut. 12:2f.; 16:21f.

[45]This is the most probable meaning of the phrase *wyśm lw ḥq wmšpṭ bškm* (24:25B); cf. M.Weinfeld, "The Period of the Conquest and of the Judges as Seen by the Earlier and the Later Sources," *VT* 17 (1967) 109f.

Yahweh, especially as that is expressed in the final speeches of Moses and Joshua.

With respect to the historical summaries, we recall that von Rad's credo theory already stressed the similarity of Deut. 6:20-24; 26:5b-9 and Josh. 24:2b-13.[46] Additional comparisons can be collected from the historical summary in the opening chapters of Deuteronomy. For example, the interest in Esau and Seir in Deut. 2:5,22 is comparable to Josh. 24:4.[47] The formulation of Josh. 24:8bB-C, *wtyršw 't-'rṣm w'šmydm mpnykm*, has its closest counterpart in Num. 33:52; Deut. 2:12,21f.; 4:26; 9:3; 28:63; 31:3. Deuteronomy and Joshua have a common interest in the two kings of the Amorites (Deut. 3:8; Josh. 24:12).[48] And the resemblance of Deut. 6:10 and Josh. 24:13 has also already been discussed.[49]

Obvious affinities exist between the farewell speeches of Moses and Joshua.[50] Since a comparison of Josh. 23 with the concluding chapters of Deuteronomy would take us too far afield, the present discussion must be restricted to a selection of elements from Josh. 24:1-28 which are paralleled in Deut. 29ff. The caveat in Deut. 29:23ff. against abandoning Yahweh to serve other gods bears striking semblance to Josh. 24:20.[51] The affinity of the witness formula in Josh. 24:27 to those of Deut. 29:19,21,26 should not be overlooked.[52] Deut. 31:19 stresses that Moses taught Israel a song for a witness against themselves, which in certain respects is comparable to the function of the people's oath of witness against themselves in Josh. 24:22. Moreover, both Moses and Joshua are presented as law-givers in the final assemblies that they lead (Deut. 31:24-29; Josh. 24:25-27).[53] And the emphasis in Deut. 32:15f. upon Yahweh's jealous nature in the event of Israel's disobedience has close affinity to Josh. 24:19.

[46]See 1.4.2.

[47]See 4.3.1.3.

[48]Cf. Josh. 2:10; 9:10; 12:2,4,5; 13:10,12,21,27; see also 4.3.3.3.

[49]See 4.3.3.4.

[50]For a discussion of many similarities between Deut. 31-34 and Josh. 23-24 consult E.von Nordheim, *Die Lehre der Alten. II Das Testament als Literaturgattung im Alten Testament und im Alten Orient* (Leiden, 1985) 65-72.

[51]Compare Deut. 29:24f. ("...*'zbw 't-bryt yhwh 'lhy 'btm ... wylkw wy'bdw 'lhym 'ḥrym...*") and Josh. 24:20a ("*ky t'zbw 't-yhwh w'bdtm 'lhy nkr*"). On Deut. 29:23ff. see also Moran, "Ancient Near Eastern Background," 83f.

[52]See our initial comments in 2.3.7.2.

[53]Note too that the prediction in Deut. 31:28f. makes a close parallel with Judg. 2:10 (see below).

The word *ywm* in reference to the time of covenant ratification occurs frequently in Deut. 28-31 and is used similarly in Josh. 24:15,25.[54] Additional similarities could be documented, but these examples are sufficient to demonstrate that Josh. 24:1-28 has many thematic emphases in common with Deuteronomy. We have argued extensively above that Josh. 24:1-28 is not literarily dependent upon Deuteronomy. The present considerations reinforce the conclusion that these passages nevertheless do have many linguistic and thematic affinities.

### 5.3.4 Josh. 24:1-28 and the Sinaitic covenant in Exodus

A literary critical analysis of Josh. 24:1-28 demonstrates a number of close connections with material from Exodus. This is true of the narration of the events involving the exodus as described in Josh. 24:5-7. The formula *kh 'mr yhwh 'lhy yśr'l* finds a direct counterpart in Ex. 5:21; 32:27, and it does not appear elsewhere in the Pentateuch. Similarly, in the Pentateuch, the designation *yhwh 'lhy yśr'l* is restricted to Exodus. The expression *śym ḥq wmšpṭ*, with the nouns in the singular, is an infrequent formulation but found in both Ex. 15:25 and Josh. 24:25. The gathering narrated in Ex. 18:12 and the establishment of law in vss.16,20 have been compared with Josh. 24:1,25f. These similarities show that it is worth pursuing a comparison of Josh. 24:1-28 with material from Exodus.

Despite the significance of the parallels mentioned above, and the possibility of finding other correlations with material throughout Exodus, the present comparison will be restricted primarily to those narratives focusing upon the Sinaitic covenant. It is worth recalling that the literary character of the decalogue has often been recognized as having a poetic quality.[55] However, since a literary comparison with material from Exodus would lead us too far afield, the following observations are restricted primarily to matters of content and terminology. It has long been suggested that the structure of Josh. 24:1-28 forms a general parallel with the organization of material in Ex. 19-24.[56] But it is imperative to move beyond general considerations of

[54]See too 3.6.3 regarding the LXX variants in Josh. 24:27. Note especially our proposed retroversion to *b'ḥryt hymym*, cf. Deut. 29:31. Josh. 24:27 LXX and Deut. 29:31 show a similar emphasis upon the testamental dimension of the respective farewell speeches.

[55]G.Fohrer, "Über den Kurzvers," *ZAW* 66 (1954) 199-236, 214f.

[56]Rendtorff, "Der Kultus im alten Israel," 95.

content, form and structure, to more specific details.

The concern of the first commandment[57] in Ex. 20:2f. is comparable to the central emphasis of Josh. 24:1-28.[58] The motivation for serving Yahweh alone has been thought to bear a striking similarity to the demand for allegiance in ancient suzerain-vassal treaties.[59] Whether the first commandment is explained in comparison with allegiance demanded in treaty contexts or upon other grounds, there are strong reasons for accepting the antiquity of this concept in the earliest stages of Israel's religious traditions.[60]

The central emphasis in Josh. 24:1-28 upon worship of Yahweh alone can also be compared to the framework of the covenant rituals in Ex. 24:1-11 and the related narrative in Ex. 32. The golden calf[61] is heralded as the god who brought Israel out of Egypt (vss.4,8; cf. Josh. 24:17; 1 Kgs 12:28). Its worship is celebrated in a festival (Ex. 32:5f.) in deliberate contrast to the sacrificial meal (24:5-8).[62] The antiquity of Ex. 24:3-8 has been vigorously contested, with numerous recent claims to find here a composition from a Dtistic hand,[63] but these attempts to ascribe Ex. 24:3-8 to a Dtist are not convincing.[64]

[57]According to the Christian tradition; according to the Jewish tradition the first two commandments of the decalogue.

[58]In addition to the emphasis upon sole allegiance to Yahweh, compare the use of *yṣ'* in Josh. 24:5f.; and cf. 24:17. Note too the grammatical shift in both texts from 1st sing. to 3rd sing. references to Yahweh in the middle of divine discourse.

[59]Beyerlin, *Herkunft und Geschichte*, 62f. Another parallel to the vassal-treaties is often identified in Ex. 34:14-17, which Fensham and Baltzer view, in connection with the first commandment, as a renewal of the covenant (Fensham, "Clauses of Protection," 139; Baltzer, *Bundesformular*, 48ff.).

[60]De Moor, *Uw God*, 64f.; for literature see his n.212.

[61]It is worth noting the connection made between Gen. 35:4 and Deut. 32:2f. and Judg. 8:24-26 on the basis of the earings. In Gen. 35:4 the people are purified by putting them away; in the latter two cases they are condemned for iconic impropriety.

[62]Cf. the sacrificial meal (*šlmym*) in 24:5 and 32:6. In contrast to the burnt-offering (*'lh*), the *šlmym* were in part consumed by the people (Gray, *Legacy*, 192; "Social Aspects of Canaanite Religion," in *Volume du Congrès, Geneve 1965*, SVT 15 [Leiden, 1966], 171: "...its primary purpose was the reintegration of the sacral community with the god...."). See also J.C.de Moor, "The Peace-Offering in Ugarit and Israel," in *Schrift en Uitleg* (Fs W.H.Gispen; Kampen, 1970) 112-117.

[63]Perlitt, *Bundestheologie*, 190-203; E.Zenger, *Die Sinaitheophanie. Untersuchungen zum jahwistischen und elohistischen Geschichtswerk* (Würzburg, 1971), 72-76.

[64]Eichrodt, "Darf man heute," 197f; Gurney, *Hittite Religion*, 30; Nicholson, "The Covenant Ritual," 74-86 (modifying his previous stance); A.Phillips, "A Fresh

There is no explicit indication in Josh. 24:1-28 that Israel engaged in a ritual sacrifice and meal. Nevertheless, the narrative presents merely a selection of details germane to the author's intention, and it is possible that the ceremony described so summarily in Josh. 24:25-27 included additional elements such as a sacrificial meal to accompany the erection of the stone of witness.[65]

The connections between *'l 'lhy yśr'l* of Gen. 33:20, altar-building near Shechem, and the worship of *yhwh 'lhy yśr'l* at Shechem in Josh. 24:1-28, have been discussed above. Vriezen sought to link the worship of *'lhy yšr'l* in Ex. 24:9-11 with the traditions of Shechem.[66] He states, "It is nearly impossible not to think first of all of Shechem as the place from which a tradition of *'Èlōhē Yiśr'ēl* as a covenantal God, as we find it in Ex. xxiv 9-11, is originating."[67]

Numerous similarities between Josh. 24:1-28 and Ex. 23:20-33 have been mentioned above. A compilation of comparable elements is provided by Schmitt,[68] including the list of nations (Josh. 24:11; Ex. 23:23); sending the hornet[69] (Josh. 24:12; Ex. 23:28); protection on the way (Josh. 24:17, Ex. 23:20); not forgiving sins (*l' nś' l*, Josh. 24:19; Ex. 23:21); use of the verb *grš* for expulsion of the Canaanites (Josh. 24:12,18; Ex. 23:28-31 [4x]);[70] *šm' bql*, (Josh. 24:24; Ex. 23:21f.).[71]

In addition to these points of comparison, mention should also be made of *ym-swp*, *mdbr*, and *hnhr* in the boundary description of Ex. 23:31. The same elements are found in the macrostructure of Josh. 24:1-28 in strategic geographic progressions.[72] This connection

Look at the Sinai Pericope: Part II," *VT* 34 (1984) 285.

[65]Cf. esp. Deut. 27:7; Josh. 8:31.

[66]Vriezen, "Exodus xxiv 9-11," 121, 127-130.

[67]Vriezen, "Exodus xxiv 9-11," 128. This conclusion generally follows the lead of von Rad, who thought that the Sinaitic covenant is a derivative of the Shechem tradition.

[68]Schmitt, *Landtag*, 26f.

[69]In our opinion "panic" or "fear" (see 4.3.3.3).

[70]We have noted that there are only five verses in the MT containing both *šlḥ* and *grš*, namely Ex. 6:1; 11:1; 23:28; 33:2; Josh. 24:12.

[71]Fensham has demonstrated that Ex. 23:22 finds a direct counterpart in the Hittite vassal-treaties, and upon this basis he calls for a reassessment of the frequent tendency to consider Ex. 23:20-33 Dtistic (Fensham, "Clauses of Protection," 133-143).

[72]Cf. Weinfeld, "*Bryt* – Covenant vs. Obligation," 126. Weinfeld denies that Ex. 23:31 is Dtistic.

is reinforced by the fact that Ex. 23:31 continues with the promise "for I will give into your hand all the inhabitants of the land, and you will drive them out before you"; cf. Josh. 24:8bA,11bD,12aB,18a.

It is most natural to assert a literary dependence of Josh. 24:1-28 upon Ex. 23:20-33, though it may be necessary to consider the possibility that the direction of literary influence could also have gone, at least in part, in the other direction. Ex. 23:20-33 also has a couple of close connections with Josh. 23.[73] Due to the dependence of Josh. 23 upon material and terminology from Deuteronomy, it is most probable that Josh. 23 is secondary to Ex. 23:20-33. In any event, it is clear that Josh. 24:1-28 has a close affinity with Ex. 23:20-33. Schmitt is correct in noting that, despite the similarity of the latter passage with Deut. 7, there are numerous elements which argue against terming Ex. 23:20-33 Dtistic.[74]

The parallelism of *krt bryt* || *ktb 't-hdbrym h'lh* (Josh. 24:25f. ext. par.) is attested also in Ex. 34:27, thereby establishing a noteworthy point of comparison between these two passages. Moreover, Ex. 34:14 prohibits worship of foreign gods and stresses that Yahweh is a jealous God, employing an ancient cultic formulary[75] expressed in a poetic bicolon, *ky yhwh qn' šmw / 'l qn' hw'*. Once again the emphasis is analogous to Josh. 24:19 and its context. These similarities reinforce other correlations between Josh. 24:1-28 and Ex. 34.[76]

There are also noteworthy elements in common between Josh. 24:1-28 and Ex. 19. The latter passage too prefaces the call to covenant obedience with an appeal to the liberation from Egypt (19:4).

[73]Cf. Ex. 23:24a, *l'-tšthwh l'lhyhm / wl' t'bdm*, and Josh. 23:7bC-D, *wl' t'bdwn / wl' tšthww lhm*. See too the use of *mwqš* in Ex. 23:33; Josh. 23:13bA.

[74]Cf. Schmitt, *Landtag*, 27f. A contrary opinion is recently reasserted by W.Johnstone ("Reactivating the Chronicles Analogy in Pentateuchal Studies with Special Reference to the Sinai Pericope in Exodus," *ZAW* 99 [1987] 25). Unfortunately, Johnstone ignores the studies by Beyerlin, Schmitt, McCarthy, Weinfeld and Halbe, inter alia, demonstrating that the primary direction of dependence is from Ex. 23:20-33 to Deuteronomy and not vice versa. Consequently, the appeal to the presence of the "angel," and phrases such as *šm' bqwl*, *grš*, *yšb h'rṣ*, *krt bryt l*, *hyh lmwqš* in Ex. 23:20-33 and Judg. 2:1-5 does not make these texts Dtistic.

[75]De Moor, *Uw God*, 54f.

[76]Cf. the poetic bicolon of 7a, *nṣr ḥsd l'lpym / nś' 'wn wpš' wḥṭ'h*, the last colon of which may be compared with Josh. 24:19c. Note too the combination of *qr'* || *yṣb* (Josh. 24:1; Ex. 34:5). The similar prohibitions of *'l 'ḥr* in Ex. 34:14 (LXX has plural: θεῳ ἑτερῳ) and *'lhy nkr* in Gen. 35:2,4; Josh. 24:20,23 are of considerable significance (Wilms, *Bundesbuch*, 157).

The elders play a prominent role (vs.7), and the narrative is built upon dialogical interaction between Moses and the people in a manner comparable to that of Josh. 24:1-28.[77] Of particular importance is the joint response of the people in Ex. 19:8, which forms a direct parallel with the people's response in Josh. 24:16-24. These details in Ex. 19 and the ensuing account of the law-giving at Sinai demonstrate the close connection between the acclamation of Yahweh in Josh. 24:1-28 and in the Sinaitic covenant of Exodus.

In the light of all these connections between Josh. 24:1-28 and the Sinaitic narratives from Exodus, it is noteworthy that Josh. 24 makes no mention of the Sinaitic covenant itself. In an attempt to explain this absence, Huffmon posited an unconvincing argument that the Hittite treaties never employ a reference to previous treaties as part of the gracious acts of the sovereign.[78] Fensham employs a similar argument, but he formulates it more cautiously, noting that the historical descriptions in Hittite treaties do not necessarily mention previous treaties.[79] H.P.Harner reverses the argument, suggesting that since some of the Hittite treaties do include a reference to previous treaty arrangements as part of the prologue, von Rad's argument from silence must be taken seriously.[80] Despite the treaty examples listed by Harner,[81] which support the supposition that Josh. 24's treatment of covenant may have been expected to refer to the covenant at Sinai,[82] previous caveats against arguments from silence remain valid.[83] Polzin has observed, moreover, that the historical recital in Josh. 24:2b-13 focuses primarily upon Israel's attainment of the land;[84] it does not attempt to give a complete account of Israel's previous legal relationship to Yahweh.

[77]Cf. the comparisons raised between Josh. 24:2 and Ex. 19:3ff. in 4.3.1.1 above. See also Muilenburg, "Form and Structure," 351-365, esp. 359f.; Buis, "Les formulaires," 397f., 400, 402, 406, 408.

[78]Huffmon, "The Exodus," 108.

[79]Fensham, "Covenant, Promise," 313f.

[80]P.B.Harner, "Exodus, Sinai, and Hittite Prologues," *JBL* 85 (1966) 233-236.

[81]Other examples could be added, cf. 5.10.4.

[82]Such a reference in the speech of Joshua could have strengthened his argument considerably.

[83]Th.C.Vriezen, *Hoofdlijnen der theologie van het Oude Testament* (Wageningen, 1954), 80.

[84]Polzin, *Moses*, 142f.

## 5.4 Josh. 24 and the Book of Judges

### 5.4.1 Josh. 24:28-31 and Judg. 2:6-10

The textual relationship between Josh. 24:28-31 and Judg. 2:6-10 is crucial for the study of the literary and thematic progression of Joshua and Judges. The relationship between these passages is also important for the dating of Josh. 24:1-28. The ensuing analysis suggests that a recognition of the colometric structure of the respective passages offers important clues regarding the direction of dependence.

In its present form, Josh. 24:1-28 is a self-contained poetic unit. However, the parallel verses in Judg. 2:6-10 do not reflect a literary boundary between Josh. 24:28 and vs.29. This complicates the question of the direction of literary dependence. Is Josh. 24 modeled in part upon Judg. 2:6-10, or is the latter passage dependent upon Josh. 24:28ff.? This question has been treated frequently, but without consensus. As summarized above,[85] the priority of Josh. 24:28-31 has been defended by Richter, Smend, Rösel, and Auld,[86] but criticism was advanced by Gray, Nelson, and Mayes. The former scholars view Josh. 24 as an original portion of the Dtistic history, while the latter see its present place as a late insertion into this history, without thereby necessarily committing themselves on the question of the tradition's origin or antiquity. On the basis of the witness of the LXX and from the poetic structure which can be reconstructed, it is possible to demonstrate, contrary to Gray, Nelson and Mayes, that Josh. 24:28ff. is not a late insertion into a Dtistic history, based upon a prior text now found in Judg. 2:6-10.

To establish a medium of comparison, Judg. 2:6-10 is presented in colometric format, with a brief justification of the proposed structure. This will in turn facilitate a synoptic juxtaposition on the basis of the priority of Josh. 24:28ff. In this manner we in particular wish to refocus the question of literary priority with respect to these parallel passages.

[85] Cf. the works referred to in 2.3.7.3.

[86] To the previous references add A.G.Auld, "Judges I and History: A Reconsideration," *VT* 25 (1975) 264.

## Judg. 2:6-10

[petuchah]

**i.1**

| | |
|---|---|
| *wyšlḥ yhwš' 't-h'm* [2] | (6a) Joshua sent the people away; |
| *wylkw bny-yśr'l* [12] | (6bA) and the sons of Israel went, |
| *'yš lnḥltw* [8] | (6bB) each man to his inheritance |
| *lršt 't-h'rṣ* [1] | (6bC) to possess the land. |

**i.2**

| | |
|---|---|
| *wy'bdw h'm 't-yhwh* [5] | (7aA) And the people served Yahweh |
| *kl ymy yhwš'* [2] | (7aB) all the days of Joshua, |
| *wkl ymy hzqnym* [7] | (7bA) and all the days of the elders |
| *'šr h'rykw ymym 'ḥry yhwš'* [5] | (7bB) who outlived the days of Joshua, |
| *'šr r'w 't kl-m'śh yhwh hgdwl* [5] | (7bC) who saw all the great deeds of Yahweh |
| *'šr 'śh lyśr'l* [1] | (7bD) which he did for Israel. |

..............................................................

**ii.1**

| | |
|---|---|
| *wymt yhwš' bn-nwn 'bd yhwh* [2] | (8aA) And Joshua son of Nun, servant of Yahweh, died, |
| *bn-m'h w'šr šnym* [1] | (8aB) a son of one hundred and ten years. |
| *wyqbrw 'wtw bgbwl nḥltw* [5] | (9A) And they buried him in his inheritance |
| *btmnt-ḥrs bhr-'prym* [2] | (9B) in Timnath-heres in Mt. Ephraim, |
| *mṣpwn lhr-g'š* [1] | (9C) north of the mountain of Gash. |

**ii.2**

| | |
|---|---|
| *wgm kl-hdr hhw'* [5] | (10aA) And all of that generation |
| *n'sp 'l-'bwtyw* [2] | (10aB) was gathered to their fathers. |
| *wyqm dwr 'ḥr 'ḥryhm* [5] | (10bA) And there arose another generation |
| *'šr l'-yd'w 't-yhwh* [5] | (10bB) which did not know Yahweh |
| *wgm 't-hm'śh* [5] | (10bC) and all of his deeds |
| *'šr 'śh lyśr'l* [1] | (10bD) which he did for Israel. |

[setumah]

With respect to the justification of these four strophes, we note the following criteria:

**Strophe i.1**

Sep. ↑: *petuchah*; unicolon
Sep. ↓: rep. *l*; tricolon
Int. || : *bny-yśr'l* || *'yš*; *nḥlh* || *'rṣ*
Ext. || : *wyšlḥ* || *wylkw*; *h'm* || *bny-yśr'l*[87] and *'yš*

**Strophe i.2**

Sep. ↑: absent[88]
Sep. ↓: rep. *kl*, *ym*, *'šr*, and *'śh*; quadrocolon; refrain *'šr 'śh lyśr'l*[89]
Int. || : *h'm* || *yhwš'*; *yhwh* || *yhwš'*; *kl* || *kl*; *ymy* || *ymym*; *hzqnym* || *yhwš'* || *yśr'l*; *'šr* (3x); *m'śh* || *'śh*; *yhwš'* || *yhwh*
Ext. || : *h'm* || *hzqnym* and *yśr'l* ; *yhwh* and *yhwš'* || *yhwš'* and *yhwh* (chiastic) ; *ymy* || *ymy* and *ymym*; *kl* || *kl* (2x)

**Ext. par. between i.1 and i.2**

*h'm* || *h'm* (6a, 7aA; responsion); *yhwš'* || *yhwš'* (6a, 7aB; responsion); *bny-yśr'l* || *lyśr'l* (6bA, 7bD)

**Strophe ii.1**

Sep. ↑: change of subject;[90] rep. *bn*
Sep. ↓: tricolon; rep. prep. *b* (3x); rep. *hr*
Int. || : *bn* || *bn*;[91] *b* (3x); *tmnt-ḥrs* || *'prym* || *g'š*; *hr* || *hr*
Ext. || : *wymt yhwš'* || *wyqbrw 'wtw*[92]

**Strophe ii.2**

Sep. ↑: *wgm*;[93] *hhw'*
Sep. ↓: *setumah*; quadrocolon; refrain *'šr 'śh lyśr'l*; rep. *'šr* and *'śh*

[87]Van der Meer, *Oude woorden*, 105.

[88]However, note the thematic shift. The preceding strophe described the dispersal of the people to their inheritance; the present strophe focuses upon their obedience.

[89]Cf. 10bD with the identical refrain.

[90]Shift to 3 m.s. *waw*-consecutive form referring to Joshua.

[91]Van der Meer, *Oude woorden*, 94, 95.

[92]Cf. the framework formed by 1 Kgs 2:1,10 in the poetic testament of David (Koopmans, "The Testament,").

[93]Cf. van der Lugt, *Strofische structuren*, 521; C.J.Labuschagne, "The Emphasizing Particle *gam* and its Connotations," in *Studia Biblica et Semitica* (Fs. Th.C.Vriezen; Wageningen, 1966), 193-203; Koopmans, "The Testament."

Int. || : *dwr* || *'bwtyw*;[94] *'šr* || *'šr*; *hm'śh* || *'śh*
Ext. || : *wgm* || *wgm*; *dwr* || *dwr*; *'l-'bwtyw* || *lyśr'l*

**Ext. par. between ii.1 and ii.2**
*wymt* || *n'sp 'l-'bwtyw* (8aA, 10aB; responsion);[95] *yhwh* || *yhwh* (8aA, 10bB; responsion)[96]

**The macrostructure of Judg. 2:6-10**
The strophic divisions delineated above agree precisely with the thematic progressions of the passage. The four strophes focus respectively upon dispersal of the people to their inheritance, the obedience of the people, the death of Joshua and his burial in his inheritance, and the disobedience of the next generation. The resulting A.B.Á.B́ strophic arrangement is supported by external parallelism between the two canticles:
*yhwš'* || *yhwš'* (6a, 8aA; responsion); *bny* || *bn* (2x) (6bA, 8aA,B; responsion); *lnḥltw* || *nḥltw* (6bB, 9A; responsion); *kl ymy yhwš'* || *kl-hdwr hhw'* (7aB, 10aA; responsion); *hzqnym* || *'bwtyw* (7bA, 10aB);[97] *'ḥry* || *'ḥr 'ḥryhm* (7bB, 10bA; responsion); *'šr r'w* || *'šr l'-yd'w* (7bC, 10bB; responsion);[98] *'t kl-m'šh* || *wgm 't-hm'śh* (7bC, 10bC; responsion); *'šr 'śh lyśr'l* || *'šr 'śh lyśr'l* (7bD, 10bD; responsion of refrains).

This high degree of external parallelism demonstrates that the two canticles of Judg. 2:6-10 form a deliberate responsion with each other, culminating particularly in the refrain. The first canticle states positively that Israel was faithful during the time of Joshua's lifetime.

[94]Van der Meer, *Oude woorden*, 43.

[95]Cf. the external parallelism of *lmwt* || *yškb 'm-'btyw* in 1 Kgs 2:1,10 (Koopmans, "The Testament"). Perhaps an additional parallelism is intended between *wyqbrw 'wtw* and *wyqm dwr 'ḥr*. Joshua is buried and another generation rises up.

[96]Note the contrast between Joshua as faithful servant of Yahweh and the unfaithful generation who did not know Yahweh.

[97]For this parallelism compare Deut. 32:7, *š'l 'byk wygdk* || *zqnyk wy'mrw lk*; cf. the chiastic arrangement of Prov. 17:6 and the ext. par. in Joel 1:2 (van der Meer, *Oude woorden*, 42, 47).

[98]Talmon explains this variance as a substitution on the basis of the frequent paratactic association of these two words by means of which they become virtually synonymous, and finally interchangeable ("Synonymous Readings in the Textual Traditions of the Old Testament," in Rabin, ed., *Studies in the Bible*, 341). Recognition of the poetic nature of these texts suggests that the substitution may have been deliberate (see below).

The second canticle asserts that conversely after his death the following generation was disobedient. Both canticles end with a refrain, *’šr ‘śh lyśr’l*. This twofold emphasis is similar to the structural and theological layout of Josh. 23,[99] but for our present purpose it is more important to compare the structure with that of Josh. 24:28ff. to discern whether Judg. 2:6-10 is contracted or Josh. 24:28-31 is expanded.

| Josh. 24:28-31 | Judg. 2:6-10 |
|---|---|
| *wyšlḥ yhwš‘ ’t-h‘m* | (6a) *wyšlḥ yhwš‘ ’t-h‘m* |
| | (6bA) *wylkw bny-yśr’l* |
| *’ys lnḥltw* | (6bB) *’yš lnḥltw* |
| | (6bC) *lršt ’t-h’rṣ* |
| *wyhy ’ḥry hdbrym h’lh* | |
| *wymt yhwš‘ bn-nwn ‘bd yhwh* | (8aA) *wymt yhwš‘ bn-nwn ‘bd yhwh* |
| *bn-m’h w‘śr šnym* | (8aB) *bn-m’h w‘śr šnym* |
| *wyqbrw ’wtw bgbwl nḥltw* | (9A) *wyqbrw ’wtw bgbwl nḥltw* |
| *btmnt-srḥ ’šr bhr-’prym* | (9B) *btmnt-ḥrs bhr-’prym* |
| *mṣpwn lhr-g‘š* | (9C) *mṣpwn lhr-g‘š* |
| *wy‘bdw yśr’l ’t-yhwh* | (7aA) *wy‘bdw h‘m ’t-yhwh* |
| *kl ymy yhwš‘* | (7aB) *kl ymy yhwš‘* |
| *wkl ymy hzqnym* | (7bA) *wkl ymy hzqnym* |
| *’šr h’rykw ymym ’ḥry yhwš‘* | (7bB) *’šr h’rykw ymym ’ḥry yhwš‘* |
| *w’šr yd‘w ’t kl-m‘śh yhwh* | (7bC) *’šr r’w’t kl-m‘śh yhwh hgdwl* |
| *’šr ‘śh lyśr’l* | (7bD) *’šr ‘śh lyśr’l* |
| | (10aA) *wgm kl-hdr hhw’* |
| | (10aB) *n’sp ’l-’bwtyw* |
| | (10bA) *wyqm dwr ’ḥr ’ḥryhm* |
| | (10bB) *’šr l’-yd‘w ’t-yhwh* |
| | (10bC) *wgm ’t-hm‘śh* |
| | (10bD) *’šr ‘śh lyśr’l* |

[99] Koopmans, “Joshua 23,” 110.

The structural parallelism coalesces with the thematic intention of the respective units. Judg. 2:6-10 contrasts two different generations, the faithfulness of Joshua's day, and the infidelity of the subsequent generation. For that reason, the author of Judg. 2:6-10 places vs.7 in a sequence other than that of Josh. 24:31. The sequential shift makes the colon *wyhy 'ḥry hdbrym h'lh* (Josh. 24:29A) irrelevant, and it is accordingly dropped.[100] If retained, the phrase would create a logical problem because it would no longer refer to the covenant ceremony. This in fact is the case in the LXX of Josh. 24:29ff., which inappropriately has the wording of the MT in the order of Judg. 2:6ff.[101]

With Rofé,[102] we have noted that the *Vorlage* of the LXX in Josh. 24:28 presupposes a reading other than *nḥlh*.[103] The shift to *nḥlh* in Judg. 2:6, in turn, had a reciprocal influence upon the present reading of the MT in Josh. 24:28. This explains the different *Vorlage* of the LXX, and it agrees entirely with the difference in emphasis between Josh. 24:1-28 (legal setting) and Judg. 2:6-10 (infidelity in the land of the inheritance). The modification of Josh. 24:28, by substitution of *nḥlh* for the original reading, made Josh. 24:28 a summary of the conquest, which is different from its original emphasis narrating the termination of the covenantal gathering. Moreover, the new presence of *nḥlh* in 24:28 facilitated the establishment of external parallelism with *nḥltw* in 24:30A (= Judg. 2:9A).

The priority of Josh. 24:28-31 is confirmed by additional structural considerations. Judg. 2:7bC substitutes *r'w* for *yd'w*, bringing it in line with Deut. 11:7. It employs *yd'* in strophe ii.2 (vs.10), where the author creates an entire new strophe modeled upon i.2 (vs.7).[104] He thereby creates an example of the break-up of a word-pair,[105] distributing the components over two refrains forming responsion at the

[100]In Josh. 24:29 it is necessary to form separation upwards in the new literary unit. The similarity of this usage and the narrative style in parts of Genesis, including especially the Joseph narrative, is noted by Westermann, *Genesis*, 2:435.

[101]With Butler (*Joshua*, 281), contra Rofé ("The End of the Book," 23).

[102]Rofé, "The End of the Book," 21f.

[103]See 3.6.3; the original reading likely was *lbytw*.

[104]The manner in which the author composes a new strophe (ii.2) and places it in external parallelism with the original (i.2) provides an excellent example of how narrative poetry could create responsions between entire units.

[105]Cf. Talmon, "Synonymous Readings," 341. On the parallelism of *r'h* and *yd'* cf. Huffmon, "Treaty Background," 35; Avishur, *Stylistic Studies*, 259, 261, 293, 294.

end of the respective canticles.[106] To argue conversely, that Josh. 24:31bC substitutes *yd'w* for *r'w*, would lack an apparent reason for such a change, while there *is* an important rationale in Judg. 2:6-10. The same is true with respect to the other variations between these passages, e.g., the extra emphasis added in Judg. 2:7bC with *gdwlh*, also bringing it closer in line with Deut. 11:7. There is no reason why Josh. 24:31bC should delete *gdwlh* if it were copying Judg. 2:7. The expansion of the bicolon (Josh. 24:28) to a unicolon plus a tricolon (Judg. 2:6) enables the resulting strophe to stand alone; it thereby introduces the theological theme of the possession of the land, which also accounts for the use of *nḥlh*, contrary to the witness of the LXX in Josh. 24:28. Finally, the addition of *bny-yśr'l* makes an inclusion between 2:6aB and 2:10bD, whereas there is no reason why this should have been omitted if Josh. 24:28 was borrowing from Judg. 2:6. Directly related is the change of *yśr'l* (Josh. 24:31aA) to *h'm* (Judg. 2:7aA). The result in Judg. 2:6-10 is the responsion of *h'm* || *h'm* (6aA, 7aA), as well as avoidance of interference with *yśr'l* employed in the refrains (7bD, 10bD) and in the inclusion (6aB, 10bD). At first glance one might conclude that Judg. 2:9C (without *'šr*), offers a more original reading than Josh. 24:30C (with *'šr*). This is likely the case. However, since the presence of *'šr* in Josh. 24:30C may be a late addition in the MT, it proves nothing regarding the direction of dependence.[107]

In summary, there is only one place where Josh. 24:28-31 has a true plus in comparison to Judg. 2:6-9, namely 29aA. This colon was necessarily dropped in Judg. 2:8 because it was no longer appropriate. The expansions in Judg. 2:6-10 can all be explained theologically and structurally,[108] which is not the case if one presupposes that Judg. 2:6-10 is original and Josh. 24:28-31 dependent.[109]

[106]The same pair is used as an inclusion for Deut. 11:26-28, and less conspicuously in Josh. 23 (cf. vss.3,4,13,14). The pair *yd'* and *r'h* is employed upon numerous occasions to form a hendiadys (Muilenburg, "Intercession," 179).

[107]Cf. LXX* etc. with BHS critical apparatus.

[108]The phenomenon attested here employs the manner of expansion or contraction attested elsewhere in parallel poetic traditions, cf., e.g., M.C.A.Korpel, "The Poetic Structure of the Priestly Blessing," *JSOT* 45 (1989) 3-13.

[109]The matter of the alternate names Timnath-seraḥ (Josh. 24:30) and Timnath-ḥeres (Judg. 2:9) has been widely disputed. Even if Timnath-seraḥ were to prove secondary (Boling, *Joshua*, 469), this would not entail that Josh. 24:28-31 is dependent upon Judg. 2:6-10.

### 5.4.2 Josh. 24:2-24 and Judg. 6:7-10

In the preceding section it has been argued that Josh. 24:28ff. is literarily prior to Judg. 2:6-10. In the present comparison it is suggested that the connections between Josh. 24:2-24 and Judg. 6:7-10 reinforce the conclusion that Josh. 24 played a conspicuous role in the shaping of the present form of Judges. The message of Judg. 6:7-10 is attributed to an unkown prophet. His words are introduced with the prophetic formula *kh-’mr yhwh ’lhy yśr’l*—which is already striking because the Hexateuch reserves this formula for Moses, Aaron and Joshua.[110]

In his Judges commentary, Boling indicates that the prophetic message in 6:8c-9 is poetic.[111] There can be little doubt about the correctness of Boling's colometric presentation of vss.8c-9, and in the following analysis it will be argued that the poetic unit is not restricted to this section.

### Judg. 6:7-10

[petuchah]

| | |
|---|---|
| *wyhy ky z‘qw [21!]* | (7aA) So it was that they cried out, |
| *bny-yśr’l ’l-yhwh [2]* | (7aB) the sons of Israel to Yahweh |
| *‘l ’dwt mdyn [1]* | (7aC) on account of the Midianites. |
| *wyšlḥ yhwh ’yš nby’ [8]*[112] | (8aA) And Yahweh sent a prophet |
| *’l-bny yśr’l [2]* | (8aB) to the sons of Israel. |
| *wy’mr lhm [13]* | (8bA) And he said to them, |
| *kh-’mr yhwh ’lhy yśr’l [7]* | (8bB) "Thus says Yahweh, God of Israel, |
| *’nky h‘lty ’tkm mmṣrym [5]* | (8cA) 'I am the one who brought you up from Egypt |
| *w’ṣy’ ’tkm mbyt ‘bdym [1]* | (8cB) and brought you out of the house of bondage. |

[110]Cf. the discussion of this formula in 4.3.1.1.

[111]Boling, *Judges*, 124-127. He states, "The bulk of the speech is clearly poetic, making use of two great nuclear themes of Israel's credo and having the Sinai covenant as the presupposition of the current indictment" (126).

[112]In agreement with the Masoretic accentuation we consider *’yš nby’* to be an idiom involving apposition rather than an instance of parallelism (*’yš* || *nby’*) distributed over two cola, as is the case in, e.g., Hos. 9:7 (*hnby’* || *’yš hrwḥ* or Zeph. 3:4 (*nby’yh pḥzym* || *’nšy bgdwt*).

| | |
|---|---|
| *w'ṣl 'tkm myd mṣrym* [*5*] | (9aA) And I delivered you from the hand of the Egyptians |
| *wmyd kl-lḥṣykm* [*2*] | (9aB) and from the hand of all your oppressors. |
| *w'grš 'wtm mpnykm* [*5*] | (9bA) And I drove them out before you, |
| *w'tnh lkm 't-'rṣm* [*1*] | (9bB) and I gave you their land'." |
| *w'mrh lkm* [*7*] | (10aA) "And I said to you, |
| *'ny yhwh 'lhykm* [*5*] | (10aB) 'I am Yahweh your God.' |
| *l' tyr'w 't-'lhy h'mry* [*5*] | (10bA) Do not fear the gods of the Amorites |
| *'šr 'tm ywšbym b'rṣm* [*2*] | (10bB) in whose land you are dwelling |
| *wl' šm'tm bqwly* [*1*] | (10bC) and do not listen to their voice." |

[petuchah]

A brief justification of this structure must suffice. Judg. 6:7 is preceded by a *petuchah* and 6:10 is followed by one, which provides evidence that 6:7-10 is to be treated as a literary unit. Inclusion is formed by the pair *z'q* || *šm'* (7aA, 10bC),[113] which supports this delimitation of the literary boundaries. Furthermore, on the basis of thematic considerations and content commentators have generally recognized that 6:7-10 constitutes a unit functioning at its present setting as part of the "Rahmenwerk" of Judges.[114] These observations validate an analysis of 6:7-10 as a literary unit.

**Strophe 1**

Sep. ↑: *petuchah*; tricolon; *ky*

Sep. ↓: absent

Int. || : *bny-yśr'l* || *mdyn*;[115] *'l* || *'l*

Ext. || : *bny yśr'l* || *bny yśr'l*; *yhwh* || *yhwh*

**Strophe 2**

Sep. ↑: rep. *'mr*; beginning of prophetic discourse, with formula *kh 'mr yhwh 'lhy yśr'l*[116]

[113]Cf. the discussion of this parallelism with respect to the macrostructure of Josh. 24:1-28 as dealt with in the ext. par. between I.iii and I.iv (cf. 3.5.3).

[114]W.Beyerlin, "Geschichte und Heilsgeschichtliche Traditionsbildung im Alten Testament," *VT* (1963) 10-13; "Gattung und Herkunft," 8f.

[115]The appeal to Yahweh (as judge) is perhaps intended to make a pun on the name *mdyn*.

[116]Cf. Josh. 24:2 (at 3.4.2).

Sep. ↓: rep. *'tkm*
Int. par.: *'mr* || *'mr*; *h'lyty* || *w'ṣy'*;[117] *'tkm* || *'tkm*; *mmṣrym* || *mbyt 'bdym*[118]
Ext. || : *yhwh* || *'nky h'lty*;[119] *yśr'l* || *mṣrym*
Rhyme: formed by *m* terminating three of the four cola.[120]

**Strophe 3**
Sep. ↑: rep. *myd*
Sep. ↓: rep. *-km*[121]
Int. || : *myd mṣrym* || *myd kl-lḥṣykm*;[122] *w'grš* || *w'tnh*;[123] *'wtm* || *lkm*
Ext. par.: 2 pers. pronouns; 1 c.s. verbal forms
Rhyme: formed by *m* ending all four cola

**Strophe 4**
Sep. ↑: *'mr*
Sep. ↓: *petuchah*; tricolon; rep. *l'*
Int. || : *-km* || *-km*; *l' tyr'w* || *wl' šm'tm*.[124]
Ext. || : *yhwh 'lhykm* || *'lhy h'mry*.

Of the external parallelism between the strophes, particularly noteworthy is the close link between the central two strophes, especially as formed by concatenations, *'tkm* || *'tkm* and *mṣrym* || *mṣrym*. We also note the inclusion of *z'q* || *šm'* (7aA, 10bC); *wy'mr lhm* || *w'mrh lkm* (8bA, 10aA; responsion); *'nky* || *'ny* (8cA, 10aB).[125] The

[117]This parallelism was dealt with in connection with the macrostructure of Josh. 24:1-28 (see 3.5.5).
[118]Cf. the evidence listed regarding Josh. 24:17a.
[119]Cf. the discussion of int. par. in Josh. 24:17a.
[120]The exception is in 8bB where the formula prohibits it; cf. the following strophe as well.
[121]Separation downwards is weak here, but separation upwards is strong in the following strophe.
[122]The parallelism is evident here; cf. Ex. 3:9; 22:20; 23:9; 1 Sam. 10:18; Isa. 19:20. The similarity with the historical recital in 1 Sam. 10:18 is dealt with more extensively below.
[123]Cf. Ex. 23:31 and Ezek. 31:11, which are the only other OT texts where these two verbs are found together in a single verse. In all three cases the verbs *ntn* and *grš* are used synonymously as actions by Yahweh. See too Ex. 33:1f. and Josh. 24:11f.
[124]Cf. the poetic parallelism in Isa. 50:10; 51:7; Hab. 3:2; Ps. 55:20; 61:6; 66:16; 76:9; 145:19; Eccl. 12:13.
[125]Dahood–Penar, "Ugaritic-Hebrew Parallel Pairs," 117 no.51. Cf. the respon-

connections between strophes 1 ⇔ 4 and 2 ⇔ 3 establish a concentric macrostructure. The final strophic arrangement is therefore a very balanced 3+2 / 2+2 // 2+2 / 2+3 structure. On the basis of this analysis it appears that the entire unit of vss.7-10 is colometric.

Discernment of colometry in Judg. 6:7-10 facilitates a specific comparison with Josh. 24:2-24, which in turn reveals a telling frequence and quality of parallels. The ensuing table of comparisons follows the colometric order of Judg. 6:8b-10.

| Judg. 6:8b-10 | Josh. 24:2-24 |
|---|---|
| *wy'mr lhm* (8bA) | *wy'mr yhwš' 'l-kl-h'm* (2aA) |
| *kh-'mr yhwh 'lhy yśr'l* (8bB) | *kh-'mr yhwh 'lhy yśr'l* (2aB) |
| *'nky h'lyty 'tkm mmṣrym* (8cA) | *hw' hm'lh 'tnw* (17aB) |
| | *w't-'bwtynw* (17aC) |
| | *m'rṣ mṣrym* (17aD) |
| *mbyt 'bdym* (8cB) | *mbyt 'bdym* (17aE MT) |
| *w'ṣl 'tkm myd mṣrym* (9aA) | *w'ṣl 'tkm mydw* (10aC) |
| *wmyd kl-lḥṣykm* (9aB) | [*w'ṣl 'tkm mydw* (10aC)] |
| *w'grš 'wtm mpnykm* (9bA) | *wtgrš 'wtm mpnykm* (12aB) |
| *w'tnh lkm 't-'rṣm* (9bB) | *w'tn 'wtm bydkm* (8bA) |
| | *wtyršw 't-'rṣm* (8bB) |
| *'ny yhwh 'lhykm* (10aB) | *n'bd 't-yhwh* (18bB *ky-hw' 'lhynw* (18bC) |
| *l' tyr'w 't-'lhy h'mry* (10bA) | *w'th yr'w 't-yhwh* (14aA) |
| *'šr 'tm yšbym b'rṣm* (10bB) | *'šr 'tm yšbym b'rṣm* (15dB) |
| *wl' šm'tm bqwly* (10bC) | *wbqwlw nšm'* (24aC). |

This list demonstrates that, starting with the prophetic introduction in vs.8b, virtually every colon of 6:8b-10 finds a direct counterpart in Josh. 24:2-24.[126] The fact that the first two of these cola (8bA-B) stand at the beginning of the direct discourse, as in Josh. 24:2, may not appear significant at first because of the nature of the introductory formula. However, the scarcity of the formula prior to the prophets is already noteworthy. It is virtually always reserved for well-known leaders and prophets in the Israelite tradition. And, what surely cannot be coincidence, the final colon (6:10bC) corresponds with the

sion formed by mention of "Yahweh" in the first and last strophes.

[126]The list omits only the colon *w'mrh lkm* (10aA), which marks the beginning of the new strophe. Since *'mr* in Josh. 24:14-24 repeatedly serves to mark separation of structural units in the dialogue, even here there is a formal and thematic parallel.

final colon of discourse in Josh. 24 canticle II.iv (vs.24). This entails that the prophetic discourse in both Judg. 6:8b-10 and Josh. 24:2-24 is framed by the introductory formula *kh-'mr yhwh 'lhy yśr'l* and the concluding idiom *šm' bqwl*.[127]

The evidence linking these passages is reinforced by the relatively scarce wording of a number of the expressions. The *Masora parva* at Josh. 24:10 already notes that the precise form *w'ṣl* occurs only 3x. The third instance is in 1 Sam. 10:18, which is demonstrated below to be directly dependent upon Judg. 6:9aA. Judg. 6:7-10, along with Josh. 24:1-28, has long been recognized to contain a unique emphasis upon contacts with the gods of the Amorites. These details confirm the conclusion attained from the textual synopsis above; the similarities are not to be explained on the grounds of a common milieu or linguistic tradition. There is a textual dependence between the passages.

On the basis of these comparisons, some conclusions are warranted. All thirteen cola from 6:8b-10 have a counterpart in Josh. 24:2-24. Although the order of the respective cola is rearranged in Judg. 6:8b-10, the correspondence with the original cola in Josh. 24 is still evident. Moreover, it is precisely at the level of the cola that the connections are most apparent. This reinforces the conclusion that Josh. 24:1-28 is a colometric composition. Despite the rearrangement in Judg. 6:8b-10, the inclusion formed by the introductory formula *wy'mr ... kh-'mr yhwh 'lhy yśr'l* (8b) and the idiom *šm' bqwl* (10b) correspond precisely with the boundaries of the dialogue in Josh. 24:2-24. These details, along with the precise correspondence of certain diction (e.g., *w'šl* [Judg. 6:9aA; Josh. 24:10aC] and *'šr 'tm yšbym b'rṣm* [Judg. 6:10bB; Josh. 24:15dB]), prove a literary dependence between the two passages.

The commonality of emphasis has not gone unobserved in previous analyses,[128] but the literary connection has not been adequately pursued, perhaps due to failure to detect the colometric structure of the units. On the basis of the preceding synopsis, as well as considerations of content and context, it is evident that Judg. 6:8b-10

[127]Significantly, Josh. 24:14aA forms a contrast with serving the gods of the Amorites, see in the same canticle *w'm 't-'lhy h'mry* (15dA), and cf. Judg. 6:10bB and Josh. 24:15dB with identical references, *'šr 'tm yšbym b'rṣm*.

[128]Cf. Schmitt, *Landtag*, 17f., 22-24, 29, 44, 48, 59, 62; Beyerlin, "Geschichte und Heilsgeschichtliche Traditionsbildung," 11f.

is directly dependent upon Josh. 24:2-24. The direction of dependence is already hinted by the anonymity of the prophet in Judg. 6:7-10, while in Josh. 24:2 the speaker is specified. Furthermore, the prophetic message enters the Gideon cycle of Judg. 6 abruptly, which has long prompted speculation about its origin and history of redaction. The question of context merits further elaboration.

Commentators generally agree that this prophetic message springs into its context enigmatically.[129] Among other considerations, it has been suggested that the gods of the Amorites are awkward in the Midianite setting,[130] and, in the estimation of most scholars, vs.10 ends in an abrupt manner which leaves the concern of the passage unresolved. The relationship of these verses to the surrounding material appears to have already been problematic for ancient scribes.[131] On the basis of context, therefore, there are multiple reasons for viewing Josh. 24:2-24 as the original version upon which Judg. 6:8b-10 is dependent.

Judg. 6:7-10 is frequently attributed to a Dtistic editor, and Richter is inclined to view it as a late insertion after the main Dtic redaction.[132] Soggin regards it as an exilic insertion, but he argues that it possibly originated with Dtr in another context.[133] Arguments to the contrary have also been raised.[134] Beyerlin notes that nowhere

[129]E.g., Oettli, *Das Deuteronomium* 249; more elaborately, Beyerlin, "Gattung und Herkunft," 8f.; Gray, *Joshua, Judges, Ruth*, 283; Soggin, *Judges*, 112.

[130]On the other hand, a comparison with Gen. 15:16 and Josh. 24:15 has often been made, e.g., Oettli, *Das Deuteronomium*, 249; Keil–Delitzsch, *Joshua*, 330. Boling's approach, which calls attention to the parallelism between *bny-qdm* as Easterners and *h'mry* as Westerners, is an exception. But Boling too sees 6:3-10 as a secondary insertion into the Gideon cycle (*Judges*, 125f.).

[131]"Der Codex Vaticanus der Septuaginta, die Peschitta und Vulgata haben wohl den Übergang zu diesem Zuwachs durch die Auslasssung des Verses 7a zu glätten versucht ..." (Beyerlin, "Gattung und Herkunft," 8). "The passage is significantly wanting in 4QJudges[a], which indicates that it was recognised as redactional in a text still current in the first century AD" (Gray, *Joshua, Judges, Ruth*, 284, with reference to F.M.Cross, "The Contribution of the Qumran Discoveries to the Study of the Biblical Text," *IEJ* 16 [1966] 81-95).

[132]Cf. Richter, *Bearbeitungen*, 2, 11, 13. His main argument is the fact that vs.7 repeats vs.6b, which suggests that they come from different hands.

[133]Soggin, *Judges*, 113; cf. his "Deuteronomistische Geschichtsauslegung während des babylonischen Exils," in F.Christ, ed., *Oikonomia* (Fs O.Cullmann; Hamburg, 1967), 11-17.

[134]It has been noted, e.g., that a certain similarity exists between the present passage and a prophetic utterance from Mari (McCarthy, *Covenant and Treaty*, 169 n.23). McCarthy raises reservations about considering the language to be per

else in the "Rahmenwerk des Richterbuchs" is mention made of the gods of the Amorites.[135] The enigma of this reference disappears once one realizes its dependence upon Josh. 24:15. Any subsequent attempts to deal with the identity of the present redactor[136] will have to distinguish between terminology borrowed from Josh. 24:2-24 and terminology original to the redactor of the present composition, especially as that is found in 6:7-8a.

Despite these multiple indications that Josh. 24 is original and Judg. 6:8b-10 is derivative, one might anticipate a question whether the direction of dependence could possibly go in the other direction, perhaps even from an original composition of the Judges material somewhat different from the present form. One argument which might initially seem to support the contention that Josh. 24 is influenced by Judg. 6:7-10 can be identified in the presence of *mbyt ʿbdym* in 24:17 MT, absent in the LXX. The argument, however, does not carry much weight because it can be reversed.[137]

On the basis of these contacts, it is safe to assume that the similarity of the divine self-revelation in Judg. 6:8cA and Josh. 24:17a is not coincidental. The ensuing descriptions of the liberating actions can therefore yield clues concerning the direction of dependence. For this question the composition of Judg. 6:9 is fundamental. In the present form of the verse, the phrase *w'grš 'wtm* ... can scarcely refer to the Egyptians. The *'wtm* must therefore refer to "all your oppressors," even though upon a first reading one is inclined to view "from the hand of the Egyptians" and "from the hand of all your

se Dtistic. For example, he suggests that the expression "save from the hand of ..." (with Yahweh as subject) is common and old, with only Judg. 6:9 and 8:34 possibly belonging to Dtr, and these references are doubtful as evidence of Dtr (209).

[135]Beyerlin, "Gattung und Herkunft," 8f.

[136]This is an example of where the terms redactor and author become virtually synonymous. The compiler, redactor or author of Judges incorporated material from other sources, and in cases such as 6:7-10 this is integrated as a new composition.

[137]If on other grounds it is possible to demonstrate that Josh. 24 is prior to Judg. 6:7-10, the correlation of "from the house of bondage" in the respective texts argues for (a) the authenticity of the MT in Josh. 24:17aE contra LXX or (b) a later reciprocal influence of Judg. 6:8 upon Josh. 24:17 or (c) the influence of a third source upon both Judg. 6:8 and Josh. 24:17—or, more likely, a stage of redaction at which time the shorter formula "out of the land of Egypt" was expanded with the phrase "out of the house of bondage." Absence of a reference to the "fathers" in 6:8cA might support the reading of the Peshitta in Josh. 24:17.

oppressors" as synonymous parallelism in which "oppressors" equals "Egyptians."[138] But this would produce a conflict with the historical situation known from the Pentateuch and Joshua. And it was not the land of the Egyptians that Israel possessed as an inheritance. Accordingly, the oppressors as the referent of *'wtm* in this case must be the other nations or groups who opposed Israel from the time of the settlement and following. This is consistent with the use of *lḥṣ* in the framework of Judges (cf. 1:34; 2:18; 4:3; 10:12). The root is not used elsewhere in Judges. The colon *wmyd kl-lḥṣykm* (6:9aB) is part of a bicolon reminiscent of Josh. 24:10aC, but it employs the verb *lḥṣ*, thereby tying this verse into the framework of Judges. It is clear that Judg. 6:9aA is closer to Josh. 24:10aC than is Judg. 6:9aB. The latter colon is typical of the editor of Judges. The net result is a verse in which there is no narrated transition from the period of the Egyptian sojourn to the later oppression. The historical overview of Josh. 24 is telescoped as a précis of Yahweh's historical acts of delivery, thereby making an actualization in the context of the Gideon cycle. Along with the realization that the reference to the gods of the Amorites is central to Josh. 24:2-24, whereas in Judg. 6:10 it has been a constant stumbling block for commentators,[139] this actualization with *lḥṣ* argues for the priority of Josh. 24:2-24 as the source for Judg. 6:8b-10. Whether the *mbyt 'bdym* in Josh. 24:17aE is original or due to reciprocal influence from Judg. 6:8cB is difficult to decide with certainty from the present evidence.[140] The possibility of a reciprocal influence is by no means impossible.[141]

A couple of concluding observations are pertinent with respect to the unknown prophet and the importance of the priority of Josh. 24:2-24 for the literary composition of Judges. The degree to which the message of 6:8b-10 is dependent upon Josh. 24:2-24 suggests that the reference, "And Yahweh sent a prophet to the sons of Israel," might

[138]As attested elsewhere in Ex. 3:9.

[139]Note the abrupt transition from the introduction of the gods of the Amorites in vs.10 to the resumption of the theme of Midianite oppression in vs.11. Judg. 6:6 would make a very plausible link with vss.11ff.

[140]See further the discussion in 3.6.2, and note that a reference to *mbyt 'bdym* is not found in 1 Sam. 10:17f., which otherwise shows a colon for colon dependence upon Judg. 6:8f. (cf. below).

[141]This may be yet another example of the minor variations in different "editions" which we have repeatedly noted in the variations between the *Vorlage* of the LXX and the MT.

be a veiled allusion to Joshua. The prophetic formula is employed in reference to Joshua in Josh. 7:13; 24:2, and it is employed again for the first time in Judg. 6:8. The role of Joshua as Israel's leader played an important part in the structure of the framework of Judges (cf. 1:1; 2:6-10). These other references to Joshua in Judges demonstrate that dischronologization for thematic emphasis posed little difficulty for the author of Judges. It has been demonstrated above that Judg. 2:6ff. is dependent upon Josh. 24:28ff. And Judg. 6:7-10 is based upon Josh. 24:2-24, which demonstrates the primary role played by Josh. 24 in structuring the present form of Judges. The leadership provided by Joshua, particularly as demonstrated in the covenantal ceremony at Shechem, is viewed by the author of Judges as a definitive norm by which to evaluate the history of the period of the judges. This theme is explicit in 2:6-15. The author of the framework follows Josh. 24 in suggesting that the worship of the gods of the Amorites, which was rejected as an option in Joshua's covenant ceremony, is now the source of the difficulty which befell Israel in the time of the Midianite oppression.

The reference to Yahweh's sending of a prophet need not be read in a strictly chronological sense.[142] The fact that both Judg. 2:6ff. and 6:8bff. are dependent upon Josh. 24 suggests that these two passages of Judges may derive from the same author/compiler. Furthermore, since Judg. 2:6-10 and 6:8b-10 employs material from Josh. 24:2-31, the last chapter of Joshua must have been available in close to its definitive form to the compiler of Judges. It is not possible here to discuss the propriety of calling passages such as Judg. 6:7-10 Dtistic. However, on the basis of our conclusions with respect to Josh. 24 in the preceding chapter, and the observations by McCarthy,[143] we are forced to agree with Beyerlin[144] that Noth spoke too readily of the hand of a Dtic redactor in passages such as these.[145] There is little in these literary connections that is exclusively Dtistic. Most theories of the Dtistic history imply that the type of thematic progressions

[142]A striking corrollary to the idea defended here has been posited by others with respect to the unknown prophet in 1 Sam. 2:27 as a possible allusion to Moses (Cross, *Canaanite Myth*, 196-198). It is also possible, but less likely, that Judg. 6:7-10 does not allude specifically to Joshua but wishes rather to imply that another prophet summarized the words of Joshua, who had instigated a prior renewal.

[143]McCarthy, *Treaty and Covenant*, 169, 209.

[144]Beyerlin, "Geschichte und Heilsgeschichtliche Traditionsbildung," 10f.

[145]Cf. Noth, *Überlieferungsgeschichtliche Studien*, 51f.

outlined here are to be attributed to a specific Dtic/Dtistic school, but actual evidence to link the present passages to such a school is lacking.

### 5.4.3 Judg. 9 and kingship at Shechem

Josh. 24:1-28 is linked thematically and literarily to Judg. 9. The two narratives have a common setting in Shechem. The reference in 9:6 to an enthronement by the oak of the pillar appears to make a link not only with Josh. 24:26,[146] but also with Gen. 12:6f. Moreover, Jotham's perch on Mt. Gerizim (9:7) prompts comparison with Deut. 27:12. And the detail of the "terebinth of the soothsayer" in Judg. 9:37 has been compared to the references in Gen. 12:6 and Deut. 11:30.[147] The combination of *btmym* and *b'mt* is applied in Josh. 24:14 to service of Yahweh, and in Judg. 9:16,19 it denotes allegiance to the human king. The worship of *'l bryt* at Shechem (Judg. 9:46) is equated by the narrator with the worship of *b'l bryt* (9:4),[148] and can only lead to a contrast with the covenant ceremony in Josh. 24:1-28, where Israel pledges to serve Yahweh as God of the covenant. These various literary links between Josh. 24:1-28 and Judg. 9 reinforce the conclusion that Josh. 24:1-28 implicitly presupposes the concept of divine kingship. The comparisons are not sufficient to demonstrate a direct literary dependence one way or the other, but they do show a common emphasis upon the importance of Shechem in the period of the judges with respect to the covenant worship of Yahweh.

## 5.5 Josh. 24:1-28 and 1 Samuel

Josh. 24 exerted major influence upon the final form of Judges. Both Judg. 2:6-10 and 6:7-10 betray direct dependence upon Josh. 24. The first of these passages from Judges employs only 24:28-31, which left open the question of whether Josh. 24 was used in a form close

[146]Regarding *mṣb* cf. Boling, *Judges*, 171f.

[147]Cf. G.W.Ahlström, "*hammōreh liṣdāqāh* in Joel II 23," in *Congress Volume Rome 1968*, *SVT* 17 (Leiden, 1969), 27f.

[148]Cf. the manner in which the narrator typifies Israel's unfaithfulness in the time of the Judges (see also 8:33), in criticism of the worship of *b'l bryt*. The use of the verb *śym* in the phrase *wyśmw lhm b'l bryt l'lhym* is analogous to a technical term sometimes used in the sense "to set as king," e.g., Deut. 17:14f.; 1 Sam. 8:5; 10:19; 1 Kgs 10:9. The same verb is often used in appointment to other offices as well (cf. Weinfeld, "Covenant Terminology," 197).

to its final structure in the MT. Judg. 6:8b-10, on the other hand, is composed as a telescoped summary of 24:2-24 without mentioning the gathering in 24:1,25-28. It is now possible to take the line of dependence upon Josh. 24 a step further and trace it into 1 Samuel as well. In 1 Samuel there are in particular three passages of interest for the present study, i.e., 1 Sam. 10:17-27; 7:2-17; 11:14-12:25.

### 5.5.1 Josh. 24:1-28 and 1 Sam. 10:17-27

The importance of 1 Sam. 10:17-27 for an understanding of Josh. 24:1-28 is generally conceded. However, the question of dependence has been a matter of debate and uncertainty. Ben-Barak is of the opinion that the covenant ceremonies of Ex. 19-24 and Josh. 24 provided a model for later traditions of covenant making in Israel, e.g., as described in 1 Sam. 7:10; 2 Sam. 5:1-3; 11:12,17.[149] If it is possible to demonstrate that the enthronement narratives in 1 Samuel–2 Kings are indeed dependent upon Josh. 24, the implications are manifold. First, this would provide a degree of confirmation that one aspect of the covenant of Josh. 24:1-28 centers upon divine kingship. Secondly, it would provide some clues to a cluster of questions regarding the composition of the enthronement narratives of the early monarchy and the relative dating of Josh. 24:1-28 compared to these texts.

It is unnecessary to treat 1 Sam. 10:17-27 in its entirety. The relevant verses for the present research are 10:17f.,24f. along with a number of phrases sprinkled throughout the intervening verses. When written colometrically, it is evident that 10:17f. is dependent upon Judg. 2:8f., which in turn was based upon Josh. 24:2-24. And 1 Sam. 10:25 contains affinities to Josh. 24:25-28 which are too close to be merely coincidental. What needs to be investigated is whether the similarities reveal a literary dependence, or whether they are to be attributed to the commonality of the setting and subject matter.

The literary unit of 1 Sam. 10:17-27 is introduced by a description of the enthronement ceremony in a manner similar to the setting of Josh. 24:1. 1 Sam. 10:17-18aA is both preceded and followed by a *petuchah.* The reason for this is not difficult to ascertain. In the present Masoretic edition of Samuel the *petuchot* are frequently placed in conjunction with the beginning of a new unit of speech, especially when it is *divine* discourse. Accordingly, the first *petuchah*

[149]Ben-Barak, "The Mizpah Covenant," 30-43.

at vs.17 is motivated by the beginning of a new literary unit, and the second *petuchah* is based on the formula *kh-'mr yhwh 'lhy yśr'l.* For the purpose of the present comparison vss.17f. will be treated as a literary unit.[150]

**1 Sam. 10:17-18**

| | |
|---|---|
| *wyṣq šmw'l 't-h'm [5]* | (17aA) And Samuel called the people |
| *'l-yhwh hmṣph [1]* | (17aB) to Yahweh at Mizpah. |
| *wy'mr 'l-bny yśr'l [8]* | (18aA) And he said to the sons of Israel, |
| *kh-'mr yhwh 'lhy yśr'l [5]* | (18aB) "Thus says Yahweh, God of Israel, |
| *'nky h'lyty 't-yśr'l mmṣrym [2]* | (18bA) 'I am the one who brought Israel up from Egypt, |
| *w'ṣyl 'tkm myd mṣrym [5]* | (18bB) and I delivered you from the hand of the Egyptians, |
| *wmyd kl-hmmlkwt [5]* | (18cA) and from the hand of the kingdoms, |
| *hlḥṣym 'tkm [1]* | (18cB) those who oppressed you'." |

This unit is dependent upon Judg. 6:8f. and not vice versa. To demonstrate the parallels we list Judg. 6:8f. and 1 Sam. 10:18 synoptically.

| Judg. 6:8-9 | 1 Sam. 10:18 |
|---|---|
| *wy'mr lhm* | *wy'mr 'l-bny yśr'l* |
| *kh-'mr yhwh 'lhy yśr'l* | *kh-'mr yhwh 'lhy yśr'l* |
| *'nky h'lty 'tkm mmṣrym* | *'nky h'lyty 't-yśr'l mmṣrym* |
| *w'ṣy' 'tkm mbyt 'bdym* | |
| *w'ṣl 'tkm myd mṣrym* | *w'ṣyl 'tkm myd mṣrym* |
| | *wmyd kl-hmmlkwt* |
| *wmyd kl-lḥṣykm* | *hlḥṣym 'tkm* |

The order of the six cola in 1 Sam. 10:17f. follows precisely that of Judg. 6:8f. As in the LXX of Josh. 24:17, there is no reference to "from the house of bondage" (cf. Judg. 6:8cB). Furthermore, 1 Sam. 10:18cA-B, *wmyd kl-hmmlkwt / hlḥṣym 'tkm*, is an expansion of Judg. 6:9aB to a bicolon. The necessity for this expansion is not difficult to determine. In Judg. 6:9aB the reference to "your oppressors" (*lḥṣkm*) is controlled by other references in 1:34; 2:18; 4:3, making the referent clear. At least for the author of Judg. 6:7-10 it was clear that the Egyptians were not intended but rather the surrounding nations—as

[150]The validity of maintaining these literary boundaries is confirmed by the unity of Judg. 6:8f., upon which the present verses are based.

in Josh. 24:2-24 which he was contracting. However, when Judg. 6:8f. is re-employed in the context of 1 Sam. 10:18, the possibility of a confusion of *lḥṣykm* (as in Judg. 6:9aB) with the Egyptians (as in Ex. 3:9) necessitates that the colon *wmyd kl-lḥṣykm* (Judg. 6:9aB) be expanded to a bicolon, *wmyd kl-hmmlkwt / hlḥṣym 'tkm* (1 Sam. 10:18cA-B). These considerations demonstrate that the direction of dependence was from Josh. 24 to Judg. 6:7-10 to 1 Sam. 10:18. The preciseness of the colometric correlations rules out the possibility that the passages simply derive from a common tradition or are modeled upon a specific *Gattung*. A direct literary connection is indicated.

The situation is more difficult in the strophe formed by 1 Sam. 10:25, but here too the equivalencies are revealing. To facilitate a comparison, 1 Sam. 10:25 is first presented colometrically with a translation, and secondly it is presented with the relevant parallels from Josh. 24.

| 1 Sam. 10:25 | |
|---|---|
| *wydbr šmw'l 'l-h'm* [5] | (25aA) And Samuel recited to the people, |
| *'t mšpṭ hmlkh* [5] | (25aB) a regimen[151] of the kingship. |
| *wyktb bspr* [5] | (25bA) And he wrote it in a book |
| *wynḥ lpny yhwh* [2] | (25bB) and he placed it before Yahweh. |
| *wyšlḥ šmw'l 't-kl-h'm* [8] | (25cA) And Samuel sent all the people away, |
| *'yš lbytw* [1] | (25cB) every man to his house. |

The points of comparison with Josh. 24:25-28 are the following:

| 1 Sam. 10:25 | Josh. 24 |
|---|---|
| *wydbr šmw'l 'l-h'm* | (27aA) *wy'mr yhwš' 'l-kl-h'm* |
| *'t mšpṭ hmlkh* | (25aB) *wyśm lw ḥq wmšpṭ bškm* |
| *wyktb bspr* | (26aA) *wyktb yhwšw' 't-hdbrym h'lh* |
| | (26aB) *bspr twrt 'lhym* |
| *wynḥ lpny yhwh* | (26bD) *'šr bmqdš yhwh* |
| *wyšlḥ šmw'l 't-kl-h'm* | (28aA) *wyšlḥ yhwš' 't-h'm* |
| *'yš lbytw* | (28aB) *'yš lnḥltw* |

In the preceding comparison, numerous cola of the lengthier account in Josh. 24:25-28 have been left out because they do not have a direct counterpart in 1 Sam. 10:25. Nevertheless, it is striking that

[151] For the sense of regimen for a life see Judg. 13:12.

all six cola of 1 Sam. 10:25 have a direct correlate in Josh. 24:25-28. Furthermore, the final bicola may originally have been virtually identical if Josh. 24:28aB at one time read *'yš lbytw*, as has been suggested on the basis of the LXX.[152]

In addition to the parallels in these cola, there are a number of important similarities in additional references throughout 1 Sam. 10:17-27 and Josh. 24:1-28, and it is advisable to consider these affinities prior to summarizing the results and drawing conclusions. Both narratives begin in a similar manner with the prophetic leader summoning a gathering at a particular place (Shechem and Mizpah). However, there is an important difference in the verbs used for gathering. Whereas Josh. 24:1 has *'sp*, *qr'* and *yṣb*, 1 Sam. 10:17 has *ṣ'q*.[153] The verb *qr'* in Josh. 24:1 does not have a counterpart in 1 Sam. 10:17. Both passages contain a reference to the people stationing themselves before God (cf. 1 Sam. 10:19, *htyṣbw lpny yhwh*, and Josh. 24:1, *wytyṣbw lpny h'lhym*), but the procedure of the tribal selection in 1 Sam. 10:19-21 differs from the collective gathering in Josh. 24:1.[154] This comparison shows that although there are similarities in the terms used to describe the gatherings, both of which presuppose a national assembly, there are sufficient differences to make a strict literary dependence improbable. This demonstrates that the respective terms for gathering establish a thematic comparison but not a textual dependence.

It is also of interest to compare God's choice of Saul as king (1 Sam. 10:24) with Israel's choice of Yahweh (Josh. 24:22). In fact, as is evident from the following comparison, there is a formal similarity as well as thematic affinity.

[152]Cf. 3.6.3. Note that 1 Sam. 10:25 reads *kl-h'm* while Josh. 24:28 is without a *kl*. In Josh. 24:27aA and 1 Sam. 10:25aA the situation is reversed.

[153]In the Hiph. form it is used only here, and the related *z'q* in the Hiph., meaning "to call to assemble," is found only in Judg. 4:10,13; 2 Sam. 20:4f. These two verbs in the Niph., with the meaning "to be called to assemble," are found in Judg. 7:23f.; 10:17; 12:1; 1 Sam. 13:4; 2 Kgs 3:21 (*ṣ'q*) and Josh. 8:16; Judg. 6:34f.; 18:22f.; 1 Sam. 14:20. In short, whereas these verbs are never found in this sense in the Pentateuch, they are quite common throughout Judges and Samuel.

[154]Furthermore, in 1 Sam. 10:20 is found the synonym *qrb*, in the phrase *wyqrb šmw'l 't kl-šbṭy yśr'l*, cf. Josh. 24:1, *wy'sp yhwš' 't-kl-šbṭy yśr'l*. Cf. 4.2.1. For the poetic parallelism of the various terms for gathering, consult our structural analysis of Josh. 24:1, as well as Watson, "Word-pair *'sp* || *qbṣ*," 426-434.

| 1 Sam. 10:24 | Josh. 24:22 |
|---|---|
| *wy’mr šmw’l ’l-kl-h‘m* | (22aA) *wy’mr yhwš‘ ’l-h‘m* |
| *hr’ytm ’šr bḥr-bw yhwh* | (22aB) *‘dym ’tm bkm* |
| *ky ’yn kmhw* | (22bA) *ky-’tm bḥrtm lkm ’t-yhwh* |
| *bkl-h‘m* | (22bB) *l‘bd ’wtw* |
| *wyr‘w kl-h‘m* | |
| *wy’mrw* | (22cA) *wy’mrw* |
| *yḥy hmlk* | (22cB) *‘dym* |

Both texts describe a legal setting in which the leader calls the people to witness. In 1 Sam. 10:24 the imperative to see (*r’h*) has a legal connotation. This is evident from the response of the people (see below). It is also evident from similar employment in 1 Sam. 12:16, which is also in a legal context.[155] Both Josh. 24:22 and 1 Sam. 10:24 focus upon the choice which is made (cf. *bḥr* in both texts). That which is to be witnessed is introduced with a *ky*-clause, which leads to the demand for the people's acknowledgment, which is expressed in a cryptic oath formula. The present correspondence is not of such a nature that it would suggest a direct literary dependence in which one text copies or borrows from the other. However, for a number of reasons it is noteworthy. As is demonstrated above,[156] Josh. 24:22 is a legal formula with close counterparts in Ruth 4:9-11 and 1 Sam. 12:5. On the basis of both stylistics and content, it is now possible to add 1 Sam. 10:24 to the discussion. The climactic phrase *yḥy hmlk* (10:24) is not simply a hearty and exuberant wish; it implies an oath on behalf of the utterer.[157] Mettinger adduces evidence from the Amarna Letters for a comparable Akkadian formula, *libluṭ šarru*, where *libluṭ* is to be taken as a precative of *balāṭu*, clearly bearing the weight of an oath.[158] The form *yḥy* in 10:24 is not adequately

[155]Cf. T.Longman III, "1 Sam. 12:16-19: Divine Omnipotence or Covenant Curse?" *WTJ* 45 (1983) 168-171. The connection between 1 Sam. 10:24 and 12:16 is made explicit in 1 Sam. 12:13.

[156]Cf. 2.2 and 2.4.1.

[157]Cf. P.A.H.de Boer, "Vive le roi!" *VT* 5 (1955) 225-231; D.Michel, "Studien zu den sogenannten Thronbesteigungspsalmen," *VT* 6 (1956) 46; Lipiński, *La royauté de Yahwé*, 348-361; Mettinger, *King and Messiah*, 131-137; Kalluveettil, *Declaration and Covenant*, 61f. The oath *ḥy yhwh* "by the life of Yahweh," is attested in Lachish 6:12; 3:9 (perhaps 12:3) (J.H.Tigay, "Israelite Religion: The Onomastic and Epigraphic Evidence," in Miller et al., eds., *Ancient Israelite Religion*, 176).

[158]Mettinger, *King and Messiah*, 134.

rendered as a simple jussive.[159] The legal format of the reference in 1 Sam. 10:24 suggests that it can be read as a precative[160] with an idiomatic function as an acclamation in an enthronement ceremony. Since the acclamation was tantamount to an oath of allegiance, a parallel is evident with the declaration *'dym* in Josh. 24:22. In the latter context, the fourfold *n'bd* refrains also establish a declaration of allegiance, especially since Josh. 24:17f. builds upon the confessional acclamations *ky yhwh 'lhynw* and *ky hw' 'lhynw.*

Thus, the description of the formal assembly of 1 Sam. 10:17-25 starts with a prophetic recital of Yahweh's saving acts (introduced by the formula *kh-'mr yhwh 'lhy yśr'l*), followed by a ritual selection of a king (*bḥr*), the people are called to see (10:24), i.e., to *witness* the king whom Yahweh has chosen, and immediately following this the narrative advances to the recital of law,[161] inscription in a book, placement before Yahweh, and dispersal of the people. This all makes a striking parallel with the events in Josh. 24:1-28, where there is an assembly, prophetic recital of Yahweh's saving acts (beginning with *kh-'mr yhwh 'lhy yśr'l*), a liturgical ritual in which Yahweh is chosen (*bḥr*), the people pledge their allegiance in an acclamation ritual,[162] they are called as legal witnesses to their own choice, which is followed by law-giving in a public, juridical ceremony, the writing of the law in a book, and dispersal of the people.

The implications of these parallels warrant a number of significant conclusions. The narrative account of 1 Sam. 10:17-25 in its present form must be later than Josh. 24:1-28 because 1 Sam. 10:18 is dependent upon Judg. 6:8f., which in turn, as we have seen, was based upon Josh. 24. The entire form and flow of the narrative in 1 Sam. 10:17-27 is strikingly similar to Josh. 24:1-28. Yet, except for the dependence of 1 Sam. 10:18 upon Judg. 6:8f., there is no additional evidence to prove that 1 Sam. 10:17-25 is literarily dependent upon Josh. 24:1-28. This entails that either Josh. 24:1-28 served as the model (not source!) for 1 Sam. 10:17-25, or the similarities detected

[159]De Boer identifies the form as jussive, but he cites evidence for other places where a jussive has the strength of an indicative: "En des sens secondaires, le jussif peut équivaloir à un imperatif" ("Vive le roi!" 230 n.2.; cf. Michel, "Thronbesteigungspsalmen," 46).

[160]Williams, *Hebrew Syntax*, 34 no.184.

[161]Note that here as in Josh. 24:25 *mšpṭ* is singular.

[162]Frankena, "Vassal-Treaties," 140; Kalluveettil, *Declaration and Covenant*, 61 n.188; cf. 4.4.

in 10:17,19b,24f. are due to a common background in the description of such a legal ceremony. In either case, Josh. 24:1-28 appears to be older than 1 Sam. 10:17-25. Furthermore, whether Josh. 24:1-28 was a conscious model for 1 Sam. 10:17-25,[163] or played only a subconscious role upon the author via Judg. 6:8f., it is clear that the close correspondence between the two narratives supports the conclusion that Josh. 24:1-28 describes a covenant ceremony in which Yahweh was recognized as king. Evidence favoring an enthronement ceremony linked with a New Year festival as the background for 1 Sam. 10:17-25 has been collected by de Moor.[164] The present comparison of Josh. 24:1-28 and 1 Sam. 10:17-25 suggests that both events may represent acclamation festivals honouring the divine and human kings respectively.

It is noteworthy that Mettinger, following a very different route of analysis, concludes that 1 Sam. 10:17-27 is the "oldest tradition of a royal designation in ancient Israel."[165] He is in fact inclined to date it to the time of Solomon or possibly earlier.[166] In our present analysis we have discerned that the origin of Josh. 24:2-24 must predate 1 Sam. 10:18 and it plausibly predates the present form of the remainder of 1 Sam. 10:17-25. If Mettinger's dating of 1 Sam. 10:17-27 is acceptable and if 1 Sam. 10:18 is not a later addition, the basic form of Josh. 24:1-28 must have been intact already at an early period. However, the question of dating the respective accounts demands a more detailed analysis, which we will momentarily postpone. In the meantime we turn to a consideration of Josh. 24:1-28's connection with additional passages in 1 Samuel.

[163]The similarities listed above suggest that the author of 1 Sam. 10:17-25 may have played deliberately upon Josh. 24:1-25 in order to compare the election of Saul as king with the election of Yahweh as divine king. Note too that the description of Saul standing "a shoulder above the people" (*wygbh mkl h'm mškmw wm'lh*, 1 Sam. 10:23) is perhaps intended to form a pun on Gen. 48:22, *škm 'ḥd 'l-'ḥyk* (cf. Josh. 24:12), as well as the ill-fated attempt of Abimelech to attain kingship at *škm* (Judg. 9).

[164]Cf. de Moor, *New Year*, 1:12-16.

[165]Mettinger, *King and Messiah*, 179.

[166]His conclusion is based on a relative chronology of the descriptions in 1 Sam. 16:1-13 and 1 Sam. 9:1-10:16, which he sees to be later than 1 Sam. 10:17-27 (*King and Messiah*, 182).

### 5.5.2 Josh. 24:1-28 and 1 Sam. 7:2-17

1 Sam. 7:2-17 demonstrates a clear continuation of themes traceable from Josh. 24:1-28 through Judges and Samuel. The historical situations confronting Israel are explained in terms of their allegiance or disobedience to Yahweh. The renewal ceremony conducted by Samuel is described in terms reminiscent of the ceremonies in Gen. 35:2 and Josh. 24:23.[167]

| 1 Sam. 7:3cA-dB | Josh. 24:23 |
|---|---|
| *hsyrw 't-'lhy hnkr* | *w'th hsyrw 't-'lhy hnkr* |
| *mtwkkm wh'štrwt* | *'šr bqrbkm* |
| *whkynw lbbkm* | *whṭw 't-lbbkm* |
| *'l-yhwh* | *'l-yhwh 'lhy yśr'l* |

Whereas Josh. 24:23aB employs the preposition *bqrbkm*, in Gen. 35:2bB and 1 Sam. 7:3cB *btwkkm* and *mtwkkm* are used.[168] Mention here of the *'štrwt* may be taken as a concrete reference to the given historical situation. The same is true of the Philistines in the following portion of 1 Sam. 7:3, *wyṣl 'tkm myd plštym* which may be compared with Josh. 24:10aC, *w'ṣyl 'tkm mydw.*[169] Furthermore, the combination of the imperatives *hsyrw* and *w'bdw* is found in Josh. 24:14 and 1 Sam. 7:3 and nowhere else within a single verse of the MT.[170] As a final point of comparison, mention may be made of the stone of witness in Josh. 24 and the memorial *'bn h'zr* of 1 Sam. 7:12.

[167]Blenkinsopp, "Traces of the Gibeonite Covenant," 218; van Selms, "Temporary Henotheism," 346.

[168]The parallelism of *btwk* and *bqrb* has been defended above in the comparison of Gen. 35:2 and Josh. 24:23.

[169]Note the sudden emphasis upon Amorites in 1 Sam. 7:14. It may also be significant that Samuel's circuit included Bethel, Gilgal and Mizpah, all of which are sites known from other texts as places of worship, and all three of which come into clear focus in a comparison of texts related to Josh. 24:1-28; e.g., regarding Bethel cf. the discussion of Gen. 28:20f. above, for Mizpah cf. 1 Sam. 10:17-27, and regarding Gilgal cf. 1 Sam. 11:14f., discussed below. 1 Sam. 7:15 specifically states that in Ramah Samuel built an altar to Yahweh, which can be compared with the patriarchal altars for Elohim.

[170]For a list of the verses containing the two verbs in all forms see our structural analysis of Josh. 24:14.

### 5.5.3 Josh. 24:1-28 and 1 Sam. 11:14-12:25

Our structural and literary analyses of Josh. 24:1-28 appealed to the narrative of 1 Sam. 11:14-12:25 for comparison of closely related themes and terminology. The present section summarizes the correlations between these two passages.

Since both narratives include a summons to gather, it is desirable to determine the precise nature of the assembly at Gilgal. 1 Sam. 11:14 states that the intention was to renew the kingship.[171] Vannoy has argued that this renewal was not of the kingship of Saul but of Yahweh.[172] While he has mustered some evidence to support the conclusion that the narration of this ceremony in combination with the covenant renewal in ch.12 presupposes the kingship of Yahweh, it is certainly incorrect to downplay the centrality of the kingship of Saul in 11:14f. Vannoy gives inadequate attention to the fact that kingship in Israel likely was renewed or celebrated in accordance with Israel's festal calendar.[173] The final compilation of 1 Samuel purposely places ch.12 after the renewal of Saul's kingship in 11:14f. But this does not obliterate the evidence that 11:14f. is a brief, self-contained unit which may at one time have stood in a source independent from the material which now follows in ch.12. The predominant elements of 11:14f. become most obvious when delineated in their intended colometric format.

**1 Sam. 11:14f.**
[setumah]

| | |
|---|---|
| *wy’mr šmw’l ’l-h‘m* [*5*] | (14A) And Samuel said to the people, |
| *lkw wnlkh hglgl* [*2*] | (14B) "Come, let us go to Gilgal, |
| *wnḥdš šm hmlwkh* [*1*] | (14C) and we will renew there the kingship." |
| *wylkw kl-h‘m hglgl* [*7*] | (15aA) And all the people went to Gilgal, |
| *wymlkw šm ’t-š’wl* [*13*] | (15aB) and there they made Saul king, |
| *lpny yhwh bglgl* [*5*] | (15aC) before Yahweh in Gilgal. |

[171] *wnḥdš šm hmlwkh.*

[172] Vannoy, *Covenant Renewal*, 68.

[173] We have already referred to the suggestion by de Moor that the ceremony in 1 Sam. 10:17-25 describes Saul's enthronement in a festival. In the same study, it is suggested that Saul's kingship was renewed annually at Gilgal (*New Year*, 1:14, 15 n.174).

| | |
|---|---|
| *wyzbḥw-šm* [*12*] | (15bA) And they sacrificed there |
| *zbḥym šlmym* [*8*] | (15bB) peace offerings |
| *lpny yhwh* [*2*] | (15bC) before Yahweh. |
| *wyśmḥ šm š'wl* [*12*] | (15cA) And Saul rejoiced there |
| *wkl-'nšy yśr'l* [*8*] | (15cB) as did all the men of Israel |
| *'d-m'd* [*1*] | (15cC) exceedingly. |
| [petuchah] | |

We have presented these verses as two strophes of poetic narrative.[174] Once the colometric structure is recognized, it is apparent that the four verses are governed by the expressions *nḥdš šm* ("renew there"), *wymlkw šm* ("make king there"), *wyzbḥw-šm* ("sacrificed there"), and *wyśmḥ šm* ("rejoiced there") respectively. The first strophe explicitly states that Saul is made king in Gilgal,[175] while the second focuses upon the sacrificial meal that accompanied such events.[176] The second strophe (11:15b-c) shows a close resemblance to the altar law of Deut. 27:5-7 delineated above.[177]

[174]Note that the pericope is preceded with a *setumah* and followed by a *petuchah*. The first strophe is sructured upon the threefold repetition of "Gilgal," the threefold repetition of the root *hlk* and the parallelisms *hmlwkh* || *wymlkw*, *h'm* || *h'm*, and *šm* || *šm*. The second strophe similarly employs *šm* twice in strategic positions. It too uses the expression *lpny yhwh* in concatenation with 15ac. And an inclusion is produced by *h'm* || *kl-'nšy yśr'l* (14aA, 15cB). The structure is a well-balanced 3+3 || 3+3 colometry. A prosaic account would not be expected to contain the degree of tautological repetition found in these strophes, e.g., the fourfold presence of *šm* (once in each verse) and the threefold repetition of *glgl* in the first strophe.

[175]On the significance of *šm* and *bglgl* consult G.Buccellati, "The Enthronement of the King and the Capital City in Texts from Ancient Mesopotamia and Syria," in R.D.Biggs–J.A.Brinkman, eds., *Studies Presented to A. Leo Oppenheim* (Chicago, 1964), 54-61, esp. 56f.

[176]Regarding the connection between enthronement rituals and sacrifice cf. the examples collected by de Moor (*New Year*, e.g., 2:31—regarding KAI 214:15-22). The combination of renewing kingship and sacrificing in the extra-biblical texts suggests that Vannoy is correct that 1 Sam. 11:14 is not a redactional attempt to connect 11:15 with 10:17ff. (*Covenant Renewal*, 130). But he is wrong in stating that the renewal is of Yahweh's kingship and not Saul's.

[177]On the association of "offering" and "rejoicing" in these passages and elsewhere in the OT see the discussion of Deut. 27:7 above.

| Deut. 27:6b-7 | 1 Sam. 11:15 |
|---|---|
| *wh'lyt 'lyw 'wlt* | *wyzbḥw-šm* |
| *lyhwh 'lhyk* | *zbḥym šlmym* |
| *wzbḥth šlmym* | *lpny yhwh* |
| *w'klt šm* | *wyśmḥ šm š'wl* |
| *wśmḥt lpny yhwh 'lhyk* | *wkl-'nšy yśr'l* |
| | *'d-m'd* |

The elements in common are *zbḥ šlmym*, *śmḥ*, *šm*, and *lpny yhwh*. The connection between the building of the altar in Deut. 27:5-7 and the renewal of the kingship in 1 Sam. 11:14f. perhaps provides clues to one of the most ancient riddles of OT studies, namely the reference to Gilgal in Deut. 11:30.[178] As is noted by Eissfeldt,[179] this reference in Deut. 11:30 already perplexed Eusebius.[180] Deut. 11:30 apparently makes a connection with both Gen. 12:6[181] and 1 Sam. 11:14f. with its enthronement ritual of Saul at Gilgal. This offers a plausible explanation for what is otherwise a most enigmatic reference to Gilgal in Deut. 11:30. The author of Deut. 11:30 apparently knows the significance of Shechem and Gilgal and the ceremonies which occurred in these locations. Via the covenantal sacrificial meal described at Mt. Ebal and Mt. Gerizim, he links these ceremonies to a fulfilment of the Abrahamic promise of the land.[182]

What follows in 1 Sam. 12 is similar in some respects to a combination of the emphases of Josh. 23[183] and 24:1-28. The present farewell speech of Samuel, like that of Joshua before him, combines the elements of a final testimony with an emphasis upon faithful,

[178]Cf. Sellin, *Gilgal*, 1-60; *Geschichte*, 1:96f., 101; Eissfeldt, "Gilgal or Shechem," 90-101; E.Otto, *Das Mazzotfest in Gilgal* (Stuttgart, 1975), 12-25. See also the summaries in 1.3.6 and 1.3.8.

[179]Eissfeldt, "Gilgal or Shechem," 100f.

[180]Cf. E.Kloostermann, *Das Onomastikon der biblischen Ortsnamen* (Leipzig, 1904), 65ff.

[181]Note not only the reference to the Oak of Moreh, but the Canaanites in the Arabah as well.

[182]With respect to *zbḥ šlmym* and its covenantal implications cf. R.Schmid, *Das Bundesopfer in Israel* (München, 1964); R.de Vaux, *Studies in Old Testament Sacrifice* (Cardiff, 1964), 27-51; Vannoy, *Covenant Renewal*, 88-91. See further our discussion of Ex. 24:3-8 (5.3.4).

[183]Cf. especially Josh. 23:2b, *'ny zqnty b'ty bymym*, and 1 Sam. 12:2aB, *w'ny zqnty wśbty*.

covenant allegiance to Yahweh.[184] The structural similarity of 1 Sam. 12:5 and Josh. 24:22 has been demonstrated above. 1 Sam. 12:6f. identifies the present period with that of the fathers in a manner analogous to Josh. 24:5-7,17. The historical summary of 1 Sam. 12:8-12 has numerous parallels to that of Josh. 24:2b-13.[185] 1 Sam. 12:9-15 extends the historical summary with a description of the unfaithfulness in the time of the judges, culminating with the demand for a king, thereby jeopardizing the exclusive kingship of Yahweh.

This period is described with terms reminiscent of those used in analogous accounts in Judges and in 1 Sam. 7, e.g., the combination of *yr'* and *šm'*[186] and especially the combination of abandoning Yahweh to serve the "Baalim" and "Ashtarot." There are only four verses in the MT which contain the combination of *b'l* and *'štrwt*, namely, Judg. 2:13; 10:6; 1 Sam. 7:4 and 12:10.[187] Significantly, of these four texts, Judg. 2:13; 10:6 and 1 Sam. 12:10 also employ the parallelism of *'zb* || *'bd*. 1 Sam. 7:4 also contains the verb *'bd* but not in parallelism with *'zb*. The connection between these verses is surely not fortuitous. Judg. 2:13 is part of the description of what happened in Israel after the death of Joshua. It continues the theme of Israel's transition to unfaithfulness introduced with material modified in 2:6-10 from Josh. 24:28ff. Furthermore, 1 Sam. 12:10 quotes the speech of the Israelites in Judg. 10:10. Samuel's discourse harks back to Israel's previous appeal for a king to reign over them. This theme is present in Judg. 10:18, illustrated in a local way in the promise of the Gileadites that whoever would deliver them would be their ruler.[188] Samuel's discourse traces the present ambiguity, regarding the place and role of the divine and earthly kings respectively, back to the conflict at Gilead between the Israelites and the Ammonites (Judg. 10:17-12:7).

In short, 1 Sam. 12 summarizes a number of themes which are

[184]Cf. P.K.McCarter, *1 Samuel* (Garden City, 1980), 220f.

[185]Cf. the descent of Jacob to Egypt (in both cases without a *locale h*) and use of the verb *z'q* in the respective contexts: *wyz'qw 'bwtykm 'l yhwh* (12:8bA), *wyz'qw 'l-yhwh* (12:10aA) and *wyṣ'qw 'l-yhwh* (Josh. 24:7aA). Cf. further *wyšlḥ yhwh 't-mšh w't-'hrn* (12:8bA) and *w'šlḥ 't-mšh w't-'hrn* (Josh. 24:5aA MT); *wywṣy'w 't-'bwtykm mmṣrym* (12:8bB) and *w'wṣy' 't-'bwtykm mmṣrym* (Josh. 24:6aA).

[186]Used similarly in Judg. 6:10; 1 Sam. 12:14 (cf. 7:7).

[187]Avishur, "Word Pairs," 21, cf. KAI 14:18.

[188]Cf. Judg. 11:4ff. Jephthah's first act of sending an ambassador to the Ammonite king shows that he now functions as a king in Gilead; the message sent to the Ammonite king follows the format typical of international correspondence (Kalluveettil, *Declaration and Covenant*, 143f.).

introduced already in Josh. 24:1-28, and which function as a canon by which to measure Israel's relationship to Yahweh in the period of the judges. The central question is the worship of Yahweh rather than the gods of the surrounding nations. This worship entails in part the recognition of Yahweh as king. Josh. 24:1-28 presents a setting in which such a choice was made. Judges illustrates numerous examples of the breaking of the oath of allegiance to Yahweh, at the same time interacting with the theme of the rise of human kingship in Israel.

Our argumentation to this point has been primarily along the lines of literary affiliations rather than literary *dependence* between 1 Sam. 12 and Josh. 24:1-28. The distinction is an important one. The main focus in the analysis above is to demonstrate that, in the present form of the historical material, the arrangement and narration of the various passages follows a studied progression from Joshua to Samuel. It is a second, more difficult, question to inquire whether this advancement accords with the actual order in which the accounts were written.

We have argued that Judg. 2:6-10 is dependent upon Josh. 24:28ff. Similarly, Judg. 6:7-10 and 1 Sam. 10:18 are dependent upon Josh. 24:2-24. The renewal of the kingship in 1 Sam. 11:14 presupposes knowledge of the previous enthronement account in 1 Sam. 10:17-25. Furthermore, the issue of the relationship between the human king and the divine king is already specifically raised in 1 Sam. 10:19, in verses which very naturally proceed from the historical summary in vs.18, which in turn is later than Josh. 24:2-24. 1 Sam. 12:12-19 continues this theme. And 1 Sam. 12:9-11 is dependent upon the prior accounts of the judges as narrated in Judges, including Judg. 2:11ff., which is subsequent to Josh. 24:28ff. All this evidence points to the temporal priority of Josh. 24 to 1 Sam. 12. And it establishes a relative dating of Josh. 24 antecedent to the various passages treated above.[189] It does not yet say anything about the actual date of composition.

## 5.6 Josh. 24:1-28 and enthronement in 1-2 Kings

A detailed comparison of Josh. 24 with enthronement rituals in 1-2 Kings is beyond the scope of this study. A select comparison with 1 Kgs 12:1-17 and 2 Kgs 11 will suffice to demonstrate the similarity

[189]Contra Van Seters, "Joshua 24," 147-149.

of Josh. 24:1-28 and certain descriptions of the enthronement of the human king in ancient Israel.

### 5.6.1 Josh. 24:1-28 and 1 Kgs 12:1-17

Numerous semblances are detectable between these two gatherings at Shechem. We restrict ourselves here to a demonstration that the negotiation of the kingship[190] with Rehoboam employs deliberate poetic exchanges in the dialogue.[191] The offer of kingship is presented in vs.4.

| | |
|---|---|
| *'byk hqšh 't-'lnw* [*2*] | (4aA) Your father made it severe for us, |
| *w'th 'th* [*18*] | (4aB) but as for you now |
| *hql m'bdt 'byk hqšh* [*7*] | (4aB) lighten your father's severe toil, |
| *wm'lw hkbd* [*12*] | (4bA) and that heavy yoke, |
| *'šr ntn 'lynw* [*8*] | (4bB) which he placed on us, |
| *wn'bdk* [*1*] | (4bC) and we will serve you. |

This proposition concludes with an offer of service or vassalage employing a form of *n'bd* comparable to that which is so crucial as a refrain in Josh. 24:14-24. The poetic advice of the elders follows in vs.7, and once again the verb *'bd* is used to denote the relationship to the king.

190 Apparently, in the early stages of the monarchy it was common practice to negotiate the terms of kingship prior to the actual enthronement ceremony, cf. e.g., Judg. 9:1-4; 2 Sam. 5:1-3. See also Fohrer, "Der Vertrag," 1-22.

191 For a broader discussion of 1 Kgs 12:1-17 consult A.Malamat, "Kingship and Council in Israel and Sumer: A Parallel," *JNES* 22 (1963) 247-253; "Organs of Statecraft in the Israelite Monarchy," *BA* 28 (1965) 34-65; D.G.Evans, "Rehoboam's Advisers at Shechem, and Political Institutions in Israel and Sumer," *JNES* 25 (1966) 273-279; D.W.Gooding, "The Septuagint's Rival Version of Jeroboam's Rise to Power," *VT* 17 (1967) 173-189; H.Seebass, "Zur Königserhebung Jerobeams I," *VT* 17 (1967) 325-333; M.Aberbach–L.Smolar, "Jeroboam's Rise to Power," *JBL* 88 (1969) 69-77; E.Lipiński, "Le récit de 1 Rois XII 1-19 a la lumiere de l'ancien usage de l'hébreu et de nouveaux textes de Mari," *VT 24* (1974) 430-437; C.D.Evans, "Naram-Sin and Jeroboam: The Archetypal Unheilsherrscher in Mesopotamian and Biblical Historiography," in Hallo et al., eds., *Scripture in Context II*, 97-125; R.L.Cohn, "Literary Technique in the Literary Technique," *ZAW* 97 (1985) 23-35.

| | |
|---|---|
| *wydbr 'lyw l'mr* [*7*] | (7aA) And they spoke to him saying, |
| *'m-hywm thyh-'bd* [*13*] | (7aB) "If this day you will be a servant |
| *l'm hzh w'bdtm* [*5*] | (7aC) to this people and serve them, |
| *w'nytm wdbrt 'lyhm* [*8*] | (7bA) and you answer and speak to them |
| *dbrym twbym* [*2*] | (7bB) with good words, |
| *whyw lk 'bdym* [*8*] | (7cA) then they will be your servants |
| *kl-hymym* [*1*] | (7cB) for all days." |

The wise and balanced advice of the elders is neatly reflected in this strophe which is marked with inclusions formed by the legal terminology of *hywm* and *kl-hymym* as well as the double expression *hyh 'bd l* (7a and 7c).[192] The advice of the youths is also narrative poetry.[193]

| | |
|---|---|
| *wydbrw 'lyw* [*7*] | (10aA) And they said to him, |
| *hyldym 'šr gdlw 'tw l'mr* [*3*] | (10aB) the youths who grew up with him, saying |
| *kh-t'mr l'm hzh* [*15*] | (10bA) "Say thus to this people |
| *'šr dbr 'lyk l'mr* [*7*] | (10bB) who spoke to you saying, |

| | |
|---|---|
| *'byk hkbyd 't-'lynw* [*5*] | (10cA) 'Your father made our yoke heavy, |
| *w'th hql m'lynw* [*2*] | (10cB) now you lighten it from upon us.' |
| *kh tdbr 'lyhm* [*5*] | (10dA) Speak thus to them, |
| *qṭny 'bh* [*8*] | (10dB) 'My little one[194]is thicker |
| *mmtny 'by* [*1*] | (10dC) than my father's loins. |

| | |
|---|---|
| *w'th 'by h'mys 'lykm 'l kbd* [*5*] | (11aA) Now my father loaded you with a heavy yoke |
| *w'ny 'wsyp 'l-'lykm* [*2*] | (11aB) but I will add to the yoke upon you |
| *'by ysr 'tkm bšwṭym* [*5*] | (11bA) My father disciplined you with scourges |
| *w'ny 'ysr 'tkm b'qrbym* [*1*] | (11bB) but I will discipline with scorpions'." |

[192]Note the parallelism formed on the root *dbr* in the central verse. The strong inclusions neutralize this repetitive parallelism with regard to strophic division.

[193]Cohn, "Literary Technique," 29.

[194]On the proposals to read this as a euphemism for penis cf. Cohn, "Literary Technique," 29.

Excluding 10dB-C, Rehoboam's answer follows the same basic poetic[195] format as the advice of the youths,[196] and need not be repeated here. The answer of the people is presented in two terse bicola.[197]

| | |
|---|---|
| *mh-lnw ḥlq bdwd* [*13*] | (16cA) "What portion do we have in David? |
| *wl'-nḥlh bbn-yšy* [*7*] | (16cB) No inheritance in the son of Jesse! |
| *l'hlyk yśr'l* [*5*] | (16dA) To your tents, O Israel! |
| *'th r'h bytk dwd* [*2*] | (16dB) Look[198] to your own house, O David!" |

In these excerpts from the account of 1 Kgs 12:1-17, the enthronement negotiation is presented in successive stages of poetic narrative. This is not to deny the possibility that the intervening verses may contain additional narrative poetry, but for our present purpose it is necessary to curtail the analysis. This account is of considerable importance regarding the poetic narrative of Josh. 24:1-28 because it demonstrates that the enthronement negotiation in Shechem as narrated in 1 Kgs 12:1-17 also employs poetic discourse (cf. the enthronement negotiation at Shechem in Judg. 9). The previous relationship between the king's father and the people is narrated here, which in certain respects forms an analogy with the historical summary in Josh. 24:2b-13. But the harsh demands of the king result in his rejection by the people rather than fostering an ensuing acclamation ritual with the formula *n'bd*.

[195]Note the parallelism in these three strophes. E.g., in the first there is both internal and external parallelism built upon the verbs of speech, *dbr* and *'mr*. Between strophes 1 and 2 note *kh-t'mr l'm* || *kh tdbr 'lyhm* (responsion). In strophe 2 note, e.g., *hkbyd 't-'lynw* || *hql m'lynw*; *qṭny* || *mtny*; *'bh* || *'by* (wordplay). The third strophe builds upon the alternating parallelism of *'by* || *'ny*. Since *'byk* is already introduced in 10cA, the word *w'th* in 11aA becomes crucial for strophic division. Consider also *'lykm 'l* || *'l-'lykm*; *ysr 'tkm* || *ysr 'tkm*; *bšwtym* || *b'qrbym*; etc.

[196]Note, however, that the A-colon *w'th 'by h'mys 'lykm 'l kbd* (11aA) is shortened to *'by hkbyd 't-'lykm* (14bA) while the B-colon *w'ny 'wsp 'l-'lykm* (11aB, 14bB) is left unchanged. The revised colon softens Rehoboam's answer. It also demonstrates the impossibility of reading this narrative poetry according to classical metrical theories.

[197]The poetic character of these verses is recognized by the NIV. On *ḥlq* "portion" || *nḥlh* "inheritance" cf. Avishur, *Stylistic Studies*, 107, 126, 316, 657f.; for *'hl* || *byt* see 158, 282. If the final phrase *wylk yśr'l l'hlyw* is accepted as part of the poetry, the final verse would be a tricolon: *l'hlyk yśr'l* || *yśr'l l'hlyw*.

[198]Perhaps read with LXX: "Shepherd your own house, O David!"

### 5.6.2 Josh. 24:1-28 and 2 Kgs 11

Previous studies of OT enthronement narratives have identified various elements found in common in passages such as Josh. 24:25-28; 1 Sam. 10:25; 2 Sam. 5:1-3 and 2 Kgs 11:12-19.[199] Therefore, in support of observations made above regarding 1 Sam. 10:17-25, the present comparison is restricted to the most conspicuous affinities between Josh. 24:1-28 and 2 Kgs 11:12-19. It is significant that in 2 Kgs 11:12 the giving of the *'dwt*[200] is accompanied by the acclamation formula *yḥy hmlk*, which is the same as in 1 Sam. 10:24, demonstrated above to be comparable to Josh. 24:22. The ritual in 2 Kgs 11 took place "according to the protocol" (vs.14) for such ceremonies, which supports the theory that it is part of a longer tradition. The enthronement ritual was accompanied by a covenantal ceremony focusing upon sole allegiance of both the people and the king to Yahweh,[201] which again forms a parallel with the covenant ceremony following the oath of allegiance in Josh. 24:24f.

## 5.7 Josh. 24:1-28 and Josh. 23

The foregoing study of the connection of Josh. 24:1-28 with other passages facilitates a return to its more immediate literary context, viz., ch.23. A logical point of departure for the present investigation is the correlation of 24:1 with 23:1f. The latter verses comprise two strophes in the opening canticle of a poetic narrative spanning Josh. 23:1-16:[202]

Josh. 23:1-2

| | |
|---|---|
| *wyhy mymym rbym* [*5*] | And it was many days |
| *'ḥry 'šr-hnyḥ yhwh lyśr'l* [*12*] | after Yahweh had given rest to Israel |
| *mkl-'ybyhm msbyb* [*2*] | from all their surrounding enemies |
| *wyhwš' zqn* [*5*] | And Joshua was old, |
| *b' bymym* [*1*] | advanced in years. |

[199]See especially Ben-Barak, *Mizpah Covenant*, 30-43, plus literature cited there.
[200]Cf. our discussion in 2.3.7.2.
[201]Mettinger, *King and Messiah*, 135, 142-145.
[202]Koopmans, "Joshua 23," 90-118.

| | |
|---|---|
| *wyqr' yhwš' lkl-yśr'l* [*5*] | And Joshua called all Israel |
| *lzqnyw wlr'šyw* [*5*] | his elders and his heads |
| *wlšpṭyw wlšṭryw* [*2*] | his judges and his officers. |
| *wy'mr 'lhm* [*5*] | And he said to them, |
| *'ny zqnty* [*5*] | "I am old, |
| *b'ty bymym* [*1*] | I am advanced in years." |

It is noteworthy that the lists of leaders in 23:1f. and 24:1 include the same four categories.[203] Furthermore, the same verb (*qr'*) is used in both. Finally, at the end of Josh. 23 the emphasis turns to obedience to the covenant, which in a qualified way is comparable to Josh. 24:25. However, in addition to the similarities there is a high number of differences between the passages. Not least of these variances is a number of considerations involving Joshua's personal references in 23:1f. Commentators have frequently noted that here Joshua is depicted as very old, while in 24:1-28 no hint is given of his advanced age.[204] Josh. 23:1 ties in directly with the narrative progression of Joshua, which is not true of Josh. 24:1-28. Josh. 23 highlights obedience to the law, and it does so with repeated employment of terminology taken from Deuteronomy. The Dtistic language of Josh. 23 is universally recognized, and a few examples will suffice. The expression *k'šr dbr yhwh*, which is typical of Deuteronomy,[205] is employed strategically in Josh. 23:5bB.[206] The final strophe (23:16) is composed essentially of Deut. 11:16f., and most of the emphases of Josh. 23 are directly paralleled in Deut. 11.

The references in 23:1f.,14a to Joshua's age are not simply of historical significance; they constitute a vital dimension of ch.23's literary form. Joshua's *Abschiedspredigt* in this chapter is closely con-

[203]Cf. 4.2.1.

[204]One might wonder whether such a reference should be expected after it is already mentioned in ch.23. However, comparison with other passages suggests that Josh. 24:1-28 interrupts the reference to Joshua's advanced age and the announcement of his death and burial (see below).

[205]Hulst, "Opmerkingen over de ka'ašr-zinnen," 337, 356-360.

[206]Cf. 10aD, 14cC, 15aC (Koopmans, "Joshua 23," 107f.). In 14cC the colon *'šr dbr yhwh 'lhykm 'lykm* stands at the center of a strophe characterized by ABCB́Á chiastic parallelism. In 15aC *'šr dbr yhwh 'lhykm 'lykm* is the central colon of an ABCÁB́ arrangement. And 5bB and 10aD are refrain cola. These observations show the centrality of this Dtistic phrase in the structure of Josh. 23. Note too the use of *'šr ṣwh 'tkm* in 16aB.

nected in literary form to other *testament* narrations in the OT.[207] It is also instructive to compare the narration of other OT farewell accounts. Gen. 49:1 similarly employs the verb *qr'*. As with David, the testament of Jacob is followed by an account of his death and burial. Despite the fact that ch. 23 in its present form is a well-structured poetic unit, the absence of the death and burial account, which is postponed until after 24:1-28, gives rise to additional questions about the relationship of the two chapters and the originality of their present juxtaposition.

Reference has been made above to Deut. 31 and the commissioning of Joshua, and it is apparent that in the portrayal of Moses in Deut. 31-34 the final testament and law-giving are combined in a manner analogous to Josh. 23-24.[208] Josh. 23 stands at the conclusion of Joshua with a twofold purpose. As a testament of Joshua it serves to complete his role in the *Landnahme* motif spanning from Deuteronomy through Joshua. It also combines with Josh. 24:1-28 to anticipate the dual introduction to Judges. Not only is Josh. 23:16 modeled upon Deut. 11:16f., but Josh. 24:31 and Judg. 2:7b,10b are linked to Deut. 11:7.[209]

The literary critical analysis of Josh. 24:1-28 and the relationships to the other passages treated above reveal that there is finally only one satisfactory solution for the arrangement of Josh. 23 and 24:1-28. Josh. 24:1 is not dependent upon 23:2. On the contrary, Josh. 23:1-16 is composed in such a way that it combines with Josh. 24:1-28 to provide a literary transition from the Joshua to Judges. Josh. 23:1-16 has a narrower focus. It elaborates a demand for obedience to the *torah*, showing that such obedience would facilitate inheritance of the land as promised in Deuteronomy. By contrast, Josh. 24:1-28 stresses sole allegiance to *yhwh 'lhy yśr'l* rather than other gods. Its

[207]Particular mention may be made of the similarity to David's testament in 1 Kgs 2:1-10. For a list of the many literary connections between the two passages consult Koopmans, "Testament of David."

[208]See 5.3.3.

[209]Cf. *ky 'ynykm hr't 't-kl-m'śh yhwh hgdl 'šr 'śh* (Deut. 11:7) and *'šr r'w't kl-m'śh yhwh hgdwl 'šr 'śh lyśr'l* (Judg. 2:7bC-D). Although the expression "deeds which one has done" is conventional (cf. Gen. 44:15; 1 Sam. 8:8; 1 Kgs 13:11; Ps. 107:24; Eccl. 1:14; 3:11; 4:3; 8:17; 11:5), it is not likely that the precise correspondence between Deut. 11:7 and Judg. 2:7b is coincidental, especially so in the light of the influence of Deut. 11:16f. upon Josh. 23:16 and the correlation of Josh. 23-24 with the dual introduction to Judges.

connection with the land is not made contingent upon observance of the law but serves rather to complete essential themes introduced already in the narratives of the patriarchs and the exodus. The present combination of Josh. 23-24,[210] which is likely to be attributed to the final stages of compilation of Joshua, has little to say about the antiquity of Josh. 24:1-28, but it is of importance for understanding the role which Josh. 24:1-28 ultimately played in the shaping of the narratives of Judges–1 Samuel 12.

## 5.8 Additional incidental relationships

The acclamation formulae *ky-yhwh 'lhynw* and *ky-hw' 'lhynw* find close parallels in Ps. 99:9 and 95:7, in two Psalms exalting the kingship of Yahweh. The refrain of Ps. 99:5,9[211] appeals to the holiness of King Yahweh, cf. especially Josh. 24:19, *'lhym qdšym hw'*, and Ps. 99:5, *qdwš hw'*.[212] The phrase *ky-hw' 'lhynw* is found in Josh. 24:18 and Ps. 95:7 and nowhere else in the OT. In Ps. 95:7 it is part of the reciprocal covenant formulary "for he is our God and we are his people."[213] This covenantal formula in 95:7 makes an explicit correlation between Yahweh's kingship and his covenant relationship with his people. Various additional comparisons can be listed between Ps. 95 and Josh. 24:1-28. For example, the emphasis in 95:3 that Yahweh is king above all gods may be compared with the demand for sole allegiance in Josh. 24. Note too the emphasis upon the fathers in a historical summary and the stress upon Yahweh as a punishing God (95:11, cf. Josh. 24:19). These comparisons between Josh. 24:1-28 and two Psalms celebrating Yahweh's kingship adds to the considerable evidence adduced above to defend the thesis that Josh. 24:1-28

[210]Once the complete literary structure of 23:1-16 and 24:1-28 is recognized the admittedly awkward placement of Josh. 24:1-28 between ch.23 and the death and burial of Joshua in 24:29-31 is explainable. Given Josh. 23:1-16 and 24:1-28 as two poetic units, there was little choice. Josh. 24:1-28 could hardly be placed prior to 23:1-16 because the dispersal of the people in 24:28 is re-employed in Judg. 2:7, not in the sense of the end of an assembly but specifically as the end of the *Landnahme*. To place Josh. 24:1-28 prior to 23 would entail sending the people home and then immediately calling them again for a farewell speech.

[211]Cf. Lipiński, *La royauté de Yahwé*, 329-333.

[212]Note too the place of Moses and Aaron (99:6, cf. Josh. 24:5), and the observance of testimonies and statutes (99:7, cf. Josh. 24:25). Ps. 99:8 stresses that God not only was forgiving but also avenging, cf. Josh. 24:19.

[213]Cf. provisionally Smend, *Bundesformel*; Lohfink, "Beobachtungen," 297.

presupposes divine kingship. Lipiński has raised formidable arguments for an early dating of Ps. 99,[214] which, if acceptable, provides valuable evidence for the antiquity of the idea of Yahweh's kingship. Numerous previous studies have been prompted by von Rad's lead in comparing Josh. 24:2-13 to the historical summaries in the Psalms.[215] The present affinities demonstrate the value of extending such comparisons to kingship and festival motifs in the Psalms.[216] Additional incidental relationships could be adduced between Josh. 24:1-28 and other passages in Genesis–2 Kings, the Prophets and Psalms. Many of these are mentioned in our structural and textual analyses (chs.3-4) or in passing references in the present chapter, and it is unecessary to burden the present study with an attempt to be exhaustive.

## 5.9 Josh. 24:1-28 and ancient NE texts

### 5.9.1 Divine military intervention

Numerous references have been made above to similarities between Josh. 24:1-28 and the Mesha inscription. Both these texts emphasize that military victory is facilitated by the deity. However, the concept of divine intervention in history,[217] including divine warfare in particular,[218] is widely attested in ancient NE literature, and many of the elements in Josh. 24:2-13 have analogies in texts from other lands. For example, the description in Josh. 24:7 of the dark cloud as a divine military intervention may be compared to a Hittite parallel in the Annals of Muršiliš where the Storm-god employs a cloud of fog (IMBARU) to protect his troops from the enemy.[219] So too, Yahweh's use of the sea in waging war against the Egyptians has broad parallels

[214]Lipiński, *La royauté de Yahwé*, 333-335, esp. 335: "En conclusion, le psaume peut dater de l'époque de Salomon."

[215]Cf. Kühlewein, *Geschichte*, 159f.; Kreuzer, *Frühgeschichte*, esp. 20, 23, 32f., 183-213. Unfortunately, Kühlewein and Kreuzer are too ready to accept previous criteria for a literary dissection of Josh. 24:1-28, which in turn sharply influence the historical conclusions drawn.

[216]Cf. the initial efforts in this direction by Weiser (see 1.4.5).

[217]Cf. B.Albrektson, *History and the Gods* (Lund, 1967); H.Cancik, *Mythische und historische Wahrheit* (Stuttgart, 1970); *Grundzüge der Hethitischen und alttestamentlichen Geschichtsschreibung* (Wiesbaden, 1976); W.G.Lambert, "Destiny and Divine Intervention in Babylon and Israel," *OTS* 17 (Leiden, 1972), 65-72.

[218]See conveniently Kang, *Divine War*.

[219]Goetze, *Die Annalen des Muršiliš*, 194; Weinfeld, "Divine Intervention," 144.

in the ancient NE literature.[220] With respect to the translation *ṣrʿh* in Josh. 24:12 as panic, it is noteworthy that ancient Greek epics also mention the element of panic as part of divine intervention in warfare.[221] The Greek texts make a connection with a demon who causes the panic, while the *ṣrʿh* of Ex. 23:28; Deut. 7:20; Josh. 24:12 is associated with the angel (*ml'k*) sent by Yahweh.[222] These parallels show that the similarities between Josh. 24:2-13 and other ancient NE texts extend beyond the formal identification of a treaty or covenant prologue, which has often been the starting point for comparisons.

### 5.9.2 Ancient NE covenants with a deity

A comparison of OT covenants between Israel and Yahweh and extra-biblical covenants between human parties and their deities is unavoidable if one wishes to do justice to both the similarities and differences between Josh. 24:1-28 and comparable ancient NE texts. For decades it has been commonplace to assert that the covenant relationship of Israel with Yahweh was unique in the ancient world because other people did not covenant with their gods. Indeed, the OT expression of a covenant between Yahweh and Israel as a whole is understandably unparalleled by other examples of a single deity in covenant with an entire nation.[223] Therefore, the degree to which covenant expressions in Israel were unique will likely be a matter of discussion for years to come. However, previous claims that other individuals did not covenant with their gods must now be thoroughly modified. The investigation of extra-biblical covenants cannot with justification be restricted to the designation *bryt*, and even this term was apparently used already in Ugarit to designate a covenant relationship with a deity. The following discussion summarizes the evidence for the existence of covenant relationships between human parties and their deities in the ancient NE.

Since the Hittite texts have stood at the foreground of the treaty-covenant comparisons, it is significant that the ritual of Zarpiya, as attested in a text from Boğazköy, documents an oath ritual in the

[220] Cf. O.Kaiser, *Die mythische Bedeutung des Meeres in Ägypten, Ugarit und Israel* (Berlin, 1959); C.Kloos, *Yhwh's Combat with the Sea: A Canaanite Tradition in the Religion of Ancient Israel* (Amsterdam and Leiden, 1986).
[221] Weinfeld, "Divine Intervention," 135 n.66; 136f.
[222] Cf. Ex. 23:20-23.
[223] Cf. de Moor, *The Rise of Yahwism* (Leuven, 1990), 265.

capacity of a covenant ceremony. Gurney suggests, "In the ritual of Zarpiya blood functions as part of the symbolism of sharing a meal in order to establish a covenant relationship with a deity."[224] Here, as in many OT contexts, the implication of the oath, clothed in the sacrificial rite, bears the implication of covenant ratification.[225]

Nor does the evidence for divine-human covenant relationships in Anatolia end with this reference. In his *Apology*, Ḫattušiliš III, son of King Muršiliš, describes himself as having a covenant relationship with the goddess Ishtar as his protecting deity.[226]

The historical link between the Hittites and Israelites has been widely debated. It is not possible to delve into this matter other than to suggest that the relationships of the kingdom of Hatti with its various vassal states, e.g., the kingdom of Ugarit,[227] provides an entirely plausible avenue by which the influence could have traveled to Canaan. It is well established that the kingdom of Ugarit at various times was bound by treaty relationships with the Hittites.[228] And the significance of Ugaritic conceptions and terminology cannot be overlooked in an investigation of the origin of the OT covenant formulations,[229] especially since it now appears that in Ugarit a covenant god was worshipped as *'l brt*,[230] a designation which has quite naturally been compared to *'l bryt* and *b'l bryt* of Judg. 8:33;

[224]Gurney, *Hittite Religion*, 29. Gurney presents a translation of the relevant text and draws a comparison with Ex. 24:5-8.

[225]Gurney, *Hittite Religion*, 30.

[226]Gordon, *Before the Bible*, 95f.; A.Goetze, *Ḫattušiliš. Der Bericht über seine Thronbesteigung nebst den Paralleltexten* (MVAG 29/3; Leipzig, 1925), col. IV, 57-59.

[227]Gordon has demonstrated that certain peculiarities are shared in common by Hittite, Ugaritic and Hebrew. For example, the idiomatic use of "hand" (Hebrew *yd*) to designate a stele is paralleled in Ugaritic and Hittite but not in Sumerian and Akkadian, and its employment with this sense by Ḫattušiliš III suggests a possible direction of influence from Hittite to subsequent Ugaritic and Hebrew employment (*Before the Bible*, 93f.).

[228]Cf. Nougayrol, *Le palais royal, IV*, 29ff.; von Schuler, in *TUAT*, I/2:131-134; McCarthy, *Treaty and Covenant*, 97f., 130-132, 301f. One must also note the Bronze Age contacts between the Hittites and Egypt while Palestine was under Egyptian control. It is therefore by no means far-fetched to posit considerable influence from Anatolia upon Palestine.

[229]For a summary of the evidence from Ugarit see de Moor, *Rise of Yahwism*, 257-259.

[230]*Ugar. V*, 510 (RS 24.278 14-15). It may be significant that this Semitic designation is found in a Hurrian hymn. In Gen. 34:2 Hamor of Shechem is called a Hivite, which Speiser equates with Hurrian ("Hurrian," *IDB*, 2:665).

9:4,46.[231] In any event, it has been adequately demonstrated that Hebrew *bryt* is to be explained via West Semitic *brt* and not via recourse to Akkadian.[232] The significance of these comparisons is reinforced by a number of additional Ugaritic expressions which are related to OT terms used at times either as synonyms for covenant or treaty, or as part of the terminology employed in the establishment of such relationships.[233] In one of the closest parallels to the OT concept of covenant,[234] the alliance (*tappūtu*) with the deity is described as the alliance of the god who approaches the human party: "For (the god) Apšukka of (the city of) Irḫanta came up and demanded of me that (I enter) into his alliance."

In addition to these references to Hittite and Ugaritic material, it is noteworthy that although actual texts documenting covenant relationships between humans and their deities are relatively scarce, references widely scattered in time and geographical location can now be brought to bear upon discussions of the date at which Israel first began to speak in terms of an explicit covenant theology. A third millenium Sumerian document from Lagash describes a covenant between Urukagina and his god Ningirsu.[235] The Middle Assyrian Tukulti-Ninurta Epic has been interpreted as a prayer to the Sun-god based upon a covenant with the deity.[236] A Babylonian calendar text

[231]Cf. P.C.Craigie, "EL BRYT. EL DN (RS 24.278, 14-15)," *UF* 5 (1973) 278f.; Lipiński, "El-Berit," 50f.; Cross, *Canaanite Myth*, 39, 44; K.A.Kitchen, "Egypt, Ugarit, Qatna and Covenant," *UF* 11 (1979) 453-464; de Moor, *Uw God*, 50 n.170.

[232]Tadmor, "Treaty and Oath," 136-138.

[233]Cf. KTU 1.82:2, *'idy 'alt l 'aḥš / 'idy 'alt 'in ly*, translated by de Moor ("Contributions to the Ugaritic Lexicon," *UF* 11 [1979] 650) "Didn't I hasten to fulfill a sworn agreement? I have no sworn agreement to fulfill." Cf. J.C.de Moor–K.Spronk, "More on Demons in Ugarit (KTU 1.82)," *UF* 16 (1984) 237-250, esp. 239. Additional points of comparison between Ugaritic and OT terms and customs can be found in Kalluveettil, *Declaration and Covenant*, e.g., 34 (re *ṣmd* and *mṣmt*), 45, 123, 202 (re international treaty diplomacy), 97-106, 191 (re declaration formulae).

[234]RS 17.383:32-40, cf. Nougayrol, *PRU*, IV, 222. For a discussion of this passage see de Moor, *Rise of Yahwism*, 258f.

[235]Due to the rarity of this concept some scholars doubted the correctness of the translation, including McCarthy (*Treaty and Covenant*, 1963), but in his revised edition of 1978, McCarthy notes that "the phrase in question (INIM KA-KEŠDA) clearly refers to making an agreement between parties ..." (31 n.6), and he accepts the reading as evidence of a religious covenant. See also M.J.Buss, "The Covenant Theme in Historical Perspective," *VT* 16 (1966) 502-504; Kitchen, "Egypt, Ugarit, Qatna and Covenant," 462 plus n.77.

[236]P.C.Craigie, "The Song of Deborah and the Epic of Tukulti-Ninurta," *JBL* 88

published by R.Labat[237] includes the phrase DINGIR. MEŠ EN *sa-li-mi*[*-šu*],[238] which he translates, "les dieux seront ses amis," rendered elsewhere with the variant reading, "the gods will be his allies".[239] This reference provides a good example of how treaty and covenant terminology could overlap to describe a relationship with the deity.

A covenant with tribal deities, as recorded in a Minaean text, was discussed by Willesen.[240] And, considerable evidence has accrued regarding covenants with deities amongst southern Semitic tribes.[241] To this evidence may also be added the incantations from Phoenicia which attest to a divine-human covenant relationship.[242] The combined weight of these various texts argues against the postulation that the idea of a divine-human covenant was unique to Israel and that it developed for the first at a relatively late date in Israel's history, e.g., in a 7th cent. Dtistic movement.

### 5.9.3 The stone of witness

Josh. 24:26 places considerable emphasis upon the stone raised in the sanctuary of Yahweh. Upright stones were set for various purposes in the ancient NE,[243] and it is important to ascertain the closest parallels discernible in the extra-biblical texts. The assembly of Josh. 24:1-28 is clearly depicted as ending with a legal ceremony at the *mqdš yhwh* prior to the dispersal of the people. This location at a sanctuary intimates a cultic setting.[244] It is striking that in the Hittite rituals

(1969) 253-265, esp. 256f.

[237]R.Labat, *Un calendrier babylonien des travaux des signes et des mois (Series iqqur îpuš)* (Paris, 1965), 93-95, §32.

[238]Variant, EN. MEŠ SILIM-*mi-šú*.

[239]*Salīmu*, *CAD*, 15:103b.

[240]Willesen, "Eselsöhne," 216f.

[241]Cf. the references cited by Vriezen ("Exodus xxiv 9-11," 131 n.3) with respect to Arabian and Sabaean beliefs and customs.

[242]Cf. F.M.Cross–R.J.Saley, "Phoenician Incantations on a Plaque of the Seventh Century B.C. from Arslan Tash in Upper Syria," *BASOR* 197 (1970) 42-49; Z.Zevit, "A Phoenician Inscription and Biblical Covenant Theology," *IEJ* 27 (1977) 110-118. Gordon argues for the similarity between the OT idea of a covenant with the patriarchal deity and the early Greek attestations in Homeric traditions of covenants between people and the gods of the fathers (*Before the Bible*, 256f.). Cf. KTU 1.17 I 26f.

[243]C.F.Graesser, "Standing Stones in Ancient Palestine," *BA* 35 (1972) 34-63.

[244]The use of stelae and statues in cultic settings can be traced to great antiquity, cf. A.Spycket, *Les statues de culte dans les textes mesopotamiens des origines a la*

a festival assembly would often terminate at a *ḫuwaši*, which was either a large stone erected in a sacred place or a reference to the sacred area at the heart of which stood a stone monument ordinarily affiliated with a sacred tree.[245] The termination of Hittite festivals at an open-air shrine may itself be patterned upon ancient Babylonian festival procedures,[246] and it is in certain respects paralleled in other Canaanite traditions.[247] Furthermore, it is worth noting that such a *temenos* in the Hittite rituals was often located by a mountain,[248] which adds another point of comparison with Deut. 11:29ff.; 27; Josh. 8:30-35; 24:1-28.[249]

### 5.9.4 Covenant–treaty comparisons

The matter of comparing Josh. 24:1-28 form-critically with extra-biblical treaties has been dealt with in sections 1.5 and 2.4.2, where it was observed that vss.15-24 posed some difficulty in making a mechanical correlation with the treaty texts. On the basis of the present investigation of the structure and terminology employed in Josh. 24:1-28, it is perhaps possible to advance beyond the previous impasse.

*Ire dynastie de Babylone* (Gabalda, 1968).

[245]Singer, *The Hittite KI.LAM Festival*, 1:72, 99-101; Gurney, *Hittite Religion*, 36f., 40; H.Güterbock, "Religion und Kultus der Hethiter," *Historia* 7 (Neuere Hethiterforschung; Wiesbaden, 1964), 54-73, esp. 67, and the references to the "great assembly" (64, 66). The Hittite festival texts frequently mention the major assembly as part of the ritual. In addition to the previously listed texts, cf. H.G.Güterbock, "An Outline of the Hittite *AN.TAḪ.ŠUM* Festival," *JNES* 19 (1960) 80-89.

[246]Gurney, *Hittite Religion*, 40f (including other references), cf. especially the *akītu* festivities.

[247]Cf. KTU 1.17 I 26f., *nṣb skn 'ilibh / b qdš ztr 'mh*, translated by Loretz ("Kolometrie," 256) "der hinstellt eine Stele für seinen Vater-Gott im Heiligtum das ztr für Stamm(es-Ahnen)." For the translation of *ztr* as *marjoram* cf. de Moor, *Anthology*, 228. This text proves the customary practice of the ritual raising of a stele in a sanctuary in Ugarit. The stone and tree together in a sanctuary, as described in Josh. 24:26, has been compared previously to the Ugaritic practices, cf. de Moor, *'šrh*, 479.

[248]Cf. Gurney, *Hittite Religion*, 27; R.Lebrun, "Réflexions relatives à la complémentarité entre l'archéologie et la philogie Hittites," in R.Donceel–R.Lebrun, eds., *Archeologie et religions de l'Anatolie ancienne. Mélanges en l'honneur du proffeseur Paul Naster* (Louvain, 1983), 135-156, esp. 140.

[249]The significance of the mountain motif as cultic center is widespread in the ancient NE, cf. R.J.Clifford, *The Cosmic Mountain in Canaan and the Old Testament* (Cambridge, MA, 1972); Biran, ed., *Temples*, passim.

McCarthy placed considerable weight upon the alleged absence of an oath formula. However, in agreement with Kalluveettil's identification of acclamation formulae[250] and in comparison with 1 Sam. 10:17-25 and 12:5, it is justifiable to accept the response of the people in Josh. 24:22 as a legal oath. Moreover, we have noted the similarity of the confessional refrains (with *n'bd*) to loyalty oaths. Josh. 24:1-28 does not attempt, strictly speaking, to present a treaty document. Nevertheless, the comparisons with the extra-biblical treaties do not stop at vs.15 and suddenly reappear in vss.25-28. Much of the terminology used in vss.15-24 too finds a direct analogy in the ancient NE texts which describe or presuppose either treaty or vassal relationships. This has been documented in the literary analysis above, e.g., with respect to the verbs *'zb* and *'bd* as well as *hr' lkm* and *hyṭyb lkm.*[251] References showing the technical use of *pš'* and *ḥṭ'* in treaties have also been listed. This is true of *šm' bql* as well, and recent research has also demonstrated the employment of *šwb* as a technical term meaning to go back on a previous legal agreement in treaty context.[252]

Moreover, objections have been raised above with respect to the manner in which Weinfeld argued that the concept of witnessing in Josh. 24:1-28 is not analogous to the treaty texts.[253] In fact, the treaties between the Hittites and the Kashkeans also invoked human witnesses[254] in a manner comparable to Josh. 24:22.[255] Comparison with these treaties in which human witnesses are called upon in addition to the divine witnesses ordinarily listed towards the end of the treaty document exposes the futility of literary-critical dissections

[250]Cf. Kalluveettil, *Declaration and Covenant*, 61 n.188.

[251]In addition cf. W.L.Moran, "A Note on the Treaty Terminology of the Sefire Stelas," *JNES* 22 (1963) 173-176.

[252]Cf. M.Dijkstra, "Legal Irrevocability (*lō' yāšûb*) in Ezekiel 7.13," *JSOT* 43 (1989) 109-115.

[253]Cf. 2.4.1.

[254]E.von Schuler notes that, following the reference to human witnesses involved in the treaties with the Kashkeans, "Das vorkomen von Vereidigtenlisten ist nicht auf die Kaškäerverträge beschränkt, sondern findet sich auch anderwo, wo das Reigiment durch Edle und Älteste wahrgenommen wurde, wie in den Verträgen mis Išmerikka und den Länden Išuwa, Paḫḫuwa u.a. oder mit Ura" ("Staatsverträge und dokumente Hethitischen Rechts," *Historia* 7 [Neuere Hethiterforschung; Wiesbaden, 1964], 34-53, esp. 38). Note the role of the "Edle und Älteste" here in comparison to Josh. 24:1!

[255]P.A.Riemann, "Mosaic Covenant," *IDBSup*, 194.

of Josh. 24 on the basis of allegedly conflicting views of witnessing attested in vs.22 and vs.26.

The legal significance of *bywm hhw'* and *bškm* in vs.25 must not be overlooked with respect to the extra-biblical parallels. We have claimed that the emphasis in Josh. 24:1-28 upon sole allegiance to Yahweh implies recognition of divine kingship. It is therefore noteworthy that biblical as well as extra-biblical accounts of enthronement usually include a specific formula designating the place of enactment, such as *bškm*.[256]

These comments are not intended to wrest Josh. 24:1-28 back into a covenant-treaty format as previously conducted in form criticism. Quite the contrary. Josh. 24:1-28 has its own structural integrity, which should be recognized for what it is on its own grounds. But this does not invalidate comparison with the treaties. And, at the same time, it facilitates extension of the comparison to include the wider setting of festivals and the pledging of allegiance either at enthronement rituals or within the broader context of political correspondence in the ancient NE. Josh. 24:1-28 employs formulae and terminology from the widespread background of treaty and vassal relations to demonstrate that in the cultic pledging of loyalty at Shechem Israel accepted a position of vassalage under Yahweh. Many previous studies of Josh. 24 stress its parenetic character. For Schmitt, Perlitt and Van Seters, inter alia, its particular style is a major point of discussion regarding affinity to Dtistic parenesis and intention. What has not been previously considered is the fact that a similar "parenetic" tone is found in many of the treaty prologues. The suzerain's remonstrations to the vassal often appeal to previous beneficent acts towards the vassal and/or unfaithfulness of the vassal to the suzerain.[257]

These comparisons are strikingly reinforced by considerations of the macrostructure of Josh. 24:1-28 as poetic narrative. Josh. 24:1

[256]Buccellati, "Enthronement," 54-61; with respect to enthronement of Yahweh cf. 59. This is significant because of OT references in which *krt bryt* is an indigenous part of an enthronement ritual, cf. 2 Sam. 5:3 (cf. 1 Chron. 12:39-41); 2 Kgs 11:17 (Kalluveettil, *Declaration and Covenant*, 60-65).

[257]Note the impressive parallels to be found in the discussion by S.Morschauser, in Goedicke, ed., *Perspectives*, 123-206. For an interesting parallel from Ugarit see KTU 2.39, which is a letter from a Hittite king to Ammurapi of Ugarit (cf. de Moor, "Contributions," 650f.). As in the transition with *w'th* in Josh. 24:14; the recollections about the past are followed by *ht* "now then," followed by the demand for allegiance to the king.

(canticle I.i) establishes the setting. This is followed in canticles I.ii-I.v, beginning with the equivalent of the *umma* formula, with material paralleling the ancient NE historical prologue. Canto II begins with the transition *w'th*, which is equivalent to *anumma* or *inanna* ("now") introducing the stipulations. Canticles II.i-iv all end with the equivalent of a loyalty oath, and in canticle II.iv this is reinforced with an oath of witnessing (vs.22). In canticle II.v, the composition appropriately ends with a legal ceremony and the dispersal of the assembly. In short, the poetic form and structure supports the comparisons with the ancient NE treaty texts, especially when supplemented by texts describing loyalty oaths, land-grants, and the servitude of vassals to the king.

## 5.10 Date of composition

### 5.10.1 Introduction

We have traced and evaluated the history of interpretation of Josh. 24:1-28; we have pursued its literary structure, scrutinized its employment of phraseology from a literary-critical perspective, and endeavored to let emerge its predominant textual affiliations with other OT passages as well as its affinities to extra-biblical motifs. Yet we are left to treat what may be the most elusive rubric of analysis, namely, the matrix of questions focusing upon the passage's actual date of composition. The wide diversity of previous opinions and conclusions has been noted.[258] We have concurred with the majority of previous studies in rejecting as untenable the theory that Josh. 24:1-28 is purely a Dtic fiction. Is it now possible to draw more specific conclusions about the provenance of this passage and the date when it was given its final form? Is it warranted to suggest with Eissfeldt that it is the OT's oldest example of a political farewell speech?[259] Prior to an attempt to answer these questions, we do well to call attention to the limitations of the criteria by which one may seek to date such a passage as Josh. 24:1-28.

*a*) Since the present text is the product of a long history of transmission, arguments on the basis of philology, orthography and other linguistic criteria are of restricted value. In some passages of the

[258]See especially 2.3.

[259]Eissfeldt, *An Introduction*, 13.

OT, archaic words and forms provide valuable clues to a date *ante quem*. But an absence of such archaisms does not prove a late date for the original composition.[260] It could simply mean that later editors or transmitters were more thorough and accurate in updating[261] the language and spelling in a given text than in some other passages.[262]
*b*) Attempts to date this passage can only be relative, i.e., relative to the dates to be assigned to those parts of the Tetrateuch, Deuteronomy, and the Dtistic history which can be demonstrated to be either older or younger than our passage.
*c*) Previously suggested dates relied in part upon a discernment of the most probable situation within which to explain the particular theological intention of the passage. This emphasis is consistent with an increasing trend in OT studies to appeal to sociological contexts in evaluating the origin of Israel's traditions.[263] However, too little cognizance has been taken of the fact that the particular themes in Josh. 24:1-28 may have been equally appropriate at various times in Israel's history. Furthermore, in the search for a sociologically and theologically acceptable time period, too little attention has been given to the formative and transitionary character of Israel's social conditions in the time of the settlement and the judges, the time presented by the biblical context as the setting for these events.[264] Finally, such studies must carefully distinguish between the date of a tradition's origin and the date of its final canonical formation. The latter may at times post-date the former by centuries. Against this background, it is our intention to refocus the question of dating.

[260]Cf. the limitations in dating OT poetry listed by P.C.Craigie ("The Conquest and Early Hebrew Poetry," *TB* 20 [1969] 78-80).

[261]The opposite suggestion by G.Gerleman that the Pentateuch and Prophets were redacted by the Masoretes in order to make the language more archaic than the vulgar language of Chronicles (*Synoptic Studies in the Old Testament* [Lund, 1948]) is disproven by material from Qumran and by recent comparisons of ancient Semitic languages revealing archaic elements in the OT which were no longer comprehensible to the Masoretes.

[262]Cf. Freedman, "Archaic Forms," 7f.; Cross, "Biblical Archaeology," 10.

[263]E.g., K.W.Whitelam, "Israel's Traditions of Origin: Reclaiming the Land," *JSOT* 44 (1989) 22: "It is important to ask how far the Israelite traditions of origin in Exodus, Joshua and Judges represent the self-perceptions of later communities and have been retrojected back onto earlier history."

[264]This point is elaborated in the following chapter.

### 5.10.2 The relative date of Josh. 24:1-28

We have seen the degree to which this passage is dependent upon material now incorporated in the Pentateuch. This can be employed to suggests a relative date *post quem*. The literary inter-connections are of utmost significance for our understanding of the manner in which Josh. 24 was composed. In Josh. 24:3, God's selection (*lqḥ*) of Abraham is reminiscent of Gen. 24:7, and Josh. 24:3a must be compared with Gen. 11:31-12:9; 13:14-17. Multiplication of progeny is described with formulae found in the patriarchal blessings. Jacob's descent to Egypt in Josh. 24:4 may be dependent upon Gen. 46:3-7, though the exact formulation in Josh. 24:4 is unique. Josh. 24:5-7 apparently borrows heavily from Ex. 14-15, but here too there are sufficient differences in formulation to suggest that the composition of Josh. 24:5-7 does not simply copy from Exodus. That it either paraphrases or is dependent upon an earlier form of the exodus account is evident, for example, in the parallelism of the cola *wyb' byn mḥnh mṣrym / wbyn mḥnh yśr'l* (Ex. 14:20),[265] which must be both compared and contrasted with *wyśm m'pl bynykm / wbyn hmṣrym* (Josh. 24:7aB-C). The parallelism of *byn* || *wbyn* is retained, but the account in Josh. 24:7 compresses the more elaborate account of Exodus. Josh. 24:8 summarizes Num. 21:21-35, and Josh. 24:9f. is dependent upon Num. 22-24.

In the light of this consistent manner of compressing narratives now found in Genesis, Exodus and Numbers, it is striking that Josh. 24:11 is not dependent upon Josh. 6. Moreover, while Josh. 2:2f. relates the activity of the king (*mlk*) of Jericho, Josh. 24:11 employs the rare designation *b'ly-yryḥw*. This may indicate that Josh. 24 was composed prior to the account now found in Josh. 6. The list of nations now found in Josh. 24:11b and the reference to *hṣr'h*, as well as the verbs *šlḥ* and *grš* in this connection, all show dependence upon Ex. 23, esp. vss. 23,28. Josh. 24:12b must be compared to Gen. 48:22, but since the latter text is often thought to be secondary to its context one must not press this connection with regard to relative dating. Josh. 24:14f.,23 has been compared with Gen. 35:2-4, and Josh. 24:17c has been shown to correlate with Gen. 35:3b. Thus Josh. 24 is in all likelihood dependent upon Gen. 35, though the possibility of reciprocal influence cannot be ruled out. The combination *btmym*

[265]Identified as poetry by Althann ("Unrecognized Poetic Fragments," 14f.).

*wb'mt* is to be compared with the archaic account of Judg. 9:16,19, also located at Shechem, but there are insufficient details to prove which text is literarily prior.

From the cumulative evidence of all these connections, it is possible to conclude that where Josh. 24:1-28 appeals to historical memory it does so primarily on the basis of narratives now found elsewhere in Genesis, Exodus and Numbers. This would seem to provide a relative date *post quem*. Yet it is difficult to speak confidently with more precision. In addition to the degree of dependence noted above, there are enough minor variations from the Pentateuchal accounts to suggest that Josh. 24:2-13 either tends to paraphrase or it could have been dependent upon older traditions slightly different from the present form of the Pentateuchal accounts. Theoretically, one might even have to allow the possibility of dependence upon oral traditions antecedent to the present written form of the Pentateuchal narratives.

Not only must the date *post quem* be stated in relative terms, but the same is true regarding the date *ante quem*. We have discovered that despite some similarities in both vocabulary and content, Josh. 24:1-28 was originally composed basically independent from Dtic or Dtistic influences. In most theories of the history of compositon of the OT, this would entail that it was written *prior* to the present shaping of Deuteronomy and the final compilation of the Dtistic history. Important confirmation of the priority of Josh. 24:1-28 to the Dtistic history can be adduced from the influence of Josh. 24:28-31 upon Judg. 2:6-10, and of Josh. 24:2-24 upon Judg. 6:7-10. Both these passages from Judges demonstrate a direct, *colometric* dependence upon Josh. 24. Via Judg. 6:8f., Josh. 24 also shaped the wording of 1 Sam. 10:17f. And it also appears to have influenced the formulation of 1 Sam. 7:3; 12:5-8. Secondarily, 1 Sam. 12:8 in turn may have influenced the poetic expansion in Josh. 24:5aA of the MT. There are, therefore, indications that Josh. 24 was written prior to the final composition of Judges and 1 Samuel. These observations reinforce Brekelman's conclusion that Josh. 24:1-28 may have originally functioned in a historical corpus extending to 1 Sam. 12.[266]

The historical summary in Josh. 24:2-13 does not follow the outline of the conquest recorded in Joshua, and the covenant ceremony makes no recognition of the events listed in Deut. 11:29ff.; 27; Josh.

[266]Brekelmans, "Joshua XXIV" (forthcoming).

8:30-35. Josh. 24:13 influenced the formulation of Deut. 6:10f., not vice versa. Moreover, if Josh. 24:1-28 was composed after the Dtistic account in Josh. 23, it would have been most natural to allow it to stand as a continuation of that gathering. Our comparison of Josh. 23 and 24 revealed that ch.24 is not dependent upon ch.23, but in all likelihood antedates it. These observations are reinforced by the conclusion that on the basis of literary criticism and content Josh. 24:25-27 cannot be dated late. A national assembly of such momentous occasion, with its location at Shechem, does not fit what is known of circumstances in the time of Josiah. His expansionist policy promoted Jerusalem as the center for his national cultic gatherings, and this geographical location was of considerable political importance.[267] Josiah's intolerant attitude towards the customs of the North is evident from his imposition of the festal calendar of the South.[268]

The complexity of Josh. 24's relationship to the Pentateuch on the one hand, its influence upon the so-called Dtistic history on the other, as well as its similarity with various ancient NE texts, all coalesce to form an insurmountable obstacle for narrower attempts to explain this passage in terms of parenesis in either a 7th cent. Assyrian political context[269] or within an exilic or post-exilic setting.[270] The latter views are unable to do justice to the intricate connections with Shechem in the patriarchal period and during the time of the judges and early monarchy—emphases which tend to be highlighted by precisely those aspects which are most unique to Josh. 24:1-28.

Any attempt to posit a more specific date will only be as convincing as the relative dates proposed for the comparable portions now found in the Tetrateuch, Deuteronomy, and Dtistic history, all of which continue to be vigorously debated in OT studies.[271] Sum-

[267]Note by contrast the significance of Shechem in 1 Kgs 12. Note too that in Hezekiah's attempt at consolidation with the North, the central gathering at Jerusalem is already of strategic political importance (2 Chron. 30).

[268]S.Talmon, "Divergences in Calendar-Reckoning in Ephraim and Judah," *VT* 8 (1958) 48-74.

[269]Contrary to Kreuzer's contention on the basis of the Amorites (cf. 6.3).

[270]Contrary to Van Seters and Nicholson, who appeal to the warning against the gods of Egypt as evidence for this date (6.4).

[271]The origin of Deuteronomy continues to be called the "Archimedean point" of the documentary hypothesis and therefore also of any systematic time scheme for ordering the composition of the Dtistic history, cf. A.S.van der Woude, "De wordingsgeschiedenis van het Oude Testament," in van der Woude, ed., *Inleiding*,

marizing the present state of OT studies, Lohfink[272] notes the uncertainty in dating Dtic material and concludes that "The Deuteronomic phenomenon has a diachronic dimension, beginning probably in the premonarchic period and extending into the postexilic period." Our comparison of the MT and a postulated *Vorlage* of the LXX has demonstrated that various editions of a Hebrew text of Josh. 24:1-28 existed—perhaps one should say co-existed—until a very late date. All these considerations demonstrate that the basic form and structure of Josh. 24:1-28 must be dated later than what is now usually considered the J/E corpus of the Pentateuch and prior to the passages from Judges and 1 Samuel listed above, but minor variations and actualizations of the text were possible until a stronger emphasis upon the immutability of the canonical text precluded such modifications or actualizations. Since the evidence at present cannot be extended beyond a relative dating, it is counterproductive to speculate about a specific date of composition. Still, the considerations raised here and the parameters they indicate constitute a significant advance over the manner in which the passage has previously been dated either via alleged correlations with hypothetical documentary sources or by way of certain details extracted from the passage as a whole.

These observations naturally confront one with the question of the historical value of this passage, a topic which constitutes the focus of the ensuing chapter of our study.

17f.; M.J.Paul, *Het archimedisch punt van de pentateuchkritiek* ('s-Gravenhage, 1988).

[272]N.Lohfink, "The Cult Reform of Josiah of Judah: 2 Kings 22-23 as a Source for the History of Israelite Religion," in Miller, et al., eds., *Ancient Israelite Religion*, 459.

# 6 The Historical Value of Josh. 24:1-28

Wellhausen thought that the epic narratives about Joshua contain elements which must be based on historical facts.[1] Most subsequent scholars evaluating the historical value of Josh. 24:1-28 have echoed his basic conclusion.[2] Nevertheless, on finer details, recent scholarship has attained widely disparate conclusions regarding the historical significance of Josh. 24:1-28. This passage's role in the historical reconstructions by Sellin, Alt, Noth and von Rad—to list but a few of the most conspicuous figures—has been summarized above. In the light of the historical weight which has typically been placed upon Josh. 24:1-28, it is worthwhile to reconsider the question of its historical value.

In particular it is necessary to investigate whether the picture presented in Josh. 24:1-28 is consistent with what are now thought to have been the prevailing conditions in Palestine at the time these events are alleged to have taken place. The discussion which follows is structured according to two related but distinguishable issues. The first issue pertains to the gathering at Shechem. Particular attention is given in this regard to the historical and political significance of Shechem from the LBA to the early Iron Age, the concept of Israel as a political entity at the time of Joshua, and the role Joshua can be presumed to have played in such a gathering. The second issue relates to historical implications and details of the dialogue narrated in Josh. 24:2-24. However, it is necessary to preface our analysis of these two general concerns with a brief discussion of whether this passage's identification as poetry has major ramifications for an evaluation of its historical value.

## 6.1 Poetry and history writing

A contemporary OT scholar has claimed, "Although poetry is an end in itself, prose is significative. So we must analyse the poems but interpret the prose."[3] This citation is indicative of the widespread and enduring presupposition that OT poetry, in distinction from prose,

[1]Wellhausen, *Prolegomena zur Geschichte*, 366.

[2]Auerbach, Perlitt and Nicholson, who consider the entire passage to be a later fiction, are exceptions (see 1.6.5, 1.6.9, and 2.3.4).

[3]R.P.Caroll, *From Chaos to Covenant: Uses of Prophecy in the Book of Jeremiah* (London, 1981), 2.

should be analyzed for its aesthetic qualities rather than its historical value. The unambiguous reluctance of medieval Jewish scholars to recognize poetry in the OT was in part motivated by a gnawing fear that it would reduce historical credibility[4] and thereby mitigate the truth value of the sacred text.[5] And it is virtually a truism that contemporary OT scholars continue to emphasize that the historical value of poetry is to be judged according to different criteria than that of prose.[6] Yet it is precisely in the archaic poetry of the OT that other scholars believe to attain glimpses into Israel's most remote past, from which point they attempt a reconstruction of Israel's earliest history in its various dimensions—social and religious.[7]

While it would be tempting to delve into a study of the relative historical value of OT poetry and prose, some modest observations germane to an analysis of the historical value of Josh. 24 must suffice. Various considerations argue against a sharp dichotomy between poetry and prose as representative of aesthetic and significative categories respectively. In the first place, OT prose is no less religiously or theologically coloured than is OT poetry. OT prose, like the history writing encountered in other ancient NE documents,[8] is not an exercise in purely objective history writing. Its prose is as programmatic as its poetry. Secondly, OT poetry is not purely aesthetic without regard for historical consequences. Ancient NE writers were not constrained to be either purely aesthetic or purely historical, keeping the two apart via employment of different genres. For a recently treated extra-biblical example which clearly illustrates the present point, one could mention the late 8th cent. Aramaic memorial inscriptions of

[4]R.Brann, "The 'Dissembling Poet' in Medieval Hebrew Literature: The Dimensions of a Literary Topos," *JAOS* 107 (1987) 39-54.

[5]This is by no means the only reason that the essential characteristics of OT poetry faded from view. Comparison with Greek, Latin, and Arabic poetry also played a major role (Kugel, *Idea*, 96-134).

[6]E.g., Craigie, "Conquest," 76: "Normally, poetry would be less valuable as historical source material than prose. Whilst both are the work of writers who interpret events and necessarily express value judgments, prose is usually informative and evaluative whereas poetry is primarily emotive and aesthetic."

[7]E.g., the repeated emphasis in the Albright school upon the historical value of archaic poetry in the OT.

[8]Cf. Güterbock's discussion of "The Proclamation of Telipinu", which "is not 'pure' historiography for history's sake, but rather an account that serves the purpose of showing reason for political action" ("Hittite Historiography," 28).

Panammuwa II.[9] The fact that the deeds of Panammuwa II are memorialized in poetic compositions which are carefully structured and aesthetically pleasing does not entail that because the inscriptions are emotive they are devoid of historical signification. Clearly, they can be aesthetic, emotive, and based on historical fact.[10] The presence of impressive stylistic devices in a pleasingly arranged composition cannot legitimately be claimed to per se diminish the historical reliability of the text.[11]

The fact that the Mesha inscription is written as poetic narrative and that it contains a recurring theological perception that Moab's history is determined by the beneficence or animosity of Chemosh entails that its historical details must be weighed in light of its authorial point of view. But this does not automatically mitigate the historical reliability of the composition as such. By the same standard, that the Merenptah stele is inscribed with poetic narrative does not mean that the composition is governed strictly by aesthetic and emotive concerns and is therefore historically non-significative.[12] And recognition that the deeds of Yahweh are memorialized in Josh. 24:1-28 in an aesthetically pleasing poetic composition, as well as from a given theological perspective, does not reduce the present text to lower historical credibility than would have been the case if the text in question were to have proven to be prosaic. The historical value of OT narrative must be judged upon criteria other than whether or

[9]Cf. K.L.Younger, "Panammuwa and Bar-Rakib: Two Structural Analyses," *JANES* 18 (1986) 91-103.

[10]Younger's comparative conclusion that "the aesthetic structuring of accounts in ancient Near Eastern and biblical history writing has not been fully explored or appreciated" ("Panammuwa," 103 n.44) deserves to be taken to heart.

[11]Cf. Güterbock, "Hittite Historiography," 29. Note too W.W.Hallo's suggestion relative to the Royal Correspondence of Isin by that the literary letter developed simultaneously in prosaic and poetic formats in neo-Sumerian (Ur III-Isin) times ("Sumerian Historiography," in Tadmor–Weinfeld, eds., *History, Historiography*, 9-20).

[12]Additional examples can easily be found. In addition to the Mesha, Zakkur and Kilamuwa inscriptions, de Moor also called attention to the historical poetry of the Statue of Idrimi and the historical tablet of Shalmaneser as Akkadian examples ("Book of Ruth, I," 269, 271). Consider too the legendary poems concerned with historical heroes, e.g., the Sargon Legend (cf. B.Lewis, *The Sargon Legend* [Cambridge, Mass., 1980]) and the Babylonian Historical Epics (cf. A.K.Grayson, *Babylonian Historical-Literary Texts* [Toronto, 1975], 41ff.). See also A.Livingstone, *Court Poetry and Literary Miscellanea* (State Archives of Assyria III; Helsinki, 1989), 43ff.

not it is poetry or prose.

Nor is it methodologically acceptable to maintain that the question of historical value is irrelevant to dialogue.[13] Here a comparison with the treaty form is relevant. The historical accounts in the Hittite texts are generally introduced with the *umma* formula, which is followed by the direct discourse of the Great King.[14] The exploits of Anittas son of Pitkhana, king of Kussar in early second millenium Anatolia, are known primarily from the sometimes bombastic first-person narration. One may also compare the first-person accounts of Babylonian dedicatory inscriptions, in which history is recounted in the dialogue of the king.[15] In fact, if one were to dismiss from consideration all historical references in Mesopotamian, Anatolian and Egyptian texts couched in first-person dialogue, the historical study of the ancient NE would suddenly be drastically impoverished. In all these cases, the reliability of the historical descriptions must be evaluated with caution, but it would be unwarranted to dismiss such historical references from consideration simply because they are couched in dialogue. For this reason, it is necessary in Josh. 24:1-28 to consider details of possible historical relevance in both the setting (vss.1,25-28) and the dialogue (vss.2-24).

## 6.2 Joshua's gathering at Shechem

Josh. 24:1,25 asserts that at Shechem Joshua conducted a gathering of national importance. Prior to our discussion of the historical value of this assertion, a few introductory observations are warranted. In contemporary OT scholarship, the period of the settlement is probably the most divergently treated era of Israel's history.[16] Various

[13]It was for this reason that Schmitt and Jaroš restricted their analyses of historical value to vss.1,25-28 (see 1.6.3 and 1.7.3). Similarly, Perlitt stressed the high percentage of dialogue in contrast to narrated action, suggesting thereby that this phenomenon supports his claim that the passage was Dtic fiction (cf. 1.6.5).

[14]Güterbock, "Hittite Historiography," 22.

[15]S.Mowinckel, "Die vorderasiatischen Königs-und Fürsteninschriften," in *Eucharisterion, I. Fs H.Gunkel* (*FRLANT* 19; Göttingen, 1923), 278-322.

[16]Cf. Noth, *History*, 53-163; de Vaux, *Early History*, 393-824; J.Bright, *A History of Israel*, 3rd ed. (Philadelphia, 1981), 107-182. The historical complexity of these issues is clearly evident in a comparison of the approach advocated by Eissfeldt ("The Exodus and Wanderings," *CAH*$^3$, II/2, 307-330), and the response to his methodology by Kitchen ("Historical Method," 63-97).

models for Israelite settlement in Palestine have been proposed.[17] It is beyond the scope of our study of Josh. 24:1-28 as narrative poetry to discuss these various models, and such a discussion is in fact not essential here because the conclusion is highly probable that Shechem and its surroundings must have played a conspicuous role in the early stages of the establishment of Israel as a nation in Palestine regardless of which model one accepts.[18] It is our intention in the following section to summarize the evidence which supports this conclusion. Subsequently, a number of considerations will be discussed regarding the alleged goal of Joshua's gathering. In our opinion, the combined evidence from these areas of research supports rather than counters the historical likelihood of the contention that Joshua held an assembly at Shechem to impress upon the Israelites the need to affirm exclusive allegiance to Yahweh.

### 6.2.1 Shechem as setting for the gathering

Shechem is conspicuously present in the patriarchal narratives in conjunction with the promise of the land. It is significantly absent in the conquest narratives of Joshua. And it makes a dramatic reappearance in Judg. 9 and 1 Kgs 12 with respect to kingship in Israel. We have noted that the manner in which Josh. 24:1-28 narrates a covenant gathering at Shechem makes a link between the possession of the land motif on the one hand and the divine kingship motif on the other. For this reason, it seems safe to conclude that the present narrative was written with this purpose in mind; it was not primarily intended as a historical documentation of the events of the gathering

[17]For examples, commentary, and bibliography see C.F.Burney, *Israel's Settlement in Canaan* (London, 1918); Alt, *Kleine Schriften*, 1:89-175; M.Weippert, *Die Landnahme der israelitischen Stämme* (Göttingen, 1967); "Canaan, Conquest and Settlement of," *IDBSup*, 125-130; N.K.Gottwald, "Domain Assumptions and Societal Models in the Study of Pre-Monarchic Israel," *Congress Volume Edinburgh 1974*, *SVT* 28 (Leiden, 1975), 89-100; "Two Models for the Origins of Ancient Israel: Social Revolution or Frontier Development," in H.B.Huffmon et al., eds., *The Quest for the Kingdom of God* (Fs G.E.Mendenhall; Winona Lake, 1983), 5-24; Halpern, *The Emergence of Israel*; Yadin, "The Transition," 57-68; Freedman–Graf, eds., *Palestine in Transition*; Amitai, ed., *Biblical Archaeology Today*; Lemche, *Early Israel*; de Moor, *Rise of Yahwism*, 216-221.

[18]This is true whether one's methodology places primary emphasis upon the archaeological data, upon the biblical accounts, or upon an effort to correlate the two.

itself. This obviously complicates the question of how the narrative is to be employed in a reconstruction of the historical circumstances at Shechem in the days of Joshua. Is the narrated gathering at Shechem only a literary creation to connect the patriarchal narratives to the kingship motif, or are the details narrated in Josh. 24:1,25-28 based upon an actual historical event? In our opinion the latter conclusion is warranted.

A survey of the history of Shechem from the MBA to the early IA supports the theory that this area was of major importance in Israel's earliest sedentarization. After a period of what appears to have been flourishing independence, Shechem was captured and destroyed, likely by the Egyptian Eighteenth Dynasty.[19] The subsequent infamous insurrections of Lab'ayu and his questionable relationship to Egypt during the Amarna period have often been discussed with regard to the history of Shechem.[20] Finally, there is no evidence of destruction in the period of transition from the LBA to the IA,[21] which entails that the Israelite settlement in this area at the time of Joshua appears to have been without destructive conquest. Significantly, the absence of evidence for violent destruction in the transition from the LBA to the IA also suggests that Shechem was not captured by the invading Sea Peoples.

The significance of Shechem in the period of Israel's settlement is confirmed by archaeological data and by demographic-historical surveys in the central hill country.[22] These studies show a popu-

[19]Campbell–Ross, "Excavation of Shechem," 9; L.E.Toombs, "The Stratification of Tell Balâṭah (Shechem)," *BASOR* 223 (1976) 57-59, esp. 59; J.M.Weinstein, "The Egyptian Empire in Palestine: A Reassessment," *BASOR* 241 (1981) 10.

[20]J.A.Knudtzon, *Die El Amarna Tafeln*, vol. 1 (Leipzig, 1915), nos. 252-254; E.F.Campbell, "The Amarna Letters and the Amarna Period," *BA* 23 (1960) 2-22; "Shechem in the Amarna Archive," 191-207; "Two Amarna Notes," 39-54; H.Reviv, "The Government of Shechem in the el-Amarna Period and in the Days of Abimelech," *IEJ* 16 (1966) 252-257; Toombs, "Shechem," 74f.; de Vaux, *Early History*, 103-105.

[21]Wright, "Shechem," 362; Toombs, "Stratification," 59. On the ceramic evidence see R.S.Boraas, "Iron IA Ceramic at Tell Balatah: A Preliminary Examination," in L.T.Geraty–L.G.Herr, eds., *The Archaeology of Jordan and Other Studies Presented to Siegfried H. Horn* (Berrien Springs, MI, 1986), 249-263.

[22]I.Finkelstein, in Amitai, ed., *Biblical Archaeology Today*, 80-83; *Archaeology of the Israelite Settlement*, 336-348; "The Emergence of the Monarchy in Israel: The Environmental and Socio-Economic Aspects," *JSOT* 44 (1989), 43-74. Cf. previously E.F.Campbell, "The Shechem Area Survey," *BASOR* 190 (1968) 19-41; B.Mazar, *The Early Biblical Period: Historical Essays*, edit. S.Aḥituv and

lation influx from east to west. This picture agrees with what is known of the early settlement of the Israelites in the neighborhood of Shechem.[23] Since Israelite sedentarization of this area apparently took place without major destruction,[24] this accords well with the claim made in Josh. 24:13 that the Israelites possessed a land which they did not work, cities which they did not build, and vineyards and olive groves they did not plant.[25] The demographic statistics and archaeological data from the vicinity of Shechem and Shiloh support the conclusion that the central hill country was of utmost historical significance for the earliest stages of Israelite settlement.

Possible additional evidence for this conclusion comes from the Merenptah stele, which reveals that in 1207 B.C.[26] it was internationally known that a restricted group living in Canaan at that time bore the name "Israel". Various scholars have indicated that the other geographical names included on the stele suggest that this "Israel" may have been located in the area of Shechem.[27] The determinative shows

B.A.Levine (Jerusalem, 1986), 35-48 (revised from *BASOR* 241 [1981] 75-85).

[23]J.A.Callaway, "A New Perspective on the Hill Country Settlement of Canaan in Iron Age I," in J.N.Tubb, ed., *Palestine in the Bronze and Iron Ages: Papers in Honour of Olga Tufnell* (London, 1985), 31-49, esp. 36; W.G.Dever, "The Contribution of Archaeology to the Study of Canaanite and Early Israelite Religion," in Miller et al., eds., *Ancient Israelite Religion*, 234f. Cf. the summary by Ahlström, *Who Were the Israelites?* 25-28, 65-83.

[24]In Josh. 8:30-35 the Israelites are suddenly present at Shechem. Some have concluded from this that there were Israelite tribes already living in the area (cf. H.Schmid, "Erwägungen zur Gestalt Josuas in Überlieferung und Geschichte," *Judaica* 24 [1968] 47, 52f.). However, one must be cautious about drawing such historical conclusions from the chronological ordering—which often appears to be programmatic—of the MT. Regarding the different placement of Josh. 8:30-35 in the LXX, see E.Tov, "Some Sequence Differences between the MT and LXX and their Ramifications for the Literary Criticism of the Bible," *JNSL* 13 (1987) 152-154.

[25]For an agricultural study see D.G.Hopkins, *The Highlands of Canaan: Agricultural Life in the Early Iron Age* (Sheffield, 1985). In addition to the cautious appraisal by Hopkins (228-232), there is evidence for the domesticated use of grapes and olives in Bronze Age Palestine, cf. L.E.Stager, "The Firstfruits of Civilization," in Tubb, ed., *Palestine*, 176f.

[26]Earlier treatments of the Merenptah stele often dated it to c. 1220 B.C., but current theories of the New Kingdom chronology suggest that Merenptah reigned from 1212-1202 B.C. (L.E.Stager, "Merenptah, Israel and Sea Peoples: New Light on an Old Relief," in B.Mazar–Y.Yadin, eds., *ErIs* 18 [Fs N.Avigad; Jerusalem, 1985], 56).

[27]E.g., de Vaux, *Early Israel*, 389f.

that a people, not a country, is intended.[28] Unfortunately, the exac location and political extent of this group cannot be determined.[29]

Various references in the OT also support the conclusion tha the hill country of Ephraim and Manasseh was crucial for Israelit settlement in Palestine. For example, Shiloh is referred to repeatedl as the central location of the tent of meeting in the time of Joshua,[30] and there is no reason to doubt the claim that it served as a sacra center in Ephraim at that time.[31]

In Judges the question of kingship in Israel is first raised in regar to territory belonging to Manasseh and Ephraim, for this is the setting of the narratives involving Gideon[32] and Abimelech.[33] The loca rule of the latter in Shechem is said *pars pro toto*—in the manne of Judges—to be a rule over Israel (*wyśr ’bymlk ‘l-yśr’l*). The loca extent of his rule is already proven by the detail that it was negotiated with leaders of the city (Judg. 9:1-6) and not with the head of Israel.[34] For this reason, the use of "Israel" in Judg. 9:22 cannot be equated with the political extent of Israel in the time of th true monarchy. However, the fact that the author of Judg. 9 considered Shechem to be a center of political activity crucial for the earl stages of Israelite settlement is significant in comparison with the importance attributed to this same geographical area in the narrativ of Josh. 24.

Although the foregoing considerations support the historical credibility of an Israelite assembly at Shechem in Joshua's time, a mor precise identification of its intended location may not be possible Previous attempts to locate the assembly of Josh. 24:1-28 at a sacrec precinct inside the city proper are inconclusive,[35] and the mass gath-

[28]Cf., e.g., Stager, "Merenptah," 61.

[29]Noth, *History*, 3.

[30]Josh. 18:1,8-10; 19:51; 21:2; 22:9,12. For a recent discussion of these references cf. Schley, *Shiloh*, 101-126, 191f., 201.

[31]Cf. M.Weinfeld, "The Pattern of the Israelite Settlement in Canaan," in Emerton, ed., *Congress Volume Jerusalem 1986*, 273f.; Finkelstein, "Emergence," 61. The significance of Shiloh as the location of an Israelite sanctuary prior to Jerusalem is visible in various references in Judges and 1 Samuel as well as Ps. 78:60.

[32]Cf. Z.Kallai, *Historical Geography of the Bible: The Tribal Territories of Israe* (Jerusalem and Leiden, 1986), 422ff.

[33]Note too that Deborah is said to have judged Israel between Ramah and Bethel in the hill country of Ephraim (Judg. 4:5).

[34]Bettenzoli, "Gli 'Anziani di Israele'," 47-73; "Gli 'Anziani' in Giuda," 211-224.

[35]See 1.7.5.

ring of representatives of the people likely took place in open air.[36] Crisler has demonstrated that the acoustic qualities of the valley between Mt. Ebal and Mt. Gerizim make it a natural choice for an open air theater.[37] However, Josh. 24:1-28 does not provide sufficient details to determine the exact setting intended.

### 6.2.2 The goal of the Shechem gathering

Josh. 24:1-28 implies that the main goal of the gathering was to impress upon the people the need to express their collective and sole allegiance to Yahweh. In many theories of the development of Israelite monotheism such an emphasis in Joshua's time stands as a stark anachronism.[38] It is therefore imperative to reconsider the appropriateness of such an emphasis in Joshua's day. In the present section an attempt will be made to demonstrate that the biblical role attributed to Joshua as successor of Moses in the promulgation of exlusive Yahwism is entirely plausible. Our discussion is focused upon the following three areas: (a) The OT depicts Joshua as the successor of Moses with respect to the emphasis upon worshipping Yahweh alone. (b) Joshua's time period provides a plausible setting for such an emphasis upon exclusive Yahwism. (c) The assertion that Joshua played an important role in the promotion of exclusive Yahwism receives support from a consideration of theophoric names in the OT.

#### Joshua as successor of Moses

The Israelite reception of exclusive worship of Yahweh has been the subject of considerable study in recent years.[39] One of the issues re-

[36]See 2.5.

[37]Crisler, "Acoustics and Crowd Capacity," 128-141.

[38]Cf. Ahlström's insistence that normative Yahwism is a late monarchic phenomenon (*Who Were the Israelites?*, 83 n.89).

[39]E.g., Brekelmans, "Exodus xviii," 215-224; G.W.Anderson, "Hebrew Religion," in H.H.Rowley, ed., *The Old Testament and Modern Study*, reprint ed. (Oxford, 1961), 283-310; R.Knierim, "Das erste Gebot," *ZAW* 77 (1965) 20-39; R.Rendtorff, "El, Ba'al und Jahwe: Erwagungen zum Verhaltnis von kanaanaischer und israelitischer Religion," *ZAW* 78 (1966) 272-292; Albright, *Yahweh and the Gods*, esp. 133-180; "From the Patriarchs to Moses II. Moses out of Egypt," *BA* 36 (1973) 48-76; F.Stolz, "Monotheismus in Israel," in O.Keel, ed., *Monotheismus im Alten Israel und seiner Umwelt* (Freiburg and Göttingen, 1980), 143-184; de Moor, *Uw God*; *Rise of Yahwism*; P.D.Miller, "Israelite Religion," in Knight–Tucker, eds., *The*

peatedly raised is whether Yahwism predates Moses.[40] Most recently this question has been answered affirmatively by de Moor.[41] However, for the present discussion it is not necessary to discuss the role of Moses beyond his connection with Joshua and the emphasis upon knowledge of Yahweh as the one true God of Israel.[42]

Particularly important in this respect is Ex. 17:14-16, where Moses is commanded to write a memorial of Yahweh's actions against the Amalekites. This memorial is to be recited in the hearing of Joshua. Ex. 17:16 has been defended as poetry by Althann,[43] and upon the basis of a more detailed investigation there is adequate reason to include 17:14f. as part of the poetic unit. The designation *yh* in reference to Yahweh occurs elsewhere exclusively in poetry.[44] The phrase *mdr dr* is a stock poetic expression (see below). Ex. 17:14-16 is both preceded and followed by a *petuchah*, which shows that in the Masoretic tradition these three verses were treated as a literary unit. It can profitably be scanned as two strophes of 3+2 || 2+3 colometry.

*Hebrew Bible*, 201-237; Miller et al., eds., *Ancient Israelite Religion*, passim.

[40]Cf. Eissfeldt, "Jakobs Begegnung," 325-331; H.H.Rowley, *Worship in Ancient Israel: Its Form and Meaning* (London, 1967), 41, 45, 61; Freedman, "The Name," 155; Campbell, "Moses and the Foundations," 145. Moses's role in Israel's history has been assessed with radically diverse conclusions, cf., e.g., C.A.Keller, "Vom Stand und Aufgabe der Moseforschung," *ThZ* 13 (1957); R.Smend, *Das Mosebild von Heinrich Ewald bis Martin Noth* (Tübingen, 1959); E.Osswald, *Das Bild des Mose* (Berlin, 1962); A.H.J.Gunneweg, "Mose in Midian," *ZThK* 61 (1964) 1-9; H.Schmid, "Der Stand der Moseforschung," *Judaica* 21 (1965) 194-221; *Mose. Überlieferung und Geschichte* (Berlin, 1968); *Die Gestalt des Mose. Probleme alttestamentlicher Forschung und Berücksichtigung der Pentateuchkrise* (Darmstadt, 1986); F.Cornelius, "Mose urkundlich," *ZAW* 78 (1966) 75-78; G.Widengren, "What Do We Know about Moses?" in Durham–Porter, eds., *Proclamation and Presence*, 21-47; Nielsen, "Moses and the Law," 87-98; G.W.Coats, *Moses: Heroic Man, Man of God* (Sheffield, 1988).

[41]De Moor, *Rise of Yahwism*, 111f., 236.

[42]For discussion of the broader issue of Joshua as successor of Moses cf. N.Lohfink, "Die deuteronomistische Darstellung des Übergangs der Führung Israels von Moses auf Josue," *Scholastik* 37 (1962) 32-44; D.J.McCarthy, "An Installation Genre?" *JBL* 90 (1971) 31-36.

[43]Althann, "Unrecognized Poetic Fragments," 19-21. We agree with the claim that this verse is poetry, but we offer another colometric division. Althann's study is influenced by syllable counting, which causes him to drop *wy'mr* from the colometry and to unnecessarily divide the final cola contrary to the Masoretic accentuation.

[44]Cf. Ex. 15:2; Isa. 12:2; 26:4; 38:11, plus in the Psalms, passim.

**Ex. 17:14-16**

| | |
|---|---|
| [*petuchah*] | |
| *wy'mr yhwh 'l-mšh* [*7*] | (14aA) And Yahweh said to Moses, |
| *ktb z't zkrwn bspr* [*5*] | (14aB) "Write this memorial in a book, |
| *wśym b'zny yhwš'* [*2*] | (14aC) and recount it in Joshua's hearing, |
| *ky-mḥh 'mḥh 't zkr 'mlq* [*5*] | (14bA) for I will surely destroy the remembrance of Amalek |
| *mtḥt hšmym* [*1*] | (14bB) from under the heavens." |
| *wybn mšh mzbḥ* [*2*] | (15A) And Moses built an altar, |
| *wyqr' šmw yhwh nsy* [*1*] | (15B) and he called its name "Yahweh is my banner." |
| *wy'mr ky-yd 'l-ks yh* [*5*] | (16A) He said, "a hand upon the throne of Yah; |
| *mlḥmh lyhwh b'mlq* [*2*] | (16B) Yahweh at war with Amalek |
| *mdr dr* [*1*] | (16C) from generation to generation." |
| [*petuchah*] | |

**Justification of strophe 1:**

Sep. ↑: *petuchah*; *'mr*; rep. *b*; imperatives; *z't*; tricolon
Sep. ↓: *ky*; rep. *mḥh*
Int. || : *'mr* || *ktb*[45] || *sym b'zn*;[46]; *b* || *b*; *mšh* || *yhwš'*[47]
Ext. || : *zkrn* || *zkr*.

**Justification of strophe 2:**

Sep. ↑: change of subject
Sep. ↓: *petuchah*; *'mr*; *ky*; rep. *dr*;[48] tricolon
Int. || : *wybn* || *wyqr'* (formal); *mšh* || *šmw* (assonance); *yh* || *yhwh*;[49]
Ext. || : *qr'* || *'mr*; *yhwh* || *yh*[50]

[45]For *'mr* || *ktb* see above, ext. par. between II.v.1 and II.v.2 (Josh. 24:26f.).

[46]For *'mr* || *śym b'zn* cf., e.g., the comparable parallelism in Jer. 2:2; Job 36:10.

[47]This parallelism receives incidental support from the attribution of the title *'bd yhwh* to both Moses and Joshua, cf. e.g. Deut. 34:5; Josh. 1:1; Josh. 24:29, etc., placing Moses and Joshua in a category together.

[48]Cf. van der Lugt, *Strofische structuren*, 521.

[49]Listed by Althann ("Unrecognized Poetic Fragments," 20f.), with appeal to Ps. 122:4; 135:1,3; (Isa. 12:2; 26:4), to which add Ps. 89:9 and cf. many verses in the Psalms with *yhwh* || *hllw yh*.

[50]Perhaps the original composition included an additional ext. par. of *nsy* || *ns yh*. Childs has summarized the evidence in which the etiological accounts regarding naming follow a certain form, and on that basis he argues there should be a wordplay

There is external parallelism between the strophes, e.g., *mšh* || *mš* (14aA, 15A; responsion); *yhwš'* || *yhwh* (14aC, 15B; responsion); perhaps *mḥh 'mḥh* || *mlḥhmh*[51] (14bA, 16B; responsion); *'mlq* || *b'm* (14bA, 16B; responsion); *mtḥt hšmym* || *mdr dr*[52] (14bB, 16C; responsion); *zkrwn* and *zkr* || *šm* and perhaps *yd* (14aB, 14bA, 15B 16A; responsions)[53]

Most important for the present discussion, Ex. 17:14-16 link both Moses and Joshua to the wars of Yahweh. It makes an external parallelism between Joshua and Yahweh, thereby playing upon Joshua's Yahwistic name in a manner comparable to what we repeatedly noted in Josh. 24:1-28. The composition of Ex. 17:14-1 antedates Deut. 25:17-19[54] and it is presupposed by the narrative c 1 Sam. 15, all of which suggests that Ex. 17:14-16 cannot be considered a late tradition.[55] Freedman accepts Ex. 17:16 as a premonarchi

between the name and the explanation, which he sees as support for emending *k* to *ns* (*Exodus*, 311f.). Childs makes a strong case for his suggestion; the concep of a banner as a memorial would not be unrelated to other usages of *ns* in the O to signify a sign of remembrance. See Ps. 60:6, and in Isaiah cf. 5:26; 11:10, 1 13:2; 18:3; 30:17; 31:9; 49:22; 62:10. In Num. 26:10 the death of Korah, Datha and Abiram is called a *ns* for Israel; cf. the pole in Num. 21:8f., which shows tha *ns* can be a rather flexible term. For a recent attempt to defend the reading *ks* c C.Houtman, "YHWH Is My Banner," *OTS* 25 (Leiden, 1989) (forthcoming).

[51]Signifying destruction of Amalek by Yahweh. The lack of an article wit *mlḥhmh* is noted by Althann ("Unrecognized Poetic Fragments," 20).

[52]The phrase *mdr dr* is treated as meristic by Krašovec (*Der Merismus*, 92 no.68 and Althann ("Unrecognized Poetic Fragments," 21). Polzin considers the construc tion *dr wdr* "a stock poetic phrase" (*Late Biblical Hebrew: Toward an Historic Typology of Biblical Hebrew Prose* [Missoula, 1976], 50), and his opinion receive considerable support from a survey of the distribution of all occurrences of *mdr d ldr dr* or *dr wdr*, etc., in the OT, where the thirty-eight juxtaposed *dr* construction are found virtually exclusively in poetry, cf. Deut. 32:7; Isa. 13:20; 34:10,17; 51:8 58:12; 60:15; 61:4; Jer. 50:39; Joel 2:2; 4:20; Psalms (22x); Prov. 27:4; Eccl. 1:4 Lam. 5:19; Ex. 3:15 (poetic, *zh-šmy l'lm* || *wzh zkry ldr dr*) and Esth. 9:28. On the question of dating raised by Polzin, cf. G.Rendsburg, "Late Biblical Hebrew and the Date of 'P'," *JANES* 12 (1980) 65-80, esp. 68f.; S.Gevirtz, "Of Synta and Style in the 'Late Biblical Hebrew'–'Old Canaanite' Connection," *JANES* 1 (1986) 25-29.

[53]Cf. Avishur, *Stylistic Studies*, 3, 11, 83, 317, 579, 598f., 600.

[54]Von Rad, *Deuteronomy*, 155. While earlier commentators usually attributed i to E, recent scholarship ordinarily assigns it to J. De Vaux, for example, claims "The text is certainly very early and is attributed to the Yahwist" (*Early History* 422).

[55]The use of *Yh* here may also be suggestive of a relatively early date of compo

poetic fragment.[56] Most commentators defend the unity of this passage, but some consider vs.14 to be a later addition.[57] Our structural observations support the conclusion that it is a unity. Accordingly, Ex. 17:14-16 provides valuable evidence for Joshua's role in the early perpetuation of the knowledge of Yahweh as the God of Israel. It is also noteworthy that Ex. 17:14-16 reflects a striking affinity to the actions of writing in a book and setting up a stone as a witness as in Josh. 24:26. Surely the reason why Moses had to recite these events in the hearing of Joshua was so that he would perpetuate them after Moses's death.

The succession from Moses to Joshua has been termed one of the most important themes in Deuteronomy.[58] It would take us too far afield to trace this theme in detail in Deuteronomy, partly because the question of dating various portions of Deuteronomy continues to be vigorously debated. As a single example we call attention to the manner in which Deut. 3:23-29 is deliberately structured to emphasize the role of Joshua as the successor of Moses. It makes a literary link between the mighty acts of Yahweh and the mighty acts of Joshua, Israel's leader with a Yahwistic name. The chiastic structure of these verses can be summarized as follows:

a. temporal setting (vs.23)
  b. Yahweh's great works (vs.24)
    c. request to see land across Jordan, and Mt. Lebanon (vs.25)
      d. Yahweh's refusal of Moses's request (vs.26)
    ć. go to Mt. Pisgah, see land across the Jordan (vs.27)
  b́. Joshua's great works (vs.28)
á. geographical setting (vs.29)

ition. Cf. the comments on Ex. 15:2 by de Moor, *Uw God*, 62 n.206.

[56]D.N.Freedman, "'Who Is Like Thee among the Gods?': The Religion of Early Israel," in Miller et al, eds., *Ancient Israelite Religion*, 316. Since this account is known to the author of 1 Sam. 15, there is little reason to contest the claim that this reminiscence about the Amalekites is premonarchic. Because of the manner in which it legitimates Davidic kingship, 1 Sam. 15 may have been written in the time of the united monarchy (cf. H.Tadmor, "Autobiographical Apology in the Royal Assyrian Literature," in Tadmor–Weinfeld, eds., *History, Historiography*, 36, 56).

[57]Childs, *Exodus*, 313.

[58]Craigie, *Deuteronomy*, 125.

The picture attained from Ex. 17:14-16 and from Deuteronomy is consistent with the broader outline of the Pentateuchal narratives as well as with certain details mentioned in particular. In Num. 13:8,16, Hoshea son of Nun is renamed "Joshua." This suggests that he received his Yahwistic name from Moses and not from his parents.[59] The task of promulgating knowledge of Yahweh was carried on by Joshua as Moses's successor.[60]

## Yahwism at the time of the settlement

We have mentioned above that in some theories of the development of Israelite religion it would appear to be anachronistic that Joshua is said to have stressed the need to worship Yahweh alone. However, OT tradition repeatedly emphasizes that Joshua inherited this task from Moses. It is our intention in the present section to demonstrate that the main emphases of Josh. 24:1-28 are not out of place in the setting the passage itself assigns to them.

Recent studies have demonstrated that there existed a religious crisis in the polytheistic religions of Egypt and Canaan in the LBA.[61] This situation is already suggestive that the religious climate at the time of Joshua would provide a plausible setting for the injunction for Israel to worship only one God, as well as for the preference to worship him as Yahweh rather than as El, especially since El had a sordid reputation in the Canaanite religion.[62] A similar conclusion

[59]For an explanation of the name change in Num. 13:16, in connection with the theology of the spy narrative, cf. E.Noort, "De naamsverandering in Num. 13:16 als facet van het Jozuabeeld," in F.García Martínez et al., eds., *Profeten en profetische geschriften* (Kampen, [1987]), 55-70.

[60]Cf. de Moor, *Rise of Yahwism*, 176f., where it is demonstrated that the appointment of Joshua as Moses's successor in Num. 27:16f. is described in poetic format. There is little reason to view Joshua as the initiator of exclusive Yahwism, contrary to the opinion of J.Dus ("Mose oder Josua? [Zum Problem des Stifters der israelitischen Religion]," *ArOr* 39 [1971] 16-45]. Dus follows many previous commentators in viewing the Sinai narrative of Exodus as a later expansion of Shechemite tradition. However, in our foregoing analysis we have noted numerous examples of the dependence of Josh. 24 upon material now found in Exodus, which counters the manner in which Dus seeks to employ Josh. 24 in his analysis.

[61]Cf. J.Assmann, *Re und Amun. Die Krise des polytheistischen Weltbilds im Ägypten der 18.-20. Dynastie* (Göttingen, 1983); de Moor, *Uw God*, 8-46; "The Crisis of Polytheism in Late Bronze Ugarit," in A.S.van der Woude, ed., *Crisis and Perspectives*, *OTS* 24 (Leiden, 1986), 1-20; *Rise of Yahwism*, 42-100.

[62]See de Moor, *Rise of Yahwism*, 80f. On the contrast between the descrip-

has been accepted previously by some scholars,[63] but many others consider it unlikely that the type of exclusive Yahwism described in Josh. 24:1-28 could have already been present in the time of Joshua. For this reason it is necessary to reconsider the alleged goal of Joshua's admonition in the light of its historical context.

We have seen above that the employment of *bḥr* with respect to Israel choosing Yahweh (Josh. 24:15,22) may be compared with the circumstances described in Judg. 5:8aA, in which the people are said to have chosen new gods. Scholars have repeatedly suggested that the choice offered in Josh. 24:15 should be viewed as a real choice[64] and not dismissed as rhetorical embellishment. Josh. 24 envisions a setting in which Israel was confronted with a concrete decision regarding the God or gods they would worship. At the same time, it is undeniable that the author of Josh. 24:1-28 has the firm conviction that the only true choice is acceptance of Yahweh as the one God of Israel.

Nicholson suggests that such an emphasis upon choosing Yahweh fits the circumstances of the exile.[65] However, the objections raised by Sperling in response to the setting proposed by Van Seters apply equally to Nicholson's proposal.[66] A literary-critical analysis of Josh. 24:1-28 reveals that this passage is not the Dtistic composition assumed by Nicholson. And, specifically in regard to the choice, the verb *bḥr* with Israel as subject and Yahweh as object would be entirely unique in Dtic or Dtistic literature where the emphasis is always upon Yahweh's election of Israel. But Judg. 5:8 suggests that this is precisely the type of thing which occurred in the time of the judges. Furthermore, as is demonstrated below on the basis of theophoric names, the period of the judges must have marked a critical period in the dissemination of the conviction that the one true God of Israel was Yahweh. Accordingly, the formulation of the choice to serve Yahweh alone, employing the verb *bḥr* as it does, is less problematic in the context of Israel's settlement in Canaan than at the time of Josiah's reform or during the exile. Schmitt is surely correct in con-

tion of God in Israel, and Ilu in Ugarit, see also a forthcoming monograph by M.C.A.Korpel.

[63]Cf. Gordon, *Before the Bible*, 119. See also Albright, *From the Stone Age*, 150ff.

[64]Nicholson, *His People*, 160f.; cf. McCarthy, *Treaty and Covenant*, 228.

[65]Nicholson, *His People*, 160-163.

[66]Sperling, "Joshua 24," 135f.

cluding that the emphasis upon true worship of Yahweh cannot be extracted from the consideration that Israel had just been settled in their promised land.[67]

However, the imperative to choose Yahweh is often judged to stand in direct conflict with the claim in vs.19 that Israel is not able to serve him. Kreuzer accordingly wishes to solve the alleged difficulty by viewing Josh. 24:19 as an elaboration of the theology of Josh. 23.[68] Yet a detailed comparison of terminology in Josh. 23 and 24 casts doubt upon the idea that there is any direct dependence of Josh. 24 upon ch.23. Furthermore, we have noted that while Josh. 23 is clearly dependent upon Deuteronomy, that is not the case with Josh. 24. Kreuzer's treatment of vss.1-15 and vss.16ff. as two originally independent sections is also countered by the deliberate structure of the present composition.

This conclusion is not refuted by the emphasis in Josh. 24:19f. upon the inability of the Israelites to serve Yahweh. The concept of serving Yahweh exclusively makes a significant contrast with the polytheism which was prevalent in Palestine. It is therefore not surprising that Yahweh's nature as a jealous God is brought to the forefront here.[69] Yahweh would not tolerate the worship of other gods, and in the event of disobedience his people would be punished severely. The emphasis found in Josh. 24:19f. is precisely what one might expect in the event of exclusive worship of a single deity when viewed against the background of Canaanite polytheism.[70]

We have already raised reservations about the contention that Josh. 24:20 should be read as a *vaticinium ex eventu.*[71] Without reviewing all of the examples of exile—both threatened and real—in the ancient NE,[72] it will suffice to note that defeat in battle was universally equated with punishment by the gods. In the ancient world of political turmoil and natural disasters, the gods were perceived as

[67]Schmitt, *Landtag*, 41.

[68]Kreuzer, *Frühgeschichte*, 193f.

[69]Cf. already Deut. 32:16.

[70]Regarding the antiquity of the emphasis upon Yahweh as a jealous God cf. de Moor, *Rise of Yahwism*, 227-229.

[71]See 2.3.7.2 above.

[72]For examples see Kitchen, "Ancient Orient, 'Deuteronism'," 5-7. Deportation, whether real or threatened in the treaty curses, was a common theme already in texts from the second millenium B.C. See also H.D.Galter, "28.800 Hethiter," *JCS* 40 (1988) 217-235.

oscillating between beneficence and castigation as regularly as cities were built and destroyed and as frequently as bumper crops were followed by devastating drought. In the light of the many similarities between Josh. 24:1-28 and the international treaties, and with a view to the curses of the treaties in particular, attention can be called to the common threats they contain of punishment for disobedience.[73] It is not surprising that some scholars have weighed the comparisons with the treaties so heavily that they find here an explanation for why Yahweh is considered to be a jealous God who will not tolerate the worship of other gods.[74] However, Fensham correctly notes that additional influences may also have been at work.[75] It would appear to have been an indigenous aspect of the worship of Yahweh from the very beginning that his veneration was exclusive and intolerant of other gods, as is seen already from the epithet "jealous" used with *'l* in Ex. 34:14.[76]

The assertion that the future will be conditioned by the degree of obedience to the sovereign deity is, in certain respects, not far removed from similar claims in polytheistic contexts in which a single deity can be associated with both blessing and punishment. The reciprocity of good and evil in the relationship to the deity is clearly evident in the Mesha inscription. When Moab is subjected by Israel the explanation lies in the fact that Chemosh was angry with his country,[77] but when Moab is successful it was Chemosh who brought prosperity.[78] As Licht has observed,

> "All ancient Near Eastern deities of some standing interfere in the affairs of their peoples. Victories, defeats and much else are quite regularly explained in the literature of the region as manifestations of divine benevolence and wrath."[79]

[73]E.g., regarding the threat of exile, cf. Hillers, *Treaty-Curses*, 34; Weidner, *Politische Dokumente*, 55.

[74]Beyerlin, *Herkunft und Geschichte*, 63; Fensham, "Clauses of Protection," 138.

[75]Fensham, "Clauses of Protection," 138.

[76]De Moor, *Uw God*, 54f.; *Rise of Yahwism*, 228.

[77]KAI 181:5f.

[78]KAI 181:4, 8f., 19, 33.

[79]J.Licht, "Biblical Historicism," in Tadmor–Weinfeld, eds., *History and Interpretation*, 110.

By comparison, the emphasis in Josh. 24:19f. is a perfectly understandable conclusion to be drawn from the demand of a total commitment to one God. This deduction would have been as apparent during the political turbulence of the LBA and early IA as it was after 722 or 586 B.C. Since the God of blessing also punished in times of disobedience, those who chose to worship him could be forewarned of the consequences which would follow in the event of unfaithfulness to their jealous sovereign.

## Yahwism and theophoric names

The emphasis of exclusive worship of Yahweh as an alternative to Canaanite polytheism fits the religious context of Joshua's time. Moreover, it also receives support from a study of theophoric names in the OT.[80] Recent studies by J.H.Tigay[81] and J.D.Fowler[82] affirm the value of studying theophoric names. Via the study of theophoric names among people who regularly reflect the name(s) of their deity in the names given to their children, it is possible to get a picture of which gods they worshipped. It is therefore striking that the first Yahwistic name encountered in the OT is that of Jochabed,[83] the mother of Moses. The only other Yahwistic name in Israel attested to the time of the settlement in Canaan is that of Joshua.[84] This suggests that in the time of the exodus the employment of Yahwistic theophoric names was rare.

Whereas at the time of the exodus and settlement the Israelites unequivocally preferred to use names composed with the element *El* rather than *Yahweh* or *Yah*, by the time of David Yahwistic names were firmly established.[85] Therefore, the period of the judges was critical for the transition from worship of Israel's one God as El to the recognition that their God was to be worshipped as Yahweh. As

[80]The present writer was privileged to assist professor J.C.de Moor in a study of theophoric names in the OT to the time of the early monarchy, with a particular emphasis upon tribal distribution. For a summary of the conclusions see de Moor, *Rise of Yahwism*, 10-41.

[81]J.H.Tigay, *You Shall Have No Other Gods: Israelite Religion in the Light of Hebrew Inscriptions* (Atlanta, 1986); "Israelite Religion," 157-194.

[82]J.D.Fowler, *Theophoric Personal Names in Ancient Hebrew* (Sheffield, 1988).

[83]De Moor, *Uw God*, 157f., following the vocalization of the LXX.

[84]De Moor, *Uw God*, 59. Cf. already B.J.Oosterhoff, *Israëlitische persoonsnamen. Exegetica* 4 (Delft, 1953), 23.

[85]De Moor, *Rise of Yahwism*, 33.

is noted by Oosterhoff,[86] Yahwistic names are still relatively rare in the earlier period of the judges. But the names which are recorded may be of considerable significance.

Joash, the father of Gideon, is involved in the struggle between Baalism and Yahwism (Judg. 6:11-32). He was a Manassite, from Ophrah.[87] Gideon's son Jotham (Judg. 9:5) is inextricably connected with the struggle climaxing in Shechem at the sanctuary of *'l bryt* or *b'l bryt* (8:33; 9:4,46). Jonathan, the grandson of Moses (Judg. 18:11), serves as a priest in the house of Micah, which significantly is also in the hill country of Ephraim (Judg. 18:2). Is it coincidental that the Danites ask him to inquire of *Elohim*, and he responds that they may go in peace because *Yahweh* is watching over them?[88] This Ephraimite, Micah, is presented in 17:1,4 with the explicitly Yahwistic name *mykyhw*. Samuel, whose lineage is listed alternatively with Levi or Ephraim, gives Yahwistic names to two of his sons, Joel and Abijah (1 Sam. 8:2). The name Joel is a form which either deliberately identifies Yahweh and El or is to be read "Yahweh is God." Moreover, 1 Chron. 6:36(21) mentions an *'zryh* as an ancestor of Samuel. What these various accounts all have in common is a setting in the hill country of Ephraim and Manasseh, precisely in the area where Joshua is said to have impressed upon Israel the necessity of unequivocally embracing Yahweh as their exclusive God. These observations reinforce conclusions drawn by other scholars with respect to the establishment of the Mosaic faith in the hill country and the struggle there of Yahwism against polytheism.[89]

The foregoing considerations support the claim that Joshua had an important part in the dissemination of the knowledge of Yahweh as the one God of Israel. During the period of the judges Israel did not worship Yahweh alone. Many worshipped the one God of Israel as El and others venerated other deities. The extent of cultic syncretism in the pre-monarchical period is a matter of ongoing study.[90] However,

[86]Oosterhoff, "Israelitische persoonsnamen," 23.

[87]Cf. above, re Gideon.

[88]Judg. 18:5f.

[89]Cf. D.N.Freedman, "Early Israelite History in the Light of Early Israelite Poetry," in H.Goedicke–J.J.M.Roberts, eds., *Unity and Diversity* (Baltimore, 1975), 12-19, especially re Judg. 5:8. See also Albright, *Yahweh and the Gods*, 172.

[90]W.G.Dever, "Material Remains and the Cult in Ancient Israel: An Essay in Archaeological Systematics," in Meyers–O'Connor, eds., *Word of the Lord*, 571-587; "Contribution of Archaeology," 209-247; J.A.Emerton, "New Light on Israelite

the fact that the period between Joshua and David marked a critical transition to the employment of theophoric names with Yahweh, rather than almost exclusively with El, provides important verification of the historical likelihood that Joshua played an important part as Moses's successor in the promulgation of exclusive Yahwism. Although these considerations remain circumstantial evidence regarding the historical reliability of the account of a Yahwistic gathering at Shechem in the time of Joshua, they do demonstrate how well the primary emphasis of Josh. 24:1-28 fits the history of the hill country of Ephraim and Manasseh as far as it can now be reconstructed from biblical and archaeological evidence.

## 6.3 Details in the dialogue of Josh. 24:2-24

We have suggested that there are good reasons for accepting the conclusion that Joshua was instrumental in emphasizing the exclusive worship of Yahweh at the time of Israel's settlment in Canaan. We turn now to a consideration of various historical references and implications entailed in the dialogical portions of Josh. 24:2-24. Since the historical summary in vss.2b-13 is largely dependent upon narratives from the Pentateuch, a full discussion of the historical value of these verses would ideally be conducted in the broader context of the parallels in Genesis, Exodus and Numbers. However, such a discussion is clearly beyond the scope of this study.

### 6.3.1 Foreign gods beyond the river

Josh. 24:2 places a unique emphasis upon patriarchal worship of other gods. Since one might presuppose that later traditions would rather exculpate than incriminate Israel's early ancestors, this can scarcely be attributed to a very late tradition. The probability that the patriarchs indeed worshipped foreign deities is reinforced by a study of possible theophoric elements in their names.[91]

Religion: The Implications of the Inscriptions from Kuntillet 'Ajrud," *ZAW* 94 (1982) 2-20; R.Wenning–E.Zenger, "Ein bäuerliches Baal-Heiligtum im samarischen Gebirge aus der Zeit der Anfänge Israels," *ZDPV* 102 (1986) 75-86; R.Rosen, "Early Israelite Cultic Centres in the Hill Country," *VT* 38 (1988) 114-117; Shanks, "Two Early Israelite Cult Sites," 48-52.

[91] Cf. Gibson, "Light from Mari," 54, 58; de Vaux, *Early History*, 191ff.; W.T.Pitard, *Ancient Damascus* (Winona Lake, 1987), 86.

## 6.3.2 Yahweh and Mt. Seir

Josh. 24:4 states that Yahweh gave Mt. Seir to Esau. In recent years, certain archaeological discoveries have been enthusiastically received as evidence linking the region of Seir to the name Yahweh. Egyptian documents such as the topographical list of Amenhotep III found in the Temple of Amon at Soleb in Nubia, and the list of Ramses II from Amarah-West were thought to make a possible connection between *yhwh* and the names "Seir" and "Laban."[92] Asserting the significance of these Egyptian references with the geographic denomination, Mazar concludes, "They lend support to the supposition that the worship of Yahweh existed there already in the time of Amenhotep III, towards the end of the 15th and the beginning of the 14 centuries BCE."[93]

However, the topographical locations included in the Egyptian lists have been the subject of different interpretations. M.C.Astour[94] has argued extensively that these locations were in the area stretching through Phoenicia and Syria, rather than in Edom. Although his interpretation has been rejected by some scholars,[95] it certainly demonstrates that future attempts to employ the Shasu references to prove a relationship between Yahweh and Seir will have to be more cautious.

[92] W.Helck, *Die Beziehungen Ägyptens zu Vorderasien im 3. und 2. Jahrtausend v. Chr.*, 2nd ed. (Wiesbaden, 1971), 266; R.Giveon, *Les bédouins Shosou des documents égyptiens* (Leiden, 1971), 26-28; M.Weippert, "Semitische Nomaden des zweiten Jahrtausends. Über *Š3šw* der ägyptischen Quellen," *Bibl* 55 (1974) 270f.; B.Mazar, "Yahweh Came Out from Sinai," in Biran, ed., *Temples*, 5-9, esp. 7; S.Aḥituv, *Canaanite Toponyms in Ancient Egyptian Documents* (Jerusalem, 1984), 121f., 128f., 169.

[93] Mazar, "Yahweh Came Out," 7.

[94] M.C.Astour, "Yahweh in Egyptian Topographical Lists," in M.Görg–E.Pusch, eds., *Festschrift Elmar Edel* (Ägypten und Altes Testament Studien zu Geschichte, Kultur und Religion Ägyptens und des Alten Testaments, vol. I; Bamberg, 1979), 17-34.

[95] Cf. Aḥituv, *Canaanite Toponyms*, 122 n.295, 169 n.491; M.Weinfeld, "The Tribal League at Sinai," in Miller et al., eds., *Ancient Israelite Religion*, 312 n.8. An evaluation of the references to the Shasu in both the Eyptian topographical lists and the Amarna correspondence leads Weinfeld to the conclusion that Seir refers to territory south of Palestine in the Sinai (303-305). On the other side of the debate, Astour's opinion has been accepted by Ahlström (*Who Were the Israelites?* 59f.).

### 6.3.3 Conflict in Transjordan

Josh. 24:8-10 summarizes the opposition encountered by Israel in Transjordan. It is not our intention to pursue the broader historical value of the contacts between Israel and Ammon or Moab, whether as implied here or in the fuller accounts offered in Numbers. However, recent archaeological activity in Transjordan has necessitated modification[96] of N.Glueck's original theory of an extensive MBA-LBA occupation gap, as postulated on the basis of his surface surveys.[97] J.A.Sauer concludes, "The occupational gap which Glueck claimed to exist during the Middle and Late Bronze Ages in much of Transjordan has been disproved in northern and central Transjordan, although the situation in southern Transjordan is still unclear."[98] This entails that Glueck's gap theory must be questioned as a criterion by which to evaluate the historical plausibility of an Israelite conflict with Moabites and Ammonites in, e.g., the period of LB IIB and/or Iron IA.[99]

Discovery of the Balaam inscription from Deir ʻAlla has added a new dimension to the evaluation of the historical value of OT accounts mentioning Balaam.[100] Contrary to the claim by some recent scholars that the late 8th cent. date for the Balaam inscriptions from Deir ʻAlla provides a probable context for the Israelite traditions regarding Balaam,[101] the Balaam tradition in Transjordan could have been per-

[96]J.M.Miller, "Archaeological Survey of Central Moab, 1978," *BASOR* 234 (1979) 43-52; Weippert, "Israelite 'Conquest'," 15-34; Boling, *Early Biblical Community*, 13-35, 51.

[97]N.Glueck, *The Other Side of the Jordan* (New Haven, 1940); "Transjordan," in Thomas, ed., *Archaeology*, 429-453.

[98]J.A.Sauer, "Ammon, Moab and Edom," in Amitai, ed., *Biblical Archaeology Today*, 206-214, esp. 209. For an earlier criticism of the manner in which Glueck described some of the pottery evidence consult S.Mittmann, *Beiträge zur Siedlungs- und Territorialgeschichte des Nörlichen Ostjordanlandes* (Wiesbaden, 1970), 2-4.

[99]Cf. Weippert, *Die Landnahme*, 64 n.4.

[100]J.Hoftijzer–G.van der Kooij, eds., *Aramaic Texts from Deir ʻAlla* (Leiden, 1976); H.-P.Müller, "Einige alttestamentliche Probleme zur aramäischen Inschrift von Dēr ʻAllā," *ZDPV* 94 (1978) 56-67; H.Weippert–M.Weippert, "Die Bileam-Inschrift von Tell Der ʻAlla," *ZDPV* 98 (1982) 77-103; B.A.Levine, "The Deir ʻAlla Plaster Inscriptions," *JAOS* 101 (1981) 196-205; "The Balaam Inscription from Deir ʻAlla: Historical Aspects," in Amitai, ed., *Biblical Archaeology Today*, 326-339; J.Hackett, *The Balaam Text from Deir ʻAlla* (Chico, 1984); "Some Observations on the Balaam Tradition at Deir ʻAllā," *BA* 49 (1986) 216-222; "Religious Traditions in Israelite Transjordan," in Miller et al., eds., *Ancient Israelite Religion*, 125-128.

[101]E.g., M.D.Coogan, "Canaanite Origins and Lineage: Reflections on the Religion

petuated for many centuries[102] and it does not provide clear evidence by which to date the biblical accounts.[103] Thus far, no consensus has been attained on the significance of the Deir 'Alla inscriptions for the historical analysis of the biblical traditions.[104] The references in Josh. 24:8-10,12 to activities in the Transjordan do not cast doubt upon the chapter's general historical accuracy. In a recent summary of his conclusions regarding the historical value of the Transjordan traditions Boling states:

> "When all is said and done, the returns from archaeology in Jordan plotted and the stories of Moses and his followers restudied, the conclusion is inescapable that Numbers 21ff. cannot be dismissed as pious anachronism."[105]

In addition to the encounter with Balaam and the Moabites, Boling's conclusion includes the conflict with Amorites, i.e., Sihon king of Heshbon and Og king of Bashan (Num. 21:21-35). In our opinion Josh. 24:12 is an allusion to these two kings of the Amorites. Kreuzer favours the LXX reading of twelve kings, in part on the basis of the symbolic value of twelve in later history writing.[106] However, this argument could also be employed as a partial explanation for why either the LXX or a *Vorlage* to it may have preferred a reading of

of Ancient Israel," in Miller et al., eds., *Ancient Israelite Religion*, 1987, 116-118.

[102]Note that Millard observes concerning the Deir 'Allah Inscription, "Whatever its origins, it is apparently the reproduction of a column of a scroll" ("Evidence for Writing," 307).

[103]For attempts to defend an early dating on linguistic grounds cf. W.F.Albright, "The Oracles of Balaam," *JBL* 63 (1944) 207-233; S.Gevirtz, *Patterns in the Early Poetry of Israel* (Chicago, 1963), 48-71; D.A.Robertson, *Linguistic Evidence in Dating Early Hebrew Poetry* (Missoula, 1972), 145, 150; A.Tosato, "The Literary Structure of the First Two Poems of Balaam," *VT* 29 (1979) 98-106; Boling, *Early Biblical Community*, 57ff. For a different approach, dating the composition of the Balaam cycle to shortly before the overthrow of Judah, cf. L.Rost, "Fragen um Bileam," in Donner et al., eds., *Beiträge*, 377-387, and cf. already S.Mowinckel, "Der Ursprung der Bileamsage," *ZAW* 48 (1930) 233-271.

[104]Cf. the skepticism of J.C.Greenfield, "Suffice it to say that the Deir 'Alla inscription remains for me a pagan text totally outside of the Israelite orbit, despite the efforts of B.Levine to bring it under the wings of 'El" (Amitai, ed., *Biblical Archaeology Today*, 369f.).

[105]Boling, *Early Biblical Community*, 62.

[106]Kreuzer, *Frühgeschichte*, 195f.; cf. 1.6.11.

twelve kings in Cisjordan rather than of two in Transjordan.[107] Reconstruction of the historical situation in Transjordan at the time of the exodus is complicated by the fact that the selection of details in the various accounts of the Amorite kingdoms appears to be influenced by concerns of later tribal allotment and boundaries.[108] While such concerns are elaborated in Num. 32; Deut. 3:1-22; Josh. 12:1-6; 13, Josh. 24 refers only summarily to the conflict with the two Transjordanian Amorite kings.

The historical reality of a battle with Sihon has been doubted by some scholars,[109] while others think that the Sihon account preserves some form of an actual military clash, but may originally have involved local tribal groups rather than a consolidated Israelite offensive.[110] De Vaux accepts the historical reality of a battle between Sihon and a group led by Moses,[111] but he denies that Og was a historical person. He argues that the description of the battle with Og was modeled upon the Sihon account.[112] On the basis of the claim in Deut. 3:11 that Og was the last of the Rephaim, and following other scholars in interpreting the "bed" mentioned in Deut. 3:11 as a dolmen, de Vaux assumes that Og was mythological and not historical.[113] The dolmen explanation for Og's bed is attractive,[114] The name Og, and his identification with the Rephaim, is attested in a Phoenician inscription on a sarcophagus found at Byblos and dating from the Persian period.[115] However, contrary to de Vaux's opinion, Og's con-

[107]See the discussion of Josh. 24:12 in 3.6.3 and 4.3.3.3.

[108]Kallai, *Historical Geography*, 248-259.

[109]Cf. J.Van Seters, "The Conquest of Sihon's Kingdom: A Literary Examination," *JBL* 91 (1972) 182-197; "Once Again–The Conquest of Sihon's Kingdom," *JBL* 99 (1980) 117-119; Schmitt, "Das Hesbonlied," 40. In a response to Van Seters, it was argued by J.R.Bartlett that Num. 21:21-25 is not dependent upon Deut. 2:26-37; Judg. 11:19-26 ("The Conquest of Sihon's Kingdom: A Literary Re-Examination," *JBL* 97 [1978] 347-351).

[110]J.R.Bartlett, "The Historical Reference of Numbers 21:27-30," *PEQ* 101 (1969) 94ff.; Kang, *Divine War*, 134.

[111]De Vaux, *Early History*, 566f.

[112]De Vaux, *Early History*, 567. In our opinion this argument is not conclusive because many OT battle reports contain stereotypical elements which give them a close literary form (cf. D.G.Gunn, "Narrative Patterns and Oral Tradition in Judges and Samuel," *VT* 24 [1974] 286-290; "The 'Battle Report': Oral or Scribal Convention?" *JBL* 93 [1974] 513-518).

[113]De Vaux, *Early History*, 567.

[114]Cf. Spronk, *Beatific Afterlife*, 228.

[115]For bibliography see Spronk, *Beatific Afterlife*, 210f.

nection with the cultus of the dead does not preclude the possibility that the later traditions were based originally upon an actual historical figure. The Rephaim in Ugarit were the dead ancestors of the royal dynasty.[116] Of the Ugaritic Rephaim, Gathru-and-Yaqaru was said to dwell in *ʿṯtrt* and *hdrʿy*, making an unmistakable parallel with the claim that Og lived in Ashtarot and Edrei.[117] It is possible that the enduring association of Bashan with the domain of the Rephaim caused the king of the Amorites in that area to be identified with the last of the Rephaim. As is suggested by de Moor,[118] such an understanding could have been prompted by an inscription on the tomb of Og.

While it is probable that Josh. 24:12 has the kings Sihon and Og in mind, the names are not mentioned. The question of an exodus period encounter with two Amorite kings in the Transjordan is inevitably pursued in connection with the matter of sedentarization. Excavations at Tell Ḥesbān provide no support for the biblical traditions regarding Heshbon.[119] This has led various scholars to posit that biblical Heshbon must have been located elsewehere.[120] The paucity of Egyptian references to Transjordan in the LBA is well-known, and for this reason it is significant that Ramses II claims to have plundered Dibon,[121] which demonstrates occupation of this site at that particular time period. In his recent summary of LBA and early Iron I settlement in Transjordan, Finkelstein is wisely cautious because "the overall picture is currently quite foggy."[122]

[116]M.H.Pope, "Notes on the Rephaim Texts from Ugarit," in M.de Jong Ellis, ed., *Essays on the Ancient Near East in Memory of Jacob Joel Finkelstein* (Hamden, Conn., 1977), 163ff.; de Moor, *Anthology*, 187.

[117]Deut. 1:4; Josh. 13:12. Cf. Spronk, *Beatific Afterlife*, 183.

[118]De Moor, *Anthology*, 187 n.3.

[119]See S.H.Horn, "Heshbon," in M.Avi-Yonah, ed., *Encyclopedia of Archaeological Excavations in the Holy Land* (London, 1976) 2:510-514; "Heshbon," *IDBSup*, 410; Finkelstein, *Archaeology*, 113.

[120]For example, Horn suggests Jalul as a possible candidate ("Heshbon," *IDBSup*, 410). Cf. Weippert, "The Israelite 'Conquest'," 22 n.25; Boling, *Early Biblical Community*, 47. Such an approach is rejected by Schmitt ("Das Hesbonlied," 40f. n.137).

[121]De Vaux, *Early History*, 392, with reference to K.A.Kitchen, "Some New Light on the Asiatic Wars of Ramesses II," *JEA* 50 (1964) 47-70.

[122]Finkelstein, *Archaeology*, 117.

### 6.3.4 Conflict at Jericho

The reference in Josh. 24:11 to military conflict with Jericho is employed by Sperling to argue for a date of composition considerably later than the events described.[123] We do not wish to attempt an apologetic defense of the biblical traditions regarding Jericho and Joshua. However, it would appear that Sperling's argument in this regard is inconclusive. Josh. 24:11 simply speaks of a battle with the *bʿly-yryḥw*, asserting that they were given by Yahweh into the hand of Israel. Sperling agrees with Soggin[124] in asserting that it contradicts the narrative of Josh. 6. If this is the case, the historical value of Josh. 24:11 must be evaluated independently from the full-scale account of Josh. 6,[125] and it is therefore not acceptable to equate the two as "the fall of Jericho," as is done by Sperling. Technically, Josh. 24:11 never mentions a fall of Jericho. Sperling argues that it would have taken some time for these traditions to develop, but this too indicates that he does not differentiate between Josh. 6 and Josh. 24:11. While archaeological activity at Tell es-Sulṭân casts doubt upon the existence of any LBA fortification at that site,[126] the question of the occupation of the site at this period is archaeologically more elusive.[127] Moreover, a recent attempt by J.J.Bimson to offer another chronology[128] suggests minimally that caution is in order before one dismisses all references to Jericho in connection with the settlement as later fiction. For these reasons Josh. 24:11 lies outside the realm of archaeological verifiability; when contrasted with Josh. 6 it is not possible to demonstrate that Josh. 24:11 shows growth of tradition.

[123]"The chapter cannot be contemporary with the events it describes because it accepts the fall of Jericho to the Israelites as a real event and views Joshua as a full-fledged leader of all Israel" (Sperling, "Joshua 24," 136).

[124]Soggin, "Conquest of Jericho," 215-217.

[125]Note too that Josh. 24 makes no mention of Ai, which follows upon the Jericho account of Josh. 6 and has proven to be archaeologically more enigmatic than Jericho with respect to the biblical claim of opposition in the time of Joshua.

[126]K.M.Kenyon, *Digging Up Jericho* (London, 1957), esp. 170f., 263; "Jericho," in Thomas, ed., *Archaeology*, 264-275; H.J.Franken, "Tell es-Sultan and Old Testament Jericho," *OTS* 14 (Leiden, 1965), 189-200.

[127]J.R.Bartlett, *Jericho* (Guildford, Surrey, 1982), 96-98; P.Bienkowski, *Jericho in the Late Bronze Age* (Warminster, 1986).

[128]J.J.Bimson, *Redating the Exodus and Conquest*, 2nd ed. (Sheffield, 1981), 106-136.

### 6.3.5 Land as inheritance

Culminating in Josh. 24:13, the historical summary in vss.2b-13 places particular stress upon gift of the land of inheritance as the product of Yahweh's historical intervention. Some scholars have argued that the OT's motif of the land as an inheritance is owing largely to the experience of exile.[129] Indeed, there can be little doubt that the exile had a formative influence upon the present form of Israel's history writing in which the occupation of the land holds a central place.[130] But it would be premature to conclude that the OT emphasis upon the land as a divine gift from Yahweh must be viewed primarily in this connection. The significance of a land in which to dwell forms a universal theme in ancient NE texts,[131] and it is historically reinforced by many mass migrations in early civilizations, e.g., of the Amorites or the Sea People, to list but two examples which directly affected Palestine.[132] Even a cautious appraisal of the ancient NE employment of a term such as *nḥlh* reveals examples of the widespread "land-consciousness,"[133] which cannot be separated from the awareness of the people's relationship to their deity. This is not to deny that some of the formulations in the OT are unattested in other ancient NE literature.[134] The wording of Josh. 24:13, which reads like the reversal of ancient treaty curses, does not imply an awareness of later loss of the land during exile. The land grant is amply documented already in ancient Hittite and Syro-Palestinian texts.[135] It is therefore significant that consideration of both content and literary structure demonstrates the appropriateness of this emphasis in Josh.

[129]Cf. M.Weippert, "Fragen des Israelitischen Geschichtsbewusstseins," *VT* 23 (1973) 415-442.

[130]W.Brueggemann, *The Land* (Philadelphia, 1977).

[131]For an Ugaritic example of a gift of land from a deity to a human see de Moor, *Rise of Yahwism*, 231.

[132]Cf. Am. 9:7.

[133]Cf. M.Malamat, "Pre-monarchical Social Institutions in Israel in the Light of Mari," in Emerton, ed., *Congress Volume Jerusalem 1986*, 165-176, esp. 174-176.

[134]Regarding the particularity of certain OT formulations cf. H.O.Forshey, "The Construct Chain *naḥᵃlat YHWH/ᵉlōhîm*," *BASOR* 220 (1975) 51: "There is no parallel elsewhere in the ancient Near East to this use of *naḥᵃlāh* as an appellative of the covenant community." Cf. S.E.Loewenstamm, "Nḥlt h'," in Japhet, ed., *Studies in Bible (1986)*, 155-192, e.g., Ugaritic *nḥhlh* as residence of the gods, which is only one step removed from an identification by metonymy of the people as *nḥlh* of the deity.

[135]Weinfeld, "The Covenant of Grant," 185, 189f.

24:13. Structurally, Canto I culminates in a focus upon land received from the hand of the sovereign, which is naturally followed in Canto II with a dialogical ceremony climaxing in a fourfold loyalty oath employing *n'bd* "we will serve," and a final, covenantal scene entirely appropriate to the loyalty ritual.[136]

### 6.3.6 Re-evaluating von Rad's credo theory

To this point we have commented upon the major elements of the historical summary in Josh. 24:2-13. We may now ask whether it is legitimate to speak of this summary in terms of an historical creed in the manner proposed by von Rad.[137] Previous responses have objected that von Rad's assertion of ancient terminology and formulations in some of the key passages was unsubstantiated. Others have insisted that form-critical comparison of the OT covenant texts with ancient treaty documents casts doubt upon his separation of the exodus tradition from the Sinai events.[138]

Von Rad's treatment of Josh. 24:2b-13 as an example of an ancient credo asserts that details of the Reed Sea event and the conflict with Balaam constitute later accretions into the basic form.[139] He sees these details as embellishments deriving from the hexateuchal presentation of history, arguing that they in no way influence the original form, which is not an *ad hoc* composition but is based upon a credo genre. It is precisely in this assertion that the concerns of three areas of study merge, namely, source-critical, form-critical and historical factors. Since his initial assessment of Josh. 24:2b-13 is crucial for the role that this text is allotted in his credo theory, the claim demands careful consideration. Our analysis of the historical summary in Josh. 24:2b-13[140] reveals that it is not correct to assert that the details regarding the Reed Sea event or the conflict with Balaam are incidental to the original form of the passage. It

[136]Cf. Weinfeld, "Loyalty Oath," 405, where Weinfeld notes that elements of the loyalty oath are to be detected in the background of Josh. 24:24-26. His accompanying claim that the form is less clear than in Deuteronomy must be tempered by our criticisms of this contention as delineated above in 2.4.1.

[137]For a summary of von Rad's theory of a small historical credo, including literature questioning the validity of his proposal, see 1.4.2.

[138]See 1.5.3; D.J.Wiseman, "Archaeology and Scripture," *WTJ* 33 (1970-71) 143.

[139]Von Rad, *Problem of the Hexateuch*, 7.

[140]See chs.4-5 above.

is not only in a few minor details that this passage is influenced by parallel accounts in Genesis, Exodus and Numbers. The bulk of the accounts of the calling of Abraham, the descent to Egypt, the exodus, the conflict at the Reed Sea, and the conflict with the Amorites and Moabites follows the antecedent Pentateuchal traditions ordinarily attributed to the Yahwist and Elohist corpus. Accordingly, the similarities are not found only in alleged accretions or embellishments but are more the rule than the exception.[141] Von Rad claimed, "There can, however, be no possible doubt that this speech is not an *ad hoc* composition."[142] But this assertion is unable to withstand a more detailed textual analysis of the relationship between these accounts and the antecedent traditions in the Pentateuch. Therefore, if Josh. 24:2b-13 is accepted as creedal, this designation must be qualified by the recognition that this creed is a paraphrase of various incidents now found in the Pentateuch. As such it is not evidence of a more archaic creedal genre.

Von Rad's most notable contention focused upon the absence of the Sinai event. In our discussion of comparable material in Exodus we have noted a high number of similarities between Josh. 24:1-28 and the Sinai complex, and in numerous instances Josh. 24:1-28 appears to be dependent upon that material. These observations undergird the skepticism expressed by previous scholars with respect to von Rad's argument from silence to deduce that the Sinaitic covenant would have been originally separate from the exodus account. If the absence of any direct mention of Sinai or of Moses as law-giver is to be accorded historical significance for the analysis of Josh. 24:1-28, one can scarcely go beyond the conclusion that at the time of composition it was not deemed necessary to include these details.[143]

[141]Note too, von Rad's proposal of accretions and embellishments is also countered by the deliberate structure which was discerned in our analysis.

[142]Von Rad, *Problem of the Hexateuch*, 7. He saw Josh. 24:2b-13 as a reflection of an ancient creedal form rather than as later composition dependent upon the Pentateuchal parallels.

[143]This in turn might lend limited support to a relatively early date of composition (Sperling, "Joshua 24," 135f.).

### 6.3.7 The Amorites in Josh. 24

The significance of the Amorites has been referred to in our summary of Kreuzer's position[144] and in our evaluation of the claim that the designation of the inhabitants of Canaan as "Amorites" is a particular characteristic of E.[145] Various recent studies have appealed to the presence of Amorites in Josh. 24 to argue for a late date of composition.[146] Kreuzer suggests that the generalized designation of the inhabitants of Palestine as Amorites derives from an idiom which had its apex in Assyrian texts of the 8th cent. B.C.,[147] and which by the 7th cent. was becoming archaic.[148] Therefore, if Kreuzer is correct, the mention of Amorites in a speech by Joshua is an anachronism.

The extra-biblical evidence regarding the Amurru has been researched extensively and is summarized in a most helpful manner in recent studies.[149] Liverani notes that the term Martu/Amurru was employed in Sumerian and Akkadian from early antiquity, with either a geographical or an ethnic designation of "west" or "westerner."[150] In Syria itself, the term later took on additional meanings, notably in the Amarna period when it designated a specific kingdom in the Lebanon range.[151] It has been suggested that in Egyptian, Hittite

[144]See 1.6.11.

[145]See 2.3.7.1.

[146]Cf. Van Seters, "The Terms 'Amorite' and 'Hittite' in the Old Testament," *VT* 22 (1972), 64-81; "Joshua 24," 145; Kreuzer, *Frühgeschichte*, 197, 200, 208-210. For previous reservations about Van Seters' conclusions consult Sperling, "Joshua 24," 126.

[147]Note, however, that this is in part an argument from silence because there is a substantial break in Assyrian documentation regarding Syria and Palestine after the LBA, with reports beginning again at the time of Ashur-naṣir-apli II (883-859 B.C.), at which time the designation of all Syria-Palestine as Amurru was already a general usage (M.Liverani, "The Amorites," in D.J.Wiseman, ed., *Peoples of Old Testament Times* [Oxford, 1973], 119f.).

[148]Kreuzer, *Frühgeschichte*, 209f.

[149]Cf. A.Haldar, *Who Were the Amorites?* (Leiden, 1971); Liverani, "The Amorites," 100-133 (extensive bibliography); K.Nashef, *Répertoire Géographique des Textes Cunéiformes, Bd. 5: Die Orts- und Gewässernamen der mittelbabylonischen und mittelassyrischen Zeit* (Wiesbaden, 1982), 30f.

[150]Liverani, "The Amorites," 102ff.; cf. G.Buccellati, *The Amorites of the Ur III Period* (Publicazioni del seminario di semitistica 1; Naples, 1966), esp. 352; H.B.Huffmon, *Amorite Personal Names in the Mari Texts: A Structural and Lexical Study* (Baltimore, 1965), 280.

[151]H.Klengel, *Geschichte und Kultur Altsyriens*, 2nd ed. (Leipzig, 1979), 82-84.

and Ugaritic texts Amurru sometimes retained a broader meaning in reference to all of Syria,[152] but this is uncertain.[153] The Syrian state of Amurru was taken from Egypt by Hatti in c. 1200 B.C.[154] and destroyed by the Sea Peoples in c. 1190 B.C.[155] Assyrian texts continue to designate that part of Syria as Amurru,[156] and there is evidence that by the ninth century all Syria-Palestine was known as "Amurru."[157]

An important conclusion arising from the foregoing survey of the history of Amurru is that if the Amorites in the Transjordan (Josh. 24:8,11f.) and in Cisjordan (Josh. 24:15,18) are to be associated with groups dispersed from Amurru after its destruction c. 1190 B.C. by the Sea Peoples, we are faced with an apparent anachronism. Josh. 24:15,18 not only mentions Amorite presence contemporary with the settlement of Israel in the area of Shechem, but it in fact also designates the land there as belonging to the Amorites, which suggests that they were settled there *before* the Israelites came. Moreover, the Amorites are already viewed as having established kingships in Transjordan by the time the Israelites arrived on the scene. Assuming that the Merenptah stele of c. 1207 B.C. does not predate the exodus, the lowest date of the exodus hardly allows sufficient time for the dispersion of the Amorites from Amurru c. 1200-1190 B.C. and their settlement in Canaan, both in Transjordan and in Cisjordan, prior to Joshua's gathering at Shechem. For these reasons it is understandable that Kreuzer looks to the Neo-Assyrian context to explain Josh. 24's use of Amorites.

However, in the opinion of the present writer, the Neo-Assyrian

[152]Liverani, "The Amorites," 118.

[153]E.g., one of the texts appealed to by Liverani ("Amorites," 131 n.64) is found in J.Nougayrol, *PRU* III, 183 ll.10f., but note the geographical determinatives (*mat*) which suggest that the reference is to the land of Amurru.

[154]Cf. K.A.Kitchen, "Interrelations of Egypt and Syria," in M.Liverani, ed., *La Siria nel tardo bronzo* (Orientis antiqvi collectio IX; Rome, 1969), 81.

[155]As reported by Ramses III, cf. *ANET*, 262; Liverani, "Amorites," 119, 131 n.67.

[156]E.g., under Tiglathpileser I (c. 1115-1077 B.C.); cf. P.Dhorme, "Les Amorrhéens, VIII, Amourrou et l'Assyrie," *RB* 40 (1939) 172-181 (= *Receuil Edouard Dhorme* [Paris, 1951], 152-162); Noth, *Aufsätze*, 1:99 n.74. He conducted expeditions as far as the Mediterranean (cf. W.von Soden, "Assyrien," *RGG*$^3$, 1:650-655, esp. 651; Liverani, "The Amorites," 119; D.J.Wiseman, "Assyria and Babylonia c. 1200-1000 BC," in *CAH*$^3$, II/2, 443-481, esp. 454-457, 461.

[157]Liverani, "The Amorites," 120.

explanation is unable to adequately clarify the OT employment. In the OT, the term Amorite is usually applied to groups resident specifically in highland areas both in Transjordan and Cisjordan. This is stated explicitly in Num. 13:29.[158] If this usage was derived from the Neo-Assyrian idiom, in which Amorite means westerner as a general designation for all inhabitants of Syria and Palestine, one is at a loss to explain why the OT carefully distinguishes between Amorites living as enclaves in the hill country and, e.g., Canaanites living in the lower areas. If the use of the term Amorite in Josh. 24 is consistent with its employment in other OT passages, it would follow that if its employment in Josh. 24 is to be attributed to Neo-Assyrian influence the same must be posited for the other OT references. This matter deserves further elaboration.

As is noted by Kallai,[159] the Amorites are said to have offered major opposition to the Israelites in the time of the settlement, but their threat against Israel subsequently subsided. Judg. 1:34-36 relates how the Danites were unable to dispossess the Amorites from their territory in Har-heres, Aijalon and Shaalbim, but the tribes of Joseph subdued them in this area.[160] This is significant because Joshua was from the tribe of Ephraim, and the setting of Josh. 24 is at the border of Manasseh and Ephraim. The Amorites dwelt in Har-heres (Judg. 1:35) and Joshua's tribal allotment is described in Judg. 2:9 as being in Timnath-heres; the topographical affiliation of these two places is highly probable.[161] 2 Sam. 21:2 remembers the Gibeonites as part of the remnant of the Amorites.[162] Moreover, Gen. 48:22 also refers to Shechem as having been specifically of the Amorites.[163] The multiple references to Amorites in the hill

[158] K.M.Kenyon, *Amorites and Canaanites* (London, 1966), 1-4.

[159] Kallai, *Historical Geography*, 24f., 108.

[160] Kallai, *Historical Geography*, 108, 145.

[161] Cf. Kallai, *Historical Geography*, 145, 361 n.65; "The Settlement Traditions of Ephraim," *ZDPV* 102 (1986) 68-74.

[162] Cf. 1 Sam. 7:14 and its geographical location.

[163] Note that 34:2 calls Hamor a Hivite (LXX Horite, cf. Josh. 9:7). Perhaps Gen. 48:22 uses the designation "Amorite" in the sense noted above of the various groups living in the hill country. Numerous scholars have suggested that the reference to the Shechemites as sons of Hamor (Semitic, "ass") can be compared to the Amorite attestation in Mari of a covenant established by slaughtering an ass, cf. Noth, "Covenant-making," 108-117; Campbell–Ross, "Excavation of Shechem," 7f.; G.R.H.Wright, "Shechem and League Shrines," *VT* 21 (1971) 575. However, these efforts to link the inhabitants of Shechem with the Amorites mentioned in Mari on

country of Ephraim argue against viewing all these texts as a reflection of Neo-Assyrian terminology.[164] The various accounts connecting Joshua with Timnath-heres or Timnath-serah and with Shechem in the hill country of Ephraim have been considered by others to be historically trustworthy.[165]

In view of these various OT accounts specifically noting Joshua's military role in appropriating the land from these Amorites, it cannot be surprising that precisely the ***gods of the Amorites*** are singled out for special attention in Josh. 24:15. Similarly, reference to the ***land of the Amorites*** in Josh. 24:15 cannot be treated in abstraction from the other OT references to land previously inhabited by Amorites. If one attributes the role of the Amorites in Josh. 24 to Neo-Assyrian influence, the same approach is necessary for all of the related references to Amorites in the the description of the settlement.

It is noteworthy that Josh. 5:1 and 10:6 describe as Amorite the southern coalition of kings West of the Jordan, up to the Philistine lowlands. Noth argued that these references to the Amorites are derived from reworked Benjaminite accounts dating to not later than the 10th cent. B.C.[166] Whether this date is acceptable is of secondary importance to the present argument that here too the reference to Amorites does not fit the Neo-Assyrian usage because it does not have the meaning "westerner" and it is not a general designation for the entire population of Syria-Palestine. On the other hand, it does agree with other OT descriptions of the conquest and settlement of land previously occupied by Amorites.[167] There is, therefore, no convincing evidence that the mention of Amorites in the OT was informed by the Neo-Assyrian idiom.[168]

the bases of an ass-covenant are tenuous (cf. Tadmor, "Treaty and Oath, 134ff.).

[164]The Samaritan Pentateuch of Gen. 22:2 reads "land of the Amorites" rather than land of Mt. Moriah. Some scholars are inclined to see this too, along with Gen. 12:6f., as evidence for a location near Shechem. If this was the case it appears to be later contradicted by 2 Chron. 3:1, which, if referring to the same Mt. Moriah, makes an identification with Jerusalem.

[165]Weinfeld, "The Pattern," 270-283; "Historical Facts behind the Israelite Settlement Pattern," *VT* 38 (1988) 324-332.

[166]Noth, *Aufsätze*, 1:101 n.78.

[167]In addition to the texts discussed above cf. Am. 2:9f.

[168]Liverani states, "The significance of 'Amurru' as 'west' is also out of the question, because it is only relevant from one point of view, the Mesopotamian point of view, certainly not the Palestinian one, Palestine having the sea to the west" ("The Amorites," 123).

This entails that another explanation must be sought for the presence of the Amorites in Josh. 24. Two options deserve consideration. (a) Reference to Amorites already firmly established in Transjordan and Cisjordan hill country in the time of Joshua is an anachronistic reference to inhabitants dispersed from Amurru c. 1200-1190 or later. (b) The term Amorite was employed, whether correctly or not, to designate groups already resident in Canaan prior to the arrival of the Israelites, and these groups did not arrive from Amurru after the invasion by the Sea Peoples.

It might be significant that Amurru of the LBA was an Aramaic kingdom with Tadmor (= Palmyra) as its capital.[169] Since the patriarchs originated in the same area and are repeatedly designated as Arameans,[170] it is possible that the reference in Josh. 24:15 to the gods of the Amorites is another expression for Aramaic gods similar to those of the ancestors (cf. Gen. 31; 35).[171] However, such an identification is questionable. Josh. 24:14f. presents "the gods served by the fathers beyond the river" and "the gods of the Amorites in whose land you are now living" as distinct options rather than as synonymous designations. For this reason Josh. 24:15 does not prove an Aramaic background for the Amorites mentioned there.

Although it is possible that the OT references to the presence of Amorites in the time of the settlement is owing to conditions or memories prevalent at the time of the composition of the narratives and for this reason speak anachronistically of the previous inhabitants as Amorites (cf. the first option above), it is also possible that these so-called Amorites had nothing to do with a migration from Amurru after the invasion of the Sea Peoples. According to Huffmon, "The antiquity of the Amorites in Palestine and Transjordan is unclear, but Amorite elements must have been there at least by 1900 B.C."[172] There is evidence for an Amorite identity of various groups in MB IIA (2000–1800 B.C.) and MB IIB-C (1800–1500 B.C.) Palestine,[173] e.g.,

[169]Cf. de Moor, *Anthology*, 118 n.9; D.Arnaud, *Recherches au pays d'Aštata, Emar VI.3* (Paris, 1986), No.21:16,18 (Palmyrenians pay each other in the currency of Amurru).

[170]Cf. R.T.O'Callaghan, *Aram Naharaim* (Rome, 1948), 29f.; Pitard, *Ancient Damascus*, 86.

[171]Note that McCarthy sought a setting for Josh. 24:1-28 in an Aramaic connection (*Treaty and Covenant*, 283).

[172]H.B.Huffmon, "Amorites," *IDBSup*, 21.

[173]W.G.Dever, "The Patriarchal Traditions," in Hayes–Miller, eds., *Israelite and*

from Amorite theophoric names appearing in the Egyptian Execration texts,[174] as well as references in the Mari documents.[175] Although these references are admittedly from centuries prior to the Israelite settlement, it is generally held that "the transition from the Middle Bronze to the Late Bronze Age represents neither an abrupt nor a complete break in culture."[176] This entails minimally that the OT use of the term Amorite is not necessarily an anachronistic reference to groups dispersed from Amurru after the invasion of the Sea Peoples.[177]

In the light of the various considerations summarized above, there remains little reason to maintain that Josh. 24's employment of the term Amorite betrays a 7th cent. origin. This conclusion is not countered by texts such as 1 Kgs 21:26 and 2 Kgs 21:11, which employ a standard idiom to condemn Ahab and Manasseh for engaging in the idolatry of the Amorites. As is noted above, the command in Josh. 24:14f.,23 to put away foreign gods differs significantly from the violent iconoclasm prescribed in Deuteronomy and enacted in the reforms of Hezekiah and Josiah.

### 6.3.8 The gods of Egypt

Josh. 24:14f. warns against the gods of the Amorites, but it also commands the people to put away the gods worshipped by the fathers in Egypt. The latter emphasis is frequently dismissed as secondary.[178] Such a rejection forms a link in Perlitt's attempt to find a plausible *Sitz im Leben* for the emphasis not to worship foreign gods.[179] The emphasis upon gods worshipped in Egypt is ignored in McCarthy's proposal of an Aramaic setting.[180] By contrast, both Van Seters[181]

*Judaean History*, 84-89.

[174]Cf. J.Gray, *The Canaanites* (London, 1964), 28f., 35; *Legacy*, 152f.

[175]Haldar, *Who Were the Amorites?*, 58.

[176]Dever, "Patriarchal Traditions," 89.

[177]With regard to the expression "the land of the Amorite," Y.Aharoni concludes that it "derived from the ancient name which in its day had included Palestine and at least a part of Syria" (*The Land of the Bible: A Historical Geography*, revised ed. [Philadelphia, 1979], 66).

[178]Noth, *Das System*, 139; *Josua* 1953, 135; Möhlenbrink, "Landnahmesagen," 252 n.1; Mölle, *Landtag*, 65.

[179]Perlitt, *Bundestheologie*, 257 n.1.

[180]McCarthy, *Treaty and Covenant*, 282f.

[181]Van Seters, "Joshua 24," 149.

and Nicholson[182] compare Josh. 24:14-15 to Ezek. 20 and 23, and argue, in part upon this basis, that the origin for this emphasis is exilic.

While Nicholson is quite correct that the previous reasons for rejecting mention of Egypt as secondary are inconclusive,[183] it is necessary to reconsider whether the comparison with Ezek. 20 and 23 provides legitimate grounds for claiming that only the exilic period provides a probable historical setting for such an emphasis to put away the gods worshipped in Egypt. It is understandable that in the time of Ezekiel the gods from Egypt could have been a concern.[184] However, Nicholson's conclusion that the time of the exile is the most probable setting for a warning against the gods worshipped in Egypt does not discuss the influence of Egypt in Palestine at the time of Israel's origins, or the contacts which continued to intermittently exist between Egypt and Palestine down into the period of Israel's monarchy.[185] In our opinion, the latter considerations are of considerable importance. Although Josh. 24:14 speaks of gods which were worshipped *in Egypt*, the present imperative to put away such gods has its claimed setting in Shechem in the time of Joshua. For this reason it is necessary to question whether this setting is really less plausible than the exilic setting suggested by Nicholson.

We have already presented arguments in support of the contention that Joshua promoted the exclusive worship of Yahweh. It is understandable that such an emphasis in the end of the LBA would have included a rejection of the gods worshipped in Egypt. It would be incorrect to conclude on the basis of their new location in Palestine that the gods worshipped in Egypt would automatically be relegated to the past. Extensive connections between Egypt and Shechem are attested both literarily and through additional archaeological evidence.[186]

[182]Nicholson, *His People*, 161.

[183]Structural considerations also argue for its integral place in the composition, cf. above, ext. par. of strophe II.i.1, as well as considerations of macro-structure of Canto II, e.g., 14bC, 17aD, responsion; note too in the relationship of Canto I and Canto II, e.g., 4bC, 14bC, responsion.

[184]It is known, for example, that Jews on Elephantine Island were involved in syncretistic cultic activities (E.G.Kraeling, "Elephantine Papyri," *IDB*, 2:84). For a contrary opinion see U.Cassuto, "The Gods of the Jews of Elephantine," *Biblical and Oriental Studies*, 2:240-249.

[185]K.A.Kitchen, "Egypt and Israel during the First Millenium B.C.," in Emerton, ed., *Congress Volume Jerusalem 1986*, 107-123.

[186]Harrelson, "Shechem," 2-10; R.Giveon, *The Impact of Egypt on Canaan*

The vacillating political subservience of Palestine to Egypt was accompanied by social, religious and cultic influence. Of considerable significance for our study of Shechem are the Egyptian cylinder-seals, scarabs and impressions from various Egyptian periods. A survey of the seventy-seven scarabs and impressions published by Horn[187] adds considerable support to a theory of Egyptian contact and influence at this site.[188] As is more often the case in Palestinian sites, a high percentage of scarabs is from the Hyksos period.[189] However, Horn summarized his survey of the first thirty-eight scarabs with the conclusion, "The fairly large number of New Kingdom scarabs found at Shechem—twenty-five per cent of the total—clearly indicates that this city must have maintained a reasonably good contact with Egypt."[190] In his second article,[191] he notes that a much higher frequency of scarabs was found in Palestine in coastal cities, in the Shephelah, and

(Göttingen, 1978), 30. Perhaps the significance of Egyptian relations with Palestine during the Middle Kingdom has sometimes been exaggerated, as is argued by J.M.Weinstein, "Egyptian Relations with Palestine in the Middle Kingdom," *BASOR* 217 (1975) 1-16. However, soon thereafter trade relations with Egypt increased (Weinstein, "Egyptian Relations," 13f.), and in the New Kingdom, following the expulsion of the Hyksos, Palestine was often subject to Egyptian political control, and it always stood within the shadow of her social and religious influence. See A.Malamat, "Campaigns of Amenhotep II and Thutmose IV to Canaan," in Rabin, ed., *Studies in the Bible*, 218-231; W.W.Hallo–W.K.Simpson, *The Ancient Near East: A History* (New York, 1971), 255-283; de Vaux, *Early Israel*, 82-123; R.Hachmann, "Die ägyptischen Verwaltung in Syrien während der Amarnazeit," *ZDPV* 98 (1982) 17-49; D.B.Redford, "The Relations between Egypt and Israel from El-Amarna to the Babylonian Conquest," in Amitai, ed., *Biblical Archaeology Today*, 192-205.

[187]S.H.Horn, "Scarabs from Shechem I," *JNES* 21 (1962) 1-14; "Scarabs and Scarab Impressions from Shechem II," *JNES* 25 (1966) 48-56; "Scarabs and Scarab Impressions from Shechem III," *JNES* 32 (1973) 281-289. Cf. Campbell–Ross, "Excavation of Shechem," 4f.; G.E.Wright, "Selected Seals from the Excavations at Balâṭah (Shechem)," *BASOR* 167 (1962) 8-10; R.J.Bull, "Field V. The Temple," *BASOR* 161 (1961), 38.

[188]Horn, "Scarabs, I," 2f., notes the number would likely have been higher if tombs had been found (cf. C.Klamer, "A Late Bronze Age Burial Cave near Shechem," *Qad* 14:1-2 [1981] 30-34, esp. 34 [Hebrew]), and secondly, many artifacts from Shechem are said to have been lost in the destruction of Sellin's house in 1943.

[189]Cf., e.g., R.Giveon, *Scarabs from Recent Excavations in Israel* (Göttingen, 1988); Weinstein, "Egyptian Empire," 8-10. On contacts in the Hyksos period, cf. W.G.Dever, "Relations between Syria-Palestine and Egypt in the 'Hyksos' Period," in Tubb, ed., *Palestine*, 69-87.

[190]Horn, "Scarabs, I," 14.

[191]Horn, "Scarabs, II," 48.

the plain of Megiddo, than in the mountainous area around Shechem; he concludes that, despite its prominence in Palestine, Shechem lay off of the main-stream of influence from Egypt.[192] Subsequent to the scarabs published by Horn, two additional Egyptian style scarabs, one from the time of Ramses II and one from either Ramses II or Ramses III, were recovered in archaeological excavations of a cultic site at Mt. Ebal.[193] We do not wish to exaggerate the historical value of the scarabs. A recent authority stresses, "The discovery of a royal scarab at a site merely indicates that there had, in fact, been *contact* between Egypt and the early settlement—no more than that."[194] Nevertheless, the Egyptian scarabs appear to have had religious value in Palestine[195] and Egypt. The cumulative evidence from all the scarabs found at Shechem and its surroundings reinforces the conclusion that, although the degree of Egyptian influence may have been less here than in certain other cities in Palestine,[196] polytheism in the neighborhood of Shechem may plausibly have included influence from the gods of Egypt.[197] Retrospective to the influence of Egyptian polytheism upon the religious metabolism of Palestine from

[192]Cf. I.Singer, "Merneptah's Campaign to Canaan and the Egyptian Occupation of the Southern Coastal Plain of Palestine in the Ramesside Period," *BASOR* 269 (1988) 1-10.

[193]See Zertal, "Joshua's Altar," 42 (cf. 1.7.4 above); Finkelstein, *Archaeology*, 84.

[194]Giveon, *Impact of Egypt*, 101.

[195]O.Tufnell, "Seals and Scarabs," *IDB*, 4:254-259; Horn, "Scarabs, I," 1, 9; "Scarabs, II," 54, noting that a high majority of the scarabs in Palestine are found in tombs, and they often functioned as amulets.

[196]G.R.H.Wright ("Fluted Columns in the Bronze Age Temple of Baal-Berith at Shechem," *PEQ* 97 [1965] 66-84) argues for Egyptian style architectural influence, but this does not yet prove that an Egyptian god was worshipped here, as was the case, e.g., in the Ramesside Hathor temple at Timna (B.Rothenberg, *Timna: Valley of the Biblical Copper Mines* [London, 1972], 125-207). For additional evidence of Egyptian temples in Palestine cf. Giveon, *Impact of Egypt*, 22-30; Weinstein, "Egyptian Empire," 19.

[197]Cf., with reservations, G.R.H.Wright's argument that Joseph was actually a Hebraïsed Egyptian god ("An Egyptian God at Shechem," *ZDPV* 99 [1983] 95-109). More plausible is the possibility that the descriptions of Joseph's connections with Shechem reflect ancestor veneration. Note that Joseph and Joshua, both of whom were buried at Shechem (Josh. 24:30,32), are said to have died at the age of 110 (Gen. 50:22; Josh. 24:29), which was considered "l'âge idéal pour les Egyptiens" (J.Bergmann, "Discourse d'adieu–testament–discourse posthume. Testament juifs et enseignements égyptiens," in *Sagesse et religion* [Colloque de Strasbourg, octobre 1976; Paris, 1979], 21-50, esp. 47).

the time of the Eighteenth Dynasty[198] and during the Amarna Age and Iron I period,[199] the least we can conclude is that it cannot be considered anachronistic or contextually inappropriate that Joshua is said to have warned the Israelites to put away the gods which had been worshipped in Egypt.

From the formulation of Josh. 24:14f. it is uncertain whether these gods worshipped by the forefathers in Egypt were the same as those from the period in which they lived "beyond the river" or whether they were more indigenously Egyptian deities. Since Egyptian polytheism was tolerant and readily assimilated Asiatic gods into its already vast pantheon, it is possible that the gods worshipped in Egypt by the Hebrew fathers included their own earliest Semitic gods. In either case, the stress placed in Josh. 24:14f. upon putting away the foreign gods worshipped in Egypt need not be explained in comparison with Ezek. 20 and 23 as an exilic incrimination of Israel's early ancestors. The charge could already have had a very plausible setting in the LBA or in Iron I as a necessary component of the acceptance of Yahweh as the only true God of Israel.

[198]The contact of the Eighteenth Dynasty was followed by an even greater influence during the Nineteenth and Twentieth Dynasties, cf. Weinstein, "Egyptian Empire," 18-21; E.D.Oren, "Respondents," in Amitai, ed., *Biblical Archaeology Today*, 224. See also W.Helck "Die ägyptischen Verwaltung in den syrischen Besitzungen," *MDOG* 92 (1960) 1-13.

[199]The religious exchange between Egypt and Palestine went in both directions, cf. J.A.Wilson, "Egypt," *IDB*, 2:49, 62-64; R.Stadelmann, *Syrisch-palästinensische Gottheiten in Ägpten* (Leiden, 1967), 141ff.; Redford, "Relations between Egypt and Israel," 196-200.

# 7 General Conclusions

The present analysis of Josh. 24:1-28 has confirmed the intuition voiced by von Rad that OT source criticism had come to a stalemate, and had perhaps exceeded its legitimate bounds, while questions of literary form and content were left underdeveloped.[1] The historical survey offered in ch.1 of this study demonstrates that a century of source criticism from approximately the last half of the 19th century through the first half of the 20th treated Josh. 24:1-28 as the final knot at the termination of those documentary strands thought to have been intertwined to form a Hexateuch. The broadest consensus was that this passage in particular bore the stamp and seal of the Elohist. However, one can speak only in a qualified manner of a consensus, for it became apparent in our research that the source-critical analyses had actually produced a startling variety of conclusions. According to some scholars the only true source discernible was E; additional material, whether Yahwistic, Priestly or Dtistic, was due to editing. Numerous other scholars defended the need to recognize both J and E as fully discernible sources, and at times these were further subdivided into various levels. Eissfeldt, for example, thought that Josh. 24 provided important evidence for his theory that part of the earliest J material was to be attributed to his L source. Noth initially also accepted both J and E as two independent sources. Möhlenbrink attempted to divide the passage between a *Josuarezension* and a *Jahwerezension*. By contrast, Rudolph denied the existence of E altogether and attributed the whole passage to J and later redacting or glossing. This is but a small sampling of the various source-critical positions.

Once one has surveyed the diversity of conclusions produced by these analyses, it can no longer come as a surprise that von Rad spoke of a stalemate, ventured the opinion that source criticism had tried to do too much, and sought restlessly for a new method of handling the passage's literary form and content. Yet it is readily apparent that von Rad too, like his contemporaries, was unable to extricate his own study from the source-critical presuppositions inherited from previous generations. His evaluation of the form and content of Josh. 24:2-13 began with the simple assumption that the passage was replete with accretions and embellishments,[2] but his theory of the composition of

[1] Von Rad, *Problem of the Hexateuch*, 1.
[2] Von Rad, *Problem of the Hexateuch*, 7.

Josh. 24:2b-13 cannot withstand a critical testing. Contemporaneous with the work of von Rad, Noth was developing his theory of a twelve-tribe amphictyony, and soon thereafter he began his systematic attempt to supplant previous Hexateuchal theories with a new analysis of Dtistic history. Although for a number of decades Noth's view of an amphictyony influenced scholarly opinion regarding the historical value of Josh. 24:1-28, this theory too proved inadequate as an explanation for the historical setting of Josh. 24:1-28.

Following von Rad and Noth it was impossible to return to the previous style of source criticism. Refocused questions of local traditions and possible influence of the cultus upon the present form of the text had gained a permanent foothold. Yet some of the most basic questions were left unasked and unanswered. No one adequately questioned the fundamental criteria upon which the previous source-critical divisions had been made in Josh. 24:1-28. Earlier assertions that repetitions in the text, alleged grammatical difficulties, shifts in person or number, or different theological emphases could be employed to detect either parallel strands or later glossing and redacting of earlier tradition remained largely unchallenged. As a result, the conclusions of previous source criticism and textual criticism began to be used eclectically. It became commonplace to assert that Josh. 24:1-28 contained ancient tradition which had been heavily redacted and had undergone major revision at the hand of a Deuteronomist in order to give the passage its present place in the Dtistic history. These allegations of a secondary presence of a considerable portion of Dtistic material were ambiguous enough to allow Josh. 24:1-28 to be appealed to at times as evidence for ancient Northern traditions describing a covenant gathering at Shechem, while others could simultaneously assert that the heavily redacted Josh. 24 received its present shape and prominence precisely because of its value for the Dtistic history, which for many scholars entailed that it was added to Joshua as a secondary Dtistic addition.

There are multiple reasons why some of these presuppositions regarding sources and glosses could be influential for such a prolonged time period. The complexity of the chapter was universally acknowledged and stressed. Realizing this complexity, it would be precarious on the basis of such a difficult chapter to challenge long-standing methods of interpretation developed in other passages. In many previous treatments of Josh. 24, one senses a resignation to the possibility that the evidence regarding the chapter's provenance, structure and purpose might prove to be so complex and ambiguous that it would finally be impossible to come much closer to certainty on these matters. Moreover, Josh. 24:1-28 was usually handled either as part of the commentaries on Joshua, or as one of many passages treated in a given monograph. But to significantly advance the study, a more comprehensive and more detailed analysis would be necessary. Previous approaches were constrained by either a Hexateuchal scheme or a scheme of a consistent Dtistic history. For these reasons the actual extent of contradictions and incongruencies present in the previous history of interpretation has only been exposed in the most recent analyses. And perhaps most important of all, at the time of the studies up to and including those of von Rad and Noth, there did not yet exist an alternative method of interpretation which would necessarily call into question the fundamental tenets of the previous source-critical evaluations.

This picture changed dramatically with the introduction of the new treaty and covenant comparisons. Here, finally, there appeared to be an alternative method which could demonstrate the form and unity of the text rather than attempt a fragmentation into sources. Particularly influential in this area of research were, inter alia, Mendenhall, Baltzer, Beyerlin, L'Hour, Kline, and Kitchen. However, it soon became apparent that this new form-critical approach also produced ambiguous results. Scholars could not even agree on the extent to which Josh. 24:1-28 reflected the form of ancient NE treaty texts, let alone the implications this might entail for exegesis. And, once again, the reasons for this failure were multiple. The diversity of treaty texts entailed that there was not a single, unambiguous form with which to draw comparisons. Moreover, the comparison between biblical and extra-biblical texts was always a matter of correlating elements which were similar, never exactly identical. It was universally recognized that the biblical covenant accounts were not treaty documents. But how close did the similarities have to be to warrant comparison? This question became a matter of vigorous disagreement, and the manner in which it was answered often led to controversial conclusions. Studies by Weinfeld and McCarthy argued that the comparisons revealed significant points of contact. But they also claimed the absence of various elements considered indigenous and indispensable to the treaty form.

The failure of these form-critical analyses to provide convincing answers to the riddles of Josh. 24:1-28, along with the questions produced by a number of decades of intensive study of those matters generally falling under the category of Dtistic history, led to a reappraisal of Josh. 24:1-28 with a view to discerning the extent of Dtic or Dtistic influence upon the passage. The significance of such studies was heightened by the fact that there was a long-standing series of questions regarding the nature and antiquity of the covenant theology in Israel. Accordingly, numerous studies, climaxing especially in the work of Perlitt, questioned the antiquity of both Josh. 24:1-28 and the concept of a covenant relationship between Israel and Yahweh in general. The literary-critical conclusions by Perlitt that Josh. 24:1-28 is a Dtic composition influenced numerous attempts to defend an even later date—e.g., by Van Seters, Nicholson and Blum. However, Jaroš and Kreuzer, inter alia, while willing to accept much of Perlitt's literary criticism, argued that the passage contained at least a kernel of historical tradition not fabricated by a Dtic movement. On the other hand, the literary-critical conclusion by Perlitt that the language and theology is Dtic was vigorously challenged by a brief literary-critical reanalysis by Sperling.

In ch.2 of the present study the previous methods of treating Josh. 24:1-28 are subjected to a detailed scrutiny. It is argued that the incongruity of previous literary-critical dissections necessitates a rigorous re-evaluation of the criteria by which others have attempted to interpret this passage. Previous efforts in the areas of textual criticism, literary criticism, form criticism, archaeological comparisons, and structural analysis are therefore all re-evaluated.

Textual criticism has made significant advances in attempts to deal with the relationship between the LXX and the MT of Joshua. A growing consensus of opinion suggests that many of the pluses in the MT bear evidence that an originally shorter text has been expanded. Additional research in this area may help to clarify the relative weight of pluses and minuses in the MT and LXX respectively, which in turn will facilitate advancement beyond the previous situation in which commentators employed the various textual traditions far too eclectically.

With respect to literary criticism, it was argued that efforts to link Josh. 24:1-28 with an E, J or JE strand in the Pentateuch are not convincing. Also untenable is the theory that Josh. 24:1-28 is a late, Dtic or Dtistic composition. Similarly, the idea that a covenant theology first arose in Israel in the 7th century must be rejected upon the basis of the OT evidence.

Regarding form-critical comparisons with the treaty texts, particular attention was given to an evaluation of claims by Weinfeld and McCarthy. They suggested that similarities with the treaty form are undeniable but do not yet provide adequate explanations for the final form and structure of Josh. 24:1-28. Nor can they explain the passage's purpose, its connection to related passages in the Pentateuch or Dtistic history, its date, or its historical provenance. The present analysis argued that Weinfeld's methodology is adversely affected by a desire to show that Deuteronomy stands closer to a treaty form than does Josh. 24:1-28. Weinfeld's effort to classify produced a somewhat artificial distinction between the Sinaitic and Shechem covenants as examples of covenant by law and by vassalship respectively. Similarly, crucial weaknesses also surfaced in the scholarly treatment by McCarthy, whose analysis has been viewed by many as near definitive. For example, McCarthy's treatment of vs.22 is incorrect, and his assertion regarding the absence of an oath is unfounded. These weaknesses in the treatments by Weinfeld and McCarthy did not help to clarify the ambivalence of previous conclusions. Subsequent efforts in form criticism must advance beyond initial classification in order to account for both similarities and differences in the treaty and covenant texts. Moreover, the corpus of literature for comparison must be expanded beyond the treaty texts.

If previous methods of literary criticism and form criticism were inadequate to provide a satisfactory treatment, the situation was hardly rectified by an appeal to archaeological results at Shechem as a new means of attaining objective data by which to evaluate the historical value of Josh. 24:1-28 and related passages. Archaeological results at Shechem, illuminating as they are, do not answer the literary questions raised in an exegesis of Josh. 24:1-28.

Finally, it was demonstrated that all the various previous approaches appeal, whether implicitly or explicitly, to the literary form of the passage, be it with claims about a disrupted or glossed, sophisticated or simple, original or secondarily modified composition. Evidently, however, if such assertions regarding the form and structure of Josh. 24:1-28 are permitted to occupy a formative place in the passage's evaluation, it is imperative to employ a method of structural analysis based upon objectively verifiable criteria rather than on subjective opinions concerning what is aesthetically pleasing or whether "simple" structures are older than "sophisticated" ones. The necessity of developing a new method of structural analysis is exemplified by the contradictions arising in previous *ad hoc* opinions regarding literary unity or diversity. This need is reinforced by the inherent methodological weaknesses of previous studies of structure. Giblin's analysis of Josh. 24:1-28 on the basis of numerical schematizations, for example, neither adequately defined the boundaries of the literary unit to be treated nor demonstrated the validity of the method to be employed. An effort to develop a more objective structural analysis of Josh. 24:1-28 accordingly constitutes the agenda for the third chapter of the present volume.

Recently developed methods of analyzing OT poetry have demonstrated that careful attention to parallelism frequently facilitates a recognition of poetry in passages previously treated as prose. In the light of these methodological advancements, and the fact that there are numerous clues in Josh. 24:1-28 that its many repetitions may be structurally significant as stylistic devices, the present study argues that it is worth pursuing the possibility that Josh. 24:1-28 is representative of a particular genre of poetry, namely, poetic narrative. In defense of this novel thesis an introductory analysis of the relationship between poetry and prose is offered. A survey of the ever increasing recognition of previously unidentified poetry in biblical as well as extra-biblical literature is provided. Efforts to distinguish poetry from prose on the basis of metrical analysis or so-called prose particle counts are rejected as inadequate. A more defensible method must focus upon various types of parallelism, which can be exposed only via a colometric division of the text into cola, verses, strophes, canticles and cantos. A final evaluation of whether the text is poetic must be conducted upon the cumulative evidence produced at these various levels.

A colometric division of Josh. 24:1-28 is therefore presented in strict accordance with principles which have been previously developed in the analysis of Semitic poetry. In the opinion of the present writer, application of this approach to Josh. 24:1-28 produces results which are affirmative of a poetic identity. Treating the passage as if it were poetry reveals a high frequency of parallelism and word-pairs in Josh. 24:1-28. The defense of internal and external parallelism is supported in this analysis via recourse to previous studies identifying word-pairs and the employment of a computer concordance program to discern additional occurrences of a given parallelism in OT poetry.

On the basis of the Kampen method of structural analysis, Josh. 24:1-28 divides into strophes, canticles and cantos to produce a noteworthy uniformity of structural totals at the various poetic levels. It is composed of two cantos of five canticles each. The first canto (24:1-13) consists of the setting (24:1), followed by four canticles of historical summary: I.ii (24:2-4), dealing with the patriarchal period; I.iii (24:5-7), the exodus from Egypt; I.iv (24:8-10), conflict in Transjordan and with Jericho; I.v (24:12-13), acquisition of the land. In canticle I.v, detection of the literary structure of the canticle assists in reconstructing a text which has been universally recognized as a literary crux.

The second canto also divides into five clearly marked canticles: II.i (24:14-15), the imperative to put away other gods and serve Yahweh; II.ii (24:16-18), the people's confessional response; II.iii (24:19-21), Joshua's warning regarding the choice to serve Yahweh; II.iv (24:22-24), witnessing of the people's choice; II.v (24:25-28), the concluding covenantal ceremony. The correctness of these colometric divisions is reinforced by the resulting patterns of external parallelism, especially the emergence of confessional refrains terminating canticles II.i-II.iv. From the level of internal parallelism of the cola to the macrostructure of the entire cantos, Josh. 24:1-28 reveals characteristics which are typical of poetry. The preciseness of the resulting external parallelisms and repetitions cannot be coincidental.

However, since it is not desirable to base one's conclusions exclusively upon the MT—especially since numerous recent text-critical studies of the LXX suggest that the MT of Joshua often tends to expand an originally shorter version—the colometric division, justification, and analysis of macrostructure in the Masoretic text is followed by a detailed analysis of all pluses, minuses and other variations between the LXX and the MT. The most significant result of this investigation is the conclusion that those textual differences which cannot be attributed to either errors in transmission or harmonization by a translator reveal numerous examples where LXX pluses can with probability be retroverted to a Hebrew *Vorlage* testifying to a variant poetic edition honouring basically the same poetic structure attested in the MT. The theory of multiple editions of the same basic poetic structure, with minor variation of detail in emphasis, agrees entirely with the principle of poetic expansion and contraction attested in other parallel poetic traditions both in the OT and in extra-biblical literature. By this means, it is possible to explain, for example, why Josh. 24:5aA and 17aE-b can be poetic expansions which nevertheless function purposely in the internal and external parallelism of the present structure of the MT. Textual variants in vss.4,10,14,15,27,28 can also be explained on the basis of slightly divergent poetic editions.

The net results of this investigation of structure warrant the conclusion that Josh. 24:1-28 is *narrative poetry*. A distinction is hereby made from the type or genre of Psalmic poetry, which capitalizes more profusely upon employment of predominantly internal parallelism. In the justification of some of the word-pairs, as well as the claim that such a genre as poetic narrative did in fact exist, numerous comparisons are made with the Mesha inscription, which has been demonstrated by de Moor to also be a composition in narrative poetry, as can be seen in the scribe's own employment of vertical slashes to punctuate the end of the poetic verses.

In our search for additional texts proving the presence of a given word-pair or poetic parallelism, many additional verses of narrative poetry in the OT are identified. In ch.5 of our study more extensive comparison has been made with some of the related passages, a number of which can also profitably be read as poetic narrative. These results provide an important avenue for evaluating the literary form and content of the respective passages, and this approach promises to open a new means of tracing some of the literary relationships or connections between select texts. This also illustrates the fact that synchronic and diachronic concerns need not be mutually exclusive in a close reading of the text with a view to literary structure.

At this point an important caveat is warranted. The number of OT texts suggested in this study to belong to a category of narrative poetry[3] might create the impression that this method of analysis is thought to suddenly transform all OT prose into poetry. But this is certainly not the case. A valid claim that a given text is poetry can only be made after the passage has been successfully divided colometrically and the presence of parallelisms, word-pairs, and other phe-

[3]See the appendix listing passages treated in BHS as prose but viewed in this study as poetry.

nomena typical of OT poetry provide sufficient cumulative evidence to justify a conclusion that the text is in fact poetic. The Masoretic accents often can contribute to the endeavor to divide the text colometrically. A similar observation is valid regarding the *petuchah* and *setumah*. But it is surely false to conclude that all OT prose can by this method be scanned as poetry. Only detailed and extensive research will finally provide a more conclusive picture of the percentage of narrative poetry incorporated in the OT. Such research may be anticipated to bring important advancements in the present discussion of the extent to which OT history writing has been influenced by previous poetic traditions, traditions which are viewed by many as remnants of ancient epic. On the basis of the various samples of narrative poetry exposed in the present study, it is already clear that OT narrative poetry is not necessarily epic poetry.

In chs.4-6, building upon both previous research and our new approach to the passage as poetic narrative, we have refocused attention upon the matter of literary criticism, relationship to other biblical and extra-biblical material, and the historical value of this passage. Since our structural analysis revealed an intricate and well-balanced composition, which reinforces reservations about the legitimacy of dissecting the passage into sources in the manner of previous literary criticism, it was necessary to question whether a rigorous analysis of vocabulary would support recent assertions that the passage is either to be attributed to the hand of a Dtist or was radically reshaped by Dtistic editing. The conclusion became inescapable that there are many lexicoghraphical obstacles to the theory that Josh. 24:1-28 is either Dtic or Dtistic, or that it underwent major redaction from a Dtistic perspective. Therefore, our detailed analysis of vocabulary clearly supports the conclusion published by Sperling that recent attempts to explain Josh. 24:1-28 as Dtic or Dtistic are not convincing. This result is of considerable importance in an attempt to move beyond the ambivalence of previous attempts to determine the provenance of this difficult text.

A careful comparison of Josh. 24:2-13 with parallel material elsewhere in the OT shows that the historical survey is heavily dependent upon accounts now incorporated into Genesis, Exodus, and Numbers. Various central motifs of the Pentateuch, especially with regard to the patriarchs, worship of Yahweh, the themes of the exodus, and the gift of the land find a culmination and resolution in Josh. 24:1-28. This suggests that the present passage may have been deliberately intended to literarily complete those themes.

The matter is somewhat different when one pursues the influence of Josh. 24 upon select texts in Judges and 1 Samuel. It has been argued in this study that Judg. 2:6-10 is colometrically dependent upon Josh. 24:28-31. Furthermore, the poetic composition of Judg. 6:7-10 is directly dependent upon the poetic format of Josh. 24:2-24. This is significant because it demonstrates textual influence. Moreover, *the influence is of such a nature that it presupposes the poetic format of the respective passages.* Correlations such as these illustrate the valuable exegetical contribution derived from a new recognition of poetic structure. Judg. 6:7-10 has always been a riddle to commentators, but its origin becomes clearer once the colon for colon dependence upon Josh. 24:2-24 is exposed. The cumulative evidence of the influence exerted by Josh. 24:1-28 upon the present shape of numerous passages in Judges and 1 Samuel is important for establishing a relative date of composition. It is also important for tracing the progression of certain themes in the Dtistic history, both with respect to the exclusive worship of Yahweh and the concept of his kingship. The various textual affiliations elaborated in ch.5 suggest that justice cannot be done to Josh. 24:1-28 in either a strict adherence to classical theories of a Hexateuch or many present views of the composition of the so-called Dtistic history. The various comparisons which are facilitated by recognition of its poetic structure illustrate the important contribution that can be made by structural analyses, not only for discerning the present, synchronic structure of the text, but also for investigating the diachronic relationship of literarily dependent passages.

Recognition of the dependence of Josh. 24:1-28 upon what is now considered to be a J/E corpus in Genesis, Exodus, and Numbers on the one hand and its influence upon certain passages in Deuteronomy, Judges and Samuel on the other makes it possible to speak more accurately regarding a relative date of composition. This marks a considerable advancement over previous methods of dating on the basis of certain details abstracted from the cumulative evidence of the chapter as a whole.

Moreover, recognition of the literary structure of Josh. 24:1-28 provides new critieria by which to advance beyond previous form-critical comparisons with ancient NE treaty texts. The present study affirms the validity of such comparisons but stresses that both the similarities and the differences must be accounted for. Such comparison should be made not only with the treaties but also with other texts describing vassalage, loyalty oaths, land grants, and cultic festivals. Such comparisons produce results which coincide well with the poetic structure defended above.

On the basis of our findings in chs.1-5, it is possible to refocus questions concerning the historical value of Josh. 24:1-28. The fact that Josh. 24:1-28 is poetic narrative does not entail that it is of less historical value than if it had proven to be prose. The question of historical value is relevant to both the claim that a gathering took place at Shechem and the dialogue which is presented as having taken place there. However, since the dialogue is dependent upon material found elsewhere in the OT, it is advisable to treat the setting and the dialogue separately.

Archaeological and historical considerations support the contention that Shechem was an important center for early Israelite settlement. Demographic surveys and research regarding the pattern of Israelite settlement demonstrate the significance of the hill country of Ephraim and Manasseh in Israel's earliest history. This accords well with the location of a Yahwistic assembly at Shechem in the time of Joshua. Emphasis upon exclusive Yahwism in the time of Joshua is compatible with what can be deduced from both biblical and extra-biblical evidence. This contention can be supported by a study of the cultural, political and religious milieu of the LBA in Palestine, as well as a specific study of theophoric names in the OT.

The historical value of details in the dialogue can be summarized as follows. Patriarchal worship of other gods is supported by attested theophoric elements in various of the names. Greater caution than has often been the case must be exercised in an evaluation of the Shasu texts as possible proof of a LBA relationship between Yahweh and Seir. Conflict with Moabites in Transjordan at the time of the exodus is not disproven by archaeological data, but the very nature of the accounts makes historical verifiability a tenuous endeavour. Archaeological data from Tell Ḥesbān provide no support for the biblical account of a conflict with Sihon. Extra biblical evidence demonstrates that Og and the area of Bashan had an enduring association with the Rephaim. Since archaeological activity in Transjordan has not yet produced a clear picture, archaeological data must be employed with extreme caution in discussions of the historical value of the biblical traditions. Israel's conflict with the inhabitants of Jericho alluded to in Josh. 24:11 has at times been considered historically doubtful on the basis of Josh. 6, but such a conclusion depends upon a questionable methodology.

Employment of the term "Amorite" for groups in Transjordan and Cisjordan cannot be adequately explained by the theory that it is borrowed from the Neo-Assyrian idiom for "west" or "westerner". However, a possible relationship of the OT Amorites to people dispersed from Amurru at the end of the LBA is also uncertain in light of earlier Amorite groups in Palestine. Israel's early relationship with Egypt makes it unnecessary to look to the time of the exile for a plausible historical setting for Joshua's imperative to put away the gods which had been worshipped in Egypt.

The present treatment may finally prove to provide few if any definitive answers to the plethora of questions pertaining to the literary structure, history of transmission, date and historical value of Josh. 24:1-28. Hopefully it has been demonstrated that, by building upon the work of previous scholarship and by employing new methods of analysis, it is possible to advance the study of this fascinating chapter. It is to be readily acknowledged that the complexity of the issues treated and the vast quantity of literature relevant to these areas of research has entailed that our discussion of Josh. 24:1-28 as narrative poetry necessarily has left out of purview various other significant aspects of study which ultimately should be applied to this passage. For example, we have made only passing reference to the function which Josh. 24:1-28 may be presumed to have had in subsequent stages of Israel's worship. And insights to be gleaned from Josh. 24 with respect to the significance of kerygma in the OT[4] confront one with equally relevant concerns regarding the manner in which the message of this passage ought to be conveyed to God's people today, as a reassertion of the necessity for communal and individual pledging of fidelity to their one true God. Josh. 24:1-28 provides an important background for the instructions of Jesus regarding true worship (John 4:20-26).[5] As long as believers seek to worship the Father in spirit

[4]Cf. F.N.Jasper, "Preaching in the Old Testament," *The Expository Times* 80 (1968-69), 359.

[5]O.Betz, "'To Worship God in Spirit and in Truth': Reflections on John 4, 20-26," in A.Finkel–L.Fizzell, eds., *Standing Before God* (Fs J.M.Oesterreicher; New

and in truth, Josh. 24:1-28 will continue to challenge God's people to renew their commitment with the refrain:

| | |
|---|---|
| *gm-'nḥnw* | So as for us too, |
| *n'bd 't-yhwh* | we will serve Yahweh, |
| *ky-hw' 'lhynw* | for he is our God. |

York, 1981), 53-72.

# Appendix

Throughout this study, numerous OT passages have been treated as part of a wider genre of poetic narrative. For convenience we here provide a catalogue of passages which appear in BHS as prose but in the present volume are presented colometrically as narrative poetry.

Gen. 26:4 (192 n.95)
Gen. 35:2 (350)

Ex. 17:14-16[1] (424-427)
Ex. 34:27 (298)

Lev. 26:14-15 (220 n.282)

Deut. 7:12 (221 n.282)
Deut. 27:5-7 (354-356)
Deut. 29:9 (284)

Josh. 23:1-2[2] (396-397)
Josh. 24:1-28 (passim, esp. 165-270)
Josh. 24:28-31 (367-369)

Judg. 2:6-10 (363-369)
Judg. 6:7-10[3] (370-378)
Judg. 11:25 (200)

Ruth 4:9-11[4] (99-100)

1 Sam. 7:3 (387)
1 Sam. 10:17-18,24-25 (380-385)
1 Sam. 11:14-15 (388-390)
1 Sam. 12:5 (100)

1 Kings 12:4,7,10,11,16 (393-395)

[1]Discussed in conjunction with Althann's identification of 17:16 as poetry ("Unrecognized Poetic Fragments" 19-21).

[2]Following a previous analysis of Josh. 23:1-16 as narrative poetry (cf. Koopmans, "Joshua 23," 83-118).

[3]Cf. Boling's identification of 6:8c-9 as poetry (*Judges*, 124-127).

[4]Following de Moor's identification of the whole of Ruth as poetic narrative ("Book of Ruth, I," 262-283; "Book of Ruth, II," 16-46.).

# Selected Bibliography


AALDERS, G.CH. *Oud-Testamentische kanoniek.* Kampen, 1952.

ACKROYD, P.R.–LINDARS, B., eds. *Words and Meanings: Essays Presented to David Winton Thomas.* Cambridge, 1968.

AḤITUV, S. *Canaanite Toponyms in Ancient Egyptian Documents.* Jerusalem, 1984.

AHLSTRÖM, G.W. *Who Were the Israelites?* Winona Lake, 1986.

ALBERTZ, R. et al., eds. *Werden und Wirken des Alten Testaments. Festschrift für Claus Westermann zum 70. Geburtstag.* Göttingen, 1980.

ALBRIGHT, W.F. *From the Stone Age to Christianity.* Baltimore, 1946.

— . *Yahweh and the Gods of Canaan.* London, 1968.

ALONSO-ASENJO, J., "Investigación crítica sobre Jos 24,19-20. Análisis de tres expressiones raras y significativas," *EstBib* 32 (1973) 257-270.

ALONSO-SCHÖKEL, L. *A Manual of Hebrew Poetics.* (*Subsidia biblica* 11) Rome, 1988.

ALT, A. *Die Staatenbildung der Israeliten in Palästina.* Leipzig, 1930.

— . "Die Wallfahrt von Sichem nach Bethel," in *Piam memoriam A.von Bulmerincq.* Riga, 1938, 218-230 (= *Kleine Schriften,* 1:79-88).

— . *Kleine Schriften zur Geschichte des Volkes Israel.* 3 vols. München, 1953-59.

ALTER, R. *The Art of Biblical Narrative.* New York, 1981.

— . *The Art of Biblical Poetry.* New York, 1985.

ALTHANN, R. "Unrecognized Poetic Fragments in Exodus," *JNSL* 11 (1983) 9-27.

AMITAI, J., ed. *Biblical Archaeology Today: Proceedings of the International Congress on Biblical Archaeology, Jerusalem, April 1984.* Jerusalem, 1985.

ANBAR, M. "The Story about the Building of an Altar on Mount Ebal," in N.Lohfink, ed. *Das Deuteronomium. Entstehung, Gestalt und Botschaft.* (*BETL* 68) Leuven, 1985, 304-309.

ANDERSEN, F.I. *The Sentence in Biblical Hebrew.* The Hague and Paris, 1974.

ANDERSEN, F.I.–FORBES, A.D. "'Prose Particle' Counts of the Hebrew Bible," in C.L.Meyers and M.O'Connor, eds. *The Word of the Lord Shall Go Forth: Essays in Honor of David Noel Freedman in Celebration of His Sixtieth Birthday.* Winona Lake, 1983.

AUERBACH, E. "Die grosse Überarbeitung der biblischen Bücher," in *Congress Volume, Copenhagen 1953.* (*SVT* 1) Leiden, 1953, 1-10.

AUGUSTIN, M. AND SCHUNCK, K.-D., eds. *"Wünschet Jerusalem Frieden": Collected Communications to the XIIth Congress of the International Organization for the Study of the Old Testament, Jerusalem 1986.* Frankfurt am Main, 1988.

AULD, A.G. "Textual and Literary Studies in the Book of Joshua," *ZAW* 90 (1978) 412-417.
— . "Joshua: The Hebrew and Greek Texts," in J.A.Emerton, ed. *Studies in the Historical Books of the Old Testament.* (*SVT* 30) Leiden, 1979, 1-14.
— . *Joshua, Moses and the Land.* Edinburgh, 1980.
AVISHUR, Y. "Word Pairs Common to Phoenician and Biblical Hebrew," *UF* 7 (1975) 13-47.
— . *Stylistic Studies of Word-Pairs in Biblical and Ancient Semitic Literatures.* (*AOAT* 210) Neukirchen-Vluyn, 1984.
BALTZER, K. *Das Bundesformular, sein Ursprung und seine Verwendung im Alten Testament.* (*WMANT* 4) Neukirchen, 1960 (= *The Covenant Formulary in Old Testament, Jewish and Early Christian Writings.* Oxford, 1971).
BEGRICH, J. "Berit. Ein Beitrag zur Erfassung einer alttestamentlichen Denkform," *ZAW* 60 (1944) 1-11.
BEN-BARAK, Z. "The Mizpah Covenant (I Sam 10:25)–The Source of the Israelite Monarchic Covenant," *ZAW* 91 (1979) 30-43.
BERLIN, A. *The Dynamics of Biblical Parallelism.* Bloomington, 1985.
BETTENZOLI, G. "Gli 'Anziani di Israele'," *Bibl* 64 (1983) 47-73.
— . "Gli 'Anziani' in Giuda," *Bibl* 64 (1983) 211-224.
BEYERLIN, W. *Herkunft und Geschichte der ältesten Sinaitraditionen.* Tubingen, 1961 (= *Origins and History of the Oldest Sinaitic Traditions.* Oxford, 1965).
— . "Gattung und Herkunft des Rahmens im Richterbuch," in E.Würthwein and O.Kaiser, eds. *Tradition und Situation. Studien zur alttestamentlichen Prophetie.* (Fs A.Weiser) Göttingen, 1963, 1-29.
— . "Geschichte und Heilsgeschichtliche Traditionsbildung im Alten Testament," *VT* 13 (1963) 1-25.
BIRAN, A. ed. *Temples and High Places in Biblical Times.* Jerusalem, 1981.
BLENKINSOPP, J. "Are There Traces of the Gibeonite Covenant in Deuteronomy," *CBQ* 28 (1966) 207-219.
DE BOER, P.A.H. "Vive le roi!" *VT* 5 (1955) 225-231.
BOLING, R.G. "'Synonymous' Parallelism in the Psalms," *JSS* 5 (1960) 221-255.
— . *Judges.* (*AB* 7) New York, 1975.
— . *Joshua: A New Translation with Notes and Commentary.* (*AB* 6) New York, 1982.
— . *The Early Biblical Community in Transjordan.* Sheffield, 1988.
BREKELMANS, C.H.W. "Exodus xviii and the Origins of Yahwism in Israel," (*OTS* 10) Leiden, 1954, 215-224.
— . "Het 'historische credo' van Israel," *TvT* 3 (1963) 1-11.

— . "Die sogenannten deuteronomischen Elemente in Gen.–Num. Ein Beitrag zur Vorgeschichte des Deuteronomiums," in *Volume du congrès Genève 1965.* (*SVT* 15) Leiden, 1966, 90-96.

— . "Joshua XXIV: Its Place and Function," (forthcoming).

BREKELMANS, C.H.W., ed. *Questions disputées d'Ancien Testament. Méthode et Theologie. 23e session des Journées Bibliques de Louvain.* (*BETL* 33) Gembloux, 1974.

BRIGHT, J. *Covenant and Promise: The Prophetic Understanding of the Future in Pre-Exilic Israel.* Philadelphia, 1976.

BRONGERS, H.A. "Bemerkungen zum Gebrauch des Adverbialen *We'attāh* im Alten Testament," *VT* 15 (1965) 289-299.

BROWNLEE, W.H. "The Aftermath of the Fall of Judah According to Ezekiel," *JBL* 89 (1970) 393-404.

BRUEGEMANN, W. "Amos iv 4-13 and Israel's Covenant Worship," *VT* 15 (1965) 1-15.

BUCCELLATI, G. "The Enthronement of the King and the Capital City in Texts from Ancient Mesopotamia and Syria," in *Studies Presented to A. Leo Oppenheim.* Chicago, 1964, 54-61.

BUIS, P. "Les formulaires d'alliance," *VT* 16 (1966) 396-411.

BUSS, M.J. "The Covenant Theme in Historical Perspective," *VT* 16 (1966) 502-504.

BUTLER, T.C. *Joshua.* (*WBC* 7) Waco, 1983.

CALVIN, J. *Commentaries on the Book of Joshua.* Translated by H.Beveridge, Grand Rapids, 1949.

CAMPBELL, A.F. *Of Prophets and Kings: A Late Ninth-Century Document (1 Samuel 1–2 Kings 10).* (*CBQMS* 17) Washington, 1986.

CAMPBELL, E.F. "The Amarna Letters and the Amarna Period," *BA* 23 (1960) 2-22.

— . "Shechem in the Amarna Archive," in G.E.Wright, *Shechem: The Biography of a Biblical City.* New York, 1965, 191-207.

— . "Moses and the Foundations of Israel," *Interp* 29 (1975) 141-154.

— . "Two Amarna Notes: The Shechem City State and Amarna Administrative Terminology," in F.M.Cross et al., eds. *Magnalia Dei: The Mighty Acts of God.* New York, 1976, 39-54.

— . "Judges 9 and Biblical Archaeology," in C.L.Meyers and M.O'Connor, eds. *The Word of the Lord Shall Go Forth.* Winona Lake, 1983, 263-271.

CAMPBELL, E.F.–ROSS, J.F. "The Excavation of Shechem and the Biblical Tradition," *BA* 26 (1963) 2-27.

CASSUTO, U. *A commentary on the Book of Genesis.* 2 vols. Translated by I.Abrahams. Jerusalem, 1961-64. [Heb. orig. 1944-49].

— . *Biblical and Oriental Studies.* 2 vols. Translated by I.Abrahams. Jerusalem, 1973-75.

CHILDS, B.S. "Deuteronomic Formulae of the Exodus Traditions," in *Hebräische Wortforschung.* Fs W.Baumgartner. (*SVT* 16) Leiden, 1967, 30-39.

— . *Biblical Theology in Crisis.* Philadelphia, 1970.

— . *The Book of Exodus: A Critical, Theological Commentary.* (*OTL*) Philadelphia, 1974.

CLINES, D.J.A. "The Parallelism of Greater Precision,"in E.R.Follis, ed. *Directions in Biblical Hebrew Poetry.* (*JSOTS* 40) Sheffield, 1987, 77-100.

— . *The Theme of the Pentateuch.* Sheffield, 1978.

COATS, G.W., "The Traditio-Historical Character of the Reed Sea Motif," *VT* 17 (1967) 253-265.

COHN, R.L. "Literary Technique in the Jeroboam Narrative," *ZAW* 97 (1985) 23-35.

— . "The Conquest and Early Hebrew Poetry," *TB* 20 (1969) 76-94.

— . *The Book of Deuteronomy.* (*NICOT*) Grand Rapids, 1976.

CRISLER, B.C. "The Acoustics and Crowd Capacity of Natural Theaters in Palestine," *BA* 39 (1976) 128-141.

CROSS, F.M. *Canaanite Myth and Hebrew Epic.* Cambridge, MA., 1973.

— . "The Epic Traditions of Early Israel," in R.E.Friedman, ed. *The Poet and the Historian: Essays in Literary and Historical Biblical Criticism.* (*HSS* 26) Chico, CA, 1983, 13-39.

— . "Biblical Archaeology Today: The Biblical Aspect," in J.Amitai, ed. *Biblical Archaeology Today.* Jerusalem, 1985, 9-15.

CROSS, F.M., ed. *Symposia Celebrating the Seventy-fifth Anniversary of the Founding of the American Schools of Oriental Research (1900-1975).* Cambridge, MA, 1979.

CROSS, F.M.–FREEDMAN, D.N. "The Song of Miriam," *JNES* 14 (1955) 237-250.

— . "Some Observations on Early Hebrew," *Bibl* 53 (1972) 413-420.

— . *Studies in Ancient Yahwistic Poetry.* (*SBL Diss* 21) Reprint ed. Missoula, 1975.

CROSS, F.M. et al., eds. *Magnalia Dei: The Mighty Acts of God.* New York, 1976.

DAHOOD, M. *Psalms.* 3 vols. (*AB* 16, 17, 17a) Garden City, NY, 1966-1970.

— . "Ugaritic-Hebrew Parallel Pairs, II," in L.R.Fisher, ed. *RSP, II.* (*AnOr* 50) Rome, 1975, 1-39.

— . "Ugaritic-Hebrew Parallel Pairs," in S.Rummel, ed. *RSP, III.* (*AnOr* 51) Rome, 1981, 1-206.

— . "The Minor Prophets and Ebla," in C.L.Meyers–M.O'Connor, eds. *The Word of the Lord Shall Go Forth.* Winona Lake, 1983, 47-67.

DAHOOD, M.–PENAR, T. "Ugaritic-Hebrew Parallel Pairs," in L.R.Fisher, ed. *RSP, I.* (*AnOr* 49) Rome, 1972, 71-382.

DANIELS, D.R. *Hosea and Salvation History: The Early Traditions of Israel in the Prophecy of Hosea.* Hamburg, 1987.

DEVER, W.G. "The Patriarchal Traditions," in J.H. Hayes–J.M. Miller, eds. *Israelite and Judaean History.* London, 1977, 70-120.

—. "The Contribution of Archaeology to the Study of Canaanite and Early Israelite Religion," in P.D.Miller et al., eds. *Ancient Israelite Religion.* Philadelphia, 1987, 209-247.

DILLMANN, A. *Numeri, Deuteronomium und Josua.* 2nd ed. (*KeH* 13) Leipzig, 1886.

DONNER, H. "Balaam Pseudopropheta," in H.Donner et al., eds. *Beiträge zur Alttestamentlichen Theologie.* Göttingen, 1977, 112-123.

DONNER, H. et al., ed. *Beiträge zur Alttestamentlichen Theologie.* (Fs W.Zimmerli) Göttingen, 1977

DURHAM, J.I.–PORTER, J.R., eds. *Proclamation and Presence: Old Testament Essays in Honour of G.H.Davies.* London, 1970.

EICHRODT, W. "Bund und Gesetz. Erwägungen zur neueren Diskussion" in H.Graf Reventlow, ed. *Gottes Wort und Gottes Land.* Fs H.W.Hertzberg. Göttingen, 1965, 30-49 (= "Covenant and Law: Thoughts on Recent Discussion," *Interp* 20 [1966] 302-321).

—. "Darf man heute noch von einem Gottesbund mit Israel reden?" *ThZ* 30 (1974) 193-206.

—. *Theology of the Old Testament.* 2 vols. Translated by J.A.Baker. (*OTL*) Philadelphia, 1961, 1967.

EISSFELDT, O. *Hexateuch-Synopse: Die Erzählung der fünf Bücher Mose und des Buches Josua mit dem Anfange des Richterbuches.* Leipzig, 1922; reprinted Darmstadt, 1962.

—. "El and Yahweh," *JSS* 1 (1956) 25-37.

—. "Jakobs Begegnung mit El und Moses Begegnung mit Jahwe," *OLZ* 58 (1963) 325-331.

—. *Einleitung in das Alte Testament.* 3rd ed. Tübingen, 1964 (= *The Old Testament: An Introduction.* Translated by P.A.Ackroyd. Oxford, 1965).

—. "Gilgal or Shechem?", in J.I.Durham and J.R.Porter, eds. *Proclamation and Presence.* London, 1970, 90-101.

ELLIGER, K. *Leviticus.* (*HAT* 4) Tübingen, 1966.

EMERTON, J.A., ed. *Congress Volume Jerusalem 1986.* (*SVT* 40) Leiden, 1988.

FENSHAM, F.CH. "Malediction and Benediction in Ancient Near Eastern Vassal-Treaties and the Old Testament," *ZAW* 74 (1962) 1-9.

—. "Clauses of Protection in Hittite Vassal-Treaties and the Old Testament" *VT* 13 (1963) 133-143.

—. "Psalm 21–A Covenant-Song?" *ZAW* 77 (1965) 193-202.

—. "Covenant, Promise and Expectation in the Bible," *ThZ* 23 (1967) 305-322.

—. "Notes on Treaty Terminology in Ugaritic Epics," *UF* 11 (1979) 265-274.

—. "The Marriage Metaphor in Hosea for the Covenant Relationship between the Lord and His People (Hos. 1:2-9)," *JNSL* 12 (1984) 71-78.

FINKELSTEIN, I. *The Archaeology of the Israelite Settlement.* Jerusalem, 1988.

—. "The Emergence of the Monarchy in Israel: The Environmental and Socio-Economic Aspects," *JSOT* 44 (1989) 43-74.

FISHBANE, M. "The Treaty Background of Amos 1:11 and Related Matters," *JBL* 89 (1970) 313-318.

FLOSS, J.P. *Jahwe dienen–Göttern dienen. Terminologische, literarische und semantische Untersuchung einer theologischen Aussage zum Gottesverhältnis im Alten Testament.* (*BBB* 45) Köln-Bonn, 1975.

FOHRER, G. "Der Vertrag zwischen König und Volk in Israel," *ZAW* 71 (1959) 1-22.

—. "Altes Testament–'Amphiktyonie' und 'Bund'?" *ThLZ* 91 (1966) 801-816, 893-904.

FOLLIS, E.R., ed. *Directions in Biblical Hebrew Poetry.* (*JSOTS* 40) Sheffield, 1987.

FOWLER, M.D. "A Closer Look at the 'Temple of El-Berith' at Shechem," *PEQ* 115 (1983) 49-53.

FRANK, H.T.–REED, W.L., eds. *Translating and Understanding the Old Testament: Essays in Honor of H.G.May.* Nashville and New York, 1970.

FRANKENA, R. "The Vassal-Treaties of Esarhaddon and the Dating of Deuteronomy," (*OTS* 14) Leiden, 1965, 122-154.

—. "Some Observations on the Semitic Background of Chapters XXIX-XXXI of the Book of Genesis," in *The Witness of Tradition.* (*OTS* 17) Leiden, 1972, 53-64.

FREEDMAN, D.N. "Archaic Forms in Early Hebrew Poetry," *ZAW* 72 (1960) 101-107.

FREEDMAN, D.N.–GRAF, D.F., eds. *Palestine in Transition: The Emergence of Ancient Israel.* Sheffield, 1983.

GARCIA-TRETO, F.O. "Genesis 31:44 and 'Gilead'," *ZAW* 79 (1967) 13-17.

GELLER, S.A., *Parallelism in Early Biblical Poetry.* (*HSM* 20) Missoula, 1979.

DE GEUS, C.H.J. "De richteren van Israël," *NThT* 20 (1965-66) 81-100.

GEVIRTZ, S. "On Canaanite Rhetoric: The Evidence of the Amarna Letters from Tyre," *Or* 42 (1973) 162-177.

—. "Evidence of Conjugational Variation in the Parallelization of Selfsame Verbs in the Amarna Letters," *JNES* 32 (1973) 99-104.

GIBLIN, C.H. "Structural Patterns in Jos 24:1-25," *CBQ* 26 (1964) 50-69.

GIBSON, J.C.L. "Light from Mari on the Patriarchs," *JSS* 7 (1962) 44-62.
— . *Textbook of Syrian Semitic Inscriptions.* 3 vols. Oxford, 1971-1982.
GIVEON, R. *The Impact of Egypt on Canaan.* (*OBO* 20) Göttingen, 1978.
GOEDICKE, H., ed. *Perspectives on the Battle of Kadesh.* Baltimore, 1985.
GOETZE, A. *Die Annalen des Muršiliš.* (*MVÄG* 38) Leipzig, 1933.
GORDIS, R. *Poets, Prophets, and Sages: Essays in Biblical Interpretation.* Bloomington and London, 1971.
GORDON, C.H. *Before the Bible: The Common Background of Greek and Hebrew Civilisations.* London, 1962.
GRAY, G.B. *The Forms of Hebrew Poetry.* Oxford, 1915; reprinted New York, 1972.
GRAY, J. *The Legacy of Canaan.* 2nd ed. (*SVT* 5) Leiden, 1965.
— . *Joshua, Judges, Ruth.* Revised ed. (*NCBC*) Basingstoke and Grand Rapids, 1986.
GREENSPOON, L.J. *Textual Studies in the Book of Joshua.* (*HSM* 28) Chico, CA, 1983.
GRESSMANN, H. *Die Anfänge Israels. Die Schriften des Alten Testaments,* I/2. Göttingen, 1922.
GÜTERBOCK, H.G. "Hittite Historiography: A Survey," in H.Tadmor and M.Weinfeld, *History, Historiography and Interpretation.* Jerusalem and Leiden, 1983, 21-35.
GURNEY, O.R. *Some Aspects of Hittite Religion.* Oxford, 1977.
HALBE, J. *Das Privilegrecht Jahwes Exodus 34,10-26. Gestalt und Wesen, Herkunft und Wirken in vordeuteronomischer Zeit.* Göttingen, 1975.
HALDAR, A. *Who Were the Amorites?* Leiden, 1971.
HALLO, W.W. et al., eds. *Scripture in Context II: More Essays on the Comparative Method.* Winona Lake, 1983.
HALPERN, B. *The Emergence of Israel in Canaan.* Chico, 1983.
HARRELSON, W. "Shechem in Extra-Biblical References," *BA* 20 (1957) 2-10.
HARRISON, R.K. *Introduction to the Old Testament.* Grand Rapids, 1969.
HARVEY, J. *Le plaidoyer prophétique contre Israël après la rupture de l'alliance.* (*Studia* 22) Montreal, 1967.
HATCH, E.–REDPATH, H.A. *A Concordance to the Septuagint.* Oxford, 1897; reprinted Grand Rapids, 1983.
HAYES, J.H.–MILLER, J.M., eds. *Israelite and Judaean History.* (*OTL*) London, 1977.
HEMPEL, J.–ROST, L., eds. *Von Ugarit nach Qumran.* (*BZAW* 77) Berlin, 1958.
HERTZBERG, H.W. *Die Bücher Josua, Richter, Ruth.* (*ATD* 9) Göttingen, 1953.
HILLERS, D.R. *Treaty-Curses and the Old Testament Prophets.* Rome, 1964.

—. *Covenant: The History of a Biblical Idea.* Baltimore, 1969.
HÖLSCHER, G. *Geschichtsschreibung in Israel. Untersuchungen zum Jahwisten und Elohisten.* Lund, 1952.
HOFTIJZER, J. *The Function and Use of the Imperfect Forms with Nun Paragogicum.* Assen, 1985.
HOLMES, S. *Joshua: The Hebrew and Greek Texts.* Cambridge, 1914.
HOLZINGER, H. *Einleitung in den Hexateuch.* 2 vols. Freiburg and Leipzig, 1893.
—. *Das Buch Josua.* (*KHC*) Leipzig and Tübingen, 1901.
HORN, S.H. "Scarabs from Shechem I," *JNES* 21 (1962) 1-14.
—. "Scarabs and Scarab Impressions from Shechem II," *JNES* 25 (1966) 48-56.
—. "Scarabs and Scarab Impressions from Shechem III," *JNES* 32 (1973) 281-289.
L'HOUR, J. "L'alliance de Sichem," *RB* 69 (1962) 5-36, 161-184, 350-368.
—. *La morale de l'alliance.* (*Cahiers de la RB* 5) Paris, 1966.
HUFFMON, H.B. "The Exodus, Sinai and the Credo," *CBQ* 27 (1965) 101-113.
—. "The Treaty Background of Hebrew *YĀDA'*," *BASOR* 181 (1966) 31-37.
HULST, A.R. "Opmerkingen over de *ka'ašer*-zinnen in Deuteronomium," *NThT* 18 (1963-64) 337-361.
JAPHET, S., ed. *Studies in the Bible (1986).* (*ScH* 31) Jerusalem, 1986.
JAROŠ, K. *Sichem. Eine archäologische und religionsgeschichtliche Studie mit besonderer Berücksichtigung von Jos 24.* (*OBO* 11) Göttingen, 1976.
JAROŠ, K.–DECKERT, B. *Studien zur Sichem-Aera.* (*OBO* 11a) Göttingen, 1977.
JENNI, E.–WESTERMANN, C., eds. *Theologisches Handwörterbuch zum Alten Testament.* 2 vols. 4th ed. München and Zürich, 1984.
JEPSEN, A. "Berith. Ein Beitrag zur Theologie der Exilseit," in A.Kuschke, ed. *Verbannung und Heimkehr: Beiträge zur Geschichte und Theologie Israels im 6. und 5. Jahrhundert v. Chr.* (Fs W.Rudolph) Tübingen, 1961, 161-179.
JOHAG, I. "*twb*–Terminus Technicus in Vertrags- und Bundisformularen des Alten Orients und des Alten Testaments," in H.-J.Fabry, ed. *Bausteine Biblischer Theologie.* (Fs G.J.Botterweck; *BBB* 50) Köln-Bonn, 1977, 3-23.
KALLAI, Z. *Historical Geography of the Bible: The Tribal Territories of Israel.* Jerusalem and Leiden, 1986.
KALLUVEETTIL, P. *Declaration and Covenant: A Comprehensive Review of Covenant Formulae from the Old Testament and the Ancient Near East.* (*AnBibl* 88) Rome, 1982.
KANG, S.-M. *Divine War in the Old Testament and in the Ancient Near East.* (*BZAW* 177) Berlin and New York, 1989.

KAPELRUD, A.S. "The Prophets and the Covenant," in W.B.Barrick and J.R.Spencer, eds. *In the Shelter of Elyon: Essays on Ancient Palestinian Life and Literature.* (*JSOTS* 31) Sheffield, 1984.
KARGE, P. *Geschichte des Bundesgedankens im Alten Testament.* Münster, 1910.
KEIL, C.F.–DELITZSCH, F. *Joshua, Judges, Ruth.* Translated by J. Martin. Grand Rapids, 1950.
KITCHEN, K.A. *Ancient Orient and Old Testament.* London, 1966.
—. "Historical Method and Early Hebrew Tradition," *TB* 17 (1966) 63-97.
—. "Ancient Orient, 'Deuteronism,' and the Old Testament," in J.B.Payne, ed. *New Perspectives on the Old Testament.* Waco, 1970, 1-24.
—. *The Bible in its World.* Downers Grove, 1977.
—. "Egypt, Ugarit, Qatna and Covenant," *UF* 11 (1979) 453-464.
KLENGEL, H. "Die Rolle der 'Ältesten' (LU$^{MES}$ŠU.GI) im Kleinasien der Hethiterzeit," *ZA* 57 (1965) 223-236.
KLINE, M.G. "Abram's Amen," *WTJ* 31 (1968-69) 1-11.
—. *The Structure of Biblical Authority.* Revised ed. Grand Rapids, 1975.
KNIERIM, R. *Die Hauptbegriffe für Sünde im Alten Testament.* Gütersloh, 1965.
KOCH, K. "*păḥăd jiṣḥaq* – eine Gottesbezeichnung?" in R.Albertz et al., eds. *Werden und Wirken des Alten Testaments.* (Fs C.Westermann) Göttingen, 1980, 107-115.
KOOPMANS, W.T. "The Poetic Prose of Joshua 23," in W.van der Meer and J.C.de Moor, eds. *The Structural Analysis of Biblical and Canaanite Poetry.* (*JSOTS* 74) Sheffield, 1988, 83-118.
—. "Psalm 78, Canto D – A Response," *UF* 20 (1988) 121-123.
—. "The Testament of David in 1 Kings ii 1-10," (forthcoming in *VT*).
KOROŠEC, V. *Hethitische Staatsverträge. Ein Beitrag zu ihrer juristischen Wertung. Leipziger rechtswissenschaftliche Studien* 60. Leipzig, 1931.
KORPEL, M.C.A.–DE MOOR, J.C. "Fundamentals of Ugaritic and Hebrew Poetry," *UF* 18 (1986) 173-212.
KRAETZSCHMAR, R., *Die Bundesvorstellung im Alten Testament in ihrer geschichtlichen Entwickelung untersucht und dargestellt.* Marburg, 1896.
KRAŠOVEC, J. *Der Merismus im Biblisch-hebräischen und Nordwestsemitischen.* (*BiblOr* 33) Rome, 1977.
—. "Merism–Polar Expression in Biblical Hebrew," *Bibl* 64 (1983) 231-239.
—. *Antithetic Structures in Biblical Hebrew Poetry.* (*SVT* 35) Leiden, 1984.
KRAUS, H.-J. "Gilgal: Ein Beitrag zur Kultusgeschichte Israels," *VT* 1 (1951) 181-199.
—. *Gottesdienst in Israel: Grundriss einer Geschichte des alttestamentlichen Gottesdienstes.* (*Beiträge zur evangelische Theologie* 19) München, 1954 (= *Worship in Israel.* Oxford, 1966).
—. "Gottesdienst im alten und im neuen Bund," *EvTh* 25 (1965) 172-174.

KREUZER, S. *Die Frühgeschichte Israels in Bekenntnis und Verkündigung des Alten Testaments.* (*BZAW* 178) Berlin, 1989.

KSELMAN, J.S. "Semantic-Sonant Chiasmus in Biblical Poetry," *Bibl* 58 (1977) 219-223.

—. "The Recovery of Poetic Fragments from the Pentateuchal Priestly Source," *JBL* 97 (1978) 161-173.

KÜHLEWEIN, J. *Geschichte in den Psalmen.* Stuttgart, 1973.

KÜLLING, S.R. *Zur Datierung der "Genesis-P-Stücke," namentlich des Kapitels Genesis XVII.* Kampen, 1964.

KUENEN, A. "Bijdragen tot de critiek van Pentateuch en Jozua: V. De godsdienstige vergadering by Ebal en Gerizim (Deut. XI:29,30; XXVII; Joz. VIII:30-35)," *ThT* 12 (1878) 297-323.

—. "Bijdragen tot de critiek van Pentateuch en Jozua. VIII, Israel bij den Sinai" *ThT* 15 (1881) 164-223.

—. *Historisch-critisch onderzoek naar het ontstaan en de verzameling van de boeken des ouden verbonds.* 2 vols. 2nd ed. Leiden, 1887-89.

KUGEL, J.L. *The Idea of Biblical Poetry: Parallelism and Its History.* New Haven and London, 1981.

KUTSCH, E. "Der Begriff *bryt* in vordeuteronomischer Zeit," in F.Maass, ed. *Das Ferne und Nahe Wort,*. (Fs L.Rost; *BZAW* 105) Berlin, 1967, 133-143.

—. "Gesetz und Gnade: Probleme des alttestamentlichen Bundesbegriffs," *ZAW* 79 (1967) 18-35.

—. "Von *bryt* zu 'Bund'," *KuD* 14 (1968) 159-182.

—. "'Bund' und Fest. Zu Gegenstand und Terminologie einer Forschungsrichtung," *TheolQuart* 150 (1970) 299-320.

—. "*Bryt* Verpflichtung," *THAT*, 1:339-352.

—. *Verheissung und Gesetz. Untersuchungen zum sogenannten "Bund" im Alten Testament.* (*BZAW* 131) Berlin, 1973.

LABUSCHAGNE, C.J. "Divine Speech in Deuteronomy," in N.Lohfink, ed. *Das Deuteronomium.* (*BETL* 68) Leuven, 1985, 111-126.

LAURENTIN, A. "*We'attah–Kai nun.* Formule caractéristique des textes juridiques et liturgiques," *Bibl* 45 (1964) 168-197, 413-432.

LEMCHE, N.P. *Early Israel: Anthropological and Historical Studies on the Israelite Society Before the Monarchy.* (*SVT* 37) Leiden, 1985.

DE LIAGRE BÖHL, F.M.TH. *De opgraving van Sichem. Bericht over de voorjaarscampagne en de zomercampagne in 1926.* Zeist, 1927.

LIPIŃSKI, E. *La royauté de Yahwé dans la poésie et le culte de l'ancien Israël.* 2nd ed. Brussels, 1968.

—. "*B'ḥryt hymym* dans les textes préexiliques," *VT* 20 (1970) 445-450.

LIVERANI, M. "The Amorites," in D.J.Wiseman, ed. *Peoples of Old Testament Times.* Oxford, 1973, 100-133.

LOEWENSTAMM, S.E. "*Šopeṭ* and *Šebāṭ*," in *Comparative Studies in Biblical and Ancient Oriental Literatures.* (*AOAT* 204) Neukirchen-Vluyn, 1980, 270-272

LOHFINK, N. "Zum 'kleinen geschichtlichen Credo' Dtn. 26,5-9," *ThPh* 46 (1971) 19-39.

LOHFINK, N., ed. *Das Deuteronomium. Entstehung, Gestalt und Botschaft.* (*BETL* 68) Leuven, 1985.

LORETZ, O. *Der Prolog des Jesaja Buches (1,1-2,5). Ugaritiologische und kolometrische Studien zum Jesaja-buch.* (*UBL* 1) Altenberge, 1984.

—. "Kolometrie ugaritischer und hebraischer Poesie," *ZAW* 98 (1986) 249-266.

LUCAS, E.C. "Covenant, Treaty, and Prophecy," *Themelios* 8 (1982) 19-23.

VAN DER LUGT, P. *Strofische structuren in de bijbels-hebreeuwse poëzie.* Kampen, 1980.

MCCARTHY, D.J. "Three Covenants in Genesis," *CBQ* 26 (1964) 179-189.

—. "Covenant in the Old Testament: The Present State of Inquiry," *CBQ* 27 (1965) 217-240.

—. *Old Testament Covenant: A Survey of Current Opinions.* Oxford, 1972.

—. "*Berît* in Old Testament History and Theology," *Bibl* 53 (1972) 110-121.

—. "*Bryt* and Covenant in the Deuteronomistic History," in *Studies in the Religion of Ancient Israel.* (*SVT* 23) Leiden, 1972, 65-85.

—. *Treaty and Covenant: A Study in Form in the Ancient Oriental Documents and in the Old Testament.* 2nd ed. (AnBib 21A) Rome 1978.

MALAMAT, A. "Mari," BA 34 (1971) 2-22.

MAYES, A.D.H. *The Story of Israel between Settlement and Exile: A Redactional Study of the Deuteronomistic History.* London, 1983.

MAYS, J.L. *Hosea.* (*OTL*) Philadelphia, 1969.

MAZAR, B. "Yahweh Came Out from Sinai," in A.Biran, ed. *Temples and High Places in Biblical Times.* Jerusalem, 1981, 5-9.

VAN DER MEER, W. *Oude woorden worden nieuw. De opbouw van het boek Joël.* Kampen, 1989.

VAN DER MEER, W.–DE MOOR, J.C., eds. *The Structural Analysis of Biblical and Canaanite Poetry.* (*JSOTS* 74) Sheffield, 1988.

MELAMED, E.Z. "Break-up of Stereotype Phrases as an Artistic Device in Biblical Poetry," in Ch.Rabin, ed. *Studies in the Bible.* (*ScH* 8) Jerusalem, 1961, 115-153.

MENDENHALL, G.E. *Law and Covenant in Israel and the Ancient Near East.* Pittsburgh, 1955 (reprinted from *BA* 17 [1954] 26-46, 50-76).

—. "Covenant," *IDB*, Vol. 1. Abingdon, 1967, 716.

METTINGER, T.N.D. *King and Messiah: The Civil and Sacral Legitimation of the Israelite Kigns.* (*CB OTS* 8) Lund, 1976.

MEYER, E. "Kritik der Berichte über die Eroberung Palaestinas (Num. 20,14 bis Jud. 2,5)," *ZAW* 1 (1881) 117-146.
— . *Die Israeliten und ihre Nachbarstämme.* Halle, 1906.
MEYER, R. "Bemerkungen zu den hebräischen Aussprachetraditionen von Chirbet Qumrān," *ZAW* 70 (1958) 39-48.
MEYERS, C.L.–O'CONNOR, M., eds. *The Word of the Lord Shall Go Forth: Essays in Honor of David Noel Freedman in Celebration of His Sixtieth Birthday.* Winona Lake, 1983.
MICHEL, D. "Studien zu den sogenannten Thronbesteigungspsalmen," *VT* 6 (1956) 40-68.
MILLARD, A.R. "An Assessment of the Evidence for Writing in Ancient Israel," in J.Amitai, ed. *Biblical Archaeology Today.* Jerusalem, 1985, 301-312.
MILLER, P.D. et al., eds. *Ancient Israelite Religion: Essays in Honor of Frank Moore Cross.* Philadelphia, 1987.
MÖHLENBRINK, K. "Die Landnahmesagen des Buches Josua," *ZAW* 56 (1938) 238-268.
MÖLLE, H. *Der sogenannte Landtag zu Sichem.* (*FzB* 42) Würzburg, 1980.
DE MOOR, J.C. *The Seasonal Pattern in the Ugaritic Myth of Ba'lu According to the Version of Ilimilku.* (*AOAT* 16) Neukirchen-Vluyn, 1971.
— . *New Year with Canaanites and Israelites.* 2 vols. *KC* 21-22. Kampen, 1972.
— . "Diviners' Oak," *IDBSup.* Nashville and New York, 1976, 243f.
— . "The Art of Versification in Ugarit and Israel," in Y.Avishur–J.Blau, eds. *Studies in Bible and the Ancient Near East.* Fs S.E.Loewenstamm. Jerusalem, 1978, 119-139.
— . "The Art of Versification in Ugarit and Israel, II: The Formal Structure," *UF* 10 (1978) 187-217.
— . "The Art of Versification in Ugarit and Israel, III: Further Illustrations of the Principle of Expansion," *UF* 12 (1980) 311-315.
— . *Uw God is mijn God. Over de oorsprong van het geloof in de ene God.* (*KC* 51) Kampen, 1983.
— . "The Poetry of the Book of Ruth," *Or* 53 (984) 262-283; "... (Part II)," *Or* 55 (1986) 16-46.
— . *An Anthology of Religious Texts from Ugarit.* Leiden, 1987.
— . "Narrative Poetry in Canaan," *UF* 20 (1988) 149-171.
— . *The Rise of Yahwism.* Leuven, 1990.
MORAN, W.L. "The Ancient Near Eastern Background of the Love of God in Deuteronomy," *CBQ* 25 (1963) 77-87.
— . *Les Lettres d'el-Amarna: Correspondence diplomatique du pharaon.* Paris, 1987.
MORGENSTERN, J. "The Book of the Covenant, I" *HUCA* 5 (1928) 1-151; "Part II," *HUCA* 7 (1930) 19-258; "Part III–The Ḥuqqim," *HUCA* 8-9

(1931-1932) 1-150.
MOWINCKEL, S. *Le décalogue.* Paris, 1927.
— . "'Rahelstämme' und 'Leastämme'" in J.Hempel and L.Rost, eds. *Von Ugarit nach Qumran.* (*BZAW* 77) Berlin, 1958, 129-150.
— . *Psalmenstudien.* 2 vols. Amsterdam, 1961 (= 6 vols. Oslo, 1921-24).
— . *Tetrateuch-Pentateuch-Hexateuch. Die Berichte über die Landnahme in den drei altisraelitischen Geschichtswerken. BZAW* 90. Berlin, 1964.
MUILENBURG, J. "A Study in Hebrew Rhetoric: Repetition and Style" in *Congress Volume Copenhagen 1953.* (*SVT* 1) Leiden, 1953, 97-111.
— . "The Form and Structure of the Covenantal Formulations," *VT* 9 (1959) 347-365.
— . "The Intercession of the Covenant Mediator (Exodus 33:1a, 12-17)," in P.R.Ackroyd and B.Lindars, eds. *Words and Meanings.* Cambridge, 1968, 159-191.
— . "Form Criticism and Beyond," *JBL* 88 (1969) 1-18.
MURAOKA, T. *Emphatic Words and Structures in Biblical Hebrew.* Leiden and Jerusalem, 1985.
NELSON, R.D. *The Double Redaction of the Deuteronomistic History.* (*JSOTS* 18) Sheffield, 1981.
NEWMAN, M.L. *The People of the Covenant: A Study of Israel from Moses to the Monarchy.* New York, 1962.
NICHOLSON, E.W. "The Covenant Ritual in Exodus xxiv 3-8," *VT* 32 (1982) 74-86.
— . *God and His People: Covenant and Theology in the Old Testament.* Oxford, 1986.
— . "Covenant in a Century of Study since Wellhausen," in A.S. van der Woude, ed. *Crises and Perspectives* (*OTS* 24) Leiden, 1986, 54-69.
NIEHR, H. *Herrschen und Richten. Die Wurzel špt im Alten Orient und im Alten Testament.* (*FzB* 54) Würburg, 1986.
NIELSEN, E. "The Burial of the Foreign Gods," *StTh* 8 (1955) 103-123.
— . *Shechem: A Traditio-Historical Investigation.* Copenhagen, 1955.
— . *Die Zehn Gebote: Eine Traditionsgeschichtliche Skizze.* (*AThD* 8) Copenhagen, 1965.
— . "Historical Perspectives and Geographical Horizons," *ASThI* 11 (1977-78) 77-89.
— . "Moses and the Law," *VT* 32 (1982) 87-98.
— . "The Traditio-historical Study of the Pentateuch since 1945, with Special Emphasis on Scandinavia," in *Law, History and Tradition: Selected Essays by Eduard Nielsen.* Copenhagen, 1983, 138-154.
NÖTSCHER, F. "Bundesformular und 'Ammtsschimmel'. Ein kritischer Überblick," *BZ* 9 (1965) 181-214.
NOTH, M. *Das System der Zwölf Stämme Israels.* (*BWANT* 4th series, 1) Stuttgart, 1930; reprinted Darmstadt, 1980.

—. *"Uberlieferungsgeschichtliche Studien: Die sammelnden und bearbeitenden Geschichtswerke im Alten Testament.* Halle, 1943; 2nd ed. Tübinger 1957.
—. *Das Buch Josua.* (*HAT* 7) Tübingen, 1938; 2nd ed. Tübingen, 1953.
—. *Gesammelte Studien zum Alten Testamentum.* (*ThB* 6) München, 1957.
—. "Das alttestamentliche Bundschliessen im Lichte eines Mari-Textes," in *Gesammelte Studien zum Alten Testament.* 2nd ed. München, 1960 (= "Old Testament Covenant-Making in the Light of a Text from Mari," in *The Laws in the Pentateuch and Other Studies.* Translated by D.R.Ap-Thomas. London, 1966) 108-117.
—. *The History of Israel.* Revised edition. New York and London, 1960.
—. *Könige.* (*BKAT* IX/1) Neukirchen-Vluyn, 1968.
—. *Aufsätze zur biblischen Landes- und Altertumskunde.* 2 vols. Edited by H.W.Wolff. Neukirchen-Vluyn, 1971.
NOUGAYROL, J. *Le palais royal d'Ugarit, IV. Mission de Ras Shamra, IX.* Paris, 1956.
O'CONNOR, M. *Hebrew Verse Structure.* Winona Lake, 1980.
OETTLI, S. *Deuteronomium, Buch Josua und Buch der Richter.* München, 1893.
OOSTERHOFF, B.J. *Israëlitische persoonsnamen.* (*Exegetica* 4) Delft, 1953.
OTTO, E. *Jakob in Sichem. Überlieferungsgeschichtliche, archäologische und territorialgeschichtliche Studien zur Entstehungsgeschichte Israels.* (*BWANT* 110) Stuttgart, 1979.
PARDEE, D. *Ugaritic and Hebrew Poetic Parallelism: A Trial Cut ('nt I and Proverbs 2).* Leiden, 1988.
PATTON, J.H. *Canaanite Parallels in the Book of Psalms.* Baltimore, 1944.
PAYNE, J.B. "The B'rith of Yahweh," in J.B.Payne, ed. *New Perspectives on the Old Testament.* Waco, 1970, 240-264.
PAYNE, J.B., ed. *New Perspectives on the Old Testament.* Waco, 1970.
PEDERSEN, J. Der Eid bei den Semiten in seinem Verhältnis zu verwandten Erscheinungen sowie die Stellung des Eides im Islam. Strassburg, 1914.
—. *Israel: Its Life and Culture.* 2 vols. London, 1926-40.
PERLITT, L. *Bundestheologie im Alten Testament.* (*WMANT* 36) Neukirchen–Vluyn, 1969.
PFEIFFER, R.H. *Introduction to the Old Testament.* 2nd ed. London, 1948.
PITARD, W.T. *Ancient Damascus.* Winona Lake, 1987.
POLZIN, R. *Moses and the Deuteronomist: A Literary Study of the Deuteronomic History.* New York, 1980.
PORTEN, B.–RAPPAPORT, U. "Poetic Structure in Genesis ix 7," *VT* 21 (1971) 363-369 .
RABIN, CH., ed. *Studies in the Bible.* (*ScH* 8) Jerusalem, 1961.
VON RAD, G. *The Problem of the Hexateuch and Other Essays.* Translated by E.W.T.Dicken. London, 1984.

—. *Old Testament Theology.* 2 vols. Translated by D.M.G.Stalker. New York, 1962-65.
—. *Deuteronomy.* Translated by D.Barton. (*OTL*) Philadelphia, 1966.
REDFORD, D.B. "The Relations between Egypt and Israel from El-Amarna to the Babylonian Conquest," in J.Amitai, ed. *Biblical Archaeology Today.* Jerusalem, 1985, 192-205.
RENAUD, B. *Je suis un Dieu jaloux. Lectio divina* 36. Paris, 1963.
RENDTORFF, R. "Der Kultus im Alten Israel," *JHL* 2 (1956) 1-21.
RENKEMA, J. "The Literary Structure of Lamentations," in W. van der Meer and J.C. de Moor, eds. *The Structural Analysis of Biblical and Canaanite Poetry.* (*JSOTS* 74) Sheffield, 1988, 294-396.
REVENTLOW, H.GRAF, *Wächter über Israel: Ezechiel und seine Tradition.* (*BZAW* 82) Berlin, 1962.
RICHTER, W. "Beobachtungen zur theologischen Systembildung in der alttestamentlichen Literatur anhand des 'kleinen geschichtlichen Credo'," in *Wahrheit und Verkündigung.* (Fs M.Schmaus) Paderborn, 1967, 175-212.
RÖSEL, H.N. "Erwägungen zu Tradition und Geschichte in Jos 24," *BN* 22 (1983) 41-46.
ROFÉ, A. "The End of the Book of Joshua According to the Septuagint," *Henoch* 4 (1982) 17-35.
—. "Joshua 20: Historico-Literary Criticism Illustrated," in J.H.Tigay, ed. *Empirical Models for Biblical Criticism.* Philadelphia, 1985, 131-147.
ROSE, M. *Deuteronomist und Jahwist. Untersuchungen zu de Berührungspunkten beider Literaturwerke.* (*AThANT* 67) Zürich, 1981.
ROST, L. *Die Überlieferung von der Thronnachfolge Davids.* Stuttgart, 1926.
—. *Das Kleine Credo und andere Studien zum Alten Testament.* Heidelberg, 1965.
RUDOLPH, W. *Der "Elohist" von Exodus bis Josua.* (*BZAW* 68) Berlin, 1938.
SCHLEY, D.G. *Shiloh: A Biblical City in Tradition and History.* (*JSOT* 63) Sheffield, 1989.
SCHMITT, G. "El Berit–Mitra," *ZAW* 76 (1964) 325-327.
—. *Der Landtag von Sichem.* Stuttgart, 1964.
—. *Du sollst keinen Frieden schliessen mit den Bewohnern des Landes.* (*BWANT* 91) Stuttgart, 1970.
SCHREINER, J. "Die Entwicklung des israelitischen 'Credo'," *Concilium* 2 (1966) 757-762.
—. "Vertrag zwischen Suppiluliuma I. und Niqmaddu II. von Ugarit," in *TUAT*, I/2. Gütersloh, 1983, 131-134.
SEEBASS, H. *Der Erzvater Israel und Die Einführung der Jahweverehrung in Kanaan.* (*BZAW* 98) Berlin, 1966.

SEGAL, M.H. *The Pentateuch, its Composition and its Authorship, and other Biblical Studies.* Jerusalem, 1967.

SELLIN, E. *Gilgal: Ein Beitrag zur Geschichte der Einwanderung Israels in Palästina.* Leipzig, 1917.

— . *Geschichte des Israelitisch-jüdischen Volkes.* 2 vols. Leipzig, 1924-32.

— . "Die Masseben des El-Berit in Sichem," *ZDPV* 51 (1928) 119-123.

— . "Der gegenwärtige Stand der Ausgrabungen von Sichem und ihre Zukunft," *ZAW* 50 (1932) 303-308.

VAN SELMS, A. "Temporary Henotheism," in M.A.Beek et al., eds. *Symbolae Biblicae et Mesopotamicae Fransisco Mario Theodoro de Liagre Böhl Dedicatae.* Leiden, 1973, 341-348.

SHANKS, H. "Two Early Israelite Cult Sites Now Questioned," *BAR* 14 (1988) 48-52.

SHERIFFS, D.C.T. "The Phrases *ina IGI DN* and *lipĕnēy Yhwh* in Treaty and Covenant Contexts," *JNSL* 7 (1979) 55-68.

SIMPSON, C.A. *Revelation and Response in the Old Testament.* New York, 1947.

— . *The Early Traditions of Israel: A Critical Analysis of the Pre-deuteronomic Narrative of the Hexateuch.* Oxford, 1948.

SINGER, I. *The Hittite KI.LAM Festival. Part One.* (*StBoT* 27) Wiesbaden, 1983.

SMEND, R. *Die Erzählung des Hexateuch auf ihre Quellen untersucht.* Berlin 1912, 334-339.

SMEND, R. *Die Bundesformel.* (*ThSt* 68) Zürich, 1963.

SOGGIN, J.A. *Joshua.* (*OTL*) London, 1972.

— . *Judges.* (*OTL*) London, 1981.

— . "The Conquest of Jericho through Battle. Note on a Lost Biblical Tradition (Josh. 24:11; 5:13ff.; 2:18 LXX)," *ErIs* 16 (1982) 215-217.

SPERBER, J. "Der Personenwechsel in der Bibel," *ZA* 32 (1918-19) 23-33.

SPERLING, S.D. "Joshua 24 Re-examined," *HUCA* 58 (1987) 119-136.

SPRONK, K. *Beatific Afterlife in Ancient Israel and in the Ancient Near East.* (*AOAT* 219) Neukirchen-Vluyn, 1986.

STAGER, L.E. "Merenptah, Israel and the Sea Peoples: New Light on an Old Relief," in B. Mazar and Y. Yadin, eds. *ErIs* 18 (Fs N.Avigad) Jerusalem, 1985, 56-64.

STEUERNAGEL, C. *Übersetzung und Erklärung der Bücher Deuteronomium und Josua, und allgemeine Einleitung in den Hexateuch.* Göttingen, 1900.

— . *Jahwe und die Vätergötter.* Stuttgart, 1935.

TADMOR, H. "Treaty and Oath in the Ancient Near East: A Historian's Approach," in G.M.Tucker and D.A.Knight, eds. *Humanizing America's Iconic Book: SBL Centennial Addresses 1980.* Chico, 1982, 127-152.

TADMOR, H.–WEINFELD, M., eds. *History, Historiography and Interpretation: Studies in Biblial and Cuneiform Literatures.* Jerusalem and Leiden, 1983.

TALMON, S. "Synonymous Readings in the Textual Traditions of the Old Testament," in Ch.Rabin, ed. *Studies in the Bible.* (*ScH* 8) Jerusalem, 1961, 335-383.

TENGSTRÖM, S. *Die Hexateucherzählung. Ein literaturgeschichtliche Studie.* (*CB OTS* 7) Uppsala, 1976.

THOMAS, D.W., ed. *Archaeology and Old Testament Study: Jubilee Volume of the Society for Old Testament Study 1917-1967.* Oxford, 1967.

THOMPSON, J.A. "Non-Biblical Covenants in the Ancient Near East and Their Relevance for Understanding the Covenant Motif in the Old Testament," *ABR* 8 (1960) 39-45.

—, *The Ancient Near Eastern Treaties and the Old Testament.* London, 1964.

THOMPSON, T.L. "The Joseph and Moses Narratives," in J.H. Hayes–J.M. Miller, eds. *Israelite and Judaean History.* London, 1977, 149-180.

TIGAY, J.H. "Israelite Religion: The Onomastic and Epigraphic Evidence," in P.D. Miller et al., eds. *Ancient Israelite Religion.* Philadelphia, 1987, 157-194.

TIGAY, J.H., ed. *Empirical Models for Biblical Criticism.* Philadelphia, 1985.

TOOMBS, L.E. "The Stratification of Tell Balâṭah (Shechem)," *BASOR* 223 (1976) 57-59.

— . "Shechem: Problems of the Early Israelite Era," in F.M.Cross, ed. *Symposia Celebrating the Seventy-fifth Anniversary of the Founding of the American Schools of Oriental Research (1900-1975).* Cambridge, MA, 1979, 69-83.

TOV, E. "Midrash-Type Exegesis in the LXX of Joshua," *RB* 85 (1978) 50-61.

— . *The Text-Critical Use of the Septuagint in Biblical Research.* Jerusalem, 1981.

— . "The Growth of the Book of Joshua in the Light of the Evidence of the LXX Translation," in S.Japhet, ed. *Studies in the Bible (1986).* (*ScH* 31) Jerusalem, 1986, 321-339.

TUBB, J.N., ed. *Palestine in the Bronze and Iron Ages: Papers in Honour of Olga Tufnell.* London, 1985.

TUCKER, G.M. "Covenant Forms and Contract Forms," *VT* 15 (1965) 487-503.

VALETON, J.J.P., "Bedeutung und Stellung des Wortes *bryt* im Priestercodex," *ZAW* 12 (1892) 1-22

— . "Das Wort *bryt* in den jehovistischen und deuteronomischen Stücken des Hexateuchs, sowie in den verwandten historischen Büchern," *ZAW*

12 (1892) 224-260.

— . "Das Wort *bryt* bei den Propheten und in den Ketubim–Resultat," *ZAW* 13 (1893) 245-279.

Van Seters, J. *Abraham in History and Tradition.* New Haven and London, 1975.

— . *In Search of History: Historiography in the Ancint World and the Origins of Biblical History.* New Haven and London, 1983.

— . "Joshua 24 and the Problem of Tradition in the Old Testament," in W.B.Barrick and J.R.Spencer, eds. it In the Shelter of Elyon: Essays on Ancient Palestinian Life and Literature in Honor of G.W.Ahlström. (*JSOTS* 31) Sheffield, 1984, 139-158.

Vannoy, J.R. *Covenant Renewal at Gilgal: A Study of I Samuel 1:14-12:25.* Cherry Hill, New Jersey, 1977.

de Vaux, R. *The Early History of Israel.* Translated by D.Smith, Philadelphia, 1978.

Volz, P.–Rudolph, W. *Der Elohist als Erzähler. Ein Irrweg der Pentateuchkritik?* (*BZAW* 63) Giessen, 1933.

Vriezen, Th.C. "The Exegesis of Exodus xxiv 9-11," in *The Witness of Tradition.* (*OTS* 17) Leiden, 1972, 100-133.

Wächter, L. "Die Übertragung der Beritvorstellung auf Jahwe," *ThLZ* 99 (1974) 801-816.

— . "Zur Lokalisierung des sichemitischen Baumheiligtums," *ZDPV* 103 (1987) 1-12.

Wallace, H.N. "The Oracles against the Israelite Dynasties in 1 and 2 Kings," *Bibl* 67 (1986) 21-40.

Walters, P. (formerly Katz). *The Text of the Septuagint: Its Corruptions and the Their Emmendation.* Edited by D.W.Gooding. Cambridge, 1973.

Watson, W.G.E. "Fixed Pairs in Ugaritic and Isaiah," *VT* 22 (1972) 460-468.

— . *Classical Hebrew Poetry: A Guide to Its Techniques.* (*JSOTS* 26) Sheffield, 1984.

— . "The Hebrew Word-pair *'sp* || *qbṣ*," *ZAW* 96 (1984) 426-434.

Watters, W.R. *Formula Criticism and the Poetry of the Old Testament.* (*BZAW* 138) Berlin and New York, 1976.

Weidner, E.F. *Politische Dokumente aus Kleinasien. Die Staatsverträge in akkadischer Sprache aus dem Archiv von Boghazköi. Boghazköi Studien* 8-9. Leipzig, 1923.

Weinfeld, M. "Traces of Assyrian Treaty Formulae in Deuteronomy," *Bibl* 46 (1965) 417-427.

— . "The Covenant of Grant in the Old Testament and in the Ancient Near East," *JAOS* 90 (1970) 184-203.

— . *Deuteronomy and the Deuteronomic School.* London, 1972.

—. "Covenant Terminology in the Ancient Near East and Its Influence on the West," *JAOS* 93 (1973) 190-199.
—. "*Bryt* –Covenant vs. Obligation," *Bibl* 56 (1975) 120-128
—. "The Loyalty Oath in the Ancient Near East," *UF* 8 (1976) 379-414.
—. "Judge and Officer in Ancient Israel and in the Ancient Near East," in *Israel Oriental Studies*, 7. *Annual Publication of the Faculty of Humanities*, Tel-Aviv University, 1977, 65-88.
—. "Divine Intervention in War in Ancient Israel and in the Ancient Near East," in H.Tadmor and M.Weinfeld, eds. *History, Historiography and Interpretation.* Jerusalem and Leiden, 1983, 121-147.
—. "The Emergence of the Deuteronomic Movement: The Historical Antecedents," in N.Lohfink, ed. *Das Deuteronomium.* (*BETL* 68) Leuven, 1985, 76-98.
WEINSTEIN, J.M. "The Egyptian Empire in Palestine: A Reassessment," *BASOR* 241 (1981) 1-28.
WEIPPERT, M. *Die Landnahme der israelitischen Stämme in der neueren wissenschaftlichen Diskussion.* Göttingen, 1967.
—. "The Israelite 'Conquest' and the Evidence from Transjordan," in F.M.Cross, ed. *Symposia Celebrating the Seventy-Fifth Anniversary of the Founding of the American Schools of Oriental Research (1900-1975).* Cambridge, MA, 1979, 15-34.
WEISER, A. "Das Deboralied," *ZAW* 71 (1959) 67-97.
—. *Einleitung in Das Alte Testament.* Stuttgart, 1939.
—. *The Psalms.* Translated by H.Hartwell. *OTL.* Philadelphia, 1962.
WELLHAUSEN, J. *Geschichte Israels, I.* Berlin, 1878.
—. *Prolegomena zur Geschichte Israels.* 5th ed. Berlin, 1899.
—. *Die Composition des Hexateuchs und der Historischen Bücher des Alten Testaments.* 3rd ed. Berlin, 1899; reprinted Berlin, 1963.
WESTERMANN, C. *Genesis.* 3 vols. (*BKAT* I/1-3) Neukirchen, 1979.
WEVERS, J.W. "Exegetical Principles Underlying the Septuagint Text of 1 Kings ii 12-xxi 43," *OTS* 8. Leiden, 1950, 300-322.
WHITLEY, C.F. "Covenant and Commandment in Israel," *JNES* 22 (1963) 37-48.
WIJNGAARDS, J., "*Hwṣy'* and *h'lh*: A Twofold Approach to the Exodus," *VT* 15 (1965) 91-102.
WILDBERGER, H. *Jesaja.* (*BKAT* X/1) Neukirchen-Vluyn, 1965.
WILLESEN, F., "Die Eselsöhne von Sichem als Bundesgenossen," *VT* 4 (1954) 216-217.
WILLIAMS, R.J. *Hebrew Syntax: An Outline.* 2nd ed. Toronto, 1976.
WILLIS, J.T. "Alternating (ABÁB́) Parallelism in the Old Testament Psalms and Prophetic Literature," in E.R.Follis, ed. *Directions in Biblical Hebrew Poetry.* (*JSOTS* 40) Sheffield, 1987, 49-76.
WILMS, F.-E. *Das Jahwistische Bundesbuch in Exodus 34.* München, 1973.

WISEMAN, D.J. "The Vassal-Treaties of Esarhaddon," *Iraq* 20 (1958) 1-99.

WOLFF, H.W. *Hosea.* (*BKAT* XIV/1) Neukirchen-Vluyn, 1961.

WOLFF, H.W., ed. *Probleme biblischer Theologie.* (Fs G.von Rad) München, 1970.

VAN DER WOUDE, A.S., ed. *Inleiding tot de studie van het Oude Testament.* Kampen, 1986.

WOUDSTRA, M.H. *The Book of Joshua.* (*NICOT*) Grand Rapids, 1981.

WRIGHT, G.E. "The Lawsuit of God: A Form-Critical Study of Deuteronomy 32," in B.W.Anderson and W.Harrelson, eds. *Israel's Prophetic Heritage: Essays in Honor of James Muilenburg.* London, 1962, 26-67.

— . *Shechem: The Biography of A Biblical City.* New York and Toronto, 1965.

— . "Shechem," in D.W.Thomas, ed. *Archaeology and Old Testament Study.* Oxford, 1967, 355-370.

WÜRTHWEIN, E.–KAISER, O., eds. *Tradition und Situation. Studien zur alttestamentlichen Prophetie* (Fs A.Weiser) Göttingen, 1963.

WYATT, N. "Sea and Desert: Symbolic Geography in West Semitic Religious Thought," *UF* 19 (1987) 375-389.

YADIN, Y., "The Transition from a Semi-Nomadic to a Sedentary Society in the Twelfth Century B.C.E.," in F.M.Cross, ed. *Symposia Celebrating the Seventy-fifth Anniversary of the Founding of the American Schools of Oriental Research (1900-1975).* Cambridge, MA, 1979, 57-68.

YODER, P.B. "A-B Pairs and Oral Composition in Hebrew Poetry," *VT* 21 (1971) 470-489.

YOUNGER, K.L. "Panammuwa and Bar-Rakib: Two Structural Analyses," *JANES* 18 (1986) 91-103.

ZERTAL, A. "Has Joshua's Altar Been Found on Mt. Ebal?" *BAR* 11 (1985) 26-43.

ZURRO, E. *Procedimientos iterativos en la poesía ugarítica y hebrea.* Rome, 1987.

# Index of Authors

# Selected Index of Scriptural References

# Index of Subjects

# Selected Hebrew Words and Parallelisms